Why You Need This New Edition

Here are 6 good reasons to give the ninth edition a close look!

1. **Finding your voice theme:** The new subtitle for this edition focuses on a theme that has been implicit in the book from the beginning: Helping our readers develop as speakers and as people as they gain presentation skills and confidence and discover causes that interest and engage them. This theme is evident in each chapter, from the **opening scenarios** that describe speakers in the process of finding their voice to the **"Final Reflections" summary sections** that connect the chapter content specifically to the process of finding your voice. A new **"Finding Your Voice" boxed feature,** which appears several times in each chapter, offers brief exercises and activities that challenge students to think about and apply key chapter concepts.

2. **Numerous new speeches:** The ninth edition offers many new sample student informative, persuasive, and ceremonial speeches, some of which appear in full, *with annotations* **at the end of chapters,** and some of which appear in **Appendix B: Speeches for Analysis.**

3. **Updated information and research:** The new edition provides significantly revised discussions throughout, such as a review of newer presentation media including Prezi, VUE and other cutting-edge technologies, and the potential pitfalls of computer-generated presentations such as PowerPoint™ in Chapter 10, "Presentation Aids."

4. **Restored order of the two persuasion chapters:** In response to reviewers' requests, we have reorganized these two chapters, 14 and 15, to return to their original focus, first presenting the basic principles of persuasion and persuasive design strategies, and building to a discussion of reasoned persuasion and how to develop strong arguments to support a position.

5. **Streamlined coverage:** While retaining the breadth and depth of coverage that our readers have valued over the years, judicious editing throughout has eliminated extraneous discussions and outdated information, making the overall content more succinct and selective. Material has been reorganized and recast for greater clarity and to accommodate today's diverse learning styles, such as the former two chapters on "Organizing" and "Outlining," which have now been combined into **one concise chapter** (Chapter 9).

6. **Enhanced design and study tools:** This edition boasts a striking new design and photographs, and includes fresh pedagogical aids. In addition to the running glossary at the bottom of each page, there is now a full glossary at the end of the book. A new feature, **"Your Ethical Voice,"** increases ethical sensitivity and points out ethical concerns.

NINTH EDITION

PUBLIC
Speaking
FINDING YOUR VOICE

Michael Osborn
University of Memphis

Suzanne Osborn
University of Memphis

Randall Osborn
University of Memphis

with Kathleen J. Turner, *Davidson College*

Allyn & Bacon

Boston   Columbus   Indianapolis   New York   San Francisco   Upper Saddle River
Amsterdam   Cape Town   Dubai   London   Madrid   Milan   Munich   Paris   Montreal   Toronto
Delhi   Mexico City   São Paulo   Sydney   Hong Kong   Seoul   Singapore   Taipei   Tokyo

Editor-in-Chief, Communication: Karon Bowers
Director of Development: Meg Botteon
Development Editor: Hilary Jackson
Associate Development Editor: Angela G. Mallowes
Editorial Assistant: Megan Sweeney
Marketing Manager: Blair Tuckman
Media Producer: Megan Higginbotham
Project Manager: Anne Ricigliano
Project Coordination, Text Design, and Electronic Page Makeup: Nesbitt Graphics, Inc.
Cover Design Manager: Anne Nieglos
Cover Designer: Ilze Lemesis/T–9
Cover Images: ©Fancy Collection/SuperStock; Fenton/Shutterstock.Images
Manufacturing Buyer: Mary Ann Gloriande
Printer and Binder: R.R. Donnelley/Willard
Cover Printer: Lehigh-Phoenix Color/Hagerstown

Library of Congress Cataloging-in-Publication Data
Osborn, Michael.
  Public speaking / Michael Osborn, Suzanne Osborn, Randall Osborn.—9th ed.
    p. cm.
  ISBN-13: 978-0-205-77844-7
  ISBN-10: 0-205-77844-5
  I. Public speaking. I. Osborn, Suzanne. II. Osborn, Randall. III. Title.
  PN4129.15.O83 2012
  808.5'1—dc22

                                        2010046660

Printed in the United States of America
1 2 3 4 5 6 7 8 9 10 DOW 13 12 11 10

Allyn & Bacon
is an imprint of

www.pearsonhighered.com

ISBN-13: 978-0-205-77844-7
ISBN-10:   0-205-77844-5

AIE ISBN-13: 978-0-205-00009-8
AIE ISBN-10: 0-205-00009-6

This edition is dedicated to the memory of Keith Kennedy and Michael Leff, two colleagues of exceptional ability with whom we shared much joy and the challenges of building a communication program at the University of Memphis from the civil rights era up to recent times.

Brief Contents

Contents

4 Becoming a Better Listener 60

PART TWO   Preparation for Public Speaking 80

5 Adapting to Your Audience and Situation 80

6 Developing Your Topic 106

7 Building Responsible Knowledge   122

8 Supporting Your Ideas   146

9 Structuring and Outlining Your Speech 168

PART THREE   Developing Presentation Skills 200

12 Presenting Your Speech 252

PART FOUR   Types of Public Speaking 278

13 Informative Speaking 278

14 Persuasive Speaking 300

Preface

Those familiar with *Public Speaking* through its first eight editions may wonder about its new subtitle and its contemporary look. "Finding Your Voice" means that the book continues to grow and evolve toward its primary purpose of helping students become better communicators in their classrooms, workplaces, and communities. The subtitle focuses a theme that has been implicit from the beginning: that developing as a speaker can help one develop as a person with a sense of purpose and mission. With this edition, *Public Speaking* has found its own voice.

What's New in This Edition

Finding your voice in the public speaking class means developing on at least three levels. On the first and most basic level, the student gains technical competence by learning how to analyze audiences, find good topics, conduct research, design messages, word them for maximum effect, and present them so that they achieve desired communication goals. The second level of finding your voice involves self-discovery: gaining confidence that you can communicate successfully and finding those causes that most deserve your personal commitment. The third level begins the process of finding your place in society, developing a sense of the communication roles that you might play in your community or in the global workplace.

The new theme resonates throughout the book. Each chapter begins with stories and examples that illustrate finding your voice and concludes with a "Final Reflections" section that places in context the importance of what you have learned.

FINDING YOUR

voice

Persuasion in the Raw

The letters-to-the-editor section of the Sunday newspaper is often a rich source for the study of persuasive material. Using a recent Sunday paper, analyze the persuasion attempted in these letters. You might also check blogs with which you're familiar or that discuss a topic of interest to you. Do you find the ideas expressed in these persuasive? Why or why not? Do you evaluate these comments differently from letters to the editor or from other media sources? Which do you think are most and least effective, and why? Report your findings in class discussion.

■ As each chapter develops, the new "Finding Your Voice" feature offers short exercises and applications that challenge students to think about and apply what they are learning, providing opportunities for class discussion and a stimulus to learning.

■ The ninth edition offers many new informative, persuasive, and ceremonial student speeches presented at the University of Arkansas, Davidson College, the University of Memphis, and the University of Texas at Austin. Offered in their entirety at the ends of chapters or in Appendix B, these speeches provide creative models for emulation. Throughout the book, fresh examples from student and professional speakers join with old favorites to enliven the illustration of particular points.

But consider this: In today's society, huge corporations like Coca-Cola, Pepsi, and Nestle are marketing their own "ice cubes" to us with immense success. Water, a natural resource that has historically been viewed as free and open to the public, is now being bottled and sold for profit by large multinational corporations.

Katie sets up a refutative design which first identifies the shallow attitudes about bottled water that are induced by advertisers. She will then proceed to challenge these attitudes. ▶

Why are we buying water? And what are the consequences of it? These are the questions I want to consider today. We will examine marketing strategies, consumer misconceptions, and the environmental impact of our behavior.

Let's begin by considering how the bottled water industry sells its own "ice cubes" to us. Consumers gravitate towards bottled water instead of tap water for two reasons: what's in it and what's not in it. What could possibly be inside a 20-ounce bottle of water that would compel someone to pay $3 and beyond for it? According to *The Journal of Consumer Culture*, "bottled water is a form of cultural consumption, driven by everything from status competition to a belief in magical curing." Clever advertisers feed these feelings. Since bottled water has become an affordable status symbol in today's society, companies can appeal to social distinctions of wealth and class to sell their product.

Katie makes effective use of humor to debunk buying behaviors, and connects her speech to the "god terms" used by advertisers to make bottled water seem ▶

Take a look at some of the brands currently on the market: There are vitamin waters, nicotine waters, caffeine waters, electrolyte enhanced SmartWater, the "orbtastic" Aquapods that target kids, Bling H$_2$O which sells for $35 a bottle, "Hello Kitty" water for cats, and yes, even a "diet" water called "Skinny." And according to *The Journal of Consumer Culture*, "new water brands are entering the US market at the rate of about eight per month." Now tell me, how can

speaking. Use the longer pauses in your speech to breathe, and make note of your breathing pattern as you practice your speech.

Vary the loudness of words and phrases in your speech, just as you change your pitch and rate of speaking to express ideas more effectively. Changes in loudness are often used to express emotion. The more excited or angry we are, the louder we tend to become. But don't let yourself get caught in the trap of having only two options: loud and louder. Decreasing your volume, slowing your rate, pausing, or dropping your pitch can also express emotion quite effectively.

Davidson student BJ Youngerman demonstrated the importance of loudness as he re-enacted a scene from his experience as a baseball umpire. In the confrontation between himself and a coach, BJ contrasted the angry loudness of the coach with his own quieter, more controlled vocal mannerisms as an umpire. Read the scene aloud, and as you play both roles, explore your own capacity to produce louder and more quiet speech:

Me:	"He's out!" (with hand motion).
Coach:	"You've got to be kidding me, Blue! He was a good 10 feet beyond the base before the ball got there. That's horrible!"
Me:	"Coach, it's a judgment call. I called it like I saw it. Please get back to your dugout."
Coach:	"Blue, that was the worst call I've ever seen. You're totally blind."
Me:	"Coach, this is your final warning: Get in the dugout."

BJ Youngerman used changes in loudness effectively in his speeches.

talk about it. For PowerPoint presentations, use the "entrance" code to make subsequent portions appear at the click of the mouse. Keep the graphic simple, using intense colors with good contrast. In a bulleted list, have no more than six lines of information and no more than six words to a line.

Another frequently used type of textual graphic presents an **acronym** composed of the initial letters of words to help your audience remember your message. The transparency in Figure 10.10 used the acronym EMILY (adapted from Emily's List, a political network) in a persuasive speech urging students to start saving early for retirement. When preparing such a graphic, use the acronym as a title; then list the words under it. Use size and/or color to make the first letters of the words stand out.

Keep textual graphics simple, with colors that make ideas stand out. A single word or phrase is far more effective than a full sentence, which competes with you for attention.

Pictures

Photographs and illustrations can be powerful presentation aids. A good photograph can authenticate a point in a way that words cannot. It can make a situation seem more vivid and realistic. For instance, a speaker could talk about the devastating environmental effects of the collapsed oil rig in the Gulf of Mexico, which might evoke a modest response from the audience. Suppose, however, the speaker also projected the photograph in Figure 10.11 on a screen in the front of the room as she said these words. Which strategy—with or without the picture—do you think would have the greater impact?

FIGURE 10.9 Bulleted List

Marketing Task Force

- Mission Statement
- Current Image
- Target Market
- Desired Image

FIGURE 10.10 Acronym Graphic

EMILY

EARLY
MONEY
IS
LIKE
YEAST

IT MAKES

■ The new edition significantly updates the knowledge offered in important chapters, especially those that involve cutting-edge technologies. Professor Kathleen J. Turner of Davidson College, an award-winning teacher and scholar, has assumed responsibility for updating, revising, and refreshing our chapter on the use of presentation aids (Chapter 10). The successful results of her work are self-evident in the new chapter. Professor Larry Lambert of Indiana University South Bend has offered invaluable advice in helping us bring our chapter on research (Chapter 7) up-to-date. We are grateful to these colleagues, as well as to the many reviewers acknowledged later in this Preface, for their contributions to our book.

■ The new edition is more compact and more selective. For many students, this has become the Age of Multi-Tasking, a time in which many demands are being made simultaneously on their time. Partly to help such students, and partly (we admit!) because shorter is usually better, we have sought to reduce the length of our book without sacrificing the quality many have come to associate with it. An especially apt example is our new chapter on structuring and outlining, which combines what had previously been two separate chapters. We think the effort to streamline the text has made this edition more student friendly.

Some Things Don't Change; They Just Get Better

So it is, we think, with our book. For all the changes from one edition to another, core values remain. With each edition, we try to state them a little more clearly, a little more powerfully. Among these values are the following:

■ From ancient times, educators have recognized that *the study and practice of public speaking belongs at the foundation of a liberal education.* What other discipline requires students to think clearly, be attuned to the needs of listeners, organize their thoughts, select and combine words artfully and judiciously, and express themselves with power and conviction, all while under the direct scrutiny of an audience? The challenge to teach such a complex range of abilities has always been difficult, but it also suggests the potential value of the course to many students. This book represents our best effort to help teachers and students rise to this challenge.

■ Another core objective of our book is *to illuminate the role of public speaking in a diverse society.* Adjusting to a diverse audience is a challenge ancient writers could not have anticipated. The increasing cultural diversity of our society adds to the importance of public speaking as a force that can express the richness of a diverse society, as well as counter the growing division and incivility that are the disease of diversity. Our renewed emphasis on identification as the antidote to division, on the importance of shared stories that express universal values, and on the ethical importance of reasoned discourse as a preferred mode of public deliberation, all respond to the vital importance of diversity in our society. Thus, cultural diversity is a theme that remains constant in our book.

■ We continue to believe that a major goal of the public speaking course is *to make students more sensitive to the ethical impact of speaking on the lives of others.* We discuss ethical considerations throughout the book. For example, we direct the attention of students to ethical concerns as we consider listening, audience analysis and adaptation, cultural variations, topic selection, research, ways of structuring speeches, presentation aids, uses of language, and the consequences of informing and persuading others. Often we use a "Finding Your Ethical Voice" feature to highlight these concerns.

YOUR ethical VOICE   The Ethics of Topic Selection

Ethical problems can infiltrate the process of topic selection for speeches. To avoid many of these problems, follow these guidelines:

1. Do not select a topic that could be hurtful, such as "How to Make a Pipe Bomb."

2. Do not select a topic that invites illegal activity, such as "Growing Marijuana in Your Dorm Room."

3. Do not select a topic on which you cannot obtain responsible knowledge.

4. Do not purposely obscure your thesis statement in order to hide your specific purpose.

■ At the suggestion of several reviewers, we have restored the original order of the persuasion chapters so that we build from the nature of persuasion—how it works and how to accomplish it—to the ethical importance of *reasoned persuasion.* We offer this concept *as an antidote to the manipulative persuasion evident in much of contemporary communication.* The emphasis on reasoned persuasion extends a moral axiom that has characterized our book since its inception: *the speaker's obligation to communicate based on responsible knowledge.*

■ We continue to believe that *a college course in public speaking should offer both practical advice and an understanding of why such advice works.* We emphasize both the *how* and the *why* of public speaking—*how* so that beginners can achieve success as quickly as possible, and *why* so that they can manage their new skills wisely. Our approach is eclectic: we draw from the past and present and from the social sciences and humanities to help students understand and manage their public speaking experiences.

■ The Roman educator Quintilian held forth the ideal of "the good person speaking well" as a goal of education. Two thousand years later, we join him in stressing *the value of speech training in the development of the whole person.* In addition, *understanding the principles of public communication can make students more resistant to unethical speakers and more critical of the mass-mediated communication to which they are exposed.* The class should help students become both better consumers and better producers of public communication.

In addition to these core values, we continue to offer features that have remained constant and distinctive across the many editions of our book.

■ *Responsible knowledge as a standard for public speaking.* In order to develop a standard for the quality and depth of information that should be reflected in all speeches, we offer the concept of *responsible knowledge.* This concept is developed in detail in Chapter 7, in which we discuss the foundation of research that should support speeches.

■ *Special preparation for the first speech.* As teachers, we realize the importance of the first speaking experience to a student's ultimate success in the course. Yet much useful advice must be delayed until later chapters as the subject of public speaking develops systematically over a semester. Having experienced this frustration ourselves while teaching the course, we decided to include an overview of practical advice early in the book that previews later chapters and prepares students more effectively for their first speeches. This overview is provided in Chapter 3.

■ *Situational approach to communication ethics.* We have always discussed ethical issues as they arise in the context of topics. The "Finding Your Ethical Voice" feature helps highlight these concerns as they develop chapter by chapter.

■ *The importance of narrative in public speaking.* We discuss narrative as an important form of supporting material and as a previously neglected design option. This material is initially presented in Chapter 3. We also identify appeals to traditions, heroic symbols, and legends—all built upon narrative—as an important emerging form of proof (*mythos*) in persuasive speaking.

YOUR **ethical** VOICE   Guidelines for the Ethical Use of Evidence

To earn a reputation for the ethical use of evidence, follow these rules:

1. Provide evidence from credible sources.
2. Identify your sources of evidence.
3. Use evidence that can be verified by experts.
4. Be sure such evidence has not been corrupted by outside interests.
5. Acknowledge disagreements among experts.
6. Do not withhold important evidence.
7. Use expert testimony to establish facts, prestige testimony to enhance credibility, and lay testimony to create identification.
8. Quote or paraphrase testimony accurately.

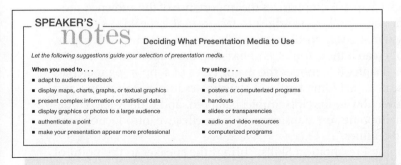

SPEAKER'S **notes**   Deciding What Presentation Media to Use

Let the following suggestions guide your selection of presentation media.

When you need to . . .
- adapt to audience feedback
- display maps, charts, graphs, or textual graphics
- present complex information or statistical data
- display graphics or photos to a large audience
- authenticate a point
- make your presentation appear more professional

try using . . .
- flip charts, chalk or marker boards
- posters or computerized programs
- handouts
- slides or transparencies
- audio and video resources
- computerized programs

■ *Speaker's Notes as a major pedagogical tool.* When our first edition appeared some twenty-five years ago we introduced to the field a feature we called "Speaker's Notes." This feature serves as an internal summary that helps highlight and bring into focus important concepts as the student reads the text. In the new edition, this traditional feature works in collaboration with the new "Finding Your Voice" and "Finding Your Ethical Voice" features to encourage learning and enrich the student's reading experience.

■ *Improving language skills.* We introduce students to the power of language, help them apply standards so that this power is not diminished, and demonstrate special techniques that can magnify this power at important moments in speeches. Among the standards is learning how to avoid grammatical errors that make listeners cringe.

■ *Enhanced understanding of ceremonial speaking.* We provide coherence and respect for the study of ceremonial speaking by pointing out the importance of such speaking in society, and by indicating how two powerful concepts, one offered by Aristotle and the other by Kenneth Burke, can combine to generate successful ceremonial speeches, especially speeches of tribute and inspiration.

Plan of the Book

Public Speaking: Finding Your Voice is designed to help beginning students build cumulative knowledge and skills. Positive initial speaking experiences are especially important. For this reason, Chapter 2 helps apprehensive students control communication anxiety as they stand to speak for the first time. Chapter 3 offers an overview of advice to help students design and present successful first speeches.

In the chapters that follow, students learn how to listen critically and constructively; analyze their audiences; select, refine, and research speech topics; develop supporting materials; arrange these materials in appropriate structures; and create effective presentation aids. They also learn how to manage words and present their messages. Students become acquainted with the nature of information and how to present it, the process of persuasion and how to engage it, and the importance of ceremonial speaking in its various forms. Appendix A, "Communicating in Small Groups," describes how to use public communication skills to participate effectively in small group interactions.

Teachers may adapt the sequence of chapters to any course plan, because each chapter covers a topic thoroughly and completely.

Detailed Plan of the Book

Part One, "The Foundations of Public Speaking," provides basic information that students need for their first speaking and listening experiences. Chapter 1 defines public speaking and the significance of "finding your voice," highlights the personal, social, and cultural benefits of being able to speak effectively in public, and emphasizes the ethical responsibilities of speakers. Chapter 2 helps students come to terms with communication anxiety, so that they can control this problem early in the course. Chapter 3 offers practical advice for organizing, practicing, and presenting first speeches. Chapter 4 identifies common listening problems and ways to overcome them, helps students sharpen critical thinking skills, and presents criteria for the constructive evaluation of speeches.

Part Two, "Preparation for Public Speaking," introduces the basic skills needed to develop effective speeches. Chapter 5 emphasizes the importance of the audience, indicating how to adapt a message and how to adjust to factors in the speaking situation. Chapter 6 provides a systematic way to discover, evaluate, and refine speech topics. Chapter 7 shows how to research these topics, emphasizing the importance of acquiring *responsible knowledge*. Chapter 8 identifies the major types of supporting materials fashioned from such research, including facts and statistics, examples, testimony, and narratives. Chapter 9 shows how to develop simple, balanced, and orderly speech designs, select and shape main points, use transitions, prepare effective introductions and conclusions, and develop outlines.

Part Three, "Developing Presentation Skills," brings the speaker to the point of presentation. Chapter 10 explains the kinds and preparation of presentation aids. Chapter 11 provides an understanding of the role of language in communication and offers practical suggestions for using words effectively. Chapter 12 offers exercises for the improvement of voice and body language. The chapter helps students develop an extemporaneous style that is adaptable to most speaking situations.

Part Four, "Types of Public Speaking," discusses informative, persuasive, and ceremonial speaking. Chapter 13 covers speeches designed to share information and increase understanding. The chapter discusses the types of informative speeches and presents the major designs that can structure them. Chapter 14 describes the persuasive process, focusing on how to meet the many challenges of persuasive situations. Chapter 15 develops the concept of reasoned persuasion, helping students develop strong, reasoned arguments to support their positions. The chapter also identifies the major forms of fallacies so that student speakers can avoid them and detect them in the messages of others. Chapter 16 explains how to prepare effective ceremonial presentations, including speeches of tribute and inspiration, speeches introducing others, eulogies, after-dinner speeches, and speeches presenting and accepting awards. The chapter revisits the use of narratives and the narrative design, often used in ceremonial speeches.

Appendix A, "Communicating in Small Groups," introduces students to the problem-solving process and to the responsibilities of both group leaders and group participants. This appendix also provides guidelines for managing informal and formal meetings, and explains the basic concepts of parliamentary procedure. Appendix B provides a number of student and professional speeches for additional analysis.

Learning Tools

To help students master the material, we offer a number of special learning tools.

- We open each chapter with a chapter outline and learning objectives that prepare students for efficient and productive reading.

- The epigrams and vignettes that start each chapter help point out the topic's significance and motivate readers to learn more.

- We use contemporary artwork and photographs to illustrate ideas, engage student interest, and add to the visual appeal of the book.

- Examples illustrate and apply the content in a clear, lively, and often entertaining way.

- Special embedded features help students read productively. "Speaker's Notes" offer guidelines to help students focus on the essentials; "Finding Your Voice" offers exercises and applications that stimulate class discussion and the learning process; and "Finding Your Ethical Voice" heightens ethical sensitivity.

- A running Glossary develops through the book, helping students focus on key terms as they are introduced. In addition, all the key terms and their definitions are gathered in a complete Glossary at the end of the book.

- Sample classroom speeches found at the end of many chapters illustrate important concepts. The annotated speech texts show how the concepts apply in actual speaking situations. Appendix B contains additional speeches that offer an interesting array of topics, contexts, and speakers.

THIS CHAPTER WILL HELP YOU

1 Understand how words can empower you
2 Apply standards to use language effectively
3 Learn how special techniques can magnify your voice

FINDING YOUR
voice Proofs in Advertising

Bring to class advertisements that emphasize each of the four forms of persuasive proof: logos, pathos, ethos, and mythos. What factors in the product, medium of advertising, or intended audience might explain this emphasis in each example? Do the advertisements combine other forms of proof as well? How effective is each advertisement? Present your findings and your answers to these questions in class discussion.

that the plot unfolds through three major scenes: (1) her family suffering in Gorazde, (2) Sabrina worrying about her parents, who had gone to seek food for

▶ **narrative design** A speech structure that develops a story in terms of a prologue, plot, and epilogue.

▶ **prologue** An opening that establishes the context and setting of a narrative, foreshadows the meaning, and introduces major characters.

▶ **plot** The body of a speech that follows narrative design; unfolds in a sequence of scenes designed to build suspense.

Resources IN PRINT AND ONLINE

Name of Supplement	Available in Print	Available Online	Instructor or Student Supplement	Description
Annotated Instructor's Edition (ISBN: 0-205-00009-6)	✓		Instructor Supplement	This instructor's version of *Public Speaking: Finding Your Voice,* Ninth Edition includes annotations written by the authors, with general and ESL teaching tips for every chapter.
Instructor's Classroom Kit, Volumes I and II (Vol. I ISBN: 0-205-00292-7 Vol. II ISBN: 0-205-11031-2)	✓	✓	Instructor Supplement	Prepared by Randall Osborn, University of Memphis, Pearson's unparalleled Classroom Kit includes every instruction aid a public speaking professor needs to manage the classroom. Organized by chapter, each volume contains materials from the Instructor's Manual and Test Bank, as well as slides from the PowerPoint™ Presentation Package that accompanies this book. The fully updated two-part Instructor's Manual can also be used for training teaching assistants. Part I of the manual includes sections on the purpose and philosophy of the course, preparing a syllabus, various sample syllabi, an assortment of speech assignment options, a discussion of evaluating and grading speeches, and a troubleshooting guide with teaching strategies for new instructors. Part II offers a chapter-by-chapter guide to teaching Public Speaking, including learning objectives, suggestions for teaching, and classroom activities. The Test Bank, also prepared by Randall Osborn, contains multiple choice, true/false, and short answer questions, with answers provided for each question. Available for download at www.pearsonhighered.com/irc (access code required).
MyTest (ISBN: 0-205-11026-6)		✓	Instructor Supplement	This flexible, online test generating software includes all questions found in the Test Bank section of the Classroom Kit, allowing instructors to create their own personalized exams. Instructors also can edit any of the existing test questions and even add new questions. Other special features of this program include random generation of test questions, creation of alternate versions of the same test, scrambling of question sequence, and test preview before printing. Available at www.pearsonmytest.com (access code required).
The Speech Preparation Workbook	✓		Student Supplement	Prepared by Suzanne Osborn of the University of Memphis especially for *Public Speaking: Finding Your Voice,* the *Workbook* contains forms to help students prepare a self-introductory speech, analyze the audience, select a topic, conduct research, organize supporting materials, and outline speeches (available for purchase).
PowerPoint™ Presentation Package (ISBN: 0-205-11029-0)		✓	Instructor Supplement	Prepared by authors Suzanne Osborn and Randall Osborn, this text-specific package provides a basis for your lecture with PowerPoint™ slides for each chapter of the book. Available for download at www.pearsonhighered.com/irc (access code required).
Pearson's ClassPrep		✓	Instructor Supplement	New from Pearson, ClassPrep makes lecture preparation simpler and less time-consuming. It collects the very best class presentation resources—art and figures from our texts, videos, lecture activities, audio clips, classroom activities, and much more–in one convenient online destination. You may search through ClassPrep's extensive database of tools by content topic (arranged by standard topics within the public speaking curriculum) or by content type (video, audio, activities, etc.). You will find ClassPrep in the Instructor's section of MySpeechLab (access code required).
Pearson's Contemporary Classic Speeches DVD (ISBN: 0-205-40552-5)	✓		Instructor Supplement	This exciting supplement includes over 120 minutes of video footage in an easy-to-use DVD format. Each speech is accompanied by a biographical and historical summary that helps students understand the context and motivation behind each speech. Speakers featured include Martin Luther King Jr., John F. Kennedy, Barbara Jordan, the Dalai Lama, and Christopher Reeve. Please contact your Pearson representative for details, some restrictions apply.

Name of Supplement	Available in Print	Available Online	Instructor or Student Supplement	Description
Pearson's Public Speaking Video Library	✓		Instructor Supplement	This collection contains a range of different types of speeches delivered on a multitude of topics, allowing you to choose the speeches best suited for your students. Please contact your Pearson representative for details and a complete list of videos and their contents to choose which would be most useful in your class. Samples from most of our public speaking videos are available on www.mycoursetoolbox.com. Some restrictions apply.
The Classical Origins of Public Speaking (ISBN: 0-205-56416-X)	✓		Student supplement	Written by Michael Osborn of the University of Memphis, this supplement offers a concise overview of classical Greek theory on the nature and importance of public speaking (available for purchase).
Public Speaking in the Multicultural Environment, Second Edition (ISBN: 0-205-26511-1)	✓		Student Supplement	Prepared by Devorah A. Lieberman, Portland State University, this booklet helps students learn to analyze cultural diversity within their audiences and adapt their presentations accordingly (available for purchase).
Multicultural Activities Workbook (ISBN: 0-205-54652-8)	✓		Student Supplement	By Marlene C. Cohen and Susan L. Richardson of Prince George's Community College, this workbook is filled with hands-on activities that help broaden the content of speech classes to reflect the diverse cultural backgrounds. The checklists, surveys, and writing assignments all help students succeed in speech communication by offering experiences that address a variety of learning styles (available for purchase).
Study Card for Public Speaking (ISBN: 0-205-44126-2)	✓		Student Supplement	Colorful, affordable, and packed with useful information, the Pearson Allyn & Bacon Study Cards make studying easier, more efficient, and more enjoyable. Course information is distilled down to the basics, helping students quickly master the fundamentals, review a subject for understanding, or prepare for an exam. Because they are laminated for durability, they can be kept for years to come and pulled out whenever students need a quick review (available for purchase).
Pearson Allyn & Bacon Public Speaking Study Site		✓	Student Supplement	This open access student Web resource features practice tests, learning objectives, and Web links organized around the major topics typically covered in the Introduction to Public Speaking course. The content of this site has even been correlated to the table of contents for your book (available at www.abpublicspeaking.com).
VideoLab CD-ROM (ISBN: 0-205-56161-6)	✓		Student Supplement	This interactive study tool for students can be used independently or in class. It provides digital video of student speeches that can be viewed in conjunction with corresponding outlines, manuscripts, note cards, and instructor critiques. Following each speech there are a series of drills to help students analyze content and delivery (available for purchase).
MySpeechLab		✓	Instructor & Student Supplement	MySpeechLab is a state-of-the-art, interactive and instructive solution for public speaking courses. Designed to be used as a supplement to a traditional lecture course or to completely administer an online course, MySpeechLab combines a Pearson eText, MySearchLab™, Pearson's MediaShare, multimedia, video clips, activities, research support, tests and quizzes to completely engage students. MySpeechLab can be packaged with your text and is available for purchase at ww.myspeechlab.com (access code required). See next page for more details.

Designed to amplify a traditional course in numerous ways or to administer a course online, **MySpeechLab** combines pedagogy and assessment with an array of multimedia activities—videos, speech preparation tools, assessments, research support, multiple newsfeeds—to make learning more effective for all types of students. Now featuring more resources, including a video upload tool, this new release of **MySpeechLab** is visually richer and even more interactive than the previous version—a leap forward in design with more tools and features to enrich learning and aid students in classroom success.

Teaching and Learning Tools

NEW VERSION! Pearson eText: Identical in content and design to the printed text, a Pearson eText provides students access to their text whenever and wherever they need it. In addition to contextually placed multimedia features in every chapter, our new Pearson eText allows students to take notes and highlight, just like a traditional book.

Videos and Video Quizzes: Interactive videos provide students with the opportunity to watch and evaluate sample speeches, both student and professional. Select videos are annotated with instructor feedback or include short, assignable quizzes that report to the instructor's gradebook. Professional speeches include classic and contemporary speeches, as well as video segments from communication experts.

MyOutline: MyOutline offers step-by-step guidance for writing an effective outline, along with tips and explanations to help students better understand the elements of an outline and how all the pieces fit together. Outlines that students create can be downloaded to their computer, emailed as an attachment, or saved in the tool for future editing. Instructors can either select from several templates based on our texts, or they can create their own outline structure for students to use.

Topic Selector: This interactive tool helps students get started generating ideas and then narrowing down topics. Our Topic Selector is question based, rather than drill-down, in order to help students really learn the process of selecting their topic. Once they have determined their topic, students are directed to credible online sources for guidance with the research process.

Self-Assessments: Online self-assessments including the PRCA-24 and the PRPSA provide students with opportunities to assess and confirm their comfort level with speaking publicly. Instructors can use these tools to show learning over the duration of the course via MyPersonalityProfile, Pearson's online self-assessment library and analysis tool. MyPersonalityProfile enables instructors to assign self-assessments, such as the PRPSA at the beginning and end of the course so students can compare their results and see where they've improved.

Study Plan: Pre- and Post-tests for each chapter test students on their knowledge of the material in the course. The tests generate a customized study plan for further assessment and focus students on areas in which they need to improve.

Speech Evaluation Tools: Instructors have access to a host of **Speech Evaluation Tools** to use in the classroom. An additional assortment of evaluation forms and guides for students and instructors offer further options and ideas for assessing presentations.

Building Speaking Confidence Center: In this special section of MySpeechLab, students will find self-assessments, strategies, video, audio, and activities that provide additional guidance and tips for overcoming their speech apprehension—all in one convenient location.

ABC News RSS feed: MySpeechLab provides online feeds from ABC news, updated hourly, to help students choose and research their speech topics.

Cutting Edge Technology

MediaShare: With this new video upload tool, students are able to upload their speeches for their instructor and classmates to watch (whether face-to-face or online) and provide online feedback and comments, including the option to include an evaluation rubric for instructors and/or students to fill out. Instructors can also opt to include a final grade when reviewing a student's video. Grades can be exported from MediaShare to a SCORM-compliant .csv spreadsheet that can be imported into most learning management systems. Structured much like a social networking site, MediaShare can help promote a sense of community among students.

AmericanRhetoric.com partnership: Through an exclusive partnership with AmericanRhetoric.com, MySpeechLab incorporates many great speeches of our time (without linking out to another site and without advertisements or commercials!). Many speeches are also accompanied by assessment questions that ask students to evaluate specific elements of those speeches.

Audio Chapter Summaries: Every chapter includes an audio chapter summary for online streaming use, perfect for students reviewing material before a test or instructors reviewing material before class.

Online Administration

No matter what course management system you use—or if you do not use one at all, but still wish to easily capture your students' grade and track their performance—Pearson has a **MySpeechLab** option to suit your administrative needs. Contact one of Pearson's Technology Specialists for more information and assistance.

A **MySpeechLab** access code is no additional cost when packaged with selected Pearson Communication texts. To get started, contact your local Pearson Publisher's Representative at **www.pearsonhighered.com/replocator.**

Acknowledgments

Many people have helped our book evolve and succeed over its twenty-five years of existence. Margaret Seawell and George Hoffman, communication editors at Houghton Mifflin, and Nader Dareshori, president of the company, were warm and helpful friends who enjoyed early good fortune with us.

More recently, we have been blessed by our relationship with two extraordinary professionals at Allyn & Bacon. Karon Bowers, Editor-in-Chief of Communication, has been responsive to our every need. She brings her sunny, constructive disposition to every challenge, and does her job exceptionally well. What can we say to her other than Thank you! And Thank you again!

For this edition especially, we offer a very large bouquet to our amazing development editor, Hilary Jackson, who has been a warm friend and trusted companion on the adventure of revising this book. Through the tough times, she has known when to pet us and when to push us. Her hands are all over this book, and if it is as successful as all of us anticipate, she must receive much of the credit. Hilary, you are simply the best!

We also thank our colleagues over all the years who have used our book and helped us to make it better. All of these people are inscribed in the Osborn family memory book. For this edition, we wish to express special gratitude to Professor Lynn Meade of the University of Arkansas, who encouraged her students to submit speeches for possible inclusion in the new edition, and with whom we exchanged ideas on the teaching of speech. Special thanks also to historian Bob Doerk, who first told us the story retold in Chapter 16 about Charlie Russell's disastrous speech in Montana, and who helped us track down the roots of the story.

We are grateful to our colleagues listed below whose critical readings have inspired improvements in the ninth edition:

Frances Brandau-Brown, Sam Houston State University

Ferald Bryan, Northern Illinois University

Monette Callaway-Ezell, Hinds Community College

Courtney Carter, Eastfield College

Laura DiBenedetto Kenyon, Monroe Community College

Alissa Duncan, Barton County Community College

Jo Anna Grant, California State University, San Bernardino

Carla Harrell, Old Dominion University

Julia Keefer, New York University

Helen Prien, Ferrum College

Cindy Stover, Metropolitan Community College

Kathleen Turner, Davidson College

Kris Willis, Appalachian State University

Mariam Willis, Appalachian State University

Public Speaking: Finding Your Voice welcomes the following new student contributors to the pages of the ninth edition:

Jess Bradshaw, Davidson College

Guy Britton, The University of Arkansas

Marty Gaines, The University of Memphis

Stephanie Lamb, The University of Arkansas

Katie Lovett, Davidson College

Elizabeth Lyles, Davidson College

Alexandra McArthur, Davidson College

Simone Mullinax, The University of Arkansas

Dolapo Olushola, Davidson College

Michael Parker, The University of Memphis

Joseph Van Matre, The University of Arkansas

Gabrielle Wallace, Davidson College

Austin Wright, The University of Texas-Austin

Benjamin Youngerman, Davidson College

PUBLIC
Speaking
FINDING YOUR VOICE

THIS CHAPTER WILL HELP YOU

1 Appreciate how this course can help you

2 Understand what this course asks of you in return

1 Finding Your Voice

> *Whenever you speak, you define a character for yourself and for at least one other—your audience—and make a community at least between the two of you.*
>
> —JAMES BOYD WHITE,
> WHEN WORDS LOSE THEIR MEANINGS

Jason was more than a little upset about having to take public speaking. He just wanted to major in nursing—what did this course have to offer him? "Just quit worrying and go to class," said his weary roommate. At the first class meeting, Jason saw twenty-five others who looked about as uncomfortable as he felt. But he decided to stick it out.

His first oral assignment was a speech of self-introduction. As he prepared his speech, it dawned on him why a career in nursing was so important to him. When he spoke, his enthusiasm for his topic helped relieve his nervousness. Although the speech was far from perfect, he had begun to build credibility for his later informative and persuasive speeches on the critical need for improved health programs.

As he listened to his classmates, Jason began to care about them and to take pleasure in their successes. As he researched his later speeches, he discovered facts, expert opinions, examples, and stories that deepened his awareness and made his listeners think. Toward the end of the term, it dawned on him: He was, in the words of one classmate, "finding his voice." He was becoming a speaker!

3

What does it mean to "find your voice"? Clearly, the phrase goes far beyond merely opening your mouth and making sounds. Rather, Jason's experience suggests at least three levels of meaning.

The first has to do with *technical competence*: To "find your voice" you have to learn how to make a speech. Despite the commonplace notion to the contrary, speakers are made, not born. They have to learn—through study, practice, and experience—the art and principles that go into speech-making. Every chapter in this book elaborates an important dimension of this knowledge.

The second level of meaning involves *self-discovery*: As you "find your voice" you become more confident in yourself. You develop self-esteem and your own style as a speaker. You also develop an increased understanding of why you are speaking. As he spoke successfully, Jason found not only his voice but a renewed appreciation for the career goals he had set for himself.

At a third level of meaning, "finding your voice" means finding your place in society, learning the value of the views and contributions of others, and discovering your ethical obligation to listeners. As you listen to others and as they respond to your words, you develop a sense of your mutual dependency. You learn, as the conservative intellectual Richard Weaver once noted, that "ideas [and the words that convey them] have consequences," and that what you say (or don't say) can be important.[1] We do live in a social world, and our speech or our silence can improve or degrade our surroundings.

"Finding your voice" is a quest that deserves your commitment. This chapter will explain further what this course has to offer and what it asks of you in return.

What Public Speaking Has to Offer You

The ability to communicate well in public settings will help establish your credentials as a competent, well-educated person. Learning to present yourself and your ideas effectively can help prepare you for some of the more important moments in your life: times when you need to speak to protect your interests, when your values are threatened by the action or inaction of others, or when you need approval to undertake some vital project.

The principles you will learn in this class should also make you a more astute consumer of public messages. They will help you sort through the barrage of information and misinformation that bombards us on a daily basis.

Beyond these important considerations, the public speaking course offers other essential practical and personal benefits. This chapter will describe them, and also will introduce you to the tradition and processes of public communication.

Practical Benefits

Your public speaking course should help you develop an array of basic communication skills, ranging from controlling your communication anxiety to expressing your ideas with power and conviction.

Developing these skills should help you succeed both in school and in your later professional life. Each year, the National Association of Colleges and Employers (NACE) surveys hundreds of corporate recruiting specialists. According to this organization,

> Employers responding to NACE's *Job Outlook 2007* survey named communication ability and integrity as a job seeker's most important skills and qualities. "Communication skills have topped the list for eight years." NACE advises: "Learn to speak clearly, confidently, and concisely."[2]

In 2009 NACE repeated its survey, during a time when the job market was much tougher. Again, as employers sought the "perfect" job candidate, the thing they prized most was communication skills.[3] Paul Baruda, who serves as an employment expert for the jobs site Monster.com, agrees that "articulating thoughts clearly and concisely will make a difference in both a job interview and subsequent job performance."

> The point is, you can be the best physicist in the world, but if you can't tell people what you do or communicate it to your co-workers, what good is all of that knowledge? I can't think of an occupation, short of living in a cave, where being able to say what you think cogently at some point in your life isn't going to be important.[4]

So unless you plan to live in a cave, what you learn in this course can be vital to your future.

These practical benefits also extend to your civic engagement throughout your life. All of us feel compelled to "speak out" from time to time to defend our vital interests and core values. Finding your voice as a speaker will help you do just that. For instance, you might find yourself wanting to speak at a school board meeting about a proposal to remove "controversial" books such as the Harry Potter series or *The Adventures of Huckleberry Finn* from reading lists or the school library. Or you may wish to speak at a city council meeting in favor of or against attempts to rezone your neighborhood for commercial development.

SPEAKER'S notes

Practical Benefits of the Public Speaking Course

This course can help you in many vital ways:

- Help you present yourself as a competent, well-educated person.
- Help you prepare for important moments in your life.
- Help you become a more critical consumer of public information.
- Help you develop basic communication skills.

- Help you control your communication anxiety.
- Help improve odds that you will succeed in college and career.
- Help you become a more effective citizen.

On campus, you might find yourself speaking for or against attempts to alter your college's affirmative admissions policy, the firing of a popular but controversial professor, or allowing religious groups to stage protests and distribute literature on school grounds. In your class, you might speak for or against stronger immigration laws, government domestic surveillance policies, allowing gay people to marry or serve openly in the military, or the right of "hate" groups such as the Ku Klux Klan to stage public rallies. As you speak on such topics, you will be enacting the citizenship role envisioned for you by those who framed the Constitution of the United States:

> Congress shall make no law respecting an establishment of religion, or prohibiting the free exercise thereof, or abridging the freedom of speech, or of the press; or the right of people peaceably to assemble, and to petition the government for a redress of grievances. (*First Amendment to the Bill of Rights*)

The political system of the United States is built on faith in open and robust public communication. Indeed, Thomas Jefferson emphasized the importance of allowing, even encouraging, the broadest range of expression as vital to the health and survival of a democratic society. He reasoned that if citizens are the repositories of political power, then our understanding must be nourished by a full and free flow of information and exchange of opinions so that we can make good decisions on matters such as who should lead us and which public policies we should support.

Public speaking classes therefore become laboratories for the democratic process.[5] Developing, presenting, and listening to speeches should help you develop your citizenship skills. Preparation for your role as citizen is a practical benefit that serves not just you but the society in which you live.

Personal Benefits

Other benefits of this course are more personal in nature. These include learning more about yourself and expanding your cultural horizons.

Learning More about Yourself. In a very real sense, we are the sum of our communication experiences with other people. As you put together speeches on topics that you care about, you will explore your own interests and values, expand your base of knowledge, and develop your skills of creative expression. In short, you will be seeking your own voice as a unique individual, a voice distinct from all other voices. As Roderick Hart has put the matter: "Communication is the ultimate people-making discipline. . . . To become eloquent is to activate one's humanity, to apply the imagination, and to solve the practical problems of human living."[6]

As you adapt to diverse audiences, you will also develop a heightened sensitivity to the interests and needs of others—what one might call an "other-orientation." The public speaking class invites us to listen to one another, to savor what makes each of us unique and valuable, and to develop an appreciation for the different ways people live. Your experiences should bring you closer to meeting one of the major goals of higher education: "to expand the mind and heart beyond fear of the unknown, opening them to the whole range of human experience."[7]

Finally, as you learn to speak and listen, you will gain a richer and more sophisticated appreciation of the world around you. You will be encouraged to seek out and consider multiple perspectives on controversial issues before committing yourself. Public speaking classes are unique in that they make you an active participant in your own education. You don't just sit in class, absorbing lectures. You communicate. And as you communicate, you help your class become a learning community. It is no accident that the words *communication* and *community* are closely connected.

Expanding Cultural Horizons. Today's typical public speaking class offers a sampling of different races, religions, and cultural backgrounds from which you can learn.

What barriers might stand in the way of expanding your cultural horizons as you listen to others in classroom speeches? One such barrier could be **ethnocentrism**, our tendency to presume that our own cultural ways of seeing and doing things are the proper standard and that other such world views and behaviors are at best suspect and at worst inferior. There is nothing inherently wrong with being a proud American or a proud Native American or a proud New Yorker. But when we allow

Public speaking is vital to the maintenance of a free society. The right to assemble and speak on public issues is guaranteed by the Bill of Rights.

FINDING YOUR

voice   The Story of Your Quest

Keep a diary in which you record your feelings and experiences as you navigate this class. As one of your first entries, consider what you think "Finding Your Voice" might mean to you. At the end of the course, bring this entry up to date, reframing the question as "What has 'finding your voice' meant to you in this class?" and "What do you think 'finding your voice' might mean to you in the future?"

▶ **ethnocentrism**   The tendency of any nation, race, religion, or group to believe that its way of looking at and doing things is right and that other perspectives have less value.

The audience in your public speaking class may represent different cultural backgrounds.

this pride to harden into arrogance, condescension, and hostility toward others, it becomes a formidable barrier to intercultural communication.

If you had attended college a few decades ago, you might have encountered the unquestioned assumption that our country is a "melting pot" that fuses the cultures of immigrant peoples into a superior alloy called "the American character." The melting pot idea may seem harmless, but the "ideal American" it suggests often had a white male face. Historically, women and certain minority groups were excluded from the public dialogue that shaped values and policies. Moreover, the idea of a melting pot does not prepare us for the diversity of audiences we encounter both in classes and in later life. Elizabeth Lozano summarizes the shortcomings of the melting pot image and proposes an alternative view of American culture:

> The "melting pot" is not an adequate metaphor for a country which is comprised of a multiplicity of cultural backgrounds . . . . [W]e might better think of the United States in terms of a "cultural bouillabaisse" in which all ingredients conserve their unique flavor, while also transforming and being transformed by the adjacent textures and scents.[8]

A public speaking class is an ideal place to savor this rich broth of cultures. As we hear others speak, we may discover the many flavors of the American experience. And as you examine your own identity and that of the people around you, you may well discover that most of us in this country are indeed "multicultural," a blend of many voices and backgrounds. If you want to speak effectively and ethically before American audiences, a sensitivity toward and appreciation for cultural diversity is truly necessary.

A second barrier rises in the form of **stereotypes**, those generalized assumptions that supposedly represent the essential nature of races, genders, religious affiliations, sexual orientations, and so on. Before we get to know the individual members of our audience, we may invoke stereotypes to anticipate how they will react to our words. Even seemingly positive stereotypes—Asian Americans are good at math, Mexican Americans have a strong devotion to family—can be hurtful if they block us from experiencing the unique humanity of someone who just happens to be an Asian American or Mexican American. As a general rule, nobody likes to feel that he or she is being addressed as an "other" by another "other." So pack your stereotypes away as you enter the public speaking class. You may discover that they are not very useful after all.

One of our favorite ways of depicting the complex culture of the United States was introduced in the conclusion of Abraham Lincoln's first inaugural address, as Lincoln sought to hold the nation together on the eve of the Civil War:

> The mystic chords of memory, stretching from every battlefield, and patriot grave, to every living heart and hearthstone, all over this broad land, will yet swell the chorus of the Union, when again touched, as surely they will be, by the better angels of our nature.[9]

Lincoln's image of America as a harmonious chorus implied that the individual voices of Americans will create a music together far more beautiful than any one voice alone.

▶ **stereotypes** Generalized pictures of a race, gender, or group that supposedly represent its essential characteristics.

FINDING YOUR

voice
Ways of Thinking about American Identity

Is it better to think of American culture as a "bouillabaisse" or "chorus" rather than as a "melting pot"? Can you think of other desirable ways of expressing American identity?

Lincoln's vision holds forth a continuing dream of a society in which individualism and the common good not only will survive but will also enhance each other.

In your class and within this book, you will hear many voices: Native Americans and new Americans, women and men, conservatives and liberals, Americans of all different colors and lifestyles. Despite their many differences, all of them are a part of the vital chorus of our nation. Public speaking gives you the opportunity to hear these voices and add yours to them.

Introduction to Communication

The study of public speaking also offers an entrance into the larger subject of how people communicate, both to the tradition of the study and to the elements that interact within the communication process.

The Tradition of the Study

Some people are surprised to learn that the study and practice of public speaking rests upon a rich intellectual history that extends back over two thousand years to the ancient Greeks—the same people credited with introducing democracy to Western civilization. In an age long before the printing press, Internet, and 24-hour cable-news service, public speaking served as the major means of disseminating ideas and information, resolving legal disputes, and debating political issues.

In those long-ago years, there were no professional lawyers, and citizens were expected to speak for themselves in legal proceedings and as active participants in the deliberations that shaped public policy. Most of all, the Greeks considered the power and eloquence of the spoken word as necessary to virtuous behavior.[10] One of their greatest leaders, Pericles, reflects this attitude in a much-celebrated speech:

> For we alone think that a man that does not take part in public affairs is good for nothing, while others only say that he is "minding his own business." We are the ones who develop policy, or at least decide what is to be done, for we believe that what spoils action is not speeches, but going into action without first being instructed through speeches. In this too we excel over others: ours is the bravery of people who think through what they will take in hand, and discuss it thoroughly; with other men, ignorance makes them brave and thinking makes them cowards.[11]

We are heirs to this tradition of "participative democracy" enabled by "participative communication."[12] When citizens gather today in virtual or actual rooms to discuss and debate together the policies that shall govern their lives, they are re-enacting Pericles' dream of an empowered citizenship. Not only do they exercise their individual voices, but they also seek together to find and create what the National Issues Forums Institute has called "the Public Voice," a collective position that represents an informed majority position on issues of the day.[13] We may feel compelled to speak out about an issue in our communities or on campus, or we may join the national debate about health care or the environment. As we communicate with others, either face-to-face or on the Internet, we learn what techniques work or don't work in different situations. We explore ideas together, and often enrich our options. We learn what causes are important to us and what messages we want to convey. "Finding your voice" remains as relevant today as it was in the time of Pericles.

Throughout this book, we shall draw upon the classic rhetorical tradition to help us understand both *how to communicate* and *how we ought to communicate*. In short, the ancients should help us grasp both the techniques and ethics of speaking in public, whether in the marketplace or in cyberspace.

Pericles' speech left a vital question unresolved: *What is the well-rounded communicator, the citizen ready to perform his or her vital role in self-government and in society?* The Greek philosopher who stepped up to the challenge of this question was Aristotle, who first explored systematically the study of public speaking. In his *Rhetoric*, Aristotle implies that the well-rounded communicator reasons with listeners in full knowledge of our communication natures (read the *Rhetoric* online at http://classics.mit.edu/Aristotle/rhetoric.html). We like to think we are creatures of reason: The able speaker offers us arguments based upon evidence and logic. We are also moral beings who commit ourselves to private, public, and often religious values: The able speaker must prove to our satisfaction that certain courses of action will respect and advance these values while other options would subvert or defeat them. We are also creatures of strong self-interest: What's in it for us is a powerful consideration, and able speakers must show exactly that. Moreover, we are creatures of feeling and affection for others: The able speaker must appeal to this emotional side of our nature as part of an overall communication strategy. Finally, we are cautious creatures who judge the motives and character of those who speak to us: we trust or distrust them in light of their perceived abilities, character, and personalities—whether they seem stable, likable, and attractive people who have our interests at heart. In short, Aristotle makes it abundantly clear that "finding your voice" means not only finding yourself but also grasping the complexities of those with whom we communicate. He also recognized that unlike pure logic, reasoning on public problems usually involves uncertainties and—at best—probabilities. In the murky waters of everyday problems, absolute certainty can be hard to come by. But the constructive public speaker helps listeners arrive at an informed judgment on troublesome issues. When considering issues on which reasonable people can differ, well-informed listeners are in a better position to evaluate the different options that are open to them.

Raphael's painting shows *The School of Athens* where rhetorical skills were part of the basic curriculum.

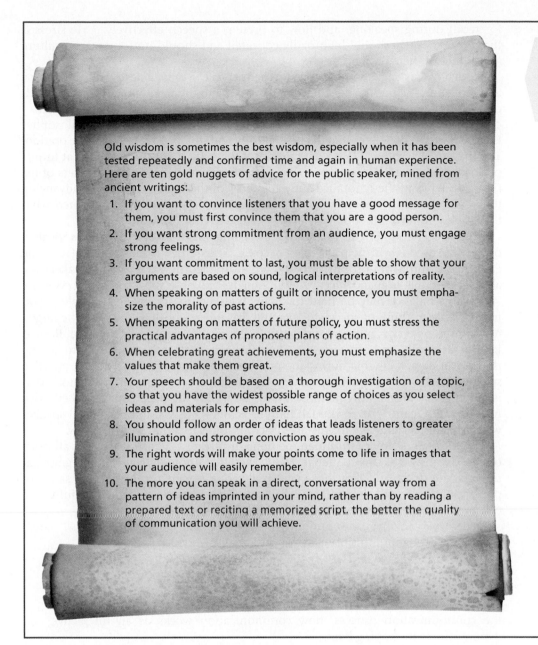

FIGURE 1.1 Ten Timeless Lessons from the Ancient World

Old wisdom is sometimes the best wisdom, especially when it has been tested repeatedly and confirmed time and again in human experience. Here are ten gold nuggets of advice for the public speaker, mined from ancient writings:

1. If you want to convince listeners that you have a good message for them, you must first convince them that you are a good person.

2. If you want strong commitment from an audience, you must engage strong feelings.

3. If you want commitment to last, you must be able to show that your arguments are based on sound, logical interpretations of reality.

4. When speaking on matters of guilt or innocence, you must emphasize the morality of past actions.

5. When speaking on matters of future policy, you must stress the practical advantages of proposed plans of action.

6. When celebrating great achievements, you must emphasize the values that make them great.

7. Your speech should be based on a thorough investigation of a topic, so that you have the widest possible range of choices as you select ideas and materials for emphasis.

8. You should follow an order of ideas that leads listeners to greater illumination and stronger conviction as you speak.

9. The right words will make your points come to life in images that your audience will easily remember.

10. The more you can speak in a direct, conversational way from a pattern of ideas imprinted in your mind, rather than by reading a prepared text or reciting a memorized script, the better the quality of communication you will achieve.

As he explored the versatility required of the speaker, Aristotle described three prominent forms of speaking: political, legal, and ceremonial, which we encounter, respectively, when we gather to decide on future policy, judge the past, and celebrate the moment. We may "find our voice" in any or all these arenas of public speaking.

Aristotle's *Rhetoric* laid the groundwork for the Romans, who would further develop the education of speakers.[14] Cicero, one of the most celebrated orators of antiquity, described rhetoric as "an art made up of five great arts." In his *De Oratore*, he concentrated on how to think through and defend positions, how to arrange and organize arguments, how to use language effectively, how to store ideas in the mind for recall during speaking, and how to present a speech effectively.[15] He stressed that ideal speakers should be broadly educated and should understand the culture and values of their audiences.

Much of this ancient knowledge focused on *how to communicate*, teaching the art and techniques of public speaking. The second major theme that developed in classical writings concerned *how we ought to communicate*, which considers the power of communication and how it might be managed ethically. The Greek philosopher Plato wrote two dialogues that deal specifically with the power of the public oration. The first, *Gorgias*, offers Plato's dark vision of the subject (read the *Gorgias* at http://philosophy.eserver.org/plato/gorgias.txt). He charged that the public speakers of his time pandered to the ignorance and prejudices of the masses instead of advancing their own visions of what was right. These orators too often told their listeners what they *wanted* to hear rather than what they *needed* to hear.[16] Sound familiar?

In the second dialogue, *Phaedrus*, Plato paints his ideal of the virtuous speaker, one whose words will help listeners become better citizens and people (read the *Phaedrus* at http://philosophy.eserver.org/plato/phaedrus.txt).[17] Such speakers are able to be both ethical and effective, even though Plato observed—somewhat cynically—that this balance may be hard for many speakers to achieve. Nevertheless, you may be able to think of successful examples of those who have hit near the target, depending on your political orientation. Many, for example, describe Ronald Reagan's rhetoric as both virtuous and effective, while others may point to the rhetoric of Barack Obama during the political campaign of 2008. Indeed, effective speaking that is not ethical may quickly lose its influence, while ethical rhetoric that is not effective may simply be futile. Plato's goal of being both ethical and effective may be quite realistic, even though hard to achieve. His vision of the ideal speaker would remain a challenge for the ages of communicators that would follow.

The Roman scholar Quintilian, perhaps the greatest speech teacher of all time, offered an answer to this challenge. He insisted that immediate effects and gratifications fade quickly, and that those who build their careers on the shifting sands of public popularity will soon fall into disfavor. To be a good speaker whose influence endures, he argued, *one must be a good person*.[18]

These two themes from antiquity—"What works?" and "What's right?"—will occupy us throughout this book as you seek your own voice as a speaker.

Knowledge of the Communication Process

Contemporary scientists and philosophers continue to enrich our understanding of the communication process: how communication works as an interactive and dynamic force in shaping lives.

Public Speaking as an Interactive Process. A speech is not an art object produced for the admiration of onlookers. Instead, *a speech is an interactive process that attempts to do important work: to introduce the speaker to listeners, to share knowledge with them, to convince them of the rightness or wrongness of certain attitudes and actions, or to celebrate with them some special moments.* A speech is an action performed with the help of listeners, and gets its job done when the audience learns, accepts the speaker's point of view, and/or joins the celebration. In short, the meaning of speeches is a joint production, a collaborative process that requires the work of both speakers and listeners. As others respond to your words, they will help you find your voice.

Examining a public speech closely, we can identify six elements that are critical to its nature: speaker, message, occasion, audience, interference, and feedback.

Speaker. There can be no speeches without **speakers**, those who present oral messages for public consumption. Because the fate of speeches turns especially on how listeners respond, speakers are audience-centered. Ethical speakers believe that their messages will improve listeners, and help them think critically, creatively, and constructively about issues.

Whether listeners accept a speaker as credible is clearly crucial to the interaction: If listeners think a speaker is competent, likable, and trustworthy, and shares their interests and goals, they will be more likely to accept the speaker's message. We discuss establishing yourself as a credible speaker in Chapter 3.

Message. A speech must have a **message**, a clear conception of what it wishes to accomplish. To establish its message, a speech follows a design and a strategy. To make its message clear and attractive, a speech uses words artfully and often employs presentation aids such as graphs, charts, or photographs projected on a large screen. To make its message credible, a speech will offer convincing evidence and reasoning. To make its message forceful and impressive, a speech will call upon all the speaker's presentational skills—his or her voice, body language, and platform presence. How to convey messages successfully is the major business of this book.

Occasion. The **occasion** of a speech is the reason why speakers and listeners gather in certain places at certain times for certain purposes. Some occasions are obvious: You will be speaking at certain times and places because your class requires it of you. On the job, you may speak at certain meetings because you have ideas to contribute or have been asked to report on an issue.

At other times, arranging the occasion for a speech may be far more challenging. One of your authors, while managing an election campaign, wanted to use the "free speech" platform on a nearby university campus as the dramatic setting for his candidate's speech on education reform. To make this happen he (1) had to obtain permission from university officials for an "outsider" to use the platform, (2) arrange for sound equipment so that the candidate might be heard, (3) decorate the platform so that it would be visually appealing, (4) ask some colleagues to announce the event in their classes to assure a "live" audience, and (5) urge local media—especially television stations—to "cover" the event, thereby providing access to the much larger, intended audience for the speech. In this case, arranging for the speech occasion was itself an exhausting, difficult challenge.

This example suggests that the **setting** for a speech can be an important part of the occasion. The setting often affects how messages are constructed, presented, and received. The *physical setting* includes such factors as the actual place where the speech is presented, the time of day, and the size and arrangement of the audience. The open and outdoor physical setting of the free speech platform called for a speech with a simple structure of ideas, vivid and concrete language, colorful examples that would catch and hold attention from passersby, and good sound amplifiers. Similarly, but on a much grander scale, when Martin Luther King, Jr., described his "dream" of people of color participating fully in the promise of America, he spoke under the watchful eyes of Lincoln's statue to a vast audience gathered at the Lincoln Memorial in Washington, D.C. The very setting of the speech entered its text and affected profoundly how these listeners—hundreds of thousands of them in the actual audience and millions more listening on radio or watching on television —would respond.

Speeches can also have a *psychological setting* that includes such considerations as the inclinations that listeners bring to the speaking situation and the context of recent events. For instance, if you have planned a speech attacking oppressive campus security

▶ **speakers** Those who present oral messages for public consumption.

▶ **message** What speakers wish to accomplish.

▶ **occasion** Why speakers and listeners gather to present and listen to speeches.

▶ **setting** Physical and psychological context in which a speech is presented.

measures, and right before your speech a frightening and well-publicized crime is committed on your campus, the psychological setting for your speech may suddenly be less receptive. We shall say more about the occasion and setting of a speech in Chapter 5.

Audience. Questions concerning the **audience** for speaking—those who hear but don't really listen, those whom the speaker would like to listen, and those who actually do listen—can quickly become complicated. For example, in planning the free speech platform occasion, it was necessary to arrange for a live audience as the excuse for having the speech to begin with. But this apparent audience of a few students was not the actual target audience for the speech. Rather, the intended audience was the much larger group of viewers who might catch a few soundbites from the speech on the evening news.

Similarly, in our time "speakers" may broadcast their overheated messages on YouTube, hoping to engage a portion of the global audience that congregates on the world wide web. They cast their speeches like nets into that vast undifferentiated sea of listeners, and occasionally enjoy spectacular catches. Rep. Alan Grayson (D-FL) reproduced on YouTube his congressional speech accusing Republicans of offering one health plan on the theme "Don't get sick," and another plan for the sick: "Die quickly." Ten thousand viewers offered a total of more than $250,000 to his re-election campaign after that effort. According to *Time*, Rep. Michele Bachmann (R-MN) wondered whether health reform "would allow a 13-year-old girl to use a school 'sex clinic' to get a referral for an abortion and 'go home on the school bus that night.' She raised the question of whether President Obama "may have anti-American views" and accused him of creating a "gangster government." She received a cascade of contributions after these rhetorical efforts.[19]

Such speakers obviously hope to carve out audiences for themselves from the limitless possibilities offered on the Internet. They offer an unconscious parody of the words offered by John Milton as he presented his great epic poem, *Paradise Lost*: "Fit readers find, though few." Rather, their implied mantra is "Unfit viewers find, though many."

Questions about the nature of the audience—who are the actual, virtual, and intended listeners and what ethical constraints should govern listening—abound. Even when those actually present are the intended audience, ethical questions persist. All teachers know that students can sometimes feign listening, while absorbing little of what they are hearing. Are they an audience, just because they are seated in front of the speaker? Occasionally, speakers may "perform" a speech. They seem to care little about whether others are actually listening or might benefit from what they are saying. So do these speakers constitute their own audience?

Finding your voice as a speaker can also require that you discover your ears as an audience member. If you want others to give you encouragement and a fair hearing, you must be a good listener in return. What are others saying that you can use? How can you help them grow as a speaker by being a good listener? We shall say more about what constitutes a fit audience later in this chapter and in Chapter 4.

Interference. Occasionally, the flow of a message can be interrupted by distractions. These distractions function as **interference** that can disrupt the communication process.

Outside the classroom, in cyberspace or in community meetings, interference in the form of relentless heckling and even verbal abuse has become an occasional but appalling feature of the communication practices of our time. Such lack of civility is an enemy of the free and open flow of communication that is essential to democratic forms of government.

Fortunately, you will experience little if any such hostile interference in your classroom presentations. But what if you have just started your speech, and you

▶ **audience**   Includes those whom speakers would like to listen, as well as others who actually listen.

▶ **interference**   Distractions that can disrupt the communication process.

are drowned out by laughter in the hall? What if the classroom door opens, and someone late for class walks up to a seat on the front row? Whatever happens, don't let such thoughtless interference disturb your composure. Usually, if you pause and smile, the distractions will fade. Often a little impromptu humor will disarm the situation, and show that you are still in control. We discuss interference problems in greater detail in Chapters 4 and 5.

Feedback. As you speak, you should be picking up cues from your audience that will help you adjust to the ongoing situation. These cues constitute **feedback** that helps you monitor the immediate effectiveness of your message. The need for feedback is one reason why you should maintain eye contact with listeners and not be focusing on your notes or gazing out the window or up at the ceiling.

This charismatic speaker seems dynamic and likable.

What if listeners are straining forward in their seats? This suggests they may not be able to hear you. You may have to increase the loudness of your voice and raise the energy level of your presentation. What if they look puzzled? You may need to provide an example to clarify your point. What if they are frowning or shaking their heads? Offer additional evidence to convince them.

On the other hand, suppose they are smiling and nodding in agreement. You are on the right track! Sometimes you will sense that listeners are so caught up in what you are saying that you know you are getting through to them. That's the moment when you know you are finding your voice! We discuss feedback further in Chapter 12.

These six elements—speaker, message, occasion, audience, interference, and feedback—all interact in the adventure of public speaking.

Public Speaking as a Dynamic Process.   Kenneth Burke, one of the major communication theorists of our time, suggested that speakers are constantly confronting the problem of listeners who feel powerless and who don't see themselves as members of a community. A basic challenge that speakers must meet is to bring these listeners together so that they can recognize their common interests and realize what they can accomplish together.

The first day you enter your public speaking class, you encounter a group of other students. Perhaps a few of them know each other, but most are strangers. Many are frightened about the "ordeal" they believe they will soon have to endure.

FINDING YOUR

voice   Framing a Model of the Six Elements

You have been asked to give an informative speech explaining the six elements that make up the public speaking experience. Develop a visual model that displays the relationships among these elements. Compare these in class. What might be the advantages of using your model in your hypothetical speech? Might there be any disadvantages?

▶ **feedback**   Speaker's perception of audience reactions to the message.

FIGURE 1.2 Public Speaking as a Dynamic Process: When Communication Works

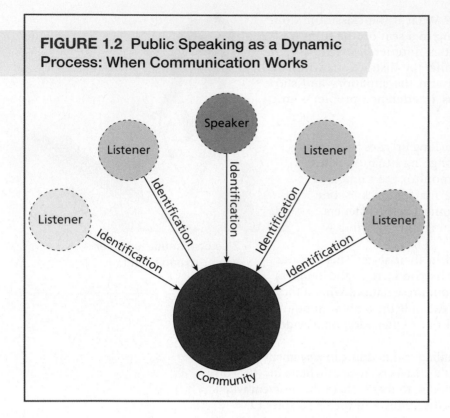

They may feel isolated and vulnerable. So when you first stand to speak, a major task may be to tear down the invisible walls that separate you from listeners and listeners from each other. Can you tell them stories that will remind them of shared experiences? Can you help them laugh together? If so, you will have begun Burke's work of **identification**, creating *the feeling that audience members share with you and with each other experiences, values, fears, desires, and dreams—that they are, in effect, a community.*[20]

Successful public speaking is a dynamic process that changes people and the relationships among them. Burke's concept of identification is a concept we draw upon throughout this book, because it helps explain so much. For example, it helps explain the power of the appeal offered in Anna Aley's speech protesting slum housing in her campus town of Manhattan, Kansas:

What can one student do to change the practices of numerous Manhattan landlords? Nothing, if that student is alone. But just think of what we could accomplish if we got all 13,600 off-campus students involved in this issue! Think what we could accomplish if we got even a fraction of those students involved! [See Anna Aley's speech in Appendix B.]

Anna, a Kansas State University student, helped her listeners realize that they were *victims* of slum housing. In other words, she pointed out their *identity*. And she offered a new, dynamic vision of themselves acting together to correct these abuses.

Identification also helps explain the power of public speaking on the wider stage of public affairs. When Martin Luther King, Jr., strove to change racial practices in America, he offered an answer for the legacy of humiliation and segregation that continued to divide Americans. In his celebrated speech "I Have a Dream," King offered a vision of identification as an answer to the old racial divisions:

I have a dream that . . . one day right there in Alabama little black boys and black girls will be able to join hands with little white boys and white girls as sisters and brothers. I have a dream today.[21]

As his leadership emerged, King's own image seemed to grow and expand. And his followers also became heroic figures as they marched through one ordeal after another. These transformations indicate how people can grow and enlarge when they interact in ethical communication that inspires and encourages them. Plato told us long ago in the *Phaedrus* about ethical communication that nourishes listeners by expanding

▶ **identification** The feeling of closeness between speakers and listeners that may overcome personal and cultural differences.

their horizons of knowledge. In your modest way, you too can contribute to this process through your classroom speeches. The connection between Kenneth Burke and Plato, identification and ethical communication, leads into our next section.

What This Course Asks of You

A course that offers so much requires a great deal in return. It asks that you make a serious commitment of time and dedication to finding your voice as a speaker. It asks also that you carefully practice **public speaking ethics**, the search for *standards*

**FIGURE 1.3
Credo for Ethical
Communication**

[*As you read this code adopted by the National Communication Association, think of situations in which one or more of these principles may have been threatened or violated. Are there other ethical principles that might be added to the list?*]

Questions of right and wrong arise whenever people communicate. Ethical communication is fundamental to responsible thinking, decision making, and the development of relationships and communities within and across contexts, cultures, channels, and media. Moreover, ethical communication enhances human worth and dignity by fostering truthfulness, fairness, responsibility, personal integrity, and respect for self and others. We believe that unethical communication threatens the quality of all communication and consequently the well-being of individuals and the society in which we live. Therefore we, the members of the National Communication Association, endorse and are committed to practicing the following principles of ethical communication.

- We advocate truthfulness, accuracy, honesty, and reason as essential to the integrity of communication.

- We endorse freedom of expression, diversity of perspective, and tolerance of dissent to achieve the informed and responsible decision making fundamental to a civil society.

- We strive to understand and respect other communicators before evaluating and responding to their messages.

- We promote access to communication resources and opportunities as necessary to fulfill human potential and contribute to the well-being of families, communities, and society.

- We promote communication climates of caring and mutual understanding that respect the unique needs and characteristics of individual communicators.

- We condemn communication that degrades individuals and humanity through distortion, intimidation, coercion, and violence and through the expression of intolerance and hatred.

- We are committed to the courageous expression of personal convictions in pursuit of fairness and justice.

- We advocate sharing information, opinions, and feelings when facing significant choices while also respecting privacy and confidentiality.

- We accept responsibility for the short- and long-term consequences for our own communication and expect the same of others.[22]

▶ **public speaking ethics** Standards for judging the rightness or wrongness of public speaking behaviors.

for judging the rightness or wrongness of public speaking behaviors, and that you apply what you learn in your speaking and listening. The National Communication Association in its "Credo for Ethical Communication" offers a list of principles that may help you begin your quest.

Specific moral questions can arise in every phase of speech-making, from topic selection to making the actual presentation. For this reason, you will encounter situation-grounded discussions and "Your Ethical Voice" features throughout this text. In this final section, we discuss three major considerations that underlie ethical public speaking: *respect for the integrity of ideas and information, a genuine concern for consequences, and the shared responsibilities of listeners.*

Respect for the Integrity of Ideas and Information

In an age when misinformation and outright lies often circulate unchallenged on the Internet, when passion and prejudice—loudly asserted—too often take the place of sound reasoning, and when people "tweet" more than they think, it is good to remind ourselves that respect for the integrity of ideas and information is a basic principle of better communication. This respect requires that you speak from responsible knowledge, use communication techniques carefully, and avoid a set of practices described collectively as plagiarism.

Speaking from Responsible Knowledge.   No one expects you to become an expert on the topics you speak about in class. You will, however, be expected to speak from **responsible knowledge**. As we discuss in detail in Chapter 7, responsible knowledge of topics includes

- knowing main points of concern about them.

- understanding what experts believe about them.

- acknowledging differing points of view on controversial topics and giving these fair treatment in speeches.

- being aware of the most recent events or discoveries concerning them.

- realizing how topics might affect the lives of listeners.

In short, *responsible knowledge* is not perfect or exact, but it is the best that might reasonably be expected, given the circumstances.

Consider how Stephen Huff, one of our students at the University of Memphis, acquired responsible knowledge for an informative speech. Stephen knew little about earthquakes before his speech, but he knew that Memphis was on the New Madrid fault and that this could mean trouble. He also knew that an earthquake research center was located on campus.

Stephen arranged for an interview with the center's director. During the interview, he asked a series of well-planned questions: Where was the New Madrid fault, and what was the history of its activity? What was the probability of a major quake in the near future? How prepared was Memphis for a major quake? What kind of damage could result? How could listeners prepare for it? What readings would he recommend?

All these questions were designed to gain knowledge that would interest and benefit his listeners. Armed with what he had learned, Stephen went online and then to the library, where he found other valuable sources of information. He was well on his way to speaking from responsible knowledge.

▶ **responsible knowledge** An understanding of the major features, issues, information, latest developments, and local applications relevant to a topic.

Responsible Use of Communication Techniques. Unethical speakers can misuse valuable techniques for communicating ideas and information in order to confuse listeners or to hide a private agenda. Consider, for instance, the practice called **quoting out of context**. In Chapter 8, we encourage you to cite experts and respected authorities to support important and controversial assertions. However, this technique is corrupted when speakers twist the meanings of such statements to support their own views and to endorse positions these respected persons would never have accepted.

Speakers sometimes invoke Martin Luther King's "dream" of a color-blind society to roll back reforms that he helped to inspire. In his "I Have a Dream" speech, for example, King offered his vision of a world in which we would judge people "not by the color of their skin but by the content of their character." One state official offered these words to justify ending scholarships targeted for minority students. A governor used the same dream to explain why he was appointing only white men to the board running the university system in his state. A well-known theater critic in New York invoked King's vision to condemn the formation of black theatrical companies.[23] These people applied King's words *out of the context* of his speech to defeat his actual purpose.

Throughout this text, we warn you in specific situations how evidence, reasoning, language, humor, visual aids, and other powerful communication techniques can be abused to deceive audiences and undermine constructive communication.

Avoiding Academic Dishonesty. In the public speaking classroom, the most disheartening form of academic dishonesty is **plagiarism**, *presenting the ideas or words of others as though they were your own.*[24] Plagiarism mutates into specific forms of intellectual abuse, such as "parroting" an article or speech from a newspaper, magazine, or Internet site without crediting the source in your speech. In effect, you offer the work as though it were your own creation.

Another corrupt form is "patchwork plagiarism," cutting passages from multiple sources and splicing them together as though they were one speech, *your* speech. Then there is a kind of "social plagiarism," in which students collude to produce one speech which they then present in different sections of the public speaking course. Sadly, we must report that outside the classroom as well, speakers and writers often falsify evidence and the sources and dates of information.

There are many good reasons for you to avoid such bad behaviors. Most colleges and universities regard them as a serious threat to the integrity of higher education, and stipulate penalties ranging from a major grade reduction to suspension or even expulsion from the university. You can probably find your university's policy in your student handbook or on your college website. Your communication department or instructor may have additional rules regarding academic dishonesty.

So the first good reason to avoid plagiarism in its various forms is that universities take it seriously and *you might get caught*. Instructors are better at spotting academic dishonesty than some students may realize. Many departments keep files of speeches and speech outlines, instructors do talk to each other, and there are Internet resources that instructors can use for looking up "stock" speeches that have been lifted from the Internet. Professional associations are constantly updating speech instructors on how to detect plagiarism.[25]

A second, even better reason for avoiding plagiarism is to realize it for what it is: *an intellectual crime*, the theft and/or abuse of other people's ideas. You would not steal the property of others; is it less wrong to steal the creative products of their minds? If you credit the thinking of others in your speech by citing your sources honestly, you honor them. If you plagiarize, you abuse them.

▶ **quoting out of context** An unethical use of a quotation that changes or distorts its original meaning.

▶ **plagiarism** Presenting the ideas and words of others as though they were your own.

YOUR ethical VOICE   Avoiding Plagiarism

Avoiding plagiarism is a matter of faith between you, your instructor, and your classmates. Be especially alert to the following:

1. Don't present or summarize someone else's speech, article, or essay as though it were your own.

2. Draw information and ideas from a variety of sources, then interpret them to create your own point of view.

3. Don't parrot other people's language and ideas as though they were your own.

4. Always provide oral citations for direct quotations, paraphrased material, or especially striking language, letting listeners know who said the words, where, and when.

5. Credit those who originate ideas as you introduce their statements in your speech:

   "Studs Terkel has said that a book about work 'is, by its very nature, about violence—to the spirit as well as the body.'"

6. Allow yourself enough time to research and prepare your presentation responsibly.

7. Take careful notes as you do your research so that you don't later confuse your own thoughts and words with those of others.

The most compelling reason for avoiding plagiarism is that *you are robbing and cheating yourself*. The plagiarized voice is a fraud. When you plagiarize, you give up your search for your authentic voice, and prevent yourself from growing into the communicator you might become. When you do not prepare your own work, you likely will not speak very well anyway. You end up compromising all the benefits we have described.

Your Ethical Voice offers a number of ways to avoid plagiarism. Study them carefully, and put them to work in your speeches.

A Concern for Consequences

Finding your voice also means finding others, listeners who share interests, dreams, and concerns, as well as finding your place in the community. You can't help but be concerned about how your words will impact the lives of your audience.

A related concern is the impact of our speaking on the quality and integrity of public communication itself. That we are undergoing a crisis of quality and civility in public communication practices seems obvious: Robust and spirited debate of ideas is a dream of democracy, but perverse practices such as the verbal abuse of opponents and shrill heckling that seeks to drown out others rather than answer their arguments are democracy's nightmare. In such a corrupt age, we need to set a higher standard of more honorable communication practices.

There can be occasions that tempt us, times when the right ends might seem to justify questionable means. In the final days of a heated political campaign, for example, when we are certain that "we're right" and "they're wrong," it may seem acceptable for our preferred candidates to rely on character attacks, fear-mongering, and fallacies of reasoning such as those we discuss in Chapter 15. But we need to ask ourselves whether these slips from grace are worth the long-term consequence of adding to a communication climate in which unethical practices are—as some might say—"justified under certain circumstances." Public speaking in democratic societies should elevate, not degrade the public mind. In a world of increasing incivility, we must preserve and protect the goal of informed and rational decision-making made possible only by open, tolerant, and respectful discussion of ideas.[26]

FINDING YOUR
voice   Becoming a Critic of Public Speaking

"Finding Your Voice: The Story of Your Quest" (p. 7) suggests that you keep a diary in which you describe your experiences during this class in finding your voice. Add a speech evaluation dimension to this diary by commenting on effective and ineffective, ethical and unethical speeches you hear both in and out of class, including local and national media, YouTube, and other sources. As you listen to speeches, ask yourself:

1. How did the speaker register in terms of credibility?
2. Was the speech well adapted to listeners' needs and interests?
3. Did the speech take into account the cultural makeup of its audience?
4. Was the message clear and well structured?
5. Was the language and presentation of the speech effective?
6. How did listeners respond, both during and after the speech?
7. Did the setting have any impact on the message?

8. Did the speech have any interference problems to overcome?
9. Did the speech promote identification between speaker and listeners?
10. Did the speaker demonstrate responsible knowledge and an ethical use of communication techniques?
11. Did listeners meet their responsibilities as critical, constructive listeners?

Toward the end of the term, complete your personal narrative on "finding your voice," and summarize and interpret what you have learned about the ethics and effectiveness of speech-making. Share these with your instructor.

FINAL
reflections   The Fate of Public Discourse

Listeners as well as speakers carry grave responsibilities for the fate of public discourse. Often we encounter people who have grown disenchanted with the quality of public conversation and the very prospect of democracy. It is disheartening to hear them cite their cynicism as an excuse for "tuning out" and ignoring public issues altogether. Nothing does more to reinforce dishonesty and demagoguery in public discussions than when good people decide to turn the other way and abandon the public forum to those who would abuse it. If public speaking is to be ethical, then listeners must play the critical and constructive roles we assign to them in Chapter 4.

When one reflects upon it, playing an honorable role as speaker and listener is a small price to pay for the fountain of benefits described in this chapter. At the outset, therefore, we urge you to accept this role and we offer a toast: Here's to a successful adventure as you find your voice as a public speaker!

THIS CHAPTER WILL HELP YOU

1 Put your fear of public speaking into perspective
2 Understand communication anxiety
3 Learn ways to manage communication anxiety

2 Managing Your Fear of Speaking

> *Bravery is being the only one who knows you're afraid.*
>
> —DAVID HACKWORTH

Betsy Lyles, shown here, enjoyed much success in her public speaking class at Davidson College. After she completed the class, she was invited to become a Speaking Center tutor so that other student speakers might benefit from her help. Certainly Betsy is the kind of speaker who never suffered from communication anxiety (CA), right? Listen to her story:

"I felt like I was experienced with public speaking—I had given speeches to peers in high school and had lots of experience reading the lectionary at church. I normally heard positive responses from people about my public speaking; however, standing up to give my first COM 101 speech made me realize that my prior experience didn't mean I was immune to CA. When I stood up to give my first informal speech, I wanted to appear confident but my face was red, my body felt really warm and I began to fidget. I was less than graceful to say the least! It was a problem for me because I didn't want to think of myself as a poor public speaker. I wanted to begin with a high standard for myself and get better from there.

"For my next speech, I knew I had to do something to work against the apprehension. One of the most noticeable things I did was pin my hair back so I couldn't fidget or mess with it. Seems simple I know, but it's amazing how much an ethos can be helped by none other than not twirling hair! Also, I made myself present first out of everyone in our class (this became what I did for every speech I gave). It helped me to come to class with the mindset that the first thing I would be doing was presenting. I found that when I sat around or listened to other speeches, I made myself nervous when I didn't need to be. As I grew comfortable with the class, I feel like I gained control of my CA, and the noticeable problems from my first speech didn't appear in my last speech.

Betsy's struggles with **communication anxiety** suggest that fearful speakers are not alone. Most undergraduates are somewhat nervous when they have to address a class. International students and those from marginalized groups often have a great deal of apprehension. Students who make strides toward overcoming this problem are well on the way to finding their voices. Many well-known people also have problems when in front of an audience. Athletes may experience anxiety before or during a competition. Sometimes they control this through rituals such as bouncing a ball three times before attempting a free throw or crossing themselves before kicking a field goal.[1] The best athletes learn to channel their nervousness into positive energy. For example, Joe Montana, the legendary San Francisco 49ers quarterback who led his team to four Super Bowl championships, noted, "Nerves are good. I want to be nervous. If you don't care, I hope you're on the other side."[2]

Actors and musicians have similar problems. When the late Michael Jackson was scheduled to perform at the World Music Awards in Great Britain, he might not have made it onto the stage had Beyoncé not gone backstage to comfort him and settle him down. He was 30 minutes late for his performance.[3] Elvis Presley had similar problems. He noted, "I've never gotten over what they call stage fright. I go through it every show."[4]

Your speech instructor may even have some communication anxiety, but you probably won't be able to detect it. Even your authors have experienced this problem. Here is our story:

> As college professors and authors, we have done a lot of speaking both in and out of the classroom. Being the authors of a public speaking text puts special pressure on us. When you earn your bread and butter by telling others how to do something, they expect you to be able to do it yourself—and do it much better than most other people. Even with all our experience, every time we face a new group—a college class, a community meeting, or colleagues at conventions—we feel this pressure.

Still think that everyone else is more confident than you are? The late Edward R. Murrow, a famous radio and television commentator, once said, "The best speakers know enough to be scared. . . . The only difference

Many celebrities have problems with communication apprehension.

▶ **communication anxiety** Those unpleasant feelings and fears you may experience before or during a presentation.

between the pros and the novices is that the pros have trained the butterflies to fly in formation."

The first step in controlling communication anxiety is understanding it. The second step is learning techniques to help you manage it. Our goal in this chapter is not to rid you of communication anxiety, but to help you train your butterflies to fly in formation so that your message reaches out to your listeners and helps them learn something new, changes their way of thinking about an important issue, or celebrates special occasions. Channeling your nervous energy into something constructive will help you find your voice.

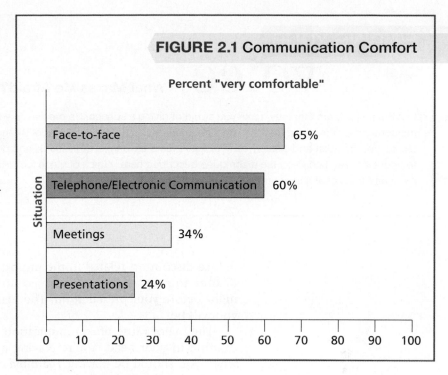

FIGURE 2.1 Communication Comfort

Percent "very comfortable"

- Face-to-face — 65%
- Telephone/Electronic Communication — 60%
- Meetings — 34%
- Presentations — 24%

(Situation)

0 10 20 30 40 50 60 70 80 90 100

Understanding Communication Anxiety

On the day of your first presentation you sit waiting for your turn to speak. You can't really listen to the speeches before yours because you feel miserable. You hear your name called. Your stomach drops. Your hands start to sweat. Your heart races. Your ears feel hot. Your mouth feels dry. You plod to the podium and look up at the audience. Your knees start to shake. You grab the lectern for support.

Any of these symptoms sound familiar? Most likely, you won't have *all of these* symptoms of communication anxiety, but you may have some of them. If you didn't, you wouldn't be normal. *Remember, a little bit of anxiety is a good thing.* It can help you "psych up" for your presentation. You can learn to channel your nervousness into positive energy that invigorates your performance.

About now you may be thinking, "Okay, so I'm not alone, but I'm still uptight." Almost everybody is somewhat ill at ease in unfamiliar situations, and addressing a large number of people face-to-face is not an everyday event for most of us. Whenever we embark on a new adventure, there is always some element of uncertainty that can cause anxiety. Fortunately, familiarity with a situation tends to reduce anxiety for most people. Practice your speech before a group of friends. If you can arrange it, practice in the room where you will give your speech. Give yourself time to adjust. You should become more confident as the term progresses. If you would like to evaluate your own communication anxiety, take the Gauge of Communication Anxiety self-examination at the end of this chapter. You may be surprised to find that you didn't score as high on this scale as you thought you might.

People also tend to feel uncomfortable when the stakes are high. Most public speaking is done in situations that are important. In school, most presentations (in this class and others) are graded. When you make presentations outside the classroom, the personal or professional consequences may be far-reaching. To help

FINDING YOUR

voice   What Makes Me Afraid?

List the major fears that may make you afraid of giving a speech. Be precise as you complete the sentences "I'm afraid that . . ." or "I'm afraid because . . ." As you work through this chapter, go over your list and classify each of these fears as rational or irrational and develop a plan to counter them, based on the techniques described here. Which of these techniques proves most and least useful in controlling your fears?

reduce discomfort related to the importance of the situation, give yourself plenty of time to prepare your speech. Do not put off preparing your speech until the night before your presentation. The better prepared you are, the more confident you will be.

The major cause of communication anxiety is that you have the wrong movie running in your head. You're playing and replaying *Titanic* or *The Perfect Storm*, when you should be playing *The Blind Side* or *It's a Wonderful Life*. Your personal catastrophe film may include such scenes as these:

> I'll be so scared I'll pass out.
> I'll embarrass myself.
> My mind will go blank.
> I won't be able to finish my speech.
> I'll shake so much my classmates will laugh at me.
> Listeners are waiting to pounce on my mistakes.
> I'm going to fail this class if my speeches aren't perfect.

If you run this movie through your head enough times, you are going to believe that it is real and that its consequences are inevitable. Thinking that it's real can make it real to you. Psychologists call such scripts self-fulfilling prophecies that literally bring about what you fear most.[5] Such scenarios lead to avoidance and procrastination. Avoidance behaviors may include putting off registering for the course, registering for the course and then dropping it before you ever attend, starting to attend the class and then disappearing from the radar, and failing to attend class on the day you're scheduled to speak. Procrastination behaviors may include waiting to prepare your speech until the night before you are scheduled to present and repeatedly asking your instructor to reschedule your speech at a later date.

Managing Your Communication Anxiety

You've probably heard a great deal of advice about how to control communication anxiety. For example, you might picture the audience sitting there naked. Another pearl of wisdom is to take a really deep breath each time you feel yourself getting anxious. Or—and this is probably the worst advice we've heard—cut back on your preparation because "in general, the more you prepare, the worse you will do."[6] The people who offer such wisdom mean well, but quick-fix techniques don't work.

You also may have been told that taking a public speaking class will cure you of your communication anxiety. *There is no cure for communication anxiety, but there are strategies that can help you keep it under control.* The techniques we discuss in this chapter do help, and they work best when used in combination. Start with one technique and move on to another until you find what helps you the most. The techniques that we will consider are reality testing, selective relaxation, attitude adjustment, cognitive restructuring, and visualization.

Reality Testing

When you engage in **reality testing** you subject the negative aspects of the movie in your head to rational scrutiny. To see things realistically you have to stand back from your emotions and look for answers to three basic questions:

1. What has actually happened in the past?
2. What is the worst thing that's actually *likely* to happen?
3. How bad would it be if it did happen?[7]

For example, suppose one of the fears in your script is "I'll be so scared I'll pass out." Have you ever passed out from fear? Is this likely to happen? How bad would this be? What would be the consequences? Let's reality test some of the other scenes in your personal horror film.

I'll Embarrass Myself.   What can you possibly do in a speech that would be all that embarrassing? Little blunders do not a catastrophe make. Save being embarrassed for the truly ludicrous things in your life. And keep in mind that you will survive even those.

> The first class one of your authors taught was held in a large auditorium. While monitoring a test one hot day, a student asked her to cut off the noisy air conditioners. She shut off the air conditioner on one side of the stage and was walking across to the other side, not looking where she was going, and tripped over the base of the free-standing chalkboard, falling flat on her face in front of 250 students.
>
> Now, that's embarrassing! To her amazement, no one was laughing. The expressions on the faces she could see showed concern. She picked herself up, brushed the dirt off her clothes, and muttered something like, "Grace is my middle name!" To her surprise, the sun rose as usual the next morning. And regardless of how embarrassed she had felt, she had to show up to teach the next class.

My Mind Will Go Blank.   A comedian once joked, "The mind is a wonderful thing. It begins working as soon as you are born and doesn't quit until you stand up to speak." Most of us can remember a time when we memorized a passage to recite in class—the Gettysburg Address, a scene from Shakespeare, or a poem—and drew a blank about halfway through our performance.

Having your mind go blank is one of the major pitfalls of memorized presentations. That is why most classroom speeches are presented extemporaneously: prepared

▶ **reality testing**   Subjecting negative messages you send yourself to rational scrutiny.

and practiced, but not memorized. And, if by chance you do forget what you were going to say next, repeat what you just said in different words. Audiences expect summaries in speeches, and going back over your material can help get you back on track.

I Won't Be Able to Finish My Speech.   On *very, very rare* occasions, a speaker may experience a panic attack. Let's say this happens to you. You're presenting your speech and everything is going well, when you suddenly feel overwhelmed with fear for no apparent reason. Not only are you afraid, but you realize that the fear is irrational and you think you're "losing it." All you want to do is bolt for the door. Don't! A panic attack seldom lasts more than a few seconds (although it may feel like it's going on for hours).

Mark Twain once said, "Courage is resistance to fear, mastery of fear, not absence of fear." Keep talking. Look for the friendliest face in the room and direct your words to that person. Accept your fear for what it is—a temporary aberration. Chances are it will never happen again.

I'll Shake So Much My Classmates Will Laugh at Me.   You may worry that everyone in the audience will know how nervous you are. Actually, most listeners won't know this unless you tell them. They are not clairvoyant! Communication consultant H. Dennis Beaver brings this point home to his clients by having them think back to a time when they felt especially nervous speaking to a group. Then he asks:

> Did a single audience member come up to you and comment on how loud your heart was beating? Or how sweaty your hands appeared? Or how dry your voice sounded? Or what an interesting sound your knocking knees made?[8]

Even if your hands are trembling or your leg is twitching, is this all that bad? If listeners do notice, what will they think? That you're incompetent? Or that you—like them—are somewhat uncomfortable in front of a group? If you think you are prone to trembling, plan some purposeful physical activity such as gesturing or walking closer to the audience. Integrate a presentation aid into your speech. As you point out the features of a model or refer to the figures in a chart, you give yourself a positive way to work off some tension.

You may feel that the audience is just waiting for you to make a mistake, but in truth, most audiences want you to succeed.

Listeners Are Waiting to Pounce on My Mistakes.   You may picture your listeners as predators lying in wait, ready to pounce on any little mistake, eager to make fun of you as though they were kids in middle school. In reality, most audiences want speakers to succeed. This is especially true in the college classroom. If you see someone frowning, that listener is more likely worried about a personal problem, an upcoming test, or his or her own presentation. Look for a friendly face. Don't second-guess your audience!

I'm Going to Fail This Class If My Speeches Aren't Perfect.   As a beginning speaker you may believe that your speech has to be perfect for it to be effective—even though no presentation is ever perfect. If you look at the

Concerned About . . .	Try This . . .
Unfamiliarity of the situation?	Practice before an audience
Importance of the occasion?	Prepare well in advance
Afraid you'll be scared?	Remember you'll be "psyched up"
Embarrassing yourself?	Don't sweat the little things
Drawing a blank?	Paraphrase what you just said
Won't be able to finish?	Keep talking, look for a friendly face
I'll shake uncontrollably?	Use gestures and purposeful movement
Predatory listeners?	Classmates want you to succeed
I'll fail if my speech isn't perfect?	No speech is perfect, cut yourself some slack

FIGURE 2.2 Coping with Your Concerns

speech evaluation forms used in your class, you probably won't see perfection anywhere in the criteria. It's all right if you make a few mistakes—if you flub a word or leave out something you meant to include. Your listeners probably won't even notice these small flaws unless you call attention to them. It's fine to want to do your best, but cut yourself some slack.

Selective Relaxation

Another technique for handling your anxiety is to master the art of **selective relaxation**. Begin practicing this technique well before your first speech. Practice relaxing several times a day until it becomes second nature to relax at the mention of your special cue word. Follow the sequence outlined here:

1. Find a quiet place where you can be by yourself. Sit in a comfortable chair or lie down, close your eyes, and breathe deeply, in through your nose and out through your mouth. You should feel yourself beginning to relax.

2. Once you feel yourself relaxing, begin slowly repeating a cue word, such as *one*, each time you exhale. Let your mind drift freely. You should soon feel quite relaxed.

3. While you are relaxed and breathing deeply, selectively tense and relax different muscle groups. Begin by tensing your feet and legs: Curl your toes, tighten your calves, lock your knees, contract your thigh muscles. Hold this tension for several seconds and think about how it feels. Not very comfortable, is it?

4. Concentrate on breathing deeply again, saying your special word and let your muscles relax.

5. Now, repeat steps 1 through 4, moving the focus of tensing and relaxing up your body: First move it to your abdominal muscles, then your hand and arm muscles, and finally your neck and head muscles. After you have done this a

▶ **selective relaxation** Practicing muscle control techniques to help you reduce physical tension by relaxing on cue.

number of times, simply repeating your selected word should trigger a relaxation response.

One good thing about this exercise is that once you have mastered the technique, you can practice it unseen in many situations. While you are sitting in class waiting to speak, tense your feet and leg muscles; then relax them. If you find yourself getting nervous while you are speaking, say your cue word to yourself. The word alone may be enough to help you relax and return your concentration to your message. If this technique doesn't work as well as you would like, try tensing and relaxing a hand as you speak. (Just be sure it's down at your side where it can't be seen.)

Attitude Adjustments

If you look over the scenes from your catastrophe movie about giving a speech, you'll find that most of them begin with "I." You think things like "I'm going to really screw this up" or "I'll never remember what I want to say." You have the focus on yourself. You are acting in an ego-centered manner. You need to change your focus. You need a new script for the movie in your head. You should try to become:

1. other-centered,
2. message-centered, and
3. communication-centered.

First, as you prepare and practice your speech, keep your audience in the forefront of your mind. What can I give to my listeners? How can I help them understand this situation? Second, focus on your message. Choose a meaningful topic that you can get excited about. Learn all you can about the topic so that you have something of value to give to your listeners. Third, become communication-centered. Public speaking is an interactive communication event between the speaker, message, and audience. When you focus mainly on yourself, you throw this interaction out of balance.

SPEAKER'S notes
Techniques for Handling Communication Anxiety

1. Reality testing allows you to apply rational scrutiny to negative aspects of the movie in your head.
2. Selective relaxation reduces tension by training you to relax on cue.
3. Attitude adjustments move the focus from you to your listeners and your message.
4. Cognitive restructuring changes negative self-messages to positive ones.
5. Visualization puts a more positive movie in your mind.

Let's look at how attitude adjustments worked for Beverly, one of the most communication-apprehensive students we ever taught. During her first presentation she actually left the room in the middle of her speech to try to compose herself.

▶ **attitude adjustment** Shifting your focus from yourself to your listeners and message.

While she was out of the room, we discussed with the class how we might help her. She came to our office after the speech and we tried to encourage her to focus on her message and her audience. Her second effort was a little better. She stopped during her presentation to try to pull herself together, but she managed to finish without leaving the room. Her third speech was a totally different story.

Beverly worked during the day as a dispatcher for a major interstate trucking firm. Her persuasive speech urged her classmates to lobby their congressional representatives to vote for a pending truck safety bill. This topic was very important to her. Her speech was filled with interesting examples of near catastrophes that this legislation would make less likely. She knew her topic. She knew it was important. She really cared about it. Consequently, she got so caught up with what she was saying that she forgot to be anxious. The audience was spellbound. When she finished, there was a moment of silence while it all sank in, then spontaneous applause—applause for a speech well given and applause for a speaker who had conquered her personal demons. During this presentation she became more other-centered, more message-centered, and more communication-centered. Beverly came up to us after the class and asked if there was an advanced public speaking class she could take. She had found her voice and felt better about herself because of it.

Cognitive Restructuring

The disaster movie in your head sends you many negative messages about your ability to present an effective speech. You need to consciously change these messages to their positive, more constructive counterparts. Psychologists call this **cognitive restructuring**. Positive messages can help boost your self-confidence.

To change the messages you send yourself, begin by making a list of the irrational negative messages that you are sending yourself. Write these out in full and then determine their positive counterparts. For example, instead of telling yourself, "I'm going to sound stupid," say, "I've done my research and I'm going to sound knowledgeable." Replace "Everyone else is more confident than I am" with "I am as confident as anyone in this class." For "I really don't want to give this speech," try "This is my chance to present my ideas to the class." Use these positive messages as a pep talk to yourself.

Visualization

Early on the morning of October 9, 2009, President Barack Obama was awakened with the news that he had won the Nobel Peace Prize. He was scheduled to make a presentation from the Rose Garden at about 11 that morning. He didn't have much time to prepare and get ready for his remarks acknowledging the award. CNN coverage was set up before he appeared to speak. In the time leading up to his speech, the television cameras zoomed in on the window where he was putting the finishing touches on his remarks and getting ready to deliver them. His head would bend down, presumably as he was looking at his manuscript; then it would rise up and his eyes would close in contemplation of what he was going to say. He was visualizing his presentation. Clearly, visualization is not simply a tool for the communication apprehensive, but a vital part of speech preparation.

▶ **cognitive restructuring** Replacing negative thoughts with positive, constructive ones.

FIGURE 2.3 Practicing Positive Thinking

Negative thoughts . . .	Constructive alternatives . . .
I really don't want to give this speech.	This is my chance to offer my ideas to others.
I'm the only one who is nervous.	Other students are just as nervous as I am.
My speech is going to be boring.	I have good examples and stories to liven up my speech.
I'm not an expert on my topic.	I've done enough research to be knowledgeable about my topic.
I know I'm going to blow it.	I'm ready and I'm going to do a good job.

Actors, musicians, and athletes also use visualization to prepare for success. During a recent Women's World Cup Soccer championship the game was tied at the end of play. China and the United States each had five penalty kicks to determine the winner. Before one of China's kicks, the camera zoomed in on the American goalkeeper. She had a look of intense concentration on her face. The announcer commented, "She's visualizing blocking this next kick."

You can help control your communication anxiety with a **visualization** of yourself as a successful speaker.[9] As you prepare your visualization script, you will be rewriting the movie that has been playing in your head. You're going to

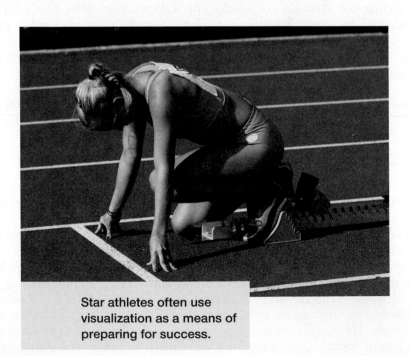

Star athletes often use visualization as a means of preparing for success.

▶ **visualization** Systematically picturing yourself succeeding as a speaker and practicing your speech with that image in mind.

move from a disaster movie to a feel-good film. Begin by going through your horror movie and write down the negative messages you are sending yourself. Do a reality check on these messages, asking yourself how likely they are to happen and what the consequences would be if they did. Restructure these messages into their positive counterparts. Use these new messages to develop your visualization script, keeping in mind that you want to be concerned mainly about reaching your listeners with a message that you communicate effectively and enthusiastically.

Putting It All Together

Think back to a time in your childhood when you acquired a new skill. It might have been learning to swim or to ride a bicycle. The more you learned and the more you practiced, the more confident you became. The more confident you became, the less afraid you were. Before too long, you were jumping into the deep end of the pool without hesitation or riding without training wheels.

The same type of learning relationship exists between knowledge, practice, confidence, and public speaking. When you learn how to prepare a speech and have practiced your presentation, you will feel more confident and have less apprehension.

Keep in mind that practicing is an important part of your preparation. Highly anxious students often spend a lot of time researching and organizing their speeches, but then they don't spend enough time actually practicing their presentations.[10] So practice, and then practice some more. The more you master the presentation of your message, the more confident you will be.

A final word of advice: When you rise to speak, *act confident* even if you don't feel that way. Walk briskly to the front of the room, look at your audience, and establish eye contact. Unless you are speaking on a very grim topic, smile at your listeners. Whatever happens during your speech, remember that your listeners cannot see or hear what's happening inside you. They only know what you show and tell them. Show them a controlled speaker presenting a

---

FINDING YOUR

voice   My Script for Success

Write out your visualization script for the presentation of your first speech in this class. Keep your message brief and positive. Provide your instructor with a copy, and then read through it as you prepare your presentation. After your speech, write a postscript on how well you followed your script, and what you must do to improve.

Your visualization script need not be long or overly dramatic. Keep it short enough to run through in your mind as you walk to the lectern to make your presentation. As you practice your speech, run through your script before you open your mouth. Practice this way several times until it becomes easy for you to conjure up your positive messages.

well-researched speech. Maintain eye contact for a short time, and then walk confidently back to your seat. Even though you may feel relieved that your speech is over, don't say "Whew!" or "I made it!" And never act disappointed with your presentation. You probably did better than you thought.

SPEAKER'S notes   Ten Ways to Control Communication Anxiety

1. Select a topic that excites you.
2. Carefully research and organize your message.
3. Master your topic so you can speak with authority.
4. Practice your presentation until it flows smoothly.
5. Focus on communicating with your audience.

6. Learn how to relax on cue.
7. Think positively.
8. Visualize success.
9. Act confident even if you aren't.
10. Take advantage of other opportunities to speak in public.

Finding your voice allows you to speak with confidence.

Do these techniques really work, and is such advice helpful? Research related to communication anxiety has established the following conclusions: (1) *Such techniques do work*, and (2) *they work best in combination.*[11] Heed the suggestions of Davidson College student Betsy Lyles, whose account of her communication anxiety opened this chapter:

> To incoming students, I would suggest a couple of things—the first being it doesn't matter how much experience you've had with speaking in the past. Taking a public speaking course and learning about the theories at work behind what you do can be illuminating. And, there's no way not to improve. If possible, have your speeches filmed so you can watch them after your presentation. Make note of what you like and also what you can improve upon. Unfortunately, communication anxiety is a universal problem faced by public speakers *without* a universal solution. Commit yourself to finding solutions that work for you. They might be different than what your classmates do.

Controlling anxiety takes time. As you become more experienced at giving speeches and at using the suggestions in this chapter, you will find your fears lessening, and you will be able to convert your mild anxiety into positive, constructive energy.

FINAL
reflections   **Victory Over Fear**

Before you can find your voice, fear is a barrier you must climb. Actually, fear is a magic mountain, because as you climb, one small step at a time, the mountain grows smaller, and you become more confident. The mountain never totally disappears, nor should it. From it you draw the energy you will need for special communication presentations. From the top of fear mountain, you can also see clearly the territory you must explore as you continue the adventure of finding your voice.

A GAUGE OF COMMUNICATION ANXIETY: A SELF-EXAMINATION

Directions: Assume that you have to give a speech within the next few weeks. For each of the statements below, indicate the degree to which the statement applies to you within the context of giving a future speech. Mark whether you strongly agree (SA), agree (A), are undecided (U), disagree (D), or strongly disagree (SD) with each statement. Circle your SA, A, U, D, or SD choices. Do not write in the blanks next to the questions. **Work quickly and record your first impression.**

___ 1. While preparing for the speech, I would feel uncomfortably tense and nervous. SA_5 A_4 U_3 D_2 SD_1

___ 2. I feel uncomfortably tense at the very thought of giving a speech in the near future. SA_5 A_4 U_3 D_2 SD_1

___ 3. My thoughts would become confused and jumbled when I was giving a speech. SA_5 A_4 U_3 D_2 SD_1

___ 4. Right after giving the speech I would feel that I'd had a pleasant experience. SA_1 A_2 U_3 D_4 SD_5

___ 5. I would get anxious when thinking about the speech coming up. SA_5 A_4 U_3 D_2 SD_1

___ 6. I would have no fear of giving the speech. SA_1 A_2 U_3 D_4 SD_5

___ 7. Although I would be nervous just before starting the speech, after starting it I would soon settle down and feel calm and comfortable. SA_1 A_2 U_3 D_4 SD_5

___ 8. I would look forward to giving the speech. SA_1 A_2 U_3 D_4 SD_5

___ 9. As soon as I knew that I would have to give the speech, I would feel myself getting tense. SA_5 A_4 U_3 D_2 SD_1

___ 10. My hands would tremble when I was giving the speech. SA_5 A_4 U_3 D_2 SD_1

___ 11. I would feel relaxed while giving the speech. SA_1 A_2 U_3 D_4 SD_5

___ 12. I would enjoy preparing for the speech. SA_1 A_2 U_3 D_4 SD_5

___ 13. I would be in constant fear of forgetting what I had prepared to say. SA_5 A_4 U_3 D_2 SD_1

___ 14. I would get uncomfortably anxious if someone asked me something that I did not know about my topic. SA_5 A_4 U_3 D_2 SD_1

___ 15. I would face the prospect of giving the speech with confidence. SA_1 A_2 U_3 D_4 SD_5

___ 16. I would feel that I was in complete possession of myself during the speech. SA_1 A_2 U_3 D_4 SD_5

___ 17. My mind would be clear when giving the speech. SA_1 A_2 U_3 D_4 SD_5

___ 18. I would not dread giving the speech. SA_1 A_2 U_3 D_4 SD_5

___ 19. I would perspire too much just before starting the speech. SA_5 A_4 U_3 D_2 SD_1

___ 20. I would be bothered by a very fast heart rate just as I started the speech.   SA$_5$ A$_4$ U$_3$ D$_2$ SD$_1$

___ 21. I would experience considerable anxiety at the speech site (room, auditorium, etc.) just before my speech was to start.   SA$_5$ A$_4$ U$_3$ D$_2$ SD$_1$

___ 22. Certain parts of my body would feel very tense and rigid during the speech.   SA$_5$ A$_4$ U$_3$ D$_2$ SD$_1$

___ 23. Realizing that only a little time remained in the speech would make me very tense and anxious.   SA$_5$ A$_4$ U$_3$ D$_2$ SD$_1$

___ 24. While giving the speech I would know that I could control my feelings of tension and stress.   SA$_1$ A$_2$ U$_3$ D$_4$ SD$_5$

___ 25. I would breathe too fast just before starting the speech.   SA$_5$ A$_4$ U$_3$ D$_2$ SD$_1$

___ 26. I would feel comfortable and relaxed in the hour or so just before giving the speech.   SA$_1$ A$_2$ U$_3$ D$_4$ SD$_5$

___ 27. I would do poorly on the speech because I would be anxious.   SA$_5$ A$_4$ U$_3$ D$_2$ SD$_1$

___ 28. I would feel uncomfortably anxious when first scheduling the date of the speaking assignment.   SA$_5$ A$_4$ U$_3$ D$_2$ SD$_1$

___ 29. If I were to make a mistake while giving the speech, I would find it hard to concentrate on the parts that followed.   SA$_5$ A$_4$ U$_3$ D$_2$ SD$_1$

___ 30. During the speech I would experience a feeling of helplessness building up inside me.   SA$_5$ A$_4$ U$_3$ D$_2$ SD$_1$

___ 31. I would have trouble falling asleep the night before the speech.   SA$_5$ A$_4$ U$_3$ D$_2$ SD$_1$

___ 32. My heart would beat too fast while I was presenting the speech.   SA$_5$ A$_4$ U$_3$ D$_2$ SD$_1$

___ 33. I would feel uncomfortably anxious while waiting to give my speech.   SA$_5$ A$_4$ U$_3$ D$_2$ SD$_1$

___ 34. While giving the speech I would get so nervous that I would forget facts I really knew.   SA$_5$ A$_4$ U$_3$ D$_2$ SD$_1$

To determine your score:
1. Fill in the blank next to each item with the NUMBER accompanying the response you circled. BE CAREFUL to enter the CORRECT NUMBER. NOTICE that the numbers printed with the responses are not consistent for every question.
2. Add up the numbers you recorded for the 34 questions. The sum is your public speaking apprehension score.

Interpretation:

34–84	low
85–92	moderately low
93–110	moderate
111–119	moderately high
120 +	high

Source: Adapted from James C. McCroskey, "Personal Report of Public Speaking Anxiety" in "Measures of Communication Bound Anxiety," *Speech Monographs 37*(4), 269-277. © 1970 National Communication Association. Reprinted by permission of Taylor and Francis Ltd., www.tandf.co.uk/journals, on behalf of the National Communication Association.

THIS CHAPTER WILL HELP YOU

1 Manage the impressions you make
2 Prepare and present your first speech
3 Develop a speech in which you introduce yourself or a classmate

3

Your First Speech: An Overview of Speech Preparation

> *Without speech there would be no community. …Language, taken as a whole, becomes the gateway to a new world.*
>
> —ERNST CASSIRER

Richard was worried about giving his first speech. He had been asked to talk about something that meant a lot to him. As he thought about this, he became frustrated. Nothing exciting or monumental had ever happened to him. He had a middle-class upbringing with loving parents. He had a part-time job as a clown, working his way through school by entertaining children at parties or special school functions. Nothing very earthshaking about that. Then he began to think about what he had learned from those children, and he shaped those thoughts into a very interesting first speech. He was beginning to find his voice.

Many of you may share Richard's concerns when faced with your first speech. You may not think you have anything interesting to say, and you may not feel prepared to speak effectively. You are not quite sure how to go about "finding your voice." You may never have thought about what is meaningful to you, what you really value enough to want to speak about it. The skills you pick up in this chapter will help start you on a journey of self-discovery that can lead to finding your voice.

We begin this journey by exploring the impressions you make on others. When speaking, it is very important to make positive first impressions. In this chapter we help you learn to manage these impressions.

Much of the information here is explored in greater detail later in the text. This chapter provides an overview of the basic skills you need to present an effective first speech. These basics, which you will build on in later speeches, include:

- Finding a subject that is right for you and your listeners.

- Focusing your topic to make your message clear.

- Using supporting materials to add interest and substance to your speech.

- Designing and outlining your speech.

- Developing presentation skills.

Managing the Impressions You Make

As you stand to speak, your listeners begin to form impressions that will influence how they respond to your message. Aristotle called these impressions **ethos**. A person with high ethos will be listened to with respect. You can build positive ethos by cultivating favorable impressions of your competence, integrity, goodwill, and dynamism.

Competence

Competent speakers are well-informed, intelligent, and well prepared. Build a perception of your **competence** by selecting topics you know something about and then by doing research to qualify you as a knowledgeable speaker. You can further enhance your competence by quoting experts and citing authorities who support your position.

For example, if you are speaking on the relationship between nutrition and heart disease, you might quote a medical specialist or a publication of the American Heart Association. Melissa Anderton introduced testimony into her speech in this way: "Dr. Milas Peterson heads the Heart Institute at Harvard University. During his visit to our campus last week, I spoke with him about this idea. He told me. . . ." Note the competence-related elements in this example:

- She points out the qualifications of her expert.

- The testimony she uses is recent.

- She made a personal contact with her expert.

- She prepared carefully for her speech.

▶ **ethos** Those characteristics that make a speaker appear honest, credible, powerful, and appealing.

▶ **competence** The perception of a speaker as being informed, intelligent, and well prepared.

When you cite authorities in this way, you are "borrowing" their credibility to enhance your own. Personal experience expressed in stories or examples also helps a speech seem authentic, brings it to life, and makes you appear more competent. Your competence is further enhanced if your speech is well organized, if you use language correctly, and if you have practiced your presentation.

Integrity

A speaker demonstrates **integrity** by being honest, ethical, and dependable. Listeners are more receptive when speakers are straightforward and concerned about the consequences of their words. You can encourage perceptions of integrity by presenting all sides of an issue and then explaining why you have chosen your position. You should also show that you are willing to follow your own advice. For example, in a speech that calls for commitment to action, it should be clear that you are not asking more of listeners than you would of yourself. The more you ask of the audience, the more important your integrity becomes.

How can you demonstrate integrity? One of our students, Antonio Lopez, was preparing a speech on urban gangs. The more he learned about the subject, the more convinced he became that gangs could better be controlled by family interventions than by increased social programs. In his speech, Antonio reviewed positions supporting and disputing his position, and then he showed listeners why he believed as he did. Finally, Antonio revealed that he had been a gang member at one time. "I know how this hurt my parents. They didn't want to see video of me shot or arrested on the evening news. I knew I had to change to live up to their expectations for me." His openness showed that he was willing to trust his listeners to react fairly to this sensitive information. The audience responded in kind by trusting him and what he had to say. He had built an impression of himself as a person of integrity.

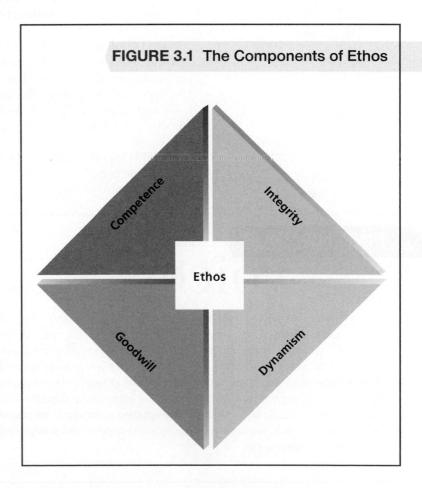

FIGURE 3.1 The Components of Ethos

Goodwill

Speakers of **goodwill** have the interests of others at heart. They are not self centered; rather, they think and act in terms of what is good for the group or community as a whole. We like such people and enjoy their company, perhaps because we feel that they like and enjoy us.

Audiences are more willing to accept ideas and suggestions from speakers who manifest goodwill.[1] A smile and direct eye contact signal listeners that you want to communicate. Sharing your feelings as well as your thoughts conveys the same message. Speakers with goodwill also enjoy laughter at appropriate moments, especially laughter directed at themselves. Being able

---

▶ **integrity** The quality of being ethical, honest, and dependable.

▶ **goodwill** The dimension of ethos by which listeners perceive a speaker as having their best interests at heart.

Smiling and engaging the audience helps speakers demonstrate goodwill.

to talk openly and engagingly about your mistakes can make you seem more human and appealing as well as more confident.

The more speakers seem to demonstrate goodwill, the more audiences want to identify with them.[2] **Identification** is the feeling of sharing or closeness that can develop between speakers and listeners. It typically occurs when you believe someone is like you—that you have the same outlook on life or that you share similar backgrounds or values. Identification is more difficult to establish when the speaker and listener have different cultural backgrounds. In such situations, speakers can invite identification by telling stories or by using examples that help listeners focus on shared experiences and beliefs.

Even though she was speaking before a class that included students from all sections of the United States and different economic circumstances, Marie D'Aniello encouraged identification in her self-introductory speech by developing a theme everyone could share—family pride. At one moment in her speech, Marie pointed out how she had drawn inspiration from her brother's athletic accomplishments:

> When I think of glory, I think of my brother Chris. I'll never forget his championship basketball game. It's the typical buzzer-beater story: five seconds to go, down by one, Chris gets the ball and he drives down the court, he shoots, he scores! . . . I'll never forget the headline, "D'Aniello saves the game!" D'Aniello, hey wait, that's me. I'm a D'Aniello. I could do this too. Maybe I can't play basketball like Chris, but I can do other things well.

After this speech, it was hard not to like Marie. Her aura of goodwill, combined with favorable impressions of her competence, integrity, and dynamism, created respect for her point of view.

FINDING YOUR
voice Ethos in Public Speeches

Locate the video of a contemporary political speech on the Internet. Evaluate the ethos of the speaker. Did the speaker seem to know what she was talking about? Did she present credible evidence to validate her points [demonstrating competence]? Did the speaker seem honest and open? Did she have something personal to gain if you followed her advice [demonstrating integrity]? Did she seem to have your best interests at heart? Was the speaker pleasant and likable [demonstrating goodwill]? Was the speaker enthusiastic about the topic of the speech? Did she seem energetic and forceful [demonstrating dynamism]? Be prepared to explain how the speaker demonstrates each of the dimensions of ethos and how you think this impacts the effectiveness of the speech.

▶ **identification**   The feeling of sharing or closeness that can develop between speakers and listeners.

Goodwill and identification can also be enhanced by shared laughter. For example, Marcos White, a point guard for his school's basketball team, endeared himself to listeners during his first speech. Marcos introduced himself as the son of an African American father and a Mexican mother: "I guess," he said, "that makes me a Blaxican."

Audiences often identify with speakers who talk or dress the way they do. They prefer speakers who use gestures, language, and facial expressions that are natural and unaffected.

Dynamism

James Norton, whose assignment was to introduce his classmate Rosamond Wolford, confessed that he was nervous before he gave his speech. He was not sure how it would be received, and he worried that he might make a mistake. But when James stood to speak, he seemed confident, decisive, and enthusiastic. In short, he exhibited **dynamism** the perception that a person is energetic, enthusiastic, and in control of the situation. Whatever he might have secretly felt, his audience responded only to what they saw—his commanding presence.

At first you may not feel confident about public speaking, but you should act as though you are. If you appear self-assured, listeners will respond as though you are, and you may find yourself becoming what you seem to be. In other words, you can trick yourself into developing a very desirable trait! When you appear to be in control, you also put listeners at ease. This feeling comes back to you as positive feedback and further reinforces your confidence.

You can gain dynamism from the enthusiasm you bring to your speech. Your face, voice, and gestures should indicate that you care about your subject and about the audience. Choose your topic carefully so that it is something you truly can get excited about. Without such a topic, your presentation will seem flat. Enthusiasm endorses your message. We discuss more specific ways of projecting confidence, decisiveness, and enthusiasm in Chapter 12.

Shared laughter can enhance audience perceptions of the speaker's goodwill.

YOUR ethical VOICE The Ethics of Ethos

Speakers may create false impressions of themselves to further their ends. When such deceptions are discovered, the speakers lose the trust of listeners. To build your ethos in ethical ways, follow these guidelines.

- Do enough research to speak from competence.
- Cite respected authorities in support of your ideas.
- Interpret information fairly.

- Be honest about where you stand on your topic.
- Have your listeners' best interests at heart.
- Don't feign enthusiasm.

▶ **dynamism** The perception of a speaker as confident, decisive, and enthusiastic.

Preparing Your First Speech

Whatever your first speech assignment, the planning, creativity, and excitement of that presentation are up to you. To effectively plan your presentation, you must work through a series of steps. Figure 3.2, Major Steps in Speech Preparation, illustrates this process.

Developing a speech is not a linear process. You may have to back up from time to time. As you work through your second step, you may find that you need to go back and modify what you planned in step one. You can't put off your preparation to the night before you're scheduled to speak. Take the first step as soon as you get your assignment. Plan your preparation so that you can work through all the steps. A speech needs time to jell, and you need time to reflect on what you want to say.

Step 1: Find the Right Topic

The nature of the first speech assignment often will suggest an appropriate topic. For example, if your instructor asks you to introduce yourself or a classmate, the topic is limited to your personal experiences or those of the other person. Other assignments may take different approaches that limit topic possibilities. Regardless of the type of

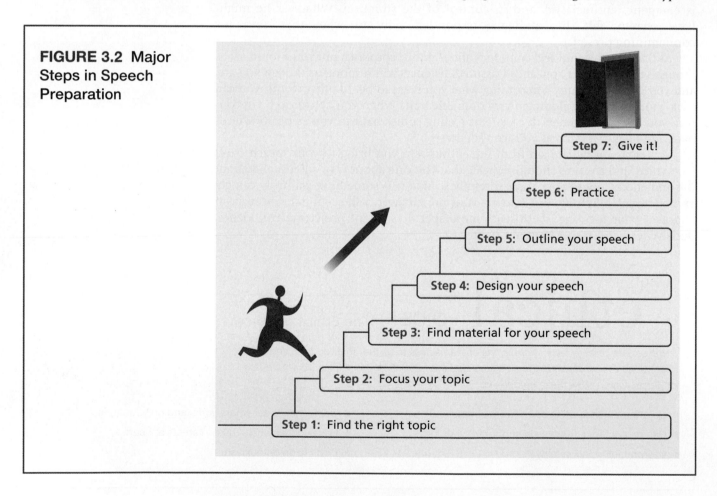

FIGURE 3.2 Major Steps in Speech Preparation

Step 7: Give it!

Step 6: Practice

Step 5: Outline your speech

Step 4: Design your speech

Step 3: Find material for your speech

Step 2: Focus your topic

Step 1: Find the right topic

assignment, the topic you select must be appropriate to you and your listeners. To find this topic, ask yourself these questions:

- What am I most interested in?
- What do I hope to accomplish by speaking on this subject?
- Do I know enough or can I learn enough to speak responsibly on this topic?
- Can I make the topic interesting and useful to my audience?
- Will my ideas or experiences enrich my listeners' lives?
- Can I present a speech on this topic in the allotted time?

Sabrina Karic's first speech, "A Little Chocolate" (which appears at the end of this chapter), grew out of her childhood experiences of living through a war. Therefore, her message seemed authentic and credible. Because children continue to be innocent victims of war, her speech was timely and useful for listeners. It helped them understand the basis for her convictions. By the end of her speech, she had established credibility for later speeches she would give on global communication.

Step 2: Focus Your Topic

Your first ideas for a topic may be too broad to cover in a short classroom speech. Beth Tidmore wanted to give her self-introductory speech on the university's rifle team. As a member of this team, Beth became an All-American during her freshman year. She knew so much about her sport that she could have talked about it for hours, but she had only five minutes to speak. Beth knew she had to narrow her topic and focus it so that it would interest her listeners. She might have talked about how rifle matches are scored or how to make a successful shot. Beth decided these were too technical to appeal to listeners who knew little about the sport.

Instead, Beth decided to talk about how and why she became a shooter. She opened by discussing the commitment her mother made when she bought Beth an expensive rifle. Beth then described the personal price she paid in terms of time, hard work, and dedication to reach the top of her sport and the satisfaction she got from her success. Beth's speech illustrates two important principles of focusing a topic:

1. *You must have a clear idea of what you want to accomplish.* Beth wanted to tell us how and why rifle competition became a central passion in her life.

2. *You should be able to state the essence of your speech in a single, simple sentence.* The essence of Beth's message was that hard work can justify faith and commitment.

Your personal experiences can provide examples and narratives for your speech.

Step 3: Find Material for Your Speech

Once you have a focused topic, you can start gathering material to make your ideas come to life. Four basic forms of supporting materials are narratives, examples, testimony, and information (facts and statistics).

Narratives.   Narratives are stories that illustrate the ideas or theme of a speech. For first speeches, narratives may be very important. They help develop a feeling of closeness between the audience and the speaker. Through the stories they tell, speakers can create desirable impressions of themselves or the classmates they introduce. Stories can make speakers seem more human. They involve the audience in the action, making it a shared adventure.

Beth Tidmore's speech, reprinted in Appendix B, offers a good example of the use of narrative in a speech. She opened her speech with a story that described her mother's commitment:

> I'm sure everybody has had an April Fool's joke played on them. My father's favorite one was to wake me up on April 1st and tell me, "School's been canceled for the day; you don't have to go," and then get all excited and say "April Fool!" . . . Well, on April 1st, 2000, my mother said three words that I was sure weren't an April Fool's joke. She said, "We'll take it." The "it" she was referring to was a brand-new Anschutz 2002 Air Rifle. Now, this is $2,000 worth of equipment for a sport that I'd been in for maybe three months—not long. That was a big deal! It meant that I would be going from a junior-level to an Olympic-grade rifle.
>
> Somebody outside of the sport might think, "Eh, minor upgrade. A gun is a gun, right?" No. Imagine a fifteen-year-old who has been driving a used Toyota and who suddenly gets a brand new Mercedes for her sixteenth birthday. That's how I felt. And as she was writing the check, I completely panicked. I thought, "What if I'm not good enough to justify this rifle? What if I decide to quit and we have to sell it, or we can't sell it? What if I let my parents down and I waste their money?" So later in the car, I said, "Momma, what if I'm not good enough?" She said, "Don't worry about it—it's my money."

Beth's story illustrates the use of **dialogue**, which makes listeners eavesdroppers to a conversation. Her narrative also illustrates the use of analogy as she invites listeners to compare her feelings with those of someone who just received a Mercedes. The analogy highlights the significance of the gift to her. Finally, notice how Beth builds suspense: Was she able to justify the purchase of such an expensive gift? Her narrative aroused curiosity for the rest of the speech.

Stories should be short and to the point, moving naturally from the beginning to the end. The language of stories should be colorful, concrete, and active. The presentation should be lively and interesting.

After mentioning her successes in national and international competitions, Beth concluded her speech with another narrative:

> So not long ago, I asked my mother, "How did you know?" She said, "Ah, I just knew." I said, "No, Mom—really. How did you know that you weren't going to waste your money?" She got very serious and she took me by the shoulders

Beth Tidmore's narratives helped listeners relate to her topic.

▶ **narratives** Stories used to support a point in a speech.

▶ **dialogue** Having the characters in a narrative speak for themselves, rather than paraphrasing what they say.

and she squared me up. She looked me right in the eye and she said, "When you picked up that gun, you just looked like you belonged together. I knew there was a sparkle in your eye, and I knew that you were meant to do great things with that rifle."

Examples.   Examples illustrate points, clarify uncertainty, and make events seem authentic. When listeners ask, "Can you give me an example?" they are seeking clarification and reassurance. An example says, in effect, "This really happened." It takes an idea out of the abstract and places it firmly in the concrete. To illustrate her abstract argument that it is good business to serve the needs of disabled people, Karen Lovelace described a group called Opening Doors, which encourages companies to improve travel for the disabled:

> One hotel chain that has used this program is Embassy Suites. Their staff is taught by Opening Doors to problem-solve based on guests' needs. And you'd better believe that the word gets around to disabled travelers!

You can use an extended example that goes into details, or a series of brief examples to illustrate a point. Whatever type of examples you use, remember that their function is to help listeners understand your point. As with stories, you should use colorful, concrete, and active language in your examples.

Testimony.   Testimony offered by experts or other respected people can add authority to your speech. When you quote the words of others, you call those whom you have quoted as *witnesses* to support a point. As she developed her speech supporting better service for the disabled, Karen Lovelace cited Sandy Blondino, director of sales at Embassy Suites Hotels, who confirmed that the hospitality industry is now more receptive to disabled travelers. She concluded with Ms. Blondino's exact words: "But that's just hospitality, right?" Karen followed up this *expert testimony* with *prestige testimony* by quoting former President Bill Clinton: "When I injured my knee and used a wheelchair for a short time, I understood even more deeply that the ADA isn't just a good law, it's the right thing to do."

When you quote expert testimony, be sure to mention the expert's credentials, including when and where the statement you are quoting was made.

Information.   Information in the form of **facts** and **statistics** demonstrates the legitimacy of an idea. To support her point that Native Americans are victims of social injustice, Ashley Roberson used an array of statistical comparisons:

> Did you know that Indians have one of the lowest life expectancies of any population living in this hemisphere, second only to those living in Haiti? And did you know that the suicide rate among American Indians is seventy percent higher than that of the general U.S. population? Or, did you

Christopher Reeve used personal experience to speak in favor of stem cell research.

▶ **examples** Verbal illustrations of a speaker's points.

▶ **testimony** Citing information from or opinions of others to support a point.

▶ **information** Using facts or statistics to support a point.

▶ **facts** Information that can be verified by observation.

▶ **statistics** Numerical information.

know that in 1999, Indians suffered 124 violent crimes for every 100,000 people—two and a half times the national average?

The effective use of information helps convince listeners that you know what you are talking about and that you didn't just make something up. To find such supporting materials, you will have to invest some time in the library or make careful use of the Internet.

As you do this research, be sure to record *who* said something, *where* it was said, and *when* it was said. In your speech, use this material to support your claims. For example, Ashley's facts and statistics would have been more effective if she had introduced them with the following statement: "According to a Princeton research survey reported in the *Denver Post* of March 15, 2009, 'Native Americans are our most abused Americans.'"

Taken as a whole, narratives, examples, testimony, and facts and statistics provide the substance that makes listeners take a speech seriously.

Step 4: Design Your Speech

You should develop a design for your speech that arranges your material in an orderly fashion. Your ideas should fit together so that it is easy for your listeners to follow them. Three designs often used in first speeches are narrative, categorical, and cause-effect.

Narrative Design. The **narrative design** structures your speech by developing a story from beginning to end. The narrative design in speeches differs markedly from other speech design formats. Instead of having an introduction, body, and conclusion, the narrative design features a prologue, plot, and epilogue. Figure 3.3 shows how these elements go together.

The **prologue** sets the scene for what will follow. It orients listeners to the context of the action so that they can make sense of it. It foreshadows the meaning and importance of the story that will follow. It introduces the characters who enact the story. The prologue is similar to the introduction in other speech designs. Let's look how these factors are developed in the prologue to Sabrina Karic's self-introductory speech (reprinted at the end of this chapter):

> I want you to think back to when you were six years old. Then, imagine living in a time, a place, a country, where you constantly heard the noises I just played. I am from the small, durable, and tragic country of Bosnia and Herzegovina. In 1992, while many of you were playing with toys and learning to ride a bike, I was living through a nightmare. I was six years old, not really ready to experience war. But on May 28th, I heard my first gun shots and my happy, innocent childhood ended. Almost overnight, my family of privileged Bosnians was plunged into homelessness and poverty.

The **plot** in a narrative design is where the action of the story unfolds in a sequence of scenes designed to build suspense. The characters developed in the plot gain complexity by the way they participate in the action. They may live on in our memories after the speech is over. When you read Sabrina's speech, you will find that the plot unfolds through three major scenes: (1) her family suffering in Gorazde, (2) Sabrina worrying about her parents, who had gone to seek food for

---

▶ **narrative design** A speech structure that develops a story in terms of a prologue, plot, and epilogue.

▶ **prologue** An opening that establishes the context and setting of a narrative, foreshadows the meaning, and introduces major characters.

▶ **plot** The body of a speech that follows narrative design; unfolds in a sequence of scenes designed to build suspense.

FIGURE 3.3 Outline Format for a Narrative Design

I. Prologue _____
   A. Setting and context of story: _____
   B. Foreshadowing characters: _____
   C. Foreshadowing meaning: _____

II. Plot _____
   A. Scene 1: _____
   B. Scene 2: _____
   C. Scene 3: _____

III. Epilogue _____
   A. Final scene: _____
   B. Lessons of the story: _____

the family, and (3) the ongoing horror of the situation. The plot is similar to the body of other speech designs.

The **epilogue** of a narrative reflects on the meaning of the story and is the counterpart to the conclusion of other speech designs. In her epilogue Sabrina reflects on the meaning of her ordeal. She applies her experiences so that they transcend national boundaries. Chocolate becomes a symbol for hope. The Speaker's Notes: Checklist for Developing a Narrative Design will help you plan such a design.

SPEAKER'S notes   Checklist for Developing a Narrative Design

_____ I develop my prologue by describing the setting and context for my story.

_____ My prologue introduces the characters in my story.

_____ I use colorful language and dialogue to bring my story to life.

_____ I develop interesting characters who take part in the action.

_____ I build suspense into my story.

_____ I reflect on the meaning of my story.

_____ I use vivid language that helps listeners remember my story.

Categorical Design.   The **categorical design** develops a subject according to its apparent or customary divisions. Laura Haskins used a categorical design in her speech *The Magnificent Juggler*. She discussed three aspects of her life that she had to juggle to stay on top of things. These three categories—family, work, and school—were ones that many students have to juggle in their lives as well, so they were able to identify with her.

Laura's speech also demonstrates how the introduction, body, and conclusion of a speech should work together. Her introduction opened with a carnival barker's

▶ **epilogue**   The final part of a narrative, reflecting upon its meaning.

▶ **categorical design**   A speech structure that develops a subject in terms of its apparent or customary divisions.

call, "Come one, come all, see the magnificent juggler!" She aroused interest with the novelty of her approach and told listeners how her juggling act began. In the body of her speech, Laura used examples to elaborate how she juggled taking care of her home and family, working as an RN in an intensive care unit, and attending college. Her conclusion pointed out what she learned from juggling while echoing her ideas in her introduction:

> My experience as a juggler has taught me to plan, prioritize, rearrange as necessary and pass off to my assistant juggler, my husband, without missing a beat. The International Jugglers Association is reviewing my application for membership. I'm a shoo-in because I truly am a magnificent juggler.

Cause-Effect Design.   If you want to tell about something that had a great impact on you, a **cause-effect design** might work best. This design helps you explain how something came about. Maria One Feather, a Native American student speaker, used such a design in her speech "Growing Up Red—and Feeling Blue—in White America." She treated her background, being "Red," or Native American, as the cause of her depression, and the impact on her life as the effect.

These and other designs for speeches are discussed in detail in Chapters 9, 13, 14, and 16.

Introductions, Bodies, and Conclusions.   In addition to arousing interest and preparing listeners for the rest of the speech, your **introduction** should build a good relationship between you and your audience. The best introductions are planned *after* the body of the speech has been designed—after all, it is difficult to draw a map if you don't yet know where you are going.

The **body of the speech** is where you satisfy the curiosity aroused in your introduction. The body includes the most important ideas in your message. In a cause-effect design, the body consists of two main points: the explanation of a cause of some condition and the elaboration of its effect. In a categorical design, the body develops two or three major divisions of the subject. You won't have time to cover more than that. In a narrative design, the plot becomes the body of the speech and it contains the scenes needed to carry the story.

The **conclusion** summarizes your main points and ends with reflections on the meaning of the speech. Good conclusions are easily remembered—even eloquent. Sometimes they quote well-known people who state the point very well. They may tie back to the introduction, completing a symbolic circle in a way that the audience finds satisfying. You will find more on developing introductions, bodies, and conclusions in Chapter 9.

Transitions.   As you prepare your speech, you should also be planning **transitions**. Transitions help you move from one point to another. They are generally phrases, such as "having explained the cause, I will now discuss the effect," or "let's now consider another part of this problem," or "let me tell you what happened after I warned him." Transitions also may be used to remind listeners of the point you have just made or to preview what is going to happen next in the speech. Oral connectives such as *first*, *second*, and *finally* can also work as transitions.

Step 5: Outline Your Speech

Preparing an outline allows you to put your design down on paper so that you can see how it will work. The outline should contain your introduction, the body of your speech (including your main ideas and their subpoints), and your conclusion.

▶ **cause-effect design**   A speech structure that explains a situation in terms of what originates it.

▶ **introduction to a speech**   An opening for your speech that gains attention, previews your topic, and helps establish initial ethos for a speaker.

▶ **body of a speech**   The section of a speech that contains the main points you want to make.

Full outlines help you during speech preparation, but you should not use them during presentation. During your presentation, you may wish to use a key-word outline, which we discuss later in this chapter.

In the following outline for a self-introductory speech, the introduction and conclusion are written out word for word. This can make your entrance into and exit from the speech smooth and graceful.

"The Magnificent Juggler"

Laura Haskins

Introduction

Come one! Come all! See the magnificent juggler! See her juggle family, work, and college! I wasn't always this good. My juggling act began when I enrolled in nursing school. My children were preschoolers then, and I had to learn fast. With experience, practice, and trial and error, I have become a magnificent juggler.

[Transition: Toss up the first ball, my family.]

Body

I. I had to learn to juggle family obligations related to my children's personalities.

    A. My son, Adam, is calm and cool about things.

    B. My daughter, Sara, is energetic, talkative, and sometimes frenetic.

[Transition: Toss up the second ball, my work.]

II. I'm a registered nurse working in intensive care.

    A. I must juggle the needs of my patients.

    B. I must juggle the demands of doctors.

[Transition: Toss up ball number three, college]

III. I have to keep up with my coursework.

    A. I have to read assignments.

    B. I have to write papers.

    C. I have to prepare speeches.

[Transition: So, what have I learned from this?]

Conclusion

My experience as a juggler has taught me to plan, prioritize, rearrange as needed, and pass off to my assistant juggler, my husband, without missing a beat. The International Jugglers Association is reviewing my application for membership. I'm a shoo-in, because I really am a magnificent juggler.

Step 6: Practice

After you have developed and outlined your first speech, you are ready to practice your presentation. Effective practice begins with understanding what constitutes an effective presentation. *An effective presentation focuses on the ideas, not the speaker.* It

▶ **conclusion to a speech** An ending for your speech that summarizes your main points and provides final reflections on their meaning.

▶ **transitions** Connecting elements used in speeches.

▶ **full outline** A full-sentence outline of a speech.

should sound as though you are talking with the audience, not reading to them or reciting from memory.

Focus on the Ideas.   The presentation of a speech is the climax of planning and preparation. Although presentation is important, it should not overshadow the substance of the speech. Have you ever heard this kind of exchange?

> "He's a wonderful speaker—what a beautiful voice, what eloquent diction,
> what a smooth delivery!"
> "What did he say?"
> "I don't remember, but he sure sounded good!"

As you practice speaking and as you present your speech, concentrate on the ideas you have to offer. Your thoughts should come alive as you speak.

Speak Naturally.   An effective presentation, we noted in Chapter 1, preserves the best qualities of a good conversation. It sounds natural and spontaneous yet has a depth, coherence, and quality not normally found in conversation. Always keep in mind that *audience contact is more important than exact wording.* The best way to maintain such contact is to present your speech extemporaneously. An **extemporaneous presentation** is carefully prepared and practiced but not written out or memorized.

If you write out your speech, you will be tempted either to memorize it or read it to your audience. Reading or memorizing almost always results in a stilted presentation. DO NOT MEMORIZE OR READ YOUR SPEECH! The only parts of a speech that might be memorized are the introduction and conclusion, plus a few other critical phrases, such as the wording of main points or the punch lines of humorous stories.

SPEAKER'S notes   Practicing Your Presentation

Keep these suggestions in mind as you practice your speech.

1. Visualize yourself making an effective presentation.
2. Focus on your ideas.
3. Speak naturally.
4. Present extemporaneously.

5. Maintain eye contact with your listeners.
6. Begin practicing from a key-word outline.
7. Rehearse until your speech flows smoothly.

Practice From a Key-Word Outline.   If you think you might need a cue sheet during your presentation, use a **key-word outline**, an abbreviated version of your full-sentence outline. You can use the key-word outline to practice your speech. Using the key-word outline will help you sound more conversational and spontaneous. *Never use your full outline as you present your speech.* You may lapse into reading the speech if you do.

As its name suggests, the key-word outline contains only words that prompt your memory. It may also contain presentation cues, such as *pause* or *talk slowly.* Although the full outline may require a page or more, the key-word outline should fit on a single sheet of paper or a couple of index cards. To prepare it, go through your full-sentence outline and highlight the key words in each section. Transfer

---

▶ **extemporaneous presentation**   A form of presentation in which a speech is carefully prepared and practiced, but not written out, memorized, or read.

▶ **key-word outline**   An abbreviated version of a formal outline that may be used in presenting a speech.

them to a sheet of paper or index cards to use as prompts as you speak. The following key-word outline is based on the outline presented earlier.

The Magnificent Juggler

Introduction
Carnival call

How I became a juggler

Body
I. Family obligations

    A. Adam

    B. Sara

II. Work obligations

    A. Patients

    B. Physicians

    C. Coworkers

III. School obligations

    A. Read assignments

    B. Write papers

    C. Prepare speeches

Conclusion
Learned to plan, prioritize, rearrange, and delegate to become a magnificent juggler.

Rehearse Your Speech. Many speech classrooms have a speaker's lectern at the front of the room. Speaking from a lectern makes the occasion seem formal and can create a physical barrier between you and listeners. If you are short, you might almost disappear behind a lectern. If your gestures are hidden by it, your message may lose the power of body language. For these reasons, you may wish to speak either to the side or in front of the lectern.

It helps to rehearse your speech where you will present it.

If you plan to use the lectern, place your key-word outline high on its surface so that you can see your notes easily without having to lower your head. This will help you maintain eye contact with your listeners. Print your key-word outline in large letters. If you decide to hold your outline or note cards, don't try to hide them or act embarrassed if you need to refer to them. Most listeners may not even notice when you use them.

Imagine your audience in front of you as you practice. Start with your full outline; then move to your key-word outline. Maintain eye contact with your imaginary listeners, just as you will during the actual presentation. Look around the room so that everyone feels included in your message. Be enthusiastic! Let your voice suggest confidence. Strive for variety in your voice. Pause to let important ideas sink in. Let your face, body, and voice respond to your ideas as you speak.

Step 7: Give It!

It's your moment to speak. You've earned it. Now enjoy the moment with your listeners.

Introducing Yourself or a Classmate: An Application

One frequent first speech assignment is to introduce yourself or a classmate. The speech of introduction helps warm the classroom atmosphere, creates a sense of community, and provides an opportunity for the speaker or the one introduced to develop ethos.

The self-introductory assignment also has practical applications beyond the classroom. In later life, you may be called on to introduce yourself or an organization to which you belong. Typically, this introduction will be part of a longer speech. When he spoke to the Democratic National Convention in 2004, Barack Obama, then candidate for the U.S. Senate from Illinois, introduced himself as "a skinny kid with a funny name who believes that America has a place for him, too."[3] In the process, he established his potential for future national leadership.

A classroom speech of introduction is usually short. Since there is no way to tell an entire life story in a brief speech, you have to be selective. However, you should avoid simply reciting a few superficial facts, such as where you went to high school or what your major is. Such information reveals little about a person and is usually not very interesting. One tried-and-true way to introduce yourself or others is to answer this question: *What is the one thing that defines me (or the other person) as a unique individual?*

Begin by conducting a **self-awareness inventory** in which you consider the following possibilities:

1. *Is your cultural background the most important thing about you?* How has it shaped you? How can you explain this influence to others? In her self-introductory speech, Sandra Baltz described herself as a unique product of three cultures. She

▶ **self-awareness inventory** A series of probes that allow speakers to explore their individuality so they can prepare a speech of self-introduction.

felt that this rich cultural background had widened her horizons. Note how she focused on food to represent the convergence of these different ways of life:

> In all, I must say that being exposed to three very different cultures—Latin, Arabic, American—has been rewarding for me and has made a difference even in the music I enjoy and the food I eat. It is not unusual in my house to sit down to a meal made up of stuffed grape leaves and refried beans and all topped off with apple pie for dessert.

The text of this speech may be found in Appendix B.

2. *Is the most important thing about you the environment in which you grew up?* How were you shaped by it? What stories or examples illustrate this influence? How do you feel about its effect on your life? Are you pleased by it, or do you feel that it limited you? If the latter, what new horizons would you like to explore? In his self-introductory speech, "My Life as a River Rat," Jimmy Green concluded by saying:

> To share my world, come with me to my part of the Tennessee River. We'll take a boat ride to New Johnsonville, where Civil War gunboats still lie on the bottom of the river. You'll see how the sun makes the water sparkle. You'll see the green hills sloping down to the river, and the rocky cliffs, and I'll tell you some Indian legends about them. Then, we'll "bump the bottom" fishing for catfish as we drift with the current. And if we're lucky, we might see a doe and her fawn along the shoreline, or perhaps some great blue herons or an eagle overhead.

Jimmy's words conveyed his feelings about his childhood home without his having to tell us about them.

SPEAKER'S notes   Self-Awareness Inventory

1. Was your *cultural background* important in shaping you?
2. Was your *environment* a major contributor to who you are?
3. Did a *special person* have a lasting impact on your life?
4. Were you shaped by an unusual *experience*?
5. Does a favorite *activity* add meaning to your life?
6. Does your *work* help define you as an individual?
7. Were you shaped by a special *goal* or *purpose* in life?
8. Do your values help define who you are?

---

3. *Was there some particular person—a friend, relative, or childhood hero—who had a major impact on your life?* Why do you think this person had such influence? Often you will find that some particular person was a great inspiration to you. Here is a chance to share that inspiration, honor that person, and in the process, tell us much about you. In her self-introductory speech, Marty Gaines explained how her two grandmothers had meant so much to her:

> Margaret Hasty was my "Memma." She was the kind of grandmother that everybody knows and loves. The kind that when you visit her house, she's waiting for you at the back door and you walk up the steps and she grabs you, and she gives you a big hug. And she's always got your favorite cookies hidden in the cabinet.

Martha Clark Akers was my other grandmother. And that's what she was, my Grandmother. Grandmother was very formal, very strict, very well educated. And when you went to visit Grandmother's house, she was at the door. But she didn't yank you up and give you a big hug. She held the door open so that you could walk in, file past, and give her a gentle kiss on the cheek. And then you would go to the couch and sit down. And she would say, "Well, how are your grades?" or "What books have you read lately?"

I didn't understand Grandmother for years. I finally realized that she loved me just as much as Memma, but in a different way. Where Memma loved me for who I was, Grandmother loved me for what she knew I could become and for what she wanted me to be. Both have given me a great blessing.

Now, when I come home from work, there are some days that I'll just grab my children up, give them a big hug, and tell them I love them. And I think to myself, "Thank you, Memma." And then there are days when I come home and there may be a nasty note from the teacher, and I know I'm going to have to be strong and strict. And I say to myself, "Give me strength, Grandmother."

4. *Have you been marked by some unusual experience?* What was it? Why was it important? How did it affect you? What does this experience tell us about you as a person? The speech at the end of this chapter emphasizes the power of experience in shaping lives. Sabrina Karic tells how she survived war and ethnic cleansing as a child. Her experiences have made her appreciate the small things in life that many of us may take for granted—things like a chocolate bar.

5. *Are you best characterized by an activity that brings meaning to your life?* Remember, what is important is not the activity itself but how and why it affects you. When you finish, the audience should have an interesting picture of you or the person you are introducing. When he conducted his self-awareness inventory, David Smart decided that playing golf had taught him useful lessons:

I don't let the little frustrations bother me and I keep going, no matter what happens. In golf, even though you hit a bad shot, you still have to go on and hit the next one. You can't walk off the course just because things aren't going your way. College life is the same way. If you have a bad day or do poorly on a test, you can't just give up and go home. You have to get up the next day and keep trying.

6. *Is the work you do a major factor in making you who you are?* If you select this approach, focus on how your job has shaped you rather than simply describing what you do. What have you learned from your work that has changed you or made you feel differently about others? Richard Bushart was quite a spectacle as he stood to present his self-introductory speech, wearing a big red nose, a coat with a floppy bow tie, and a yellow wig that spiked in all directions. Actually, it was his work outfit—Richard was a clown! But those who were expecting a trivial or lighthearted speech were in for a surprise: Richard wanted to talk about how being a clown had admitted him into the wise and wonderful world of children.

An adult will think I'm foolish, weird, or just insane. But to a child I'm funny, caring, and a friend. Children have taught me so much. . . . They have inspired me to dream again and be creative. A child playing in the backyard can take a broom and turn it one way and it's a horse waiting to ride. Turn it another way, and it's a hockey stick. Turn it still another, and it becomes a telescope that she can see the universe through.

Richard's work had taught him "never to lose that childlike heart no matter how old I get."

7. *Are you best characterized by your goals or purpose in life?* Listeners are usually fascinated by those whose lives are dedicated to some purpose. If you choose to describe some personal goal, be sure to emphasize why you have the goal and how it affects you. Tom McDonald had returned to school after dropping out for eleven years. In his self-introductory speech, he described his goal:

> Finishing college means a lot to me now. The first time I enrolled, right out of high school, I "blew it." All I cared about was sports, girls, and partying. Even though I have a responsible job that pays well, I feel bad about not having a degree. My wife's diploma hangs on our den wall. All I have hanging there is a stuffed duck!

As he spoke, many of the younger students began to identify with Tom. They saw a similarity between what caused him to drop out of school and their own feelings at times. Although he wasn't "preachy," Tom's description of the rigors of working forty hours a week and carrying nine hours a semester in night school carried a clear message.

8. *Are you best described by a value that you hold dear?* How did it come to have such meaning for you? Why is it important to you? Values are abstract, so you must rely on concrete applications to make them meaningful to others. As she described her commitment to family values, Velma Black discussed growing up in a large family on a small farm in Missouri:

> When you are one of thirteen, you have to learn to get along with others. You have no choice. You learn to work together without whining and complaining. And you learn to love—not noisy shows of affection—just quiet caring that fills the house with warmth and strength.

As she told stories of her early life, Velma was able to reveal her family values and why they meant so much to her.

As you explore your own background or that of a classmate, we suggest that you ask all the probe questions in the Self-Awareness Inventory. Don't be satisfied with

Your early environment and favorite activities can be a rich source of ideas for speeches.

FINDING YOUR
voice   The Adventure of Preparing Your First Speech

Write out a summary of your personal adventure of preparing your first speech. What steps identified in this chapter were most difficult for you? Why? What mistakes did you make? What could you have done to avoid such problems? What have you learned about speech preparation that might be useful for your next speech? Submit your report and analysis to your instructor. Keep a copy for yourself so you can review it as you prepare later speeches.

the first idea that comes to mind. You should find this thorough examination of yourself and others to be quite rewarding. You will be discovering yourself and finding your voice through the process.

One word of caution: Remember, you are not on a tabloid talk show. You don't want to embarrass listeners with personal disclosures they would just as soon not hear. If you are uncertain about whether to include such personal material, discuss it with your instructor. The general rule to follow is, *When in doubt, leave it out!*

FINAL
reflections   Exploration through Preparation

Preparing and presenting your first speech should help you find your voice as others around you are finding theirs. You can explore what is important to you, what you are most interested in, and what values are most vital. You will discover some basic ways of organizing your speech materials to effectively convey your ideas to others. And you will grow in self-confidence as you stand and make a successful presentation.

A Little Chocolate

SABRINA KARIC

Sabrina Karic gave this self-introductory speech to her class at the University of Nevada–Las Vegas. Her speech is built round a narrative that features a personal experience as the shaping force in her life. She tells about surviving the ethnic cleansing that took place in Bosnia and Herzegovina during the early 1990s when she was a child. As she described this situation, her listeners were intrigued by her power and passion.

In her prologue, Sabrina ▶ ducked beneath the table as she played the sounds of an explosion and gunfire which startles the audience, then she establishes her credibility to speak from personal experience.

I want you to think back to when you were six years old. Then, imagine living in a time, a place, a country, where you constantly heard the noises I just played. I am from the small, durable, and tragic country of Bosnia and Herzegovina. In 1992, while many of you were playing with toys and learning to ride a bike, I was living through a nightmare. I was six years old, not really ready to experience war. But on May 28th, I heard my first gun shots and my happy, innocent childhood ended. Almost overnight, my family of privileged Bosnians was plunged into homelessness and poverty.

In the first major scene of ▶ her story, as her family begins to starve in Gorazde, Sabrina uses concrete detail to help her listeners visualize and share the horror of her experience.

After the Serbs forced us out of our home, we had to endure endless nights sleeping under trees while rain poured down on us and mice crawled over our bodies. We finally made our way to Gorazde, a city that was surrounded by the Serbians and held under siege for months. The local authorities kept us all barely alive by distributing food among the families. Typically each week we would receive thirty pounds of flour, three pounds of beans, one pound of sugar, and two liters of oil. Every day, my mom made bread that was one inch thick. She divided it in half; one half for breakfast and the other for dinner. Then each half was divided in five even pieces, one piece for me, my mom, my dad, my sister, and my cousin, who lived with us.

This was incredibly hard for us. We often ran out of food before the next week's food distribution. Sometimes the supplies were delayed or not available. I can tell you that nothing etches itself more in a child's memory than the pain of hunger. During those days, I never dreamed of living in a big house, or having a pool, or even a doll to play with. I simply prayed to God for chocolate.

On January 31st of 1993, my parents decided to leave for Grebak, where the Bosnian army was situated. They would have to sneak through enemy lines to get there. If they made it, the Bosnian army would give them food to bring back to us. If they didn't make it—well, we didn't talk about that. If they didn't try, we were all going to starve anyway.

When my parents departed, they had to leave my sister and me on our own. Luckily, we had cousins who lived in Gorazde long before the war began. They took us in, and I can tell you that if it hadn't been for them, we would have starved to death. Days passed, and each day we waited for our parents. And our fears began to grow. We heard rumors that they had run into mine fields and been killed. We felt very much alone and scared.

Then on February 7th, a miracle happened. The door opened, and there were our parents! I remember the crying and hugging and kissing. And I remember hope flooding back into our hearts. Our parents explained that although many people had died, God had spared them.

That day I learned the meaning of gratitude, as well as sorrow for those whose parents would not return. But then our thoughts turned to food. My parents had brought so much of it to us! For those of you who celebrate Christmas, I'm sure I can compare my happiness on that one day to all of your holidays, added together. My parents had brought us one unforgettable treasure: Can you guess what it was?

Yes, it was chocolate, a small chocolate bar, broken into pieces during the trip. But my sister and I treasured each tiny piece, and ate it very slowly.

After the joy of that reunion, we returned to the reality of life around us. It seemed that every day, the explosions were getting closer, louder, and more frequent. I remember one particular day when I was playing with my friends outside our building. Suddenly we heard a nearby explosion, and all of us dashed for the building. We knew that we had only a few seconds at best. I just got inside the door and closed it, when a grenade exploded right where we had been playing. I fell to the floor and put my hands over my ears, waiting for the ringing to go away. After a few minutes, I peeked outside to see if any of my friends had been hurt. Thank God, all of us had been spared.

I can't remember how this nightmare ended, but somehow it did. Clearly, that whole experience left a huge scar on my heart. To this day, I vividly remember everything, and the experience has made me the person I am today. Now, I appreciate small things in life. I find satisfaction just taking a walk in the park, thanking God I survived. The experience also made me a fighter, and gave me strength and a will to live that has carried me through life, and brought me here to share my story with you.

And even today, my experience makes me weep for all the children everywhere—Muslim, Jewish, and Christian—in Africa, the Middle East, and elsewhere—all the six-year-olds who experience prejudice and hatred and violence they can't understand. I weep for the loss of their innocence, for the loss of their happiness, for the loss of their lives. Can't we reach out to them and make their world a little more liveable? Can't we bring them a little chocolate?

◄ In the second major scene, waiting for the return of her parents, Sabrina describes her growing despair. This dark feeling sets up the happiness she feels over their safe return. She uses an analogy to Christmas to help her listeners appreciate her joy. In this scene chocolate begins to develop its larger symbolic meaning.

◄ In the third scene of her plot, Sabrina jerks listeners back into the daily horror of her situation. The image of a hand grenade interrupting the play of children is especially graphic and memorable.

◄ In her epilogue Sabrina reflects on the meaning of her ordeal and invites listeners to look for ways to counter such inhumanity. Note how she applies her experience in global, contemporary ways. At this final point in the speech, chocolate has become a universal symbol for hope.

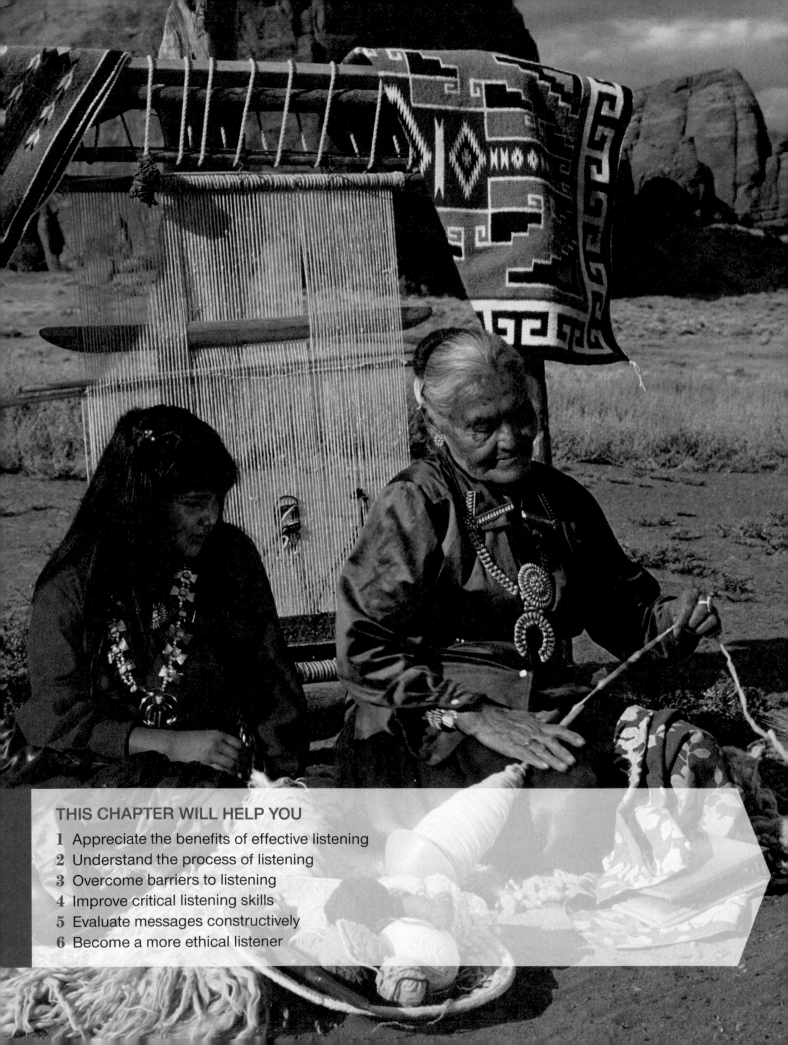

THIS CHAPTER WILL HELP YOU

1 Appreciate the benefits of effective listening
2 Understand the process of listening
3 Overcome barriers to listening
4 Improve critical listening skills
5 Evaluate messages constructively
6 Become a more ethical listener

4 Becoming a Better Listener

Know how to listen, and you will profit even from those who talk badly.
—PLUTARCH

Jacobs was silent for a while, thinking about it, her face full of sympathy. She was a talented listener. He had noticed it before. When you talked to this woman, she attended. She had all her antennae out, focused on the speaker. The world was shut out. Nothing mattered but the words she was hearing. Listening was ingrained in the Navajo culture. One didn't interrupt. One waited until the speaker was finished, gave him a moment or two to consider additions, or footnotes or amendments, before one responded. But even Navajos too often listened impatiently. Not really listening, but framing their reply. Jean Jacobs really listened.[1]

It would be nice if everyone listened this intently, this effectively. Unfortunately, good listeners are rare. Legend has it that President Franklin Delano Roosevelt was bemused by the poor listening behavior of people who visited the White House. To test his notion that people didn't really listen, he once greeted guests in a receiving line by murmuring, "I murdered my grandmother this morning." Typical responses ran along the lines of "Thank you," "How good of you," and other platitudes of polite approval. Finally he met someone who had actually listened and who responded, "I'm sure she had it coming to her."[2]

Poor listening can exact a large price. Leaders may make up their minds about the intentions of other nations and then refuse to listen to information that does not support their conclusions. People in groups, swayed by the power of one member's personality, may make poor decisions. Juries may not render fair verdicts because they have not used critical listening skills. If you are not listening effectively in a classroom, you may find it hard to do well in a course.

Fortunately, listening skills can be learned. In this chapter we consider why you should want to become a better listener, and describe the listening process. We then consider some of the causes of poor listening and suggest ways to overcome them. Next, we tie these skills into the evaluation of speeches, especially in the classroom. Finally, we consider your ethical responsibilities as a listener.

The Benefits of Effective Listening

Why should you want to become a better listener? Becoming a more effective listener will help you become a more effective speaker in at least four ways:

1. You will develop a sense of your audience. As you listen to their speeches you will get a feel for what types of topics and examples might interest them, what authorities they will respect, and how they feel about important issues. Effective listening tunes you in to such factors.

2. You will become sensitive to which techniques work and don't work in different situations. Not all speaking techniques work well all the time. Some that you hear will seem brilliant, while others fall flat. You will develop a sense of which techniques work best with your audience in various situations.

3. You will learn how to evaluate what you hear, what constitutes a credible source of information, and whether appropriate types of supporting materials are used.

4. You can use what you learn from listening to others to help you find your voice. You may hear speeches on topics you never thought you would find interesting, thus expanding your horizons. And, you can learn to evaluate your personal positions on issues to see if they will stand up to critical scrutiny.

All of these skills can help you develop and present more effective speeches.

Listening in the Workplace

John was a truck driver hauling a load of lettuce. He called his dispatcher early in the morning. "Where do you want me to take the load?"

"Jackson," she answered, and gave him the street address.

Around lunchtime, John called her back, "Well, I'm in Jackson, and I can't find the address."

"I've got it here, just as clear as can be. It says, get off I-40 at exit 82 and . . . ."

"Wait a minute," John interrupts. "I came down on I-55."

"I-55? In Jackson, Tennessee?"

"Hold it. You didn't tell me that. I'm in Jackson, Mississippi."

"Well, why didn't you ask me?" she countered. And while they argued over who was more to blame, the poor speaker or the poor listener, a load of lettuce wilted under the Mississippi sun.

Variations of this story are played out in different forms every day. Most employees spend about 60 percent of their workday listening.[3] Who can say how much time and money are lost because of poor listening. This is one reason companies assign great importance to listening ability in their hiring, promotion, and firing decisions. As former President Calvin Coolidge noted, "No man ever listened himself out of a job."

Effective listening skills are valued in almost all jobs in an organization. This may be because ineffective listening leads to ineffective performance. If you listen effectively on the job, you will improve your chances of having a successful career.

Listening in the Classroom

It is a brilliant fall day. Marvin is sitting in his human relations class, but his mind is wandering somewhere off in space as he thinks about Saturday's football game and his date for the weekend. Then, he texts his girlfriend to check on their plans. The instructor's voice drones on in the background of his mind, but the words don't register until she says: "Now, I know that Marvin has worked in this kind of challenging environment. Marvin, please tell us what it was like."

The ability to listen effectively can help you in your other classes.

If you have ever lived through this kind of nightmare, we won't have a hard time convincing you how important listening is in the classroom. Effective listeners read assignments ahead of time to familiarize themselves with new words and to build a basis for understanding. They take careful notes that help them to review effectively for tests.

SPEAKER'S notes   Guidelines to Improve Your Notetaking

Following these guidelines will help you listen more effectively both to instructors and to classroom speeches:

1. Study background material ahead of time.
2. Come prepared with paper and a pen or pencil.
3. Leave a 3-inch margin on the left side of your notes to add comments after class.
4. Take your notes in outline form, leaving space between main points.
5. Don't try to write down everything you hear. Write down verbs and nouns; omit adjectives, adverbs, and prepositions.
6. Be alert for signal words such as:
   a. *for example,* which suggests that supporting material will follow.
   b. *the three steps,* which suggests a list you should number.
   c. *before* or *after,* which suggests that the order is important.
   d. *therefore,* which suggests a causal relationship.
   e. *similarly* or *on the other hand,* which suggests that a comparison or contrast will follow.
   f. *above all* or *keep in mind,* which means that this is an important idea.
7. Summarize what you hear and jot questions in the large left margin.
8. Review and correct your notes the same day that you take them.

The Chinese symbol for listening suggests the complexity of the process.

Effective listening is particularly important in the public speaking class. Earlier we mentioned ways that listening can help you become a better speaker. Additionally, good listeners provide feedback that helps speakers adjust their messages. An attentive audience can help ease a speaker's anxiety by creating a supportive environment. Give speakers your undivided attention, and show respect for them as people, even if you disagree with their ideas.

The Process of Listening

The Chinese symbol for the verb *listen* has four basic elements: attention, ears, eyes, and heart. These elements are reflected in the dynamic listening process, which is made up of interacting and mutually supportive phases. Although these phases seem separated when they are discussed in print, they are not separable in practice. Any "apparent" separation among these phases tends to recede as they blend, overlap, or occur simultaneously. The major phases in the listening process include:

- *Threshold listening*, which involves being able to distinguish and interpret the words in a message and to pick up on the cues to meaning intended by speakers.

- *Critical listening*, which adds appreciation and evaluation to the reception of a message.

- *Empathic listening*, which moves beyond recognizing the rationality of a speech to encompassing the human and humane aspects of a message.

- *Constructive listening*, which involves an active search for the value that messages have for your life.

Threshold Listening

Threshold listening involves finding meaning in the sounds you hear. This includes not only the words in a message, but the way the words are spoken and the nonverbal messages that accompany them. Because we listen not only with our ears but with our eyes as well, threshold listening also includes being able to interpret a speaker's body language. Threshold listening involves the attention, eyes, and ears of the Chinese symbol for listening.

Critical Listening

Critical listeners are skeptical listeners. They accept nothing at face value. The major function of **critical listening** is to enable us to detect problems in the message or in the apparent intention of the speaker. Developing critical listening skills helps protect us from manipulative persuasion. To listen critically you must be able to sort through the evidence and arguments, determine the credibility of sources

▶ **threshold listening** Phase of listening in which we focus on, understand, and interpret the verbal and nonverbal aspects of messages.

▶ **critical listening** Listening for careful appreciation and evaluation of a message.

cited, detect logical fallacies, and wade through emotional language and appeals (see Chapters 14 and 15).

A second function of critical listening involves understanding the ways in which esthetically pleasing language can beguile us into accepting messages without actually evaluating them. For example, we may get so caught up in the beauty of language or the grace of delivery that we tend to ignore the power and effectiveness of such factors (see Chapters 11 and 12).

Empathic Listening

Empathic listening is based on listening with your heart. It goes beyond critical listening in that you try to see things from the speaker's perspective. Empathic listening is important in public speaking courses when your classmates are trying to cope with communication anxiety. It creates a supportive environment for speaker development. It searches for the humanity in a message.

Constructive Listening

Constructive listening involves an active search for the value that messages may have for your life. It presumes that all messages have some value, even if they only serve as negative examples. Constructive listeners participate with speakers in the construction of meaning. For example, in response to a speech urging the importance of mathematics education, constructive listeners may ask questions such as, "Does mathematics education contribute to the development of logical thinking? Should math education be adapted to the needs and goals of local students?" Discussion on such questions following a speech can create a constructive dialogue in which the ultimate meaning of a message develops out of the interaction of the participants.

Effective Listening Behaviors

Even those of us who think we listen well often fall victim to one or more of the barriers to effective listening. We sometimes let our minds wander, or get sidetracked thinking about personal matters, or may make up our mind about what is being said before we have heard the speaker out. We may let our personal emotions and biases become a problem. Figure 4.1 can help you identify some of the problems that act as your personal barriers to effective listening.

How can we overcome these barriers? Some of them can arise from problems in the speaking situation or with particular speakers. These are often easily corrected. However, listening problems that occur within the listener may require more effort to overcome.

Overcoming External Barriers

External listening barriers are those based on the circumstances of speaking or on speaker problems. They include physical noise, flawed messages, and presentation problems.

Physical Noise. You really are trying to listen attentively to your comparative literature professor describe the contrasting rhyme schemes in English and Italian

---

▶ **empathic listening** Phase of listening in which we go beyond rationality to encompassing the human and humane aspects of a message.

▶ **constructive listening** Search for the value that messages may have for your life, despite their defects.

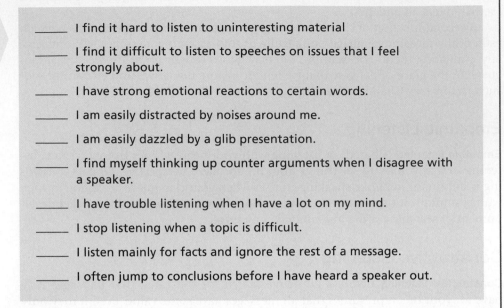

**FIGURE 4. 1
Listening Problems
Checklist**

_____ I find it hard to listen to uninteresting material

_____ I find it difficult to listen to speeches on issues that I feel strongly about.

_____ I have strong emotional reactions to certain words.

_____ I am easily distracted by noises around me.

_____ I am easily dazzled by a glib presentation.

_____ I find myself thinking up counter arguments when I disagree with a speaker.

_____ I have trouble listening when I have a lot on my mind.

_____ I stop listening when a topic is difficult.

_____ I listen mainly for facts and ignore the rest of a message.

_____ I often jump to conclusions before I have heard a speaker out.

sonnets. Suddenly his words are lost in the noise of students horsing around in the hall outside your classroom. "Oh, no," you think. "I can't hear with all this racket!" While you are fuming about that and the professor talks on, you lose track of his message entirely and abandon the attempt to listen.

What we have described is a crisis of threshold listening. Speakers and listeners must work together to solve such noise problems. The speaker should talk louder in order to be heard. Listeners can provide feedback to let the speaker know there is a problem. Cup your hand by your ear or lean forward, obviously straining to hear. If you still can't hear, move to a seat closer to the front of the room. If the noise comes from outside, get up and close the window or door.

Flawed Messages.   Before the noisy students intervened, your instructor had just enlightened you with this blockbuster: "The Petrarchan octave and sestet are replaced by the three Shakespearean quatrains and a rhyming couplet." "Yeah, sure," you think. Messages that are full of unfamiliar words or that are poorly organized interfere with comprehension. When speakers are insensitive to this problem, listeners must make a special effort to overcome it. If you know that there may be unfamiliar words in a class lecture, read about the subject ahead of time. If a message is poorly organized, taking notes can help. Try to pick out the main points. See if you can identify key words, and look for a pattern among them. Differentiate these points and words from supporting materials such as examples or narratives. Finally, by all means, ask questions.

Presentation Problems.   Speakers who talk too fast may be difficult to follow, while speakers who talk too slowly or too softly may lull you to sleep. Speakers also may have distracting mannerisms, such as swaying to and fro or fiddling with their hair. Simply realizing you are responding to irrelevant cues may help you listen more attentively. If you find yourself drifting away because of such problems, remind yourself that what speakers say is what is most important.

SPEAKER'S
notes   Improving Your Listening Skills

Use these suggestions to help improve your listening skills.

1. Identify your listening problems so that you can correct them.

2. Look for something of value in every speech.

3. Put biases and problems aside when listening.

4. Control reactions to trigger words.

5. Control reactions to general distractions.

6. Reserve judgment until you have heard a speech all the way through.

7. Don't try to write down everything a speaker says.

8. Listen for main ideas.

Overcoming Internal Barriers

By far, the greatest barriers to listening arise within listeners themselves. Chief among these barriers are inattention, bad listening habits, emotional reactions to words, and personal biases.

Inattention.   One of the most common barriers affecting listening is simply not paying attention. One cause of this problem is that our minds can process information faster than people speak. Most people talk at about 125 words per minute in public, but listeners can process information at about 500 words per minute. This "communication gap" provides an opportunity for listeners to drift away to more interesting concerns or personal problems.

Chance associations with words may also cause inattention. For example, a speaker mentions the word *table*, which reminds you that you need a lamp table by your bed—which starts you thinking about going to the mall—which reminds you that you didn't eat breakfast and you're hungry. By the time your attention drifts back to the speaker, it's too late.

Personal concerns are a third cause of inattention. When you are tired, hungry, angry, worried, or pressed for time, you may find it difficult to concentrate. Your personal problems may take precedence over listening to a speaker. Or, you simply may have "listening burnout" from too much concentrated exposure to oral material. If you've ever attended three lecture classes in a row, you will know what this means.

Overcoming inattention requires some work. Bridge the speaking–listening gap by paraphrasing to yourself what the speaker has just said. Leave personal worries at the door. Establish eye contact with the speaker, and consciously commit to listening.

Bad Listening Habits.   It is all too easy to acquire bad listening habits. You probably know how to fake attention while tuning out a speaker. You may listen just for facts. Too much television viewing may lead you into the "entertainment syndrome," in which you want speakers to be lively, funny, and engaging at all times. Unfortunately, not all subjects lend themselves to entertainment.

FIGURE 4.2
Differences Between Good and Poor Listeners

Good Listeners	Poor Listeners
1. Focus on the message	1. Let their minds wander
2. Control emotional reactions	2. Respond emotionally
3. Set aside personal problems	3. Get sidetracked by personal problems
4. Listen despite distractions	4. Succumb to distractions
5. Ignore speaker's mannerisms	5. Get distracted by speaker's mannerisms
6. Listen for things they can use	6. Tune out dry material
7. Reserve judgment	7. Jump to conclusions
8. Consider ideas and feelings	8. Listen only for facts
9. Hold biases in check	9. Allow biases to interfere
10. Realize listening is hard work	10. Confuse listening with hearing

Overcoming bad habits requires effort. If you find yourself faking attention, remember that honest feedback helps speakers, while faking misleads them. Differentiate between main ideas and supporting materials. Pay attention to nonverbal cues. Does the speaker's tone of voice change the meaning of the words? Are the gestures and facial expressions consistent with the words? If not, what does this tell you? Remember, not all important messages will or should be fun. Focus on what you can get out of a speech beyond enjoyment.

To become effective listeners, we may have to work to overcome boredom and fatigue.

Emotional Reactions to Words. Certain words may set off such powerful emotional reactions that they become a barrier to effective listening. We call these **trigger words**. Trigger words can evoke either positive or negative reactions. Positive trigger words generally relate to values and traditions that we hold dear. Negative trigger words often relate to racial, ethnic, sexist, or religious slurs.

Positive trigger words can blind us to flawed or dangerous messages. Our reactions to them are usually subtle, and we may not realize that we are being influenced. How many times have people been deceived by such trigger words as *freedom*, *democracy*, or *progress* to justify certain courses of action? Negative trigger words may invoke extreme emotional reactions in us, thus lowering our estimation of a speaker's ethos and making us less likely to give her message a fair hearing.

How can you lessen the power of trigger words? To help you gain control over them, Professor Richard Halley of Weber State University and past president of the International Listening Association suggests that you observe your own behavior

▶ **trigger words** Words that arouse such powerful feelings that they interfere with the ability to listen critically and constructively.

FINDING YOUR

voice   Identifying Trigger Words

List three positive and three negative trigger words that provoke a strong emotional reaction when you hear them, including ideals, political terms, sexist or ethnic slurs, and so on. Consider why these words have such a strong impact and how you might control your reactions to them. Share your insights with your classmates.

over a period of time and make a list of words that cause you to react emotionally.[4] Then, ask yourself the following questions:

- Do I let these words affect the way I respond to messages?
- Could the speaker be using these words to test or manipulate me?
- What can I do to control my reactions?

Train yourself to listen to the entire message before allowing yourself to react. By listening before reacting, you can avoid jumping to conclusions that may not be grounded in the reality of the situation.

Personal Biases.   All of us have biases of one kind or another. Unfortunately, they can sidetrack effective listening. Like trigger words, biases may be difficult to

Problem	Try this
Physical Noise	Alert speaker, move closer, shut door or window
Complex message	Familiarize yourself with topic ahead of time, take notes, provide honest feedback
Presentation style	Keep your focus on the message, not the manner
Inattention	Paraphrase what you hear, check personal concerns at the door
Bad habits	Don't fake attention or give irrelevant feedback, don't always expect to be entertained.
Responses to trigger words	Identify your trigger words, don't jump to conclusions
Personal biases	Admit you have these, delay judgement, look for something of value in message

**FIGURE 4.3
Overcoming Barriers
to Effective Listening**

control. The first step in controlling biases is to recognize that you have them. Next, decide to listen as objectively as you can. Being objective does not mean that you must agree with a message, only that you will reserve judgement until you have heard the entire speech. Decide that you will look for something of value in every speech that you hear.

To learn more about how to overcome external and internal barriers to listening, visit the excellent Web site "Effective Listening Skills," presented by the Elmhurst College Learning Center, www.elmhurst.edu/library/learningcenter/Listening/effective_listening_skills.htm. See the "Suggestions for Active Listening" link.

Becoming a Critical Listener

Critical listening involves developing a healthy skepticism about what you hear. It can protect you from manipulative messages, yet it requires you to give a fair hearing to ideas you disagree with. Critical listening is a skill that can be acquired. To develop this skill, you must learn to apply certain vital questions to all that you hear:

- Do speakers support the claims that they make?

- Do they document the sources of their information within the speech, and are these sources credible?

- Is language used to clarify the subject and aid understanding, or does it function more to mystify and intimidate critical listening?

- What strategies are speakers using to make me more vulnerable to their messages?

Do Speakers Support Their Claims?

The claims and proposals within a speech should be justified by facts, testimony, examples, or narratives. To measure the adequacy of this justification, remember the four R's: supporting material should be *relevant, representative, recent,* and *reliable.*

Evidence is *relevant* when it relates directly to the issue at hand. The speaker who declares, "The Internet is destroying family values!" and then offers statistics that demonstrate a rising national divorce rate has not established the connection between the Internet and family values. The information is not relevant to the claim.

Supporting materials should also be *representative* of a situation rather than an exception to the rule. The speaker who asserts, "Young people have no sense of values," based on a study of juvenile delinquents in London, has violated this particular "R."

Information should be the most *recent* available. This is particularly important when knowledge about a topic is changing rapidly. Information should also be *reliable*—we must be able to depend on it. The more significant and controversial the claim, the more reliable the evidence must be. Reliability means that the claims should be confirmed by more than one source, that the sources of information should be independent of each other, and that the sources possess impeccable credentials.

Information should also be evaluated in terms of how well it fits with what you already know. Information that is inconsistent with what you know or believe should set off an alarm in your mind. You should always evaluate such material very carefully before you accept it.

When evaluating supporting ideas, be sure the speaker avoids confusing facts, inferences, and opinions. **Facts** are verifiable units of information that can be confirmed by independent observation. **Inferences** are assumptions or projections based on incomplete data. **Opinions** add judgments to facts and inferences. For example, "Mary was late for class today" is a fact. "Mary will probably be late for class again tomorrow" is an inference. "Mary is an irresponsible student" is an opinion. Be alert to possible confusions among facts, inferences, and opinions as you listen to messages.

Do Speakers Rely on Credible Sources?

Evidence and supporting material should come from sources that are trustworthy and competent in the subject area. Speakers should document these sources carefully, demonstrating that they are expert and authoritative on the topic. If these credentials are left out or described only in vague terms, a red flag should go up in the minds of critical listeners. We recently found an advertisement for a health food product that contained "statements by doctors." A quick check of the current directory of the American Medical Association (AMA) revealed that only one of the six "doctors" cited was a member of AMA and that his credentials were misrepresented. Always ask yourself, *Where does this information come from?* and *Are these sources really qualified to speak on the topic?*

Do Speakers Use Words to Reveal or Befuddle?

When speakers want to hide something, they often use incomprehensible or vague language. Introducing people who are not physicians as "doctors" to enhance their testimony on health subjects is one form of vagueness. Another ruse is using pseudoscientific jargon, such as "This supplement contains a gonadotropic hormone similar to pituitary extract in terms of its complex B vitamin methionine ratio." Huh? If it sounds impressive but you don't know what it means, be careful. In addition, if speakers use trigger words or inflammatory language, be careful about accepting their ideas.

SPEAKER'S

notes   Critical Thinking Red Flags

These red flags should alert you to potential problems in a message.

1. No objective evidence provided
2. Sources of information not identified
3. Questionable sources of information
4. Information inconsistent with what you know
5. Claims of exclusive knowledge

6. Opinions or inferences passed off as facts
7. Vague or incomprehensible language
8. Overdone emotional appeals
9. Outlandish promises or guarantees

What Strategies Do Speakers Use?

You can pretty well anticipate that skillful speakers will paint their positions in the best possible light. There is nothing inherently wrong with that tendency, but as a critical listener you have to take it into account when you assess the merits of a message.

▶ **facts** Information that can be verified by observation or expert testimony.

▶ **inferences** Assumptions based on incomplete information.

▶ **opinions** Expressions of personal attitude or belief offered without supporting material.

Be sure emotional appeals are backed with sound information.

Consider, for instance, the speaker's appeal to your feelings. Emotional appeals are useful for moving people to action, but they can easily be misused. Vivid examples and compelling stories demonstrate the speaker's passion for a subject and invite the listener to share these feelings. However, if speakers do not justify such feelings with good reasons and sound evidence, you should be careful about accepting what they have to say.

You should be equally skeptical of speakers who ignore the emotional aspects of a situation. You cannot fully understand an issue until you understand how it affects others, how it makes them feel, how it colors the way they view the world. Suppose you were listening to a speech on global warming that contained the following statement:

The United States has 5 percent of the world's population but produces 25 percent of the world's carbon dioxide emissions.

Although these numbers are impressive, what do they tell you about the human problems of global warming? Consider how much more meaningful this material might be if accompanied by stories of what this problem can mean for our coastal cities.

The reasoning used in a speech should also make good sense. Conclusions should follow from the points and evidence that precede them. The basic assumptions that support arguments should be those that most rational, unbiased people would accept. Whenever reasoning doesn't seem plausible, question the speaker or consult with independent authorities before you commit yourself.

Speakers who try to rush you into accepting their position or sell you something you don't need often use exaggeration. If an offer sounds too good to be true, it probably is. The health food advertisement previously described contained the following claims:

The healing, rejuvenating and disease-fighting effects of this total nutrient are hard to believe, yet are fully documented. Aging, digestive upsets, prostrate [*sic*] diseases, sore throats, acne, fatigue, sexual problems, allergies, and a host of other problems have been successfully treated . . . . [It] is the only super perfect food on this earth. This statement has been proven so many times in the laboratories around the world by a chemical analyst that it is not subject to debate nor challenge.

Maybe the product is also useful as a paint remover and gasoline additive! As you build effective listening skills, you also develop resistance to persuasive scams from charlatans who try to mask a lack of substance or faulty reasoning with a glib presentation and irrelevant emotional appeals.

Finally, you should consider whether a speaker acknowledges alternative perspectives on issues. Ask yourself, *How might people from a different cultural background see the problem? How might someone of the other gender see it? Would their solutions or suggestions be different?* Whenever a message addresses a serious topic, try to consider the issue from various points of view. New and better ideas often emerge when we look at the world through a new lens.

Evaluating Classroom Speeches

Listening to speeches in the classroom offers you a laboratory to develop skills that are both constructive and critical.

Your Role as a Constructive Listener

Constructive listening invites you to contribute to the meaning and value of messages by seeking their usefulness in your life. It also means helping speakers become more effective through honest, but tactful oral feedback in the form of questions you ask, appreciation you express for effective techniques, or suggestions you offer for improvement.

There is an important difference between criticizing a speaker and offering a **critique** of a speech. *Criticism* suggests focusing on what someone did that was wrong. A *critique* is helpful and supportive, emphasizing strengths as well as weaknesses, showing consideration for the speaker's feelings, and focusing on how a speaker might improve.

A critique harnesses the power of constructive listening to the benefit of both speaker and listener. You can begin to find your own voice by helping others find theirs.

Your Role as a Critical Listener

To develop an orientation to listening that is critical as well as constructive, you need a set of standards to help you answer the question, *What makes a good speech?* The application of standards may vary with the assignment; for example, the critique of an informative speech might focus on the adequacy of statistics and examples, and that of a persuasive speech might emphasize evidence and reasoning. Nevertheless, there are four general areas of concern for evaluating all speeches: overall considerations, substance, structure, and presentation.

SPEAKER'S notes   Guidelines for Giving Constructive Critiques

Follow these guidelines to give helpful feedback to speakers.

1. Be constructive and supportive.
2. Begin with a positive statement.
3. Avoid vague comments such as, "I didn't like this speech."
4. Don't criticize the speaker: analyze the speech.

5. If you point out a specific problem, offer suggestions for improvement.
6. Word criticism tactfully.
7. End with a positive statement.

▶ **critique** An evaluation of a speech that emphasizes strengths as well as weaknesses and that focuses on how a speaker might improve.

Overall Considerations

Overall considerations include issues that apply to the speech as a whole: commitment, adaptation, purpose, freshness, and ethics.

Commitment.   Commitment means caring. You must sense that the speaker truly cares about the subject and about listeners. Committed speakers invest the time and effort needed to gain responsible knowledge of their subject. Commitment also shows up in how well a speech is organized and whether it has been carefully rehearsed. Finally, commitment reveals itself in the energy, enthusiasm, and sincerity the speaker projects. Commitment is the spark in the speaker that can touch off fire in the audience.

Adaptation.   For a speech to be effective, it must meet the requirements of the assignment and be adapted to its audience. An informative speech should extend our understanding of a topic, a persuasive speech should influence attitudes or actions, and a ceremonial speech should celebrate shared values on special occasions. The speech should also conform to the specified time limits, have at least the minimum number of references required for the assignment, and be presented in the style required for that assignment (such as using a presentation aid or making an extemporaneous delivery).

Effective speakers consider each technique in terms of its appropriateness for the audience. Will listeners find this example interesting? Is this information important for them to know? How can I best involve my listeners?

Purpose.   Speeches should have a clear purpose, such as increasing listeners' knowledge of the actions to take when a tornado is imminent or how to make healthy food choices in the cafeteria. The purpose of a speech should be evident by the time the speaker finishes the introduction. A speech that lacks a clear purpose will drift and wander like a boat without a rudder, blown this way and that by whatever random thoughts occur to the speaker. Developing a clear purpose requires speakers to determine what they want to accomplish: what they want listeners to learn, think, or do as a result of their speeches.

Freshness.   Any speech worth listening to brings something new to listeners. The topic should be fresh, or at least the approach to it should be innovative. When speakers rise to the challenge of overused topics such as drinking and driving, they can't simply reiterate the common advice "If you drink, don't drive" and expect to be effective. The audience will have heard that hundreds of times. To get through to listeners on such a subject, speakers must find a new way to present the material. One of our students gave a speech on "responsible drinking and driving" that stressed the importance of understanding the effects of alcohol and of knowing one's own limitations. Her fresh approach provided a new perspective on an old problem.

Ethics.   Perhaps the most important measure of a speech is whether it is good or bad for listeners. As we noted in Chapter 1, *an ethical speech demonstrates respect for listeners, responsible knowledge, and concern for the consequences of exposure to the message.*

Respect for listeners means that speakers are sensitive to the cultural diversity of their audience and accept that well-meaning people may hold varying positions on an issue. Ethical speakers are considerate even as they refute the arguments of others. Ethical speakers also ground their messages in responsible knowledge. They

YOUR ethical VOICE   Evaluating the Ethical Dimensions of a Speech

Public speeches can give rise to a host of ethical problems. To test the ethical dimensions of speech, ask yourself these questions:

1. Does the speaker have responsible knowledge of the topic?
2. Does the speaker show respect for the audience?
3. Does the speaker demonstrate concern about the impact of the speech?

4. Does the speaker document sources of information?
5. Does the speaker avoid inflammatory language?
6. Does the speaker avoid exaggerating claims?

provide oral documentation for the vital information in their speeches and offer a capsule summary of the credentials of experts they cite. They are alert to potential biases in their perspective. Ethical speakers do not pass off opinions and inferences as facts, nor do they make up data or present the ideas or words of others without acknowledging those contributions.

Finally, ethical speakers are aware that words have consequences. Inflammatory language can arouse strong feelings that discourage critical listening. Ethical speakers think through the potential effects of their messages before they present them. The greater the possible consequences, the more carefully speakers must support what they say with credible evidence and temper their conclusions in keeping with listener sensitivities.

Evaluating Substance

A speech has substance when it has a worthwhile message that is supported by facts and figures, testimony, examples, and/or narratives. The starting point for a substantive presentation is a topic that interests both speaker and listeners. When speakers already know something about the topics they select, their knowledge serves as the foundation for further research, which is what enables them to speak responsibly. Although personal experience gives a good start to speech preparation, speakers should always expand such experience with research.

Skillful speakers combine different types of supporting material to demonstrate their points. Combining statistics with an example will make ideas clearer. For instance, a speaker might say, "The base of the Great Pyramid at Giza measures 756 feet on each side." Although precise, this information may be difficult for listeners to visualize. But by adding, "More than eleven football fields could fit in its base," the speaker has made the material more understandable by providing an illustration that most listeners might relate to.

Evaluating Structure

A good speech carries listeners through an orderly progression of ideas that makes it easy to follow. Without a clear design, a speech may seem to be a random collection of thoughts, and the message can get lost in the confusion.

FINDING YOUR

voice   Listening in Challenging Situations

Identify speakers or speaking situations outside your class—in other classrooms, on the Internet, on television, etc.—that challenge you as a critical and constructive listener. What external or internal barriers in the speaker, the situation, or yourself make it hard for you to listen effectively? What might you miss as the result of impaired listening? How might you overcome this problem? Be prepared to share your thoughts in classroom discussion.

The introduction may begin with an example, a quotation, or a challenging question that draws listeners into the topic: "So you think there's no need in Idaho to worry about climate change? After all, you're not subject to hurricanes like those that hit the Gulf Coast. But what about forest fires? And what about the overall impact of global warming on our world?" Once speakers gain attention, they can prepare listeners for what will come by previewing the main points.

The way the body of a speech is organized will vary with its subject and purpose. A speech that tells you how to do something—such as how to plan a budget—should follow the order of the steps in the process it describes. If the subject breaks naturally into parts, such as the three major types of wine (red, white, and blended), speakers might use a categorical design.

The conclusion of a speech should summarize the points that have been made and offer a final statement that helps listeners remember the essence of the message.

Effective speeches also contain transitions that link together the various parts. Transitions bridge ideas and aid understanding. During the speech, they signal listeners when one thought is ending and a new one is beginning. "Having shown you this, I will now show you that" is a common formula for transitions. They help the speech flow better and help listeners focus on the major points. Transitions are especially vital between the introduction and body of a speech, between the body and conclusion, and among main points within the body.

Evaluating Presentation Skills

No speech can be effective unless it is presented well. Both the actual words speakers use and the way they convey these words are important factors in presentation.

The Language of Speaking. The oral language of speeches must be instantly intelligible. This means that speakers' sentences should be simple and direct. Compare the following examples:

> Working for a temporary employment service is a good way to put yourself through school because there are always jobs to be found and the places you get to work are interesting—besides, the people you work for treat you well, and you don't have to do the same thing day after day—plus, you can tailor the hours to fit your free time.

or

> Working for a temporary employment service is a good way to put yourself through school. Jobs are readily available. You can schedule your work to fit in with your classes. You don't stay at any one place long enough to get bored. And, you meet a lot of interesting people who are glad to have your services.

Which is easier to follow? The first example rambles, with the speaker pausing only to catch a breath. The second example uses short sentences, inviting the use of pauses to separate ideas. As a result, the meaning is clearer.

Concrete words are generally preferable to abstract ones because they create vivid pictures for listeners and clarify meaning. Consider the following levels of abstraction:

most abstract	my pet
	my cat
	my kitten
	my eight-week-old kitten
	my eight-week-old white kitten
most concrete	my eight-week-old white Angora kitten

As the language becomes more concrete, it is easier to visualize what is being said and there is less chance of misunderstanding.

The Art of Presentation. An effective presentation sounds natural and enthusiastic and is free from distracting mannerisms. Most class assignments call for an extemporaneous presentation in which the speech is carefully prepared and practiced but not written out or memorized. Extemporaneous speakers do not read from a script: they focus less on exact wording and more on the flow of ideas, which they constantly adapt according to audience comprehension and interest. If listeners look confused, extemporaneous speakers can rephrase what they have just said or provide an additional example. They speak from an outline that has become embedded in their minds during rehearsal, or at most from a brief outline on a card that cues them to the flow of ideas by mentioning a few key words or phrases. A speech that flows smoothly indicates that the speaker has practiced well.

Strong presentation skills encourage listeners to be attentive.

Speakers should talk loud enough to be heard easily in the back of the room. Their posture should be relaxed but not sloppy. Movements should seem natural and spontaneous as speakers gesture in response to their own ideas and to emphasize the points they are making.

Figure 4.4 summarizes these criteria for evaluating speeches. You may use it as a checklist for critiquing the speeches that you hear in class and in everyday life.

FIGURE 4.4
Guidelines for
Evaluating Speeches

Overall Considerations

Was the speaker committed to the topic?
Did the speech meet the requirements of the assignment?
Was the speech adapted to the audience?
Did the speech promote identification among topic, audience, and speaker?
Was the purpose of the speech clear?
Was the topic handled with imagination and freshness?
Did the speech meet high ethical standards?

Substance

Was the topic worthwhile?
Had the speaker done sufficient research?
Were main ideas supported with information?
Was testimony used appropriately?
Were the sources documented adequately?
Were examples or narratives used effectively?
Was the reasoning clear and correct?

Structure

Did the introduction arouse interest?
Did the introduction preview the message?
Was the speech easy to follow?
Were the main points of the speech evident?
Were transitions used to tie the speech together?
Did the conclusion summarize the message?
Did the conclusion help you remember the speech?

Presentation

Was the language clear, simple, and direct?
Was the language colorful?
Were grammar and pronunciation correct?
Was the speech presented extemporaneously?
Were notes used unobtrusively?
Was the speaker appropriately enthusiastic?
Did the speaker maintain good eye contact?
Did body language complement ideas?
Was the speaker expressive?
Were the rate and loudness appropriate?
Did the speaker use pauses?
Did presentation aids enhance the message?
Were presentation aids integrated into the speech?
Was the presentation free from distracting mannerisms?

Your Ethical Responsibilities as a Listener

The concept of constructive listening is incomplete without considering the importance of listening ethics. Ethical listeners do not prejudge a speech but rather keep an open mind. John Milton, a great seventeenth-century English intellectual, observed

YOUR ethical VOICE   Guidelines for Ethical Listening

The ethical behavior of listeners is often overlooked. Keep these guidelines in mind to help you become an ethical listener.

1. Turn off all electronic devices.
2. Give the speaker your undivided attention.
3. Open your mind to new information and ideas.
4. Park your biases outside the door.

5. Provide honest feedback to listeners.
6. Look for what is useful in a message.
7. Consider how the speech might affect others.
8. Listen to others as you would have them listen to you.

that listening to our opponents can be beneficial. We may learn from them, thus gaining a new perspective on an issue. Or, as we argue with them, we may discover *why* we believe as we do.

Just as we should be open to new ideas, we should also be open to speakers who represent different lifestyles or cultural backgrounds. We should not deprive ourselves of the chance to explore other worlds. In comparing and contrasting our ways with those of others, we learn more about ourselves.

Finally, keep in mind the impact of your listening on others. Good listeners help develop good speakers. Good listeners are also concerned about the ethical impact of messages on others who may not be present. In the sense that they represent all who might be affected by the message, they are the **universal listener**. Such listeners practice their own version of the Golden Rule: "Listen to others as you would have them listen to you." All sides benefit when speakers and listeners take their ethical roles seriously.

FINAL reflections   The Golden Rule of Listening

If we practice the art of blending constructive and critical listening, we are putting into effect the Golden Rule of Listening: *to listen to others as we would have them listen to us.* As you learn to become a better listener, you will also learn to become a better speaker. Listening to your classmates make presentations, you will learn what things interest them, how they feel about certain issues, and what techniques might work best with them. The free flow of ideas in the classroom can also give rise to novel topics and issues you may want to explore in the process of finding your voice.

In the end, there is something mystical and circular about the relationship between speaker and listener: As we listen well to others, we help them become better communicators. Their becoming better communicators makes them easier to listen to. As we experience this mystical relationship, we also make the fascinating discovery that finding your voice can be contagious: In a positive classroom setting, class members may find their voices together.

▶ **universal listeners** Listening as though one represents all who might be affected by a message.

THIS CHAPTER WILL HELP YOU

1 Understand audience dynamics
2 Adapt your message to fit your audience
3 Meet the challenges of audience diversity
4 Adjust your message to the speaking situation

5 Adapting to Your Audience and Situation

" Orators have to learn the differences of human souls."

—PLATO

You've decided to run for the state legislature. On Friday you are scheduled to present your idea for a voluntary wellness program that you believe will reduce the state's unreimbursed medical expenses. You will speak to three different groups that day. At noon you will speak at the senior citizens' center to a group of about seventy-five older adults who gather there for lunch in the cafeteria. They are not very interested in exercising or changing their eating habits. At 2 o'clock you will speak at a local college to the Gay and Lesbian Coalition. You anticipate an audience of about twenty-five students. You think they will be most concerned about AIDS prevention, but you don't believe they think abstinence is the answer. Friday evening you will address a group of about fifty members of the county medical association at an upscale restaurant. The physicians should be receptive to the idea of wellness programs as preventive medicine.

The general topic of your speeches will not change, but the different audiences and situations will require different approaches. Your listeners must be at the center of your thinking as you plan and develop your speeches. For example, with the senior citizens, you might want to stress how exercise and healthy eating can improve their lifestyle. With the students you might discuss how regular exercise enhances their immune systems. With the physicians, your focus might be on what they can do to develop wellness awareness in the community.

The focus of your speech is not the only thing you might want to adjust with respect to your audience. As you consider the size of the audience and the settings for your speeches, you might decide to change the way you present them. Your manner of presentation, as well as the language you choose, may vary from the cafeteria to the campus meeting room to the restaurant.

Why Audience Analysis Is Important

You can never really find your voice until you understand your audience. Each message must be tailored to reach listeners. If a message does not connect with listeners, it is like the conundrum about a tree that falls in the forest when no one is around. Does it make a noise, if there is no one there to hear it? Can your message make an impact if it doesn't reach your listeners?

The more you know about your listeners, the more effective your speech will be. A good audience analysis helps you find answers to four important questions:

1. How interested is my audience in my topic?

2. What does my audience know about my topic?

3. How does my audience feel about my topic?

4. How can I best reach my listeners?

You gain insight into the first question by listening constructively to your classmates as they present their own speeches. A demographic analysis of your audience that considers such factors as age, education, occupation, and group memberships can then provide some information about what they know. Understanding audience dynamics, such as the attitudes of your listeners and the factors that motivate them, helps you answer the third and fourth questions. An effective audience analysis can also help you focus your topic and select the most effective supporting materials.

Is it ethical to adapt a message to fit a particular audience? You have probably heard about political speakers who "waffled"—taking one position with one audience and a different position with another. Such maneuvering is clearly unethical. But it is possible and ethical to adapt a message without surrendering your convictions. You can vary the language you use, the examples you provide, the stories you tell, the authorities you cite, and your manner of presentation without compromising the integrity of your message.

To help you better understand your audience, we first consider *demographic factors*, such as age, political and religious preferences, and gender. Then, we cover *audience dynamics*, which includes the motivations, attitudes, and values of listeners. Next, we discuss some of the major challenges speakers face when addressing a *diverse audience*. Finally, we cover some aspects of the *communication situation* that may call for adaptations in your presentation.

YOUR ethical VOICE   Adaptation or Pandering?

You have been asked to speak to the Community Club at your old high school about immigration problems in your area. You believe that most of the students you will address have strong negative feelings about immigrants coming into the area. Your own feelings on the topic are more complex. You recognize the economic problems that might result from a large influx of immigrants, but at the same time you understand that our country is a nation of immigrants who came to our shores searching for opportunity. In addition, while in college you have become involved with your campus ministries work in helping immigrants find housing and jobs. While teaching English as a second language, you have come to know many of these newcomers and have come to both like and respect them. What could you do to prepare a speech that would both reach your audience and stay true to your own feelings on the subject? What resources might you call on?

Understanding Audience Demographics

What people know about a topic can often be determined by considering their age, gender, education, group affiliations, and sociocultural background. Such factors are called **audience demographics**. With your classroom audience, demographic information is fairly obvious. Start by looking around. How old are your classmates? What kinds of diversity are represented? Listen carefully to the first round of speeches to identify topics listeners find interesting. Keep an ear tuned for the political and social issues your classmates feel are important. If you are speaking to a group outside the classroom, the person who invites you may be able to supply such information.

Your demographic analysis of your audience can also provide insights into their attitudes, beliefs, and values. Much demographic and attitude information is available on public opinion Web sites sponsored by such groups as the Gallup Organization (www.gallup.com), the National Opinion Research Center (www.norc.uchicago.edu), and the Roper Center for Public Opinion Research (www.ropercenter.uconn.edu).

Although the data from national polls provides interesting and thought-provoking information, you should be cautious about using it in your speeches. First, much of this information is gathered through self-reports. In such surveys, people tend to give "socially appropriate" responses to questions. This doesn't mean that they lie, but it can mean that they report "what they think they ought to say" or "how they think they ought to feel." Be especially cautious with information from "polls" that local television stations or Internet sites conduct. Such material is rarely produced from a random sample of respondents: It may simply reflect the feelings of those prompted to reply or the agenda of those who have an ax to grind.

Don't assume that what is true in general about a population will automatically be true of the particular people who will be listening to your speeches. Demographic analyses can supply you with a list of tendencies, but you must confirm whether this list applies to your listeners. With these cautions in mind, we turn now to the various elements of audience demographics: age, gender, educational level, and group affiliations. Keep in mind that these demographic variables should not be considered

▶ **audience demographics** Observable characteristics of listeners, including age, gender, educational level, group affiliations, and sociocultural background.

FINDING YOUR

voice   Where Do Your Listeners Fit In?

Look up polling information on today's college students. Excellent material may be found on-line at any of the major polling sites. Some helpful resources include the Pew Research Center, www.people-press.org; the Polling Report, www.pollingreport.com; or the Higher Education Research Institute, www.geis.ucla.edu. From what you have observed in your classroom, consider how your audience compares with the demographic and attitude information that you find in national polls. Which demographic factors in your audience are similar to those in the polls? Which factors differ?

in isolation. As you look at polling data you will find that it is generally cross-referenced across a variety of these factors, i.e., age by gender, gender by educational level, group affiliations by sociocultural level, and the like. Though we can isolate these factors in discussion, in practice they tend to cluster together.

Age

Age has been used to predict audience reactions since the time of Aristotle, who suggested that young listeners are pleasure-loving, optimistic, impulsive, trusting, idealistic, and easily persuaded. Older people, he said, are more set in their ways, more skeptical, cynical, and concerned with maintaining a comfortable existence. Those in the prime of life, Aristotle argued, present a balance between youth and age, being confident yet cautious, judging cases by the facts, and taking all things in moderation.[1]

Contemporary communication research supports the relationship between age and persuasibility that Aristotle identified. Maximum susceptibility to persuasion occurs during childhood and declines as people grow older. Most research also suggests that younger people are more flexible and open to new ideas and that older people tend to be more conservative and less receptive to change.[2] You can change the minds of older adults, but you'll have to work harder to do it.

Age can be an important factor in the selection of speech topics. For example, an audience consisting mainly of eighteen- and nineteen-year-old college freshmen might be interested in a speech on campus social activities. To an audience of older, nontraditional students, this topic might seem trivial or uninteresting. Age can also be important in terms of the language you use and the people, places, things, or events you refer to in your speeches.

The typical college student audience falls into what has been called the Millennials. A detailed account of this age group can be found in a 2010 Pew Research Center report titled "Millennials: Confident. Connected. Open to Change." The report is available online at http://pewsocialtrends.org/pubs/751/millennials-confident-connected-open-to-change. You might also wish to access the annual report of the Higher Education Research Institute at UCLA on first-year college students, available online at www.gseis.ucla.edu/heri/pr-display.php?prQry=42. As you read this material, keep in mind that the national norms may not fit your particular classroom audience. Interpret the results in light of other information you have gathered about your classmates.

Gender

In the 1950s, *Life* magazine interviewed five male psychiatrists, who suggested that women's ambitions were the "root of mental illness in wives, emotional upset in husbands, and homosexuality in boys."[3] Needless to say, we have come a long way from that era!

In our time, ideas about gender differences continue to change rapidly. The changes are especially marked in the areas of "gender appropriate" roles and interests, where the lines are becoming blurred. Some of the greatest changes in gender roles have come in the areas of education and work. This is especially true in traditional male major areas such as science and engineering.[4] In 1960, 38 percent of females between the ages of twenty-five and fifty-four were in the labor force; by 2009, this number had risen to about 60 percent.[5]

The more you know about your audience, the better you can adapt your message to meet their needs and expectations.

From this data, we can safely conclude that the importance of women in the workforce—and the importance of their occupations—has risen dramatically over the past fifty years. Therefore, we suggest caution in making adjustments based on the gender of your listeners. Be certain that any assumptions you make are based on the most current data available, because the differences are often a matter of "now you see them, now you don't." Differences that seem true as we write may be only illusions by the time you read this text. Finally, be especially careful to avoid sexism and gender stereotyping. These two topics are covered in detail later in this chapter.

Educational Level

You can better estimate your listeners' knowledge of and interest in a topic from their educational level than from their age or gender. The more educated your audience, the more you can assume they know about general topics and current affairs, and the broader their range of interests is apt to be. Research suggests that better-educated audiences are more interested in social, consumer, political, and environmental issues. They are more curious, and they enjoy learning about new ideas, new things, and new places. If your speech presents a fresh perspective on a problem, they should be avid listeners. Finally, better-educated audiences tend to be more open-minded. They are more accepting of social and technological changes and more supportive of women's rights and alternative lifestyles than are less educated listeners.[6]

Educational differences can also affect the strategies you use in a speech. For example, if there are several positions on an issue, you should assume that a better-educated audience will be aware of them. Therefore, you should be especially careful to acknowledge other viewpoints and to explain why you have selected your position. Although you should always speak from responsible knowledge, knowing that your listeners are highly educated places even more pressure on you to prepare carefully. A well-educated audience will require that you supply evidence and examples that can stand up under close scrutiny. If you are not well prepared, such listeners will question your credibility.

FINDING YOUR

voice   The Importance of Groups

Of the groups you belong to, consider the one that means the most to you. What is it about being a part of this group that brings you the greatest satisfaction? Is it the social interaction? The opportunity to do something of value for society? The prestige it confers on you? Share this information with your classmates. What does your membership say about you as a person? What do their own memberships say about your classmates? As a class, make a list of all of your group affiliations. Are there more similarities than differences? How might this information be useful to you as you choose speech topics and prepare your speeches?

Group Affiliations

The groups people belong to reflect their interests, attitudes, and values. Knowing the occupations, political preferences, religious affiliations, and social group memberships of an audience can provide useful information. This knowledge can help you design a speech that better fits the interests and needs of your listeners. It can make your message more relevant and can help promote identification between listeners and your ideas.

Occupational Groups. Knowing your listeners' occupational affiliations or career aspirations can provide insight into how much your listeners know about a topic, the vocabulary you should use, and which aspects of a topic should be most interesting to them. For example, speeches on tax-saving techniques given to college students and then to certified public accountants (CPAs) should not have the same focus or use the same language. With the students, you might stress record keeping and deductions they can take for educational supplies and avoid using technical jargon. With the CPAs, you might concentrate on factors that invite audits by the IRS, and you would not have to be so concerned about translating technical terms into lay language. Knowledge of listeners' occupations also suggests the kinds of authorities that listeners will find most credible. If many of your classmates are business majors, for instance, they may find information from the *Wall Street Journal* more convincing than information from *USA Today*.

Political Groups. Members of organized political groups tend to be interested in problems of public life. Knowing your listeners' political party preferences as well as how interested in politics they are can be useful in planning and preparing your speech. It may even suggest what might be positive and negative trigger words for your audience.[7] For example, while "socialism" is a negative trigger word for Republicans, it is less negative for Democrats. Similarly, "capitalism" is a positive trigger word for Republicans, but is less positive for Democrats.

To see how these factors can work in a speech, let's look at how Amanda Miller handled them as she planned her speech attacking the U.S.-sponsored School of the Americas as a hotbed of ultra-right subversion in the Western hemisphere. Her audience analysis revealed that many of her listeners described themselves as conservative Republicans. If they sensed that she was a leftist critic, they might dismiss her arguments as exaggerated and unwarranted. Therefore, Amanda decided on the following opening to her speech:

> "If any government sponsors the outlaws and killers of innocents, they have become outlaws and murderers themselves, and they will take that lonely path at their own peril." President Bush spoke these words to the world shortly after the attacks on the World Trade Towers.

By citing a person who was held in high regard by many of her listeners, Amanda invited them to look into an ironic mirror: Once they knew what many graduates of the School of the Americas had actually done, they could only conclude that the United States was the kind of rogue government the president had described. Her speech had a powerful impact that day because of the way she adapted it to the political leanings of her audience.

People with strong political ties usually make their feelings known. Look for indications in discussions in class. Some of your classmates may be active members of the Young Democrats or Young Republicans. Your college may conduct mock elections or take straw votes on issues of political interest, reporting the results in the campus newspaper. Be on the alert for such information.

Religious Groups. Knowing the religious affiliations of listeners can provide useful information, because religious training often underlies many of our social and cultural attitudes and values. Members of fundamentalist religious groups are likely to have conservative social and political attitudes. Baptists tend to be more conservative than Episcopalians, who in turn are often more conservative than Unitarians. In addition, a denomination may advocate specific beliefs that many of its members accept as a part of their religious heritage. Since religious affiliation may be a strong indicator of values, it is wise not to ignore its potential importance.

A word of caution must be added here. You can't always assume that because an individual is a member of a particular religious group he or she will embrace all of the teachings of that group. One thing you can count on, however, is that audiences are usually sensitive about topics related to their religious convictions. As a speaker, you should be aware of this sensitivity and be attuned to the religious makeup of your audience. Appealing to "Christian" values before an audience that includes members of other religious groups may offend listeners and diminish the effectiveness of your message.

Social Groups. Typically, we are born into a religious group, raised in a certain political environment, and end up in an occupation as much by chance as by design. But we choose our social groups on the basis of our interests. Membership in social groups can be as important to people as any other kind of affiliation. Photographers may join the campus Film Club, businesspeople may become involved with the local chamber of commerce, and environmentalists may be members of the Sierra Club.

Knowing which social groups are represented in your audience and what they stand for is important for effective audience adaptation. A speech favoring pollution control measures might take a different focus, depending on whether it is presented to the chamber of commerce or to the Audubon Society. With the chamber of commerce,

Knowing the group affiliations of your listeners can help you adapt to their interests, concerns, and needs.

you might stress the importance of a clean environment in persuading businesses to relocate in your community; with the Audubon Society, you might emphasize the effects of pollution on wildlife. People tend to make their important group memberships known to others around them. Be alert to such information from your classmates, and consider it in planning and preparing your speeches.

Sociocultural Background. People often are grouped by their sociocultural background, a broad category that can include everything from the section of the country in which they live to their racial or ethnic identity to their economic status. Demographic Web sites provide access to a wide array of information relevant to a variety of sociocultural groups. Although such material may be fascinating, remember it is *your* audience for *your* speech that is important.

People from different sociocultural backgrounds often have different life experiences, interests, and viewpoints. Consider, for example, the different perspectives that urban and rural audiences may have on gun control. Urban audiences may associate guns with crime and violence in the streets; rural audiences may associate guns with hunting and recreation. A white, middle-class audience might have difficulty understanding what it means to grow up as a member of a minority. Midwesterners and Southerners may have misconceptions about each other.

With diverse audiences, your appeals and examples should relate to those experiences, feelings, values, and motivations that people hold in common. It also may be helpful to envision smaller audiences within the larger group. You may even want to direct specific remarks to these smaller groups. You might say, for example, "Those of you majoring in the liberal arts will find computer skills just as important in your work as they are for business majors," or "Those of you majoring in business may discover that large corporations are looking for employees with the breadth of perspective that comes from a liberal arts education." Direct references to specific subgroups within the audience can keep your speech from seeming too general.

Understanding Audience Dynamics

Once you have factored in the demographic characteristics of your audience, you are ready to consider the final two questions: *How does my audience feel about my topic?* and *How can I best reach my listeners?* To discover the answers to these questions, you must understand some of the psychological forces at work in listeners. While you may never attain a complete understanding of these factors, the more you know about how your audience feels and what moves them, the better your speech will be.

Audience dynamics are the attitudes, beliefs, values, and motivations that affect how listeners receive a message. An understanding of how these dynamics work is vital for adapting your message. The more you understand what makes people tick, the better you can tailor your message so that it serves their interests and needs.

▶ **audience dynamics** The motivations, attitudes, beliefs, and values that influence the behavior of listeners.

Attitudes, Beliefs, and Values

Attitudes typically refer to our *feelings* about things—whether we like or dislike, approve or disapprove of people, places, events, or ideas. Our **beliefs** express what we *know* or *think we know* about subjects. Our important social attitudes are anchored by our **values**, the moral *principles* we live by that suggest how we should behave or what we see as an ideal state of being. To be an effective speaker, you must consider your listeners' attitudes, beliefs, and values as you plan and prepare your speeches.

Attitudes.   Your audience's feelings toward your topic can affect the way it receives your message. For example, suppose you are preparing a speech favoring amnesty for illegal immigrants. You know that many members of your audience strongly oppose this policy. An audience that disagrees with you may distort your message, discredit you, or even refuse to listen to you.

Knowing how listeners feel about your topic allows you to plan your strategies to minimize the impact of negative attitudes. It can suggest what sources you might use to support your ideas, the types of examples you might choose, or even what your specific purpose might be. For example, with a reluctant audience, you should work hard to establish identification early in your speech, perhaps pointing out the values that you and your audience share. You might also want to avoid emotional appeals and limit what you want to accomplish. These and other techniques for persuading a reluctant audience are covered in more detail in Chapter 14.

Beliefs.   Beliefs are acquired through experience and education. Some beliefs may be learned through direct contact: "The waiters at that restaurant are very attentive and helpful." Other beliefs may be acquired indirectly from family, friends, and authority figures as we grow up: "My Aunt Leslie says the Democratic Party thinks about the average man." Or "Well, my Uncle Fred says that the Republicans are always against things."

Many beliefs are based on verifiable facts, such as, "The price of digital cameras has dropped dramatically over the past five years." Other beliefs are based more on faith or even legend: "You should always buy a Ford truck" or "Southerners are good cooks." At their worst, beliefs may express demeaning stereotypes about races, religions, or cultures. Information about your listeners' beliefs can suggest what additional information you need to provide or what misinformation you may need to correct.

Values.   Values may include such ideals as honesty, equality, peace, freedom, and salvation. Our personal, social, religious, and political values guide much of our thinking and behavior. They are the foundation for our most important beliefs and attitudes, providing us with standards for evaluation.

Values are at the core of our identity. As principles that govern our behavior and our way of seeing the world, they are highly resistant to change. Information that clashes with a listener's values is likely to be rejected without much thought. Speakers don't normally try to change values. Rather, they try to show how values relate to a topic in order to justify certain interpretations and recommendations. References to shared values can increase identification between a speaker and the audience and strengthen the persuasive impact of a speech.

Insight into the attitudes, beliefs, and values of your audience can help you plan your messages. It can aim you in the proper direction so that you select the most effective appeals, decide which authorities to cite, and determine which examples and stories might work best in your speeches.

▶ **attitudes**   Feelings we have developed toward specific kinds of subjects.

▶ **beliefs**   What we know or think we know about subjects.

▶ **values**   The moral principles that suggest how we should behave or what we see as an ideal state of being.

Gathering Information about Attitudes

How can you find out about attitudes toward your topic? In the classroom, this is not difficult because people reveal this kind of information readily as they take part in class discussions. Outside the classroom, you might question the person who invites you to speak about those aspects of the audience's attitude that are related to your topic.

**FIGURE 5.1
Sample Attitude
Questionnaire**

For each question, please circle the number that most clearly represents your position.

1. How interested are you in the topic of capital punishment?

Very Interested		Unconcerned			Not Interested
7	6	5	4	3	2	1

2. How important do you think the issue of capital punishment is?

Very Important		No Opinion			Very Unimportant
7	6	5	4	3	2	1

3. How much do you know about capital punishment?

Very Little		Average Amount			Very Much
7	6	5	4	3	2	1

4. How would you describe your attitude toward capital punishment?

Total Opposition		"On the Fence"			Total Support
7	6	5	4	3	2	1

5. Please place a check beside the sources of information on capital punishment that you would find the most acceptable.

_____ Attorney general's office

_____ FBI

_____ Local police department

_____ Criminal justice department of the university

_____ American Civil Liberties Union

_____ Local religious leaders

_____ Conference of Christians and Jews

_____ NAACP

_____ Other (please specify)_____

Comments:

To understand more fully how your listeners' attitudes may relate to your topic, you can conduct a survey to explore what your listeners know about your topic, how they feel about it, and how they might respond to different sources of information. Figure 5.1 shows a sample audience survey questionnaire on the subject of capital punishment that may be used as a guide to developing a questionnaire on your subject.

When preparing an attitude survey questionnaire, you should use the following guidelines:

- Use simple sentences with a single idea.

- Use clear, concrete language.

- Keep questions short.

- Avoid words such as *all, always, none,* and *never.*

- Keep your own biases out of the questions.

- Keep the questionnaire short.

- Provide room for comments.

Finally, keep in mind that any questionnaire results you get, either from one you conduct yourself or from one that is professionally administered, provide only a general snapshot of where your audience stands on a topic. Compare what you learn from a questionnaire with what you hear as you listen to others talking about the issue in question.

Motivation

To answer the question *How can I best reach my audience?* you must explore what motivates your listeners. **Motivation** is the psychological force that moves people to action and directs their behavior toward certain goals. Motivation helps explain *why people behave as they do.*

Motivation is important in both informative and persuasive speeches. People will listen, learn, and remember a message only if it relates to their needs, wants, or wishes. Moreover, people will change their attitudes or behavior only if they are motivated to do so. Understanding motivation can also help a speaker appeal to the common humanity in listeners that crosses cultural boundaries.

Motives can vary in importance according to the person, situation, and culture. *People are motivated by what they don't have that they need or want.* If you have recently moved to a new town, your need to make friends may attract you to places where you can meet others. Even when needs are satisfied, people still respond to wants. Suppose you have just eaten a very filling meal. You're not hungry, but if someone enters the room with a tray of freshly baked brownies, the sight and smell can make your mouth water.

Psychologists have been studying human motivation since the early twentieth century. Social scientists first concentrated on identifying different types of human motivation. In a pioneering study published during the 1930s, Henry A. Murray and his associates at Harvard identified more than twenty-five human needs.[8] Several decades later, psychologist Abraham Maslow arranged needs in a five-tiered hierarchy of potency with the lower-level needs (physiological and safety/security) having to be satisfied before the higher-level needs (belonging, esteem, and self-actualization) come into play.[9]

▶ **motivation** An energizing psychological dynamic that explains why people behave as they do.

Appealing to your listeners' needs and motivations helps you reach your audience and find your voice. Consider how you might frame appeals for use in your speeches based on the following types of motivation.

Comfort.   The need for comfort involves such things as having enough to eat and drink, keeping warm when it's cold and cool when it's hot, and being free from pain. Most middle-class Americans take comfort for granted, so speeches appealing to this need level must awaken an awareness of potential problems. One student speaker caught the attention of his classmates as he appealed to this need in the introduction of his speech on the benefits of yoga:

> No pain, no gain! Right? No, wrong. If workout routines leave you heading for the medicine cabinet, look for another way to get your body and heart in shape. An exercise program that combines yoga and power walking improves both your body tone and your cardiovascular system.

Other speech topics that focus on comfort might include "Perfect Posture: It Keeps Your Back from Hurting" and "Who Turned Down the Thermostat? Keeping Warm in the Dorm."

Safety.   We all need to feel free from threats. Crimes on campus, unhealthy water, accidents, and natural disasters such as tornadoes are major sources of concern. Appeals to the need for safety are usually based on arousing a sense of fear. You should be cautious when using fear appeals in speeches. If fear appeals are too obvious, your listeners may feel you are trying to manipulate them. This may cause them to resent you and reject your message. Should you decide to use appeals to safety in your speech, be sure to provide clear instructions on how the dangers can be averted or avoided. Stephanie Lamb used an appeal to safety in her speech, "Cell Phones and Driving: The Killer Combination." Other topics that might relate to this need include "Setting Up a Campus-Wide Emergency Notification System" and "Is Bottled Water Safer than Tap Water?"

DONT TEXT AND DRIVE! relies on an appeal to safety.

Belonging.   People need other people who provide acceptance, affection, companionship, approval, and support. Our friends and families help define who we are and make the world a less lonely place. Our need to belong explains our desire to join groups and take pride in our membership. The need to belong may be the most prevalent motivational appeal in contemporary American advertising. How many advertisements have you seen that suggest that if you don't use the "right" deodorant or drive the "right" car, you risk losing friends? Some speech topics based on this need might include "Love Makes the World Go 'Round: A Look at Online Dating Services" and "Overcoming Loneliness: Volunteers Help Themselves While Helping Others."

Independence.   Although we need other people, we also need independence. The desire to feel that "I can do it myself" is strongly embedded in the American culture. This need is especially strong in young adults who are in the process of finding themselves. The quest for independence allows young people to develop into fully functioning adults, to make decisions on their own, and to take responsibility

FINDING YOUR

voice   Tailoring Motivational Appeals to Your Audience

You are working on a speech urging your classmates to vote in the upcoming election. What supporting materials might you use to appeal to the following audience needs?

- Safety
- Belonging
- Achievement
- Variety

What other motivational appeals do you think you should consider? Why?

for their own lives. Consequently, college audiences may be especially responsive to speeches that stress the need for freedom from arbitrary constraints on their ideas, actions, or lifestyles. Speeches that teach listeners how to "do it yourself" rather than pay someone to do it for you appeal to this need.

Nurturance.   It makes people feel good to be able to care for, protect, and comfort others. Appeals to this need can be especially strong when speakers discuss children who have problems. Beth Tidmore used this appeal when she described the benefits disabled children receive from the Special Olympics:

> They experience courage and victory—and, yes, they also experience defeat. They get to interact with others with disabilities and with people without disabilities. And their mental disability is not a problem. It's not weird. Their biggest achievements aren't recognized with a medal. Their biggest achievements take place over time in the growth they make through being a part of the Special Olympics.

Fairness.   The need for fairness envisions a moral balance and justice in the world. We like to feel that we deserve what happens to us, both the good and the bad. For idealistic college audiences, fairness can be a strong source of motivation. Speeches that express outrage over human rights abuses, racism in the workplace, or the past and present treatment of Native Americans draw heavily on this need. In a speech urging students to buy the fair trade coffee available on campus, Betsy Lyles cited these reasons: more of the money involves goes directly to the farmers and makes it easier to maintain a sustainable lifestyle.

Tradition.   People place a premium on things that give them a sense of roots. There are some things we don't want to change. For example, Thanksgiving dinner means turkey and dressing, sweet potato casserole, cranberry sauce, and pumpkin pie. People often rely on traditions to anchor their beliefs and sustain them in times of trouble. Showing listeners that you share their traditions and values can help create identification in speeches. In a speech explaining the

Appeals to tradition can help bridge cultural differences.

similarities and differences between holidays in the United States and Mexico, Stephanie Herrera shared the following:

> Christmas in Mexico is not really a gift-giving holiday like it is in the United States. It's more of a religious observance. People walk through the neighborhood in a *posada*. This means "where they stop." The stops along the way are beautifully decorated homes where the walkers sing carols and are given gifts of food—like cookies and candies. The *posada* is a parade to honor Niño Dios, which means "baby God" in English.

Variety.   Too much of anything, even a good thing, can be dull. The need for variety can include a longing for adventure, a desire to do something different and exciting, or a yen to travel to exotic places or to meet new and interesting people. Although she couldn't take her listeners to her native Nigeria, Davidson College student Dolapo Olushola's speech describing the native dress of the three major regions of her country fulfilled this desire in her listeners. The speech was also helped with presentation aids including both PowerPoint slides and samples of the different materials. It helped listeners see Nigeria as an interesting and colorful place. Speeches that focus on fresh topics or that offer a vicarious adventure also tap into this appeal.

Understanding.   People are by nature curious. They want answers: What is it? How does it work? Why is it happening? When we satisfy curiosity, we increase our understanding. The quest for understanding has never been more important than in today's workplace, which demands that we adapt to rapid changes in knowledge. Joseph Van Matre described some aspects of video games that were not familiar to his audience (see this speech in Appendix B). By showing them how such simulations are being used in medical fields, education, the military, and business, he increased their understanding of this familiar but often misunderstood topic.

Achievement.   The need for achievement, accomplishment, and success is one of the most thoroughly studied human motives. Although winning may not be everything, most of us feel that losing does not have much to recommend it. You can tap this need for achievement when you present speeches that show listeners how they can improve themselves and increase their chances for success.

Recognition.   Most people like to be treated as valuable and important. They like others to acknowledge their existence and accomplishments. Advertisements that associate products with visible symbols of success and recognition, such as elegant homes or expensive cars, appeal to this need. Speakers tap into the need for recognition when they find ways to compliment the audience in their introductory remarks. Sincere compliments put listeners in a positive frame of mind, making them more attentive and more receptive to the speaker's message.

Consider these motivational appeals as you plan your speeches	
Comfort	Having enough to eat and drink, maintaining a comfortable temperature, being free from pain
Safety	Feeling physically safe and psychologically secure, having a sense of stability and order in your life
Belonging	Having warm relationships with others, being a member of a group, being accepted by others, having someone to love and be loved by
Independence	Being self-sufficient, making your own decisions, being your own person
Nurturance	Taking care of others, providing comfort and aid, giving to charities, volunteering service, promoting the well-being of others
Fairness	Trying to establish or restore moral balance in the world so that people get the treatment they deserve
Tradition	Having a sense of roots, doing things as they have always been done, honoring ancestors, appreciating your history
Variety	Longing for change and adventure, trying different things, exploring different majors, meeting new people
Understanding	Investigating the world around you, learning more about yourself, understanding others, questioning why things happen
Achievement	Accomplishing something of significance, overcoming obstacles in pursuit of goals, doing better than expected
Recognition	Being treated as valuable and important, being praised for accomplishments, receiving awards, being the center of attention
Enjoyment	Having fun, taking a vacation, pampering yourself, pursuing a hobby

FIGURE 5.2
Motivational Appeals for Use in Speeches

Enjoyment.   People need to have some fun in their lives, especially college students, who often find themselves overwhelmed with assignments, tests, speeches to give, and papers to write, not to mention full- or part-time work. Speeches that introduce listeners to new activities or places can fill this need. Here are some sample topics: "Fifteen-Minute Time Outs: Life's Short Pleasures" and "Weekend Break-Aways: The Alternative to Long Vacations."

All of these motivational appeals can be useful in speeches. They are summarized in Figure 5.2, "Motivational Appeals for Use in Speeches."

Well-Being.   **Well-being** describes the general sense of satisfaction that people have with their lives. A recent study by the Gallup Organization suggests that there are five essential elements of well-being.[10] These elements, which seem to tie in nicely with many of the motivational appeals, include (1) career

▶ **well-being**   A sense of satisfaction with one's life.

well-being, (2) social well-being, (3) financial well-being, (4) physical well-being, and (5) community well-being. While each element is discussed discretely, in practice they overlap and blend in with each other. Although different cultures may place more emphasis on one element than another, they are found across all cultures.

Career well-being includes liking what you do every day in work or school or even in volunteer activities. In some ways it ties into achievement and recognition, but goes beyond these to describe a unique fit between a person and his or her daily activities. It is what makes people want to get up and face the day because they have something to do that is satisfying to them. Speeches that help others discover their personal fit with both vocational and avocational activities will find an eager audience.

Social well-being involves positive interactions with others. It is similar to the need for belonging described earlier. Important social relationships may include family ties, best friends, casual friends, and work associates. For each hour of satisfying social relations, your odds of having a good day increase. And, who doesn't want to have a good day?

Financial well-being is often confused with simply making a lot of money; however, this is not what it really means. Once people feel financially secure in terms of meeting their basic needs, it is how they use their money that makes a difference. For example, more happiness is associated with experiential purchases, such as adventure and education, than with material purchases. Material purchases can wear out or go out of fashion, but experiential purchases endure in our memory.

Aside from being free of debilitating disease, physical well-being is tied into healthful eating patterns and exercise, which give a person increased energy to enjoy life. Speeches on topics such as "Avoiding the Freshman Fifteen" or "Tailoring a Personal Exercise Plan" will appeal to most audiences.

The final sense of well-being is related to the needs for nurturance and service. Betsy Lyles' speech "Locks of Love" urged students to contribute their hair to this organization, which provides wigs for children who have lost their hair because of illness. Simone Mullinax presented a speech on "The Impact of Mentoring," describing the personal satisfaction one gets from helping at-risk students.

Meeting the Challenges of Audience Diversity

Diversity in the classroom is an important factor in audience analysis. Just look around you. Learning to communicate with others from different backgrounds and cultures can be one of the most rewarding experiences of your public speaking class. You can learn from others and expand your horizons. At the same time, diversity offers a challenge to the speaker, who must adapt a message so that it crosses the cultural boundaries represented in the typical classroom audience. This cultural diversity is deeply rooted in different experiences: different attitudes, different loyalties, different goals, different religions, different fears, and what may seem to be different values. These differences can become barriers to communication. You can overcome these barriers by calling on universal values, making strategic use of speaking resources, and avoiding rhetorical land mines that could destroy the effectiveness of your efforts.

Apply Universal Values

The Institute for Global Ethics has identified a number of universal values that you can use in your speeches to help build common ground.[11] Like the elements of well-being, these values transcend cultural differences. These universal values are shown in Figure 5.3.

The first thing you may notice is how closely this list parallels the motivational appeals we discussed earlier. At times, the parallels are exact (tradition, achievement, enjoyment). At other times, they are almost identical (independence/self-direction, safety/security, nurturance/benevolence). This is good news for the speaker, because it suggests that at the same time you are developing general appeals, you can also be reaching across the cultural divide.

How can you ground your speech in universal values? Consider how effectively Anna Aley used them in her speech asking for reform in the housing laws that governed rental properties in Manhattan, Kansas (see her speech in Appendix B). First, Anna found a subject that concerned practically all of her listeners, however diverse their backgrounds. They either rented such properties themselves or had friends who rented them. Anna had found common ground that united them in a shared problem.

By depicting the dangers of this situation, Anna first appealed to *safety*—in this case, the lack of it. She asked them to come together to protest (appeal to *power*) and to take control of their lives (appeal to *independence/self-direction*). Implicitly, she appealed to their sense of adventure (taking on the slumlords would provide excitement in their lives). And she envisioned their success (*achievement*). Is there little wonder that Anna was able to establish common ground among her listeners or that she delivered such an effective persuasive speech?

Use Speaking Resources Skillfully

A second way that speakers can rise to the challenge of cultural diversity is to make strategic use of communication resources, such as supporting materials and language.

Supporting Materials. Supporting materials, discussed in detail in Chapter 8, provide the substance of all speeches. Their skillful use is essential when speaking to diverse audiences. Diverse audiences may have different expectations in terms of support for ideas or suggestions. Some listeners may be fact-oriented, priding themselves on their respect for reality. Others may rely more on authority, depending on the advice of elders, religious leaders, or respected others. Still

FIGURE 5.3 Universal Values

Power	Social power, authority, recognition from others, wealth
Achievement	Success, ambition, influence
Tradition	Acceptance of one's fate, devoutness, humility, respect for cultural heritage
Enjoyment	Pleasure
Self-Direction	Freedom, independence, choice of own goals, self-respect, curiosity, creativity
Security	National security, social order, family security, sense of belonging, personal health, reciprocity in personal relationships
Unity	Unity with nature, protecting the environment, inner harmony, social justice, equality, tolerance, a world at peace
Benevolence	Honesty, helpfulness, forgiveness, loyalty, responsibility, friendship, love, spiritual life, meaning in life
Conformity	Politeness, obedience, self-discipline, honoring parents and elders
Stimulation	Variety, excitement, daring

others may see themselves as participants in ongoing stories that give meaning to their lives.

Such diversity may suggest different strategies for the use of the facts, examples, testimony, and narratives in a speech. The primary strategy is to *provide variety*. Present facts and expert testimony from unbiased sources for those who see themselves as reality-minded. Offer quotations from respected leaders who support your point of view to reach those most influenced by authority. Avoid citing people who might set off extreme negative reactions. Develop stories for those attracted to narratives. Match the diversity of your audience with the variety of your supporting material.

A second strategy for the use of supporting materials is to *emphasize the use of narratives*. Nothing can bring diverse people together more effectively than stories that help them discover their common humanity. Al Gore suggests that storytelling can even help old enemies make peace. On one occasion, when he was vice president, he met with Palestinian, Israeli, Jordanian, and Syrian leaders to discuss a peace treaty. Gore saw the negotiations faltering. The situation looked hopeless. But then a "miracle" happened. In Gore's words, "The breakthroughs came when they told stories about their families. I have seen time and time again how storytelling brings people together."[12] Stories give meaning and life to universal values.

Avoid Language Pitfalls

The language you use can help or impede communication with diverse audiences (see Chapter 11). When audience members are unfamiliar with your topic, you should use lay language and define any terms that might be misunderstood. Consider using presentation aids to make your ideas clearer.

If your audience includes listeners for whom English is a second language, avoid slang terms that may confuse them. Our colloquial language uses many idioms drawn from sports, such as "he left it all out on the floor" or "she hit the wall." These and similar expressions can bring utter confusion to those who are new to our language or who do not share the speaker's enthusiasm for sports.

Another problem arises from cross-cultural language blunders. In the spring of 2007, a presidential candidate presented a speech that he hoped would win the support of the Cuban expatriate community in Florida. As he concluded, he shouted: *"Patria o muerte, venceremos!"* ("Fatherland or death, we shall overcome"). He did not understand the icy reaction until someone explained that those words were the trademark signoff of Fidel Castro. The lesson to you? Treat words like explosives: Don't play with them when you're not sure what you're doing!

Common values and interests can help bring groups together despite differences of age, gender, race or ethnicity.

Avoid Rhetorical Land Mines

The discussion of cross-cultural language blunders is similar to the third major consideration for reaching diverse audiences: Avoid stepping on land mines that can explode your efforts to communicate. These land mines include stereotypes and the three troublesome *-isms*: ethnocentrism, sexism, and racism.

Stereotypes. All of us use our past experiences to make sense of new information and to guide our interactions with others. To use our experiences efficiently, we react in terms of categories. For example, having heard about poisonous reptiles, we may be leery of all snakes. However, problems arise when we group people into categories. Then the categories can harden into **stereotypes**, rigid sets of beliefs and expectations about people in a certain group that reflect our attitudes toward the group. When stereotypes dominate our thinking, we react more to them than to the people themselves. For example, we may stereotype the elderly as frail and impoverished, or athletes as unintelligent and insensitive.

Stereotypes also may be related to ethnicity, religion, occupation, or place of residence. We may form positive or negative stereotypes based on direct experiences with a few individuals which we then generalize to the group as a whole. Most stereotypes, however, are learned indirectly from our families and friends, schools and churches, or media exposure. For example, our stereotype of Native Americans may come from exposure to Western movies, or our stereotype of Italian Americans may have been shaped by TV shows like *The Sopranos*.

Regardless of how we acquire them, stereotypes can have a strong and lasting influence on our thinking. We may judge people on the basis of stereotypes rather than on their merits as individuals. We are reluctant to give up our stereotypes, especially when they agree with those held by our friends and families. When we

▶ **stereotypes** Generalized picture of a race, gender, or group that supposedly represents its essential characteristics.

encounter individuals who do not fit our stereotypes, we may simply discount them as "exceptions to the rule."

Keep in mind that your listeners are individuals, and most of them will not conform to any stereotypes you may have. Respect their individuality and consciously resolve not to let stereotypes permeate your thinking. Critical listeners will detect any stereotypes in your thinking, and may reject both you and your message.

Troublesome -isms. There are three troublesome *-isms* that impede effective communication with a diverse audience: ethnocentrism, sexism, and racism.

Ethnocentrism. **Ethnocentrism** is the belief that our way of life is the "right" and superior way In its milder form, ethnocentrism reveals itself as patriotism or national pride. But ethnocentrism has a darker side. When ethnocentrism goes beyond pride in one's own group to include the rejection or derogation of others, it becomes a sometimes insurmountable problem in human relations that acts as a barrier to communication.

The first step in controlling ethnocentrism is to recognize any tendencies you may have to overestimate your culture and underestimate other cultures. For example, most Americans believe that over half of the world's population speaks English, when actually only about 20 percent do.[13] To avoid the impression of ethnocentrism in your speeches, *your language must show respect for the humanity of all people and recognize that this common humanity transcends both race and culture.*

Sexism. **Sexism** occurs when we allow gender stereotypes to control our interactions with members of the opposite sex. **Gender stereotyping** involves making broad generalizations about men or women based on outmoded assumptions, such as "men should be the head of a household" or "women don't know anything about sports." Gender stereotyping becomes problematic when it implies that the stereotypical differences justify discrimination.

As you plan and prepare your message, be aware of any gender stereotypes you have that could interfere with effective communication. Be careful not to portray gender roles in ways suggesting superiority or inferiority. For instance, when you use examples or stories to illustrate a point, don't make all your authority figures male.

Gender stereotyping often reveals itself through **sexist language**, which involves making gender references in situations in which the gender is unknown or irrelevant, such as talking about a male nurse or a female game warden. It also can involve the generic use of masculine nouns or pronouns, such as referring to "man's advances in science" or using "he" when the intended reference is to both sexes. You can avoid this problem simply by saying "she or he" or by using the plural "they."

Racism. Just as stereotyping and sexist language can block communication, so also can racism. Even though *blatant* racism and discrimination are no longer socially acceptable in most circles, a more subtle form of such prejudice can still infect our thinking. Although we may pay lip service to the principles of racial equality, we may still engage in **symbolic racism**, which is expressed more subtly or covertly. For example, if we say, "In *our* neighborhood, *we* believe in family values," the unspoken message may be, "*You* don't, and therefore *we* are superior." Or we might say, "*We* believe in hard work and earning *our* way," when we really mean, "Why don't *you* get off welfare?" Thus we may excuse the vestiges of racial stereotypes by appeals to values like family stability or the work ethic. In such cases, our underlying message may be, "*We* honor such values, and *you* don't."

▶ **ethnocentrism**   The tendency of any nation, race, religion, or group to believe that its way of looking at and doing things is right and that other perspectives have less value.

▶ **sexism**   Allowing gender stereotypes to control interactions with members of the opposite sex.

▶ **gender stereotyping**   Generalizations based on oversimplified or outmoded assumptions about gender roles.

As you take the factor of race into consideration in your audience analysis, examine your thinking for any lurking bias. Such biases may inadvertently break through in unexpected ways even though you don't intend them to. Stay away from examples that cast members of a particular ethnic group into stereotypical roles that imply inferiority. And, of course, avoid racist humor.

SPEAKER'S notes   Avoiding Racist and Sexist Language

To avoid racist and sexist innuendos in your speeches, keep these guidelines in mind.

1. Do not use slang terms to refer to racial, ethnic, religious, or gender groups.

2. Avoid using the generic "he" and gender-specific titles such as "meter maid."

3. Avoid stereotypic references that might imply inferiority or superiority.

4. Stay away from sexist, racist, ethnic, or religious humor.

Adjusting to the Communication Situation

Last, we consider the setting for your speech. You must account for the time, place, occasion, size of the audience, and overall context of recent topic-related events as you make final adjustments to your presentation.

Time

The time of day, day of the week, time of the year, and the amount of time allotted for speaking should all be taken into account. If you are speaking early in the morning, you may need to be more energetic to awaken listeners. Since we tend to grow drowsy after we eat, after-dinner speeches (discussed in Chapter 16) need lively examples and humor to hold an audience's attention. Speeches presented in the evening also present a problem. Most listeners will have completed a day's work and will have left the comforts of home to hear you. You must justify their attendance with good ideas well presented.

If your speech is scheduled for a Monday, when people have not yet adjusted to the weekend's being over, or a Friday, when they are thinking of the weekend ahead, you may need especially interesting material to hold attention. Similarly, gloomy winter days or balmy spring weather can put people in a different frame of mind, and their mood can color how they receive your speech. Your materials and presentation style will have to be bright and engaging to overcome the blahs or to ward off daydreaming.

The amount of time allotted for your presentation is also critical. *A short speech does not necessarily mean shorter preparation time.* Actually, shorter speeches often require longer preparation. Short speeches require you to focus and streamline your topic so that it can be handled in the time allotted. You must limit the number of main points and use supporting materials selectively. Choose the most relevant and

---

▶ **sexist language**   Making gender references in situations in which the gender is unknown or irrelevant, or using masculine nouns or pronouns when the intended reference is to both sexes.

▶ **symbolic racism**   An indirect form of racism that employs code words and subtle, unspoken contrast to suggest that one race is superior to another.

Speaking before a large audience requires adjustments in presentation style.

impressive facts, statistics, and testimony, the most striking examples and stories. Plan your speech so that you begin with a burst and end with a bang.

Place

The place where you will speak can also be a factor. When speaking outside, you may have to cope with distractions. When speaking inside, you need to know the size and layout of the room and whether a lectern or electronic equipment is available.

Even in the classroom, speakers must learn to cope with distractions. As we noted in our discussion of listening disruptions in Chapter 4, noise may filter into the room. How can you handle such problems? If the noise is temporary, you should pause and wait until it stops, then repeat your last words and go on with your message. If the noise is constant, you may have to speak louder to be heard. You may even have to pause and close a window or door. The important thing is to take such problems in stride and not let them distract you or your audience from your message.

Occasion

As you plan your message, you must take into account *why* people have gathered to listen. When audience attendance is mandatory, you may have to work hard to arouse interest and sustain attention. When attendance is voluntary, people are usually more motivated to listen. Understanding why your audience is present is especially important for speeches given outside the classroom setting. If your topic has been publicized and you have factored in audience dynamics and demographics, you should have a good idea of why listeners are present and the needs they expect you to meet. When a speaker does not offer the kind of message listeners expect, they may be annoyed. For example, if they are expecting an informative presentation on investment strategies and instead get a sales pitch for a particular mutual fund, they may feel exploited, which could result more in irritation than in persuasion.

SPEAKER'S notes   Checklist for Analyzing the Speaking Situation

Use this checklist to be sure you don't overlook anything important when analyzing the speaking situation.

1. Will the time or timing of my speech pose any problems?

2. How might audience expectations affect my speech preparation?

3. Is there any late-breaking news relevant to my topic?

4. How large will my audience be?

5. Does the place where I will speak call for any adjustments?

Size of Audience

The size of your audience can also affect how you speak. A small audience provides feedback and an opportunity for interaction. Generally, a small group of listeners invites a more casual presentation. On the other hand, large audiences offer less feedback. Because you cannot make or sustain eye contact with everyone, you should choose representative listeners in various sections of the audience and change your visual focus from time to time. Establishing eye contact with listeners in all sections of the room helps more people feel included. With large audiences, your gestures should be more emphatic so that everyone can see them. Presentation aids must be large enough for those in the back of the audience to see without strain.

Context

Anything that happens near the time of your presentation becomes part of the context of your speech. Both recent speeches and recent events can influence how the audience responds to you.

Recent Speeches. Any speeches presented before yours create an atmosphere in which you must work. This atmosphere has a **preliminary tuning effect** on listeners, preparing them to respond in certain ways to you and your message. At political rallies, patriotic music and introductions prepare the audience for the appearance of the featured speaker. At concerts, warm-up groups put listeners in the mood for the star.

Preliminary tuning may also influence classroom presentations, either positively or negatively. Earlier speeches may affect the mood of the audience. For example, if the speech right before yours aroused strong emotions, you may need to ease the tension in the introduction to your speech. You can make such an impromptu adjustment by acknowledging listeners' feelings and using them as a springboard into your own speech:

> Obviously, many of us feel very strongly about the legalization of same-sex marriages. What I'm going to talk about is also very important—but it is something I think we can all agree on—the challenge of finding a way to stop children from killing other children in our community.

Another technique might be to begin with a story that involves listeners and refocuses their attention. At times, humor can help relieve tension, but people who are upset may be in no mood for laughter. Your decision on whether to use humor must be based on your reading of the situation: the mood of listeners and the subject of your speech.

In addition to dealing with the mood created by earlier speeches, you may also have to adapt to their content. Suppose you have spent the past week preparing a speech on the *importance* of extending endangered species legislation. Then the speaker before you makes a convincing presentation on the *problems* of extending endangered species legislation. What can you do? Try to turn this to your advantage. Point out that the earlier speech established the importance of the topic but that—as good as that effort was—it did not give the total picture: "Now you will hear the *other* side of the story."

▶ **preliminary tuning effect**   The effect of previous speeches or other situational factors in predisposing an audience to respond positively or negatively to a speech.

FIGURE 5.4 Audience Analysis Worksheet

Topic: _____

Audience: _____

	Factor Description	Adaptations Needed
Audience Dynamics	Audience Attitude: _____ _____	_____ _____
	Relevant Values: _____	_____ _____
	Motivational Appeals: _____ _____	_____ _____
Audience Demographics	Age: _____	_____
	Gender: _____	_____
	Education: _____	_____
	Group Affiliations: _____ _____	_____ _____
	Sociocultural Background: _____ _____	_____ _____
	Interest in Topic: _____ _____	_____ _____
	Knowledge of Topic: _____ _____	_____ _____
Speaking Situation	Time: _____	_____
	Place: _____	_____
	Occasion: _____	_____
	Audience Size: _____	_____
	Context: _____	_____

Recent Events.   When listeners enter the room the day of your speech, they bring with them information about recent events. They will use this knowledge to evaluate what you say. If you are not up on the latest news concerning your topic, your credibility can suffer. A student in one of our classes once presented an interesting and well-documented speech comparing public housing in Germany with that in the United States. Unfortunately, she was unaware of a local scandal involving public housing. For three days before her presentation, the story had made the front page of the local newspaper and had been the lead story in area newscasts. Everyone expected her to mention it. Her failure to discuss this important local problem weakened her credibility.

YOUR ethical VOICE   Guidelines for Ethical Audience Adaptation

Keep the following guidelines in mind as you consider adapting your message to your audience.

1. Change your strategies, not your convictions.
2. Appeal to shared needs and values to bridge cultural differences.
3. Resist stereotypes and biases that may lead you to misjudge others.
4. Suppress any impulses toward ethnocentrism.
5. Avoid sexist, racist, ethnic, or religious humor.
6. Show respect for the common humanity of your listeners.

Finally, we need to return again to the ethics of audience adaptation. It is possible to give a speech on almost any topic that will both reach your listeners and be aligned with your personal convictions. Use the "Guidelines for Ethical Audience Adaptation" to help you bridge the gap between these two areas of potential conflict.

Bringing It All Together.   The Audience Analysis Worksheet in Figure 5.4 will help you consider all the factors we have discussed in this chapter as you plan for the audience and situation of your speech. When you have sized up the situation, adding this knowledge to your analysis of audience dynamics and demographics, you will be ready for your next challenge—choosing a suitable topic for speaking.

FINAL reflections   Keeping Your Audience in Mind

Understanding your audience helps you put together a speech that people will want to listen to. When you don't pay attention to the demographic and psychological makeup of your audience, your speeches will fall on deaf ears. You may think that you have found your voice on an issue, but if no one is listening to your message, your work has all been for naught.

Understanding audiences and understanding speaking situations are primary considerations as you prepare your speech and should govern the entire process, from selecting your topic to choosing supporting materials, making judicious word choices, and tailoring the rhetorical techniques you use. It takes time to analyze your audience, but it is well worth the effort.

THIS CHAPTER WILL HELP YOU

1 Discover a promising topic
2 Explore your topic
3 Refine your topic for speaking
4 Test your topic before your audience

6 Developing Your Topic

The life of our city is rich in poetic and marvelous subjects ... but we do not notice it.

—BAUDELAIRE

Preparing to speak before an audience can seem somewhat overwhelming, and simply getting started may be the most difficult part of all. If the task before you seems formidable, take it in small steps, advises Robert J. Kriegel, a performance psychologist. While working as a ski instructor, Kriegel found that beginners would look all the way to the bottom of a slope. The hill would seem too steep and the challenge too difficult, and the skiers would back away. However, if he told them to think only of making the first turn, their focus would change to something they knew they could do.[1]

On the "first turn" in speech preparation, you will decide on a topic that is right for you and your listeners and that fits the assignment and the time you have to speak. You will find that five minutes goes by very quickly when you are talking about something that really interests you. On the "second turn," you will focus and explore your topic and develop a clear sense of purpose for your speech. This chapter will help you negotiate these first two vital turns.

Only in the public speaking classroom, of course, can you select the topic for your speech. In the communication world that awaits you beyond the class, topics impose themselves upon you: work concerns, community concerns, and political issues of the moment may all provide the agenda for your speaking. But the "unreal" world of the public speaking classroom offers a great advantage: it allows you to explore the universe of topic possibilities to find just those best suited to help you find your voice. This freedom of topic selection helps exercise your creativity and realize your potential.

As the ski slope image suggests, other turns will soon await you: researching the topic you discover and develop, gathering supporting materials for the content of your speech, arranging these materials into effective order, creating presentation aids, selecting appropriate language, and practicing your presentation. All these turns, and the chapters that will help prepare you for them, await you on the communication ski slope over the next six chapters of this book.

What Is a Good Topic?

A good topic is one that involves you and that you care about. It allows you to express convictions that are important to you or to explore something you find fascinating. A good topic invites you to find your voice, and in the process, enrich the lives of your listeners by sharing new information or a new perspective. Finally, a good topic is one that you can speak about responsibly, given the time allotted for the preparation and presentation of your speech.

A Good Topic Involves You

Imagine yourself speaking successfully:

> You're enthusiastic about what you're saying. Your face shows your involvement in your topic. Your voice expresses your feelings. Your gestures reinforce your meaning. Everything about you says, "This is important!" "This is interesting!" or "This will make a difference in your lives!"

Once you can identify a subject that makes you feel this way, you know you have found your topic.

Your topic does not have to be on an earth-shaking issue, but it should be something your listeners ought to know more about. Trivial topics such as "how to twirl a baton" or "how to kick a football" waste the time of both the speaker and the listeners. Overworked topics such as "don't drink and drive" also waste time unless they offer listeners a new and fresh slant.

Above all, your topic should be important to you personally and should help you develop as a speaker. It takes time to think through your ideas, research them, organize what you discover, and practice your presentation. If your topic is not important to you, you will find it hard to invest the time and effort required to speak responsibly.

A Good Topic Involves Your Listeners

Picture an audience of ideal listeners:

> Their faces are alive with interest. They lean forward in their seats, intent on what you are saying. They nod or smile appropriately. At the end of your speech, they want to ask you questions about your ideas or voice their reactions. Long after your speech, they are still thinking about what you said.

What topic will help you create this kind of audience response? By now, you probably have heard the first speeches in your class, and you know something about your listeners. Ask yourself, What are my audience's interests? What do they care about? What do they need to know more about?

A Good Topic Is One You Can Manage

The final test of a good topic is whether you can acquire the knowledge you will need to speak responsibly upon it. The time you have for the preparation and presentation of your speech is limited. Consequently, you should select a *manageable part* of your topic area to develop for your presentation. For example, instead of trying to cover the entire subject of terrorism—its causes, sources, kinds, purposes, leaders, etc.—it would be much better to focus on one aspect, such as your community's plan to counter terrorism. This more limited topic would focus more closely on your audience's particular interests and should help you prepare a responsible presentation.

A passion for sports can prompt ideas for speech topics.

Think of your search for the right topic as a process that goes through phases of discovery, exploration, and refinement.

- In the **discovery phase**, you uncover promising topic areas.

- In the **exploration phase**, you focus on specific speech topics within these areas.

- In the **refinement phase**, you identify the general and specific purposes of speeches you might give on these topics and write out your thesis statements.

It is important to realize that *this process takes time*. Give yourself at least a week to select your topic, do your research, outline your speech, and practice your presentation. You will find that this time is well invested. Nothing comforts you more on the eve of a presentation than knowing you are well prepared.

Discovering Your Topic Area

Three techniques—brainstorming, interest charts, and media and Internet prompts—can help you discover promising speech topics.

Brainstorming

Brainstorming is a technique that encourages free associations in quest of topic areas. Ask yourself, If I had to pick one topic area to explore for my next speech, what would it be? At the top of a legal pad, write down the first idea that occurs to you. Below this idea, write down at least six more ideas that occur to you in association with this topic. Do not try to think critically about these ideas until you have a sizable list. Let your mind wander. You may discover, as did a student of ours, that such "daydreaming" can be productive and creative.

▶ **discovery phase** Identifying large topic areas that might generate successful speeches.

▶ **exploration phase** Examining large topic areas to pinpoint more precise speech topics.

▶ **refinement phase** Framing the general and specific purposes of a speech topic and a thesis statement.

▶ **brainstorming** Technique that encourages the free play of the mind.

Zachary came to our office one day early in the term with a serious case of topic anxiety. After we convinced him that his symptoms were not terminal, he accepted our invitation to participate in brainstorming. Zachary wrote down "Wyoming" at the top of his legal pad. He then wrote down the following associations: trout, Yellowstone, fire, drought, George Anderson (a well-known fly fisherman), catch and release, and wolves. He paused for a moment and studied this list closely. "You know," he said, "I could speak on 'Fire and Water in Yellowstone: Too Much of One, Too Little of the Other.'" And eventually he did. Zachary ultimately found his voice—not only selecting a topic of interest, but also one with an important message.

Interest Charts

The classical writers on rhetoric were the first to discover that the mind follows certain habitual paths that are productive in creative thinking. You already followed such paths when you developed the Self-Awareness Inventory in Chapter 3. The productive possibilities you explored in that chapter can be easily adapted and enlarged here. They appear in the form of questions that guide the mind:

1. What *places* do you find interesting?

2. What *people* do you find fascinating?

3. What *activities* do you enjoy?

4. What *things* do you find interesting?

5. What *events* stand out in your mind?

6. Which *ideas* do you find intriguing?

7. What *values* are important to you?

8. What *problems* concern you most?

9. What *campus concerns* do you have?

You can use these queries to develop an **interest chart** that projects a comprehensive visual display of your interests. To create such a chart, write out brief responses to the probe questions. Try to come up with at least five responses for each question. Your interest chart might then look like that in Figure 6.1.

Once you have completed your personal interest chart, make a similar chart of audience interests as revealed by class discussion and your audience analysis. What places, people, events, activities, objects, ideas, values, problems, and campus concerns seem to spark discussions in class? Study the two charts together, looking for shared interests. To do this systematically, make a three-column **topic area inventory chart**. In the first column (your interests), list the subjects you find most appealing. In the second column (audience interests), list the subjects that seem most interesting to your listeners. In the third column, match columns 1 and 2 to find the most promising areas of speech topics. Figure 6.2 shows a sample topic area inventory chart.

In this example, your interests in cycling and hiking coincide with the audience's interest in unusual places and suggest a possible topic area: "weekend adventures close to campus." Similarly, your concern for physical fitness pairs with the audience's interest in deceptive advertising to generate another possibility: "exercise spa rip-offs." Your concern over tuition costs intersects with audience interests in economic problems, leading to "keeping college affordable." Finally, your interest

▶ **interest chart**   Visual display of a speaker's interests, as prompted by probe questions.

▶ **topic area inventory chart**   A means of determining possible speech topics by listing topics you and your listeners find interesting and matching them.

FIGURE 6.1 Your Interest Chart

Places
The Four Corners
Cuba
New Orleans
Route 66
New York City

People
Osama Bin Laden
Michael Phelps
Hillary Clinton
Rush Limbaugh
Nelson Mandela

Problems
adequate water
climate change
substance abuse
airport security
religious conflicts

Ideas
Second Amendment
Libertarianism
social protest
social networking
creation stories

Objects
Kachinas
movie posters
old cars
political cartoons
gang graffiti

Events
Olympic games

Activities
hiking
cycling
gourmet cooking

Campus Concerns
race relations
student rights
date rape
campus security
tuition costs

Values
service
tolerance
physical fitness
respect
tradition

New Year's celebrations
canoeing the Grand Canyon
Mardi Gras
rites of passage

hosteling
scrapbooking

in gourmet cooking resonates with audience concerns over good health to suggest the topic area "eating well and living healthy."

Media and Internet Prompts

If brainstorming and interest charts don't produce enough promising topic discoveries, **media and Internet prompts** provide another excellent source. When using such prompts, you jump-start the creative process by scanning newspapers, magazines, and the electronic media for ideas. Go through the Sunday paper, scan *Time* and *Newsweek* or quality periodicals such as *The Atlantic* or *Smithsonian*, or read the daily headlines of the *New York Times* online.

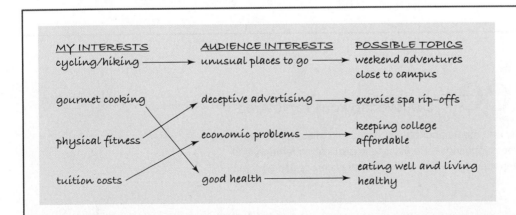

MY INTERESTS
cycling/hiking
gourmet cooking
physical fitness
tuition costs

AUDIENCE INTERESTS
unusual places to go
deceptive advertising
economic problems
good health

POSSIBLE TOPICS
weekend adventures close to campus
exercise spa rip-offs
keeping college affordable
eating well and living healthy

FIGURE 6.2 Topic Area Inventory Chart

▶ **media and Internet prompts** Sources such as newspapers, magazines, and the electronic media that can suggest ideas for speech topics.

The Internet also offers some special resources, if you are selective. For example, if you type in the words "speech topics" on a search engine, you may find a few gems among the garbage. In addition, some sites are especially helpful. See for example the "Topic Selection Helper" developed by Ron St. John of the University of Hawaii's Maui Community College Speech Department (www.hawaii.edu/mauispeech/html/public_speaking.html).

As you scan media resources, consider the headlines, advertisements, and pictures. What catches your attention? The headline "Travel Money Tips Offered" might inspire you to speak on "Champagne Travel on a Beer Budget." Or the personals section in the classified ads might prompt a speech on "The Dangers of Internet Dating Services."

The media-prompts technique has one great advantage: The topics it generates are timely. But be careful not to misuse this technique. The media and Internet can suggest ideas for speeches, but you can't simply summarize an article and use it as a speech. The article should be only a starting point for your thinking. *Your* speech must be *your* message, designed to appeal to *your* specific audience. You should always bring something new to your topic—a fresh insight or a special application for your listeners.

Exploring Your Topic Area

What you typically discover as you brainstorm, develop interest charts, and employ media and Internet prompts are not actual topics for speeches, but topic *areas*. Topic areas are promising but broad subjects that often cover too much ground for typical classroom speeches. You must explore topic areas carefully and then narrow and focus them until they become specific enough to handle in the time allotted for your speech. As Winston Churchill once noted, "A speech is like a spotlight; the more focused it is, the more intense the light."[2] The two primary techniques available to you as you explore promising topic areas are mind mapping and topic analysis.

Mind Mapping

Mind mapping disrupts customary patterns of thinking in order to free our minds for creative exploration.[3] These habitual patterns can produce what communication theorist Kenneth Burke once called a "trained incapacity" to think fully and freely about subjects. For example, most of us, when we write our thoughts out on a tablet, start at the top of the page and work down. Mind mappers turn the tablet on its side and, instead of starting at the top of the page, begin at the center, where they place the topic area they wish to explore. Instead of flowing down the page, thinking radiates out from

FINDING YOUR

voice   Discovering Your Topic Area

Use brainstorming, interest charts, and media and Internet prompts to discover at least three promising topic areas on which you might speak. Rank these in order of preference, and explain either in class or in a written report how you discovered these areas and why you ranked them this way.

▶ **mind mapping**   Changes customary patterns of thinking to encourage creative exploration.

this center so that it forms a circular rather than a linear pattern of subordinate, satellite ideas. These satellites can be ringed by even more particular associations that relate to them.[4] This novel mode of thinking is illustrated in the Sun Studio figure (Figure 6.3).

Let us assume that you have carefully completed the interest charts. You have discovered that your strongest interest is in American popular music. You think this interest will be shared by many of your listeners. This convergence of interests has produced a promising topic area, the innovative music that flowed out of Sun Studio in Memphis, Tennessee, during the last half century. You have already begun to read about this subject, and have started to accumulate information. To explore this topic area using mind mapping, place it at the center of your page, as indicated in Figure 6.3.

As your mind roams freely around this central idea, you come up with five major satellite ideas: "Early Artists," "Later Artists," "Business Practices," "Musical Significance and Birth of Rock-and-Roll," and "Cultural Significance." As you reflect on each of these satellite ideas, you develop even more specific associations that radiate from each.

Looking at these ideas as they form a spatial pattern, you can see any number of speech topic possibilities. One of these might connect three of the major satellite ideas. You could focus on the early artists who performed the first significant rock-and-roll hits and show how they blended elements of blues, country, and gospel music into rock-and-roll. You might title this speech "Sun Studio: Birthplace of an American Musical Form." You could develop presentation aids using photographs and selections from the music to make the speech truly colorful, enjoyable, and informative.

Mind mapping is a free-form exploratory technique that can be highly creative. The following technique, topic analysis, offers a more systematic, disciplined way to explore topic areas.

Topic Analysis

The beginning college course in journalism introduces fledgling reporters to the topoi of their craft: *what? why? when? how? where?* and *who?* Rudyard Kipling once described these questions as follows:

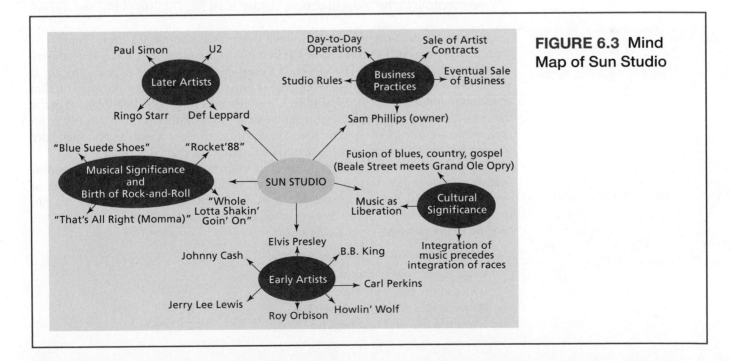

FIGURE 6.3 Mind Map of Sun Studio

> I keep six honest serving-men
> (They taught me all I knew):
> Their names are What and Why and When
> And How and Where and Who.[5]

The idea is that if reporters ask these questions as they explore a story, the odds increase that they will not neglect anything important.

The noted scholar Wayne Booth has endorsed these questions as a more general method of exploring the value of topics: "Decide which questions stop you for a moment, challenge you, spark some special interest."[6] For the public speaker who is exploring the possibilities of a topic area, these "honest serving-men" constitute the technique we call **topic analysis**. Let's consider climate change as a topic area and see how these questions might prompt inquiry:

- *What* is climate change? What are the major causes of it? What are the contributing causes in our community? What part can individuals play in reducing it? What can government do to control it? What is the role of international organizations?

- *Why* do we have climate change? Why do some countries and some companies resist reducing greenhouse emissions?

- *When* did climate change first become an issue? When was the first important book about climate change published? When were the first U.S. laws relating to climate change passed?

- *How* can climate change be controlled? How can companies be encouraged to cooperate in this effort? How can individuals help the cause?

- *Where* is climate change of most concern? Where are endangered species most susceptible? Where are human health problems most acute? Where have cities or states done the most to control climate change?

- *Who* suffers most from climate change? Who is responsible for enforcing emission controls? Who brought climate change most forcefully to public awareness?

As you consider the six prompts, write down as many specific ideas about your topic area as you can. What would be the best topic for your speech, if you indeed were to address climate change? That depends a great deal on your audience and locale. If you live in an area with an obvious emissions problem, a speech that zeroes in on that situation might have specific local appeal. Your listeners might also be interested in the history of relevant legislation in your city or state. On the other hand, if you live in an area where the impact of climate change is not immediate or apparent, you may have to work hard to convince listeners that they should be concerned about it.

The preceding topic analysis was geared to exploring what are primarily informative speech topics, but the technique can easily be adapted to the analysis of persuasive topics. Because persuasion asks us to change or not change certain behaviors, you simply adjust the focus of the questions and add a few that are specific to the persuasive perspective:

> **Who** is affected by this problem?
> **What** are the most important issues?
> **Why** did the problem arise?
> **Where** is this problem happening?
> **When** did the problem begin?

▶ **topic analysis** Using questions often employed by journalists to explore topic possibilities for speeches (who, what, why, when, where, and how).

voice   Exploring Your Topic Area

Use mind mapping and topic analysis to explore the preferred topic area you identified in "Finding Your Voice: Discovering Your Topic Area." List in order of preference three promising speech topics that emerge from this exploration. Explain in class or in a written report how and why these topics emerged and why you ranked them in the order selected.

How is this problem like or unlike previous problems?

How extensive is the problem?

What options are available for dealing with the problem?

After you have discovered and explored topic areas, one or several topics should emerge as promising possibilities for your speech. As you ponder these options, keep in mind how well they fit the assignment, whether you could speak on them in the time available, whether you will be able to research them responsibly, and how useful they might be for listeners.

Refining Your Topic

Having discovered and explored topic areas, let us assume you have decided on a promising topic. Now you move to the final phase of topic selection: refining and focusing the topic in preparation for speaking. To complete this phase, you must consider the general purpose of your speech, determine your specific purpose, and prepare a thesis statement.

General Purpose

Invitations to speak outside class will usually specify the **general purpose** of your speech: "Could you help us understand changes in the tax code?" or "Would you tell us why you are opposed to changes in the tax code?" or "Will you help us thank the senator for her leadership in changing the tax code?" Speeches that would address such questions seek understanding, offer a position on a controversial issue, or express appreciation. They correspond to the general purposes of *informing, persuading,* and *celebrating.*

■ *The general purpose of a speech to inform is to share knowledge with listeners.*

■ *If your general purpose is to persuade, you will advise listeners how to believe or act and offer them reasons to follow such advice.*

■ *A speech of celebration emphasizes the importance of an occasion, event, or person, often with the intention of amusing or inspiring listeners.* Speeches of celebration include eulogies, toasts, after-dinner speeches, and tributes.

Your instructor may specify the general purpose of your speech as part of your assignment.

▶ **general purpose**   The speaker's intention to inform or persuade listeners, or to celebrate some person or occasion.

Specific Purpose

Determining your **specific purpose** helps you narrow your topic until it comes into sharp focus. It states precisely what you want your listeners to understand, believe, feel, or do. Having your specific purpose clearly in mind helps direct your research so that you don't waste valuable time wandering around the library or surfing the Internet for irrelevant material. You should be able to state your specific purpose clearly in a single phrase. Let's look at how a specific purpose statement can give focus to a speech:

Topic area:	The Artistry of Dr. Seuss
General purpose:	To inform

Jessica Bradshaw had been entertained by the books of Dr. Seuss when she was a little girl. Now as an undergraduate student, she remained fascinated with his books, suspecting that their simplicity might result from a quite sophisticated creative process. However, her topic area, as stated here, would be much too vast and general to cover in a five- to six-minute speech. She would never be able to consider the entire range of ideas that might be associated with it, much less provide examples and supporting content. After all, Dr. Seuss wrote many books, any number of which might well be mentioned in developing such a topic. And "artistry"? That's certainly a quite vague and probably quite extensive subject. If there was ever a topic area that needed to be refined, narrowed, and focused in a specific purpose statement, this was surely it! As Jess read more about Dr. Seuss, she found a really interesting interview with him that spelled out how he had created *The Cat in the Hat*. This book, she decided, would be her point of focus. And the incredible story of how he labored to create such a simple-seeming text would be a further point of refinement. Jess came up with the following:

Specific purpose:	To inform my audience of Dr. Seuss's creative persistence as he composed *The Cat in the Hat*.

Jess had just made a major move in refining her topic. Now she was ready to test and possibly improve this specific purpose statement.

Testing Your Specific Purpose Statement. Developing a successful specific purpose statement is one of the most important steps in topic refinement. The following tests should help you:

1. *Does the specific purpose promise new information or fresh advice?* You may be greeted with yawns if you propose "to inform listeners that drunk driving is dangerous." You will have tied yourself to a tired topic. When you tell listeners something they have already heard many times, you simply waste their time and yours.

2. *Can you accomplish your specific purpose in the allotted time?* If you propose "to persuade listeners that health care in the United States is too costly and inefficient," you will have bitten off far more than you can chew. Remember, in a five-minute speech you have only about seven hundred words to get your message across. You may need to limit your remarks to the health care crisis in your community in order to meet time restrictions. That strategy might also be more interesting to your listeners.

3. *Have you avoided the double-focus trap?* It is sometimes difficult to make that final decision to narrow your topic to a single focal point. It may be tempting to fall into the trap of double focus: "to inform my listeners of hiking *and* camping opportunities in Shenandoah National Park." If you attempt to address both these subjects in any meaningful way, you may go beyond your time limits. The "and" in such statements is often a red flag that signals a double-focus problem.

▶ **specific purpose** The speaker's particular goal or the response that the speaker wishes to evoke.

4. *Have you avoided the triviality trap?* When you speak to twenty-four people for five minutes, you will be taking up two hours of their collective time. What are you offering them in return? If you promise to inform them about "how to mix a martini" or "how to punt a football," you may well leave your listeners feeling short-changed. They may react with a blunt "So what?" You must convince listeners that you have a specific purpose that promises them important information, insights, or advice so that by the end of the speech they feel they have invested their time wisely.

5. *Have you avoided the technicality trap?* Sometimes speakers forget that listeners may not share their technical vocabulary. They are puzzled when listeners respond with dazed, bewildered looks and the question, "Huh?" Speakers who promise "to inform listeners of the principles of thermonuclear energy" or "to inform my audience about the intellectual evolution of Kant's meta-ethics" are stepping directly into this trap. They have not factored audience background into their topic selection. This failure becomes evident when they write out their specific purpose statements.

Improving Your Specific Purpose Statement.   Let's look at an example of a flawed specific purpose statement and see how it might be improved:

Flawed: To persuade my audience that driving while distracted is dangerous

Improved: To persuade my audience not to text while driving

The flawed specific purpose is vague, and it tells the audience nothing new. Who would argue that driving while distracted is not dangerous? The improved version focuses more precisely on a contemporary problem.

Thesis Statement

Writing your **thesis statement** or central idea is the final refinement in preparing a topic for a speech. The thesis statement summarizes in a single sentence the message of your speech. For example, Jess Bradshaw's speech began with this thesis statement: "*The Cat in the Hat* is the incredibly simple product of an incredibly complicated creative process." B. J. Youngerman focused his persuasive speech in defense of Walmart on the following thesis statement: "Walmart is a positive force in American public life." Such sentences, notes scholar Booth, "state a potential claim" that the speeches themselves must demonstrate or prove.[7] They are usually worked into your introduction so that listeners will know your intentions from the outset.

Most of the time, your specific purpose will be revealed in your thesis statement, but the two are not identical. The specific purpose expresses what you want to accomplish; the thesis statement summarizes what you intend to say. Another student speech developed a relationship between the specific purpose and thesis statement as follows:

Specific purpose: To persuade listeners that binge drinking is a serious problem on our campus

Thesis statement: Today I want to discuss a major problem on campus—binge drinking—and what we can do about it.

In ethical speaking, the thesis statement will usually reveal the speaker's specific purpose; at the very least, it will not disguise it. *But let the listener beware!* Speakers sometimes hide their actual intentions. If you consider the hidden motives of cult leaders or sometimes even leaders of nations, you can see how serious this problem can become. *The greater the distance between the hidden specific purpose and the thesis statement disclosed in the speech, the larger the ethical risk.*

▶ **thesis statement**   Summarizes in a single sentence the central idea of your speech.

YOUR ethical VOICE   The Ethics of Topic Selection

Ethical problems can infiltrate the process of topic selection for speeches. To avoid many of these problems, follow these guidelines:

1. Do not select a topic that could be hurtful, such as "How to Make a Pipe Bomb."

2. Do not select a topic that invites illegal activity, such as "Growing Marijuana in Your Dorm Room."

3. Do not select a topic on which you cannot obtain responsible knowledge.

4. Do not purposely obscure your thesis statement in order to hide your specific purpose.

At times, ethical speakers may omit the thesis statement from their presentations, leaving it to be constructed by listeners from cues within the speech. Cecile Larson left the thesis statement implicit in her speech "The 'Monument' at Wounded Knee," which appears in Appendix B. Her intent was to create a dramatic effect as listeners discovered her thesis statement for themselves. But this technique also entails considerable risk. Listeners may miss the point!

In most cases, speakers should integrate the thesis statement into the introduction of their speeches. The thesis statement should arouse interest, and should provide sharp focus for the speech. Effective speeches are structured to develop a central idea. When that idea is obscure, there is no central focus to hold the structure of thoughts together. The speech then rambles about in a disorganized way and leaves no lasting impression on the audience. When listeners ask, "What exactly are you trying to say?" or "What would you like us to do?" chances are the thesis statement has not been clearly realized or well stated.

An Overview of the Topic Selection Process

Let us now look at the entire process of moving from general topic area to thesis statement to see how these steps can evolve in actual speech preparation. Jess Bradshaw's experience provides a good example.

FINDING YOUR voice   Refining Your Topic

Refine the preferred topic identified in "Finding Your Voice: Exploring Your Topic Area" until you have determined its general purpose, specific purpose, and thesis statement. What are the strengths and limitations of the speech you might give on this topic? As you answer this question, be sure to consider the assignment, your time limits, and audience needs and interests as well as the intrinsic value of the topic.

FINDING YOUR
voice
Developing a Topic Briefing

Present a proposal introducing a topic or series of topics you would like to explore in classroom speeches. Explain why you want to give these speeches and how listeners might benefit from them. Identify any communication problems you might have, and how you plan to deal with them. List at least five sources of information you plan to draw upon in preparing your speeches.

At the discretion of your teacher, present your topic briefing either as a written proposal or as an oral presentation to a small group or to the class as a whole. Your presentation should invite questions and suggestions. For more on topic briefings, and a sample speech, read the supplementary material offered in MySpeechLab.

Topic area:	The Artistry of Dr. Seuss
General purpose:	To inform
Specific purpose:	To inform my audience of Dr. Seuss's creative persistence as he composed *The Cat in the Hat*.
Thesis statement:	*The Cat in the Hat* is the incredibly simple product of an incredibly complicated creative process.

The refinement phase of topic selection is like looking at a topic successively through the lenses of a microscope. When you identify the general purpose, specific purpose, and thesis statement of a speech topic, you bring the topic into sharper and sharper focus. At the end of the process, what was at first vague has now become precise. You are now ready to complete the vital research and planning that will develop the topic into a successful speech.

FINAL
reflections
The Great Chain of Communication

Cicero, the renowned Roman orator and communication theorist, once wrote that public speaking is an art made up of five great arts: creating the content of a speech, organizing its ideas, expressing them in effective language, committing the speech to memory, and presenting the speech powerfully. These arts are obviously all connected, and form the great chain of the communication process. This chapter helps form the first link in the chain, which extends from the first tentative moments of preparation to the final dramatic moments of presentation. Until you have a clear, compelling idea of what you want to talk about, it is useless to discuss any of the other arts. Finding your topic—one that fascinates and excites you, that you can commit to and become passionate about, that justifies your investment of time and energy—is also an essential step in finding your voice.

"PULLING A CAT OUT OF A HAT"

NFL linebacker Keith Bulluck reads to children as a part of the Read Across America campaign

At various moments in this chapter we have referenced the experience of Jess Bradshaw in developing her topic concerning the artistry of Dr. Seuss. What follows is the final product of her careful preparation, as the speech was presented to her Davidson College class. Concerning how she came up with her topic, Jess reports that she had loved the Seuss books since childhood, and suspected that many in her audience would share her fond memories of them. Her biggest problem in topic development, she says, was narrowing the topic, making the hard decision to get rid of interesting but irrelevant information.

▶ The speech follows a narrative pattern, telling the story of how a classic work was composed. In developing the story, Jess makes effective use of expert testimony. This paints a favorable impression of her ethos as a competent, responsible person whose information can be relied on. This impression would create a positive presumption in favor of speeches she would later give on other topics.

JESSICA BRADSHAW

Have you read *The Cat in the Hat?*
Of course you have. I'm sure of that!
And how about *Green Eggs and Ham?* Did you dig that Sam-I-Am?
Or *Yertle, the Turtle* you got from Aunt Myrtle?
And, did you like the book 'bout the Grinch?
You silly goose, that was a cinch!

What Dr. Seuss gave you, as he proclaims in his opening of *The Cat in the Hat*, was good fun that is funny. His books may not seem all that complex, realistic, or even deep, but it was not without much work that Theodore Seuss Geisel, otherwise known as Dr. Seuss, was able to make you laugh and smile. Indeed, *The Cat in the Hat* is the incredibly simple product of an incredibly complex creative process. Geisel was amazingly persistent in developing, writing, and editing what would become a classic in children's literature.

The idea behind *The Cat in the Hat* did not come in one great moment of inspiration; instead, it was the result of over four months of brainstorming, drafting, rejecting, and brainstorming again. As told by Philip Nel, in *Dr. Seuss: American Icon*, William Spaulding, the educational director of Houghton Mifflin publishing company, challenged Geisel to write a story using only 225 words from a list of 348 words that first graders were able to recognize by sight or phonics. Geisel accepted the challenge, expecting to spend a few weeks on the project, according to Ruth MacDonald, author of the book *Dr. Seuss*.

Geisel, writing in *The New York Times Book Review*, reported searching for weeks for a topic before finally receiving his answer in a dream. Rushing off to his typewriter, he wrote thirty-two pages of *The Queen Zebra* before realizing that the words "queen" and "zebra" were not on the list. Four months later,

Geisel was still working on the assignment, this time attempting to write a story about a bird without using the word "bird"—because it too wasn't on the list! But without the word, he was unable to get the project off the ground. Sorry. Bad pun!

By then, according to *The New Yorker* article "Cat People: What Dr. Seuss Really Taught Us," Geisel had reached a moment of crisis:

> I thought it was impossible and ridiculous and I was about to get out of the whole thing; then I decided to look at the list one more time and to use the first two words that rhymed as the title of the book—cat and hat were the ones my eyes lighted on.

But writing *The Cat in the Hat* took as much persistence as the brainstorming for it required. "You got an idea and then found out you had no way to express yourself," Geisel states in *American Icon*. But Geisel worked through the difficulties in a complex process that he described in *The New York Times Book Review*:

> The method I used is the same method you see when you sit down to make apple strudel without the strudel. . . . You take your limited, uninteresting ingredients and day and night, month after month, you mix them up into thousands of combinations. You make a batch. You taste it. Then you hurl it out the window. Until finally one night, when it is darkest just before dawn, a plausible strudel-less strudel begins to take shape before your eyes!

And for nine months, Geisel worked at editing the strudel-less strudel that is the beloved *The Cat in the Hat*. Later in *American Icon* he described the process: "To produce a 60-page book, I may easily write more than 1,000 pages before I'm satisfied. The most important thing about me, I feel, is that I work like hell—write, rewrite, reject, re-reject, and polish incessantly." According to Seussentennial, the official website for the Dr. Seuss Enterprises, Geisel purchased an old observation tower in La Jolla, California, where he worked eight hours a day for nine months manipulating the 225 words he used in *The Cat in the Hat*. That amounts to 67 hours per word!

To reports of his genius, Geisel retorted, "If I'm a genius, why do I have to work so hard? I know my stuff looks like it was all rattled off in 28 seconds, but every word is a struggle and every sentence is like the pangs of birth."

But eventually his persistence paid off. According to *Publisher's Weekly*, *The Cat and the Hat* is the sixth best-selling children's book of all time. So the next time you're sitting in your tower, on the third floor of the library, working on that paper idea, remember the persistence of Theodore Seuss Geisel in developing, writing, and editing *The Cat in the Hat*. And even in your gloom, maybe you will smile, remembering what Dr. Seuss himself went through.

◀ The use of direct quotations from Geisel is much more striking and colorful than if Jess had used paraphrase to summarize his thoughts. The exact, colloquial words give the speech an air of freshness and authenticity it otherwise would have lacked.

◀ Having completed the remarkable narrative of how Dr. Seuss pulled a cat out of a hat, Jess ties her speech directly to the experience of her listeners. A little Seuss-like persistence might help them develop their assigned papers, she suggests. This lighthearted turn in the speech brings it to a graceful close.

7 Building Responsible Knowledge

> *Learn, compare, collect the facts! Always have the courage to say to yourself, 'I am ignorant'.*
>
> —IVAN PETROVICH PAVLOV

Last night I was up late, just fooling around on the Internet, when I saw all the shocking stories about oil spills. I got really angry just reading them. We've known for a long time that we need to develop cleaner sources of energy. How many disasters will it take to convince us to act? I think we need to enforce stricter environmental regulations on the giant energy companies. Ones that hold them accountable! That's what I want to give my speech on. I already know what I'm going to say. I don't really need to do any more research. Why read more about such a depressing subject?"

"That's a good, timely, and important topic," agreed Jonathan's instructor, "but if you want to give a speech on that topic, you absolutely have to do some more, in-depth research. Your personal feelings just aren't enough."

"Why?" asked Jonathan. "I know what I'm talking about. I've been concerned with the environment for a long, long time. I've even witnessed some of the disasters. Why do I have to do more research?"

This chapter answers Jonathan's question and starts you off on the path to building responsible knowledge for your speeches. Developing research skills and becoming more informed on the issues and subjects we care about is a crucial part of finding your voice. It provides you with that base of knowledge for speaking ethically, credibly, and effectively. Even though strong feelings suggest a strong commitment, and personal experiences add authenticity, they are rarely adequate as the basis for public speaking. Even more important, doing research actually overlaps the processes of focusing, developing, and even rethinking and revising your ideas before you open your mouth to speak. Simply put, becoming personally enlightened is a prerequisite to speaking as a source of authoritative information and ethical persuasion. Acquiring responsible knowledge also helps satisfy one of the demands of ethical communication mentioned in Chapter 1: respect for the integrity of ideas and information.

One of the major goals of an education is to help students become information literate. At a time when information seems to grow exponentially, you need a way to break through the "data smog" that occurs when too much information comes at you too fast. **Information literacy** provides you with the skills you need to locate information efficiently and to evaluate what you learn.[1] It helps you find your voice both in your academic world and your professional life after college. Unfortunately, most college students think of research as a rote process and tend to use the same small set of information resources no matter what the subject area or what questions they may have. Instead of studying a topic carefully, they look for "satisficing" information—seeking just enough information that is "good enough" to complete course assignments.[2]

A word of caution as we begin this chapter: Information resources are changing rapidly. What we write about libraries and the Internet may change before this book goes to press. What we hope to teach you is the ability to wade through the morass and become a lifetime learner who can investigate ideas from a variety of perspectives by locating, evaluating, and using sound sources of information.

Developing a Research Strategy

To make the most of the time you have for researching a speech topic, begin by developing a strategy to guide your efforts. Fill out the Research Strategy

▶ **information literacy**   The skills one needs to locate information efficiently and to evaluate what one learns.

Worksheet shown in Figure 7.1. Begin finding your materials, and then prepare research notes until you are satisfied that you have acquired responsible knowledge. As you move from top to bottom of the worksheet, you will be following these steps:

1. Developing an overview of your subject

2. Building a bibliography on your topic

3. Acquiring in-depth knowledge from reputable sources

4. Checking to see that your information is up to date

5. Discovering local applications for your topic

Prepare an Overview

You should begin developing a comprehensive picture of your subject by accessing sources of background information about it. Even if you have extensive personal experience, you may find that your knowledge is incomplete, or you may discover areas of the topic that you had overlooked. The reviews also can help you focus your speech by pointing out the most important ideas concerning your topic.

Review articles are found mainly in encyclopedias and specialized dictionaries, housed in the reference section of the library. On the Internet, go to the Library Spot (www.libraryspot.com) for links to most of the major encyclopedias online. General encyclopedias contain background information, specify keywords to use in your search for in-depth information, and often list references for additional research. The articles are brief and written in lay language.

Specialized encyclopedias, such as the *International Encyclopedia of the Social and Behavioral Sciences*, cover specific topics in greater detail. Specialized dictionaries, available on diverse subjects ranging from American slang to zoology, provide more than definitions and pronunciations. For example, the *Oxford English Dictionary* presents the origin, meaning, and history of English words.

Once you have found sources of general information that are relevant to your topic, read the background material, take notes on what you find, and identify at least four keywords you can use to access in-depth information.

Build a Bibliography

Because your preparation time for speeches is limited, you must know how to access information quickly. The major sources of access to information in the library include periodical indexes, newspaper indexes, and the online catalog. Some of the periodical indexes, such as the *Reader's Guide to Periodical Literature*, cover publications of general interest. Others, such as the *Business Periodicals Index*, are specific to a subject area. Many indexes are now available on computers in the library or through your school's online resources databases. To access information from an index, you must enter the keywords you have identified for your topic.

On the Internet, the major sources of access to information are the search engines discussed in detail later in this chapter. Use all these materials to build a

FIGURE 7.1 Research Strategy Worksheet

Topic: _____

Specific Purpose: _____

General Information Sources: (List sources of general information applicable to your topic) _____

Key Terms and Access to Information Sources: (List the key terms you will use and 2 sources of access to information you will use to identify specific and/or in-depth references)

Key Terms   1. _____   2. _____

            3. _____   4. _____

Access   1. _____   2. _____

Specific and/or In-Depth Information References: (List 3 or 4 references to specific and/or in-depth information applicable to your topic, of which at least 2 must be from periodicals or books)

1. _____
   _____

2. _____
   _____

3. _____
   _____

4. _____
   _____

Current Information References: (List 1 or 2 sources of current information if applicable to your topic)

1. _____
   _____

2. _____
   _____

Local Applications Sources: (List 1 or 2 sources for local applications material if applicable to your topic)

1. _____
   _____

2. _____
   _____

bibliography on your topic. From your bibliography, identify those articles or books that seem most relevant to your specific purpose.

Acquire In-Depth Knowledge

Most of the facts and figures, testimony, examples, ideas for narratives, and materials for presentation aids will come from in-depth sources of information, such as periodicals and books. As you research your speech, try to use a variety of sources representing different perspectives on your topic. Some, such as *Scientific American*, are perceived as highly credible and objective, whereas others may be less acceptable to critical listeners. As you read articles in periodicals, you may discover that one book is frequently mentioned. Read it, and check the *Book Review Index* for summaries of reviews of it.

When you need facts and figures, consult an almanac, yearbook, or atlas. Almanacs and yearbooks provide accurate, up-to-date compilations of information on a wide range of topics. Such materials go beyond simple lists and often include graphics that you can adapt for presentation aids. They may include data on such things as population density or industrial production and are a good source of materials for presentation aids. Biographical resources can provide information about the qualifications of experts you might cite in a speech. Books of quotations can offer material for the introductions and conclusions of speeches.

A word of caution: *The articles you find do not provide you with a speech.* Rather, they provide ideas, information, opinions, examples, and narratives for use in the speech that *you* prepare for *your* particular audience. If you simply summarize an article and present it as though it were your own, you are committing plagiarism. Although we discussed plagiarism in Chapter 1, these guidelines for avoiding plagiarism bear repeating:

- Introduce authors of quotations.

- Identify sources of information.

- Give credit to the originators of important ideas.

Be Sure Your Information Is Up to Date

The timeliness of information is important for topics that change rapidly, such as medical research and electronic technology. In addition, if you are not aware of current happenings related to your topic, your credibility will suffer. The best source of timely information is the Internet. By logging on to local newspapers and television stations throughout the world, you can keep abreast of what is happening during crisis situations. One of the best library sources for current information is *Facts on File*, a weekly publication that reports on current events by topics. Additional sources of current information include the most recent issues of weekly newsmagazines and newspapers.

Browsing through current periodicals can spark up-to-date ideas to enrich your speech.

Include Local Applications

An effective way to involve listeners with your subject is to show them how it relates to them and their community. For example, if you were discussing methods of disposing hazardous waste, it would be especially effective to talk about how that problem affects the local area. Your library may index local newspapers and may subscribe to regional magazines. Local newspapers may have archives that you can search online.

Many libraries maintain a **vertical file** that contains newspaper clippings, pamphlets, and other materials about important local people or issues. These materials may contain names of people you could interview to hear the kind of personal stories and inside information that might really make your speech come to life.

Acquiring Responsible Knowledge

Responsible knowledge entails a comprehensive understanding of your topic that allows you to speak effectively and ethically. It includes information on

- the main issues of your topic.
- what respected authorities say about it.
- the latest developments relevant to it.
- local applications that might interest your audience.

To develop responsible knowledge, you must leave yourself enough time to do research thoroughly and carefully. You should also keep an open mind. Even if you are convinced that one side of a controversial issue is correct, try to discover why others might feel differently. Being open-minded will help you develop speeches that reach out to more people.

Having responsible knowledge earns you the right to speak. It allows you to enrich the lives of listeners with good information or advice. Whenever you speak, you put your mind and character on display. If you haven't made an effort to acquire responsible knowledge, you are saying, in effect, "I don't have much to offer, and I really don't care." On the other hand, having responsible knowledge may enhance your ethos in terms of both competence and character.

Although you cannot become an authority on most topics with ten hours or even ten days of research, you can certainly learn enough to speak responsibly. Because your research time will be limited, you should follow these three simple steps:

1. Assess your personal knowledge and experience.

2. Enrich your knowledge using library and Internet resources and interviews with experts.

3. Take careful notes for use in preparing your speech.

The "Speaker's Notes: Checklist for Acquiring Responsible Knowledge," offers a systematic approach to becoming responsibly informed. Keep in mind that not every source will be appropriate for every topic, and some sources will be more appropriate than others for a particular speech.

▶ **vertical file**   A library resource containing local materials.

▶ **responsible knowledge**   An understanding of the major features, issues, information, latest developments, and local applications relevant to a topic.

SPEAKER'S notes

Checklist for Acquiring Responsible Knowledge

Use this checklist to assure that you have covered all the bases in your research.

1. _____ I have explored my personal knowledge of the topic.

2. _____ I have consulted general and/or specialized dictionaries or encyclopedias.

3. _____ I have checked newspaper indexes and recent newsmagazines to ensure that my information is up to date.

4. _____ I have used library and Internet search services to identify books and articles on my topic.

5. _____ I have looked for materials in periodicals to enrich my speech.

6. _____ I have considered the usefulness of the following sources:

   _____ atlases

   _____ biographical resources

   _____ almanacs

   _____ government documents

7. _____ I have looked for local materials relevant to my topic.

8. _____ I have interviewed experts about my topic.

Drawing on Personal Knowledge and Experience

Personal knowledge and experience add credibility, authenticity, and interest to a speech. Although you may not be an acknowledged authority on a subject, personal stories or examples suggest that you have unique insights. They also make it easier for an audience to identify with you and your topic.

If you lack direct experience with a topic, you can arrange to acquire some. Suppose you are planning a speech on how local television stations prepare newscasts. You have gathered information from books and periodicals, but it seems rather dry and lifeless. How can you make this information interesting? Call a local television station and ask the news director if you might visit the newsroom so that you can get a feel for what goes on during that hectic time right before a newscast. Take in the noise, the action, and the excitement before and during a show. This experience can help enrich your speech. You might also schedule an interview with the news director while you are at the station.

As valuable as it is, personal experience is seldom sufficient to provide all the information that you will need for your speech. Your personal knowledge may be limited, the sources from which you learned may have been biased, or your experiences may not have been typical. Even people who are acknowledged authorities on a subject look to other experts to give added authority to their messages. Use your personal knowledge as a starting point and expand it through research.

Prepare a personal knowledge summary sheet similar to the one shown in Figure 7.2. Include what you know (or think you know) about the topic, where or how you learned it, and what additional information you might need to find. Jot down any examples or narratives from personal experience so that you can remember them as you develop your speech. Use your summary sheet to direct your research.

FIGURE 7.2 Personal Knowledge Summary

Topic: Eating Right on Campus

What I Know (or Think I Know)	Where/How I Learned It	What I Need to Find Out
College students don't eat right	Gained 15 lbs on junk food Note what friends & I eat	Average frosh gain Average college diet
Lack time and opportunity	Always rushed so choose fast foods	What sells best in student center
Cafeteria food unhealthy	Choices limited, I eat there	What is offered each day
Fresh fruit & veggies good	High school life skills class Mom's wisdom	Nutritional recommendations for balanced diet

Examples/Narratives I Might Use in Speech:

Today I grabbed a slice of pizza, a can of cola, and a chocolate bar for lunch. Not really nutritious, but it was all I had time for. I had just 25 minutes to get from my work-study job in Roslyn Hall to this class. At least the student center is on the way! But that's not enough time to sit down and eat a good meal. And even if I had the time, choices are limited. Yesterday the main options were sliced pizza, hamburgers, spaghetti and meat balls, and macaroni and cheese. Heavy on the starches and fats. No wonder the average freshman here gains 10 pounds.

Doing Research in the Library

After assessing your personal experience and expertise, you should familiarize yourself with the resources in your school's library. In this age of the Internet, you may not realize how much libraries have to offer beyond books. Here you will find local resources and publications, high-quality reference materials and paid databases, unique archives and special collections, and the invaluable assistance of professional librarians. Moreover, many schools now make many of their popular and academic publications available in full-text electronic format, which students can access 24 hours a day from their personal computers.

As you use library resources, read for both breadth and depth. That is, first gain a broad appreciation for your general topic area, most likely through news articles, popular periodicals, and quick-reference resources. Specialized references, journals, and government reports can provide depth and detail for supporting and illustrating your main and supporting ideas. Your library's Web site may offer a virtual tour or tutorial for accessing and researching these materials, and many libraries offer their students guided tours on a regular basis. We encourage you to visit your library in person. Most college and large municipal libraries provide the following resources:

- *Reference or research librarian:* This person is the most valuable resource in the library. Most academic libraries have at least one professionally trained librarian, who can help steer you to the most useful materials for researching your topics.

- *Reference area:* This section contains encyclopedias, yearbooks, dictionaries, almanacs, atlases, print indexes to periodicals, and often computer terminals for searching electronic resources. While many specialized references are still available in print form only, other more popular materials, such as *Encyclopedia Britannica, Merriam-Webster's Collegiate Dictionary,* and the *Reader's Guide to Periodical Literature* are now available in electronic format through most libraries.

- *Online catalog:* The online catalog lists the books and periodicals available in the library and also tells you whether an item is available, has been checked out, or has been placed on reserve.

- *Electronic databases:* Most universities provide free access to a variety of paid databases that allow you to search and download full text versions of popular, scholarly, and government publications. You should check to see what your particular library offers. LexisNexis Academic, ProQuest, Ethnic Newswatch, and Reader's Guide Full Text provide search engines for locating articles in news resources and popular periodicals. EBSCOhost provides links to special databases covering scholarly journals and publications. Among these databases are Academic Search Premier, Humanities Abstracts, JSTOR, and Communication and Mass Media Complete.

Library materials are an excellent source of information for speeches.

- *Government documents area:* Most libraries still maintain collections of federal, state, and local government publications in hard copy, although most current documents are now available and more readily accessible in electronic form.

- *Nonprint media archives:* Collections of films, videos, DVDs, CDs, recordings, and microfilms can be found in the nonprint media archives.

- *Special collections area:* Many libraries have areas that provide access to local publications, resources, and unique archives that can help you adapt your speeches to the needs and interests of your surrounding community.

Doing Research on the Internet

The Internet represents an increasingly valuable resource for researching speech topics. Available 24 hours a day, it is especially useful for accessing the latest information in local news and government documents. Web sites are available from nonprofit, academic, activist, and corporate organizations. You will also find a growing number of free publications and databases for searching both popular and scholarly sources of information. The most basic tools for researching the Internet are search engines and subject directories.

Search Engines.   A **general search engine** such as Google (www.google.com) or Yahoo! (www.yahoo.com) allows you to search the World Wide Web for sites containing a given keyword or phrase. The results are typically organized in terms of relevance, popularity, or date of placement on the Web. We encourage you to use a variety of search engines, as they will differ in terms of what they find. Using more

▶ **general search engine**   An Internet search engine that allows you to enter a keyword and find related Web sites.

than one search engine will yield a broader variety of responses. Always make sure your anti-virus and spyware programs are up to date and running whenever you explore new Web sites and services.

A note of caution: Both Google and Yahoo! are commercial enterprises that sell initial placements that appear as "sponsored links" at the beginning of your search results. For example, British Petroleum created quite a stir when at the height of the Gulf oil crisis it purchased the right to preferentially place its materials on "oil spill" and other similar terms. To see this premium placement as anything other than a commercial enterprise can lead your carefully planned research astray.

Perhaps the greatest challenge in conducting responsible research is the sheer amount of posted materials and the lack of editorial oversight and quality control. Indeed, searching topics by keyword alone on the Web is a bit like shopping thrift stores. There are plenty of gems out there, but you usually end up sifting through a lot of junk finding them, and you don't always find what you're looking for. You can either expand or focus your searches on both Yahoo! and Google by using their advanced search options, and by consulting the advice we outline in the "Speaker's Notes: Tips for Refining Internet Searches."

Subject Directories.   You can also focus your searches by using free online subject directories. A **subject directory** organizes links on topic-specific materials such as the humanities, politics, entertainment, or sports. Because they are compiled and screened by humans, they tend to yield more selective and often higher-quality results than general search engines. Google Directory (http://directory.google.com) and Yahoo! Directory (http://dir.yahoo.com) are both useful for searching popular topics and searching by category. Infomine (http://infomine.ucr.edu/Main.html), Internet Public Library (www.ipl.org), and Google Scholar (http://scholar.google.com) can help you locate a wealth of high-quality materials and publications that general search engines will usually not uncover.

Perhaps the greatest shortcoming of conducting research on the Internet is that many of the most authoritative magazines, journals, reference materials, and newspapers are no longer available free of charge. As discussed earlier, you should be able to access most of them through your school library's electronic databases. Some Web resources you might find particularly valuable are:

Google News (http://news.google.com): offers an archive of news stories that can be searched by topic, date, source, and location.

Merriam-Webster Online (www.merriam-webster.com): provides a highly credible online dictionary with links to a thesaurus, Spanish–English translations, medical terms, and even audio pronunciations.

About.com (www.about.com): provides a database with over two million entries written by experts on a wide variety of topics ranging from travel and product reviews to science, philosophy, and history.

Intute (www.intute.ac.uk): provides links (compiled by librarians in the United Kingdom) by topic to a wealth of high-quality scholarly information representing pretty much every subject of academic inquiry.

Hulu (www.hulu.com): offers an impressive archive of informative documentaries that might help you to gain a broader appreciation for your topic area. You may also wish to access clips from YouTube as visual aids, but be warned that this is a very unstable medium; what's there the night before may not be there the next morning when you make your actual presentation. Try to download the material to your personal computer so that you can access it when you need it.

▶ **subject directory**   An organized list of links to Web sites on specific topics.

SearchGov.com (www.searchgov.com): can help you navigate and access the millions of free federal, state, and local government documents that are posted online.

American Fact Finder (www.factfinder.census.gov): provides a wealth of information gathered by the U.S. Census Bureau regarding the demographic, social, and economic makeup of your community.

FedStats.gov (www.fedstats.gov): allows access to statistics developed by various agencies of the federal government on just about every subject.

WhiteHouse.gov (www.whitehouse.gov): provides access to all major speeches, press releases, and position statements by the president. Web sites hosted by both the U.S. House of Representatives (www.house.gov) and the Senate (www.senate.gov) provide information on their proceedings as well as links to their respective members.

American Rhetoric (www.americanrhetoric.com): provides access to advanced materials and readings on public speaking, and the most thorough and authoritative online anthology of historic and current American speeches available.

When you access information from Internet sources, be sure to take careful notes so that you can document the sources later on. Note the author's name and credentials, the Web site's sponsoring source, and the complete URL (universal resource locator), also known as the Web address. These source materials are often long and must be accurate, so it is best to copy and paste the URLs. Because Web sites and news stories are routinely removed or revised or reposted with new addresses, you must record the date you accessed a site from the Web as well as the date the information was posted or last revised. Remember to be careful when cutting and pasting information from Internet documents to your research notes. Unless you specify the source of the material and indicate in some way that a passage is a direct quotation, you could find yourself inadvertently committing plagiarism. It may be helpful to highlight direct quotes in yellow so that you don't confuse them with your personal summaries or reactions.

For more information on researching your topics online, we recommend that you visit "Finding Information on the Internet: A Tutorial," posted by the University of California, Berkeley, Library (www.lib.berkeley.edu/TeachingLib/Guides/Internet/FindInfo.html).

SPEAKER'S notes   Tips for Refining Internet Searches

The following tips can help you expand or focus your searches:

1. Use AND to focus your search to only sites that include both terms or phrases: mammogram AND ultrasound.

2. Use OR to broaden your search to access all sites including either term: Memphis OR barbecue.

3. Use a minus sign (a space followed by a hyphen) to restrict your search by excluding sites containing the term or phrase following the sign: Lions -Detroit.

4. Use NEAR when words should be close to each other in the document: pollution NEAR global warming.

5. Use quotation marks to restrict your searches to a given phrase: Baltimore Preparatory School gives 2,765 hits, whereas "Baltimore Preparatory School" gives 275 hits.

6. Use "site:" following a term or phrase to restrict your search to a given site or domain. For example, typing "oil spill" site:whitehouse.gov will limit search results to presidential statements on the topic; Afghanistan site:edu will limit your search to articles posted on educational Web sites.

7. When all else fails, read the instructions under "Advanced Search Tips" on your search engine home page.

FINDING YOUR

voice

Expanding Your Sources of Information

Go to the current periodicals area of the library and find a magazine with which you are not familiar. Read an article in the magazine and evaluate it in terms of its credibility. Report your findings to the class.

Evaluating Research Materials

You should evaluate information carefully before using it in your speeches. As you research sources of information, ask yourself the following questions:

- Does this source contain relevant factual and statistical information?
- Does this source cite experts whom I can quote or paraphrase in my speech?
- Does this source provide interesting examples that can help illustrate my main ideas?
- Does this source provide narratives that can bring my topic to life?

Beyond determining what an individual source has to offer, you should consider all researched information for use in your speeches in terms of the four R's of relevance, representativeness, recency, and reliability:

- **Relevance** concerns the extent to which supporting materials apply directly to your topic and purpose for speaking.
- **Representativeness** means the extent to which supporting materials depict a situation or reality as it typically exists.
- **Recency** refers to the timeliness or currency of supporting materials.
- **Reliability** concerns the overall credibility of supporting materials.

Evaluating Material from Library Resources

As you do research in the library, keep the list of the four R's in mind. Beyond relevance and representativeness, you should consider the credibility of your sources, including both the author and the publication. Also remember that the timeliness of information is critical for topics addressing current events, disputed issues, and latest developments in science and technology, so seek out the most up-to-date information available.

As you assess the credibility of an author, ask yourself, *Is this author an expert on my topic?* Remember that scientists and college professors are not necessarily experts on every subject. You should be able to assess the credentials of most experts by searching their names (enclosed in quotation marks) to determine their professional associations and what other experts have to say about them. When assessing authors who are journalists, evaluate the credibility of the "experts" cited in their articles.

You should also consider the publication in which the material appears. Professional journals are generally seen as more credible than popular periodicals such as magazines and newspapers. In turn, popular periodicals themselves vary in terms of their credibility. For most audiences, mainline newspapers are considered more credible than tabloids, and upscale magazines such as *Atlantic Monthly* are more credible than *Reader's Digest*. Popular periodicals may also reflect political or social biases. For example, *The Nation* offers a liberal perspective on contemporary issues, and the *National Review* presents a conservative outlook. Consequently, as you select authors and publications to cite in your speeches, you should consider how their reputations might affect the way your listeners receive your message.

The more sensitive or controversial your topic, the more important the credibility of your sources. For example, let us assume that you wish to present a speech supporting a ban on semiautomatic weapons. From previous class discussions, you suspect that many in your audience may not be friendly to any ideas related to "gun control." For these listeners, citing information or opinions that support your case from highly respected "mainstream" sources such as the American Medical Association might surprise them and get them to listen more sympathetically.

Evaluating Material from the Internet

You must be especially careful while evaluating information you find on the Internet. Remember that pretty much anyone can put anything on the Internet. Sometimes sites are taken down for various reasons (copyright infringements, repugnant content, etc.), but Internet materials are generally subject to few if any editorial constraints. This makes it especially important to use your critical thinking skills. Start by determining what kind of site you are looking at. As you "surf" in search of information, consciously distinguish between advocacy, information, and personal Web sites.

Advocacy Web Sites. The purpose of an **advocacy Web site** is to raise consciousness and influence attitudes or behaviors on a given issue or promote a special agenda. An advocacy site might ask for contributions, try to influence voting, or simply strive to promote a cause. The URL of a nonprofit advocacy site often ends with .org. Some examples of advocacy sites include the Sierra Club (www.sierraclub.org), the National Rifle Association (www.nra.org), and the Southern Poverty Law Center (www.splcenter.org).

FINDING YOUR

voice   Discovering Advocacy Web Sites

Use the World Advocacy Web site (www.worldadvocacy.com) to locate a Web site for a cause or controversial issue that interests you, such as immigration laws, health care reform, or clean energy alternatives. Locate an information Web site on the same topic, then describe the differences between the two sites. Do you detect an agenda beyond being informative in either or both sites?

▶ **advocacy Web site** A Web site whose major purpose is to change attitudes or behaviors.

The Southern Poverty Law Center (SPLC) home page, shown in Figure 7.3, illustrates many of the features of an advocacy Web site. The top ribbon bears a truncated mission statement: "Fighting Hate – Teaching Tolerance – Seeking Justice." "Who We Are" and "What We Do" windows at the top of the left-hand menu document the organization's past and continuing work promoting tolerance and fighting hate groups like the Ku Klux Klan. A "Get Informed" window provides links to news stories and other sources of information, and a subsequent "Get Involved" window provides information on joining the group, receiving its "e-news," and making donations.

Like the SPLC home page, many advocacy Web sites contain credible information and links to other credible sources of information, although such sources typically present only one side of an issue. Therefore, you should carefully evaluate what you read, strive for balance by finding out what opposing groups and advocates have to say, and corroborate any information that is especially compelling or important by cross-referencing it with other, less partisan sources.

Information Web Sites.   The purpose of an **information Web site** is to provide factual information on a specific topic. Information Web sites may include research reports; current world, national, or local news; government statistics; or simply general information such as you might find in an encyclopedia or almanac. The URLs of information Web sites may have a variety of suffixes, such as .edu, .gov, or .com. For example, both the Mayo Clinic (www.mayoclinic.com) and MEDLINEplus Web sites (www.medlineplus.gov) are excellent sources of information about health issues. The material on the Mayo Clinic Web site has been prepared by physicians and scientists affiliated with the clinic; the material

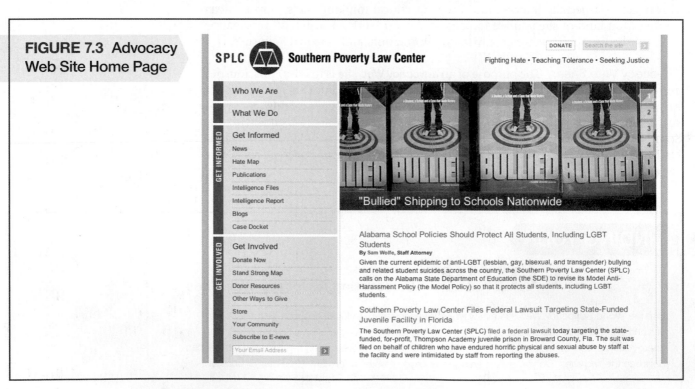

FIGURE 7.3 Advocacy Web Site Home Page

▶ **information Web site**   A Web site designed to provide factual information on a subject.

on the MEDLINEplus Web site comes from the government-sponsored National Library of Medicine.

Figure 7.4 shows the Mayo Clinic home page. Even though this Web site is registered in the commercial domain (.com), the focus is primarily on providing health-related information. Note some of the differences between this information home page and the advocacy home page shown in Figure 7.3. While you are subjected to the occasional advertisement, you are not asked for a donation, and the only thing you can sign up for is a free electronic newsletter.

It is not always easy to differentiate between advocacy and information Web sites. Some nonprofit sites walk a fine line between informing and advocating without damaging their credibility. For instance, the home page of the American Red Cross (www.redcross.org) offers links to a wealth of extremely credible information on disaster relief efforts, but it is presented in a manner that is obviously calculated to arouse your sympathies and financial generosity. Some advocacy sites seek to mask their persuasive agendas behind the appearance of informative expertise and objectivity. You should be especially wary of anonymous studies, "fact sheets," and news stories posted by partisan activist groups, and watch out for blatant disinformation that fabricates or distorts information beyond reason to advance a hidden agenda.

Personal Web Sites.   The purposes of a **personal Web site** are many and varied. They represent the work or opinion of a single individual who may or may not be affiliated with an official organization. They can contain anything from a list of a person's favorite restaurants in Boston to a professor's supplemental course material to incoherent ramblings about conspiracy theories. Because there are no controls over what can be published on personal Web sites, you should be very careful about evaluating and using material from them.

Evaluating Web Sites.   Regardless of what kind of sites you visit, you should evaluate any information you intend to use in terms of the same four R's of relevance,

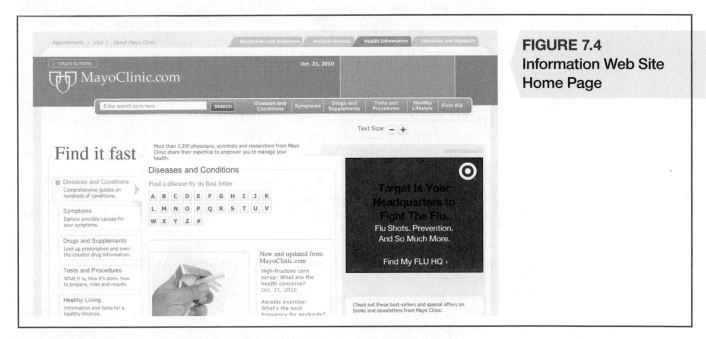

**FIGURE 7.4
Information Web Site
Home Page**

▶ **personal Web site**   A Web site designed and maintained by an individual; contains whatever that person wishes to place on it.

To ensure responsible knowledge in your speeches, carefully evaluate materials you find on the Internet.

representativeness, recency, and reliability. Of course information should be relevant to your topic, your main ideas, and your purpose for speaking. And information should be representative of the larger reality or situation you are addressing. But you cannot know whether information is relevant or representative until you have consulted a variety of sources and have read for breadth and depth.

No single article or Web site can provide all the information you need on a topic. Reputable Web sites will contain links to additional information or research that should be useful. When you are visiting advocacy sites, remember that you are reading one side of an issue, so you should read another for balance. In general, you should assume that any single source offers only a partial view.

Again, recency is crucial when addressing current events, disputed issues, and topics relating to science and technology. With such topics most of your online information will likely come from news sources and popular periodicals, information and advocacy Web sites, and government documents. Most reputable sites will date archived information. When they don't, you must rely on the date the site was last updated or depend on the credibility of the host site or sponsoring agency.

Reliability is especially important when evaluating information retrieved from Internet sources. Janet E. Alexander and Marsha Ann Tate, information specialists at the Wolfgram Memorial Library of Widener University, critique the reliability of Internet information in terms of authority, accuracy, and objectivity.[3]

Authority refers to the credibility and expertise of a given source of information with respect to a given issue or subject area. Be wary of anonymous studies, news reports, and "fact sheets" posted by activist groups. As a general rule, Web sites posted by credible organizations cite their sources and make it easy for you to identify their sponsoring agency. You can search most organizations by their URL address. If they make it hard to determine who they are, you should probably not use them. Again, you can assess the "recognized" authority of most experts and organizations by simply searching their names and/or titles, enclosed in quotation marks. Finally, be warned that many instructors have issues with Wikipedia because its entries are user-contributed and not always reviewed by recognized experts. Be sure that any Wikipedia information you use is carefully documented, and that you can access the sources the contributor has listed to double-check their authenticity.

Accuracy refers to the precision or truthfulness of information. The best way to ensure the accuracy of the information you research is to use sites posted by credible sources such as recognized experts, reference materials, and "mainstream" news organizations. Again, credible sites usually document sources and provide links to other credible information. Watch out for statistical information and studies generated by activist organizations and commercially funded "think tanks" with an obvious interest in the outcome. Be wary of information that seems purposefully obscure and inaccessible to the average reader. As always, check any information on advocacy sites that seems "too good to be true" by consulting other, less partisan sources of information.

▶ **authority** Criterion for evaluating the credentials of the author.

▶ **accuracy** Criterion for evaluating the correctness of information by checking it against other information.

YOUR ethical VOICE   Clues to Internet Shenanigans

Consider any experiences with "disreputable" Web sites you may have inadvertently encountered in terms of what you found especially offensive about these sites. What tipped you off to their unethical intent? Use your findings to help direct your research.

Objectivity concerns the extent to which information on Web sites is free from personal feelings, bias, and hidden agendas. Most recognized experts and "mainstream" news organizations have a vested interest in maintaining their ethos as objective sources of ideas and information. Most reputable advocacy and commercial Web sites are honest about their biases and strive to present information reliably and accurately. However, knowing that a source has an agenda should cue you to look for additional information from differing perspectives. As mentioned earlier, the advocacy sites that try to hide their objectives are the ones you really must watch out for. The lack of an "About Us" or "Mission Statement" link on the site should be a clear indication that it may be peddling disinformation. For example, there are racist and anti-Semitic groups that have been known to disguise their messages of hatred by developing what look like benign informative Web sites.

We close this section with a caveat that bears repeating. *Because literally anyone can put anything on the Internet, it is very important for you to be a thoughtful and critical consumer of online ideas and information.* For an excellent tutorial on assessing the quality of Web sites, we recommend "Evaluate Web Sources" (http://www.widener .edu/libraries/wolfgram/evaluate), which is posted by the Widener University Library. The Annenberg Center for Public Policy has a site titled "FactCheckEd.Org" (www.factchecked.org) that lists and assesses informative and advocacy Web sites dealing with public issues in terms of reliability and objectivity.

SPEAKER'S notes   Checklist for Evaluating Internet Materials

If you are using the Internet to do research, you should use the following checklist to evaluate the information you find.

1. What type of Web site have I accessed? Advocacy? Information? Personal?

2. Is the author or sponsoring agency identified?

3. Does the author or sponsoring agency have appropriate credentials to address the issue?

4. Does the material contain links to other information on the subject or citations of available print resources?

5. Is the material objective, or does it seem biased?

6. Do other authorities confirm the information on the Web site?

7. Is the material up to date on time-sensitive topics?

8. Is the material covered with enough breadth and depth?

▶ **objectivity** Criterion for evaluating whether or not a source is free from bias.

Interviewing for Information

Personal interviews can be an excellent source of information and opinions that add credibility to your speech. The additional work also impresses listeners with your commitment to creating a speech with value for your audience. If you can say, "Carina Del Gados, the director of research and development at Biomedical Products, told me . . .," your audience will sit up and listen. Interviews often yield stories and inside information that make speeches come to life.

As valuable as they can be, interviews also pose some challenges. Finding the right person to interview can be difficult. Once you find the person and are granted an interview, you may feel so grateful that you simply accept what the person says without critically evaluating the information. If you don't know a great deal about the subject, it may be hard for you to judge what you hear. However, the potential benefits of a good interview far outweigh any possible shortcomings. To minimize problems, use these strategies:

- Make interviews the final phase of your research preparation.

- Check your library's vertical file or local newspaper archives to help you identify nearby prospects for interviews.

- Through your initial research, identify widely recognized experts for possible telephone or e-mail interviews.

- Although it is generally preferable to conduct an interview face to face, e-mail and telephone interviews can be used to verify information, acquire a brief quotation, or discover a person's opinion.

- Don't overlook the possibilities on your campus. Every college and university has faculty members with expertise on a wide array of topics, and they are often willing to grant interviews to students.

Once you have identified prospects for interviews, you must establish contact, prepare for the interview, conduct the interview, and record what you learn so that it is readily accessible for speech preparation.

Establish Contact

The best way to initiate contact with interviewing prospects is to write them a letter in which you explain why you would like to interview them. You might even include a list of the questions you would like to ask. Such a letter helps the prospects evaluate your motives, builds your credibility, and sets the agenda for the interview. It also gives the experts, who probably are busy people, some idea of how much time you will need. Even though time is of the essence, a letter of request sent via snail mail may receive more attention than one sent via e-mail.

In your letter, express your sincere interest in the subject, and explain the significance of your request: You are preparing a public speech on a topic that is important to both them and you. Follow up the letter with a telephone call to schedule the interview. If time is short, initiate contact directly through a telephone call. Don't be shy. A request for an interview is a compliment because it suggests that you value the person's information.

Consider whether to record your interview. A recorder can free you from having to take notes to get down the exact wording of answers. However, many people do not like being recorded, so always get your expert's permission. A good time to ask is during your initial contact. If the expert seems reluctant, don't press the issue. *Never tape an interview unless you have permission.*

Prepare for the Interview

Complete most of your library and Internet research before you conduct the interview so that you know what questions to ask and can converse intelligently on the subject. Also learn as much as you can about the person you will interview. This knowledge helps you establish rapport with your expert. Write out interview questions that are relevant to your specific purpose.

Plan open questions that invite discussion, not yes-or-no answers. Suppose you are interviewing the president of the local Sierra Club. Don't ask questions that may seem obvious or actually supply the answer you want, such as "Don't you think that air pollution is a problem that demands attention?" Arrange your questions in a sequence so that the answers form a coherent line of thought:

- What are the causes of air pollution in Farmington?

- How does air pollution affect the citizens of Northern New Mexico?

- What is being done to minimize air pollution?

- What can be done to keep solutions from damaging the local economy?

- What can students do to help the effort?

Plan your wording so that your questions don't sound abrasive. Save any controversial questions for late in the interview, after you have established rapport. Ask such questions tactfully: "Some people say that environmental groups lose track of the economic impact of their plans on jobs and workers. How do you respond to such criticism?" If asked with sincerity rather than hostility, this type of question can produce the most interesting part of your interview.

Conduct the Interview

Dress appropriately to show that you take the interview seriously, and arrive on time. Take time for a little small talk before you get into your prepared questions. Talk about things you may have in common. This might include such things as where the person lives, where he or she went to school, or simply your mutual interest in the topic.

Let the expert do most of the talking while you do the listening. Allow the person you are interviewing to complete the answer to one question before you ask another. Don't interrupt and jump in with another question every time your expert pauses. Your expert may go from one point to another and may even answer a question before you ask it. You should adapt to the flow of conversation.

Be alert for opportunities to follow up on answers by using probes, mirror questions, verifiers, or reinforcers. **Probes** are questions that ask a person to elaborate on

The skills you learn in your public speaking class can help you in many ways. Learning to present yourself well can be an asset in job interviews.

▶ **probes**   Questions that ask someone being interviewed to elaborate on a response.

a response: "Could you tell me more about the part played by auto emissions?" **Mirror questions** reflect part of a response to encourage additional discussion. The sequence might go as follows:

> "So I told Anthony, 'If we want people to change their attitudes, we're going to have to start marching in the front of the movement.'"

> "You felt you were moving toward a leadership role?"

A **verifier** confirms the meaning of something that has been said, such as "If I understand you correctly, you're saying, . . ." A **reinforcer** provides encouragement for the person to communicate further. Smiles, nods, or comments such as "I see" are reinforcers that can keep the interview moving.

If you feel the interview beginning to drift off course, you can often steer it back with a transition. As your expert pauses, you can say, "I believe I understand now the causes of air pollution. But can you tell me more about how this level of pollution affects our health?"

Don't overstay your welcome. As the interview draws to a close, summarize the main points you heard and how you think they may be useful in your speech. A summary allows you to verify what you have heard and reassures the expert that you intend to use the information fairly and accurately. Thank your expert for his or her time, and follow up with a thank-you note in which you report the successful results of your speech.

SPEAKER'S notes

Guidelines for Interviewing for Information

To conduct an effective information interview, follow these guidelines:

1. Locate and contact an expert on your topic.
2. Research your topic before the interview.
3. Plan a series of questions that relate to your specific topic.
4. Act professional: be on time, dress nicely, be courteous.
5. Don't ask leading questions.
6. Let the expert do most of the talking.

Record What You Learn

If you plan to take notes during an interview, tell your expert you want to be sure to quote him or her correctly in your speech. If you are not certain you wrote down an answer correctly, read it back for confirmation. After you have completed the interview, find a quiet place to go over your notes and write out the answers to important questions while your expert's wording is still fresh in your mind.

Taking Notes on Your Research

The best research in the world will not do you any good unless you take notes that help you prepare your speech. Take notes on anything you read or hear that might be

---

► **mirror questions**   Questions that repeat part of a previous response to encourage further discussion.

► **verifier**   A statement by an interviewer confirming the meaning of what has just been said by the person being interviewed.

► **reinforcer**   A comment or action that encourages further communication from someone being interviewed.

usable in your speech. It is better to have too much material to work with than to know you read something important about a point but can't remember where.

Preparing Source and Information Cards

In this time when almost everything is done electronically, you might find it weird to be putting your notes on plain old index cards. However, note cards are easy to handle and sort by categories. The 4×6 index cards often work best because they provide adequate space for any information you want to record. You can spread them out on a table or on the floor and see every piece of information you've gathered. This helps you gain an overview of everything you have in one visual frame, rather than having to navigate through multiple screens.

Once you have your cards organized, you can consider the connections between information. You can discover the connections in your material by seeing things you had not thought of while gathering your information. You can even create connections such as developing parallel wording for your main points. These types of ideas might come more readily to mind when you are working with hard copy. Preparing research cards also may help you avoid cut-and-paste plagiarism. You should prepare both source and information cards for each article or book you might use.

A **source card** should contain standard bibliographical information (see Figure 7.5). You also may wish to include a short summary of the material, information about the author's credentials, and any of your own comments or reactions to the material. Use an **information card** to record facts and figures, examples, or quotations (see Figure 7.6). Include only one idea on each information card to make it easier to sort the cards later. Label the top of each card with a heading that includes an abbreviated identification of the source.

FIGURE 7.5 Source Card

> **Source Card**
>
> Kennedy Warne, "Organization Man," Smithsonian (May 2007) 105–111.
>
> Describes the work of Carl Linnaeus, an 18th century scientist, who classified and named more than 4,000 animals and 8,000 plants long before Darwin.
>
> Author was the founding editor of New Zealand Geographic, and frequent contributor to National Geographic.

FIGURE 7.6 Information Card

> **Information Card**
>
> Warne, "Organization Man," p. 109
>
> "Many of his ideas now seem ludicrous. He believed epilepsy could be caused by washing one's hair, and leprosy caught by eating herring worms."
>
> direct quote!

▶ **source cards** Records kept of the author, title, place and date of publication, and page references for each research source.

▶ **information cards** Research notes on facts and ideas obtained from an article or book.

Taking Notes on Your Computer

An alternative to using index cards is taking notes on your computer. For each paragraph in your notes, include a heading and an identification of its source, just as you would for an index card. You can rearrange these paragraphs in the same way that you sort index cards. It is usually wise to download and print Internet materials as you access them to be certain you have the correct URL. Make a backup copy of your notes to store on a CD or other device so that you don't accidentally lose them.

Know What Information to Record

The following checklists indicate the type of information you need to record about each source you consult:

For each book, record the

_____ Author
_____ Editor (if listed)
_____ Edition number (if listed)
_____ Full title, including subtitle
_____ Name and location of publisher
_____ Copyright date
_____ Page numbers for passages that you quote, summarize, or paraphrase

For each article, record the

_____ Author
_____ Full title, including subtitle
_____ Title of periodical
_____ Volume number
_____ Issue number
_____ Issue date
_____ Page numbers for passages that you quote, summarize, or paraphrase

For each computer-based source, record the

_____ Author
_____ Full title of the page or article, including subtitle
_____ Sponsor of the site
_____ Dates the document was posted and/or revised
_____ Date you accessed the source
_____ URL for Web pages (Web site address)
_____ Volume, issue number, and date for online journals

For each interview, record the

_____ Name of the person you interviewed
_____ Professional title of the person you interviewed
_____ Contact information: mailing address, phone number, e-mail address
_____ Date of the interview

FINAL
reflections   Your Substantive Voice

Acquiring responsible knowledge helps you add substance to your voice. It can make you more credible and authoritative as you speak. It takes time to do effective research, but it is worth every minute you spend on it. Not only will you be able to present a speech that is of value to your listeners, but learning more about any topic yields positive personal rewards. You may learn things that help clarify your thinking on an issue. What's more, you will be acquiring a specialized skill that you can use throughout your life to help you understand and verify what is going on in your world.

THIS CHAPTER WILL HELP YOU

1 Frame facts and statistics to substantiate ideas
2 Develop expert, lay, and prestige testimony to add interest and credibility
3 Build examples and narratives to involve listeners and bring your speech to life
4 Select the most appropriate supporting material for your speech
5 Combine and interpret information effectively and ethically

8 Supporting Your Ideas

> *The universe is made up of stories, not of atoms.*
>
> —MURIEL RUKEYSER

Even if you haven't seen one in person, you've probably seen a railroad trestle in an old western movie. These magnificent examples of architectural and engineering excellence must carry many times their own weight as they span deep canyons and cross fast-flowing rivers. To bear such a burden they need strong supports that are braced and cross-braced. Not only do the supports and braces add strength, but they also add beauty to the structure.

As you discover and develop your voice as a public speaker, picture yourself as an architect—a builder of ideas. Think of your speeches as thought-structures built on solid pillars of supporting materials. To be a good architect or builder, you must know your materials and what they can support. You need to know how to select and use them wisely. Just as a train trestle is built to carry heavy weights and withstand storms and high winds, your speech must withstand doubt and controversy. When you rise to speak, you must be confident of its structural integrity.

Supporting materials—facts and statistics, testimony, examples, and narratives—are the pillars, braces, and cross-braces of serious speech-making. The effective and ethical use of supporting materials helps to establish the reality and meaning of your assertions, adds credibility and human interest to your presentations, and generally distinguishes engaging and convincing messages from mere "knee jerk" assertions. Such materials contribute directly to finding and establishing your voice. As you learn to use and interpret information in support of your ideas, you sharpen your appreciation for the topics and issues you care about, elevate your ethos or credibility before your peers, and reinforce a respect for intelligent dialogue, enlightened decision-making, and the integrity of ideas and information.

At this point, you should have gathered a wealth of information and generated your main ideas as discussed in the previous two chapters. In this chapter, we discuss four forms of supporting materials that make use of this information, point out how to put them to work in your speeches, and discuss how to combine them to maximum advantage.

Facts and Statistics

As we discussed in the previous chapter, your first objective when researching any topic is to get your facts straight. Richard Weaver, a noted rhetorical theorist, has suggested that Americans honor facts and statistics as the highest form of knowledge, much as some societies respect divine revelation.[1] As the most authoritative form of supporting information, facts and statistics are indispensable to responsible speaking—especially when addressing informative or persuasive topics. When audience members get the impression that "the facts are in your favor," they believe that your message deserves their attention and respect.

Framing Facts

Facts are statements that can be verified by independent observers as true or false. For instance, on April 4, 1968, Dr. Martin Luther King Jr. was assassinated in Memphis, Tennessee. In 2009, a new form of "swine flu" emerged and quickly achieved "pandemic" status. As of January 2010, approximately one out of every ten members of the American labor force was out of work.

Conspiracy theorists aside, very few people would question the factual validity of these statements. What these truths "mean" and what we should do about them are vigorously and rightfully debated, but few would question their factual validity.

Developing Statistics

Statistics are facts measured mathematically. In our "show me the numbers" culture, statistics are useful for describing size precisely, making predictions, illustrating trends, or demonstrating important comparisons. For instance, speakers might use statistics to document the unemployment rate in a given city or area as well as to explain how those rates compare to other cities or areas and the extent to which those rates have risen or declined over recent years. Statistics can also be used to predict future developments of ongoing trends in various areas. Especially in democratic societies, public opinion polls used to characterize the will of the majority can strongly influence policy decisions.

▶ **supporting materials** The facts and figures, testimony, examples, and narratives that are the building blocks of substantive speech-making.

▶ **facts** Statements that can be verified as true or false by independent observers.

▶ **statistics** Facts that are measured mathematically.

Constructing Facts and Figures

"The art of the fact" may seem a strange expression. Don't facts stand alone, without need for further help from the speaker? Despite that commonplace assumption, the truth is that facts don't speak for themselves. *You must speak for them.* You select them to make some point, and place them within some context of interpretation. Developing the ability to frame facts effectively is vital to finding your voice

Consider the statement: "According to a U.S. Department of Labor report issued on February 5, 2010, the unemployment rate in this country was 9.7%." That is certainly a factual statement, but what point is it trying to make? In this case, the statement was linked to and followed immediately by a dependent clause: "down a mere fraction from the historic highs of 10% the previous fall."[2] That clause provides a **context of interpretation** that shapes the meaning of a fact by offering a way of looking at it. We learn that the rate is "down," but the reduction is small, described here as a "mere fraction." The significance of this reduction is further minimized by emphasizing that it is down from a "historic high."

On the other hand, if *you* were one of the hundreds of thousands of new job holders represented by the reduction in the unemployment rate, the fact might not seem so insignificant—not "mere" at all. The point is clear: *you must explain to listeners how the facts are linked to your message, and what precisely it is that they demonstrate.*

The preceding example illustrates another important decision you must make as you practice the art of the fact: whether to state your fact in general or precise terms. You will recall our earlier general statement that one in ten people in the American labor force was unemployed as of January 2010. Presenting statistics in such a "rounded off" manner can pack a real punch and be quite impressive for most audiences and situations, when listeners may not be interested in knowing or remembering exact numbers. What they may very well remember is the overall magnitude of the unemployment problem at that point in time. On the other hand, there are some audiences and situations for which the exact numbers and sources of data could be critical issues. Your college audience of careful listeners might well be such an audience. You must make the decision as to whether the general or precise manner of expressing facts will work best for you. If you are uncertain on this point, our advice is to err on the side of precision.

Because facts and figures are so vital to responsible knowledge and to ethical speaking, we may have a tendency to overemphasize them. Remember to use a variety of supporting materials, and pick the spots in your speech at which the use of facts and figures will be most necessary and be most effective. Don't drown your listeners in a sea of numbers that will numb them to your underlying ideas. Again, be selective.

Remember also the possible efficacy of presentation aids. As we discuss in Chapter 10, presentation aids can be very effective for communicating factual and statistical information. Simple bulleted textual graphics can help to emphasize the importance of one or a few particularly compelling facts. For instance, if you really want your audience to know and remember that 10% of Americans are unemployed, simply displaying that point in bold letters could be very effective.

Journalists are taught to seek more than one source for information before they rush into print with a story. This search for corroborating sources is the key to responsible reporting, but it is also the way to satisfy critical listeners when statements are controversial and vital to the well-being of the audience. Before such

▶ **context of interpretation** Helps shape the meaning of a fact by offering a way of looking at it.

audiences especially, cite several credible sources to establish the validity of your points. As Austin Wright built his case against the government's use of faulty data-bases in the War on Terror, he carefully supported each of his vital points with at least two credible sources of information (see his speech at the end of Chapter 15).

Finally, select your facts carefully for their relevance to your topic. No matter how inherently fascinating they may seem, be ruthless! If they don't fit your message, don't use them.

It becomes increasingly clear that to practice the "art of the fact" skillfully, you must also become a critic of your own work as well as the communication practices of others. It is to this facet of finding your voice that we now turn our attention.

Testing Facts and Figures

For almost any speech topic, your research notes should contain a good array of facts and statistics. To test facts and figures for their usefulness in your speech, you must subject them to the four R's, learn how to assess the value of sources, and develop the ability to distinguish fact-based interpretations from opinions.

The Four R's. In Chapter 7 we discussed the importance of evaluating information in terms of relevance, representativeness, recency, and reliability. The factual information you present in your speeches should pertain to the point you are making, should be representative of the larger reality or situation you are addressing, should be fresh and timely, and should come from sources that are highly credible.

We have already discussed the importance of weeding out fascinating but irrel-evant facts. On the other hand, you should not ignore information that contradicts your position by claiming it is irrelevant when actually it may not be. Acknowledge such facts, but be ready to explain them and to defend the way you regard them.

You should also resist the temptation to describe some event or accomplish-ment as representative of reality, when actually it is an exception to the rule. Be wary as well of whether a general conclusion actually applies to the situation you are describing. If you talk, for example, about the "crisis of unemployment" in your area, basing your claim on a national average, you could have a problem if someone in the audience points out that the local rate is quite different.

Be mindful that statistical predictions represent probability, not certainty, and that even credible statistics can be distorted by partisan interest groups. Every four years, spokespersons for both major presidential campaigns "spin" the same or similar polls to reach opposing conclusions as to who will eventually win in November. Be wary of comparative statistics provided by such groups, and of attempts to characterize the "average American" from such numbers.

The Sources of Your Data.   The facts and statistics you use in your speeches obviously should come from credible sources, recognized experts, scientists, and reputable news outlets that wish to maintain a reputation for balance and objectivity.

Especially with controversial or disputed topics, you should also consider the predisposition of your audience, and avoid sources that critical listeners might find biased. Audiences that lean liberal can be expected to scoff at Fox News, whereas many conservatives have issues with MSNBC. If you cited the latter station before a conservative audience, many listeners might discredit your argument simply be-cause of the source of the information. On the other hand, if you cited Fox before such listeners, some might be pleased, but critical listeners might suspect you of

FINDING YOUR

voice   Detecting Disinformation

Look in newspapers or magazines for "news" stories or statements by public officials that claim to be factual but that may actually contain distortions or fabrications. What tips you off to the distortion? In your judgment, would most readers be likely to detect this bias? Share your findings with your class.

pandering to listeners' media preferences. You must take the ethos of your sources into careful consideration.

Remember also that there are many pseudo news sources, especially on the Internet. Don't use them until you have checked out their credentials and are convinced of their reliability. Finally, be alert for **disinformation**, sometimes sensational pseudo-discoveries that have been willfully fabricated and packaged as "news" to advance a hidden agenda.[3]

Interpretation vs. Opinion.   There is a real difference between **opinions**, which are expressions of personal feeling and conviction that lack supporting material, and fact-centered interpretations. As speakers and listeners, we must learn to value interpretations over opinions.

Consider, for example, this claim: "Ford Escape Hybrid is a superior small SUV." Offered without any fact or statistical support or expert testimony, the statement is an opinion. It may or may not be true. But contrast its value with the following: "According to ConsumerSearch of 2009, an online evaluation service offered by the *New York Times*, Ford Escape Hybrid is a superior small SUV. Its mileage performance of 34 miles-per-gallon on the highway, 31 miles in the city, tops its class." This is a fact-based interpretation. You could argue with it, perhaps on grounds that it is somewhat dated or that factors other than gas mileage must be considered, but its value far exceeds mere opinion.

SPEAKER'S

notes   Constructing Facts and Statistics

Follow these guidelines for using facts and figures in your speeches.

1. Demonstrate how facts fit the points you are making.

2. Decide whether to present your facts in general or precise terms.

3. Don't overwhelm your listeners with facts.

4. Support your controversial claims with facts from more than one source.

5. Test facts for the four R's: relevance, representativeness, recency, and reliability.

6. Avoid using sources that are obviously biased.

7. Carefully distinguish between fact-based interpretations and opinions.

▶ **disinformation**   Information that has been fabricated or distorted beyond reason in order to advance a given agenda.

▶ **opinions**   Expressions of personal feeling and conviction that lack supporting material.

voice Critiquing Statistics

Of course, there is nothing inherently wrong with expressing our honest convictions and feelings in a speech. Freedom of speech assures us of the right to do just that. But our expressions should have some justification in facts and statistics—they should be anchored in reality. Problems can occur when we fail to distinguish between such fact-justified interpretations and loosely based opinion. We may undervalue the one, and overvalue the other.

As speakers, we can also make the mistake of assuming that facts do speak for themselves, and that the meaning we think is so self-evident does not require further demonstration on our part. As consumers of information, failing to distinguish adequately between interpretations and opinions can make us more susceptible to distortions by omission, loaded language, and outlandish claims offered by unscrupulous or partisan sources.

For more on such uses and misuses of statistics, see the brief but excellent primer compiled and maintained by Robert Niles, "Statistics Every Writer Should Know," at http://www.robertniles.com/stats/. See also our discussion of fallacies in Chapter 15.

Testimony

Testimony involves citing the words or ideas of other people or institutions to support and illustrate your ideas. Using testimony is like calling witnesses to testify on behalf of your position. You add their ethos to yours. The three most prominent forms in public speaking are expert, lay, and prestige testimony.

Framing Expert Testimony

Expert testimony comes from people who are qualified by training or experience to speak as authorities on a subject. Citing sources your audience will recognize as experts is generally the most authoritative form of testimony for establishing the validity of your assertions, explaining concepts or processes, attributing causes, and making predictions. It can be especially useful when you yourself are not an expert, and when the topic is complicated, unfamiliar, or controversial.

When you use expert testimony, remember that competence is area-specific: your experts can speak as authorities only within their area of expertise. As you introduce such experts in your speech, stress their credentials. If their testimony is

▶ **testimony** Citing the words of others to support your ideas and their relevance to your listeners.

▶ **expert testimony** Citing the words of people (or institutions) qualified by training or experience to speak as authorities on a subject.

recent, mention that as well. If the testimony appears in a prestigious journal, book, or newspaper, let listeners know where you found it. Note how Gabrielle Wallace, whose speech appears at the end of Chapter 13, wove the testimony of *three* experts together to support her speech comparing French and American eating customs:

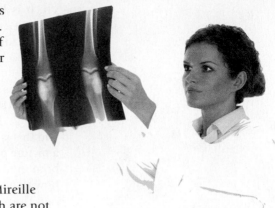

> According to Paul Rozin, a nutritionist at the University of Pennsylvania, French portion sizes on average are about 25% smaller than American portions—which might explain why Americans are roughly three times more likely to become obese than French people.
>
> A factor that might account for this is the French upbringing. Mireille Guiliano, author of *French Women Don't Get Fat*, says that the French are not conditioned to overeat. Instead, they are taught to eat only until they are full, and then stop! A recent University of Pennsylvania study confirmed this tendency. The study compared the eating habits of students from Paris and Chicago. It found that French students stopped eating in response to internal cues, like when they first started feeling full or when they wanted to leave room for dessert. The American students, on the other hand, relied more on external cues. They would, for example, eat until the TV show they were watching ended, or until they ran out of a beverage. There's no question that eating habits are a vital point of difference between the French and American cultures.

Citing expert testimony adds substance to your speech.

This was powerful testimony indeed, enhancing the credibility of both the speaker and the speech. Just think of how much weaker the speech would have been had Gabrielle *not* cited these authorities, relying simply on her own assertions. Much of its power lay in how Gabrielle established the credentials of her experts.

It's important that you guard against bias as you select expert testimony. Also be aware, however, that on some occasions, the perception of bias can actually enhance the usefulness of a source. One of the most powerful forms of testimony, **reluctant testimony**, occurs when experts testify against and despite their apparent self-interest.[4]

One of the most dramatic examples of such testimony in recent memory occurred when David Kay, head of a commission appointed by President Bush to locate weapons of mass destruction in Iraq, issued a report less than a year after the invasion suggesting there was *no evidence of such weapons or even of programs for developing such weapons*. Predictably enough, critics of the war seized upon the "Kay revelations" as powerful evidence against one of the key administration arguments for going to war in the first place. Kay's testimony was all the more compelling because it was reluctant—as evidenced by his continued support for both the Bush administration and the war in Iraq.[5]

Developing Lay Testimony

Lay testimony represents the wisdom of ordinary people. It may come from people with firsthand experience with a topic or issue, or who simply have strong feelings about it. While not appropriate for validating complex or disputed ideas, lay testimony helps to illustrate real-life consequences and adds authenticity to your

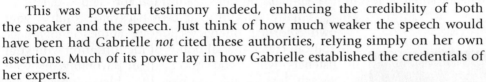

▶ **reluctant testimony** Invoking the words of sources who appear to speak against their own interests.

▶ **lay testimony** Citing the words or views of everyday people on a subject.

speech. It is highly regarded in democratic societies in which the experiences and opinions of everyday folk are generally esteemed.

As he addressed the annual meeting of the Public Broadcasting System, Bill Moyers used lay testimony to emphasize the value of public radio and television:

> There was a cabbie [in New York City] named Youssef Jada. He came here from Morocco six years ago. . . . Youssef kept his car radio tuned to National Public Radio all day and his television set at home on Channel Thirteen. He said— and this is a direct quote—"I am blessed by these stations." He pointed me to a picture on the dashboard of his 13-month-old son, and he said: "My son was born in this country. I will let him watch Channel Thirteen so he can learn how to be an American."
>
> Think about that. . . . Why shouldn't public television be the core curriculum of the American experience?[6]

There are many sources of lay testimony for use in your speeches. Stories featuring lay testimony are a common staple of both television and print journalism. The "letters to the editor" section of most newspapers, and even the opinion threads that follow many online news stories, can be colorful if somewhat dubious sources of popular opinion. Popular opinion polls can serve as a powerful form of collective lay testimony by representing the voice of the people, especially in societies in which "the people" is a positive symbol that represents the final repository of political power.[7] See, for example, Gallup International's "The Voice of the People" (www.voice-of-the-people.net). If you decide to use such testimony from survey data, be sure that it is from a reputable polling organization and is up-to-date.

Finally, look in your own backyard: conduct your own informal interviews among audience members. You can create special bonds of identification with your listeners when you quote them favorably in your speech. Just be sure you have their blessing before you cite them, and never quote them in a way that belittles or insults them.

Bill Moyers used testimony to illustrate the importance of public radio.

Constructing Prestige Testimony

Prestige testimony associates your message with the words of an admired figure—for example, Thomas Jefferson— or text, such as the Declaration of Independence. Such sources include celebrities, noted authors and journalists, and activists and politicians as well as important historical figures and revered religious and political documents. While such sources do not typically provide expertise with respect to your particular topic, the extent to which their words seem relevant can lend a heightened elegance and wisdom to your speeches. Because of this quality, prestige testimony is often used as a source of inspiration in ceremonial speaking.

Barack Obama, in his much-admired "Speech on Race" delivered during his campaign for the presidency, found it advantageous to cite prestige testimony. In the course of that speech he cited the Constitution of the United States ("We the

▶ **prestige testimony**   Citing the words of a person who is highly admired or respected but not necessarily an expert on your topic; similarly, citing a text in this way.

FIGURE 8.1 Checklist for Evaluating Testimony

General

_____ Is this testimony relevant to my purpose?

_____ Am I quoting or paraphrasing accurately?

_____ Am I using the appropriate type of testimony for my purpose?

Expert Testimony

_____ Have I verified the credentials of my source?

_____ Are my expert's credentials appropriate for my topic?

_____ Will this expert be acceptable to my listeners?

_____ Is my expert free from vested interest?

_____ Is this testimony consistent with that of other authorities?

_____ Does this testimony reflect the latest knowledge on my topic?

Lay Testimony

_____ Does this testimony demonstrate the human applications of my topic?

_____ Does this testimony enhance identification with my topic?

_____ Are the people cited likable and attractive?

_____ Is polling data from a reputable organization?

_____ Is polling data recent?

Prestige Testimony

_____ Do my listeners believe this person is prestigious?

_____ Does this testimony add grace and dignity to my speech?

_____ Does associating with this person enhance my credibility as a speaker?

_____ Does associating with this person enhance the credibility of my speech?

---

people, in order to form a more perfect union"), William Faulkner ("The past isn't dead and buried. In fact, it isn't even past"), and the Bible (We are commanded "to do unto others as we would have them do unto us. Let us be our brother's keeper, Scripture tells us. Let us be our sister's keeper.").[8] This combined prestige testimony from an iconic political document, a noted author, and a sacred text lent considerable eloquence to Obama's already eloquent argument. One newspaper enthused at the time, "Here's hoping speech students all across the country are studying it even now, and learning something not just about the art of rhetoric but about the nature of their country."[9]

If you are using prestige testimony, think about how your listeners might feel about the person you are citing. You should also consider whether associating with this person will increase your credibility as a speaker and the credibility of your message. As with lay testimony, prestige testimony should not be used to verify facts.

Designing Testimony: Other Considerations

As you frame testimony for use in your speech, you must decide whether to use the exact words of a source or to summarize what they say. When you repeat the exact words of others, you are using a **direct quotation**. Generally speaking, direct quotations are the more powerful form of citation. They are useful for statements that are brief and eloquent, or when the exact wording is important for the point you are making. They are also effective for supporting complex or controversial assertions before skeptical or discriminating audiences.

Write out quotations on separate note cards to preserve the exact wording. Give some thought to how you will blend them into your speech, for example, "According to . . ." or "In the words of. . . ." Pause as you read the words to increase their impressiveness, and maintain eye contact with listeners during the pauses.

When quotes are too long or complex to present word for word, you may **paraphrase** or restate what others have said in your own words. If your sources are experts on current topics or issues, stress their credentials and the timing of their testimony.

As you use testimony, be sure that the quotation you select reflects the overall meaning and intent of its author. Never twist the meaning of testimony to make it fit your purposes—this unethical practice is called **quoting out of context**. Political campaign advertising is often rife with this abuse. For example, during a political campaign in Illinois, one state representative sent out a fundraising letter that claimed he'd been singled out for "special recognition" by *Chicago* magazine—and, indeed, he had. He had been cited as "one of the state's ten worst legislators."[10]

SPEAKER'S notes   Using Testimony

Keep these guidelines in mind as you plan the use of testimony in your speeches.

1. Use expert testimony to validate information.

2. Use lay testimony to build identification and add authenticity.

3. Use prestige testimony to enhance the stature of your message.

4. Select sources your audience will respect.

5. Quote or paraphrase materials accurately.

6. Point out the qualifications of experts as you cite them.

Examples

Examples bring a speech to life. Just as pictures serve as graphic illustrations for a printed text, **examples** serve as verbal or sensory illustrations that help to clarify your points and ground them in reality. Listeners reveal the importance of these illustrations when they ask, "Can you give me an example?" Examples involving people help listeners relate to your message by showing the human side of situations.

▶ **direct quotation** Repeating the exact words of another to support a point.

▶ **paraphrase** Rephrasing or summarizing the words of another to support a point.

▶ **quoting out of context** An unethical use of quotation that changes or distorts the source's intended meaning to suit the speaker's own purpose.

▶ **examples** Verbal illustrations that clarify and humanize speeches with tangible applications of abstract ideas and issues.

When these examples are drawn from your personal experience, they help establish your ethos to speak on the topic. When listeners have had similar experiences, a bond is created between you and them. You share understanding, which can lead in turn to identification.

Because of the power of examples in communication, speakers often use them to open speeches. Austin Wright began the speech that appears at the end of Chapter 15 with the following example:

> On September 26, 2002, Canadian citizen Maher Arar boarded a flight home from a family vacation in Tunisia. During a layover in New York City, American authorities detained Arar, interrogating him for the next twelve days. After repeatedly denying any connection to Al Qaeda, Arar was shackled and loaded onto a private, unmarked jet headed for Syria, where he was tortured for the next ten months.

Because they are more concrete and colorful than abstract words, examples can more easily arouse emotions. They can touch people with the humanity of situations, even though listeners may come from different cultural backgrounds. When Dolapo Olushora wanted to reach out to her American listeners concerning the plight of AIDS orphans in sub-Saharan Africa, she used photos as visual examples.

Finally, examples provide emphasis. When you make a statement and follow it with an example, you are pointing out that what you have just said is *important*. Examples amplify your ideas. They say to the audience, "This deserves your attention." Examples are especially helpful when you introduce new, complex, or abstract material. Not only can they make such information clearer, but they also allow time for the audience to process what you have said before you move on to your next point.

Types of Examples

The most commonly recognized types of examples for use in public speaking are brief, extended, factual, and hypothetical. A **brief example** mentions a specific instance to demonstrate a more general statement. Brief examples are concise and to the point. Sometimes a series of brief examples can help to drive home a point. In a speech to the National Prayer Breakfast, rock star and social activist Bono used a series of brief examples while exhorting American leaders to set aside 1 percent of the federal budget for African relief programs:

> One percent is not merely a number on a balance sheet. One percent is the girl in Africa who gets to go to school, thanks to you. One percent is the AIDS patient who gets her medicine, thanks to you. One percent is the African entrepreneur who can start a small family business, thanks to you. One percent is not redecorating presidential palaces or money flowing down a rat hole. This one percent is digging waterholes to provide clean water.[11]

Bono cited brief examples in support of African relief programs.

An **extended example** provides more detail, which allows speakers to more fully develop the example. Jane Goodall, the noted naturalist and United Nations Messenger

---

▶ **brief example** A concise reference to an example to illustrate or develop a point.

▶ **extended example** A more detailed example that speakers develop with their messages.

of Peace, made good use of the technique when she described the collective response of New Yorkers after the attacks of 9/11:

> I was in New York when the World Trade Towers were destroyed, and I felt with everyone in New York the shock, the numbness, the terrible grief, the mounting anger of the city as it struggled in the aftermath of 9/11. . . .
>
> But we also saw this amazing heroism, the people who risked and lost their lives to rescue those trapped in the rubble. . . . And there was this outpouring of generosity; people gave whatever they had to give. . . . They opened their homes, they gave clothes, they gave blood, they gave what they could. And for a while people questioned their values: Were we spending too much time searching for more and more wealth and not enough time with our families? And even today . . . there are still people who tell me that they have much more contact with their families than they did before.[12]

A **factual example** is based on an actual event or the experiences of a real person. Factual examples provide strong support for your ideas because they actually did happen: they authenticate the point you are trying to make. University of Memphis student Michele Wieland used the following factual example in a speech in favor of judicial reform:

> Let me tell you about Earl Washington. Earl was easy pickings for the police when they could not solve a difficult rape and murder case. Agreeable and eager to please, with the mental age of a young child, Washington was quick to confess. It didn't seem to matter to the police or prosecutors that Earl did not have the basic facts straight. Earl said the victim was black—she was white. He said she was stabbed two or three times—she had been stabbed thirty-eight times. He said he kicked in a door—the door was found intact. The police were willing to overlook all of this to solve their case. Earl Washington was convicted and sentenced to death. He spent eighteen years behind bars before he was cleared through DNA evidence.

A **hypothetical example** is not offered as "real" so much as representative of actual people, situations, or events. This kind of example can be useful when factual examples are either not available or when their use would not be appropriate. While generally not as authoritative as their factual counterparts, hypothetical examples can still be very effective. They can be the fiction that reveals reality. Consider the following hypothetical example, which illustrates the growing problem of childhood obesity:

> Let me introduce you to Madison Cartwright. Madison is twelve years old. She's four feet eleven inches tall. She weighs 155 pounds. Her body mass index is over 29. This means that Madison is one of the more than nine million children and teenagers who can be classified as obese.
>
> How does this affect her? Not only is she a prime candidate for health problems such as childhood diabetes, but she also has other problems. She loves softball, but has difficulty playing because she gets short of breath. So she sits in the bleachers and watches her classmates. Madison is very smart, but she hates school. She is often the butt of "fat" jokes and teasing by her classmates. Instead of playing outside or socializing with friends after school, Madison goes home and watches TV by herself. Her self-esteem is very low.

▶ **factual example**   An example based on something that actually happened or really exists.

▶ **hypothetical example**   An example not offered as real but as representative of actual people, situations, or events.

Is Madison a real person? Well, yes and no. You may not find someone with her name at the middle school you attended, but you will find many Madisons in the seventh grade there. Childhood obesity in the United States has reached epidemic proportions.

Be careful that your hypothetical examples are representative of the issue or situation you are addressing. Don't distort the truth just to make your point. Always alert your listeners to the hypothetical nature of your example. You can do this as you begin presenting your example with introductory phrases such as "Imagine yourself . . ." or "Picture the following. . . ." Or, as in the preceding example, you can let listeners know near the end.

Fashioning Powerful Examples

The first thing you must do in fashioning powerful examples is to accept the need for them—it is the rare speech that can not be improved by examples. Then you must decide which kind of example will best serve the needs of your speech—brief example, extended example, factual example, or hypothetical example.

Once you choose the kind of examples you will use, you can begin their actual construction. Examples should be colorful and lively, so select details that will make them come to life. Keep them brief and to the point, even when you are using extended examples. Cut out all unimportant details.

One of the great lessons Ernest Hemingway learned as a developing writer was that the more selective he was in describing scenes, the more effective they were. When you keep examples brief but striking, listeners are stimulated to provide details on their own, and their imaginations are engaged more closely with your message.

Emphasize concrete details. Name the people, times, places, and groups in your examples. Listeners will relate more to Luis Francesco with the United Postal Service than they will to some unnamed delivery person.

Pick your spots. Examples can work well to open and close speeches, to clarify your principal ideas, and to ground your speech in reality. But don't make your speech a running series of examples when what you really need are a combination of facts, statistics, and testimony affirming that your examples are valid and representative of situations.

Finally, use transitions to move smoothly from statement to example and from example to statement. Phrases such as "For instance . . ." or "As you can see . . ." work nicely.

SPEAKER'S notes   Using Examples

Let the following suggestions guide your use of examples in speeches.

1. Use examples to emphasize major points.
2. Use examples to attract and hold attention.
3. Use examples to clarify abstract ideas.

4. Name the people and places in your examples.
5. Use factual examples whenever possible.
6. Keep examples brief and to the point.

FIGURE 8.2 Checklist for Testing Examples

____ Is this example relevant to my topic and purpose?

____ Does this example fairly represent the reality of a situation?

____ Will this example make my ideas more understandable?

____ Will this example make my point more memorable?

____ Will my listeners find this example believable?

____ Is this example appropriate for this audience?

____ Is this example in good taste?

____ Is this example interesting?

Testing Your Examples

Test the examples you are constructing in terms of whether they fit your point, are representative, and will be believable. If an example does not fit your specific purpose or help clarify the point you wish to make, it will more likely distract and confuse listeners. Avoid examples that are actually exceptions to the rule. If your examples seem farfetched, listeners will grow suspicious of both you and your speech. You may have to use other supporting materials to prove the legitimacy of your examples.

Keep in mind that what works well with one audience may not click with another. Ask yourself if the example will fit well with the experience, motivations, and interests of your listeners. Examples should meet the tests of good taste and propriety. You should risk offending listeners only when they must be shocked into attention before they can be informed or persuaded.

Last, but certainly not least, be sure any example you use is interesting. Dull examples never help a speech.

Narratives

We humans are natural storytellers.[13] Since the dawn of time—probably beginning long before we started putting together abstract arguments and linear chains of thought—we've been using stories to entertain each other, to celebrate heroic deeds, to teach and reaffirm shared values, and to make sense of the often chaotic ebb and flow of human experience. In the words of noted author and storyteller Norman Mailer:

> We tell stories in order to make sense of life. Narrative is reassuring. There are days when life is so absurd, it's crippling—nothing makes sense, but stories bring order to the absurdity.[14]

A **narrative** is a story that conveys an idea or establishes a mood. Like examples, narratives provide concrete illustrations of abstract ideas and issues, engage listeners in the speech, and help to cross the barriers that often separate people. But more than examples, they describe a sequence of actions that unfolds over

▶ **narrative** A story that conveys an idea or establishes a mood.

time. We use narratives to remember the past, illustrate our ideals, and transmit our cultural traditions from one generation to another. Americans, for instance, have long been fond of "rags to riches" stories celebrating our commitment to hard work and individual responsibility—not to mention riches! Stories such as these help to define who we are and what we're about.

You can draw narratives from many sources. You might tell stories you have made up or that document "real life" experiences. The incredible story of how Dr. Seuss wrote *The Cat in the Hat* is central to Jessica Bradshaw's "Pulling a Cat Out of a Hat," the speech that concludes Chapter 6. Speakers might adapt well-known stories from history, folklore, literature, and even popular television shows. As discussed in Chapter 3, narratives documenting personal experiences are common to self-introductions, but they also can be useful in all forms of public speaking for establishing identification and credibility to speak on a topic. In any case, your narratives should be fresh and directly relevant to your topic and purpose for speaking.

Maya Angelou often uses narrative to illustrate ideas in her speeches.

Types of Narratives

The forms of narrative often found in speeches are embedded, vicarious experience, and master narratives. **Embedded narratives**—which occur at specific points within the overall structure of a speech—are the most commonly used form. Such narratives are often included as part of the introduction or conclusion of a speech. You should use pauses and transitions to signal listeners that you are beginning or ending the story. Your narratives might be solemn and serious or humorous and lighthearted, but the story should make a point that supports your speech. Former Senator Dale Bumpers of Arkansas offered the following embedded narrative in his final defense at the impeachment trial of President Bill Clinton:

> I remember, Chaplain, the—the chaplain's not here, is he? That's too bad. He ought to hear this story [*laughter*]. This evangelist was holding this great revival meeting, and at the close of one of his meetings, he said, "Is there anybody in this audience who has ever known anybody who even comes close to the perfection of our Lord and Savior, Jesus Christ?" Nothing. He repeated the challenge, and finally a little bitty guy in the back of the audience kind of held up his hand, and the evangelist said, "You. Are you saying you've known such a person? Stand up." He stood up, and the evangelist said, "Tell us, share it with us. Who was it?" The little bitty guy said, "My wife's first husband" [*sustained laughter*].[15]

Speakers who want to maximize the involvement of the audience often use a **vicarious experience narrative**. Such a narrative invites listeners into the action so that they imagine themselves participating in the story. A vicarious narrative will often begin with a statement such as "Come along with me . . ." or "Picture yourself. . . ." Dan Rader used this type of a narrative in the introduction to his persuasive speech

▶ **embedded narrative** A story inserted within the overall structure of a speech.

▶ **vicarious experience narrative** A narrative that invites listeners to imagine themselves as participants in a story.

urging University of Memphis students to protest proposed cuts in state spending in Tennessee higher education:

> Imagine that instead of being here in this nice facility, in a class of twenty-five students, you are sitting in a large lecture hall with 250 students around you. And instead of paying $3,300 per semester in tuition, you are now paying $3,600. So for the privilege of getting less personal attention, and a worse education, you get to pay about three hundred dollars more per semester. Sounds like a pretty raw deal, doesn't it? I tell you this story because it's about to happen, and next year it will be even worse. Over the past ten years our tuition has just about tripled while state support has dwindled. The results are bad for our state and bad for us, and we need to do something about it.

Finally, sometimes a speech will develop a single **master narrative**. In this case, the use of narrative does not support your speech—it *is* your speech. Your entire speech is told in the form of a story. Master narratives are common with testimonials and introductory speaking, as we saw illustrated in Sabrina Karic's "A Little Chocolate." This speech, which narrates Sabrina's experiences as a child in war-torn Bosnia, concludes Chapter 3. Review that chapter for its discussion of how to design your presentation around a master narrative.

Building Narratives

Even though storytelling may come naturally to us as humans, there is an art to presenting stories orally. They should be carefully planned and carefully rehearsed. We recently had a student who "teased" his listeners with vague promises of stories that never materialized in his speech. He would say, "This one was really funny," and then ramble on without telling us the story. At best, he would simply paraphrase the story or present a punch line without any preparation. Listening to him was a frustrating experience.

In Chapter 3 we described how to develop the prologue, plot, and epilogue in longer narratives. But these elements occur as well in miniature in embedded narratives. Note how vividly—even though briefly—Sandra Baltz described the setting in her prologue for the story opening her speech on scarce medical resources:

> On a cold and stormy night in 1841, the ship William Brown struck an iceberg in the North Atlantic.

Her plot continued Sandra's compact but vivid account of what happened:

> Passengers and crew members frantically scrambled into the lifeboats. To make a bad disaster even worse, one of the lifeboats began to sink because it was overcrowded. Fourteen men were thrown overboard that horrible night. After the survivors were rescued, a crew member was tried for the murders of those thrown overboard.

In her epilogue, Sandra reflected on the meaning of this action, relating it to her speech:

> Fortunately, situations like this have been rare in history, but today we face a similar problem in the medical establishment: deciding who will live as

▶ **master narrative** A speech that is structured around a single, well-developed narrative.

we allocate scarce medical resources for transplants. Someday, your fate—or the fate of someone you love—could depend on how we resolve this dilemma.

The art of the story boils down to how you use language and how you present the story. The characters and action must come alive through your words. Let listeners see things by using colorful language that is pictorial. Use voice and dialect changes to signal that a "character" is speaking.

As you tell a story, let yourself get caught up in it. The more "into it" you appear, the more likely your audience will also engage and experience your narrative with you. Pause to increase the impact of important moments in your story, especially when something you say evokes astonishment or laughter.

Because storytelling is a more intimate form of communication, you should move out from behind the lectern and closer to your listeners. Stories invite informality. If your story evokes laughter, wait for it to die down before going on. Practice telling your story so that you get the wording and timing just right. Polish and memorize the punch lines of humorous tales: the story exists for them. They are the gem at the center, the capstone at the top.

Use dialogue rather than paraphrasing what someone says. Paraphrasing can save time, but it robs a story of power. Let your characters speak for themselves!

Finally, a well-told narrative can add much to a speech, but too many stories can turn a speech into a rambling string of tales without a clear focus. Save narratives for special moments. For more on the art of storytelling, see the tutorial on the Web site "Effective Storytelling," developed by Barry McWilliams (http://www.eldrbarry.net/roos/eest.htm).

Testing Your Story

Narratives should not exist for themselves, but rather should serve a real purpose in your speech. Some speakers have the mistaken notion that they should start with a joke, whether relevant or not. It's a rather cheap trick, and most listeners see through it. As a result, they usually don't take such speakers or their messages very seriously. Other speakers betray their own ethos by using offensive language in stories that foster and reinforce negative stereotypes. Don't make their mistake.

FINDING YOUR

voice   Your Favorite Story

Think back to your childhood and remember your favorite story. Prepare a brief (less than three minutes) presentation of this story. Practice presenting it as if you were telling it to a group of first graders. Working in small groups, share your story with other group members. Listen to their stories. What storytelling techniques seemed most effective? What made some of the stories less effective?

SPEAKER'S notes

Using Narratives

Keep the following suggestions in mind as you plan narratives to use in a speech.

1. Use stories to involve the audience with your topic.
2. Practice telling your stories so that they flow smoothly.
3. Make the characters in your stories come to life.

4. Use voice and dialect changes for different characters.
5. Use dialogue rather than paraphrase.
6. Use colorful, vivid language.

According to Walter Fisher, stories should be evaluated in terms of narrative probability and fidelity. By **narrative probability**, he means the extent to which a narrative fulfills the attributes of a good story—how well it hangs together.[16] A good story offers a vividly described scene, character development and interaction, and a plot that moves toward some sort of climax or—in the case of humorous narratives—a punch line. All of these elements—scene, action, characters—must seem consistent with each other to satisfy the requirement of narrative probability.

By **narrative fidelity**, Fisher means the extent to which your story rings true for listeners, whether it fits the world they have experienced and whether its characters act in ways that seem believable. When the story passes the test of truth and authenticity, it helps listeners make sense of problems and situations to which it is applied. It helps illuminate the experience of the past and options for the future.

FIGURE 8.3 Evaluating Narratives

____ Is the narrative relevant to my topic and purpose?

____ Does the narrative fairly represent the situation?

____ Will the story help listeners make sense of things?

____ Will the narrative draw listeners into the action?

____ Is the narrative appropriate for this audience?

____ Will the story provide appropriate role models?

____ Will the story enhance identification among listeners, topic, and speaker?

____ Will the narrative make my speech more memorable?

____ Does the story set an appropriate mood for my message?

____ Is the narrative fresh and interesting?

____ Does the story flow well?

____ Is the narrative believable?

____ Is the narrative in good taste?

▶ **narrative probability**   Measures the *skill* of the speaker in blending scene, characters, and action into a compelling story.

▶ **narrative fidelity**   Measures the *authenticity* of the story, the likelihood that it happened or might happen.

Selecting and Combining Supporting Materials

One point becomes increasingly clear: in responsible speaking, the four forms of supporting materials—facts and statistics, testimony, examples, and narratives— are rarely sufficient when used by themselves. If you combine the types of supporting materials, they form a much more powerful alloy that can lend great strength to your speech. Facts and figures affirm that your message is grounded in reality, while expert testimony provides credibility to your claims. Lay testimony brings your message home to ordinary folks and adds the wisdom of the streets, while prestige testimony aligns you with respected authority figures. Examples reinforce facts and figures by focusing on the experiences of representative individuals and situations. Narratives tell stories that add drama and sometimes humor to your message. Examples and narratives can also engage audience feelings in support of your position.

How you combine these forms of supporting materials leaves a lot of room for your individual artistry. Sandra Baltz began her speech on scarce medical resources by telling the dramatic story we quoted earlier in this chapter. Having aroused audience interest, she went on to introduce facts and figures that established the real dimensions of the problem she was discussing. She followed this by telling the moving story of an individual whose fate was very much affected by the medical resources problem. She concluded by offering a solution proposed by experts in the medical resources field. This particular alloy of supporting materials created great strength for her message and gave considerable resonance to her voice. In terms of our chapter opening analogy, her train had crossed the trestle.

Your use of such materials can sometimes raise ethical questions, as we see in "Your Ethical Voice: The Ethical Use of Supporting Materials."

YOUR *ethical* VOICE The Ethical Use of Supporting Materials

To be certain that you are using supporting materials in ethical ways, follow these guidelines.

1. Provide the date, source, and context of information cited in your speech.
2. Don't present a claim or opinion as though it were a fact.
3. Remember that statistics are open to differing interpretations.
4. Protect your listeners from biased information.
5. Don't quote out of context to misrepresent a person's position.
6. Be sure examples are representative of the situation or reality you are addressing.
7. Don't present hypothetical examples as though they were factual.

Different situations will call for different emphases as you combine supporting materials. Your choice of materials should reflect careful consideration of the challenges posed by your particular speech.

1. If your ideas are *controversial*, rely primarily on facts, statistics, factual examples, or expert testimony from sources your audience will respect and accept.

2. If your topic and ideas seem *distant* or *abstract*, bring them to life with examples and narratives.

3. If a point is highly *technical*, define key terms and supplement facts and statistics with expert testimony.

4. If you need to *excite emotions*, use lay testimony and vividly described examples or narratives.

5. If you need to *defuse emotions*, emphasize facts, statistics, and expert testimony.

6. If your ideas are *novel or unfamiliar*, provide key facts and illustrative examples, define and explain basic terms and concepts, and provide analogies to help your listeners better understand them.

Above all else, keep your audience at the center of your thinking and ask yourself these critical questions:

- Which of these materials will make the biggest impression on my listeners?

- Which of these materials will listeners be most likely to remember?

- Which of these materials will listeners find most credible?

- Which materials will most likely make listeners want to act?

FINDING YOUR

voice   Deciding What to Use

Which types of supporting materials in what combinations might help you build a case for or against the following claims?

A. We should increase spending on preschool education.

B. We should cut taxes paid by small business owners.

C. Security measures on campus are not adequate.

D. In deciding government priorities, we should emphasize restoring the environment over creating jobs and providing health care.

Explain and defend your choices.

FINAL
reflections   Developing a Strong Voice

At the beginning of this chapter we likened the structure of a well-supported speech to that of a railroad bridge. Like the trestles that bear many times their own weight, the right choice and use of facts and statistics, testimony, examples, and narratives can make for an overall message that is considerably stronger and more compelling than the sum of its parts. And if you've ever watched somebody present an obviously suspect piece of information to support an important or disputed claim, you also know that like a bridge, a speech is only as strong as its weakest support.

This theme of strength is certainly a quality you would like to have associated with the voice you are discovering. Think of other desirable qualities you might like to add as well to that emerging voice: Would "credible," "colorful," "appealing," "moving," and "interesting" be among them? All of these can be created as well by selecting and constructing effective supporting materials. Develop these materials, and you can add these qualities to your voice.

THIS CHAPTER WILL HELP YOU

1 Develop speeches that are simple, well ordered, and balanced
2 Construct and outline the body of your speeches
3 Plan transitions to make your speeches flow smoothly
4 Prepare effective introductions and conclusions for your speeches
5 Prepare a formal outline

9 Structuring and Outlining Your Speech

> *Every discourse ought to be a living creature; having a body of its own and head and feet; there should be a middle, beginning, and end, adapted to one another and to the whole.*
>
> —PLATO

Overheard at the Student Union:

"I've got to take Intro Biology this semester. I can take Professor Forsyth or Professor Bennett. Have you had either of them?"

"Yes, both. Forsyth is a really funny guy. Keeps you laughing."

"Sounds like my kind of guy."

"Well, there is one small problem: Dude is totally disorganized. Jumps all around in his lectures. Hard to take notes. Hard to learn from him."

"Hmmm. How about Bennett?"

"Not so funny. But she knows her stuff. She's easy to follow and makes it easy to learn."

"Okay. I think I know my choice."

Any real doubt who this student selected? Everyone likes to be entertained, but most people prefer well-organized speakers, especially when the message is important. Indeed, studies suggest that students learn more from teachers who are well-focused, and are annoyed by instructors who ramble and jump from one idea to another.[1]

Well-organized speeches are easier for listeners to follow, understand, and remember. Being well-organized will enhance audience perceptions of your credibility, and also will help you cope more effectively with communication anxiety. Clearly, developing a well-organized speech is an important phase in the process of finding your voice.

Developing organizational skills is also important to finding your voice as an ethical speaker. As we noted in Chapter 1, ethical speaking engages and encourages responsible listening. You have invested much time in finding a good topic, refining and researching it, and gathering vital information about it. But until you can focus all these discoveries in a well-structured speech that listeners will find valuable and easy to grasp, you will not have found your voice. Worse still, the cause that calls you to speak will not have been served well.

In this chapter, we discuss some basic principles of a well-structured speech. We then take you step by step through the process of constructing such a speech from generating, arranging, and outlining main ideas to adding transitions, writing effective introductions and conclusions, and developing formal outlines.

Principles of a Well-Structured Speech

The principles of a well-structured speech reflect the importance of simplicity, order, and balance.

Simplicity

A simple speech is easier for listeners to grasp and remember and for speakers to present effectively. To achieve **simplicity** in your speeches, you should limit the number of your main ideas, repeat them for emphasis, and keep your wording direct and to the point.

Number of Main Points. As a general rule, the fewer the main points in a speech, the better. It takes time to develop each point with supporting ideas and materials, and audience members can only absorb so much. Short classroom speeches rarely develop more than three main points, and longer presentations rarely develop more than five.

These considerations encourage a disciplined process of thinking that prioritizes and subordinates main and supporting ideas and materials. This process further emphasizes the importance of focus and depth over breadth of coverage. For instance, if you were researching and developing a speech in favor of welfare reform, you might initially come up with several ideas and impressions:

- we have too many welfare programs,
- most of our programs are underfunded,
- some programs spend money wastefully,
- others duplicate coverage,
- people who genuinely need assistance are sometimes denied,

▶ **simplicity** Suggests that a speech has a limited number of main points and that they are short and direct.

- recipients have little input as to what is needed, and

- traditional welfare programs can create a culture of dependence that stifles initiative and fosters a lack of self-respect.

Each of these points may be important. However, presented in such random fashion, they may confuse and overwhelm your listeners. As you engage in the process of prioritizing and subordinating ideas and information, you might begin to hammer out the following simpler and more coherent train of thought:

Thesis statement:	Our approach to welfare doesn't work.
First main point:	I. It doesn't work because it's inadequate.
Subpoints:	A. Existing programs are not sufficiently funded.
	B. People who genuinely need help are left out.
Second main point:	II. It doesn't work because it's inefficient.
Subpoints:	A. There are too many duplicate programs.
	B. There is too much waste of money.
Third main point:	III. It doesn't work because it's insensitive.
Subpoints:	A. It creates dependence that stifles initiative.
	B. It robs recipients of self-respect.
	C. Recipients have little input.

This simpler structure makes the message easier to follow. The thesis statement offers an overview of the message. Each main point elaborates and develops the thesis statement. The subpoints organize and focus the secondary ideas so that they support the major ideas. Important but overlapping ideas might be combined, while interesting but irrelevant ideas and materials might be discarded. In the process of simplifying your ideas and information, you have already begun developing a structurally coherent answer to the question of why approaches to welfare are not working.

Repeating Key Points for Emphasis.   Repeating key ideas and information helps simplify the structure of a speech and reinforce its central ideas and information. Consider our preceding revised example. The central message, "Our approach to welfare doesn't work," is reinforced by repeating the point, "It doesn't work because . . . ," while introducing each of the system's three main shortcomings. This method of repeating much of the wording of main points while emphasizing their different points of focus is called **parallel construction**.

Repetition is literally built into the standard format of well-organized speeches. Speakers preview their messages in the introduction, repeat these messages as they develop them in the body, and repeat the messages again as they review them in the conclusions of their speeches.

A well-organized speech is easy to follow.

Phrasing Main Points.   Learning to express your ideas and information as simple, direct statements is crucial to developing your communication skills. Again, consider

▶ **parallel construction**   Wording points in a repeated pattern to emphasize their importance and to show how they are both related and contrasted.

our revised example. Not only has the wording been simplified, but the use of the same word pattern to introduce each main point creates a message that is easy to understand. The repeated phrase, "It doesn't work because" suggests that these are the main points and makes them easy to remember.

Order

Order in a speech requires a consistent pattern of development from beginning to end. A well-ordered speech opens by introducing the message and orienting the audience, continues by developing the main ideas in the body of the speech, and ends by summarizing and reflecting upon the meaning of what has been said. In addition, the main points within the speech body should be developed and organized within a design scheme (categorical, problem-solution, narrative, etc.) as discussed later in this chapter. To build an orderly speech, we suggest that you design and construct the body of your speech first, because that is where you will present, illustrate, and substantiate your message. Once you have structured the body, you can prepare an introduction and a conclusion that are custom-tailored for your message.

Balance

Balance means that the major parts of your speech—the introduction, the body, and the conclusion—receive appropriate development. For most speaking occasions, and certainly for classroom speeches, you will be given specific time requirements, which you should keep in mind as you plan your message. It can be very upsetting to finish your first main point only to find out that you have one minute left to finish two main points and the conclusion. The following suggestions can help you plan a balanced presentation:

1. *The body should be the longest part of your speech.* This is where you develop your main ideas in full. If you spend two minutes introducing your speech, and then a minute and a half on the body, your speech will come across as unbalanced and underdeveloped. Again, since this is the most important part of your speech, we suggest you construct it first before developing your introduction and conclusion.

2. *Balance the development of each main point in your speech.* If your main points seem equally important, strive to give each point *equal emphasis*. This strategy would seem appropriate for the message outlined earlier on the three I's of welfare—inadequate, insufficient, insensitive—in which each point seems to merit equal attention. If your points differ in importance, you might start with the most important point, spending the most time on it, and then present the other points with a *descending emphasis*, according to their importance. For example, if you are presenting a problem-solution speech in favor of health care reform before an audience of listeners who do not believe we need health care reform, you should probably spend most of your time establishing the existence of a problem and then just touch upon prospective solutions. However, to the extent your audience already agrees that we need health care reform, you might use an *ascending emphasis* that touches briefly on the problem, and focuses primarily on prospective solutions and how audience members might become actively involved in promoting them.

▶ **order** A consistent pattern used to develop a speech.

▶ **balance** Suggests that the introduction, body, and conclusion receive appropriate development.

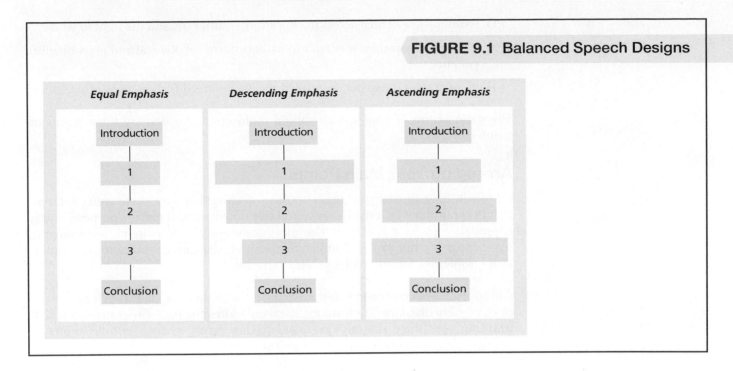

FIGURE 9.1 Balanced Speech Designs

3. *With short presentations, your introduction and conclusion should be brief and approximately equal in length.* Introductions often run slightly longer, but the combined length of both should be less than the body of your speech.

Structuring the Body of Your Speech

The **body** of your speech should develop your main ideas and materials that support them. The process of structuring the body involves the following:

- Selecting, arranging, and developing your main and supporting points and materials.
- Developing a working outline.
- Adding transitions that connect the various points of your speech.

Selecting Your Main Points

The **main points** of your speech are those most vital to establishing your thesis statement and satisfying your specific purpose. As discussed in Chapter 6, your thesis statement articulates your central idea, and your specific purpose specifies what you want your listeners to understand, agree with, do, or appreciate as a result of your speech. Your main points should emerge from general ideas that rise repeatedly as you research your topic and that seem unavoidable in discussing it.

For instance, if you were researching a speech on the mistreatment of women in Afghanistan under the Taliban, you would quickly discover a broad range of possible considerations, more than you could ever hope to cover in a single speech. But rising repeatedly in this unfortunate plenitude would be three points of emphasis:

▶ **body** That part of a speech where main points are developed and the message is supported.

▶ **main points** The most prominent ideas of the speaker's message.

(1) Women were denied access to education, health care, and the right to work.

(2) Women were routinely subject to barbaric forms of physical and psychological violence.

(3) Women who spoke out or asserted themselves faced frightening recriminations.

The main points of your speech should build upon and develop these points of emphasis.

Arranging Your Main Points

Once you have chosen your main points, you should arrange them using a design that fits your material, establishes your thesis statement and specific purpose, and is appropriate to your audience. The most commonly used patterns for arranging main ideas are categorical, comparative, spatial, sequential, chronological, causation, problem-solution, refutative, and narrative.

Categorical.   A **categorical design** arranges the main ideas of a speech by natural or customary divisions. For instance, speakers addressing the "three causes of global warming" or "three strategies to avoid paying excessive taxes" would probably arrange their main ideas using a categorical design.

Comparative.   A **comparative design** explores the similarities or differences among things, events, and ideas. For example, an informative speaker might compare the San Andreas and New Madrid fault zones in terms of the frequency and severity of major earthquakes. Similarly, persuasive speakers might compare the Republican and Democratic Party positions on important issues like health care reform or deficit spending. Speakers often try to explain the meaning of current events with comparisons to the past. For example, critics of our military involvement in Afghanistan and Iraq often invoke comparisons to the 1960s conflict in Vietnam. In that they often relate the unknown to the known, comparative speeches can be especially useful for topics that are new or difficult for audience members to understand.

Spatial.   A **spatial design** arranges the main points of a speech as they occur in physical space, often taking listeners on an imaginary tour. For example, if you were asked to address a group of incoming freshmen on the resources available to them in the library, you might use a floor plan as a presentation aid as you point out where different departments are located. An effective spatial design provides your listeners with a verbal map.

Sequential.   A **sequential design** explains the steps of a process in the order in which they should be taken. Most "how to" speeches use a sequential design scheme. For instance, if you were to give a speech on how to calibrate a piece of high-tech equipment or how to brew your own beer, you would probably use a sequential design. Sequential designs are most effective when speakers offer a "step-by-step" procedure that makes it easy for audience members to follow.

Chronological.   A **chronological design** explains events or historic developments in the order in which they occurred. Chronological designs often survey the pattern of events that led up to a present-day situation. For example, speakers favoring

---

▶ **categorical design**   Arranges the main ideas of a speech by natural or customary divisions.

▶ **comparative design**   Explores the similarities or differences among things, events, or ideas.

▶ **spatial design**   Arranges the main points of a speech as they occur in physical space.
▶ **sequential design**   Explains the orderly steps of a process.

reforms to social security often trace the financial history of the program to suggest that it simply will not be there for future generations. Chronological presentations are effective when speakers keep their presentation of events simple, in the order in which they occurred, and related to the message of the speech. Never present a history lesson for its own sake. Use the past to illuminate your specific purpose in the present.

Causation. A **causation design** addresses the origins or consequences of a situation or event, proceeding from cause to effect or from effect to cause. Causation designs are often used for explaining current developments and forecasting future events. For instance, you might give a speech explaining the causes of a budget shortfall on your campus and predicting larger class sizes, cuts in student services, and tuition increases as a consequence.

Problem-Solution. The **problem-solution design** focuses attention on a problem and then provides an answer to it. Because life constantly confronts us with difficulties, the problem-solution pattern is one of the most frequently used speech designs. To make it work, you must first convince listeners that they do have a problem that they must deal with. Then you must show them that you have a solution that makes sense, that is practical and affordable, and that will very much improve their lives.

The **motivated sequence** offers an elaborate version of the problem-solution pattern. This popular design, first developed years ago by Professor Alan Monroe, follows five steps: (1) drawing *attention* to a situation, (2) demonstrating a *need* to change it, (3) explaining how a plan might *satisfy* this problem, (4) *visualizing* the results of following or not following the speaker's advice, and (5) issuing a call for *action*.[2] Several generations of student speakers have used the motivated sequence variation to great advantage.

Refutative. The **refutative design** proceeds by defending a disputed thesis and confronting opposing views with reasoning and evidence. Found in debates over public policy, this pattern of thought proceeds by identifying an opposing argument and then showing why it is mistaken or logically flawed. Those who follow this design should be careful not to let their refutations degenerate into personal attacks. You must respect your opponents and their feelings by pointing out the problems in their arguments tactfully, while also defending your position with robust arguments that are grounded in reality and wisdom. If you were to give a speech favoring universal health care reform, opposing a specific type of immigration reform, or fighting attempts to rezone your neighborhood before a local city council meeting, you might well use a refutative design.

Narrative. The speech that follows a **narrative design** tells a story. In contrast with designs that follow a linear, logical pattern of development, a narrative design follows a dramatic pattern that proceeds from prologue to plot to epilogue, as we discussed in Chapter 3. From that discussion you will recall that the prologue introduces the story by setting the scene for action. It foreshadows the meaning of the story and introduces the main characters. The plot is the body of the narrative, in which the story unfolds through a scene or series of scenes that build to a climax. The epilogue reflects on the meaning of the story by drawing a lesson from it that audience members can apply. While commonly used in introductory and ceremonial speeches, a narrative design can be incorporated into informative and persuasive presentations to help illustrate and add human interest to a speech.

▶ **chronological design** Explains events or historical developments in the order in which they occurred.

▶ **causation design** Considers the origins or consequences of a situation or event.

▶ **problem-solution design** Focuses attention on a problem and offers an answer for it.

▶ **motivated sequence** Expanded version of the problem-solution design that emphasizes attention, need, solution, visualization, and action steps.

The preceding designs are often used in combination. For example, our earlier identification of three forms of oppression suffered by Afghan women suggests that a speech on this subject might follow a categorical design. But such a speech might also incorporate a cause-effect pattern to explain how such oppression originated, or could combine with a problem-solution design to encourage support for changes in policy. We discuss these designs in more detail as they become particularly relevant to informative, persuasive, and ceremonial speaking, as indicated in Figure 9.2.

Developing Your Main Points

Once you have selected and arranged your main points, you need to develop the subpoints and sub-subpoints that will support them. Main points are general claims, while **subpoints** supply more specific materials that flesh out these claims, make them credible, and bring them to life. In complex units of thought, **sub-subpoints** perform the same kind of service for subpoints. Thus, subpoints and sub-subpoints answer basic questions any critical listener might ask, such as, How do I know this is true? What does it mean? Why should I care?

To illustrate these thoughts, imagine that you are developing one of the earlier main points concerning the mistreatment of Afghan women. To support the general claim that Afghan women under the Taliban were routinely subjected to barbaric forms of physical and psychological violence, you should probably cite the two or three most widely reported specific forms of violence, such as domestic abuse with impunity, gang and honor rapes, and horrific forms of public punishment. Even more specific information, examples and stories, and quotations from survivors and perpetrators might well become sub-subpoints.

FIGURE 9.2 Design Options

Categorical	Arranges points by their natural or customary divisions (Chapter 13).
Comparative	Compares different ideas to reveal their similarities and differences (Chapter 13).
Spatial	Arranges points as they occur in physical space, taking listeners on an imaginary tour (Chapter 13).
Sequential	Arranges points in order of their occurrence, as in the steps of a process (Chapter 13).
Chronological	Arranges points in terms of their historical development in time (Chapter 13).
Causation	Presents the causes and/or effects of a problem (Chapter 13).
Problem-Solution	Discusses a problem, then offers a solution (Chapter 14).
Refutative	Persuades listeners by answering opposing arguments (Chapter 14).
Narrative	Follows the form of a story with a prologue, plot, and epilogue (Chapters 3, 16).

▶ **refutative design** Defends a disputed claim and attacks the reasoning and evidence of opposing views.
▶ **narrative design** Tells a story.

▶ **subpoints** The major divisions of a speech's main points.

▶ **sub-subpoints** Strengthen subpoints by supplying relevant supporting materials.

In short, to strengthen both main points and subpoints you must use supporting materials. As we discussed in Chapter 8, *facts*, *figures*, and *expert testimony* help to support ideas that are disputed, complicated, or new to your audience. *Examples* and *narratives* engage listeners by showing how your ideas apply to specific situations.

The different forms of supporting information are usually most effective when used in combination. An ideal model of support includes the most relevant facts and statistics, the most authoritative testimony, and at least one story or example that clarifies your ideas and brings them to life. Again, if you were supporting our point about violence against women under the Taliban, you might look for credible statistics and expert testimony to document the extent of the violence, and "real life" examples and narratives to put a human face on the women's oppression.

Developing a Working Outline

At this point, you should begin developing a rough or **working outline**—a *tentative* plan illustrating the pattern of your main and supporting points and information, their relative importance, and how they fit together. Outlining is a disciplined process that allows you to see the structure and interrelation of your

---

Statement:_____

_____

Transition into facts or statistics: _____

    1. Factual information or statistics that support statement: _____

_____

_____

Transition into testimony: _____

    2. Testimony that supports statement:_____

_____

_____

Transition into example or narrative: _____

    3. Example or narrative that supports statement: _____

_____

_____

_____

Transition into restatement:_____

Restatement of original assertion: _____

_____

FIGURE 9.3 Format for Supporting a Point

▶ **working outline** A tentative plan showing the pattern of a speech's major parts, their relative importance, and the way they fit together.

News accounts of Afghan mistreatment of women prompted an interesting speech.

ideas and materials as you develop them. It is an invaluable tool for untangling your thoughts and information, getting them down on paper where you can work with them, and shaping them into a coherent pattern.

The two most basic and interrelated principles of outlining are coordination and subordination. The principle of **coordination** suggests that all statements at a given level of your outline should be of similar importance; thus the three main points concerning the mistreatment of women in Afghanistan appear to share the same approximate significance. The principle of **subordination** requires that supporting ideas and materials descend in importance from the general to the specific as the outline moves from main points to sub-subpoints. Use indentation to show in your outline that subpoints are subordinate to main points, and indent again to show the subordinate status of sub-subpoints. Note how this process of indentation is indicated in the "Format for a Working Outline" (Figure 9.4).

Our main point outlining the various forms of violence against women under the Taliban might take the following form:

Main point: Afghan women were subject to various forms of violence under the Taliban.

Subpoint A: Women were subject to high rates of domestic abuse.

Sub-subpoint 1: Wives and daughters were generally regarded as the property of their husbands and fathers.

Sub-subpoint 2: Taliban officials routinely ignored attempts to report abuse.

Subpoint B: Women were subject to high rates of sexual assault.

Sub-subpoint 1: Young girls were forced into arranged marriages with older men.

Sub-subpoint 2: Gang and honor rapes were perpetuated by rival factions.

Sub-subpoint 3: Victims who reported assaults were branded social outcasts.

Subpoint C: Women who resisted or asserted themselves faced frightening recriminations.

Sub-subpoint 1: Arbitrary humiliation and flogging by Taliban officials.

Sub-subpoint 2: Macabre forms of public punishment.

As you zero in on a working outline of the body of your presentation, consider whether you've adequately supported your thesis statement and satisfied your purpose for speaking, whether your main ideas are arranged in a sensible design scheme, and whether the overall structure of your body is balanced and appropriately developed. Be honest with yourself. It's better to be frustrated and revising now than regretful later. Outlining is a corrective as well as creative process, and you will often go through several drafts as you polish and develop your speeches.

▶ **coordination**   The requirement that statements equal in importance be placed on the same level in an outline.

▶ **subordination**   The requirement that material in an outline descend in importance from the general to the specific—from main points to subpoints to sub-subpoints, etc.

Topic: _____
Specific purpose: _____

INTRODUCTION
Attention material: _____
Thesis statement: _____
Preview: _____

(**Transition** to body of speech)

BODY
First main point: _____
   Subpoint: _____
      Sub-subpoint: _____
      Sub-subpoint: _____
   Subpoint: _____

(**Transition** to second main point)

Second main point: _____
   Subpoint: _____
   Subpoint: _____
      Sub-subpoint: _____
      Sub-subpoint: _____

(**Transition** to third main point)

Third main point: _____
   Subpoint: _____
   Subpoint: _____

(**Transition** to conclusion)

CONCLUSION
Summary statement: _____
Concluding remarks: _____

FIGURE 9.4 Format for a Working Outline

Adding Transitions

Once you have found, developed, and outlined your main ideas, you should plan transitions. **Transitions** are verbal and nonverbal cues that let your audience know you are finished making one point and are moving on to the next. Effectively planned transitions connect the main points of the body of your speech and tie the body to the introduction and conclusion. They serve as signposts that help your audience see and follow the overall structure and direction of your message. They also tend to make for a smoother presentation.

Some transitions are quite subtle. A brief pause coupled with a change in vocal inflection can effectively cue your audience that you are moving on to the next point or part of your speech. Short, simple phrases such as *for my next point* and *having said that, consider this* can help your audience see the connections between your ideas. Phrases such as *until now* and *just last week* point out time changes. Transitions such as *in addition* show that you are expanding on what you have already said. The use of the word *similarly* indicates that a comparison follows. Phrases such as *on the other hand* cue listeners to a contrast. Cause and effect

▶ **transitions** Connecting elements that cue listeners that you are finished making one point and are moving on to the next.

relationships can be suggested with *as a result, consequently,* and similar phrases. Introductory phrases such as *traveling north* can indicate spatial relationships. Phrases or words such as *in short, finally,* or *in conclusion* signal that the speech is coming to an end.

Preview and summary statements can also serve as effective transitions connecting the major parts of a speech—previews into the body; summaries into the conclusion. Especially with longer, complicated presentations, an **internal summary** within the body of a speech can help remind listeners of the points you have already covered before you move on. Internal summaries are especially useful in problem-solution speeches, where they signal that you have finished your discussion of the causes or problem and are now moving on to solutions. They should be brief and to the point so that they highlight only major ideas. Consider the following example from a student speech supporting caps on greenhouse gas emissions:

> So now we know that global warming is real and getting worse. We know it exacts a frightening economic and environmental toll. And we know that human pollution and greenhouse gas emissions are a major contributing cause of global warming. The only question is, what are we going to do about it? Experts agree that the following measures could help make a real difference.

Parallel construction, which occurs when speakers begin related points with the same or similar wording, can also serve as a transition. Dr. Martin Luther King Jr.'s famous "I Have a Dream" speech used the repeated phrase "We can never be satisfied . . ." to outline his critique of racial prejudice in America, and "I have a dream . . ." to expound his redemptive vision of a new America. Not only did these parallel constructions help to cue his audience that he was moving from point to point, but they also helped to build his entire presentation to a powerful climax.

Whatever techniques you use, plan your transitions carefully. If you are having trouble coming up with fresh ideas, look back over the structure of your message. Because they are so vital to the flow of your presentation, transitions should be written out verbatim just as they will be presented. Otherwise, you may ramble awkwardly or over-rely on vocalized pauses such as "uh" and "you know."

▶ **internal summary** A transition that reminds listeners of major points already presented in a speech before proceeding to new ideas.

FIGURE 9.5 Common Transitions

To Indicate	Use
Time Changes	until, now, since, previously, later, earlier, in the past, in the future, meanwhile, five years ago, just last month, tomorrow, following, before, at present, eventually
Additions	moreover, in addition, furthermore, besides
Comparison	compared with, both are, likewise, in comparison, similarly, of equal importance, another type of, like, alike, just as
Contrast	but, yet, however, on the other hand, conversely, still, otherwise, in contrast, unfortunately, despite, rather than, on the contrary
Cause-Effect	therefore, consequently, thus, accordingly, so, as a result, hence, since, because of, due to, for this reason
Numerical Order	first, second, third, in the first place, to begin with, initially, next, eventually, finally
Spatial Relations	to the north, alongside, to the left, above, moving eastward, in front of, in back of, behind, next to, below, nearby, in the distance
Explanation	to illustrate, for example, for instance, case in point, in other words, to simplify, to clarify
Importance	most importantly, above all, keep this in mind, remember, listen carefully, take note of, indeed
The Speech Is Ending	in short, finally, in conclusion, to summarize

Introducing and Concluding Your Speech

Once you have structured the body of your speech, you should prepare an introduction and a conclusion. Introductions and conclusions are important because listeners tend to be most affected by what they hear at the beginning and end of a speech. Introductions and conclusions set the tone of the entire message, and often contain its richest language and clearest statement of the speaker's main ideas and purpose. In this section, we identify some basic functions and techniques and offer advice for effectively introducing and concluding your speeches.

Introducing Your Speech

The **introduction** to your speech should capture your audience's attention, establish your ethos as a credible speaker, and preview your message to make it easier for your audience to follow.

▶ **introduction** That part of your speech that should capture listeners' attention, establish your ethos, and preview your message.

Capturing Attention.

All too often, speakers open their presentations with something like "Good morning, my speech is on . . . ," which actually has the effect of turning listeners off. The opening lines of a speech should arouse attention and curiosity, convincing listeners that they have something to gain from the speaker's message.

Among the most commonly used strategies for capturing attention are acknowledging the audience, location, or occasion; invoking shared interests and values; soliciting audience participation; using appropriate humor; opening with a narrative; starting with a quotation; and startling your audience.

Acknowledging the audience, location, or occasion. In speeches given outside the classroom, speakers often begin with a few remarks acknowledging the audience, the location, or the purpose or meaning of the occasion. Such references are usually brief, and should convey a touch of eloquence. Consider the following words from the introduction of a speech by President John F. Kennedy at a White House dinner honoring Nobel Prize winners:

> I think this is the most extraordinary collection of talent, of human knowledge, that has ever been gathered together at the White House, with the possible exception of when Thomas Jefferson dined alone.[3]

The introduction of your speech must immediately engage your audience. If you don't get their attention within the first minute of speaking, they may be lost to you forever.

Invoking shared interests and values. Invoking shared interests and values is another stock strategy for capturing audience attention. Appeals to audience needs for material and financial security are common in "sales pitch" presentations. Speakers addressing controversial social or political issues often open by associating their speeches with shared moral commitments. Consider the opening lines from Dr. King's "I Have a Dream":

> Five score years ago, a great American, in whose symbolic shadow we stand today, signed the Emancipation Proclamation. This momentous decree came as a great beacon of light and hope to millions of Negro slaves, who had been seared in the flames of withering injustice. It came as a joyous daybreak to end the long night of their captivity. But one hundred years later, the Negro is still not free.[4]

Urging audience participation. Another common technique is to solicit the participation of audience members. A well-worded series of questions, a requested "show of hands," or getting your audience to repeat a catchphrase aloud can be very effective. However, not all such strategies require a direct response. The simple use of inclusive pronouns such as "we" and "our" can help to promote identification and involvement. Another technique is the use of **rhetorical questions** that are not intended to provoke a response so much as to engage curiosity. For instance, knowing well that most of his classmates were familiar with popular video games, University of Arkansas student Joseph Van Matre opened his speech on their constructive applications with the following rhetorical questions:

> If I say the word "gamer," what words come to mind? Antisocial? Geek? Dropout? Well, how about fighter pilot? Fitness guru? Or intelligence analyst? I'm not a

▶ **rhetorical questions**   Questions that have a self-evident answer, or that provoke curiosity that the speech then proceeds to satisfy.

hard-core gamer, but I do enjoy the company of my Wii from time to time, as well as an occasional round of Madden football with my friends. So when I heard in a radio interview that video games actually have many constructive educational and professional applications, I was intrigued and decided to do some reading. What I learned was highly surprising.

Appropriate humor. Appropriate humor, especially at the beginning of a speech, offers some real advantages. Listeners are usually grateful to speakers for the pleasure of laughter. Because laughter is shared, it can also function as identification, drawing speakers and listeners together. As Henri Bergson, the French philosopher, once noted, "Laughter appears to stand in need of an echo. . . . Our laughter is always the laughter of a group."[5] Another advantage is that successful humor at the beginning of a speech can put both listeners and speakers at ease with the speaking situation, and can sometimes make it easier for speakers to tackle difficult or obscure topics.

Unfortunately, humor can also be one of the most abused techniques for opening a speech. Some speakers have the mistaken notion that if they will just tell a joke at the beginning of their speeches—any joke—listeners will like them and listen to their message. There's no way of knowing how many listeners have suffered, and how many speakers have bombed, over this misapprehension!

The truth is, humor may not work well for everyone, and it can be grossly inappropriate for some topics on some occasions. Keep in mind that audience members tend to be especially sensitive to "politically incorrect" humor. Avoid any kind of humor based on ethnicity, gender, religion, or sexual orientation. Such usage will almost always undermine the effectiveness of your speech and can do lasting harm to your ethos.

Should you decide to open your speech with humor, keep it fresh, relevant, and brief so that it does not upstage your message. Be cautious about relying on humor to cope with communication anxiety. While effective humor can put both speaker and audience at ease, humor that falls flat can have just the opposite effect. Remember that there are other good ways to come across as likable and to capture audience attention. Explore your strengths as a speaker and play to them—this is a vital part of finding your voice and gaining confidence as a speaker.

The use of humor in an introduction gains attention.

SPEAKER'S notes

Using Humor

Keep the following in mind when considering the use of humor in your speeches.

1. Don't use humor just to be funny. Keep it relevant to your topic.

2. Use humor to put the audience at ease and make them receptive to your ideas.

3. Avoid religious, ethnic, racist, or sexist humor, all of which speak poorly of you.

4. If you must poke fun at someone, let it be yourself.

5. Don't use humor that might trivialize a serious topic.

6. Avoid planned humor if you are really anxious about speaking.

Opening with a narrative. Storytelling can be a powerful means of creating identification with your audience. Narratives educate us by helping us remember the past and shared moral commitments. Effective narratives use vivid, graphic language to help us envision abstract topics and issues in concrete human terms. Stories may be imaginary or based on real-life experiences and historic events. Depending on your purpose for speaking, they can be lighthearted and humorous or somber and serious.

In either case, introductory narratives should be brief. Consider the opening narrative to Ashlie McMillan's introductory speech on scuba diving:

> Imagine you're sitting aboard a dive boat. It's rocking back and forth, you can feel the sun beating down on you. You can feel the wind blowing on you. You smell the ocean, the salt water. You can hear the waves crashing up against the boat. You put on your dive pack with your heavy oxygen tank and you walk unsteadily across the deck of the rocking boat. And all of a sudden you plunge into a completely different environment. All around you is vast blueness and infinite space, a world completely different from the one you left above. But all you have to do is turn on your back and look above and you see the sunlight streaming in through the top of the water. And you can see the world that you left behind.

Ashlie's skillful use of action words—such as *rocking, blowing, crashing*—and her vivid appeals to the senses made this scene come alive for her listeners and placed them in the middle of it. See Chapter 3 for more advice on developing narratives in your speeches.

Opening with a quotation. Starting with a striking quotation or paraphrase from a highly respected text or figure can both arouse interest and dignify your speech. For instance, references to revered political documents such as the Declaration of Independence or well-known authors such as George Orwell and Maya Angelou can be very effective.

However, opening quotes need not come from such elevated sources. University of Arkansas student Guy Britton introduced his speech concerning illegal immigration with the following ironic quotation: "An anonymous author once said: 'The early North American Indian made a great mistake by not having an immigration bureau.'"

Quotations should be short, to the point, and relevant to your purpose for speaking. Several excellent collections of quotations are available online, including quoteland.com, creativequotations.com, and bartleby.com/quotations.

Startling the audience. Sometimes speakers open with a shocking piece of information intended to startle listeners into close attention. For instance, if you were giving a speech urging your classmates to contribute to Haitian relief efforts in the wake of the 2010 earthquake, projected pictures of the devastation might well arouse attention. You could also begin by citing the numbers of dead and injured, accompanied perhaps by the narrative of a child orphaned by those catastrophes. You might also startle your audience by citing expert testimony on the sheer extent of the damage, how long it will take to rebuild the island nation, or how much it all will cost.

You should use this technique quite carefully. You don't want your introduction to arouse more interest or expectations than the remainder of your speech can possibly satisfy. If your opening is too sensational, you run the risk of it upstaging the rest of your speech, Keep your use of startling information within the boundaries of good taste. Remember, the point is to startle your audience into listening, not to traumatize and offend them.

SPEAKER'S notes   Capturing Attention

Try the following strategies to gain attention in the introduction of your speech.

1. Acknowledge the audience, location, or occasion.
2. Invoke shared interests and values.
3. Solicit audience involvement and participation.
4. Open with a narrative that relates to your topic.

5. Engage your listeners with appropriate humor.
6. Begin with a striking quotation.
7. Startle your audience with powerful information or a novel approach.

Establishing Your Credibility. The second major function of an effective introduction is to establish your ethos as a credible speaker. People tend to form first impressions of you that color their later perceptions. In Chapter 3, we discuss the importance of listeners forming favorable initial impressions of your competence, integrity, goodwill, and dynamism. Outside the classroom, you enter a speaking situation with some initial ethos based on what listeners know or have heard of your reputation and experience. A good introduction before you stand and speak can help "prime" listeners to give you a favorable hearing. In classroom situations, listeners may have formed impressions based on previous presentations or what you have said in class discussions.

You can enhance perceptions of your competence by being well organized, using language effectively and correctly, and demonstrating that you know what you are talking about. You will seem more competent if you select a topic you already know something about and have done additional research to deepen and update your knowledge of it.

Citing personal expertise and experience at the beginning of your speech can be extremely effective. Speakers without such expertise and experience can enhance perceptions of competence by citing respected sources of quality information early in their speeches.

To strengthen impressions of integrity, you should come across as straightforward, sincere, and genuinely concerned about the consequences of your words. You can accomplish this by demonstrating respect for those who hold differing opinions, even as you make clear your personal commitment. It should also be clear to listeners that you are not asking more of them than you are willing to offer yourself.

You should also strike others as a likable and confident speaker, someone who is pleasant and tactful. Likable speakers treat listeners as friends, inspiring affection in return. They share their feelings and are able to laugh at themselves. To enhance impressions of confidence, you should appear in control of the situation from the outset. Your introduction should reflect your enthusiasm for your message. A smile and eye contact signal listeners that you want to communicate. These qualities build an overall impression of dynamism that should make you more effective.

Calling on personal experiences can help to create credibility.

When you establish favorable ethos in the introduction of your speech, you lay the foundation for establishing identification with your audience and for building the impression that you have found your voice. As discussed in Chapter 1, identification helps people overcome the personal and cultural differences that separate them and share thoughts and feelings as though they were one. When you seem likable, sincere, competent, and dynamic, your listeners want to identify with you. Your effectiveness as a speaker and your value as a spokesperson for your cause are magnified.

Previewing Your Message.   The final function of an introduction is to preview the body of your speech. The **preview** indicates the main points you will cover and offers your listeners an overview of the speech to come. Common to persuasive and informative presentations, preview statements are especially useful for speeches addressing unfamiliar, complicated, or technical topics. They help listeners follow what you are saying and serve as effective transitions into the body of your speech.

Preview statements need not be of the mundane "In this speech I'm going to talk about three points" variety. For her speech informing her Davidson classmates of how French people can eat indulgent foods while still remaining healthy, Gabrielle Wallace offered the following preview: "To understand the French paradox, we must take a close look at how they combine food choices, their consumption of beverages, and the cultural attitude they have developed towards food."

In speeches developing a narrative design as discussed in Chapter 3, the preview may take the form of a prologue using a foreshadowing technique: "I never expected that my life would be forever changed by what would happen that day." When speakers foreshadow their stories, they don't tell their listeners exactly what will happen, but they do alert them that something important will happen. Thus, they prepare them to listen intently to the story.

Concluding Your Speech

Just as you should not begin a speech with "Hello, my speech is about . . . ," you should not end it with "Well, that's it!" Your conclusion is your last opportunity to reinforce your central message, make a lasting impression, and when appropriate, move listeners to action. An effective **conclusion** should summarize your message and provide some concluding remarks.

Summarizing Your Message.   The more complicated your topic, the more important a summary becomes. A brief summary of your main points can serve as a transition between the body of your speech and your final remarks. It signals the audience that you are about to finish.

A summary should not be a simple repetition of main points so much as a chance to reflect on and reinforce the central message of your speech. Consider the conclusion to Gabrielle Wallace's speech:

> For the French, eating is an important part of their lives. It is engrained in their culture and permeates their daily existence. The three factors of eating correctly, drinking wisely, and making a meal an enjoyable experience are what keep the French paradox alive.

▶ **preview**   The part of the introduction that identifies the main points to be developed in the body of the speech and presents an overview of the speech to follow.

▶ **conclusion**   Summarizes your message and offers concluding remarks.

Concluding Remarks.   Although a summary statement can offer listeners a sense of closure, to seal that effect you need to provide concluding remarks that stay with your listeners. Many of the techniques that create effective introductions can also be used to develop memorable conclusions.

Echoing your introduction. Sometimes called a "bookend," a conclusion that applies the same technique used in the introduction can help to provide a nice sense of closure. For example, you might finish a story that you started in the introduction, or refer back to your startling information, rhetorical question, or opening quotation. Referring back to the introduction can be an effective means of letting listeners know that you are bringing your message full circle. For instance, the student speaker who opened with the example of Earl Washington's wrongful conviction for murder concluded her plea for judicial reforms by stating: "There are more Earl Washingtons out there, and they're counting on us!"

Restating the relevance of your message to your audience. At the beginning of a speech, you should involve the audience by showing them how your message relates directly to their lives. In the conclusion, you should remind them of what they personally have at stake. Consider Doneal McGee's closing plea for a speech opposing "abstinence only" sex education in American high schools:

> These kids are our future, and their problems will become ours in many ways. Babies having unplanned babies out of wedlock are more likely to end up quitting school and on welfare, producing expensive wards of the state and swelling the ranks from which a vast majority of troubled children arise. We have no choice but to support the responsible teaching of sex education in our high schools. They're our kids, and our future may well hang in the balance!

Issuing a call to action. In persuasive speeches, concluding remarks often urge listeners to take the first step to confirm their commitment to action and change. Beth Tidmore used this technique to conclude her speech urging her classmates to volunteer for the Special Olympics:

> Becoming a volunteer is the best way that you can help. If you can't give a weekend, give a couple of hours. If you can't become a leader, just become a cheerleader. Show up. Be a happy smiling face. It's the best way to give to charity, because you can see the results right in front of you. You can see the shiny medals, the triumphant finishes, the happy faces, the screaming fans. And you know that you're helping someone else and giving of yourself to them. . . . Can drives need cans. Blood drives need blood. And, the Special Olympics need volunteers. They need warm hearts and open minds. In Special Olympics, everyone is a winner—especially the volunteers!

Asking rhetorical questions. When used in an introduction, rhetorical questions can help arouse attention and curiosity. When used in a conclusion, they give your listeners something to think about after you have finished. Elinor Fraser opened a speech attacking the use of cell phones while driving in the following way: "How many of you were chatting on your cell phones while driving to class this morning?" After a speech that established the danger of such behavior in graphic terms, her final words were,

Persuasive speeches designed to recruit volunteers often end with a call to action.

"So, now that you know the risk you are running, are you going to use your cell phones again while you're on the way home? If so, let me know so I can drive in a different direction."

Closing with a story. Just as stories can effectively introduce a speech, concluding narratives can help your audience experience the meaning of your message. To end her speech on dangerous off-campus housing conditions, Anna Aley told the following story about her neighbor:

> I got out of my apartment with little more than bad memories. My upstairs neighbor was not so lucky. The main problem with his apartment was that the electrical wiring was done improperly; there were too many outlets for too few circuits, so the fuses were always blowing. One day last November, Jack was at home when a fuse blew—as usual. And, as usual, he went to the fuse box to flip the switch back on. When he touched the switch, it delivered such a shock that it literally threw this guy the size of a football player backwards and down a flight of stairs. He lay there at the bottom, unable to move, for a full hour before his roommate came home and called an ambulance. Jack was lucky. His back was not broken. But he did rip many of the muscles in his back. Now he has to go to physical therapy, and he is not expected to fully recover.

Closing with a quotation. Brief quotations that capture the essence of your message can make for effective conclusions. For example, if you open a speech with a historical quotation, another on the same theme or from the same person might provide an elegant sense of closure. Be sure to quote someone the audience respects. Arkansas student Guy Britton, who opened his speech on illegal immigration with a humorous quotation, achieved a nice bookend effect by closing with another example of the same technique: "Jay Leno once said: 'This problem with illegal immigration is nothing new. In fact, the Indians had a special name for it. They called it white people.'" Guy's sly humor took some of the ethnocentric steam out of a hot-button issue.

Closing with a metaphor. A memorable metaphor can end your speech effectively. As we discuss in Chapter 11, metaphors combine things that are apparently unalike so that we see unexpected relationships. In the conclusion of a speech, an effective metaphor may reveal hidden truths about the speaker's subject in a memorable way. Another University of Arkansas student, Simone Mullinax, closed her classroom tribute to her grandmother by concluding a metaphor that had run throughout her speech:

> Years from now I will be teaching my granddaughter to build the perfect key lime pie. And I will be thinking about my grandmother, whose love seeps into all the crust that holds me together. We will work the fillings together and we will know just what to top it off with to make it perfect. And we will bake pies like friends hold conversations, the intricacies hidden beneath the taste and the impressions lasting beyond the words.

Using strategic repetition. Repetition helps implant ideas in the minds of your listeners. The form of repetition discussed earlier called parallel construction—in which certain phrases are repeated in close succession for added emphasis—can

FINDING YOUR
voice   Critiquing Through Outlining

Select one of the speeches from Appendix B and prepare a working outline of it. Does the outline clarify the structure of the speech? Does it reveal any structural flaws? Can you see any different ways the speaker might have developed the speech? Write an alternative introduction and conclusion, using a different technique. Compare the new with the original. Which works better and why?

make for conclusions that are both elegant and dramatic. Probably the greatest orator of our time in the use of strategic repetition was Dr. Martin Luther King Jr. His repeated "I have a Dream" refrain near the end of his celebrated speech of the same name is of course famous. Two months before he died at the hand of an assassin in Memphis, Dr. King gave another remarkable speech called "The Drum Major Instinct," in which he talked about how he might like his funeral service to be held.

> I don't want a long funeral. And if you get somebody to deliver the eulogy, tell them not to talk too long. (*Yes*) . . . If you want to say that I was a drum major, say that I was a drum major for justice. (*Amen*) Say that I was a drum major for peace. (*Yes*) I was a drum major for righteousness. And all of the other shallow things will not matter.[6]

Dr. King's repeated use of the drum major refrain invited audience participation and helped underscore his important values near the end—not just of his speech, but of his life.

Selecting and Using Introductory and Concluding Techniques

Because introductions and conclusions are so crucial in shaping audience impressions and setting the tone for your speech, you should give them considerable thought. Because they should be elegant and perhaps even eloquent, we suggest that you write them out just as they will be presented, and that you commit them to memory.

Beyond that, there are no hard-and-fast rules for determining how to open and close your speeches. As you review your research notes, look for materials that might be effective openers and closers. The following guidelines may help:

- Consider relevance to your message and the mood you wish to establish. Some messages and occasions call for a light touch, while others are more serious.

- Consider your audience and what techniques might best tune your message to their needs and interests. We discuss audience analysis and adaptation in Chapter 5.

- Keep it brief! Again, the combined length of your introduction and conclusion should be considerably less than the body of your speech.

- Do what you do best. Some people are natural storytellers, others are funny, still others are better with striking statistics or quotations. Play to your strengths.

SPEAKER'S notes

Checklist for a Working Outline

You can trust your working outline if the following statements accurately describe it:

1. My topic, specific purpose, and thesis statement are clearly stated.

2. My introduction contains attention-getting material, establishes my credibility, and focuses and previews my message.

3. My main points represent the most important ideas on my topic.

4. I have an appropriate number of main points for the time allotted.

5. Each subpoint supports its main point with more specific detail.

6. My conclusion contains a summary statement and concluding remarks that reinforce and reflect on the meaning of my speech.

7. I have planned transitions to use between the introduction and body, between each of my main points, and between the body and conclusion of my speech.

Preparing Your Formal Outline

Once you have developed your working outline and a good idea of how you will introduce and conclude your speech, you can put together your **formal outline**. The formal outline represents the completed plan of your speech, offering an overview of its major components and how they fit together and listing the research sources that support it.

Most formal outlines offer the following :

- a heading with a title, topic, and specific purpose statement,

- an introduction including attention material, a thesis statement, and preview,

- the fully developed body of your speech,

- a conclusion offering a summary statement and concluding remarks, and

- a list of works consulted or cited.

Figure 9.6 offers a formal outline format. See also the sample formal outline at the end of this chapter.

Heading

The heading offers your title, topic, and specific purpose statement. Again, your specific purpose statement should specify what you want your audience to understand, agree with, do, or appreciate after hearing your speech. Remember: Do not begin your actual speech with statements such as "My topic is . . ." or "My specific purpose is. . . ." These are vital parts of the plan of your speech, but may not appear in the speech itself.

▶ **formal outline** Represents the completed plan of your speech, offering an overview of its major components and how they fit together and listing the research sources that support it.

HEADING

Title: _____
Topic: _____
Specific Purpose: _____

INTRODUCTION

Attention material: _____
_____

Thesis statement: _____
_____

Preview: _____
_____

(**Transition** into body of speech)

BODY

I. First main point: _____
   A. Subpoint or supporting material: _____
   B. Subpoint or supporting material: _____
      1. Sub-subpoint or supporting material: _____
      2. Sub-subpoint or supporting material: _____

(**Transition** into next main point)

II. Second main point: _____
   A. Subpoint or supporting material: _____
      1. Sub-subpoint or supporting material: _____
      2. Sub-subpoint or supporting material: _____
   B. Subpoint or supporting material: _____

(**Transition** into next main point)

III. Third main point: _____
   A. Subpoint or supporting material: _____
   B. Subpoint or supporting material: _____
      1. Sub-subpoint or supporting material: _____
      2. Sub-subpoint or supporting material: _____
         a. Sub-sub-subpoint or supporting material: _____
         b. Sub-sub-subpoint or supporting material: _____

(**Transition** into conclusion)

CONCLUSION

Summary statement: _____
_____

Concluding remarks: _____
_____

WORKS CONSULTED

FIGURE 9.6 Format for a Formal Outline

Note that in contrast with working outlines, formal outlines often offer a title for the speech. If mentioning a title helps you arouse curiosity and attention, it can really help you. Consider the way Elizabeth Lyles wove references to her title, "The Abused Women of Afghanistan," into the introduction of her speech on the continued oppression suffered by Afghan women:

Of course, such brutalities are hardly unknown to *the abused women of Afghanistan*. But this was the Spring of 2009—nearly eight years after the so-called liberation of the Afghan people by a U.S.-led coalition of forces. *The abused women of Afghanistan* need your support now for efforts to defend their basic human rights.

A title should not promise what the speech itself can't deliver. Titles that promise everything from eternal peace of mind to the end of taxation often disappoint listeners. To frame an effective title, wait until you have finished outlining the rest of your speech.

Introduction

Your introduction performs vital work. Here is where you gain the attention you want to sustain throughout the speech. Here also is where your meaning should come into sharp focus with your thesis statement. And here is where you offer listeners a map of the territory ahead as you preview the remainder of your speech. Again, we recommend you write out your introduction and commit it to memory. This will help you get into and out of your speech gracefully and effectively. There certainly may be moments when you wish to change your introduction slightly to take advantage of a situation (we discussed such moments in Chapter 5). But knowing exactly what you want to say and how you want to say it gets you off to a good start and helps you build confidence.

Body

The body of your outline should consist of main points, subpoints, and sub-subpoints in the order of their presentation. In contrast with working outlines, formal outlines adopt a more precise and abbreviated system for indicating coordination and subordination. Roman numerals (I, II, III) typically are used for main points, capital letters (A, B, C) for subpoints, Arabic numbers (1, 2, 3) for sub-subpoints, and—should you need them—lowercase letters (a, b, c) for sub-sub-subpoints.

The entries in a working outline are often sentence fragments, indicating their status as tentative, emerging ideas that are subject to change and revision. By the time you are ready to prepare your formal outline, these entries should have evolved into more confident and finished form. To indicate this evolution, *each main and supporting point of a formal outline should be worded as complete, simple sentences containing only one idea.* Qualifying and dependent clauses and supporting information should be subordinated as subpoints and sub-subpoints. For example, the statement "Bad eating habits are harmful because they are unhealthy and can damage your self-image" might be outlined to read:

I. Bad eating habits are harmful.

    A. They are unhealthy.

    B. They can damage your self-image.

Breaking down complex sentences into outlined format helps you to focus what you are going to say. It suggests what you should emphasize, and simplifies and clarifies both the structure and logic of your speech.

As noted earlier, we recommend that you write out your transitions between main points and commit them to memory as well. Make sure that you support every assertion in your speech that is new, complicated, or disputed with research and illustrative examples or stories. Include abbreviated **source citations** within the formal outline for each piece of supporting information you use (you will provide full references at the end of the outline in your list of works consulted or cited).

▶ **source citations** Abbreviated references in a formal outline that show how research supports the points made.

The sample formal outline offered at the end of this chapter provides a model of these abbreviated source citations. Note that in most cases the author's last name or an abbreviated source or title will suffice, included in parentheses at the ends of the points or subpoints to which they apply. List the last name of the author plus the page number when you refer to different pages in the same source. List the author's last name with an abbreviated title in quotation marks if you are citing more than one work by the same author. If the author is a group or organization, list its name in abbreviated form. If the author is not provided, provide an abbreviated title in quotation marks as the source of the information.

Placement of an abbreviated source citation at the end of a main point means that this source supports all claims in the subpoints and sub-subpoints below it. If the citation were placed at the end of a subpoint or sub-subpoint, it would apply only to that more specific sub or sub-subpoint. Again, for illustrations of these points see the sample outline.

Documenting your sources in your outline does not satisfy the need for **oral citations** to support your points as you present your speech. Your listeners are not privy, of course, to your formal outline and list of works cited—they know only what you decide to tell them. Don't overwhelm them with citations, but *do* use such citations to support your most important and possibly controversial statements and claims. "Speaker's Notes: Guidelines for Oral Documentation" will help you construct effective oral citations.

SPEAKER'S notes
Guidelines for Oral Documentation

To develop effective oral documentation, follow these guidelines:

1. Identify the publication in which the material appears.
2. Identify the time frame of the publication (usually the year is sufficient, unless the material is time-sensitive).
3. Offer "highlight" credentials for the experts you cite.
4. Select direct quotations that are brief and that will have an impact.
5. Avoid presenting every detail of the written citation.
6. Controversial and time-sensitive material requires fuller oral documentation.

Conclusion

Your conclusion brings your speech to a satisfying completion. It includes a summary statement, which helps your listeners remember your major points in a final overview, and concluding remarks, which integrate your speech into larger patterns of meaning. You should end on a high note.

Works Cited or Consulted

You should conclude your formal outline with a list of works cited or consulted, depending on your instructor's preference. **Works cited** lists just those sources you actually refer to in your speeches. **Works consulted** lists all the works you used while preparing your speech, whether you cite them or not.

In either case, your list of referenced sources is crucial to documenting your research and demonstrating your acquisition of responsible knowledge in support

---

▶ **oral citations** References to supporting materials during the speech that strengthen the credibility of the speech and support controversial and surprising claims.

▶ **works cited** List that supplies complete relevant information about sources of research actually cited in the speech.

▶ **works consulted** List that supplies complete relevant information about all sources of research considered in the preparation of the speech.

of your claims. Provide full and proper citations so that you can refer curious listeners or your instructor to the exact sources of information.

The two most popular style manuals for citing researched sources are published by the Modern Language Association (MLA) and the American Psychological Association (APA) (some instructors might prefer *The Chicago Manual of Style* or the *Turabian Manual for Writers of Term Papers, Theses, and Dissertations*). We illustrate the MLA format here, and provide you with an abbreviated guide to forms of citation most relevant for student speaking. See the guide at the end of this chapter.

If your instructor prefers APA, or if you simply want more comprehensive overviews of both styles, we recommend the tutorial posted by the University of Purdue at http://owl.english.edu/.

Formal Outlines: A Caution

Formal outlines have one great advantage. They impose a discipline on the preparation process that can help you develop a substantive speech—one that rises to the high standards of responsible knowledge. They also have one great disadvantage: if used during presentation, they can suck the life right out of a speech. You can end up reading from them rather than speaking in a fresh and apparently spontaneous way with the listeners in front of you. The only time you should read during your speech is when you are quoting the words of someone else because the exact wording is dramatic, impressive, and vital. Emblazoned across the bottom of every formal outline should be, in large red letters, "WARNING: Do Not Use During Presentation!"

At this point you should refer back to Chapter 3's advice on key-word outlines. These outlines, you may recall, are skeletal versions of the formal outline that you could take with you to the podium. They trace the flow of the speech through the main points and subpoints, but rather than full sentences they offer single words or at most simple phrases to highlight the essential ideas of the speech. At the point of presentation these ideas should be in your head, not on paper. Repeated practices and rehearsals should have made the outline part of you. The key-word outline serves as a reminder, should you wander off the track of the speech during presentation.

FINAL
reflections   Value of the Twin Disciplines

Finding your voice is more than discovering a topic that fascinates and excites you. It is more also than the hard work of researching your topic and learning how to separate good knowledge from false claims, genuine nuggets from fool's gold. It is even more than reflecting on what you have learned and developing your own position from which you must speak. It is now clear that finding your voice must also mean understanding how to arrange what you have learned into attractive patterns of knowledge that listeners will find easy to absorb and hard to forget. It means justifying your position by building a structure of reasons so compelling that the conclusion that rests upon it will seem irresistible to fair-minded listeners. As you find your voice, you will come to place great value on the twin disciplines of structuring and outlining.

Guide to Citation Format for Works Cited and Works Consulted

All entries in your list of works cited or consulted should be arranged alphabetically. The following sample references are based upon the latest revision of the Modern Language Association (MLA).[7]

Books

Frank, Thomas. *What's the Matter with Kansas?: How Conservatives Won the Heart of America*. New York: Henry Holt and Company, 2004. Print.

Osborn, Michael, Suzanne Osborn, and Randall Osborn. *Public Speaking: Finding Your Voice*. 9th ed. Boston: Pearson Education, Inc., 2012. Print.

Entries in Anthologies or Collections

Ivie, Robert L. "Eisenhower as Cold Warrior." *Eisenhower's War of Words: Rhetoric and Leadership*. Ed. Martin J. Medhurst. East Lansing: Michigan State UP, 1994. 7-25. Print.

Stanton, Elizabeth Cady. "The Solitude of Self." *Man Cannot Speak For Her: Volume II Key Texts of the Early Feminists*. Comp. Karlyn Khors Campbell. New York: Greenwood Press, Inc., 1989. 371-84. Print.

Entries in Reference Works

"Expressionism." *Dictionary of Theories*. Ed. Jennifer Bothamley. Canton: Visible Ink Press, 2002. Print.

Wilson, Charles Reagan. "Reconstruction." *History: The New Encyclopedia of Southern Culture*. Ed. Charles Wilson Reagan. Vol. 3. Chapel Hill: U of North Carolina P, 2006. Print.

Magazine Articles

Bourne, Joel K. Jr. "Redwoods: Super Trees." *National Geographic* Oct. 2009: 28-59. Print.

Newspaper Articles

Grabell, Michael, and Sebastian Jones. "Some Jets Fly Under Public's Radar." *USA Today* 9-11 Apr. 2010: A1. Print.

Journal Articles

Hariman, Robert. "Political Parody and Public Culture." *Quarterly Journal of Speech* 94.3 (2008): 247-72. Print.

Personal Interviews

Hogan, Michael. Personal interview. 19 Feb. 2004.

Speeches and Lectures

Leff, Michael. "Metaphoric Clusters in King's 'I Have a Dream' Speech." Introduction to Human Communication. U of Memphis. 20 Oct. 2008. Lecture.

Government Publications

United States. Environmental Protection Agency. *New Motor Vehicles and New Motor Vehicle Engines Air Pollution Control: Voluntary Standards for Light-Duty Vehicles*. Washington: GPO, 1998. Print.

Guide to Citation Format for Works Cited and Works Consulted *(Continued)*

News/Organization/Course/Government Web Sites
When citing online sources, your instructor may require you to provide full URL
Web sites. If so, they should be added at the end of your citation in angle brackets
"<>" followed by a period. See the first sample entry below for an illustration.
When publishers or sponsors of Web sites are not available, enter "n.p." When
dates posted are not available, enter "n.d."

Mooney, Alexander. "Palin Rallies Tea Partiers in Boston." *CNN.com*. Cable News
   Network, 14 Apr. 2010. Web. 14 Apr. 2010. < http://politicalticker.blogs
   .cnn.com/2010/04/14/palin-rallies-tea-partiers-in-boston/
   ?iref=allsearch&fbid=uTSp7AzJJsa >.
"Red Cross Issues Three Month Progress Report for Haiti Earthquake." *American*
   Red Cross. The American National Red Cross, 12 Apr. 2010. Web. 14 Apr.
   2010.
Martin, Angela. *U.S. History Since 1877*. U of Memphis, Fall 2008. Web. 14
   Apr. 2010.
United States. Dept. of State. "Advancing the Rights of Women and Girls: Keys to
   a Better Future for Afghanistan." The Office of Electronic Information,
   Bureau of Public Affairs, 29 Jan. 2009. Web. 27 Mar. 2010.

Sample Formal Outline

Adapted from a speech by Elizabeth Lyles, Davidson College

HEADING

Title: The Abused Women of Afghanistan
Topic: Plight of the Women of Afghanistan
Specific Purpose: To win support for efforts to protect women in Afghanistan.

INTRODUCTION

Attention Materials: Orbal could hardly believe the news from her native homeland. A nineteen-year-old girl had just been executed in public for adultery. That same month, a public gathering of women had been attacked by an angry mob and pelted with stones, an outspoken advocate for women's issues had been gunned down in broad daylight, and the president had just signed a law making it illegal for women to refuse sex on demand to their husbands (Taylor). Of course, such brutalities are hardly unknown to the abused women of Afghanistan. But this was the Spring of 2009 – nearly eight years after the so-called liberation of the Afghan people by a U.S.-led coalition of forces.

Thesis Statement: The abused women of Afghanistan need your support now for efforts to defend their basic human rights.

Preview: We will consider how the U.S. invasion brought hope to Afghanistan's women, how these hopes are now being dashed, and finally, how you might help in this struggle for human dignity.

(**Transition:** "First, let's revisit the hour of their promised liberation.")

BODY

I. The U.S.-led invasion in 2001 brought great promises and hopes for the women of Afghanistan.
    A. President George Bush and other Western leaders emphasized liberation in making their case for war to the Afghan people.
        1. American bombers dropped leaflets depicting the mistreatment of Afghan women ("Silent Scream").
        2. UN Secretary General Kofi Annan insisted there could be no real peace and recovery in Afghanistan without restoring basic human and civil rights for women (United Nations).
        3. First Lady Laura Bush explicitly associated the invasion with advancing their cause. "Because of our recent military gains in much of Afghanistan women are no longer imprisoned in their homes. The fight against terrorism is also a fight for the rights and dignity of women" ("An Overview").
    B. The new Afghan constitution guarantees equal rights for women ("Women in").
        1. Women are once again voting and serving in public office.
        2. In some areas women now have access to rudimentary education, health care, and a level of freedom they have not experienced in decades.

(**Transition:** "However, the reality does not always live up to the promise.")

Sample Formal Outline *(Continued)*

II. Afghan women fear that their newly gained freedoms are already being rolled back.
    A. The central government under Hamid Karzai is incapable or unwilling to protect women.
        1. Mujahideen and Taliban connected "warlords" still control most of rural Afghanistan ("Women of").
        2. "Warlords" dominate the Loya Jirga or Afghan legislative body ("An Overview").
            a. According to the warlord chair of that assembly, "God has not given you [women] equal rights because under his decision, two women are counted as equal to one man" ("Women of").
        3. Karzai has signaled his willingness to sacrifice women's rights for reconciliation.
            a. He is engaged in talks with "moderate" elements of the Taliban ("UN Head").
            b. News has recently surfaced of a secret "reconciliation law" granting amnesty for all crimes committed before 2002 ("UN Head").
            c. In 2009, he signed the infamous "rape law" that makes it illegal for women of the Shia minority to deny their husband's sexual advances on demand (Abawi).
    B. Reports of violence and oppression against women are again on the rise ("Women of").
        1. Corrupt local officials typically ignore reports of domestic abuse and sexual assault.
        2. Many schools have been shut down by a reign of terror and violence.
            a. Girls have been harassed, mutilated, and even killed for attending classes.
            b. Less than 10% of Afghan girls in rural areas have access to education.
        3. In many areas women still live in obvious fear of harsh recrimination for behaviors deemed un-Islamic.

  (Transition: "There is a little light in all this darkness. I want to tell you now about a remarkable group of women who have been fighting for these rights for over thirty years.")

III. The Revolutionary Association of the Women of Afghanistan (RAWA) is the most prominent organization for women's rights and social justice in Afghanistan.
    A. RAWA sponsors a number of humanitarian projects.
        1. They create educational opportunities for women and their children.
            a. They operate fifteen primary and secondary schools in Afghan refugee camps.
            b. They provide home-based schooling for women and girls where it is still unsafe to attend school.
        2. They provide health care to abused women and children.
            a. They operate small hospitals that provide free care.
            b. They operate mobile health teams that travel throughout the troubled regions of Afghanistan and Pakistan.
        3. They provide vocational training and financial opportunities to help Afghan women support their families and become self-sufficient.

a. They encourage chicken farms, weaving shops, and bee-fostering projects.

b. They offer small loans to start small businesses.

IV. So how can you light a small candle in the Afghan darkness?

A. Go to the RAWA website (RAWA.com) and find out how you can get involved.

B. Demand that our President and our legislators not abandon the women of Afghanistan.

(Transition: So we see that the view of Afghanistan through the eyes of women is not a happy one.)

CONCLUSION

Summary statement: It's a story that started with high hopes as the U.S. invaded Afghanistan. Then those hopes and promises began to shrivel as fundamentalist values once again spread and stained the fabric of Afghan culture. But RAWA holds high the beacon of hope for the abused and forgotten women of Afghanistan. These heroic fighters for women's rights deserve your commitment, because, as Martin Luther King Jr. said right before he died, "We are all tied together in a single garment of destiny." Go to RAWA.com and find out how you can help.

Concluding remarks: My friend Orbal, herself a RAWA activist, choked back tears as she relayed the story of an eleven-year-old neighbor that had been abducted, beaten, raped, and then traded for a dog by a local warlord. Orbal and women like her have choked back enough tears. Get involved! We must not forget the women of Afghanistan.

WORKS CONSULTED

Abawi, Atia. "Afghanistan 'Rape' Law Puts Women's Rights Front and Center." *CNN.com/asia.* Cable News Network, 7 April 2009. Web. 27 March 2010.

"An Overview on the Situation of Afghan Women." *Revolutionary Association of the Women of Afghanistan (RAWA).* Revolutionary Association of the Women of Afghanistan (RAWA), n.d. Web. 2 April 2010.

"Letter to the United Nations." *Revolutionary Association of the Women of Afghanistan (RAWA).* Revolutionary Association of the Women of Afghanistan (RAWA), 28 April 2007. Web. 2 April 2010.

"RAWA's Social Activities." *Revolutionary Association of the Women of Afghanistan (RAWA).* Revolutionary Association of the Women of Afghanistan (RAWA), n.d. Web. 5 April 2010.

"Silent Scream." *BBC News World Edition.* BBC, 8 April 2002. Web. 27 March 2010.

Siun. "McChrystal Digs In, Afghan Women Say Get Out." *Rethink Afghanistan.* Brave New Foundation, 13 July 2009. Web. 14 Apr. 2010.

Taylor, Rupert. "Women's Rights Abused in Afghanistan: Ancient Prejudice Against Females is Hard to Defeat." *Middle Eastern Affairs.* Suite101.com, 20 April 2009. Web. 27 March 2010.

"Women in Afghanistan." *Independent Lens: Afghanistan Unveiled.* Independent Television Service, 17 November 2004. Web. 26 March 2010.

"The Women of Afghanistan." *CBC News Online.* CBC, 1 March 2005. Web. 26 March 2010.

"UN Head in Afghanistan Meets with Militant Group." *Yahoo! News.* Yahoo Inc., 25 March 2010. Web. 26 March 2010.

United Nations. "The Situation of Women in Afghanistan." *Afghan Women Today: Realities and Opportunities.* The United Nations, 2002. Web. 26 March 2010.

THIS CHAPTER WILL HELP YOU

1 Appreciate how presentation aids can help your speech
2 Understand which presentation aids work best in different situations
3 Plan, design, and prepare presentation aids
4 Use presentation aids well

10

Presentation Aids

Outline

> *Seeing ... most of all the senses, makes us know and brings to light many differences between things.*
>
> —ARISTOTLE

Alumnus of West Point and the Naval War College, former senior fellow at the Kennedy School of Government at Harvard, veteran of thirty-five years of military service, Gen. Stanley A. McChrystal sat stunned before a convoluted PowerPoint slide. The head of American and NATO forces in Afghanistan tried to decipher the eight colors, twelve labels, almost one hundred names, and dozens upon dozens of arrows detailing the dynamics affecting stability in that country. Finally, he wryly observed, "When we understand that slide, we'll have won the war."[1]

Although you might not have encountered a presentation aid of quite this complexity, you surely recognize the use of aids that simply perplex and overwhelm the audience. Yet when well designed and well used, *presentation aids can really help you find your voice effectively in your speeches.*

Let's say you've chosen to speak about dyslexia. You might cite the entry from Black's Medical Dictionary, which defines it as "difficulty in reading or learning to read, . . . always accompanied by difficulty in writing, and particularly in spelling."[2] That helps your audience understand the condition on an abstract level. Imagine then taking it a step further and *showing* your audience what a dyslexic person might see when trying to read a passage (see Figure 10.1). All of a sudden, your audience gains a better understanding of what it *feels* like to be dyslexic.

Or perhaps, after a semester studying in Australia, you want to share the finer points of a didgeridoo. You could describe this instrument as a pliable mouthpiece on a long hollow tube without holes. Think of how much more vivid it would be to show a picture of one, or to play a recording or show a video clip, or even to bring one to class to demonstrate. Your verbal descriptions of the didgeridoo's distinctive droning buzz might then truly come alive for your audience.

With the advent of computer technologies, the types and uses of presentation aids are multiplying rapidly. In this chapter, we describe various kinds of presentation aids and the media used for them, identify the ways they can be used in speeches, offer suggestions for preparing them, and present guidelines for their use.

You should use presentation aids only when they increase the clarity and effectiveness of your speech. As you read this chapter, you will notice that certain suggestions are repeated time and again: Keep things simple! Be consistent! These considerations are central to whatever type of presentation aid you use.

FIGURE 10.1 The Page a Dyslexic Person Sees

—from Toni-Lee Capossela, Harcourt Brace Guide to Peer Tutoring *(New York: Harcourt Brace, 1998), p. 98*

The Advantages and Disadvantages of Presentation Aids

Presentation aids are *supplementary materials used to enhance the effectiveness and clarity of a presentation.* Whether visual, auditory, or a combination of the two, they give your audience direct sensory contact with your message. When properly prepared and used, presentation aids can help speeches in many different ways. But if they are used improperly, they can become a liability.

Advantages of Presentation Aids

Presentation aids complement words as communication tools. As powerful as words can be, they are essentially abstract. Presentation aids offer concrete and

▶ **presentation aids**   Visual and auditory materials intended to enhance the clarity and effectiveness of a presentation.

immediate images that can involve and educate listeners. Imagine how hard it would be through words alone to describe the inner workings of a computer. Even with models or charts, such a speech would still be difficult for many of us to understand. It can require both words and presentation aids, used skillfully together, to explain some topics to some audiences. The concreteness of presentation aids creates some specific advantages both for your audience and for you as a speaker.

Presentation aids help increase understanding of technical concepts.

Presentation aids can help your audience:

- **Presentation aids increase understanding.** Words are abstractions that listeners transform into mental images. Different listeners may conjure up different mental images for the same words, which may not be consistent with what you intend. As a speaker, you have more control over these images when you present both words and visuals to augment them. It is easier to give directions to someone when there is a map that both of you can see. Similarly, it is easier to explain the steps in a process when listeners are shown the numbered steps on a list.

- **Good presentation aids make your speech more memorable.** Recent research suggests that audiences recall an informative presentation better when visuals are used and that recall is even better when the visuals are in high-quality color.[3] Other research suggests that we typically remember only 20 percent of what we hear, but if we *both hear and see* something, we remember more than 50 percent.[4] Presentation aids are easier to remember than words because they are concrete. A photograph of a hungry child may linger in your memory, thus increasing the influence of a speech urging you to contribute to a cause.

- **Presentation aids add variety and interest to a speech.** Too much of a good thing, even a well-fashioned fabric of words, can seem tedious. Just as pictures and boxed materials may be used to break up long stretches of text in a book, presentation aids can be used to break up long stretches of words in a speech. Variety creates interest and helps sustain or recapture attention, as well as appealing to the different learning styles of audience members.

Presentation aids can help you as the speaker:

- **Presentation aids help establish the authenticity of your words.** When you show listeners what you are talking about, you demonstrate that it actually exists. This type of evidence is important in both informative and persuasive messages. If your audience can actually see the differences between digital cameras and film cameras, they are more likely to be convinced that one is better than the other.

- **Neat, well-designed presentation aids enhance your credibility.** They tell listeners that you put extra effort into preparing your speech. Speakers who use presentation aids are judged to be more professional, better prepared, more credible, more interesting, more concrete, and more persuasive than speakers who do not use such aids.[5] In some organizational settings, audiences expect speakers to use presentation aids, such as PowerPoint slides. If you don't have them, the audience may be disappointed and your credibility may suffer.

■ **Presentation aids can help improve your delivery skills.** Using a presentation aid encourages movement as you display your aid. Movement energizes a speech, getting you away from the "stand behind the lectern/talking head" mode of delivery that many audiences find boring. If you have problems with communication apprehension, purposeful movement—such as pointing to something on an aid as you display it—provides a constructive outlet for nervous energy. It directs your attention away from yourself and away from your problem.

Disadvantages of Presentation Aids

Despite these advantages, as the opening story about the confusing PowerPoint slide on Afghanistan illustrates, presentation aids can do your speech more harm than good. It is important to be aware of these potential problems so that you can plan to lessen their impact.

Presentation aids can be problematic for your audience:

■ **Presentation aids may distract listeners.** They can draw attention away from your message if they are not used properly. For example, if your audience has difficulty reading an aid, they may not listen to what you are saying as they strain to see it. Distributing handouts or passing around objects or pictures during your speech also creates distractions. Listeners may become so engrossed in your presentation aids that they ignore your real message.

■ **Presentation aids may confuse listeners.** As the opening example demonstrates, a complex presentation aid may leave your audience not nodding their heads but scratching them. Blurry images, unclear graphs, and overloaded slides may leave your audience more mystified than enlightened.

Presentation aids can be problematic for you as speaker:

■ **Poor presentation aids can damage your credibility.** If your aid is sloppy or inaccurate, your credibility will suffer. Listeners may think you did not care

FIGURE 10.2 Major Advantages and Disadvantages of Presentation Aids

Advantages for the Audience
1. Increased understanding
2. More memorable speech
3. Adds variety and interest

Advantages for the Speaker
1. Enhances authenticity
2. Improves credibility
3. Improves delivery

Disadvantages for the Audience
1. Can be distracting
2. Can be confusing

Disadvantages for the Speaker
1. Can damage credibility
2. Can be distracting
3. Can reduce eye contact
4. Risks uncooperative equipment

enough about your presentation to invest the time and effort needed to prepare an effective presentation aid. Worse still, they may think you are incapable of preparing one.

■ **Presentation aids can distract speakers.** If you haven't practiced your speech using your presentation aid, you may worry so much about how you are going to use it that you lose track of what you are saying. If you are not confident in your ability to use electronic equipment, this uneasiness may show up in your presentation. If something goes awry with the equipment, it might throw you completely off course.

■ **Presentation aids can reduce your eye contact with the audience.** If you look at your presentation aids more than your audience, you risk losing their attention as well as your ability to assess the audience's confusion or comprehension. That, in turn, may damage your ethos: Don't you know your material well enough to talk to the audience rather than to the aid?

■ **Presentation aids put you at the mercy of the equipment.** If the speech site is not equipped to handle computerized presentation aids, you must use other forms. Even with the best of preparations, the techno-gremlins may play havoc with your original intentions, requiring a back-up plan.

In short, presentation aids can either help or hinder your speech. An aid may be beautifully rendered, or wonderfully funny, or gorgeous to behold—but if it does not help you find your voice on this topic with this audience, you should not use it. You have a multitude of presentation aids from which to choose, as the following sections suggest. Investigate the specific options you have, as well as the benefits and challenges of each. In determining which types and media would be the best, ask yourself: *How will a presentation aid help my audience understand my thesis, main points, and supporting materials?*

Types of Presentation Aids

In considering potential presentation aids for your speech, you might be tempted to jump to media: should I use PowerPoint or a handout? (Or you might just assume that of course you will use PowerPoint—in which case, we hope you will consider the ample alternatives to this overused form.) Before determining the *media* you will use to share your presentation aid (which we'll discuss in the next section), you first need to decide what type of aid best suits your speech. In this section, we discuss some of the more frequently used kinds of presentation aids: people, objects, models, graphics, and pictures.

People

You are always a presentation aid (for good or for bad) for your speeches. Your body, grooming, actions, gestures, voice, facial expressions, and demeanor are important considerations. What you wear for a presentation can influence how your speech is received. If you will be speaking on camping and wilderness adventures, blue jeans and a flannel shirt might be appropriate. If you are a nurse discussing a medical topic, your uniform might enhance your credibility. If you are talking about how to dress for an employment interview, your own attire should illustrate your

A person's body language can act as a presentation aid.

recommendations. We discuss the importance of personal appearance in more detail in Chapter 12.

Ben Lane, one of our students, used his body during his informative speech on competitive diving to demonstrate several different kinds of dives (stopping short of diving face-first onto the floor, of course). Another, Lazetta Crawford, illustrated her speech on "stepping" (an African American dance form that combines footsteps, the spoken word, and hand claps to produce complex rhythm and sounds) by incorporating a number of the key dance steps. In each case, the demonstration added liveliness, color, and a sense of immediacy.

You can also use other people as presentation aids. John Kache was a freshman in college when he contracted meningococcal meningitis, a life-threatening disease for which immunizations are available. John survived his illness, but he lost his right leg and all of the fingers on his hands. After his recovery, he often spoke to high school students, urging them to get their shots before they went off to college. Typically, he would use a volunteer from the audience to demonstrate what life without fingers was like for him. As he put it, "I'd wrap up one of the student's hands in an Ace bandage, then throw him a bag of candy and tell him to open it and pass the candies around."[6] This demonstration dramatically illustrated the seriousness of this disease and the importance of being immunized.

Your use of people as a presentation aid does not need to be this dramatic to be effective. One of our students, Neomal Abyskera, used two of his classmates to illustrate the lineup positions in the game of rugger, as played in his native Sri Lanka. At the appropriate moment, Neomal said, "Pete and Jeff will show you how the opposing players line up." While his classmates demonstrated the shoulder grip position, Neomal explained when and why the position was assumed. The demonstration was more understandable than if he had simply tried to describe the positioning verbally or had used stick-figure drawings.

The people you ask to function as a presentation aid should be willing to do so. They should understand that their role is to illustrate your message, *not draw attention away from it*, and should agree to meet with you to rehearse the presentation. During the presentation, they should sit in the front row so that they can come forward when you need them.

Objects and Models

Displaying the actual objects you are discussing can gain attention, increase understanding, and add authenticity to your speech. If using actual objects is a problem, models can be used.

Objects. Specific objects may exemplify the concepts in your presentation, whether the objects are ingredients for a simple meal, your favorite fly-fishing rod, or a set of decorations used to celebrate Dia de los Muertos, the Mexican holiday honoring the deceased.

Listeners should be able to see the object for a presentation aid clearly without straining. The object should be portable, and you should be able to keep it out of sight when you are not talking about it. If you display the object throughout your speech, listeners may pay more attention to it than to your message. If you will be using more than one object, display them one at a time, and then conceal them when you have finished. One student speaker brought in six different objects to illustrate her talk. She lined them up across the front of the desk before beginning to speak. A classmate in the front row was so fascinated with them that he scooted his chair closer to the desk and picked up one to examine. The speaker had to stop and ask him to put it back. Concealing the objects until she was ready to use them would have avoided this problem.

Inanimate objects work better than living things, which you can't always control. One of our students brought a small puppy to use in a speech on caring for young animals. At the beginning of her speech, she spread out some newspapers on the table and placed the puppy on them. We are sure you can imagine what happened. The first thing the puppy did was wet on the papers (including her note cards, which she had put on the table while trying to control the puppy). The first thing the audience did was giggle. From there it was all downhill. The puppy squirmed, yipped, and tried to jump on the speaker the whole time she was talking. She was totally upstaged by her presentation aid.

Presentation aids meant to shock the audience into attention can cause serious problems. *Objects that are dangerous, illegal, or potentially offensive, such as guns, drugs, or pornography, must not be used in classroom speeches.* One speaker unwisely chose to demonstrate fire safety by setting fire to paper in a trash can, resulting in the arrival of the fire department and the evacuation of the building. Even replicas of dangerous materials can cause problems. One of our students brandished a very realistic-looking "toy" semiautomatic weapon that he pulled from beneath the lectern during the introduction of a speech on gun control. Several audience members became so upset that they could not concentrate on his message.

In this age of electronic wizardry, using a simple object can be all the more effective. When Andrew Evans brought a glass of water to the front of the room for his persuasive speech on faith and reason, we thought he just wanted it in case his throat got dry. Instead, in the middle of his speech he picked it up to suggest that the water represented human reason and the glass, faith. Noting that the water could be transferred from one container to another, but cannot stand on its own without any support, he suggested that reason has to have some kind of faith—in God, in science, in something—to support it.

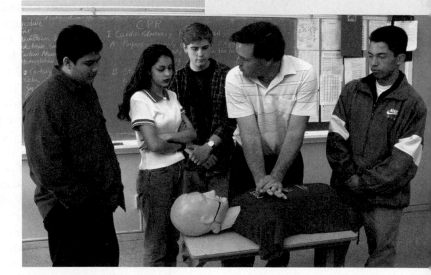

Models are useful as presentation aids when the real object would be difficult to exhibit.

Most how-to speeches require objects as presentation aids to demonstrate procedures. In a classroom speech on how to carve a jack-o'-lantern, the speaker showed listeners how to draw the face on a pumpkin with a felt marker and then how to make a beveled cut around the stem so that the top wouldn't fall in. As she exhibited these techniques, she told stories of the ancient myths surrounding jack-o'-lanterns. Her presentation aid and her words helped each other: The demonstration enlivened her speech, and the stories gave the demonstration depth and meaning. When she came to her closing remarks, she reached under the lectern and produced a finished jack-o'-lantern complete with a lighted candle. The effect was memorable.

Models.   Sometimes an object is too large, too small, very rare, expensive, fragile, or simply unavailable for class use. In these cases, a replica of the object can work well as a presentation aid. George Stacey brought a slightly smaller-than-life-sized model of a person to demonstrate cardiopulmonary resuscitation (CPR). The model folded into a suitcase so that it could be kept out of sight when not in use. When using a model as a presentation aid, it should be constructed to scale and large enough for all listeners to see. Any presentation aid that the audience must strain to see will distract the audience more than help them.

Graphics

Graphics are visual representations of information, such as sketches, maps, graphs, charts, and textual materials. Because graphics will be displayed for only a short time during your speech, they must be instantly clear. Each graphic should focus on one idea. Because the graphics will be viewed from a distance, their colors should be intense and should contrast sharply with the background. We cover such considerations more fully under "Preparing Presentation Aids" later in this chapter.

Sketches.   Sketches are simplified representations of what you are talking about. If you don't draw well, look for clip art on your computer or search children's coloring books for drawings that you can trace. If you are drawing a sketch, make it first on paper; then enlarge it or transfer it onto a transparency on a copier. One student speaker used a sketch transferred to a transparency to illustrate the measurements one should take before buying a bicycle. While talking about making bar-to-pedal and seat-to-handlebar measurements, he pointed to them as he said, "Let me show you how to take some basic measurements."

Maps.   As a representation of physical space, a map can show listeners the locations of occurrences and put problems into perspective. Because commercially prepared maps typically contain too much detail, the best maps are those that you make specifically for your speech so that they are simple, relevant to your purpose, and uncluttered. To illustrate the size of an oil slick in the Gulf of Mexico, you might superimpose the maps of Rhode Island and Delaware, with lots of room left over. To show which areas have the longest commuting times, you could show Figure 10.3. Another student speaker used a simplified map to help his listeners see where a series of earthquakes occurred along the New Madrid fault and understand how a recurrence of such earthquakes might endanger his mid-South classmates.

Maps are also useful for illustrating speeches based on spatial relationships. It is hard to give people instructions on how to get somewhere with words alone. In a speech on the major attractions in Yellowstone Park, Tiffany Brock used an outline map of the park showing the route from the South Visitor's Center to Old Faithful, Mammoth Hot Springs, and the Grand Canyon of the Yellowstone River. Seeing the map helped listeners put the locations and distances into perspective.

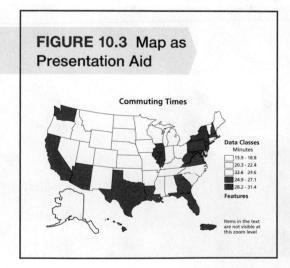

FIGURE 10.3 Map as Presentation Aid

▶ **graphics**   Visual representations of information, such as sketches, maps, graphs, charts, and textual materials.

Whether a map works well as a presentation aid depends on how effectively you integrate it into your presentation. Elizabeth Walling used a map of the wilderness canoe area in northern Minnesota to familiarize her Memphis audience with that area. She made a double-sided poster that she kept hidden behind the speaker's table until she was ready to use it. On one side, she highlighted the wilderness canoe area on an outline map of northern Minnesota, pointing out various places of interest. To illustrate how large the area is, Elizabeth said, "Let me put this in a more familiar context for you." She turned the poster over, revealing an outline map of western Tennessee on which she had superimposed the wilderness area. At a glance, we could see that the area would extend from Memphis to beyond Jackson, Tennessee, some eighty miles away. Elizabeth's artful use of the two maps created a striking visual comparison. The same type of effect can be obtained by overlaying transparencies.

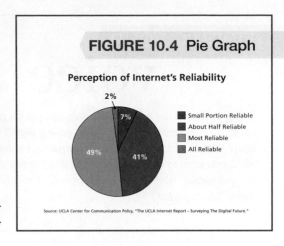

FIGURE 10.4 Pie Graph

Perception of Internet's Reliability

■ Small Portion Reliable
■ About Half Reliable
■ Most Reliable
■ All Reliable

Source: UCLA Center for Communication Policy, "The UCLA Internet Report – Surveying The Digital Future."

Graphs.   Mrs. Robert A. Taft, wife of a prominent former senator and lioness of Washington society, once commented, "I always find that statistics are hard to swallow and impossible to digest. The only one I can ever remember is that if all the people who go to sleep in church were laid end to end, they would be a lot more comfortable."[7] Many people share Mrs. Taft's feelings about statistics. As we noted in Chapter 8, masses of numbers presented orally can be overwhelming. But a well-designed graph can make statistical information easier for listeners to understand.

A **pie graph** shows the size of a subject's parts in relation to one another and to the whole. The "pie" represents the whole, and the "slices" represent the parts. The segments, or slices, are percentages of the whole, and must add up to 100 percent. The most effective pie graphs for use as presentation aids have six or fewer segments, because too many segments make a graph difficult to read. The pie graph in Figure 10.4 shows Internet users' perceptions of the reliability of information from Internet Web sites.

A **bar graph** shows comparisons and contrasts between two or more items or groups. Bar graphs are easy to understand because each item can be readily compared with every other item on the graph. Bar graphs can also have a dramatic visual impact. Figure 10.5 is a horizontal bar graph that illustrates the relative popularity of three major social networking sites. Figure 10.6 offers a vertical bar graph prepared by Dolapo Olushola for her speech illuminating a tragic crisis created by the HIV/AIDS epidemic in Africa.

Some bar graphs make use of pictographs, or stylized drawings, in place of linear bars. One student's speech on the relationship between college students' consumption of alcohol and the grades they earned, for example, showed three and a half bottles to represent the number of drinks per week for "A" students, as compared to ten and a half bottles for "D" students. If you plan to use pictographs in place of bars, be sure they are simple depictions that do not distract from the impact of your material.[8]

A **line graph** demonstrates changes across time, and it is useful for showing trends in growth or decline. Figure 10.7 shows the number of

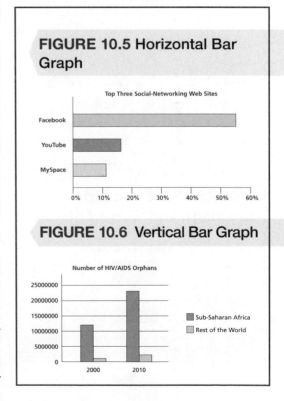

FIGURE 10.5 Horizontal Bar Graph

Top Three Social-Networking Web Sites

Facebook
YouTube
MySpace

0%   10%   20%   30%   40%   50%   60%

FIGURE 10.6 Vertical Bar Graph

Number of HIV/AIDS Orphans

25000000
20000000
15000000
10000000
5000000
0

■ Sub-Saharan Africa
■ Rest of the World

2000   2010

▶ **pie graph**   A circle graph that shows the size of a subject's parts in relation to each other and to the whole.

▶ **bar graph**   A graph that shows comparisons and contrasts between two or more items or groups.

▶ **line graph**   A visual representation of changes across time; especially useful for indicating trends of growth or decline.

FINDING YOUR voice   Exploring Graphs

Using the same set of statistical data, prepare a pie graph, a bar graph, and a line graph. What aspects of the data does each version highlight? What aspects are less evident in each version? Which version makes the information clearest and most striking for an audience? Which version seems to best represent the data? If the version that seems best for the audience is not the version that seems most representative of the data, what ethical questions does that inconsistency raise?

college graduates by gender from 1950 through 2000. The upward-sloping lines confirm the dramatic increases in the numbers of both male and female graduates across this time span, especially among women. When you plot more than one line on a graph, use distinct colors. To avoid confusing listeners, never try to plot more than three lines on a graph.

FIGURE 10.7 Line Graph

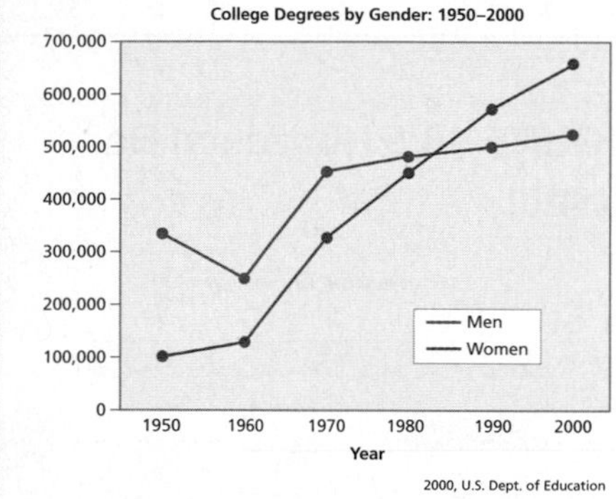

College Degrees by Gender: 1950–2000

— Men
— Women

2000, U.S. Dept. of Education

FIGURE 10.8 Flowchart: Creating a Web Site

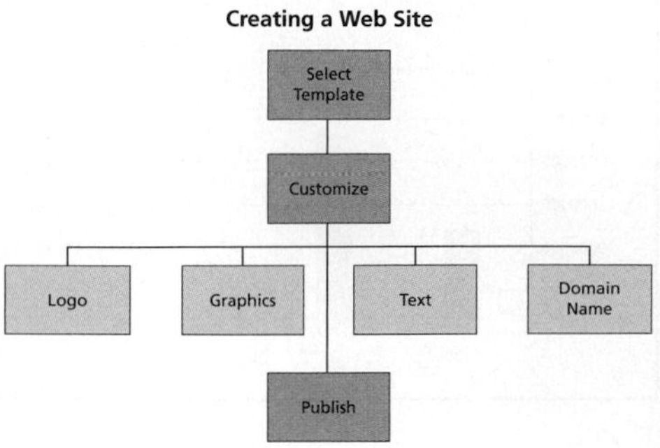

Creating a Web Site

Charts.   Charts provide visual summaries of relationships that are not in themselves visible. Charts can be quite complex, so the speaker's challenge is to simplify them without distorting their meaning. The listener must be able to understand a chart instantly and to read it from a distance.

One frequently used type of chart is a flow chart. A **flow chart** can show the steps in a process, the hierarchy and accountability in an organization, or the genealogy of a family tree. In a flow chart that explains a process, the levels, lines, and arrows indicate what steps occur simultaneously and what steps occur sequentially. Figure 10.8 is a flow chart that indicates the process of developing a Web site.

To avoid the problem of overloading charts with too much information, consider using a series of charts, presented in succession. It is much better to have several clean, clear charts than one that tries to do too much.

Textual Graphics.   **Textual graphics** are visuals that contain words, phrases, or numbers. Unfamiliar material is clearer and easier for listeners to remember when they can both hear and see the message. Presenting the key words in a message visually can help an audience follow complicated ideas more easily. For example, in an informative speech that describes the process of applying for graduate school, you might use a series of posters or slides that show numbered steps in the process and contain a key word or phrase for each step.

The most frequently used textual graphics contain **bulleted lists** of information such as that shown in the computer-generated slide in Figure 10.9. When you make a bulleted list, begin with a title, and then place the material under it. Unless you are discussing all of the elements in quick succession, you should reveal each element as you

▶ **flow chart**   A visual method of representing power and responsibility relationships, or describing the steps in a process.

▶ **textual graphics**   Visuals that contain words, phrases, or numbers.

▶ **bulleted list**   A presentation aid that highlights ideas by presenting them as a list of brief statements.

talk about it. For PowerPoint presentations, use the "entrance" code to make subsequent portions appear at the click of the mouse. Keep the graphic simple, using intense colors with good contrast. In a bulleted list, have no more than six lines of information and no more than six words to a line.

Another frequently used type of textual graphic presents an **acronym** composed of the initial letters of words to help your audience remember your message. The transparency in Figure 10.10 used the acronym EMILY (adapted from Emily's List, a political network) in a persuasive speech urging students to start saving early for retirement. When preparing such a graphic, use the acronym as a title; then list the words under it. Use size and/or color to make the first letters of the words stand out.

Keep textual graphics simple, with colors that make ideas stand out. A single word or phrase is far more effective than a full sentence, which competes with you for attention.

Pictures

Photographs and illustrations can be powerful presentation aids. A good photograph can authenticate a point in a way that words cannot. It can make a situation seem more vivid and realistic. For instance, a speaker could talk about the devastating environmental effects of the collapsed oil rig in the Gulf of Mexico, which might evoke a modest response from the audience. Suppose, however, the speaker also projected the photograph in Figure 10.11 on a screen in the front of the room as she said these words. Which strategy—with or without the picture—do you think would have the greater impact?

A picture may be "worth a thousand words," but as with all presentation aids you must use them carefully in speeches. Pictures should be selected for their relevance. Small photographs cannot be seen by anyone beyond the first row, and passing them around during a presentation is distracting. Over-reliance on pictures may detract from the speaker's main points. Moreover, pictures with disturbing content can be distracting. One student who was a paramedic showed pictures of child abuse victims taken in a local

---

FIGURE 10.9 Bulleted List

Marketing Task Force

- Mission Statement
- Current Image
- Target Market
- Desired Image

FIGURE 10.10 Acronym Graphic

EMILY

EARLY
MONEY
IS
LIKE
YEAST

IT MAKES
DOUGH GROW!

FIGURE 10.11 Projected Photograph

▶ **acronym**   A word composed of the initial letters of a series of words.

emergency room. Some members of the audience became so upset that they were not able to concentrate on her message.

Digital photographs can be used as PowerPoint projections or be made into transparencies on most computer printers. Color copiers can turn photos into inexpensive 11-by-17-inch enlargements, the minimally acceptable size for use in most classroom settings. Mount these pictures on poster board for ease of presentation.

Presentation Media

The many *types* of presentation aids can be shared with your audience through a variety of presentation *media*. Traditional media include flip charts, posters, handouts, chalk or marker boards, transparencies, videotapes, and audiotapes. Newer presentation media use computer programs, such as PowerPoint and Prezi, that can incorporate slides, films, DVDs, and sound. These newer media are rapidly becoming the standard for presentations in organizational and educational settings. Although you may be best acquainted with newer media, familiarity with other media allows you greater creativity as well as options when technology may not be available.

Traditional Media

Flip Charts.   A **flip chart** is a large, unlined tablet placed on an easel so that each page can be flipped over the top when you are done with it. Most flip charts are newsprint pads that measure about 2 feet wide by 3 feet high. Flip charts are convenient, inexpensive, and adaptable to many settings. Because flip charts are meant to be used spontaneously, they are especially useful when subjects come up that should be written out so that they can be analyzed and understood. Business meetings, decision-making groups, and organizational training sessions often use flip charts in addition to more sophisticated types of presentation tools.

Although flip charts can be effective in some group communication settings, they don't work as well in classroom speeches. Their use suggests that the speaker did not care enough to prepare a polished presentation aid. Writing on a flip chart also forces speakers either to stop speaking while they write or to speak while facing away from the audience, which may offset any gain from using the charts.

When using flip charts, keep each page as simple as possible. Use wide-point felt markers in strong colors, and print or write legibly in large letters. If you prepare a flip chart in advance, leave several pages in front of and in between your pages so that the writing does not show through.

Chalk and Marker Boards.   A chalk or marker board is available in almost every classroom and corporate conference room. Like flip charts, these boards are best used spontaneously. Despite careful speech preparation, you may sometimes realize that some of your listeners have not understood what you have just said. One way you can respond to the

Computerized slide presentations and flip charts are frequently used as presentation aids in business meetings.

▶ **flip chart**   A large, unlined tablet, usually a newsprint pad, that is placed on an easel so that each page can be flipped over the top when it's full.

apparent confusion is by writing a few words on the board or by drawing a simple diagram. Because you inevitably lose eye contact with listeners while writing on a board, do not use this medium for anything that will take more than a few seconds to write or draw. Never use chalk or marker boards simply because you did not want to take the time to prepare a polished presentation aid.

When you write on a board, use large letters so that people in the back of the room can read them without straining. Write or print legibly. Clear the board before you begin, and, as a courtesy to later speakers, erase the board when you are finished.

Posters.   Posters can be used to display pictures, sketches, maps, charts, graphs, or textual graphics. In an average-size room with a small audience, posters about 14 by 17 inches may work best; they are easier to handle than larger posters. You can place the posters face down on the lectern or table and display them as you refer to them. You can also use the back of a poster to remind you of names of people or to cue you to the next point in your presentation.

When using a series of posters, be sure to number them on the back so they don't get out of order. Keep posters simple and neat. Use large letters in strong colors that are easy to read. Keep a lot of white space. Rehearse your speech using the posters so you can integrate them smoothly into your presentation.

Handouts.   Handouts are useful when your subject is complex or your message contains a lot of statistical information, and they can extend the impact of your speech and validate the information you have presented. Pass out these handouts *after* your speech so listeners have something to remind them of what you said. If you distribute a handout before you speak, it will compete with your words for attention. The audience may read the handout rather than listen to you. Therefore, you should distribute handouts before your speech *only* when it is absolutely necessary for listeners to refer to them during your presentation. Never distribute handouts during your speech. This is a sure-fire way to disrupt your presentation and confuse or lose listeners. Multi-paged handouts are multi-distracting.

Transparencies, Projections, and Slides.   Transparencies, projections by document cameras, and slides allow audiences to see graphics or photographs more easily, especially when audiences are large or spread out in a large room. Business speakers often prefer them to posters or flip charts because they look more professional.

Transparencies are easier to use than slides because you don't have to darken the room when you show them. They are simple to make and inexpensive. You can write on a transparency while it is being shown, adding spontaneity to your presentation. You can also use a pencil as a pointer to direct listeners' attention to features you want to emphasize.

Document cameras can project either transparencies or hard copy onto a large screen. To explain how to read music, for example, you might show the score of Handel's *Messiah* while playing a recorded section, pointing to the various parts in the score as they enter in the piece.

When you show slides with a carousel projector, the room usually has to be darkened. Unfortunately, this means that the illuminated screen becomes the center of attention rather than you. One major disadvantage of using transparencies, document cameras, or slides is that often you must speak from where your equipment is located. If you have to stand behind listeners or in the middle of the audience to run the projector, you will be talking to someone's back. If remote-controlled equipment is not available, your best solution may be to practice having a classmate change the projections or slides on cue.

Most transparencies and slides are now prepared on personal computers. You can purchase transparency sheets for use with most printers. You also can draw or print your material onto plain paper and convert it to a transparency on a copying machine. If you have access to only a black-and-white copier or printer, you can add color with opaque markers. Framing your transparencies will avoid glare from light showing around the outside edges of the projection.

When you arrange slides in a carousel, be sure they are in the proper order and that none of them are upside down. Today, most personal computers are packaged with software that allows you to prepare and present slides without a carousel projector. We discuss this in greater detail in our section on new media.

If you decide to use transparencies, projections, or slides, check the equipment ahead of time and become familiar with its operation. You may need a long extension cord to position the equipment where you want it. Practice using the equipment in the room as you rehearse your speech. One final caution: Don't use too many slides or transparencies in a short speech. A presentation aid should do just that—*aid* your speech, not compete with it or replace it.

Video and Audio Resources.

Such video resources as DVDs and videotapes and such audio resources as MP3 or computer recordings and audiotapes can add variety to your presentation. Be sure in advance that the place where you will be making your presentation has the proper equipment to work with your materials.

Video resources are useful for transporting the audience to distant, dangerous, or otherwise unavailable locations. Although you could verbally describe the beauty of the Montana Rockies, your word-pictures might come to life if reinforced with actual scenes projected electronically.

Using videos poses some special problems for speakers. Moving images attract more attention than does the spoken word, so they can easily upstage you. Moreover, a videotape segment must be edited so that splices blend cleanly. Such editing takes special skill and equipment. Transferring this material onto CDs is simpler, easier to handle, and can be done on most personal computers with a DVD/CD burner. Finally, in a short speech, a clip should be no more than thirty seconds long.

For certain topics, however, carefully prepared videos can be more effective than any other type of presentation aid. A student at Northwest Mississippi Community College who was a firefighter used videotape in an informative speech on fire hazards in the home. By customizing the video to fit the precise needs of his speech, he was able to show long shots of a room and then zoom in on various hazards.[9] He prepared the video without sound so that his speech provided the commentary needed to interpret and explain the pictures. Using this technique, he made his subject much more meaningful for listeners.

Audio resources may also be useful as presentation aids. Sabrina Karic started her self-introductory speech on growing up in war-torn Bosnia and Herzegovina with a recording of a loud explosion and gunfire, during which she ducked beneath the table as the audience jumped (see "A Little Chocolate" at the end of Chapter 3). When in doubt about the wisdom or practicality of using such aids, consult your instructor.

SPEAKER'S notes

Deciding What Presentation Media to Use

Let the following suggestions guide your selection of presentation media.

When you need to . . .	try using . . .
■ adapt to audience feedback	■ flip charts, chalk or marker boards
■ display maps, charts, graphs, or textual graphics	■ posters or computerized programs
■ present complex information or statistical data	■ handouts
■ display graphics or photos to a large audience	■ slides or transparencies
■ authenticate a point	■ audio and video resources
■ make your presentation appear more professional	■ computerized programs

New Media

Computer-generated presentations have become ubiquitous. When properly designed and used well, they can bring together text, numbers, pictures, music, video clips, and artwork, all of which can be made into slides, videos, animations, and audio materials, in a polished, compelling way. Used poorly—as with the complicated slide of Afghanistan war strategy described in our opening vignette—they will bore, confuse, and annoy your audience, and perhaps you as well. Rebecca Ganzel in *Presentations* magazine pictured the following scenario:

> It's that nightmare again—the one in which you're trapped in the Electronic Presentation from Hell. The familiar darkness presses in, periodically sliced in half by a fiendish light. Bullet points, about 18 to a slide, careen in all directions. You cringe, but the slides keep coming, too fast to read, each with a new template you half-remember seeing a hundred times before: Dad's Tie! Sixties Swirls! Infinite Double-Helixes! A typewriter clatters; brakes squeal. Somewhere in the shadows, a voice drones on. Strange stick people shake hands and dance around a flowchart. Typefaces morph into Word Art.
>
> But the worst is yet to come. As though you're watching a train wreck in slow motion, you look down at your hand—and *you're holding the remote.*[10]

If swirling backgrounds and flashy transitions attract more attention than do your ideas, they are a hindrance instead of a help. Yet electronic presentation aids can provide vivid, engaging enhancements that bring your ideas alive for your audience. Moreover, in certain settings such presentation formats are simply expected. Using them well will set you apart from the countless speeches that commit "Death by PowerPoint."

PowerPoint Presentations. More than 90 percent of all computerized presentations in the United States are created using the PowerPoint program, which is distributed as part of the Microsoft Office software.[11] Why is PowerPoint so popular? For starters, it is the most widely available software of its type and is prepackaged on many computers sold to businesses and educational institutions.

▶ **computer-generated presentation** The use of commercial presentation software to join audio, visual, textual, graphic, and animated components.

PowerPoint is also fairly easy to use. The software contains templates and comes with a step-by-step online tutorial; see http://office.microsoft.com/en-us/powerpoint/default.aspx.

PowerPoint may also be the most frequently misused type of presentation aid, in part because of that ease of use. Who has not been subjected to poor PowerPoint presentations that annoy the audience, mask the message, and harm the speaker's credibility? A survey conducted by technology specialist Dave Paradi identified the most irritating elements of PowerPoint presentations:

1. Reading slides to the audience.

2. Using text too small to be easily read.

3. Writing full sentences instead of bulleted points.

4. Making poor color choices that make slides hard to see.

5. Projecting complex diagrams or charts.

6. Using moving or flying text or graphics.

7. Interjecting annoying sounds.[12]

After enduring one too many of these suffocating speeches, Peter Norvig, the director of research for Google, created a tongue-in-cheek PowerPoint version of the Gettysburg Address that "captured the main phrases of the original, while losing all the flow, eloquence, and impact."[13]

Using PowerPoint well requires an understanding that it is fundamentally a *visual* medium. Moreover, it is a design medium rather than a brainstorming medium. If your first instinct is to create your speech in PowerPoint, step away from the computer and reconsider. If your second instinct is to type in your key-word outline, step away from the computer and reconsider. Presentation designer Garr Reynolds observes that if you attempt to merge a slide for an oral presentation with a document for a written presentation, all you end up with is a "slideument" that doesn't serve either purpose well.[14]

When Gabrielle Wallace presented an informative speech on the apparent contradiction of the French eating and drinking well but rarely gaining weight, she could have used PowerPoint to list her thesis, detail her main points, and repeat her quotations. Instead of this language-heavy approach, she paired her discussion of how the French dine with photographs of red wine, fruits, vegetables, and bread. Instead of putting her pre-lunch audience to sleep, she had us drooling over her vibrant visual images and hanging on her every word.

To create effective PowerPoint presentations, start by avoiding the seven deadly sins as identified by Paradi (see the preceding list). Note that as the speaker, you can control all of these problems! Most importantly, do **not** put your outline on PowerPoint slides and then read it to the audience. They can read faster than you can speak, and in the process all of you will be bored. In addition, basic principles include these:

■ Follow the basics of preparation detailed in the next section, with particular attention to using a simple template, contrasting colors, clear images, and minimal language. Avoid the temptation of using the numerous overwrought templates available.

- Be sure to proofread your slides carefully—and have others proofread for you as well. It's really embarrassing, and distracting, to have major typos projected for all to see.

- If one slide contains material that you will discuss sequentially, such as before-and-after pictures, use the "entrance" code to make subsequent portions appear at the click of the mouse.

- At the points in your presentation when you do not need an aid, use blank slides so that your audience will not be distracted.

- Check your presentation in the room. What's clear when it's right in front of you on the computer may appear murky when it's projected.

- After you've finalized your presentation, save it as "PowerPoint Show" so that you can immediately open to the first slide, rather than having to click your way into it.

Follow these guidelines, and you will give a good name to PowerPoint. As *Slate*'s technology columnist Farhad Manjoo observes, "when people write annoying e-mails or make inscrutable spreadsheets, we don't blame Outlook and Excel; we blame the people. But for many of us, PowerPoint software is synonymous with the terrible output it often generates."[15] Figure 10.12 offers an example of a PowerPoint slide that would send your audience reeling. The tutorials accompanying PowerPoint may encourage the use of busy templates, bullet points, animation schemes, and other distractions; choose wisely, with your audience in mind.

Prezi Presentations.   Whereas PowerPoint uses a linear approach with one slide appearing after another, a new challenger called Prezi enables a three-dimensional approach to explore the interconnections. As Dr. Scott Titsworth of Ohio University explains,

> Prezi allows you to visually travel inside ideas. As a child did you ever go into your back yard and use a magnifying glass to look at things? You get a

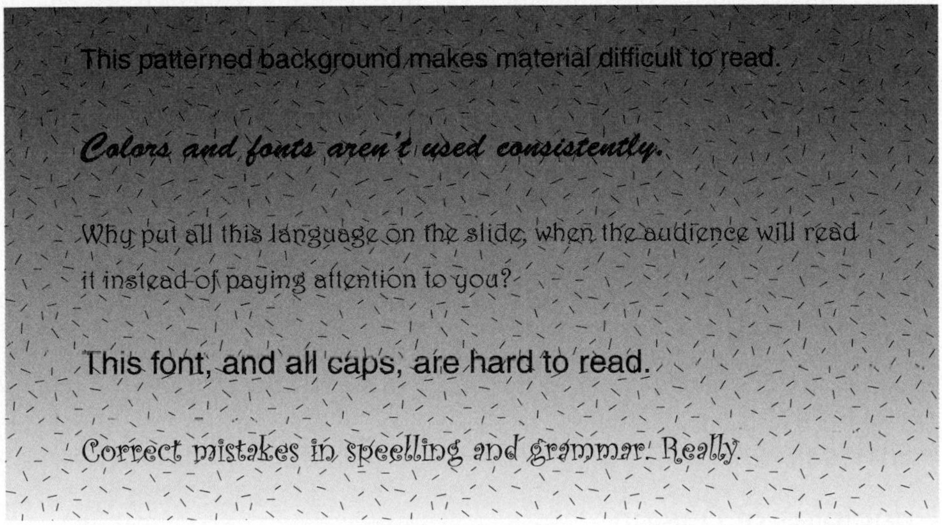

FIGURE 10.12 How NOT to Use PowerPoint

broad view and then zoom down to see very fine details to learn more
about the big picture. Prezi does that for you in presentations. You create
everything for your presentation on a big canvas, and can embed smaller
pictures or clusters of ideas within that larger picture (this can create some
very cool surprises for those in the audience). . . . Prezi allows you to think
about ways in which holistic visual designs can enhance and augment a
spoken narrative.[16]

Instead of a set of slides, Prezi uses a "canvas" on which you place your concepts. You can group ideas, layer concepts, zoom in to focus in more detail on one
aspect, and then zoom out to return to the big picture. As with PowerPoint, you
can incorporate images, videos, sound, and language. Katie Lovett developed a
powerful persuasive speech against bottled water using Prezi. She took her audience inside the marketing strategies, consumer misconceptions, and environmental effects, showing relationships and consequences in a dynamic way that had us
mesmerized.

Prezi.com contains a description, tutorials, and sample presentations on such
topics as symbolism in *The Scarlet Letter*, imperialism, and the circulatory system.
The basic format is available to the public free of charge; students and educators can
receive a more advanced free version by registering. A similar program is VUE, for
Visual Understanding Environment (see http://vue.tufts.edu/). Based at Tufts
University, VUE's metaphor is mapping, with the creation of pathways, annotated
trails, and guided walk-throughs. The drawback with VUE is that a presentation
starts with an overview, which contains so much information as to be distracting to
the audience.

As with PowerPoint, the ease of the technology can also be a trap. The guidelines
for using rather than abusing PowerPoint can also be applied to Prezi and VUE.

Preparing Presentation Aids

As the discussion so far suggests, presentation aids can either make or break a
speech. Thinking carefully about how they will contribute to your presentation
makes the difference. In addition to selecting the appropriate type and media, you
should create them following basic principles of design and color.

Principles of Design

A good presentation aid is simple, easy to see, focuses on what is important, and is
well balanced. Consider the basic principles of *simplicity*, *visibility*, *emphasis*, and

balance as you plan and prepare your materials. Look at your aids from the perspective of an audience member and see if they meet these criteria. As graphic designer Alex W. White quips, "One definition of good design is the balance between monotony and the designer's self-indulgence."[17]

Simplicity.   Many speakers—novices and professionals alike—try to cram too much information into a single presentation aid. Too much information distracts listeners as they try to figure out what everything is and what it means. We had one student divide a standard 2-by-3-foot poster into twelve segments, glue samples of medicinal herbs in each box, and then print its name and use under each sample. Needless to say, only listeners in the front row could actually read any of the print, and the aid created more confusion than illumination. He would have been better served had he used a series of smaller posters, each featuring one herb, the simple facts about it, and its basic use.

Visibility.   The size of any presentation aid must be appropriate to the setting in which it is used. Listeners in the back of the room must be able to see your presentation aid without straining. You may be able to use a poster in a room holding up to forty people, but larger rooms require projection equipment. Bringing a full-sized canoe into a small room will not only prove cumbersome for you, but overwhelming for your listeners.

When preparing a presentation aid for the standard classroom, make sure the words are clearly legible. Computer print is typically sized in terms of points (pt), while posters may use inches. Such presentation aids should use these minimum size guidelines:

	Transparencies	Slides	Handouts	Posters
Title	36 pt	24 pt	18 pt	3 inches
Subtitles	24 pt	18 pt	14 pt	2 inches
Other text	18 pt	14 pt	12 pt	1½ inches

Use a plain font that is easy to read. The following fonts work best on presentation aids: Arial Rounded Bold, Franklin Gothic, Courier, Times New Roman, Impact, and Microsoft Sans Serif Bold. Avoid script and decorative fonts such as Algerian, Brush Script, Curlz, Old English, and Snap.

Your audience needs to be able to easily read visual materials; they need to be able to easily hear audio materials. If the sound of a recording or video is so soft that your listeners can't understand, then your point about the differences in jazz styles will be lost. If it's too loud, you risk blasting them out of the room.

Emphasis.   Your presentation aids should emphasize what your speech emphasizes. Your listeners' eyes should be drawn immediately to what you want to illustrate. On the acronym chart (see Figure 10.10), the first letters of each word stand out. The map of Yellowstone Park mentioned earlier contained only the attractions the speaker planned to talk about and the route between them. Had she added pictures of bears to indicate grizzly habitats, drawings of fish to show trout streams, and mountains to designate the terrain, the presentation aid would have seemed cluttered and distracting.

Avoid cuteness! Graphics prepared for handouts may be more detailed than those used for posters, slides, or transparencies, but they should not contain extraneous material. When in doubt, leave the details out. Let your spoken words provide the elaboration.

FIGURE 10.13 Meanings of Colors

	Movie-goers	Financiers	Doctors
Blue	Tender emotions	Reliable	Cold
Green	Playful	Profitable	Infection
Yellow	Happy	Highlighted/important	Jaundice
Red	Exciting	Unprofitable	Hot/radioactive

Source: *How to Lie with Charts*, 2000

Balance. Presentation aids that are balanced are pleasing to the eye. You achieve balance when you position textual materials so that they form a consistent pattern. Don't try to use every square inch of a poster board or overload a slide. White space is important! On computer-generated slides, you should leave blank space at both the top and bottom and have equal side margins. The unbalanced and cluttered slide in Figure 10.12 violates all of the principles of design, while the slide in Figure 10.13 illustrates a balanced design. Poster boards should have a margin of at least 2 inches at the top and bottom, with side margins of about 1½ inches.

Principles of Color

As many of the illustrations in this chapter show, color adds impact to presentation aids. Most color presentation aids attract and hold attention better than black-and-white ones. Color also can convey or enhance meaning. A speech about crop damage from a drought, for example, might use an enlarged outline map showing the least affected areas in green, moderately damaged areas in orange, and severely affected areas in brown. The natural colors would reinforce the message.

Color can also be used to create moods and impressions. Figure 10.13 shows some of the reactions that various groups might have toward colors. For most Americans, blue suggests power, authority, and stability (blue chip, blue ribbon, royal blue). Using blue in your graphics can evoke these associations. Red signals excitement or crisis (in the red, red ink, "I saw red"). Such colors recently have come to connote political parties: blue for Democrats, red for Republicans. Line graphs tracing a rise in campus crimes could be drawn in red to convey the urgency of the problem. You should avoid using red when presenting financial data unless you want to focus on debts or losses. In our American culture, green is associated with both money (greenbacks) and environmental concerns (Greenpeace). When selecting colors, you should also be aware of cultural differences. In the United States, for example, white is associated with weddings, baptisms, confirmations, and other joyous rituals. In Japan, however, white is a funeral color, associated with sadness.

The way you use colors in combination can convey subtle nuances of meaning. An **analogous color scheme** uses colors that are adjacent in the color spectrum, such as green, blue-green, and blue. At the same time that this type of color scheme shows the differences among elements, it also suggests their close connection and compatibility. For example, a pie graph could use analogous colors to represent the students, faculty, and administration of a university. The different colors suggest that although these parts are separate, they belong together. In this subtle way, the presentation aid implies that these components of a university should work together.

FIGURE 10.14 Types of Color Schemes

analogous color scheme	complementary color scheme	monochromatic color scheme

▶ **analogous color scheme** Colors adjacent on the color wheel; used in a presentation aid to suggest both differences and close relationships among the components.

▶ **complementary color scheme** Colors opposite one another on the color wheel; used in a presentation aid to suggest tension and opposition.

A **complementary color scheme** uses colors that are opposites on the color wheel, such as red and green. Complementary color schemes suggest tension and opposition among elements in a speech. Because they heighten the sense of drama, they may enliven informative speaking and encourage change in persuasive speaking.

A **monochromatic color scheme** uses variations of a single color. The acronym graphic (Figure 10.10) uses a monochromatic color scheme. These schemes suggest variety within unity. A monochromatic color scheme would be inappropriate for bar graphs or line graphs, because they require more contrast to be effective. Figure 10.14 illustrates these three types of color schemes.

The colors you use for text in a presentation aid should contrast with the background. Patterned or shaded backgrounds can make words difficult to read. Generally, light-colored backgrounds contrast clearly with strong primary colors such as blue and green. However, don't use red letters against a light background. Red tends to bleed, making the words blurry and difficult to read, and a light background can create glare. Therefore, you might want to use a strong primary color for the background and have the text or other graphic elements printed in white, especially in a bright room.

Color contrast is especially important for computer-generated slides and transparencies, because the colors will appear less distinct when projected than they do when seen on a computer monitor. Colors like pastel pink, light blue, and pale yellow, or those with a grayish tinge, may not be strong enough for good graphic emphasis in any type of presentation aid.

A final word of caution concerning color: When you prepare presentation aids on a computer, the colors on your monitor will differ from the final colors when they are printed on a transparency or slide. The rich burgundy background that looks so great on your computer might look more like muddy water once it is projected. Run a sample and project it to see how the final colors will actually look to an audience. If the results are not what you expected, try other colors until you are satisfied.

Making Presentation Aids

If you use a computer to produce slides, transparencies, or handouts, experiment with several different designs. Emphasize the visual aspects of your presentation, so that the aids develop your points rather than repeating or competing with them. If you must use language, limit the amount of information on slides and transparencies to a maximum of six lines per slide and six words per line. Make sure that your words are visible from the back of the room.

To make handmade charts, graphs, or other poster aids, start with a rough draft that allows you to see how your aid will look when it is finished. If you are making a poster, prepare your draft on newsprint or butcher paper of the same size. With a light pencil, mark off the margins to frame your aid. Divide your planning sheet into four equal sections to help you balance the placement of material. Use a wide-tipped felt marker to sketch in your design and words.

Whether you are using traditional media or new media, be sure you know how your presentation aids will work in the room. Step back and inspect your presentation aid from about the same distance as the back row of your audience. Can you read it without straining? Is everything spelled correctly? Is your eye drawn to what is most important? Have you positioned your material so that it looks good? Do the images look balanced? Have you included credit for the sources of the material?

▶ **monochromatic color scheme** Use of variations of a single color in a presentation aid to convey the idea of variety within unity.

Remember, keep your presentation aid simple! Be sure your margins and borders are large enough to provide ample white space. See if there is anything you can cut. If your draft looks "busy," make a series of presentation aids instead of just one. Once you have completed a rough draft of the aid, construct the final product. If you are artistically challenged, use computers, stencils, or stick-on letters and numbers.

Limit the number of slides or transparencies you use in a speech. You probably should have *no more than four aids for a six-minute presentation and no more than six aids for a ten-minute presentation*. If you use more than this, your speech may become just a voice-over for a slide show.

SPEAKER'S notes

Checklist for Preparing Presentation Aids

Your presentation aid should meet these criteria:

_____ My presentation aid is as simple as I can make it.

_____ I have limited myself to one major idea per aid.

_____ I have ample margins at the top, bottom, and sides of my aid.

_____ My print is large enough to be read from the back of the room.

_____ My aid emphasizes a key point in my presentation.

_____ I have good color contrast on my aid.

_____ I use colors and lettering consistently.

_____ My aid is easy to see (or hear).

_____ I have checked for spelling errors.

_____ I know how I will show each aid at the appropriate point, and how I will hide it before and after.

Using Presentation Aids

Even the best-designed presentation aid requires skillful use to enhance a speech. As we discussed each type of presentation aid, we made suggestions on how to use it in a speech. Here, we bring these suggestions together and extract some general guidelines.

Be sure to practice using your presentation aids so that you don't end up fumbling around when you are making your presentation. Try them out as you practice your speech. Plan transitions such as "As you can see on this chart . . ." to integrate the material into your message. Well before your speaking time, check out the site to determine the logistics. Make sure your aid can be seen well from all points in the room. Ask your teacher if you can check out any electronic equipment you will use (e.g., computer, slide projector, overhead projector, VCR, or DVD player) in advance of your presentation, and practice using it in the room in which you will speak. What works on your personal computer, for example, might not on the classroom version. Be certain that you can operate it and that it is working properly. If you are using computerized materials on a CD, be sure that it is compatible with the equipment in the room.

For objects, models, posters, flip charts, and other physical aids, determine where or how you will conceal your aid both before and after you use it and how you will display it. Do you need an easel for a poster board or flip chart? Should you bring masking tape or push pins?

Do	**Don't**
1. Practice using your aids.	1. Try to "wing it" using your aids.
2. Display aids only when referring to them.	2. Leave aids in view throughout speech.
3. Stand to the side of aid as you speak.	3. Stand in front of aid as you speak.
4. Point to what is important on aid.	4. Make listeners search for what's important.
5. Maintain eye contact with listeners.	5. Deliver your speech to your aid.
6. Distribute handouts after your speech.	6. Distribute handouts during speech.
7. Limit the number of aids in your speech.	7. Become a voice-over for a slide show.

FIGURE 10.15 The Do's and Don'ts of Using Presentation Aids

As the previous paragraph indicates, it's important that you do not display your presentation aid until you are ready to use it; otherwise, it will distract your audience. When you have finished using the aid, once again cover or conceal it. Never stand directly in front of your presentation aid; rather, stand to the side of it and maintain eye contact with listeners. You want them to see both you and your presentation aid. As you refer to something on the presentation aid, point to what you are talking about: Don't leave your audience searching for what you are describing. Never deliver your speech to your presentation aid; instead, maintain eye contact with your listeners.

Do not distribute materials during your speech. If you have prepared handouts, the best time to distribute them usually comes after you speak. Don't pass around pictures or objects for listeners to examine. You want them to focus on your message, not on your presentation aid.

Try to anticipate what might go wrong. Consider how you will handle the situation if the techno-gremlins are at play, or the vase that is the centerpiece of your presentation breaks, or rain on the way to class smudges your charts. Foresight will enable you to address the situation more calmly.

Ethical Considerations for Using Presentation Aids

Presentation aids can enlighten a message, but they can also mislead listeners. As with any aspect of speaking, you make choices with your presentation aids, and should be aware of the ethical implications of those choices. Charts and graphs, for example, can be rigged so that they misrepresent reality.[18] As Figure 10.16 shows, one version of a graph suggests significant gains in the percentage of women partners in major accounting firms, while another version stresses the minimal nature of those gains.[19] Make sure your presentation aid presents the information in an appropriate context.

You must also remember to credit your sources on your presentation aids. Be sure to include this information in smaller (but still visible) letters at the bottom of any material you plan to display (see how this is done in Figure 10.16). Citing your source

FIGURE 10.16
Misleading Bar Graph and Same Material Presented So It Is Not Misleading

Women Partners in Accounting Firms

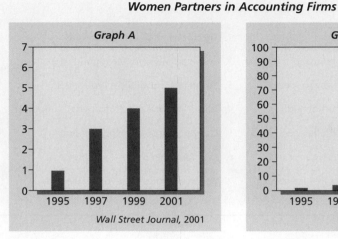
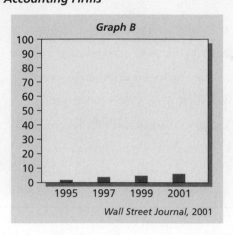

on your presentation aid verifies the information presented and reminds you to mention the source in your oral presentation.

Some of the most interesting ethical questions involve the use of film and tape materials. For example, the most famous photographer of the Civil War, Mathew Brady, rearranged bodies on the battlefield to enhance the impact of his pictures. Eighty years later, another American war photographer carefully staged the now celebrated photograph of marines planting the flag at Iwo Jima.[20] Sixty years after that, *Newsweek* placed Martha Stewart's head on a slimmer body to imply that she had lost weight during her time in prison.[21] On one hand, these famous images are fabrications: They pretend to be what they are not. On the other hand, they bring home reality more forcefully. In other words, the form of the photos may be a lie, but the lie may reveal a deeper truth. So are these photographs unethical, or are they simply artistic?

YOUR ethical VOICE   The Ethical Use of Presentation Aids

Follow these guidelines to avoid unethical use of presentation aids:

1. Be certain charts or graphs do not distort information.

2. Be aware of how the visual representation of material suggests a particular perspective.

3. Never manipulate visual images to deceive your audience.

4. If you alter an image to reveal some deeper truth, let the audience know.

5. Cite the source of your information on a presentation aid.

6. As a listener, be on guard against the power of presentation aids to trick you.

With today's technology, the potential for abuse looms ever larger. Video and audio editing easily produces illusions of reality. Consider how moviemakers depicted Forrest Gump shaking hands with Presidents Kennedy, Johnson, and Nixon. Notice how televised political commercials often use a shot from a video that catches an opponent with eyes half-shut or mouth gaping open. In movies and ads, such distortions can be easily discerned and therefore don't do much damage. In real life, however, they can be dangerous. When doctored images are passed off as actual objects or events, as when television networks or newspapers "stage" crashes to make their stories more dramatic, they can be quite deceptive.[22] We have been conditioned by experience and taught by tradition to trust the "reality" revealed by our eyes and ears. Blindly accepting the adage that "seeing is believing" can make us prey for unscrupulous manipulators.

To be an ethical communicator, you should alert your listeners to an illusion whenever you manipulate images so that they reveal your message more forcefully. You should also be able to defend your "creation" as a "better representation" of the truth. As a listener, you should develop a skeptical attitude about images and seek additional evidence if there is any question concerning their validity.

FINAL reflections   Amplifying Your Voice

When poorly conceived, designed, and used, presentation aids can overpower your voice. We once had a student who volunteered with the local rescue squad. He gave a persuasive speech urging his classmates to join the squad. After his introduction, he announced, "Now we are all going outside," where we found an emergency vehicle. While the speaker tried to tell listeners about the equipment, they were climbing in and out of the vehicle. He lost their attention completely and was never able to complete his speech.

When well conceived, designed, and used, presentation aids can empower your voice, giving nuance, power, and character to your speech. In her informative speech on the fashions typical of the three major tribes of her native Nigeria, Dolapo Olushola used an imaginative mix of a map, photographs, and fabrics to help her audience understand the cultural significance of clothing. Seeing the quality of the actual materials as well as how they created distinctive styles of dress created visual immediacy and appreciation.

Imagine yourself as a member of the audience: What kind of aid would help you as a listener? What would engage your interest, increase your understanding, and improve your retention? How could the speaker share enthusiasm for a topic in creative ways? And what would be overkill?

And always, remember the bottom line: A presentation aid should *aid* the presentation, not *be* the presentation.

THIS CHAPTER WILL HELP YOU

1 Understand how words can empower you
2 Apply standards to use language effectively
3 Learn how special techniques can magnify your voice

11 Putting Words to Work

> *Give me the right word and the right accent,
> and I will move the world.*
> —JOSEPH CONRAD

A legislator was asked how he felt about whiskey. He replied, "If, when you say whiskey, you mean the Devil's brew, the poison scourge, the bloody monster that defiles innocence, dethrones reason, creates misery and poverty—yes, literally takes the bread from the mouths of little children; if you mean the drink that topples Christian man and woman from the pinnacle of righteous, gracious living into the bottomless pit of degradation, despair, shame and helplessness, then certainly I am against it with all my power.

"But if, when you say whiskey, you mean the oil of conversation, the philosophic wine, the ale that is consumed when good fellows get together, that puts a song in their hearts and the warm glow of contentment in their eyes; if you mean Christmas cheer; if you mean the stimulating drink that puts the spring in an old gentleman's step on a frosty morning; if you mean that drink, the sale of which pours into our treasury untold millions of dollars which are used to provide tender care for our crippled children, our blind, our deaf, our dumb, pitiful, aged and infirm, to build highways, hospitals, and schools, then certainly I am in favor of it.

"That is my stand, and I will not compromise."[1]

227

The "Whiskey Speech," a legend in southern politics, was originally presented some years ago by N. S. Sweat Jr. during a heated campaign to legalize the sale of liquor-by-the-drink in Mississippi. Because about half of his constituents favored the initiative and the other half were opposed, Representative "Soggy" Sweat decided to handle the issue with humor. In the process, he provided an illustration of the magical power of words.

In this chapter, we discuss how to make this power work for you. We explain six standards you must satisfy to make language perform ethically and effectively in your speeches. We conclude by exploring some special techniques you can use to magnify the power of your voice.

What Words Can Do

Joseph Conrad's eloquent statement about the power of language at the beginning of this chapter deserves further reflection. "Give me the right word" suggests a moment in time *before* that word has been discovered. Until speakers find the right words, they will not yet have found their voice. Before speakers can "move the world"—or that small part of it that most of us address—they must first discover for themselves who they are, what they believe, and the importance of their subjects. It is words that form, frame, and express those understandings.

Words can be *windows* that reveal the world in certain ways, and words can *heat* or *chill* our feelings about what they reveal. Words can be *magnets* that draw us together or drive us apart, and words can *goad* us into action. Words can also be *rituals* that celebrate who we are. Clearly, words are vital not just in finding our voice, but in helping us express ourselves effectively (The italicized words help make our point: they are, we shall soon see, metaphors that illustrate the importance of the language choices we make).

It follows that the ability to use words effectively is one of the most important skills you will ever acquire. Most of us think in words, and the words of our language shape the way we think. For example, in most parts of the United States, we have just one word for and one conception of snow. However, in the land of the Far North, where snow is a constant phenomenon, indigenous people have devised many words to describe the different qualities of snow, and many ways to think about it.

Language, indeed, is an integral part of our cultural identity. This becomes especially evident when a language faces the possibility of extinction. D. Y. Begay, a prominent Navajo weaver and art curator, noted, "My father says when you stop speaking the language is when you stop being Navajo."[2]

What Makes the Spoken Word Special

To understand the special power of the spoken word, we must contrast it with writing.

■ **The spoken word is more spontaneous and less formal than the written word.** A journalist might write, "Eight thousand, three hundred twenty-three cases of measles have been reported in Shelby County." But a speaker, communicating the same information, would more likely say, "More than eight thousand cases of measles have been reported in Shelby County!" It's not really important that listeners know the exact number of cases. What's important is that they see the magnitude of the problem. Rounding off numbers helps listeners focus on the large picture.

■ **The spoken word is more colorful and intense than the written word.** These qualities are vital to the effectiveness of oral communication, as many studies of language intensity have demonstrated.[3] Sentence fragments and slang expressions can add to color and intensity and are more acceptable in speeches than in written discourse.

■ **Oral language is more interactive, engaging listeners directly and personally.** Speakers make much use of "us" and "we" to promote this sense of closeness with listeners. They often invite a "you are there" feeling that encourages listeners to experience the action described in the speech. Notice how Stephanie Lamb, a student at the University of Arkansas, used words to create this sense of vicarious participation at the beginning of her speech:

> We've all seen it. Driving down the road in the heat of traffic, early morning on your way to school or late afternoon during rush hour. You glance at the driver in the car beside you, and you see him talking on his cell phone and gesturing. The traffic picks up, but the driver is so absorbed in his cell phone conversation that he fails to notice that traffic has come to a stop. Wham! Another fender-bender.

Speakers often stress interactive language at the beginning of their speeches to build bridges between themselves and listeners. They may emphasize rhetorical questions that challenge listeners directly. Note how Davidson student BJ Youngerman used rhetorical questions at the beginning of his speech in defense of Wal-Mart:

> What if you could save over $900 a year on your grocery bill? What if you could save at least that much more on toys, clothes, and furniture? The fact is that if you shop at Wal-Mart on a regular basis, over the course of a year you do save that much money.

These brief examples illustrate the spontaneous, informal, intense, fragmentary, and interactive qualities of oral language. Moreover, as we discuss in detail in Chapter 12, oral language uses pauses, vocal emphasis, and pitch variations to clarify and reinforce meaning. Such resources are not available in written communication.

■ **The spoken word offers special constraints as well as opportunities.** The speaker must remain sensitive to the limitations of live audiences. Communication consultant Jerry Tarver reminds us that listeners cannot "reread" words that are spoken: Oral language must be simpler, and speakers often must repeat themselves to be understood. Speakers may need to amplify ideas more frequently with examples to ensure that listeners get the point.[4]

■ **When used skillfully, the spoken word can influence listeners in vital ways.** Words, we noted earlier, can reveal reality, heighten feelings, draw listeners together, prompt action, and celebrate cultural identity.[5] Understanding these powerful functions, and how they can be abused as well as used, is essential for both speakers and listeners. We cover this in depth later in this chapter.

Shaping Perceptions

Speakers and listeners often see subjects in different ways. The artful use of words, however, can close the gap that separates them. Consider, for example, the problem that confronted one of our students, Scott Champlin, who wanted to share an experience he'd had while serving in the military. One option was to describe the experience matter-of-factly:

Dramatic descriptions can help shape perceptions.

> While I was parachuting into Panama as part of Operation "Just Cause," I was wounded by a tracer bullet.

But Scott wished to *engage* his listeners, and those words, he thought, were flat and two-dimensional. Could he find words that would convey the *true sense* of that experience? The depiction he eventually developed allowed listeners to share his leap into danger:

> My moment came, and I jumped out into whatever destiny awaited. My parachute opened, and so did an incredible scene below me. The darkness of two o'clock in the morning was penetrated by streaks of red light marking the paths of tracer rounds as they cut their way through the night. Suddenly, I felt something hit me in the right leg with a force that spun me around like a twisted yo-yo at the end of a string.

Here the use of contrast—between "darkness" and "streaks of red light"—paints a vivid word picture. Action verbs such as *penetrated*, *cut*, and *spun* enliven the picture. The simile—"like a twisted yo-yo at the end of a string"—brings the picture into sharp focus. Scott's artful words helped his listeners see what he was talking about.

The ability of words to shape audience perceptions is particularly important when a topic is novel or unfamiliar. When astronauts walked on the moon, they had to relate what they saw to our earthbound understandings, describing what had never before been seen. The conversations from space to mission control are filled with passages such as the following:

I'm looking out here at this mountain and it's got—it looks like somebody has been out there plowing across the side of it. It's like one sort of terrace after another, right up the side.[6]

There can, however, be a negative side to this power of picturing. When listeners don't have previous experience to compare with the picture formed by the speaker's words, they can easily be deceived. For example, the so-called "moonlight and magnolias" school of Southern literature that bloomed after the Civil War offered idealized pictures of plantation life before the war. These false depictions both defended the pre-war slave society and justified post-war practices of segregation that treated the freed slaves as second-class citizens.

Such abuses of language illustrate a problem first described over four hundred years ago by the Renaissance scholar Francis Bacon. Bacon suggested that the glass in the windows of depiction can be "enchanted": the perspective may be distorted. Words can color or alter things, thus disguising or obscuring reality. This ability to shape perceptions can then become a serious ethical problem.

Arousing Feelings

Language can also arouse powerful feelings, touching listeners and changing attitudes. This power of words is used ethically when it *strengthens* sound reasoning and credible evidence. It is abused if speakers *substitute* appeals to feelings for evidence or reasoning.

To arouse emotions, language must overcome barriers of time, distance, and apathy.

Overcoming Time.   Listeners live in the present. This makes it hard to awaken feelings about events that lie in the past or distant future. But skillful speakers can use words to make the past and future come alive. Stories that recapture feelings from the past are often told at company meetings to re-create the human dimension of the business and to re-establish corporate heritage and culture. In the following story, the speaker reminds listeners of the legend of Federal Express, a pioneer in overnight delivery:

It's hard to remember that Federal Express was once just a fly-by-night dream, a crazy idea in which a few people had invested—not just their time and their money but their lives and futures. I remember one time early on when things weren't going so well. Couldn't even make the payroll that week and looked like we were going to crash. Fred [Smith, founder of the company] was in a deep funk. "What the hell," he said, and flew off to Las Vegas. The next day he flew back and his face was shining. "We're going to make it," he said. He had just won $27,000 at the blackjack table! And we made it. We met the payroll. And then things began to turn around, and Federal Express grew eventually into the giant it is today.[7]

This story enlivens the past by emphasizing the contrast of emotions—the "deep funk" versus the "shining" face. The use of lively, colloquial dialogue—"What the hell," and "We're going to make it"—re-creates the excitement and brings those feelings into the present. It would not have been as effective had the speaker simply said, "Fred was depressed, but after he got back from Las Vegas he was confident." Such a bare summary would have distanced the listener and diminished the emotional power of the scene.

Language can also make the future seem close to listeners. Because words can cross the barrier of time, both tradition and a vision of tomorrow can guide us through the present.

Overcoming Distance.   The closer anything is to us, the easier it is to develop feelings about it. But what if speakers must discuss faraway people, places, and objects? Words can act like the zoom on your computer to bring such subjects closer to your audience.

Beth Tidmore, our student who won the U.S. Junior Olympics air rifle event at Colorado Springs, demonstrated a special gift for overcoming distance between herself and her listeners. When she wanted to share her feelings about her shooting experiences, she concentrated on sensory details of touch and smell. "My friends," she said, "don't know what it's like to feel the cold, smooth wood of the cheekpiece against your face. And they don't know the rich smell of Hoppe's No. 9 [oil] when you're cleaning your rifle." Through such sensory descriptions, she was able to communicate with listeners who themselves were far removed from such experiences.

Beth was even more effective when she appealed to her listeners to become involved in Special Olympics events. To move their feelings, Beth used a technique that—when successful—collapses the distance between listeners and subjects. This technique, the vicarious experience narrative described earlier in Chapter 8, *invites listeners to imagine themselves participating in the action advocated by the speaker.*

> I've had so many great experiences, but these are hard to describe without overworking words like "fulfilling" and "rewarding." So I'm going to let you experience it for yourself. I want everybody to pack your bags—we're going to the Special Olympics summer games in Georgia!

Beth then became a tour guide for this imaginary trip, walking listeners through the moments that would move them in dramatic ways. Again, she had effectively bridged the distance between her subject and her audience.

Overcoming Apathy.   Modern audiences are beset with an endless barrage of information, persuasion, and entertainment. As a result, many of us become jaded—we may even develop a *resistance* to communication and turn away from appeals to our feelings.

Sally Duncan found an especially poignant way to overcome such apathy. Interestingly, it worked because of incompetent language usage. Sally began her informative speech by projecting a picture of her grandmother on the screen behind the lectern. She described her as a cultured, elegant woman who had a master's degree, had taught English for years, and had taken Sally to art museums and the theater. "Now," she said, "let me read my last letter from Nanny."

> Dear Sally. I am finally around to answer your last. You have to look over me. Ha. I am so sorry to when you called Sunday why didn't you remind me. Steph had us all so upset leaving and not telling no she was going back but we have a good snow ha and Kathy can't drive on ice so I never get a pretty card but they have a thing to see through an envelope. I haven't got any in the bank until I get my homestead check so I'm just sending this. Ha. When you was talking on the phone Cathy had Ben and got my groceries and I had to unlock the door. I forgot to say hold and I don't have Claudette's number so forgive me for being

so silly. Ha. Nara said to tell you she isn't doing no good well one is doing pretty good and my eyes. Love, Nanny.

Sally paused for a long moment, and then said, "My Nanny has Alzheimer's." We were riveted as she went on to describe the disease and how to cope with loved ones who have it.

The role of words in arousing feeling is also underscored by the contrast between denotative and connotative forms of meaning. The **denotative meaning** of a word is its dictionary definition or generally agreed-on objective usage. For example, the denotative definition of *alcohol* is "a colorless, volatile, flammable liquid, obtained by the fermentation of sugars or starches, which is widely used as a solvent, drug base, explosive, or intoxicating beverage."[8] How different this definition is from the two connotative definitions offered in this chapter's opening example! **Connotative meaning** invests a subject with the speaker's personal associations and emotions. Thus, the "intoxicating beverage" is no longer just a chemical substance but rather is "the poison scourge" or "the oil of conversation." Connotative language intensifies feelings; denotative language encourages detachment.

Bringing Listeners Together

In many situations, individual action is not enough. It may take many people working together to get things done, and language can bring them together. Barack Obama's campaign for the presidency depended very much on his ability to bring together many diverse audiences in support of his bid. Thus in his celebrated Speech on Race, delivered at a critical time in the campaign, he appealed directly for this togetherness:

> I believe deeply that we cannot solve the challenges of our time unless we solve them together—unless we perfect our union by understanding that we may have different stories, but we hold common hopes; that we may not look the same and we may not have come from the same place, but we all want to move in the same direction—towards a better future for our children and our grandchildren.[9]

Note the emphasis on "we" and "our." Words can also bring people together in times of grief. On April 16, 2007, a lone gunman killed 32 people at Virginia Tech University before turning his gun on himself. At a memorial ceremony the next day, the faculty and student body met to find what comfort they could during those tragic days. The honor of closing the ceremony fell to Nikki Giovanni, an acclaimed poet who was also a University Distinguished Professor. In her remarks, Giovanni combined the power of poetry and prose to bring her listeners together:

Poet and professor Nikki Giovanni's eloquent language brought listeners together.

> We are Virginia Tech.
> We are strong enough to stand tall tearlessly;
> We are brave enough to bend to cry

▶ **denotative meaning** The dictionary definition or objective meaning of a word.

▶ **connotative meaning** The emotional, subjective, personal meaning that certain words can evoke in listeners.

And sad enough to know we must laugh again.
We are Virginia Tech.
. . . We will continue to invent the future through our blood and tears,
through all this sadness. . . . We will prevail![10]

Note again the emphasis on "We," the great pronoun of inclusion. Note also how Giovanni combines opposites to create a sense of unity: sadness and laughter, "stand tall tearlessly" and "bend to cry," proposing that a promising future will grow out of the tragic past—that the past and future will come together just as her listeners are brought together by her words.

Although words can unite people, they can also drive them apart. Name calling, exclusionary language, and unsupported accusations can be notorious dividers.

Prompting Listeners to Take Action

Even when your listeners share an identity, they still may not be ready to act. What barriers might stand in their way? For one thing, they may not be convinced of the soundness of your proposal. They may not trust you, or they may not think they can do anything about a problem. They may also not be ready to invest the energy or take the risk that action demands.

Your language must convince listeners that action is necessary, that your ideas are sound, and that success is possible. In her speech urging students to act to improve off-campus housing conditions (see Appendix B), Anna Aley painted vivid word-pictures of deplorable off-campus housing. She supported these descriptions with both factual examples and her personal experiences. She also reminded listeners that if they acted together, they could bring about change:

> What can one student do to change the practices of numerous Manhattan land-lords? Nothing, if that student is alone. But just think of what we could accomplish if we got all 13,600 off-campus students involved in this issue! Think what we could accomplish if we got even a fraction of those students involved!

Anna then proposed specific actions that did not call for great effort or risk. In short, she made commitment as easy as possible. She concluded with an appeal to action:

> Kansas State students have been putting up with substandard living conditions for too long. It's time we finally got together to do something about this prob-lem. Join the Off-Campus Association. Sign my petition. Let's send a message to these slumlords that we're not going to put up with this any more. We don't have to live in slums.

Anna's words expressed both her indignation and the urgency of the problem. Her references to time—"too long" and "it's time"—called for immediate action. Her final appeals to join the association and sign the petition were expressed in short sentences that packed a lot of punch. Her repetition of "slumlords" and "slums" motivated her listeners to transform their indignation into action.

Anna also illustrated another language strategy that is important when you want to move people to action: the ability to depict dramas showing what is at stake and what roles listeners should take.[11] Such scenarios draw clear lines between right and wrong. Be careful, however, not to go overboard with such techniques. Ethical communication requires that you maintain respect for all involved in conflict. As both speaker and listener, be wary of melodramas that offer stark contrasts between good and evil. Such depictions often distort reality.

Celebrating Shared Values

It is important for people to remind themselves occasionally of the values that tie them together. To celebrate these values is to strengthen them and the communities that share them. Often these celebrations take place during ceremonies such as those that celebrate Memorial Day, Martin Luther King's birthday, or presidential inaugurals.

Aristotle noted over two thousand years ago that spoken communication serving this vital function emphasizes the *image*. When images work well, they paint vivid word-pictures that show us our values in action. They often tell stories that teach us to treasure our traditions. Such language is colorful, concrete, and graphic—it appeals to the senses. Note how President Reagan used such language in his second inaugural address to call up memories of heroes and to strengthen the image of the American heritage:

> Hear again the echoes of our past. A general falls to his knees in the harsh snow of Valley Forge; a lonely President paces the darkened halls and ponders his struggle to preserve the Union; the men of the Alamo call out encouragement to each other; a settler pushes West and sings a song, and the song echoes out forever and fills the unknowing air.
> It is the American Sound. It is hopeful, big-hearted, idealistic—daring, decent and fair. That's our heritage. That's our song.[12]

You too can use the power of words to evoke the past as you find your own voice. The right words and phrases, used in the right places, can create a lasting picture.

The power of language is great, ranging from shaping perceptions to revitalizing group culture. How can you use words in ways that will help you both find your voice and express it in powerful ways? We turn now to the standards you must apply as you seek the answers to that question.

YOUR ethical VOICE   Managing Powerful Language

To use the power of words in ethical ways, follow these guidelines:

1. Avoid depictions that distort reality: Let your words illuminate the subject, not blind the listener.

2. Use words to support sound reasoning, not substitute for it.

3. Use language to empower both past traditions and visions of the future.

4. Use images to renew appreciation of shared values.

5. Use language to strengthen the ties of community, not divide people.

6. Use language to overcome inertia and inspire listeners to action.

7. Be careful about melodramatic language that reduces complex issues and the people in disputes into good versus evil.

8. Avoid language that degrades people, especially animal metaphors.

The Six C's of Language Use

For words to work for you, they must meet certain standards: clarity, color, concreteness, correctness, conciseness, and cultural sensitivity. We call these the six C's of oral language usage.

Clarity

Clarity is the first standard, because if your words are not clear, listeners cannot understand your meaning. To be clear, you must yourself understand what you want to say. Next, you must find words that convey your ideas as precisely and as simply as possible. The standard of clarity is met when something closely approximating the idea you intend is reproduced in the minds of listeners.

One factor that impairs clarity is the use of **jargon**, the technical language that is specific to a profession. If you use jargon before an audience that doesn't share that technical vocabulary, you may not be understood. For example, as he forecasted an event in 2008 that would devastate so much of Iowa, Brian Pierce, a meteorologist with the National Weather Service in Davenport, used the following words: "We are seeing a historic hydrological event taking place with unprecedented river levels occurring."[13] Mr. Pierce would have communicated a lot more clearly to a lot more people had he simply said, "We are in for one heckuva flood."

Speakers who fall into the jargon trap are so used to using technical language that they forget that others may not grasp it. It does not occur to them that they must translate the jargon into lay language to be understood by general audiences.

A similar problem is using words that are needlessly overblown and pretentious. A notorious example occurred when signmakers wanted to tell tourists how to leave the Barnum museum. Rather than drawing an arrow with the word Exit above it, they wrote "To the Egress." There's no telling how many visitors left the museum by mistake, thinking that they were going to see that rare creature—a living, breathing "Egress."

Sometimes speakers may deliberately avoid clarity—because the truth may hurt. Such efforts to soften and obscure the truth are called **euphemisms**. At moments, these efforts may be rather lighthearted, as when a sports commentator, speaking of the quarterback on a football team, said, "He has ball security issues" when he really meant, "This guy fumbles a lot." On a slightly more serious note, politicians in Tennessee agreed to pass a new hospital tax, as long as it wasn't called a "tax." Instead, it would have to be called a "coverage fee."[14]

At its worst, such language degenerates into **doublespeak**, the use of words to deliberately befuddle listeners and hide unpleasant truths. The language of doublespeak points listeners in a direction opposite from the reality of a situation. The *New York Times* charged that the Bush administration developed what they call *ecospeak* (an apparent variation of *doublespeak*) to disguise pro-business and anti-environmental initiatives:

> Mr. Bush . . . may fairly be said to have become the master of the ostensibly ecofriendly sound bite. . . . "Healthy Forests," for instance, describes an initiative aimed mainly at benefiting the timber industry rather than the communities threatened by fire. [In another case] Mr. Bush's purpose was to defend his controversial decision in August to rewrite the Clean Air Act in ways that spared power companies the expense of making investments in pollution controls. . . . His basic argument was that the rules thwarted modernization and economic growth . . . and that his own initiative—dubbed "Clear Skies,"

▶ **jargon** Technical language related to a specific field that may be incomprehensible to a general audience.

▶ **euphemism** Words that soften or evade the truth of a situation.

▶ **doublespeak** Words that point in the direction opposite from the reality they supposedly describe.

When they say:	What they often mean is:
Marital discord	Spouse beating
Downsizing	Firing
Making a salary adjustment	Cutting your pay
Failed to fulfill wellness potential	Died
Chronologically experienced citizen	Old codger
Initial and pass on	Let's spread the blame
Friendly fire	We killed our own people
Collateral damage	We killed innocent people

FIGURE 11.1
Doublespeak

in the come-hither nomenclature favored by the White House—would achieve equal results at lower cost.[15]

How can you avoid such violations of clarity and ethics? One way is through **amplification**, which extends the time listeners have for contemplating an idea and helps them bring it into sharper focus. You amplify an idea by defining it, repeating it, rephrasing it, offering examples of it, and contrasting it with more familiar and concrete subjects. In effect, you tell listeners something and then expand what you have just said. Bill Gates used amplification effectively in a speech on reforming high school education, illustrating how definition and contrast especially can clarify an idea:

> America's high schools are obsolete. By obsolete, I don't just mean that
> our high schools are broken, flawed, and underfunded—though a case could be
> made for every one of those points.
> By obsolete, I mean that our high schools—even when they're
> working exactly as designed—cannot teach our kids what they need to
> know today.
> Training the workforce of tomorrow with the high schools of today
> is like trying to teach kids about today's computers on a
> 50-year-old mainframe. It's the wrong tool for the times.[16]

Color

Color refers to the emotional intensity or vividness of language. Colorful words are memorable because they stand out in our minds, along with the ideas they convey. Colorful language paints striking pictures for listeners that linger in the mind. In her speech urging the purchase of hybrid cars, Davidson student Alexandra McArthur framed a colorful conclusion based on a **neologism**, an invented word that combines previous words in a striking new expression. In this case, Alexandra created her new word by combining "hybrid" and "hubris":

> If you do end up buying a hybrid, as you drive around town looking trendy,
> cruising past the gas stations, you may start feeling pretty good about yourself

Colorful language and a lively presentation bring speeches to life.

▶ **amplification** The art of developing ideas by restating them in a speech.

▶ **neologism** An invented word that combines previous words in a striking new expression.

and talking about your car any chance you get. This new form of pride, commonly called *hybris*, may be annoying to your friends but is nothing incurable. I'm sure they will forgive you when they get their first hybrid.

One very special type of colorful language is **slang**, expressions that arise out of common, ordinary, everyday usage. You may have been advised not to use slang, that it is coarse, even vulgar, and that it epitomizes "bad" English. But according to general semanticist S. I. Hayakawa, slang can also be "the poetry of everyday life." Or, as the poet Carl Sandburg noted, slang is "language that rolls up its sleeves, spits on its hands, and goes to work."

Slang has its use in speeches: It can add vigor to your message and be a source of identification between you and listeners. But use it with caution. Slang is inappropriate on formal occasions when a high level of decorum is called for. Moreover, you must be certain that your audience will understand your slang expressions. You should also avoid using ethnic slang or other words that your audience might find offensive. Finally, slang should be used sparingly—to emphasize a point or add a dash of humor and color. It should supplement standard English usage in your speech, not replace it.

Using colorful language makes a speech interesting and can enhance your ethos, adding to the impression that you are a competent, likable person.

Concreteness

It is almost impossible to discuss any significant topic without using some abstract words. However, if you use language that is overly abstract, your audience may lose interest. Moreover, because abstract language is more ambiguous than concrete language, a speech full of abstractions invites misunderstanding. Consider Figure 11.2, which illustrates movement along a continuum from abstract to concrete terms.

The more concrete your language, the more pictorial and precise the information you convey. Concrete words are also easier for listeners to remember. Your language should be as concrete as the subject permits.

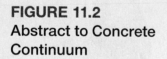

**FIGURE 11.2
Abstract to Concrete
Continuum**

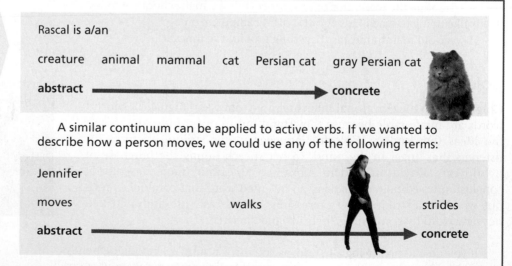

Rascal is a/an

creature   animal   mammal   cat   Persian cat   gray Persian cat

abstract ➤ **concrete**

A similar continuum can be applied to active verbs. If we wanted to describe how a person moves, we could use any of the following terms:

Jennifer

moves   walks   strides

abstract ➤ **concrete**

▶ **slang**   The language of the street.

Correctness

Nothing can damage your credibility more than the misuse of language. Glaring mistakes in grammar can make you seem uneducated and even ignorant. While touting his education plan, one prominent politician told listeners that the most important consideration should be, "Is your children learning?" Hopefully they would not miss the lesson on subject-verb agreement! Other common grammatical errors that make listeners cringe are listed in Figure 11.3.

Mistakes in word selection can be as damaging as mistakes in grammar. Occasionally, beginning speakers, wanting to impress people with the size of their vocabulary, get caught up in what we call the "thesaurus syndrome." They will look up a simple word to find a synonym that sounds more impressive. What they may not realize is that the words shown as synonyms often have slightly different meanings. For example, the words *disorganize* and *derange* are sometimes listed as synonyms. But if you refer to a disorganized person as "deranged," that person's reaction could be interesting.

People often err when using words that sound similar. Such confusions are called **malapropisms**, after Mrs. Malaprop, a character in an eighteenth-century play by Richard Sheridan. She would say, "He is the very *pineapple* of politeness," when she

---

FIGURE 11.3
Correcting Grammatical Errors

1. Using the wrong tense or verb form:
   Wrong: He *done* us a big favor.
   Right: He *did* us a big favor.

2. Lack of agreement between subject and verb:
   Wrong: *Is* your students giving speeches?
   Right: *Are* your students giving speeches?

3. Using the wrong word
   Wrong: *Caricature* is the most important factor in choosing a mate.
   Right: *Character* is the most important factor in choosing a mate.

4. Lack of agreement between a pronoun and its antecedent:
   Wrong: A hyperactive *person* will work *themselves* to death.
   Right: Hyperactive *people* will work *themselves* to death.

   or

   A hyperactive *woman* will work *herself* to death.

5. Improper type of pronoun used as subject:
   Wrong: *Him* and *me* decided to go to the library.
   Right: *He* and *I* decided to go to the library.

6. Improper type of pronoun used as object:
   Wrong: The speaker's lack of information dismayed my students and *I*.
   Right: The speaker's lack of information dismayed my students and *me*.

7. Double negative:
   Wrong: I *don't never* get bad grades on my speeches.
   Right: I *never* get bad grades on my speeches.

▶ **malapropisms** Language errors that occur when a word is confused with another word that sounds like it.

meant *pinnacle*. A prominent baseball player, trying to explain why he had forgotten an appointment for an interview, said "I must have had *ambrosia*" (which probably caused his *amnesia,* which is what he apparently meant). Archie Bunker, in the classic TV show *All in the Family*, was prone to malapropisms, such as "Don't let your imagination run *rancid*" when he meant *rampant*. William J. Crocker of Armidale College in New South Wales, Australia, collected the following malapropisms from his students:

> A speaker can add interest to his talk with an *antidote*. [anecdote]
>
> Disagreements can arise from an unintended *conception*. [Indeed they can! Inference would work better]
>
> The speaker hopes to arouse *apathy* in his audience. [sympathy? empathy?]
>
> Good language can be reinforced by good *gestation*. [gestures]
>
> The speaker can use either an inductive or a *seductive* approach. [deductive][17]

Students, ballplayers, and fictional characters are not the only ones who make such blunders. Elected officials are also not above an occasional malapropism. One former United States senator declared that he would oppose to his last ounce of energy any effort to build a "nuclear waste *suppository*" [repository] in his state (sounds like an incredible new cure for constipation!). A long-gone but not forgotten Chicago mayor once commented that he did not believe "in casting *asparagus* [aspersions] on his opponents." And the Speaker of the Texas legislature once acknowledged an award by saying, "I am filled with *humidity*" (perhaps he meant moist hot air as well as humility).

The lesson is clear. To avoid being unintentionally humorous, use a current dictionary to check the meaning of any word you feel uncertain about. For additional help, refer to the Web site developed by Professor Paul Brians of Washington State University to help students avoid common errors of usage (www.wsu.edu/~brians/errors/index.html).

Conciseness

In discussing clarity, we talked about the importance of amplification in speeches to expand understanding. Although it may seem contradictory, you must also be concise, even while you are amplifying your ideas. You must make your points quickly and efficiently.

Simplicity and directness help you be concise. Thomas Jefferson once said, "The most valuable of all talents is that of never using two words when one will do." Abraham Lincoln was similarly concise as he criticized the verbosity of another speaker: "He can compress the most words into the smallest idea of any man I know."

One way you can achieve conciseness is by using **maxims**, compact sayings that encapsulate beliefs. To reinforce his point that we need to actively (and audibly) confront the problems of racism, sexism, and homophobia, Haven Cockerham, vice president of human resources for Detroit Edison, came up with this striking maxim: "Sometimes silence isn't golden—just yellow."[18]

Maxims attract mass-media attention during demonstrations. When used on signs, they can be picked up as signature statements for movements or campaigns. Their brevity and dramatic impact make them well suited to display on television's evening news.

A caution is in order about using maxims: They should not be substituted for a carefully designed and well-supported argument. However, once you have developed

▶ **maxims**   Brief and particularly apt sayings.

a responsible and substantive speech, consider whether you might use maxims to reinforce your message.

Cultural Sensitivity

Because words can either lift and unite or wound and hurt your audience, you must exercise **cultural sensitivity** in your choice of language. Looking back into the history of human communication, you will find little about cultural sensitivity. The ancient Greeks, for example, worried only about speaking to other male Athenians who were "free men" and citizens. Today, with our increasing emphasis on lifestyles, racial diversity, and the pursuit of gender equity, cultural sensitivity becomes an important standard for effective language usage.

Cultural sensitivity requires adaptation and respect.

John Duesler, president of the Valley Swim Club in Philadelphia, might have profited from this advice. In the summer of 2009, Duesler's club accepted money from an inner-city day camp so that its children could swim once a week at the club. When the mostly minority group of children showed up, however, some club members apparently objected and the swimming privileges were revoked. Duesler's explanation? "There was concern that a lot of kids would change the complexion . . . and the atmosphere of the club." Later he admitted, "That was a terrible choice of words."[19]

A lack of cultural sensitivity almost always has negative consequences. At best, audience members may be mildly offended; at worst, they will be irate enough to reject both you and your message. Cultural sensitivity begins with being attuned to the diversity of your audience and careful about the words you choose. Don't be like the politician who singled out some audience members in wheelchairs for special praise. After lauding their accomplishments, he said, "Now, will you all stand and be recognized?"

Although you must make some generalizations about your audience, avoid getting caught up in stereotypes that suggest that one group is inferior in any way to another. Stay away from racial, ethnic, religious, or gender-based humor, and avoid any expressions that might be interpreted as racist or sexist.

How Special Techniques Can Magnify Your Voice

There are critical moments in a speech—often at the beginning, ending, or as arguments reach their conclusions—when you want your words to be most effective. At these moments, you can sometimes call on special techniques to magnify the power of your emerging voice.

The branch of communication study that deals with identifying, understanding, and utilizing these techniques is called *rhetorical style*. Over the centuries, many such techniques have been identified; they seem to be grounded in our nature and to have evolved perhaps to meet basic human needs for effective communication. Here we discuss three broad categories of techniques that are especially useful for public speaking: *figurative language*; techniques that alter the customary *order* of words; and techniques that exploit the *sounds* of words for special effects.

▶ **cultural sensitivity**   The respectful appreciation of diversity within an audience.

Using Figurative Language

Figurative language uses words in unusual ways to create fresh understandings of the subjects of communication. We focus here on seven forms of figurative language that may be especially useful for public speakers: metaphor, enduring metaphor, simile, synecdoche, personification, culturetype, and ideograph.

Metaphor. As we noted in Chapter 8, drawing comparisons is a fundamental way in which our minds work to understand unfamiliar or abstract ideas. A **metaphor** offers a brief, concentrated form of comparison that is implied, unexpected, and sometimes even startling. It connects elements of experience that are not usually related. When you use a metaphor, you pull a rabbit out of a hat. Having read that, your first reaction might be, "Wait a minute, words are not rabbits and language is not a hat!" But when a metaphor works, the listener's next reaction is, "Oooh, I see what you mean!" Good metaphors reveal unexpected similarities in striking ways. They also can add color and concreteness to your message.

Metaphors, as Aristotle once noted, may be our most useful and versatile stylistic tool. They can be especially helpful in introductions and conclusions. At the beginnings of speeches, metaphors can offer an overall frame of understanding in which a topic can develop. Note how Antoinette M. Bailey, president of the Boeing-McDonnell Foundation, used a wave metaphor to open a speech presented to the International Women in Aviation Conference:

> Suppose we have gone down to the beach on a quiet day. We are standing in the water, admiring the view. Suddenly, a speedboat zooms by at full throttle. Seconds later, we are struck by a powerful wave. This is a bow wave, and it can knock you off your feet if you aren't prepared for it. A very large and fast-moving bow wave is just now beginning to hit the aerospace industry. This morning I want to talk about what we, as an industry, and we, as women, should do to prepare for it.[20]

Eloquent language can intensify our feelings about subjects.

In a similar vein, concluding metaphors can offer a final frame of understanding that interprets the meaning of a speech for its listeners. Student speaker Alexandra McArthur used the following metaphor as she concluded a speech warning her audience not to accept at face value the pictures of foreign countries painted in travel brochures: "Tourism may be an economic Band-Aid for the gaping wound of poverty." When Martin Luther King Jr. spoke to striking sanitation workers in Memphis the night before he was assassinated, he talked of the "spiritual journey" that his listeners had traveled. He ended his speech by saying that he had climbed the mountain ahead of them—that he had "seen the Promised Land." These metaphors of the journey and the mountain lifted his listeners and allowed them to share his vision, just as he had earlier shared his "dream" with them in his famous "I Have a Dream" oration. More than just communicating in a superficial way, such metaphors may reveal and share how the speaker perceives the world.

Because metaphors can be so powerful, you should select them carefully and use them with restraint. First, *the gravity of the metaphor must match the seriousness of your subject.* Just as you would not typically wear formal attire to a basketball game, you should not use certain metaphors to express certain subjects. If you used Dr. King's mountaintop image to express your overview of the can recycling industry in a speech to a general audience, the effect might be more ludicrous than persuasive.

▶ **figurative language** Words used in surprising and unusual ways that magnify the power of their meaning.

▶ **metaphor** Brief, concentrated form of implied comparison. Often connects subjects that are not usually related in order to create a surprising perspective.

Second, *mixing metaphors by combining images that don't fit together can confuse listeners and lower their estimation of your competence.* The politician who attacked an opponent saying, "You can't take the high horse and then claim the low road," mixed his metaphors.

Third, *you also should avoid trite metaphors,* such as "that person [or idea or practice] is so cool" or "I was on an emotional roller coaster." Overuse has turned these metaphors into clichés that no longer have any impact. Not only are they ineffective, but using them may again damage your ethos. Tired comparisons suggest a dull mind.

As useful and powerful as metaphor may be, it can also be quite dangerous. Certain animal metaphors, for example, can project and justify dehumanizing, scornful attitudes about groups of people. Consider this recent statement from the lieutenant governor of South Carolina about government assistance to the poor:

> My grandmother was not a highly educated woman, but she told me as a small child to quit feeding stray animals. You know why? Because they breed! You're facilitating the problem if you give an animal or a person ample food supply. They will reproduce, especially ones that don't think too much further than that.[21]

Enduring Metaphor. One special group of metaphors taps into shared experience that persists across time and that crosses many cultural boundaries. These **enduring metaphors**—or "archetypal metaphors" as they are sometimes called—are especially popular in speeches, perhaps because they invoke experience that has great meaning and that can bring people together. They connect their particular, timebound subjects with timeless themes, such as light and darkness, storms, the sea, disease, and the family. A brief look at three of these metaphors demonstrates their potential power to magnify meaning.[22]

Light and Darkness. From the beginning of time, people have made negative associations with darkness. The dark is cold, unfriendly, and dangerous. On the other hand, light brings warmth and safety. It restores control. When speakers use the light–darkness metaphor, they usually equate problems or bad times with darkness and solutions or recovery with light. The speaker's proposal may offer the "dawn," a "candle to light our way," or a "beacon of hope."

Storms and the Sea. The storm metaphor can be used to describe serious problems. Often the storm occurs at sea—a dangerous place under the best of conditions. When political problems are the focus of the speech, the "captain" who "steers the ship of state" can reassure us with his programs or principles—and make them seem very attractive in the process. In his first inaugural address, George W. Bush said that "through much of the last century, America's faith in freedom and democracy was a rock in a raging sea."[23]

Light and darkensss and storms and the sea are enduring metaphors.

The Family. Family metaphors express the dream of a close, loving relationship among people through such images as "the family of humanity."[24] As he asked listeners to transcend race, Barack Obama appealed to such images: "Let us be our brother's keeper, Scripture tells us. Let us be our sister's keeper."[25] Such metaphors can be especially useful when listeners may feel alienated from each

▶ **enduring metaphors** Metaphors of unusual power and popularity that are based on experience that lasts across time and that crosses many cultural boundaries.

other and from their surroundings. In such situations, family metaphors can be a powerful force to bring listeners together and to effect identification. Wade Steck demonstrated the potential of such metaphors as he was describing his experiences at the University of Memphis Frosh Camp Program, his introduction to college life:

> When I got to Frosh Camp, they made me feel at home. First thing they did was to break us into "families" of ten to twelve people who would share the same cabin for those few days. Each "family" had its counselors, carefully selected juniors and seniors who were really called your "mom" and "dad." . . . The thing I liked most were the Fireside Chats. At night under the stars, watching the logs burn . . ., people would just relax and talk. I discovered that many of those in my family shared my concerns and anxieties.

Similarly, the *disease* metaphor pictures our problems as illness and offers solutions in the form of cures.[26] Metaphors of *war and peace* can frame conflict situations and our quest for their resolution.[27] The *building* metaphor, as when we talk about "laying the foundation" for the future, emphasizes our impulse to shape and control the conditions of our lives. And *spatial* metaphors often reflect striving upward and moving forward toward goals.[28]

Similes. A **simile** is a variation of metaphor that warns listeners that a comparison is coming. Words such as *like* or *as* function as signals that soften the impact of the expression. The result is to offer a more controlled form of figurative language in which the speaker guides the comparison in order to create certain planned effects. One such effect is to help listeners imagine things that are far removed from their experience. Remember Scott Champlin's words, "a force that spun me around *like* a twisted yo-yo at the end of a string"? Most of us, we hope, will never be hit by a tracer bullet while parachuting, but we may well have played with a yo-yo as children. Helped by the simile, we can imagine the experience.

A second intended effect is to heighten interest in and familiarize such experience. A particularly engaging example occurred in a speech by Davidson student Jessica Bradshaw concerning how Dr. Seuss composed the children's classic, *The Cat in the Hat*. Jess quoted Dr. Seuss as follows:

> The method I used is [like] the method you see when you sit down to make apple strudel without the strudel. . . . You take your limited, uninteresting ingredients and day and night, month after month, you mix them up into

FINDING YOUR

voice   Enduring Metaphors in Contemporary Communication

Look for examples of enduring metaphors as used in contemporary public communication (speeches, editorials, advertising, visual, and televisual communication). Why do you think they are used in these ways? Are they effective? Might they connect with motivation as it is explained in Chapter 5? How so?

▶ **simile**   A language tool that clarifies something abstract by comparing it with something concrete; usually introduced by "as" or "like."

thousands of combinations. You bake a batch. You taste it. Then you hurl it out the window. Until finally one night, when it is darkest just before dawn, a plausible strudel-less strudel begins to take shape before your eyes![29]

Simile can also be used to express feelings. Notice how one critic used it to focus her feelings about a proposal to send astronauts on an expedition to Mars: "Spending billions in outer space is *like* buying a new Lexus when the fridge is empty and the roof is leaking."[30]

Synecdoche.   One of the great classic forms of figuration, **synecdoche** (sin-eck'-duh-key), is grounded in an ancient tendency of our nature: representing a subject by focusing on a vivid part of it or on something closely associated with it. Thus, the nautical expression "all hands on deck" represents a group of people by focusing on a useful part of them. "The pen is mightier than the sword" compares two great human activities, communication and warfare, by focusing on instruments traditionally associated with them.

Memphis student Sandra Baltz explained how three cultures interact harmoniously in her life by focusing on a food synecdoche that offered a simple, colorful, and concrete illustration of her point:

> In all, I must say that being exposed to three very different cultures—Latin, Arabic, and American—has been rewarding for me and has made a difference even in the music I enjoy and the food I eat. It is not unusual in my house to sit down to a meal made up of stuffed grape leaves and refried beans and all topped off with apple pie for dessert. [See the rest of her speech in Appendix B].

Synecdoche can be easily abused. If we focus on one feature of a subject and ignore others, we may distort the picture we present about the subject and cause listeners to draw warped or incomplete conclusions. Thus "all hands on deck" may cause us to miss a larger picture—that these are human beings who also have hearts and heads, thoughts and feelings, and who deserve to be treated as such.

Personification.   One kind of figurative speech, **personification**, treats inanimate subjects, such as ideas or institutions, as though they had human form or feeling. The Chinese students who demonstrated for freedom in Tiananmen Square carried a statue they called the "Goddess of Liberty." They were borrowing a personification that has long been used in the Western world: the representation of liberty as a woman.[31] When those students then had to confront tanks, and their oppressors destroyed the symbol of liberty, it was easy for many, living thousands of miles away in another culture, to feel even more angry over their fate. Personification makes it easier to arouse feelings about people and values that might otherwise seem abstract and distant.

Culturetypes.   **Culturetypes**, sometimes stated in the form of metaphor, express the values, identity, and goals of a particular group and time.[32] In 1960, John F. Kennedy dramatized his presidential campaign by inviting Americans to explore with him "new frontiers" of national possibility. That metaphor worked well in American culture, but it probably would not have made much sense in other countries. For Americans, the frontier is a unique symbol that stands for freedom, challenge, and opportunity.

▶ **synecdoche**   Represents a subject by focusing on a vivid part of it or on something clearly associated with it.

▶ **personification**   A figure of speech in which nonhuman or abstract subjects are given human qualities.

▶ **culturetypes**   Terms that express the values and goals of a group's culture.

Some culturetypes include what rhetorical critic Richard Weaver once described as "god and devil terms."[33] Weaver suggested that *progress* has been a primary "god term" of American culture. People often seem willing to follow that word as though it were some kind of divine summons. Tell us to do something in the name of "progress," and many will feel prompted to respond. Other terms, such as *science*, *modern*, and *efficient*, are similarly powerful, Weaver argued, because they seem rooted in American values. If something is "scientific," we are apt to listen respectfully. If something is "modern," many of us think it is better, probably because it has benefited from "progress." If something is "efficient," many Americans will more often select it over options that are perhaps more ethical or beautiful. On the other hand, words like *terrorist* and *terrorism* are "devil terms." They can make a person, group, or action seem repulsive and threatening.

Culturetypes can change over time: In recent years, words like *natural*, *communication*, and *environment* have become more compelling; *liberalism* and *pollution*, if not devil terms, seem increasingly undesirable to many people.

Ideographs. Communication scholar Michael Calvin McGee identified an especially potent group of culturetypes that he called **ideographs**. These words express in a concentrated way a country's basic political values.[34] McGee suggested that words like *freedom*, *liberty*, and *democracy* are important because they are shorthand expressions of political identity. It is inconceivable to us that other nations might not wish to have a "democratic" form of government or that they might not prize "liberty" over every other value. Expressions such as "*freedom* fighters" and "*democracy* in action" have unusual power for us because they utilize ideographs.

As an audience, we can be especially vulnerable to such language, and it can be dangerous. After all, one person's "freedom fighter" can be another person's "terrorist." We must look behind such glittering generalities to inspect the agendas they may hide. You may recall that in Chapter 4 we discussed "trigger words" that can trigger our emotional responses and short-circuit reflection. Ideographs and culturetypes can function as widely shared, cultural trigger words. They are capable of honorable work: They can magnify the appeal of sound arguments, remind us of our heritage, and suggest that we must be true to our values. But the potential for abusing such words in unethical communication is considerable. You must prove that they apply legitimately to your topic. As a speaker, use them sparingly, and as a listener, inspect them carefully.

To develop a healthy resistance to such words, we should respond to them with a series of critical questions:

1. *Is this really what it claims to be?* For example, does the development of increasingly more powerful weapons of mass destruction really represent "progress"? Are "freedom fighters" actually thugs?

FINDING YOUR

voice   The Culturetypes of Our Time

What words would you nominate as culturetypes in contemporary society? Remember to look for "devil" as well as "god" terms. Find examples of how these words are actually used in public communication. What work do they do? Are there any ethical problems with these uses?

▶ **ideographs** Compact expressions of a group's basic political faith.

2. *Are those who make these claims legitimate sources of information?* For example, are those who advance the "science" of cryonics, the preservation of bodies by freezing them in hopes of discovering how to restore life to them on some future occasion, really "scientists"? Or are they simply exploiters?

3. *Do these claims reflect a proper hierarchy of values?* For example, lopping off the top of a mountain to strip-mine coal may be a highly "efficient" form of mining, but should we be featuring efficiency here? Could protection of the environment be a more important consideration?

4. *What kinds of actions are these words urging me to endorse or undertake?* For example, should I be asked to support and even die for "democracy" in a nation whose citizens may prefer some other form of government?

Changing the Order of Words

We grow accustomed to words falling into certain patterns in sentences. Strategic changes in this customary order of words violate these expectations and call attention to themselves. Why, we ask ourselves, has the speaker made these changes? What do they signify?

Antithesis, inversion, and *parallel construction* are techniques that change the way words are ordered in messages. Their primary functions are to magnify the speaker as a leader and to enhance appeals to action.

Antithesis.   **Antithesis** arranges different or opposing ideas in the same or adjoining sentences to create a striking contrast. Beth Tidmore used the technique well in her speech on Special Olympics: "With the proper instruction, environment, and encouragement, Special Olympians can learn not only sport skills but life skills."

Antithesis can suggest that the speaker has a clear, decisive grasp of options. It magnifies the speaker as a person of vision, leadership, and action. Consider, for example, how President John F. Kennedy used antithesis in his Inaugural Address:

> Ask not what your country can do for you—ask what you can do for your country.

Kennedy said essentially the same thing during a campaign speech in September 1960:

> The new frontier is not what I promise I am going to do for you. The new frontier is what I ask you to do for your country.

Same message, different words. The first is memorable; the second is not. The difference is effective antithesis (as well as effective inversion and parallel construction).[35] In its entirety, the passage from the inaugural developed as follows:

> And so, my fellow Americans: Ask not what your country can do for you—ask what you can do for your country.
> My fellow citizens of the world: Ask not what America will do for you, but what together we can do for the freedom of man.

Inversion.   **Inversion** reverses the expected order of words in a phrase or sentence to make a statement more memorable and emphatic. Consider how the impact of Kennedy's statement would have diminished had he used "Do not ask" instead of "Ask not."

Paul El-Amin concluded his criticism of internment practices after the 9/11 disaster by adapting the same passage from a meditation by the great theologian John Donne: "Ask not for whom the bell tolls. It tolls for thee. And it tolls for me. For all

---

▶ **antithesis**   A language technique that combines opposing elements in the same sentence or adjoining sentences.

▶ **inversion**   Changing the normal order of words to make statements memorable.

of us who love the Bill of Rights, it tolls." The "ask not" that begins this statement and the final sentence are both inverted from their usual order. The unusual order of the words gains attention and makes the statement impressive. Moreover, the "thee" adds to the impression that this is old, authentic wisdom. Used in student speeches, inversion works best as a beginning or ending technique, where it can gain attention, add dignity to the effort, and/or frame a memorable conclusion.

At times, inversion goes beyond reversing the expected order of words. In a baccalaureate address presented at Hamilton College, Bill Moyers commented on the many confusions of contemporary life and concluded: "Life is where you get your answers questioned."[36] Here the inversion of the conventional order of thoughts, in which answers usually follow questions rather than the other way around, makes for a witty, striking observation.

Parallel Construction. **Parallel construction** repeats the same pattern of words in a sequence of phrases or sentences for the sake of impact. We discussed the use of parallel construction for framing the main points in a speech in Chapter 9, but parallel construction can occur at any critical moment in a speech. As the Kennedy example illustrates, the repetition of the pattern of words can stamp its message into the mind and make its statement memorable. Perhaps the most famous examples in American public address are Martin Luther King's repeated phrase "I have a dream . . ." in his classic March on Washington speech and Lincoln's "of the people, by the people, and for the people . . ." near the end of the Gettysburg Address.

Using the Sounds of Words to Reinforce Their Sense

As they are pronounced, words have distinctive sounds. Part of the appeal of parallel construction is that it repeats these sounds, adding a sense of importance to the thoughts it conveys. At least two other techniques, alliteration and onomatopoeia, also arrange these sounds in distinctive ways. Both techniques magnify the language of feeling.

Alliteration. **Alliteration** repeats the initial sounds in a closely connected pattern of words. One student speaker who criticized the lowering of educational standards paused near the end of her speech to draw the following conclusion: "We don't need the doctrine of dumbing down." Her repetition of the *d* sound was distinctive and helped listeners remember her point. It expressed her strong feelings about practices she condemned.

Onomatopoeia. **Onomatopoeia** (on' uh mah' uh pay'uh) is the tendency of certain words to imitate the sounds of what they represent. For example, suppose you were trying to describe the scene of refugees fleeing from war and starvation. How could you bring that scene into focus for listeners who are far removed from it? One way would be to describe an old woman and her grandson as they *trudge* down a road to nowhere. The very sound of the word "trudge" suggests the weary, discouraged walk of the refugees. Memphis student Hannah Johnston also used the technique when she described packinghouse workers as "literally drenched in a river of blood." By its very sound, *drenched* suggests the unpleasant idea of being soaked with blood as you work. Combined with the "river of blood" metaphor, the technique draws listeners close to what the language describes. Onomatopoeia has this quality of conveying listeners into a scene by allowing them to hear its noises, smell its odors, taste its flavors, or touch its surfaces. The technique awakens sensory experience.

▶ **parallel construction** Wording points in the same way to emphasize their importance and to help the audience remember them.

▶ **alliteration** The repetition of initial consonant sounds in closely connected words.

▶ **onomatopoeia** Words that sound like the subjects they signify.

These various ways to magnify the power of language are summarized in Figure 11.4. As you consider how you might use them, remember that your words must not seem forced or artificial. For these techniques to work, they must seem to arise naturally and spontaneously in your speaking, and they must seem to fit both you and your subject. Use them sparingly so that they stand out from the rest of what you say. Employed artfully, and in accord with the six standards discussed earlier, they can both increase and harness the power of words so that they reinforce your message and help make your voice significant.

FIGURE 11.4 Magnifying the Power of Language

Using Figurative Language

Technique	Definition	Example
Metaphors	Unexpected figurative comparisons	An *iron curtain* has descended across the continent.
Enduring metaphors	Metaphors that transcend time and cultural boundaries	The development of the Internet marked the *dawn* of a new way of learning.
Similes	Figurative comparisons using *like* or *as*	The jellyfish is *like a living lava lamp*.
Synecdoche	Focusing on part to represent the whole	All *hands* on deck.
Personifications	Attributing human characteristics to things or events	Liberty *raises her flame* as a beacon.
Culturetypes	Words that express the values, identity, and goals of a group	This company is devoted to the ideals of *modern, efficient, progressive science.*
Ideographs	Words that express a country's basic political beliefs	All we ask is *liberty* and *justice*.

Manipulating the Order of Words

Technique	Definition	Example
Antithesis	Presenting contrasting ideas in parallel phrases	There is a *time to sow* and a *time to reap*.
Inversion	Changing the expected word order	This insult *we did not deserve,* and this result *we will not accept.*
Parallel construction	Repetition of words/phrases at beginning or end of sentences	*It's a program that … It's a program that … It's a program that …*

Exploiting the Sounds of Words

Technique	Definition	Example
Alliteration	Repetition of initial sounds in closely connected words	Beware the *nattering nabobs* of *negativism.*
Onomatopoeia	Words that imitate natural sounds	The creek *gurgled* and *babbled* down to the river.

FINDING YOUR
voice　Do Words Work for You?

Analyze how you used the power of language in your last speech. Did you have to overcome any barriers to perception or feeling among your listeners? Did you measure up to the standards suggested by the six C's? Did listeners respond to your message? What special techniques did you use? Could you have done better? How?

FINAL
reflections　Give Me the Right Word

It may be helpful to end this chapter where we began it, reflecting on Joseph Conrad's eloquent "Give me the right word and the right accent, and I will move the world." Words, we now see, can also enlighten us or blind us, enflame us or benumb us, bring us together or drive us apart, inspire us to act or discourage action, and define who we are and are not. Words can heal us or injure us: There is no greater lie than the nursery maxim you may have chanted as a child, "Sticks and stones may break my bones but words can never harm me."

At their best, words can help us experience that "ah-hah" moment of illumination when we suddenly can see more clearly the world in which we live, who we are or must become in that world, and what we must do and say through our actions and our words. In short, words can help us come to focus, find our voice, and give it power.

A SAMPLE SPEECH

*In her self-introduction presented at Vanderbilt University, Ashley Smith used three contrasting photographs—each representing a different lifestyle—to structure her speech. This device also illustrates the cooperation of the visual and the verbal—pictures and words—to complete a very effective **synecdoche**. The photographs offer the surface details, but the words explain how they are representative of ways of life and what she learned from these exposures. In effect, they bring the photographs into focus for her speech.*

Three Photographs
ASHLEY SMITH

Photographs often tell stories that only a few can hear. I would like to tell you the story told to me by three snapshots that hang in my room in suburban Jacksonville, Florida. If you saw them, you might think them totally unrelated; together, they tell a powerful tale.

"Ashley, *levantete!*" I heard each morning for the month that I spent in Costa Rica as an exchange student. I would wake up at 5:30 to get ready for school and would stumble off to the one shower that the family of five shared. I had to wash myself in cold water because there was no warm water—that usually woke me up pretty fast! I then got dressed and breakfast would be waiting on the table. Predictably it would be fruit, coffee, and gallo pinto, a black bean and rice dish usually served at every meal.

We would then walk to school and begin the day with an hour and a half of shop class. After shop we would have about 15- to 20-minute classes in what you and I might call "regular" academic subjects: math and Spanish, for example. Those classes had frequent interruptions and were not taken very seriously. The socialization process was quite clear: These children were being prepared for jobs in the labor force instead of for higher education. Each afternoon as we walked home we passed the elite school where students were still busy working and studying. The picture in my room of my Costa Rican classmates painting picnic tables in the schoolyard reminds me of their narrow opportunities.

The second photograph on my wall is of a little girl in Botswana. She's nearing the end of her education and has finished up to the equivalent of the sixth grade. She will now return to a rural setting because her family cannot afford to continue her schooling. To add to the problem, the family goat was eaten by a lion, so she had to return to help them over this crisis.

But she didn't miss out on much—most likely, she would have gone on into the city and ended up in one of the shantytowns, one more victim of the unemployment, poverty, even starvation endured by the people. Her lack of opportunity is due not so much to class inequalities as in Costa Rica, but more to the cultural tradition of several hundred years of European exploitation. Recently there has been extensive growth there, but the natives have been left far behind.

The third photograph in my room is of four high school students, taken where I went to school in Jacksonville, Florida. We're all sitting on the lawn outside school, overlooking the parking lot full of new cars that will take us home to warm dinners and comfortable beds and large homes and privileged lives. Many of us—including myself for most of my life—took this world for granted. But now, for me, no more. I may have gained a lot in my travels, but I lost my political innocence.

One thing I gained is an intense desire to become an educator. I want to teach people to succeed on their merits despite the social and economic inequalities that they're faced with. And I want to learn from them as well. I want to teach the boy who never mastered welding that he could own the factory. And I want him to teach me how to use a rice cooker. I want to teach the girl who is exhausted each afternoon after walking to the river with a jar on her head to gather water that she could design an irrigation system. But I also want her to teach me how to weave a thatched roof. I want to travel and teach and learn.

Three photographs, hanging on my wall. They are silent, mute, and the photographer was not very skillful. But together they tell a powerful story in my life.

Ashley's sharp, clear use of images helps shape listener perceptions and arouses feelings by overcoming barriers of distance. The touch of dialogue adds action to the picture.

The Botswana picture personifies the cultural deprivation Ashley criticizes. Again, the combination of picture and words magnifies and explains her feelings and invites identification from her listeners.

The third photograph offers a transition into Ashley's personal plan of action. We see that for her it reflects a way of life that hides the reality she had found elsewhere that now calls her into a life commitment.

Again, Ashley uses synecdoche and personification to focus sharply on her life goals and to represent them to her listeners.

THIS CHAPTER WILL HELP YOU

1 Develop your voice for better communication
2 Develop more effective body language
3 Become versatile in using various presentation techniques
4 Become flexible in adapting to special situations
5 Practice for success

12 Presenting Your Speech

> "*There is no gesture that does not speak.*"
>
> —MONTAIGNE

Over the years, we remember three undergraduate student speakers whose presentations really made us want to accept their messages. Dr. Sandra Baltz, who has gone on to a distinguished career in psychiatry, conveyed an impression of incredible competence and caring when she spoke on medical issues. Marie D'Aniello exuded great warmth, character, and magnetism as she addressed problems of the family and human relationships. The excitement in Beth Tidmore's voice and body, as she moved from behind the lectern to engage her listeners more closely, established an electricity in the room that made it impossible not to listen intently to her. All three of these speakers communicated in ways that magnified their ethos: the qualities of competence, character, good will, and forcefulness that we described in Chapter 3. And that is why, years later, we still have vivid memories of their speeches.

"Finding your voice" means far more than simply sounding good and looking good at the lectern. Rather, finding your voice means finding the causes that call you to speak, discovering what you want to say about them, and framing these messages with all the skill and power they deserve. Nevertheless, all your reflection, investigation, and planning will come to naught unless your speeches come to life in the actual **presentation**.

That's what this chapter is about—preparing you for presentation by helping you develop two great resources, your physical voice and your body language. We also want to help you become versatile in using certain techniques of presentation, and flexible in special communication situations. Finally, we show you how to practice for success.

The Power of Presentation

The three speakers we have just mentioned showed how presentation can really sell a speech. We also remember, however, another student speaker who described her childhood in these terms: "I was always getting into trouble." But as she said these words, she seemed listless; she slouched at the podium and avoided eye contact. Her passive manner did not reinforce her self-portrait as a boisterous child. Instead, *there was a disconnect between what she said and what she showed.* Law enforcement interviewers often refer to such moments as "discrepancies, places where words, facial expressions, and body language do not jibe."[1]

Whenever verbal and nonverbal symbols seem out of sync, listeners typically assign more importance to the nonverbal message. One interesting explanation for this tendency is that nonverbal language is biologically older than verbal language. Psychologist Paul Ekman argues that facial expressions

> have their own evolutionary history. Smiling, for example, is probably our oldest natural expression. For humans, as for monkeys, smiling is a way to disarm and reassure those around us. . . . Some geneticists date the origin of language back as little as 50,000 years, and the richness of words actually seems to distract us from the older medium of faces.[2]

Clearly, communication goes far beyond the mere exchange of words. For presentations to be effective, listeners must be able to hear you easily, and your pronunciation must not be a barrier to understanding. Nor should listening to your voice be a painful, unpleasant experience. Your nonverbal behavior should not call attention to itself nor distract from your message. Thus, you should also avoid pompous pronunciations, an artificial manner, and overly dramatic gestures.

Instead, *an effective presentation should sound natural and conversational*—as though you were talking *with* listeners, not *at* them. Your goal should be an **expanded conversational style** that is direct, spontaneous, colorful, and tuned to the responses of listeners. Although a bit more formal than everyday conversation, such a style *sounds* natural.

Underlying the obvious requirements for an effective presentation are deeper requirements of *attitude.* As both speaker and listener, *you should want to communicate.* This point may seem obvious, but we remember another student in whom this desire to communicate seemed oddly lacking. She had done well in high school speaking contests, she told us in her first speech, and thought of herself as a good speaker. And in a technical sense, she was right. Her voice was pleasant and expressive, her manner direct and competent. But there was a false note, an overtone of artificiality. As a result, her listeners gave her a rather chilly reception. It was clear

▶ **presentation**　Delivering a speech to an audience, integrating the skills of nonverbal communication with the speech content.

▶ **expanded conversational style**　A presentational quality that, while more formal than everyday conversation, preserves its directness and spontaneity.

that, for her, speaking was an exhibition. *She* was more important than her ideas. Listeners sensed that she had her priorities wrong.

The desire to communicate produces a sense of **immediacy**, a closeness between speaker and listeners.[3] Immediacy relates to the likableness dimension of ethos, which we discussed in Chapter 3. It encourages listeners to open their minds to you and to be influenced by what you say.[4]

You can encourage immediacy by reducing the actual distance between yourself and listeners. If possible, move closer to them. Smile at them when appropriate, maintain eye contact, use gestures to clarify and reinforce ideas, and let your voice express your feelings. Even if your heart is pumping, your hands are a little sweaty, and your knees feel wobbly, the self you show listeners should be a person in control of the situation. Listeners admire and identify with speakers who maintain what Ernest Hemingway once called "grace under pressure."

To summarize, *an effective presentation makes your ideas come alive while you are speaking.* It blends nonverbal with verbal symbols so that reason and emotion, heart and head, mind and body all work together to advance your message. The remainder of this chapter helps you move closer to a presentation that reaches this goal.

An effective presentation, makes your ideas come alive.

Developing Your Physical Voice

It may seem strange to say that to find your voice you must develop your voice. But when utilized properly, the human vocal apparatus can be a rich and expressive instrument of communication. Consider the following simple statements:

> I don't believe it.
>
> You did that.
>
> Give me a break.

How many different meanings can you create as you speak these words, just by changing the ways you say them?

The quality of your voice affects your ethos as well as your message. If you sound confident and comfortable with your own identity, and if listening to you is a pleasant experience for your audience, listeners are likely to raise their estimation of you. But if you sound tentative, people may think you are not very decisive, perhaps not even convinced by your own message. If you mumble, they may think you are trying to hide something. If you are overly loud or strident, they may conclude you are not very likable.

How you talk is actually part of your identity. Someone who talks in a soft, breathy voice may be thought of as "weak"; someone who speaks in a more forceful manner may be considered "authoritative." For some speakers, a dialect is part of their ethnicity and a valued part of their personality.[5]

Although you may not want to make radical changes in your speaking voice, minor improvements can produce big dividends. As one voice specialist put it, "Though speech is a human endowment, how well we speak is an individual achievement."[6] With a little effort and practice, most of us can make positive changes. However, simple vocal exercises will not fix all physical impairments. If you have a serious vocal problem, contact a speech pathology clinic for professional help.

▶ **immediacy** A quality of successful communication achieved when the speaker and audience experience a sense of closeness.

The first step in learning to use your voice more effectively is to evaluate how you usually talk. Record yourself while speaking and reading aloud. As you listen to yourself, ask:

- Does my voice convey the meaning I intend?

- Would I want to listen to me if I were in the audience?

- Does my voice present me at my best?

If your answers are negative or uncertain, you may need to work on pitch, rate, loudness, variety, articulation, enunciation, pronunciation, or dialect. Save your original recording so that you can hear yourself improve as you practice.

Pitch

Pitch is the placement of your voice on a scale ranging from low and deep to high and shrill. For effective speaking, find a pitch level that is comfortable and that allows maximum flexibility and variety. Each of us has a **habitual pitch**, the level at which we speak most frequently. We also have an **optimum pitch**, the level that allows us to produce our strongest voice with minimal effort and that permits variation up and down the scale. You can use the following exercise to help determine your optimum pitch:

> Sing the sound *la* down to the lowest pitch you can produce without feeling strain or having your voice break or become rough. Now count each note as you sing up the scale to the highest tone you can comfortably produce. Most people have a range of approximately sixteen notes. Your optimum pitch will be about one-fourth of the way up your range. For example, if your range extends twelve notes, your optimum pitch would be at the third note up the scale. Again, sing down to your lowest comfortable pitch, and then sing up to your optimum pitch level.[7]

Record this exercise, and compare your optimum pitch to the habitual pitch revealed during your first recording. If your optimum pitch is within one or two notes of your habitual pitch, you should not experience vocal problems related to pitch level. If your habitual pitch is much higher or lower than your optimum pitch, you may not have sufficient flexibility to raise or lower the pitch of your voice to communicate changes in meaning and emphasis. You can change your habitual pitch by practicing speaking and reading at your optimum pitch.

Read the following paragraphs from N. Scott Momaday's *The Way to Rainy Mountain* at your optimum pitch level, using pitch changes to provide meaning and feeling. To make the most of your practice, record yourself so you can observe both problems and progress.

> A single knoll rises out of the plain in Oklahoma, north and west of the Wichita Range. For my people, the Kiowas, it is an old landmark, and they gave it the name Rainy Mountain. The hardest weather in the world is there. Winter brings blizzards, hot tornadic winds arise in the spring, and in the summer the prairie is an anvil's edge. The grass turns brittle and brown, and it cracks beneath your feet. There are green belts along the rivers and creeks, linear groves of hickory and pecan, willow, and witch hazel. At a distance in July or August the steaming foliage seems almost to writhe in fire. . . . Loneliness is an aspect of the land. All things in the plain are isolate: There is no confusion of objects in the eye, but one hill or one tree or one man. To look upon that landscape in the early

---

▶ **pitch** The position of the human voice on a scale ranging from low and deep to high and shrill.

▶ **habitual pitch** The vocal level at which people speak most frequently.

▶ **optimum pitch** The level at which people can produce their strongest voice with minimal effort and that allows variation up and down the musical scale.

morning, with the sun at your back, is to lose the sense of proportion. Your imagination comes to life, and this, you think, is where Creation was begun.[8]

This exercise should help you explore the full range of variation around your optimum pitch and make you more conscious of the relationship between pitch and effective communication. Record yourself reading the passage again, this time exaggerating the pitch variations as you read it. If you have a problem with a narrow pitch range, you may discover that exaggerating makes you sound more effective.

When you speak before a group, don't be surprised if your pitch seems higher than usual. Pitch is sensitive to emotions and usually goes up when you are under pressure. If pitch is a serious problem for you, hum your optimum pitch softly to yourself before you begin to speak, so that you start out on the right level.

Rate

Your **rate**, or the speed at which you speak, helps set the mood of your speech. For example, serious material may call for a slower, more deliberate rate, while lighter topics may need a faster pace. These variations may involve the duration of syllables, the use of pauses, and the overall speed of presentation.

The rate and stress patterns within a speech produce its **rhythm**, an essential component of all communication.[9] With rhythmic variations, you point out what is important and make it easier for listeners to comprehend your message. For example, if you have been speaking rapidly, and suddenly slow your pace, pausing to highlight the contrast, you will call attention what to what you are saying. This, your vocal change will suggest, is important.

Beginners who feel intimidated by the speaking situation often speed up their presentations and run their words together. What this rapid-fire delivery communicates is the speaker's desire to get it over with and sit down! At the other extreme, some speakers become so deliberate and slow that they almost put themselves and their audiences to sleep. Neither extreme lends itself to effective communication.

As we noted in Chapter 3, the typical rate for extemporaneous speaking is approximately 125 words per minute. You can check your speed by timing your reading of the excerpt from *Rainy Mountain*. If you were reading at the average rate, you would have taken about sixty seconds to complete that material. If you allowed time for pauses between phrases, which is appropriate for such formal material, your reading may have run slightly longer. If you took less than fifty seconds, you were probably speaking too rapidly or not using pauses effectively.

Pausing before or after a word or phrase highlights its importance. Pauses also give your listeners time to contemplate what you have said. They can build suspense and maintain interest as listeners anticipate what you will say next. Moreover, pauses can clarify the relationships among ideas, phrases, and sentences. They are oral punctuation marks, taking the place of the commas and periods, underlines, and exclamation marks that occur in written communication. Experienced speakers learn how to use pauses to maximum advantage. Humorist William Price Fox once wrote of Eugene Talmadge, a colorful Georgia governor and fabled stump-speaker, "That rascal knew how to wait. He had the longest pause in the state."[10] Use pause and vocal emphasis to state your main ideas most forcefully.

In her speech "Pulling a Cat Out of a Hat," reprinted at the end of Chapter 6, Jessica Bradshaw began by reading a poem written about Dr. Seuss's writing. Try your hand as well at reading the following passage, deliberately using rate and pitch variations, including pauses, to communicate the mood of the material. To fully explore and exercise your capacity to use pace variations effectively, remember to

▶ **rate** The speed at which words are uttered.

▶ **rhythm** Rate and stress patterns of vocal presentation within a speech.

exaggerate for effect. (It helps to actually read the material to young children. They usually make a wonderful audience!)

> Have you read *The Cat in the Hat*?
>
> Of course you have. I'm sure of that!
>
> And how about *Green Eggs and Ham*? Did you dig that Sam-I-Am?
>
> Or *Yertle, the Turtle* you got from Aunt Myrtle?
>
> And, did you like the book 'bout the Grinch?
>
> You silly goose, that was a cinch!

Just as pausing can work for you, the wrong use of silence within a speech can be harmful. *There is considerable difference between a pause, which is deliberate, and a hesitation, which can signal confusion, uncertainty, and/or a lack of preparation.* Moreover, some speakers habitually use "ers" and "ums," "wells" and "okays," or "you knows" in the place of pauses without being aware of it. These **vocal distractions** may fill in the silence while the speaker thinks about what to say next, or they may be signs of nervousness. They may also be signals that speakers lack confidence in themselves or their messages.

To determine if you have such a habit, record yourself as you practice presenting one of the main points for your next speech. Often, simply becoming aware of such vocal distractions is enough to help you control them. Also, don't use "okay," "well," or "you know" as transitions. Practice your presentation until the ideas flow smoothly. Finally, don't be afraid of the brief strategic silence that comes when you pause. Make silence work for you.

If your natural tendency is to speak too slowly and dully, you can practice developing a faster, more lively rate by reading light material aloud. Try reading other stories by Dr. Seuss. Such tales as *Green Eggs and Ham* should bring out the ham in you!

Different cultures have different speech rhythms. In the United States, for example, northerners often speak more rapidly than southerners. These variations in the patterns of speech can create misunderstandings. Californians, who use longer pauses than New Yorkers, may perceive the latter as rude and aggressive. New Yorkers may see Californians as too laid back or as not having much to say. Guard against stereotyping individuals on the basis of what may be culturally based speech rate variations.

Loudness

No presentation can be effective if the audience can't hear you. Nor will your presentation be successful if you overwhelm listeners with a voice that is too loud. When you speak before a group, you usually need to speak louder than you do in general conversation. The size of the room, the presence or absence of a microphone, and background noise may also call for adjustments. To develop the capacity to deal with such noise, speech teachers of ancient Greece often took their students to the beach and had them practice over the sound of crashing waves. To adjust your loudness, take your cues from audience feedback. If you are not loud enough, you may see listeners leaning forward, straining to hear. If you speak too loudly, they may unconsciously lean back, pulling away from the noise.

You should also be aware that different cultures have different norms and expectations concerning appropriate loudness. For example, in some Mediterranean cultures, a loud voice signifies strength and sincerity, whereas in some Asian and Native American cultures, a soft voice is associated with good manners and education.[11] When members of your audience come from a variety of cultural and ethnic groups, be attentive to this point.

▶ **vocal distractions** Filler words, such as "er," "um," and "you know," used in the place of a pause.

To speak with proper loudness, you must have good breath control. If you are breathing improperly, you will not have enough force to project your voice so that you can be heard at the back of a room. Improper breathing can also cause you to run out of breath before you finish a phrase or come to an appropriate pause. To check whether you are breathing properly for speaking, do the following:

> Stand with your feet approximately eight inches apart. Place your hands on your lower rib cage, thumbs to the front, fingers to the back. Take a deep breath—in through your nose and out through slightly parted lips. If you are breathing correctly, you should feel your ribs moving up and out as you inhale.

Improper breathing affects more than just the loudness of your speech. If you breathe by raising your shoulders, the muscles in your neck and throat will become tense. This can result in a harsh, strained vocal quality. Moreover, you probably will not take in enough air to sustain your phrasing, and the release of air will be difficult to control. The air and sound will all come out with a rush when you drop your shoulders, leading to unfortunate oral punctuation marks when you don't want or need them. To see if you have a problem, try this exercise:

> Take a normal breath and see how long you can count while exhaling. If you cannot reach fifteen without losing volume or feeling the need to breathe, you need to work on extending your breath control. Begin by counting in one breath to a number comfortable for you, and then gradually increase the count over successive tries. Do not try to compensate by breathing too deeply. Deep breathing takes too much time and attracts too much attention while you are speaking. Use the longer pauses in your speech to breathe, and make note of your breathing pattern as you practice your speech.

Vary the loudness of words and phrases in your speech, just as you change your pitch and rate of speaking to express ideas more effectively. Changes in loudness are often used to express emotion. The more excited or angry we are, the louder we tend to become. But don't let yourself get caught in the trap of having only two options: loud and louder. Decreasing your volume, slowing your rate, pausing, or dropping your pitch can also express emotion quite effectively.

Davidson student BJ Youngerman demonstrated the importance of loudness as he re-enacted a scene from his experience as a baseball umpire. In the confrontation between himself and a coach, BJ contrasted the angry loudness of the coach with his own quieter, more controlled vocal mannerisms as an umpire. Read the scene aloud, and as you play both roles, explore your own capacity to produce louder and more quiet speech:

BJ Youngerman used changes in loudness effectively in his speeches.

Me:	"He's out!" (with hand motion).
Coach:	"You've got to be kidding me, Blue! He was a good 10 feet beyond the base before the ball got there. That's horrible!"
Me:	"Coach, it's a judgment call. I called it like I saw it. Please get back to your dugout."
Coach:	"Blue, that was the worst call I've ever seen. You're totally blind."
Me:	"Coach, this is your final warning: Get in the dugout."

> Coach: "Well just because you got cut in Little League doesn't mean you have to take it out on these kids!"
>
> Me: "That's it! You're done!" (waves arms to signify ejection of coach)

To acquire more variety in loudness, practice the following exercise recommended by Ralph Hillman: "First, count to five at a soft volume, as if you were speaking to one person. Then, count to five at medium volume, as if speaking to ten or fifteen people. Finally, count to five, as if speaking to thirty or more people."[12] If you record this exercise, you should be able to hear the clear progression in loudness.

Variety

The importance of vocal variety shows up most in speeches that lack it. Speakers who drone on in a monotone, never varying their pitch, rate, or loudness, send a clear message: They tell us that they have little interest in their topic or their listeners or that they fear the situation they are in. Variety can make speeches come to life by adding color and interest. One of the best ways to develop variety is to read aloud materials that require it to express meaning and feeling.

As you read the following selection from Betty Ren Wright's *Johnny Go Round*, strive for maximum variation of pitch, rate, and loudness:

> Johnny Go Round was a tan tom cat.
> Would you like to know why we called him that?
> Because Johnny goes round when he's chasing a ball,
> And Johnny goes round after nothing at all.
> Silly old Johnny Go Round![13]

Record yourself while reading this and other favorite poems or dramatic scenes aloud. Compare these practices with your initial self-evaluation recording to see if you are developing variety in your presentations.

Vocal Problems

People often make judgments about others on the basis of their speech patterns. If you slur your words, mispronounce familiar words, or speak with a dialect that sounds unfamiliar to your audience, you may be seen as uneducated or distant. When you sound "odd" to your listeners, their attention will be distracted from what you are saying to the way you are saying it. In this section we cover articulation, enunciation, pronunciation, and dialect as they can detract from speaking effectiveness.

Articulation.   **Articulation** is the way you produce individual speech sounds. Some people have trouble making certain sounds. For example, they may substitute a *d* for a *th*, saying "dem" instead of "them." Other sounds that are often misarticulated include *s*, *l*, and *r*. Severe articulation problems can interfere with effective communication, especially if the audience cannot understand the speaker or if the variations suggest low social or educational status. Many of these problems may be best treated by a speech pathologist, who retrains the individual to produce the sound in a more acceptable manner.

Enunciation.   **Enunciation** is the way you pronounce words in context. In casual conversation, it is not unusual for people to slur their words—for example, saying "gimme" for "give me." However, careless enunciation causes credibility problems for

---

▶ **articulation**   The manner in which individual speech sounds are produced.

▶ **enunciation**   The manner in which individual words are articulated and pronounced in context.

public speakers. Do you say "Swatuh thought" for "That's what I thought"? "Harya?" for "How are you?" or "Howjado?" for "How did you do?" These lazy enunciation patterns are not acceptable in public speaking. Check your enunciation patterns on the recordings you have made to determine whether you have such a problem. If you do, concentrate on careful enunciation as you practice your speech. Be careful, however, to avoid the opposite problem of inflated, pompous, and pretentious enunciation, which can make you sound phony. You should strive to be neither sloppy nor overly precise.

Pronunciation. **Pronunciation** involves saying words correctly. It includes both using the correct sounds and placing the proper accent on syllables. Because written English does not always indicate the correct pronunciation, we may not be sure how to pronounce words that we first encounter in print. For instance, does the word *chiropodist* begin with a *sh*, a *ch*, or a *k* sound?

If you are not certain how to pronounce a word, consult a dictionary. An especially useful reference is the *NBC Handbook of Pronunciation*, which contains 21,000 words and proper names that sometimes cause problems.[14] When international stories and new foreign leaders first appear in the news, newspapers frequently indicate the correct pronunciation of their names. Check front-page stories in the *New York Times* for guidance with such words.

In addition to problems pronouncing unfamiliar words, you may find that there are certain words you habitually mispronounce. For example, how do you pronounce the following words?

government	athlete
ask	library
nuclear	picture

Unless you are careful, you may find yourself slipping into these common mispronunciations:

goverment	athalete
axe	liberry
nuculer	pitchur

Mispronunciation of such common words can damage your ethos. Be sure to verify your pronunciation of troublesome words as you practice your speech.

Dialect. A **dialect** is a speech pattern typical of a geographic region or ethnic group. Your dialect usually reflects the area of the country where you were raised or lived for any length of time or your cultural and ethnic identity.[15] In the United States, there are three commonly recognized dialects: eastern, southern, and midwestern. Additionally, there are local variations within the broader dialects. For example, in South Carolina, one finds the Gullah dialect from the islands off the coast, the low-country or Charlestonian accent, the Piedmont variation, and the Appalachian twang.[16] And then there's always "Bah-stahn" [Boston], where you can buy a "lodge budded pup con" [large, buttered popcorn] at the movies!

There is no such thing in nature as a superior or inferior dialect. However, there can be occasions when a distinct dialect is a definite disadvantage or advantage. Listeners prefer speech patterns that are familiar to their ears. Audiences may also have stereotyped preconceptions about people who speak with certain

Matt Damon made effective use of his natural Boston accent when speaking in New England.

▶ **pronunciation** The use of correct sounds and of proper stress on syllables when saying words.

▶ **dialect** A speech pattern associated with an area of the country or with a cultural or ethnic background.

FINDING YOUR

voice   Working for Improvement

Make a recording of your voice as you read material aloud or practice speaking, and exchange it with a classmate. Write a critique of each other's voice and articulation. Be kind and positive, but also be honest and try to make specific recommendations for improvement. Work on your classmate's recommendations for you, and then make a second recording to share with your partner. Do you detect signs of improvement in each other's performance?

dialects. For example, those raised in the South often associate a northeastern dialect with brusqueness and abrasiveness, and midwesterners may associate a southern dialect with slowness of action and mind.

> Sarah Ophelia Cannon was known throughout most of her life as Minnie Pearl of the Grand Ole Opry in Nashville, Tennessee. Her signature opening, "Hoowdee! I'm just so proud to be here!," her frumpy dress, and her straw hat with the dangling price tag, endeared her to audiences. In real life, Sarah Cannon was a well-educated, cultured woman who lived in an estate next to the Governor's mansion, founded the Sarah Cannon Cancer Center and the affiliated Sarah Cannon Research Institute. Her true dialect was soft, educated Southern. If you have a marked dialect, you may have to work hard to overcome prejudices.

You may have to work to overcome such a prejudice against your dialect.

Your dialect should reflect the standard for educated people from your geographic area or ethnic group. You should be concerned about tempering it only if it creates barriers to understanding and identification between you and your audience. Then you may want to work toward softening your dialect so that you can lower these barriers for the sake of your message.

Developing Your Body Language

Communication with your audience begins before you ever open your mouth. Your facial expression, personal appearance, and manner of movement all convey a message. Do you seem confident and determined as you walk to the front of the room to give your speech, or do you stumble and shuffle? As you begin your speech, do you look listeners directly in the eye, or do you stare at the ceiling as though seeking divine intervention?

Body language is a second great resource you must utilize to achieve a successful presentation.[18] Erving Goffman, in his classic book *The Presentation of Self in Everyday Life*, emphasizes the importance of creating consistency among the verbal and nonverbal elements of expression. To achieve a harmony of impressions, *your body language must reinforce your verbal language.*[19] If your face is expressionless as you urge your listeners to action, you are sending inconsistent messages. If you seem flustered and uncertain as you urge listeners to be confident and calm, your impressions will be badly out of sync. Be sure that your body and words both "say" the same thing. As you study this section, remember that although we discuss separate types of body language, in practice they all work together and are interpreted as a totality by listeners.[20]

▶ **body language** Communication achieved using facial expressions, eye contact, movements, and gestures.

Facial Expression and Eye Contact

> I knew she was lying the minute she said it. There was guilt written all over her face!
>
> He sure is shifty! Did you see how his eyes darted back and forth? He never did look us straight in the eye!

Most of us believe we can judge people's character, determine their true feelings, and tell whether they are honest by watching their facial expressions. If there is a conflict between what we see and what we hear, we usually believe our eyes rather than our ears.

The eyes are the most important element of facial expressiveness. In mainstream American culture, frequent and sustained eye contact suggests honesty, openness, and respect. We may think of a person's eyes as windows into the self. If you avoid looking at your audience while you are talking, you are drawing the shades on these windows. A lack of eye contact suggests that you do not care about listeners, that you are putting something over on them, or that you are afraid of them. Other cultures may view eye contact somewhat differently. In China, Indonesia, and rural Mexico, traditional people may lower their eyes as a sign of deference. In general, people from Asian and some African countries engage in less eye contact than those from the mainstream American culture.[21] Some Native Americans may even find direct eye contact offensive or aggressive. Therefore, with culturally diverse audiences especially, don't conclude that listeners who resist eye contact are necessarily expressing their distrust or refusal to communicate.

When you reach the podium or lectern, turn, pause, and engage the eyes of your audience. This signals that you want to communicate and prepares people to listen. During your speech, try to make eye contact with all sectors of the audience. Don't just stare at one or two people. You will make them uncomfortable, and other audience members will feel left out. First, look at people at the front of the room, then shift your focus to the middle and sides, and finally, look at those in the rear. You may find that those sitting in the back of the room are the most difficult to reach. They may have taken a rear seat because they don't want to listen or be involved. You may have to work harder to gain and hold their attention. Eye contact is one way you can reach them.

Smile as you start your speech unless a smile is inappropriate to your message. A smile signals your goodwill toward listeners and your ease in the speaking situation—qualities that should help your ethos.[22] From your very first words, your face should reflect and reinforce the meanings of your words. An expressionless face suggests that the speaker is afraid or indifferent. A frozen face may be a mask behind which the speaker hides. The solution lies in selecting a topic that excites you, concentrating on sharing your message, and having the confidence that comes from being well prepared.

You can also try the following exercise. Utter these statements using a dull monotone and keeping your face as expressionless as possible:

> I am absolutely delighted by your gift.
>
> I don't know when I've ever been this excited.
>
> We don't need to beg for change—we need to demand change.
>
> All this puts me in a very bad mood.

Now repeat them with *exaggerated* vocal variety and facial expression. You may find that your hands and body also want to get involved. Encourage such impulses so that you develop an integrated system of body language.

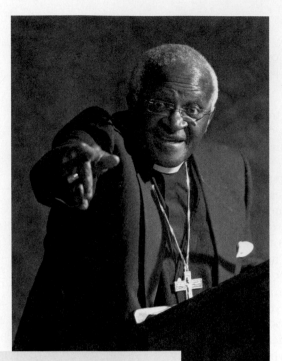

Bishop Desmond Tutu uses strong gestures that seem natural.

Movement and Gestures

Most actors learn—often the hard way—that if you want to steal a scene from someone, all you have to do is move around, develop a twitch, or swing a leg. Before long, all eyes will be focused on that movement. This cheap theatrical trick shows that physical movement sometimes can attract more attention than words. All the more reason that your words and gestures should work in harmony and not at cross-purposes! This also means you should avoid random movements, such as pacing back and forth, twirling your hair, rubbing your eyes, or jingling change in your pockets. Once you are aware of such mannerisms, it is easier to control them. Arrange for a video recording as you practice for your next speech. (You can probably do this on a cell phone or with a digital camera.) Just as audio recording can reveal aspects of your voice that are surprising, so can video recording reveal unsuspected habits of movement that you should correct.

Your gestures and movement should grow out of your response to your message.[23] You may have developed a strategic awareness of body language as you practice, such as: "When I reach this moment in the speech, I've got to stop, pause, look hard at listeners, and use gestures to really drive home my point." But body language should always *appear* natural and spontaneous. Gestures should never *look* contrived or artificial. For example, you should avoid framing a gesture to fit each word or sequence of words you utter. Perhaps every speech instructor has encountered speakers like the one who stood with arms circled above him as he said, "We need to get *around* this problem." That's not good body language!

Effective gestures involve three phases: *readiness*, *execution*, and *return*. In the readiness phase, you must be prepared for movement. Your hands and body should be in a position that does not inhibit free action. For example, you cannot gesture if your hands are locked behind your back or jammed into your pockets or if you are grasping the lectern as though it were a life preserver. Instead, let your hands rest in a relaxed position, at your sides, on the lectern, or in front of you, where they can easily obey the impulse to gesture in support of a point you are making. As you execute a gesture, let yourself move naturally and fully. Don't raise your hand halfway, and then stop with your arm frozen awkwardly in space. When you have completed a gesture, let your hands return to the relaxed readiness position, where they will be free to move again when the next impulse to gesture arises.

Do not assume that there is a universal language of gesture. Rwandans, for example, learn an elaborate code of gestures that is a direct extension of their spoken language.[24] In contrast, our "gesture language" is far less complex and sophisticated. Still, it can perform important communication functions, reinforcing, amplifying, and clarifying the spoken word and signaling your feelings and intentions.

The Factor of Distance. From **proxemics**, the study of how humans use space during communication, we can derive two additional principles that help explain the effective use of movement during speeches. The first suggests that *the actual distance between speakers and listeners affects their sense of closeness or immediacy.* Barack Obama's speeches offer an interesting illustration of this principle. At times Obama speaks in formal settings that seem to place him *above* and somewhat *distant from* his listeners. An obvious example occurs when he makes formal speeches to Congress such as the State of the Union address. These manipulations of space

▶ **proxemics** The study of how human beings use space during communication.

▶ **distance** Principle of proxemics involving the control of the space that separates speaker and audience.

emphasize the power and formality of his office, and enhance his presidential qualities. At other moments, we see him in less formal settings, responding to question-and-answer sessions, or conducting town hall meetings. In these moments he comes closer to listeners, approaches them more on their own level, and comes across more as a "regular guy" with a charming smile and appealing sense of humor. Control of proxemics in all such cases helps to establish his well-rounded identity as a citizen-leader who enjoys unusual power but is also "one of us." You can be very sure that his advisers are aware of these proxemic effects!

The greater the physical distance between speaker and audience, the harder it is to achieve identification between them. This problem gets worse when a lectern acts as a physical barrier. Short speakers can almost disappear behind it! If this is a problem, try speaking from either beside or in front of the lectern so that your body language can work for you.

A related (but quite different) problem arises if you move so close to listeners that you make them feel uncomfortable. If they pull back involuntarily in their chairs, you know you have violated their sense of personal space. To increase your effectiveness, you should seek the ideal zone of physical distance—not too far and not too close— between you and listeners.

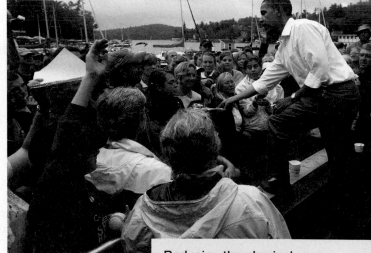

The Factor of Elevation. The second principle of proxemics suggests that *elevation also affects the sense of closeness between speakers and listeners.* When you speak, you often stand above your seated listeners in a "power position." Because we tend to associate *above* us with power over us, speakers may find that this arrangement discourages identification with some listeners. Often, they will sit on the edge of the desk in front of the lectern in a more relaxed and less elevated stance. If your message is informal and requires close identification, or if you are especially tall, you might try this approach.

Reducing the physical distance between the speaker and audience can help increase identification with the speaker.

Personal Appearance

Your clothing and grooming affect how you are perceived and how your message is received.[25] Once again, as Goffman notes, one's personal appearance should be consistent with the overall impression one wishes to give.[26] How we dress can even influence how we see ourselves and how we behave. A police officer out of uniform

▶ **elevation** Principle of proxemics dealing with power relationships implied when speakers stand above listeners.

may not act as authoritatively as when dressed in blue. A doctor without a white jacket may behave like just another person. You may have a certain type of clothing that makes you feel comfortable and relaxed. You may even have a special "good luck" outfit that raises your confidence.

When you are scheduled to speak, dress in a way that makes you feel good about yourself and that respects the audience and the occasion. How you dress reflects how you feel about the importance of the event. Think of your speech as a *professional* situation, and dress accordingly. By dressing a little more formally than you usually do, you emphasize both to yourself and to the audience that your message is important. As we noted in Chapter 10, your appearance can serve as a presentation aid that complements your message. Like any other aid, it should never compete with your words for attention or be distracting. Always dress in good taste for the situation you anticipate.

Body language is a fascinating subject. To learn more of its tactics, plus additional tips for improvement in business communication, see Carmine Gallo's "It's Not Your Mouth That Speaks Volumes," published in *BusinessWeek* in 2007 (http://www.businessweek.com/careers/content/feb2007/ca20070207_700175.htm?campaign_id=nws_insdr_feb10&link_position=link18). Gallo also offers a slide show, "The Silent Language of Success," that illustrates the do's and don'ts of body language.

Developing Versatility in Presentation

To develop more competent presentation skills, you must do more than develop your natural resources of voice and body language. You must also master the four types of presentation: impromptu speaking, memorized text presentation, reading from a manuscript, and extemporaneous speaking. You may have to use all of these forms, even in the same speech. A versatile speaker is able to move easily among them as they become appropriate in different situations.

Impromptu Speaking

Impromptu speaking is speaking on the spur of the moment in response to unpredictable situations with limited time for preparation. Such speaking is sometimes called "speaking off the cuff," a phrase that suggests you could put all your notes on the cuff of your shirt, or, if you followed the practice of a recent political speaker, in the palm of your hand (we recommend neither practice!). Even in a carefully prepared speech, there may be moments of impromptu presentation—times when you must make on-the-spot adjustments to audience feedback or respond to questions at the end of your speech.

Many situations call for impromptu speaking. At work, you might be asked to make a presentation "in fifteen minutes." Or in meetings, you may decide to "say a few words" about a new product. In both cases, you will make impromptu speeches. You can also use impromptu speaking skills in other classes—to answer or to comment on a point made by your professor.

When you have just a few minutes to prepare, first *determine your purpose*. What do you want the audience to know? Why is this important? Next, *decide on your main points*. Limit yourself to no more than three main points. Don't try to cover too much. If you have access to any type of writing material—a note pad, a scrap of paper—jot down a memory-jogging word for each idea, either in the order of importance or as the ideas seem to flow naturally. This skeletal outline will keep you from rambling or forgetting something that is important.

▶ **impromptu speaking** Speaking on the spur of the moment in response to an unpredictable situation with limited time for preparation.

Stick to the main points, using simple transitions as you go: "My first point is. . . . Second, it is important to. . . . Finally, it is clear that. . . ." Use the **PREP formula** to develop each point: State the *point*, give a *reason* or *example*, then restate the *point*. Keep your presentation short, and end with a summary of your remarks.

Point:	You should buy a hybrid car.
Reason(s):	Hybrid cars are good for the environment—and good for your pocketbook!
Example:	If you drive 10,000 miles a year, you could easily save $600 a year on gas alone.
Restatement of Point:	Drive green and keep more green. Buy a hybrid!

An impromptu speech often is one of several such speeches as people express their ideas in meetings. The earlier speeches create the context for your presentation. If others stood at the front of the room to speak, you should do so as well. If earlier speakers remained seated, you may wish to do the same. However, you should consider whether earlier speakers have been successful. If these speakers offended listeners while making standing presentations, you may wish to remain seated to differentiate yourself from them. If seated speakers have made trivial presentations, you may wish to stand to signal that what you are going to say is important.

Most impromptu speaking situations are relatively casual. No one expects a polished presentation on a moment's notice. However, the ability to organize your ideas quickly and effectively and to present them confidently puts you at a great advantage. The principles of preparing speeches that you are learning in this course will help you become a more effective impromptu speaker.

Memorized Text Presentation

Memorized text presentations are committed to memory and delivered word for word. Because the introduction and conclusion of a speech are especially important— the introduction for gaining audience attention and the conclusion for leaving a lasting impression—their wording should be carefully planned and rehearsed. You might also want to memorize short congratulatory remarks, a toast, or a brief award-acceptance speech.

In general, you should avoid trying to memorize entire speeches because this method of presentation poses many problems. Beginning speakers who try to memorize their speeches can get so caught up with *remembering* that they forget about *communicating*. The result often sounds stilted or sing-songy. Speaking from memory also inhibits adapting to feedback. It can keep you from clarifying points when the audience signals that it doesn't understand or from following up on ideas that seem especially effective.

Another problem with memorized speeches is that they often must be scripted word for word in advance. Many people do not write in a natural oral style. The major differences between oral and written language, covered in Chapter 11, bear repeating. Good oral style uses short, direct, conversational speech patterns. Even sentence fragments can be acceptable. Repetition, rephrasing, and amplification are more necessary in speaking than in writing. The sense of rhythm and saving the most forceful idea for the end of the sentence may be more important in oral style. Imagery can be especially useful to help the audience visualize what you are talking about.

▶ **PREP formula**   A technique for making an impromptu speech: state a point, give a reason or example, and restate the point.

▶ **memorized text presentations**   Speeches that are committed to memory and delivered word for word.

If you must memorize a speech, commit it so thoroughly to memory that you can concentrate on communicating with your audience. If you experience a "mental block," keep talking. Restate or rephrase your last point to put your mind back on track. If this doesn't work, you may find yourself forced into an extemporaneous style and discover that you can actually express your ideas better without the constraints of exact wording.

Reading from a Manuscript

When you make a **manuscript presentation**, you read to an audience from either a text or a teleprompter. Manuscript presentations have many of the same problems as memorized presentations. Because speakers must look at a script, they lose eye contact with listeners, which in turn causes a loss of immediacy and inhibits adapting to feedback. Moreover, as with memorized presentations, you may have trouble writing in an oral style.

Some problems are exclusive to manuscript presentations. Most people do not read aloud well. Their presentations lack variety. When people plan to read a speech, they often do not practice enough. Unless speakers are comfortable with the material, they can end up glued to their manuscript rather than communicating with listeners, even when they are using teleprompters.

President George W. Bush sometimes had trouble with making manuscript presentations, especially early in his presidency. He was far more comfortable out on the "stump," interacting with local audiences in the rough-and-tumble of politics, than he was on ceremonial occasions. For example, on the evening of the devastating terrorist attack on the World Trade Center, Bush spoke to the nation from the Oval Office in the White House, trying to bring words of comfort and reassurance. Somehow, "the president could not find the right words."[27] His language was uninspiring and flat.[28]

Later that week, however, he visited the ruins at ground zero in New York City, and there, for perhaps the first time in his presidency, he found his voice. The scene Bush encountered was like an illustration from Dante's *Inferno*. Thousands of firemen, policemen, and rescue workers were combing the scattered, smoking ruins, still looking for survivors. The president, holding a bullhorn, climbed a pile of debris above the crowd and, as he started to speak, he was interrupted:

Audience member: Can't hear you.

The President: I can't go any louder. (Laughter) I want you all to know that America today—America today is on bended knee in prayer for the people whose lives were lost here. . . . This nation stands with the good people of New York City and New Jersey and Connecticut as we mourn the loss of thousands of our citizens.

Audience member: I can't hear you.

The President: I can hear you. I can hear you. The rest of the world hears you. And the people who knocked these buildings down will hear all of us soon.

Audience members: U.S.A.! U.S.A.! U.S.A.![29]

In retrospect, these moments were charged with symbolism. The audience member who could not hear represents all those who indeed

President George W. Bush was more effective at impromptu speaking than reading from a manuscript.

▶ **manuscript presentation**   A speech read from a prepared text or teleprompter.

FIGURE 12.1 Methods of Presentation

Method	Use	Advantages	Disadvantages
Impromptu	When you have no time for preparation or practice	Is spontaneous; can meet demands of the situation; is open to feedback.	Is less polished, less well-researched, less organized; allows less use of supporting material.
Memorized	When you will be making a brief remark, such as a toast or award acceptance, or when the wording of your introduction or conclusion is important	Allows planning of eloquent wording; can sound well polished.	Must be written out in advance; can make you forget to communicate; can sound sing-songy.
Manuscript	When exact wording is important, time constraints are strict, or your speech will be telecast	Allows planning of precise wording; can be timed down to seconds.	Requires practice and an ability to read well; inhibits response to feedback.
Extemporaneous	For most public speaking occasions	Is spontaneous; encourages responding to audience feedback; encourages focusing on the essence of your message.	Requires considerable preparation and practice; experience leads to excellence.

could not "hear" the president before this crisis. Bush, obviously sensitive to the larger meaning of the moment, built on its symbolic significance—first expanding it, then giving it an ominous turn. Stephen Wayne, a presidential scholar and professor of government at Georgetown University, believes this was the first time Bush had met the "challenge of a leader," which was to have his speech "capture the needs and mood of his country."[30] Later Bush would give successful manuscript speeches, but it is interesting that he should find his voice in the give-and-take of impromptu speaking.

Manuscript presentations are most useful when the speaker seeks accuracy or eloquence or when time constraints are severe: media presentations, for example, must be timed within seconds. Extemporaneous presentations may also include quotations or technical information that must be read if the speeches are to achieve their effect. Because you will need to read material from time to time, we offer the following suggestions:

- Use a large font to prepare your manuscript so you can see it without straining.

- Use light pastel rather than white paper to reduce glare from lights.

- Double- or triple-space the manuscript.

- Mark pauses with slashes.

- Highlight material you want to emphasize by capitalizing it.

- Practice speaking from your manuscript so that you can maintain as much eye contact as possible with your audience.

As you make final preparations, ask a friend to make a video recording of your rehearsal. Review the recording and ask yourself, Do I sound as though I'm *talking with someone*, or as if I'm *reading a text*? Do I maintain eye contact with my imaginary audience? Do I pause effectively to emphasize the most important points? Does my body language reinforce my message? Revise and continue practicing until you are satisfied.

Extemporaneous Speaking

Extemporaneous speaking *is prepared and practiced, but not written out or memorized.* Rather than focusing on the exact wording of the speech, the speaker concentrates instead on the sequence of ideas that will develop in the speech, on its underlying message, and on the final impression the speech should leave with listeners. Extemporaneous speaking features a spontaneous and natural-sounding presentation and makes it easier to establish immediacy with an audience. The speaker is not the prisoner of a text, and each presentation will vary according to the audience, occasion, and inspiration of the moment.

Another large advantage is that extemporaneous speaking encourages interaction with an audience. The Vanderbilt student who distributed photographs and then instructed listeners on how to view them, and another student who asked listeners to close their eyes and to imagine themselves living as dwarfs, were playing up these advantages. Such interaction encourages the audience to participate in constructing the message of the speech. It becomes their creation as well, which is especially important when persuading listeners.

Because it requires speakers to master the overall pattern of thought within their speeches, extemporaneous speaking emphasizes the importance of preparation and practice. As you rehearse for your extemporaneous speech, put aside any manuscript or full-sentence outline you may have prepared, and use a key-word outline such as we discussed in Chapter 3. Both in practice and in actual presentation, the key-word outline will keep you on track, but also keep your focus where it belongs: on your ideas and your listeners.

At its best, such speaking combines the advantages of the other modes of speaking, the spontaneity and immediacy of impromptu speech, and the careful preparation of manuscript and memorized presentations. *It is therefore the master mode of speaking,* the best for most speaking situations, preferred by most instructors for most classroom speeches. Its special advantage is that it encourages you to adapt to audience feedback in creative and constructive ways.

Responding to Feedback from Your Audience.   As we saw in Chapter 1, **feedback** is the message listeners send back to you as you speak. Facial expressions, gestures, or sounds of agreement or disagreement let you know how you are coming across. Since most feedback is nonverbal, you should maintain eye contact with your audience so that you can respond to these signals. Use feedback to monitor whether listeners understand you, are interested, and agree with what you are saying. Negative feedback in particular can alert you that you need to make on-the-spot adjustments.

Feedback That Signals Misunderstanding.   Listeners' puzzled expressions can signal that they don't understand what you are saying. You may need to define an

---

▶ **extemporaneous speaking**   A form of presentation in which a speech, although carefully prepared and practiced, is not written out or memorized.

▶ **feedback**   Your perception of how audience members react to the message as you speak.

YOUR ethical VOICE   Persistent Questions About Presentation

Audiences often raise ethical and practical questions concerning the presentation aspects of public speaking. The following mini-scenarios offer a sampling of such questions and doubts:

1. "He talks so slow. Does he *think* slow too?"

2. "She talks so fast. Is she trying to put something over on me?"

3. "I don't like how he dresses or his hairstyle, either. Can a person with such bad taste be telling the truth?"

4. "She has a peculiar accent. Probably foreign. How can she possibly understand my problems?"

5. "He just mispronounced a word. Could his thinking be flawed as well? Can I trust such an ignoramus?"

6. "She looks uncomfortable. Kind of buried in her notes and not looking us in the eye. If she's not confident as a speaker, should I be confident in following her advice?"

7. "He sounds too good, too polished. Can I trust him?"

Assuming that you are the person to whom such questions are asked, how would you answer them? What advice would you offer to counter such distrust?

---

unfamiliar word or rephrase an idea to make it simpler. You could add an example or story to make an abstract concept more concrete. It might help to compare or contrast an unfamiliar idea with something the audience already knows and understands. When you detect signs of misunderstanding, you can say, "Let me put it another way." Then provide a clearer explanation.

Feedback That Signals Loss of Interest. Bored listeners wiggle in their seats, drum their fingers, or develop a glazed look. Remind them of the importance of your topic. Provide an example or story that makes your message come to life. Involve listeners by asking a question that calls for a show of hands. Startle them with a bold statement. Keep in mind that enthusiasm is contagious: your interest can arouse theirs. Move from behind the lectern and come closer to them. Whatever happens, do not become disheartened or lose faith in your speech. In all likelihood, some people—probably more than you think—will have found the speech interesting.

Feedback That Signals Disagreement. Listeners who disagree with you may frown or shake their heads to indicate how they feel about what you are saying. A number of techniques can help you soften disagreement. If you anticipate resistance, work hard to establish your ethos in the introduction of your speech. Listeners should see you as a competent, trustworthy, strong, and likable person who has their best interests at heart.

To be perceived as competent, you must *be* competent. Arm yourself with a surplus of information, examples, and testimony from sources your audience will respect. Practice your presentation until it is polished. Set an example of tolerance by respecting positions different from your own.

You may find that although you differ with listeners on issues, you agree with them on goals. Stress the values that you share. Appeal to their sense of fair play and their respect for your right to speak. You should be the model of civility in the situation. Avoid angry reactions and the use of inflammatory language. Think of these listeners as offering an opportunity for your ideas to have impact.

Developing Flexibility in Special Situations

To the versatility you develop as you master and integrate the various modes of speaking, you should add flexibility in special speaking situations. We address two such situations: question-and-answer sessions and video presentations.

Handling Questions and Answers

If you are successful in arousing interest and stimulating thinking, your listeners may want to ask questions at the end of your speech. You should welcome and encourage this sign of success. The following suggestions should make handling questions easier for you.[31]

- **Prepare for questions.** Try to anticipate what you might be asked, think about how you will answer these questions, and do the research required to answer them authoritatively. Practice your speech before friends, and urge them to ask you tough questions.

- **Repeat or paraphrase the question.** This is especially important if the question was long or complicated and your audience is large. Repetition ensures that everyone in the audience hears the question. It gives you time to plan your answer, and it helps verify that you have understood the question. Paraphrasing also enables you to steer the question to the type of answer you are prepared to give.

- **Maintain eye contact with the audience as you answer.** Note that we say "with the audience," not just "with the questioner." Look first at the questioner, and then make eye contact with other audience members, returning your gaze to the questioner as you finish your answer. The purpose of a question-and-answer period should be to extend the understanding of the entire audience, not to carry on a conversation with one person.

- **Defuse hostile questions.** Reword emotional questions in more objective language. For example, if you are asked, "Why do you want to throw our money away on people who are too lazy to work?" you might respond with something like, "I understand your frustration and think what you really want to know is 'Why aren't our current programs helping people break out of the cycle of unemployment?'" Don't be afraid to use such questions to help you make a closely related point.[32]

- **Don't be afraid to concede a point or to say, "I don't know."** Such tactics can earn you points for honesty and can also help defuse a difficult question or hostile questioner. Vice President Joe Biden of Delaware, while highly regarded as a foreign policy expert, entered the 2008 presidential sweepstakes with a reputation for being a compulsive talker and for putting his foot in his mouth. At the first nationally televised debate for Democratic Party hopefuls, the moderator skewered him with an unfriendly question:

Answering questions gives you a chance to extend and increase the influence of your speech.

Moderator: An editorial in the *Los Angeles Times* said, "In addition to his uncontrolled verbosity, Biden is a gaffe machine."' Can you reassure voters in this country that you would have the discipline you would need on the world stage, Senator?

Sen. Biden: Yes.

(Audience laughter. Long moment of silence)

Moderator: Thank you, Senator Biden.

(More laughter)[33]

As the *New York Times* described the moment, "The audience laughed at his brevity. Mr. Biden, looking proud of himself, said nothing else, as Mr. [Brian] Williams silently if slightly uncomfortably waited for him to expand on his remarks."[34] Commentator Chris Matthews described it as "a Johnny Carson moment." Fellow commentator Margaret Carlson added, "In a debate with that many [eight] people, a one-liner stands out. And the best one-liner is a one-word one-liner."[35] Especially, she might have added, when the one-liner comes from Senator Biden! While the Vice President seemed on the surface to concede the assumption behind the question, the brevity of his answer really worked as a refutation to the charge that he was uncontrollably verbose. His lightheartedness also drew a lot of the poison out of the question.

Joe Biden's bright moment leads directly to the next consideration:

- **Keep your answers short and direct.** Don't give another speech.

- **Handle nonquestions politely.** If someone starts to give a speech rather than ask a question, wait until he or she pauses for breath and then intervene with something like, "Thank you for your comment" or "I appreciate your remarks. Your question, then, is . . ." or "That's an interesting perspective. Can we have another question?" Stay in command of the situation.

  In a question-and-answer session he had with Congressional Republicans, President Obama was confronted with a "questioner" who actually made a long, hostile political speech. When he finally paused for a moment, the President commented, "I know there's a question in there somewhere [and]. . . . At some point I know you're going to let me answer." This rather blunt (but polite) interruption allowed Obama to control the remainder of the exchange.[36]

- **Bring the question-and-answer session to a close.** Call for a final question, and as you complete the answer, summarize your message again to refocus listeners on your central points.

FINDING YOUR

voice   Prepping for Q & A

Make a list of questions you think you might be asked following your next speech. Plan the answers you might give to these questions. Working in small groups, distribute your questions so that group members can ask them of you. Invite the group to evaluate your responses.

Making Video Presentations

It is quite likely that at some time in your life you will make a video presentation. You may find yourself speaking on closed-circuit television, recording instructions or training materials at work, using community access cable channels to promote a cause, running for public office, or even appearing on commercial television. Many video presentations utilize a manuscript printed on a teleprompter. In other situations, such as in small group discussions or question-and-answer formats, you may have to utilize impromptu or extemporaneous techniques. With some minor adaptations, the skills you are developing should help you make effective video presentations.[37]

Television encourages a conversational mode of presentation. Your audience may be individuals or small groups seated in their dens. Imagine yourself talking with another person in an informal setting. While intimate, however, television is also remote—you can't see the faces of viewers as they respond to what you're saying. Since you have no immediate feedback to help you, your meaning must be instantly clear. Use language that is colorful and concrete so that your audience remembers your points. Use previews and internal summaries to keep viewers on track. If you would like to use visual aids, be sure to confer in advance with studio personnel to be certain your materials will work well in that setting. For example, large poster boards displayed on an easel are more difficult to handle in video presentations than are smaller materials. (See related considerations in Chapter 10.)

Television magnifies all your movements and vocal changes. Slight head movements and underplayed facial expressions should be enough to reinforce your ideas. Avoid abrupt changes in loudness as a means of vocal emphasis. Rely instead on subtle changes in tempo, pitch, and inflection, and on pauses, to drive your points home.

Because television brings you close to viewers, it also magnifies every aspect of your appearance. You should dress conservatively, avoiding shiny fabrics, glittery or dangling jewelry, and flashy prints that might "swim" on the screen and distract viewers. Do not wear white or light pastels, which could reflect glare. Ask in advance about the color of the studio backdrop. If you have light hair or if the backdrop will be light, wear dark clothing for contrast. If you have a dark skin tone, request a light or neutral background and consider wearing light-colored clothes.

Both men and women need makeup to achieve a natural look on television. Have powder available to reduce skin shine or to hide a five o'clock shadow. Use makeup conservatively, because the camera will intensify it. Avoid glasses with tinted lenses, which appear even darker on the screen. Even untinted lenses can reflect glare from the studio lights. Wear contact lenses if you have them. If you can see well enough to read the monitor without glasses, leave them off.

For most televised presentations, timing is crucial. Five minutes of air time means five minutes, not five minutes and five seconds. For this reason, television favors manuscript presentations read from a teleprompter. The teleprompter controls timing and preserves a sense of direct eye contact between speakers and listeners. The rolling script appears directly below or on the lens of the camera. Practice your speech ahead of time until you *almost* have it memorized so that you can glance at the script as a whole. If you have to read it word for word, your eyes may be continually shifting (and shifty eyes do not correlate with high credibility in American culture!).

Try to rehearse your presentation in the studio with the production personnel. Develop a positive relationship with studio technicians. Your success depends in large part on how well they do their jobs. Provide them with a manuscript marked to show when you will move around or use a visual aid. Practice speaking from the teleprompter and learn how to use the microphone correctly. Remember that the microphone picks up *all* sounds, including shuffling papers and tapping on a lectern. If you use a stand or handheld microphone, position it about 10 inches below your mouth. The closer the microphone is to your mouth, the more it picks up unwanted noises like whistled *s* sounds or tongue clicks. Microphones with cords restrict your movement. If you plan to move about during your presentation, know where the cord is so you won't trip over it.

Don't be put off by distractions as you practice and present your speech. Studio technicians may need to confer with one another while you are speaking. This is a necessary part of their business; they are not being rude or inattentive. Even though they are in the room with you, they are not your audience. Keep your mind on your ideas and your eyes on the camera. The camera may seem strange at first, but think of it as a friendly face waiting to hear what you have to say. Use the time during lighting and voice checks before the actual taping begins to run through your introduction. Before you begin your speech and after you finish, always assume that any microphone or camera near you is "live." Don't say or do anything you wouldn't want your audience to hear or see.

Even though the situation may seem strange, make a conscious effort to relax. If you are sitting, lean slightly forward as though you were talking to someone in the chair next to you. The floor director will give you a countdown before the camera starts to roll. Clear your throat and be ready to start on cue. Begin with a smile, if appropriate, as you make eye contact with the camera. If several cameras are used, a red light on top will tell you which camera is on. Make smooth transitions from one camera to the other. During your presentation, the studio personnel may communicate with you using special sign language. The director will tell you what cues they will use.[38]

If you make a mistake, keep going. Sometimes "mistakes" are improvements. Do not stop unless the director says "cut." If appropriate, smile when you finish and continue looking at the camera to allow time for a fade-out.

Practicing for Presentation

It takes a lot of practice to sound natural. Although this statement may seem contradictory, it should not be surprising. Speaking before a group is not your typical way of communicating. Even though most people seem spontaneous and relaxed when talking with a small group of friends, something happens when they walk to the front of a room and face a larger audience of less familiar faces. They often freeze or become stilted and awkward. This blocks the natural flow of communication.

The key to overcoming this problem is to practice until you can respond fully to your ideas as you present them. Don't fall into the trap of avoiding practice because it reminds you that you are not confident about your upcoming speech: That is a recipe for a self-fulfilling prophecy![39] Instead, rehearse your speech until your voice, face, and body can express your feelings as well as your thoughts. On the day of your speech, you become a model for your listeners, showing them how they should respond in turn.

To develop an effective extemporaneous style, practice until you feel the speech is part of you. During practice, you can actually hear what you have been preparing and try out the words and techniques you have been considering. What looked like a good idea in your outline may not seem to work as well when it comes to life in spoken words. It is better to discover this fact in rehearsal than before an actual audience.

You will probably want privacy the first two or three times you practice. Even then, you should try to simulate the conditions under which the speech will be given. Stand up while you practice. Imagine your listeners in front of you. Picture them responding positively to what you have to say. Address your ideas to them, and visualize your ideas having impact.

If possible, go to your classroom to practice. If this is not possible, find another empty room where the speaking arrangements are similar. Such onsite rehearsal helps you get a better feel for the situation you will face, reducing its strangeness when you make your actual presentation. Begin practicing from your formal outline. Once you feel comfortable, switch to your key-word outline, and then practice until the outline transfers from the paper to your head.

Keep material that you must read to a minimum. Type or print quotations in large letters so you can see them easily, and put each quotation on a single index card or sheet of paper. If using a lectern, position this material so that you can maintain frequent eye contact while reading. If you will speak beside or in front of the lectern, hold your cards in your hand and raise them when it is time to read. Practice reading your quotation until you can present it naturally while only glancing at your notes. If your speech includes presentation aids, practice handling them until they are smoothly integrated into your presentation. They should seem a natural extension of your verbal message.

During practice, you can serve as your own audience by video recording your speech so that you can both see and hear yourself. Try to be the toughest critic you will ever have, but be a constructive critic. Never put yourself down. Rather, work on specific points of improvement. Be sure to check the length of your speech to assure you are within time limits.

As you develop confidence, you may also find it helpful to ask a friend or friends to observe your presentation and offer suggestions. Recent findings confirm that speakers who practice before audiences receive higher evaluation scores later.[40] The suggestions of others may be more objective than your self-evaluation, and you will get a feel for speaking to real people rather than to an imagined audience. Seek constructive feedback from your friends by asking them specific questions. Was it easy for them to follow you? Do you have any mannerisms (such as twisting your hair or saying "you know" after every other sentence) that distracted them? Were you speaking loudly and slowly enough? Did your ideas seem clear and soundly supported?

On the day that you are assigned to speak, get to class early enough to look over your outline one last time so that it is fresh in your mind. Visualize yourself presenting a successful speech. If you have devoted sufficient time and energy to your preparation and practice, you should feel confident about communicating with your audience. The "Speaker's Notes: Practicing for Presentation" checklist summarizes our suggestions for practicing.

SPEAKER'S notes Practicing for Presentation

To practice presentation skills, follow these suggestions:

1. Practice standing up and speaking aloud, if possible in the room where you will be making your presentation.

2. Practice first from your formal outline; then switch to your key-word outline when you feel you have mastered your material.

3. Work on maintaining eye contact with an imaginary audience.

4. Practice integrating your presentation aids into your message.

5. Check the timing of your speech. Add or cut as necessary.

6. Continue practicing until you feel comfortable and confident.

7. Present your speech in a "dress rehearsal" before friends. Make final changes in light of their suggestions.

FINDING YOUR
voice
Critiquing Presentation Practices

Attend a guest lecture or speech on campus or view a presentation on YouTube (such as Mark McGwire's "confession" or Tiger Woods's apology). Was the speaker's voice effective or ineffective? Why? How would you evaluate the speaker's body language? Did the speaker read from a manuscript, make a memorized presentation, or speak extemporaneously? Was the speaker adept at moving from one mode of presentation to another? How flexible was the speaker in answering questions? Report your observations in class.

FINAL
reflections
Taking the Stage

It is now clear that no one is going to give you your voice. You have to find it for yourself, and to convince others that you have found it as you stand before them. As you step to the front of the room when you are asked to speak, you should do so confidently. You should project the realization that you have something worthwhile and important to say that listeners should consider carefully. This confidence, this air of leadership, is what communication consultant Judith Humphrey calls "taking the stage."[41] This theatrical metaphor summarizes much of what we have said to this point about preparing for public speaking. Taking the stage, Humphrey says, implies six steps.

1. Adopt the *attitude* that every public communication situation is an opportunity to influence, inspire, and motivate others.

2. Have the *conviction* that what you bring to others will have great value.

3. Create the *character of leadership* as you speak. Humphrey says: "A leader has vision. A leader has a point of view and is not afraid to express it. A leader must also be . . . totally authentic."[42]

4. Follow a great *script*. You should have a simple, clear, positive message.

5. Use the *language* of leadership. Your words should be forceful and should avoid indirection and self-correction. Don't overuse phrases like "in my opinion" or "maybe I'm wrong but." Don't soften your point or subvert yourself.

6. Finally, *believe in your ideas*. As you rise to speak, don't shrink into yourself. Stand still and don't fidget. Establish eye contact and use strong gestures. Use pauses to emphasize your points. "Taking the stage" is your invitation and opportunity to lead others, and to convince them that you are indeed finding your voice.

13 Informative Speaking

> *The improvement of understanding is for two ends: first our own increase of knowledge; secondly, to enable us to deliver that knowledge to others.*
> —JOHN LOCKE

In ancient Greek mythology, Prometheus was punished by the other gods for teaching humans how to make fire. According to the myth, these jealous gods knew that people would now be able to keep warm, cook food, use the extended light, and share knowledge as they huddled around their campfires. Eventually they would build civilizations and challenge the gods themselves with the power of their new learning. His fellow gods had every right to be angry with Prometheus. He had just given the first significant informative speech.

This tale of Prometheus reminds us that knowledge empowers us as humans to survive and thrive in a world of our own making. Advances such as breakthroughs in medical research, new ways to improve the environment, and early detection systems that alert us to natural disasters not only help us to cope with basic challenges to our existence but contribute to the quality of our lives. Free and open exchange of information is especially crucial to democratic societies in which the fate of us all depends upon the will of an enlightened citizenry.

Learning to make effective and ethical informative presentations will contribute substantially to finding your voice as a public speaker. As discussed in Chapter 8, presenting substantive information in a balanced and responsible fashion is a skill that will benefit you regardless of whether your general purpose is to inform, persuade, or celebrate. Should you become a journalist, a teacher, a manager, or a market analyst, most of the everyday work-related presentations you will be asked to give will be primarily informative. Finally, responsible informative speaking reinforces a respect for quality dialogue and the integrity of ideas and information and facilitates enlightened decision-making, all of which are vital standards of ethical public speaking as discussed in Chapter 1.

In this chapter we examine the nature, types, and functions of informative speaking; offer advice for motivating your listeners to attend and remember your messages; and cover the design schemes most often used to structure informative presentations. We close by considering perhaps the most common form of "real world" informative speech you will be asked to present in your later professional careers: a briefing.

Informative Speaking: An Overview

Informative speaking functions to enlighten by sharing ideas and information. As an informative speaker, you want listeners to pay attention and understand. But your purpose is not to influence them to change their minds or behaviors so much as to offer a balanced presentation of relevant ideas and information so that they can more responsibly reach their own conclusions. For instance, Heide Norde presented an informative speech to her class on the dangers of prolonged exposure to ultraviolet radiation, but she did not urge her listeners to boycott tanning salons or even to wear sunscreen. What they did in response to this new knowledge was up to them.

By sharing information, an informative speech reduces ignorance. It does not simply repeat something the audience already knows. Rather, the **informative value** of a speech is measured by *how much new and important information or understanding it provides the audience.* As you prepare your informative speech, ask yourself the following questions:

- Is my topic significant enough to merit an informative speech?
- What do my listeners already know about my topic?
- What more do they need to know to accomplish my purpose?
- Do I understand my topic well enough to help others understand it?

The answers to these questions should help you plan a speech with high informative value.

It is clear that informative speakers carry a large ethical burden to communicate responsible knowledge of their topics. A responsible informative speech should

---

▶ **informative speaking** Functions to enlighten by sharing ideas and information.

▶ **informative value** A measure of how much new and important information or understanding a speech conveys to an audience.

YOUR ethical VOICE   The Ethics of Informative Speaking

As you prepare your informative speech, keep these ethical considerations in mind.

1. Be sure you can defend the morality of your choice of topic.
2. Mention all major positions on a topic when there are differing perspectives.
3. Present all information that is vital for audience understanding.
4. Do not distort information that is necessary for audience understanding.
5. Do sufficient research to speak responsibly on your subject.
6. Do not omit relevant information because it is inconsistent with your perspective.
7. Strive to be as objective as possible.

cover all major positions on a topic and present all vital information. Although speakers may have strong feelings on a subject, it is unethical to deliberately omit or distort information that is necessary for audience understanding. Similarly, speakers who are unaware of information because they have not done sufficient research are irresponsible. As you prepare your speech, you should seek out material from sources that offer different perspectives on your subject.

Forms of Informative Speaking

If it's true that we live in an Age of Information, the importance of informative speaking can hardly be exaggerated. Informative speaking arises out of three deep impulses within us:

1. *We seek to expand our awareness of the world around us.* Perhaps we sense that to stretch our horizons is also to grow in power. This impulse may account for the value of speeches of description.

2. *We seek to learn skills that are vital or enjoyable.* This impulse accounts for the importance of speeches of demonstration.

3. *We have an abiding curiosity about how things work and how they are made.* This is especially true when these things are important to our quality of life. This impulse may account for the importance of speeches of explanation.

Speeches of Description

Often the specific purpose of a speech is to describe what's "out there" or "in here" with respect to a given activity, event, object, person, or place. A **speech of description** should give the audience a clear picture of your subject. The words should be concrete and colorful to delineate the subject precisely and to convey the feeling of the message. The speech "The Monument at Wounded Knee" in Appendix B describes a *place* and

▶ **speech of description** An informative speech that uses vivid language to illustrate an activity, object, person, or place.

object by providing vivid word-pictures. Thus, the landscape is not simply desolate; it is characterized by "flat, sun-baked fields and an occasional eroded gully." Cecile Larson goes on to describe the monument:

> The monument itself rests on a concrete slab to the right of the grave. It's a typical, large, old-fashioned granite cemetery marker, a pillar about six feet high topped with an urn—the kind of gravestone you might see in any cemetery with graves from the turn of the century. The inscription tells us that it was erected by the families of those who were killed at Wounded Knee. Weeds grow through the cracks in the concrete at its base.

Can you "see" the monument? If so, Cecile's pictorial language has done its descriptive work. While she describes a place and an object, Cecile's purpose is also to deepen historical understanding of an *event* that occurred there.

As Cecile's vivid example makes clear, the key to descriptive speaking is creating in the minds of your listeners a sharp, pictorial realization of what your subject looks like. The effective use of presentation aids can be very helpful, as can the use of concrete, colorful language as discussed in Chapter 11 and in the next section of this chapter. The topic, purpose, and strategy of your speech of description should suggest the appropriate design for it. The "Monument" speech follows a spatial pattern, in that it develops a verbal map of the Pine Ridge reservation. We will discuss this and other design options for informative speaking later in this chapter.

Speeches of Demonstration

The **speech of demonstration** shows an audience how to do something. Dance instructors teach us the Texas two-step. Librarians and computer specialists teach us how to do research on the Internet efficiently. CPR instructors teach us skills and procedures that save lives. One of our students, Bonnie Marshall, took her classmates step by step through the process of putting together a living will. The tip-off to the speech of demonstration is often the phrase *"how to."* What these examples have in common is that they demonstrate a process and empower listeners so that they too can perform it.

Speeches of demonstration are often helped by the use of presentation aids, as discussed in Chapter 10. The speaker can present and discuss objects that listeners must use to accomplish something, show slides that reveal the steps in a process, or actually demonstrate how to perform an activity. When you are making such a speech, "show and tell" is usually much more effective than just telling.

Speeches of Explanation

A **speech of explanation** offers information about subjects that are abstract or complicated. Because understanding is the object of such a speech, a speech of explanation should present the critical characteristics of a subject and offer abundant examples.[1] Speeches of explanation sometimes incorporate characteristics of speeches of description and demonstration. In her speech explaining

Speeches of demonstration show the audience how to do something.

▶ **speech of demonstration** An informative speech that shows the audience how to do something or how something works.

▶ **speech of explanation** An informative speech that offers understanding of abstract and complex subjects.

Alzheimer's disease, Amanda Miller presented the critical features of her subject in the following way:

1. She justified her speech by quoting a famous victim, President Ronald Reagan, who asked for greater public awareness and understanding of the disease as he exited from public life.

2. She defined the disease.

3. She explained the significance of the disease for those afflicted with it, their families, and the nation (in terms of cost).

4. She described the process of the disease.

5. She identified the risk factors associated with it.

6. She explained how to minimize susceptibility to it.

As you present the critical features of your subject in a speech of explanation, be sure to go through the essential phases of defining your subject, explaining its significance to the lives of your listeners, and describing any processes by which it develops. Include a variety of examples and testimony.

Speeches of explanation face a considerable challenge when their information runs counter to common misconceptions. Professor Katherine Rowan provides an example of how this can work in public service campaigns:

> A particularly resilient obstacle to [seat] belt use is the erroneous but prevalent belief that hitting one's head on a windshield while traveling at 30 miles per hour is an experience much like doing so when a car is stationary. . . . If people understood that the experience would be much more similar to falling from a three-story building and hitting the pavement face first, one obstacle to the wearing of seat belts would be easier to overcome.[2]

As her example indicates, dramatic analogies—such as comparing an auto accident at thirty miles per hour to falling from a building—can help break through our resistance to new ideas. The use of such strategic comparisons and contrasts can help listeners accept new information and use it in their lives.

SPEAKER'S notes
Guidelines for Effective Informative Speaking

Keep these tips/ guidelines in mind as you develop an informative speech.

1. Speeches of description should come alive through colorful language.

2. Speeches of demonstration should present a clear, orderly sequence of steps.

3. Speeches of demonstration are helped by presentation aids.

4. Speeches of explanation need clear definitions of important terms.

5. Speeches of explanation require good examples.

Helping Listeners Learn

Having been a student for most of your life, chances are you've suffered the misfortune of taking a class from a teacher or professor who was just too boring to listen to. He or she was obviously well qualified and even well-prepared, but every time s/he started to lecture on course materials, you found yourself drifting off to oblivion. We offer advice for enhancing your listening skills in Chapter 4, but you can take comfort in knowing that we all tend to "drift off" while listening to boring speakers.

Moreover, we "hear" a great deal every day, but we can only listen to so much. We attend selectively to messages that interest us, concern us, engage us, and even alarm us. Much of the rest simply doesn't penetrate our listening barriers and filters.

So how can you enhance the chances that audience members will listen to and remember your informative messages? You can start by considering some basic audience characteristics as discussed in Chapter 5. How much do your listeners already know about your topic? How interested might they be in it? What preconceptions might they have about it that might help or hinder your purpose? How

FIGURE 13.1
Audience Considerations for Informative Speeches

Audience Type	Strategies
Interested but uninformed	• Provide basic information in clear, simple language. • Avoid jargon; define technical terms. • Use examples and narratives for amplification. • When communicating complicated information, use analogies, metaphors, and/or presentation aids. • Use voice, gestures, and eye contact to reinforce meaning.
Interested and knowledgeable	• Establish your credibility early in the speech. • Acknowledge diverse perspectives on topic. • Go into depth with information and expert testimony. • Offer engaging presentation that keeps focus on content.
Uninterested	• Show listeners what's in it for them. • Keep presentation short and to the point. • Use sufficient examples and narratives to arouse and sustain interest. • Use eye-catching presentation aids and colorful language. • Make a dynamic presentation.
Unsympathetic (toward topic)	• Show respect for listeners and their point of view. • Cite sources the audience will respect. • Present information to enlarge listeners' understanding. • Develop stories and examples to arouse favorable feeling. • Make a warm, engaging presentation.
Distrustful (of speaker)	• Establish your credibility early in the speech. • Rely heavily on factual examples and expert testimony. • Cite sources of information in your presentation. • Be straightforward, business-like, and personable. • Keep good eye contact with listeners.

do they regard you and your ethos to speak on this topic? Figure 13.1 charts these audience considerations and directs you to possible strategies you can use.

Motivating Audiences to Listen

To motivate listeners, especially those who are not initially interested in your subject, you must tell them why your message is important to them. As you consider your primary audience with respect to your main ideas and purpose for speaking, ask yourself why they would want to know what you have to tell them.

- Will it help them understand and control the world around them?

- Will it improve their health, safety, or general well-being?

- Will it give them a sense of making a contribution by caring for others?

- Will it help them establish better relations with family and friends?

- Will it give them a sense of accomplishment and achievement, thus enhancing their personal growth, power, and independence?

- Will it contribute to the restoration of moral balance and fairness?

- Will it provide them with enjoyment?

For example, a speech offering advice for that perfect first job interview would appeal to your listeners' need for achievement, whereas a speech documenting the suffering of Haitians in the wake of the 2010 earthquake would engage our need to care for others.

Hannah Johnston opened her speech on the fast-food industry by appealing to health and safety motivations: "If you had a choice, I'm sure you wouldn't choose to eat some of the stuff that can end up in processed meat." Hannah ruined lunch for some of her classmates, but they could not help but listen closely.

Maintaining Audience Attention

Once you have motivated your audience to listen, you want to hold their attention throughout your speech. In Chapter 9, we discussed how to attract audience attention in the introduction of your speech. Here we focus on how to sustain that interest. You can do so by applying one or more of the five factors that affect attention: relevance, intensity, contrast, repetition, and novelty.

Organizational training programs must combine motivation and information to help employees become more effective.

Relevance. A speech that relates to an audience's specific needs, interests, or concerns will hold its attention. Uninterested listeners may need to have this **relevance** demonstrated for them. Stephen Huff created relevance for his speech on earthquakes by concentrating on the New Madrid area in which he and his listeners lived. He dramatized this relevance by the use of contrast, pointing out that the energy

▶ **relevance** Refers to the extent to which a speech relates to an audience's specific needs, interests, or concerns.

level of the New Madrid quakes of the previous century "was over nine hundred times more powerful than the Hiroshima atomic bomb and more than thirty times more powerful than the 7.0 quake that hit San Francisco." Needless to say, Stephen had his listeners' attention as he talked about how to prepare for the next major quake in the area.

Intensity. **Intensity** in a speech refers to its boldness, colorful language, or passionate presentation. Striking examples and effective use of presentation aids can also add intensity. Josh Logan created intensity in his concluding remarks as he described the unfolding reality of global warming:

> If you want to understand why global warming has become one of the great crises of our time, you've simply got to step outside into the greenhouse. Listen for the falling trees, watch the industrial smokestacks darkening the sky, and smell that rich bouquet of exhaust fumes that we are constantly pumping into the air. The greenhouse effect is a monster we all are creating.

Contrast. **Contrast** attracts attention and sharpens perspective by highlighting the differences between opposites. In this textbook, we print important terms in boldface so that they will grab your attention. While making your presentation, you can employ contrast through abrupt changes in pitch, volume, movement, and rate of speech. Contrasting views can help to dramatize disputed issues in a way that listeners often find engaging. Speakers may define abstract concepts by contrast in a manner that attracts attention; i.e., "We Americans are definitely *not* socialists!" Finally, you can highlight contrasts by simply speaking in terms of oppositions, such as life and death, or by highlighting the highs and lows of a situation.

Alexandra McArthur used contrast as she discussed the "dream" Honduras painted in tourist brochures with the "reality" she had experienced during a longer stay in that country. Throughout his career, Martin Luther King Jr. made frequent use of rich contrasting images such as "mountaintops of jubilation" and "valleys of despair" to couch his vision of social justice and progress. "[O]nly when it is dark enough," he insisted just before his assassination, "can you see the stars."[3]

Repetition. The **repetition** of sounds, words, and phrases during a speech can attract and hold attention. Skillful speakers may use repetition to emphasize points, help listeners follow the flow of ideas, and embed messages in audience memory. As we saw in Chapter 11, repetition underlies alliteration and parallel construction. Alliteration lends vividness to main ideas: "Today, I will discuss how the *M*ississippi River *m*eanders from *M*innesota to the sea." The repetition of the *m* sound catches attention and emphasizes the statement. Similarly, parallel construction establishes a pattern that sticks in the mind. Repeated questions and answers, such as "What is our goal? It is to . . .," sustain attention.

Novelty. **Novelty** refers to the quality of being new or unusual. If you have a fresh way of seeing and saying things, uninterested or distrustful listeners may increase both their respect for you and their interest in your subject. A novel phrase can fascinate listeners and hold their attention. In a speech on environmental stewardship, Jim Cardoza found a novel way to describe the magnitude of pollution. After reporting that 19 million tons of garbage are picked up each year along the nation's beaches, he concluded: "And that's just the tip of the wasteberg." His neologism, *wasteberg*, reminded listeners of *iceberg* and suggested the enormity of the problem.

▶ **intensity** Refers to the extent to which aspects of a speech have the quality of being striking or standing out.

▶ **contrast** Attracts attention and sharpens perspective by highlighting the differences between opposites.

▶ **repetition** Repeating sounds, words, or phrases to attract and hold attention.
▶ **novelty** The quality of being new or unusual.

SPEAKER'S notes — Attention Techniques

Use the following strategies to attract and sustain the attention of your listeners.

1. *Motivate* listeners by showing them how they can benefit from your message.

2. *Speak with intensity*—develop word-pictures that vividly depict your topic.

3. *Use strategic repetition* to amplify your message.

4. *Rely on novelty* by using fresh expressions and providing new examples.

5. *Present contrasts* to show what your topic is not.

6. *Highlight relevance* to connect your subject directly to the experience of listeners.

Promoting Audience Retention

Even the best information is useless unless your listeners remember and use it. Repetition, relevance, and structural factors can all be used to promote audience **retention.** The more frequently we hear or see anything, the more likely we are to retain it. This is why advertisers bombard us with slogans to keep their product names in our consciousness. These slogans may be repeated in all of their advertisements, regardless of the visuals or narratives presented. The repetition of key words or phrases in a speech also helps the audience remember. In his famous civil rights speech in Washington, D.C., Martin Luther King Jr.'s repetition of the phrase "I have a dream . . ." became the hallmark of the speech and is now used as its title.

Relevance is also important to retention. Our minds filter incoming information, associating it with things we already know and evaluating it for its potential usefulness. *If you want listeners to remember your message, tell them why and how it relates to their lives.*

Structural factors also affect how well a message is retained. Previews, summaries, clear transitions, and a well-organized speech as discussed in Chapter 9 can help your audience retain and remember your message. Suppose you were given the following list of words to memorize:

> North, man, hat, daffodil, green, tulip, coat, boy, south, red, east, shoes, gardenia, woman, purple, marigold, gloves, girl, yellow, west

Memorization might be quite a challenge, but what if the words were rearranged like this?

> North, south, east, west
> Man, boy, woman, girl
> Daffodil, tulip, gardenia, marigold
> Green, red, purple, yellow
> Hat, coat, shoes, gloves

In the first example, you have what looks like a random list of words. In the second, the words have been organized by categories. Now you have five groups of four related words to remember. Material that is presented in a consistent and orderly pattern is much easier for your audience to retain.

▶ **retention** The extent to which speakers remember and use a message.

FINDING YOUR

voice Your Favorite Teacher

You can probably recall one or several outstanding teachers who have helped inspire you to want to learn. How did he or she do so? What techniques discussed here did they employ to motivate you to listen, maintain your attention while speaking, and help you retain their main ideas and information?

Speech Designs

Once you have selected a topic that promises new and important information for your listeners, conducted thorough and responsible research, determined your main and supporting ideas, and given some thought to how you might motivate your listeners to attend and remember your messages, you need to choose a design to arrange or structure the body of your speech. In chapter 9, we offer a brief overview of the most prominent designs used in public speaking. Here we offer more detailed discussions of six designs particularly well suited to informative speaking: categorical, comparative, spatial, sequential, chronological, and causation.

Categorical Design

A **categorical design** arranges the main ideas and materials of a speech by natural or customary divisions. Natural divisions exist within the subject itself, such as three important early warning symptoms for detecting breast cancer. Customary divisions represent conventional ways of thinking about a subject, such as past, present, and future views of it. Categories help us sort information so that we can make sense of it.

Each category in the design becomes a main point for development. For a short presentation, you should limit the number of categories to no more than five; three is often better for a short speech. Remember, you must develop these points with supporting material that details, authenticates, and illustrates what you are talking about. That takes time! You don't want to go beyond the time limits set by your instructor. Nor do you want to overtax your listeners' ability to remember and their willingness to give you their attention.

In her informative speech, Nicolette Fisk described architectural answers to a dilemma posed by terrorist attacks: how to keep our greatest monuments and buildings safe but still beautiful. Here is an abbreviated outline of the categorical design of her speech.

Preview: Architects have developed three innovative answers to the question of how to both guard and beautify our greatest buildings and shrines.

   I. Retaining walls provide one such answer.

      A. Overlapping stone walls can provide a picturesque barrier to explosive-laden vehicles.

▶ **categorical design** Arranges the main ideas and materials of a speech by natural or customary divisions.

B. Retaining walls have been erected to protect the Washington Monument.

C. Architect Laurie Olin said, "The point is to turn this security thing into a beautiful walk."

II. Collapsible concrete is a second answer to the challenge.

A. It is strong enough to support pedestrians, but collapses under the weight of heavier vehicles.

B. It both preserves open public space and creates an urban booby trap for terrorists.

C. It is widely used in New York City.

III. Adding street furniture offers a third answer to protect pedestrians along sidewalks.

A. Bollards are designed to absorb huge vehicular impacts.

1. They were first designed for military security measures.

2. Now they function as fashionable, decorative features around buildings.

B. Heavy benches and boulders along the street provide seating as well as protection for strollers.

To conclude, *categories are the mind's way of ordering the world by seeking patterns within it or by supplying patterns to arrange it.* Speech designs based upon these patterns are often quite effective in conveying information.

Comparative Design

A **comparative design** explores the similarities or differences among things, events, and ideas. Comparing the unknown to the known can be especially useful when your topic is unfamiliar, abstract, technical, or difficult to understand. Speakers often shed light on current events by comparing them to the past. Two basic variations of comparative design are literal and figurative analogies.

In a **literal analogy**, the subjects compared are drawn from the same field of experience. For instance, you might track the voting records of two different politicians on an important issue such as campaign finance reform. "The French Paradox," printed at the end of this chapter, illustrates literal analogy, comparing French and American styles of eating.

In a **figurative analogy**, the subjects are drawn from different fields of experience. For example, you might describe the complexities of the human circulatory system by way of comparison to a city traffic system. Paul Ashdown, a professor of journalism at the University of Tennessee, used an extended figurative analogy comparing the World Wide Web to America's "Wild West."[4] Both literal and figurative analogy designs can be insightful and imaginative, helping listeners see subjects in surprising, revealing ways. But if the comparison seems strained or far-fetched, the speech will collapse and the speaker's ethos will be damaged.

Comparative designs often proceed by contrast, in which case each point of difference becomes a main point. In the interest of simplicity, you should limit yourself to five or fewer points of similarity and difference in a short presentation. In her speech on healthy nutrition, Thressia Taylor used the figurative analogy of

▶ **comparative design**   Arranges a speech by exploring the similarities or differences among things, events, and ideas.

▶ **literal analogy**   A comparison drawn from subjects from the same field of experience.

▶ **figurative analogy**   A comparison drawn from subjects from essentially different fields of experience.

caring for a classic car to help her arrange her main ideas and offer a creative take on a potentially less-than-fascinating topic:

Preview: Providing your body with the right nutrients is just as important as providing your classic car with the right fuels and lubricants.

I. Getting the right proteins is like having enough octane in your gasoline.

   A. Protein builds, maintains, and repairs the tissues that keep your engine from sputtering.

   B. Three or more servings a day will help boost your octane and keep your engine running.

II. Along with proteins, you need carbohydrates for energy and quick acceleration.

   A. Most of them should come from whole grains, fruits, and vegetables.

   B. Eat four or more servings daily to keep your engine well-tuned and humming along.

III. Finally, you need fat to keep your system well-lubricated and running smoothly.

   A. Most of us get too much of the bad kind, which can gum up our systems and land us in the junkyard before our time.

   B. But the right fats are absolutely necessary for that long haul down life's highway.

Spatial Design

A **spatial design** is appropriate for speeches that develop their topics within a physical setting. The main points are arranged as they occur in physical space, the order of discussion often proceeding in terms of the relative nearness of things to one another. Most people are familiar with maps and can readily visualize directions. A speech using a spatial design provides listeners with a descriptive oral map, such as we see in Cecile Larson's "Wounded Knee" speech.

To develop a spatial design that is easy for listeners to follow, select a starting point and then take your audience on an orderly, systematic journey to a destination. Once you begin a pattern of movement, stay with it to the end of the speech. If you change direction in the middle, the audience may get lost. Be sure to complete the pattern so that you satisfy listeners' desire for closure. Suzanne Marchetti's informative speech introducing Yellowstone Park developed within a spatial design:

Preview: When you visit Yellowstone, stop first at the South Entrance Visitor's Center, then drive northwest to Old Faithful, north to Mammoth Hot Springs, and then southeast to the Grand Canyon of the Yellowstone.

I. Your first stop should be at the South Entrance Visitor's Center.

   A. Talk with a park ranger to help plan your trip.

   B. Attend a lecture or film to orient yourself.

   C. Pick up materials and maps to make your tour more meaningful.

▶ **spatial design** Arranges the main points of a speech as they occur in actual space.

II. Drive northwest through Geyser Valley to Old Faithful.

    A. Hike the boardwalks in the Upper Geyser Basin.

    B. Join the crowds waiting for Old Faithful to erupt on schedule.

    C. Have lunch at Old Faithful Inn.

III. Continue north to Mammoth Hot Springs.

    A. Plan to spend the night at the lodge or in one of the cabins.

    B. Attend the evening lectures or films on the history of the park.

IV. Drive southeast to the Grand Canyon of the Yellowstone.

    1. Take in the view from Inspiration Point.

    2. Hike down the trail for a better view of the waterfalls.

Suzanne's speech design described an approximate circular pattern that was orderly and provided her listeners with a good sense of the location of important places within the park. Each of her main points received about the same amount of attention, so that her speech seemed well balanced as it traced this circle. Speakers using the spatial pattern often use a presentation aid, such as a map, to reinforce the sense of space created in their speeches.

Landmarks, such as Old Faithful, help listeners identify the places in a spatial design.

Sequential Design

A **sequential design** explains the steps of a process in the order in which they should be taken. This design is especially useful for "how to" speeches of demonstration. You begin by identifying the necessary steps in the process and the order in which they should take place. These steps become the main points of your speech. In a short presentation, you should have no more than five steps as main points. You can assign numbers to these steps as you make your presentation.

The following abbreviated outline, developed by Jeffrey O'Connor, illustrates a sequential design:

Preview: The five steps of efficient textbook reading include skimming, reading, rereading, reciting, and reviewing.

  I. First, *skim* through the chapter to get the overall picture.

    A. Identify the major ideas from the section headings.

    B. Read any summary statements.

    C. Read any boxed materials.

    D. Make a key-word outline of major topics.

  II. Second, *read* the chapter a section at a time.

    A. Make notes in the margins on questions you have.

    B. Look up definitions of unfamiliar words.

    C. Go back and highlight the major ideas.

▶ **sequential design** Explains the steps of a process in the order in which they should be taken.

III. Third, *reread* the chapter.

    A. Fill in your outline with more detail.

    B. Try to answer the questions you wrote in the margin.

    C. Frame questions for your instructor on anything you don't understand.

IV. Fourth, *recite* what you have read.

    A. Use your outline to make an oral presentation to yourself.

    B. Explain the material to someone else.

V. Finally, *review* the material within twenty-four hours.

    A. Review your outline.

    B. Reread the highlighted material.

Presenting the steps in this orderly, sequential way helped Jeffrey "walk" his University of New Mexico classmates through the process.

Chronological Design

A **chronological design** explains events or historical developments in the order in which they occurred. Using the chronological design, you may start with the beginnings of the subject and trace it up to the present through its defining moments. Or, you may start with the present and trace the subject back to its origins. In either case, chronological presentations are generally more effective when speakers keep their presentation of events simple, in the order in which they occurred, and related to the message of the speech. Never discuss history for its own sake. Use the past to illuminate your purpose for speaking in the present.

To keep your listeners' attention and to meet time requirements, you must be selective. Choose landmark events as the main points in your message, and then arrange them in their natural order. D'Angelo Dartez presented a speech on the evolution of the T-shirt based upon the following chronological design:

Preview: The T-shirt began as an undergarment, developed into outerwear, next became a bearer of messages, and finally emerged as high-fashion apparel.

I. The T-shirt originated as an undergarment early in the twentieth century.

    A. The first undershirts with sleeves were designed for sailors, to spare sensitive people the sight of hairy armpits.

    B. They were first sold commercially in the late 1930s.

    C. During World War II, T-shirts were used as outerwear in the tropics.

II. After World War II, civilians began using T-shirts as outerwear.

    A. They were comfortable and absorbent.

    B. They were popularized in movies like *Rebel Without a Cause*.

    C. They were easy to care for.

III. T-shirts soon became embellished with pictures and messages.

    A. Children's T-shirts had pictures of cartoon characters.

▶ **chronological design** Explains events or historical developments in the order in which they occurred.

  B. Adult T-shirt designs were usually related to sports teams.

  C. T-shirts soon were used for "political" statements.

IV. Today's T-shirts are unique.

  A. You can customize a message.

  B. You can put your picture on a T-shirt.

  C. You can buy bejeweled T-shirts.

Causation Design

A **causation design** addresses the origins or consequences of a situation or event, proceeding from cause to effect or from effect to cause. The most important points of focus are the subject and how it came about, or what its results might be. The major causes or consequences become main points in the body of the speech.

In her speech "Honduras: Paradise or . . ." Alexandra McArthur holds the tourism industry up for close critical inspection. Although the industry is typically accepted without question as a blessing for underdeveloped nations, Alexandra discovered a scamier side of it. Her speech developed in the following cause-effect pattern:

Preview: While it can offer some benefits, tourism can also be a curse because of its economic, sociological, and political impact.

The causation design used by Alexandra McArthur exposed the negative side of tourism.

  I. Economic impact: the dollars generated by tourism are not an unmixed blessing.

  A. Tourism contributes to unequal distribution of wealth: the rich get richer, the poor poorer.

  B. Tourism can take money out of a country and put it into the pockets of foreign investors.

 II. Sociological impact: native populations can suffer.

  A. Native workers are often over-qualified and underpaid.

  B. Encourages child labor: tourists are more likely to buy souvenirs and crafts from children.

III. Political impact: tourism encourages class and foreign resentment.

  A. Natives are often forced off land so that tourist attractions can be built.

  B. Natives are often then banned from the beaches and restaurants created on their land.

  C. Natives can't afford these luxuries anyway.

  D. You don't have to behave badly to be an Ugly American: just show up!

Speeches that use the causation design are subject to one serious drawback—the tendency to oversimplify. Any complex situation will generally have many underlying causes, and any given set of conditions may lead to many different future effects. Be wary of overly simple explanations and overly confident predictions.

▶ **causation design**   Addresses the origins or consequences of a situation or event, proceeding from cause to effect or from effect to cause.

FIGURE 13.2 Which Speech Design to Use When

Design	Use When
Spatial	Your topic can be discussed by how it is positioned in a physical setting or natural environment. It allows you to take your audience on an orderly "oral tour" of your topic.
Sequential	Your topic can be arranged by time. It is useful for describing a process as a series of steps or explaining a subject as a series of developments.
Chronological	Your topic can be discussed as a historical development through certain defining moments.
Categorical	Your topic has natural or customary divisions. Each category becomes a main point for development. It is useful when you need to organize large amounts of material.
Comparative	Your topic is new to your audience, abstract, technical, or simply difficult to comprehend. It helps make material more meaningful by comparing or contrasting it with something the audience already knows and understands.
Causation	Your topic is best understood in terms of its underlying causes or consequences. May be used to account for the present or predict future possibilities.

Such simplified explanations and predictions are one form of faulty reasoning (fallacy), discussed further in Chapter 15.

As noted in Chapter 9, your choice of speech design should reflect your speech materials and specific purpose for speaking. Note that the designs discussed in this chapter are often used in varying degrees of combination. For instance, D'Angelo's speech tracing the modern history of the T-shirt combines elements of a chronological and categorical design. Most speeches employ some degree of categorical thinking. See Figure 13.2 for an overview of what designs to use and when to use them.

Rising to the Challenge of the Informative Speech

Informative speaking can pose a special challenge for speakers. Self-introductory speaking often reveals fascinating insights into the minds and personalities of speakers. Persuasive speeches offer the drama of controversy and the excitement of watching speakers take public stands on issues. Ceremonial speeches can

FINDING YOUR voice
Developing Strategies for Informative Speaking

As you near completion of preparing your informative speech, pair off with a classmate and critique each other's plans in terms of:

- the kind of informative speech you will be presenting;
- how you will apply the principles of motivation, attention, and retention to help audience members learn;

- what design or combination of designs you have chosen to use and why; and
- how you will meet the challenges of presenting an interesting informative speech.

After the successful presentations of your speeches, take each other to lunch to celebrate.

---

entertain and inspire. In contrast, informative speeches can sometimes come across as dull. On the other hand, many of the informative speeches we have heard in class, including those cited here, managed to be quite engaging and interesting. What can we learn from these successful speakers to help us avoid the information doldrums?

First, these speakers selected good topics. They chose topics they themselves were genuinely fascinated with, and topics that yielded information of inherent interest and importance to the lives of their listeners.

Second, these speakers used their time well. They found topics well in advance of their speaking assignments and left plenty of time for research and to reflect on what they learned.

Third, these speakers devised artful designs for their speeches. They introduced topics in ways that grabbed and held attention, establishing a clear understanding of their purposes, developing ideas so that they satisfied the expectations of listeners, and finding a conclusion that would make it hard for audiences to forget their most important themes.

Fourth, these speakers filled their designs with colorful and striking content. They provided facts and figures and testimony to confront their listeners with unexpected realities, and examples and stories to awaken feelings and stir the imagination. They used language in ways that made their ideas stick in the memory.

Fifth, they put a lot of energy into their presentations. They set a varied and lively pace, using pauses for emphasis. Their voices came alive with the importance of their messages, and their gestures emphasized what they were saying.

Briefings: an Application

A **briefing** is a specialized form of informative speaking offered in an organizational setting. It may involve description and demonstration, but usually emphasizes explanation. Briefings often take place during meetings, as when employees gather at the beginning of a workday to learn about plans or policy changes.[5] At such meetings, you might be asked to give a status report on a project. Briefings also take

---

▶ **briefing** A short informative presentation offered in an organizational setting that focuses upon plans, policies, or reports.

place in one-on-one situations, as when you report to your supervisor at work. They can take the form of a press briefing that follows a crisis or major event.[6] Often a question-and-answer period will follow the briefing.

Being asked to present briefings at school or at work provides you with the opportunity to demonstrate your leadership potential and importance to the group. Unfortunately, they are not often done well. Most how-to books on communicating in organizations deplore the lack of brevity, clarity, and directness in presentations.[7] When executives in eighteen organizations were asked, "What makes a presentation poor?" they offered the following answers:

- It is badly organized.

- It is not presented well.

- It contains too much jargon.

- It is too long.

- It lacks examples or comparisons.[8]

The following guidelines can help you prepare and present more effective briefings:

1. *A briefing should be what its name suggests: brief.* Cut out any material that is not related directly to your main points. Keep your introduction and conclusion short. Begin with a preview and end with a summary.

2. *Organize your ideas before you open your mouth.* How can you possibly be organized when you are called on without warning in a meeting to "tell us about your project"? The answer is simple: prepare in advance (also review our guidelines for making impromptu speeches in Chapter 12). *Never go into any meeting in which there is even the slightest chance that you might be asked to report without a skeleton outline of a presentation.* Select a simple design and make a key-word outline of points you would cover. Take this to the meeting with you.

3. *Rely heavily on facts and figures, expert testimony, and short examples for supporting materials.* Don't drift off into extended examples and long stories. Use comparison and contrast to make your points stand out and come alive.

4. *Adapt your language to your audience.* If you are an engineer reporting on a project to a group of managers, use the language of management, not the language of engineering. Tell them what they need to know in language they can understand. Relate the subject to what they already know.

5. *Present your message with confidence.* Be sure everyone can see and hear you. Stand up, if necessary. Look listeners in the eye. Speak firmly with an air of assurance. After all, the project is yours, and you are the expert on it.

6. *Be prepared to answer tough questions.* Be prepared to respond to likely questions forthrightly and honestly. No one likes bad news, but worse news will come if you don't deliver the bad news to those who need to know it *when* they need to know it. Review our suggestions for handling question-and-answer sessions in Chapter 12.

FINAL
reflections Your Informed Voice

When the gods punished Prometheus for giving that first informative speech teaching humans the power of fire, they did so not merely for fear of humans coming to overpower them. They knew that knowledge and enlightenment would eventually endow us with god-like powers, and they feared that we would not exercise those powers responsibly. Finding your voice as an informative speaker means considerably more than mastering the skills of descriptive, demonstrative, and explanatory speech-making, more than motivating listeners to attend and retain your messages, more than simply knowing what you are saying and saying it effectively. It means becoming a conscious and accountable source of truth in a world too often drowned by partisan discord and disinformation. It means taking seriously your role and obligation as an informed voice and as a source of enlightenment before your peers.

SAMPLE INFORMATIVE SPEECH

This colorful informative speech builds largely upon a comparative design, developing a literal analogy between French and American eating styles. It also offers a model of responsible knowledge, using facts and testimony drawn from numerous sources and experts. Gabrielle connects with audience dreams of a "give us the cake but spare us the consequences" lifestyle. In effect, she shows how these dreams might become reality. You can watch this speech as it was presented at Davidson College on MySpeechLab.

The French Paradox: A Delicious Secret Revealed

GABRIELLE WALLACE

Have any of you ever fought the dreaded "freshman 15"—those unwanted pounds that seem to show up on you out of nowhere—but noticed by everyone as soon as you go home after your first year? What if I told you of a land where people eat this, drink this, and look like this [shows slides revealing delicious foods, elegant wines, and attractive people]? Would you believe me? They live like we wish we could, but don't experience the freshman 15—at least not as many of them do. If this sounds unlikely, it is nonetheless true. I call it "the French paradox." It refers to the fact that the French eat foods on a regular basis that are every bit as rich and fattening as what we eat, yet they are not nearly as prone to rapid weight gain and other negative health consequences. In order to understand the French paradox, we must consider how they combine food choices, beverage consumption, and cultural attitudes towards eating itself.

◀ Gabrielle's opening reference to the "freshman 15" motivates audience members by appealing to their desires for health and attractiveness. Her use of presentation aids depicting rich foods, elegant wines, and beautiful young people adds colorful intensity to her speech.

◀ Gabrielle's preview of her main points and her effective transitions make for a presentation that is easy for listeners to follow and remember.

First, let's take a look at French eating habits. What they eat and how much they eat work together to make an ideal diet. The French eat as little processed food as possible. According to Roger Corder, a professor at St. Bartholomew's Hospital in London who has studied the French diet extensively, the French eat a higher quality and better variety of foods than most Americans. Like us, the French like rich fatty foods—gravies and cream sauces are common. But a much higher percentage of their diet consists of whole grains and vegetables, and they emphasize seasonally fresh and locally grown foods. This richness and variety satiates the palate and is considerably more filling than processed foods.

As a result, perhaps, the French eat smaller portions of food. According to Paul Rozin, a nutritionist at the University of Pennsylvania, French portion sizes on average are about 25% smaller than American portions—which might explain why Americans are roughly three times more likely to become obese than French people.

A factor that might account for this is the French upbringing. Mireille Guiliano, author of *French Women Don't Get Fat*, says that the French are not conditioned to overeat. Instead, they are taught to eat only until they are full, and then stop! A recent University of Pennsylvania study confirmed this tendency. The study compared the eating habits of students from Paris and Chicago. It found that French students stopped eating in response to internal cues, like when they first started feeling full or when they wanted to leave room for dessert. The American students, on the other hand, relied more on external cues. They would, for example, eat until the TV show they were watching ended, or until they ran out of a beverage. There's no question that eating habits are a vital point of difference between the French and American cultures.

The second important factor in explaining the French paradox has to do with beverage consumption. The French drink primarily two beverages: water and wine. Again according to Mireille Guiliano, they start the day with a glass of water. Water is known to have metabolic benefits: an article in *Prevention* magazine suggests that consuming 16 oz. of water increases the body's calorie burning rate as much as 30% within 40 minutes.

The second beverage of choice is red wine. According to an article published in 2008 in the *Independent*, a prominent London newspaper, the average French person drinks nearly 17 gallons of wine a year, as compared to the 7 gallons a year consumed by the average Briton. Recently scientists have discovered numerous health benefits of red wine. Studies suggest it promotes higher levels of heart-healthy HDL cholesterol, which counters the effects of bad cholesterol by preventing artery blocking plaque deposits. The World Health Organization reported that countries with the highest wine consumption—France, Italy, and Spain—had the lowest rates of heart disease. Indeed, the region of France that drinks the most wine has the highest percentage of men who live to age 90!

The third important factor in explaining the French paradox has to do with their overall attitude and approach to eating itself. Meal time in France is an elaborate event. Meals typically consist of three to four courses, including a separate course for salad, cheese, and fruit. Susan Loomis, writing in *Health* magazine, likened French meals to Thanksgiving. "[W]hat Americans

▶ Gabrielle has clearly done her research, and makes excellent use of a variety of factual information, expert testimony, and illustrative examples. The result is a highly credible as well as colorful speech. Note how she cites the sources of her knowledge to augment credibility.

do once a year," she continued, "prepare food linked to ritual and history, then gather with family and friends—the French do often, most of them at least once a week."

A meal being a social event encourages slow eating—which contributes again to less overall consumption. As Dr. Rozin argues, the French tend to eat more slowly and to include more socializing and conversation with their meals. The social etiquette of a French meal also tends to promote gradual eating. The next course is never brought out until everyone at the table has finished. Only then, usually after some delay, does eating resume.

Finally, the French thoroughly enjoy the delight of food itself. They enjoy using all five senses when eating. My stepfather, when tasting a new wine, always sticks his nose in it to take in the smell, swirls it to watch the color, and slowly takes in a small amount to absorb the flavor. The owner of a French bakery where I work back home often puts baguettes up to his ear and squeezes them to hear their crunch and test their quality. Claude Fischler, a French sociologist at the University of Pennsylvania, notes that when asked to respond to the words chocolate cake, Americans say "Guilt" whereas the French say "Celebration."

For the French, eating is about the experience of living. It is engrained in their culture and permeates their daily experience. The three factors of eating correctly, drinking wisely, and making a meal an enjoyable experience are what make the French paradox possible. It appears the French have found the secret to being able to have their cake and eat it too—along with some wine, friends, and celebration. We, as American college students, could learn from their example, especially if we want to avoid the horror of the freshman 15!

◀ Gabrielle does an excellent job summarizing her ideas with a succinct conclusion. Her reference back to the freshman 15 echoes the introduction with a "bookend" effect that brings her presentation full-circle.

THIS CHAPTER WILL HELP YOU

1 Understand the nature of persuasion
2 Learn the types of persuasive speaking
3 Understand the persuasive process
4 Adapt persuasive messages to different audiences
5 Select appropriate designs for your persuasive speeches

14 Persuasive Speaking

> *Because there has been implanted in us the power to persuade each other . . ., not only have we escaped the life of the wild beasts but we have come together and founded cities and made laws and invented arts.* —ISOCRATES

Recently we put together a "top ten" list among the thousands of student persuasive speeches we have heard or that have been sent to us. One thing especially stood out about these memorable speeches: *they arose out of strong feeling.*

- Dolapo Olushola was obviously moved as she described the plight of orphans at the Open Arms Orphanage in Malawi, Nigeria, asking her Davidson College listeners to contribute to their cause. You can see her powerful speech in MySpeechLab.

- Beth Tidmore touched the hearts of her University of Memphis audience as she invited them on an imaginary journey to the Special Olympics, urging them to join her as a chaperone and volunteer.

- Anna Aley spoke with anger and indignation as she described the lax rental laws and slum lords that victimized students at Kansas State University.

- Austin Wright of the University of Texas expressed outrage as he described the government's misuse of faulty databases, urging listeners to "help keep Big Brother off your back."

These and other fine speeches make clear that there is a real difference between having to give a persuasive speech and speaking persuasively because you feel you just have to share your passion or concern. Through their speeches these students demonstrated dramatically that they had found their voices.

When we speak persuasively, we want others to share our feelings, and to see the world as we see it. We want to influence both their attitudes and their actions. **Persuasion,** therefore, is the *art of gaining fair and favorable consideration for our points of view.* Ethical persuasion is grounded in sound reasoning and is sensitive to the needs and interests of listeners. Such persuasion gives us the chance to make the world a little better.

Many people still ask, "What difference can one person make? My words don't carry much weight." Perhaps not, but words make ripples, and ripples can come together to make waves. Such was the case with Anna Aley, who gave a persuasive speech condemning substandard off-campus student housing. Her classroom speech was later presented in a public forum on campus. The text of her speech, which appears in Appendix B, was reprinted in the local newspaper, which followed it up with investigative reports and a supportive editorial. Brought to the attention of the mayor and city commission, Anna's speech helped promote reforms in the city's rental housing policies. Her words are still reverberating in Manhattan, Kansas.

Perhaps your classroom speech will not have that kind of impact, but you never know who or what may be changed by it. In this chapter, we explore the nature of persuasive speaking in contrast with informative speaking. Then we will identify the major types of persuasive speaking, how the persuasive process works, challenges that persuaders must confront, and the major designs that serve persuasive speaking.

The Nature of Persuasive Speaking

Persuasive speaking differs from informative speaking in eight basic ways: *First, while informative speeches reveal options, persuasive speeches urge a choice among them.* For example, an informative speaker might say: "There are three different ways we can deal with the budget deficit. Let me explain them." In contrast, a persuasive speaker would urge support for one of them.

Second, informative speakers act as teachers: persuaders act as advocates. The difference is often one of passion and engagement. Persuasive speakers are more vitally committed to a cause. This does not necessarily mean that persuaders are loud; the most passionate and intense moments of a speech can be very quiet.

Third, informative speeches offer supporting material to illustrate points: persuasive speeches use the same material as evidence that justifies advice. An ethical persuader interweaves facts and statistics, testimony, examples, and narratives into a compelling case based on responsible knowledge and sensitivity to the best interests of listeners.

Fourth, the role of the audience changes dramatically from information to persuasion. Informed listeners expand their knowledge, but persuaded listeners often become *agents of change.* Their new attitudes, beliefs, and actions will affect themselves and others.

▶ **persuasion**   The art of gaining fair and favorable consideration for our points of view.

Fifth, persuasive speeches ask for more audience commitment than do informative speeches. Although there is some risk in being exposed to new ideas, more is at stake when listening to a persuasive message. What if a persuasive speaker is mistaken or even dishonest? What if her proposed plan of action is defective? Doing always involves a greater risk than knowing. Your commitment could cost you—and those who may be influenced by your actions—dearly.

Sixth, leadership is even more important in persuasive than in informative speeches. Because persuasive speeches involve risk, listeners weigh the character and competence of speakers closely. Do they really know what they are talking about? Do they have their listeners' interests at heart? As a persuasive speaker, your ethos will be on public display and will be scrutinized carefully.

Seventh, appeals to feelings are more useful in persuasive than in informative speeches. Because of the risk involved, listeners may balk at accepting recommendations, even when those recommendations are supported by good reasons. To overcome such inertia, persuaders must sometimes appeal to feelings,[1] which is why they often use emotional appeals to open their speeches. For example, the informative statement "A 10 percent rise in tuition will reduce the student population by about 5 percent next term" might take the following form in a persuasive speech:

> The people pushing for the tuition increase don't think a few hundred dollars more each semester will have that much effect. They think we can handle it.
>
> Let me tell you about my friend Tricia. She's on the Dean's List in chemistry, the pride and hope of her family. Tricia will get a great job when she graduates—if she graduates! But if this increase goes through, Tricia won't be back next term. Her dreams of success will be delayed—and perhaps denied!
>
> Perhaps you're in the same boat as Tricia—paddling like mad against the current. We all need to work together to defeat this tuition increase.

Emotional and graphic language, developed through examples or narratives, can help people see the human dimension of problems and move these listeners to the right action.

Eighth, the ethical obligation for persuasive speeches is even greater than for informative speeches. As Isocrates said in this chapter's opening quotation, persuasion can be

Informative Speaking	Persuasive Speaking
1. Reveals options.	1. Urges a choice among options.
2. Speaker acts as teacher.	2. Speaker acts as advocate.
3. Uses supporting material to enlighten listeners.	3. Uses supporting material to justify advice.
4. Audience expands knowledge.	4. Audience becomes agent of change.
5. Asks for little audience commitment.	5. Asks for strong audience commitment.
6. Speaker's credibility is important.	6. Speaker's credibility more important.
7. Fewer appeals to feelings.	7. More appeals to feelings.
8. High ethical obligation.	8. Higher ethical obligation.

FIGURE 14.1
Informative Versus Persuasive Speaking

a blessing to humankind. This great educator of the Golden Age of Greece knew that at their best, persuasive speakers make us confront our obligation to believe and act in socially and morally responsible ways. By describing how they themselves became persuaded, they model how we should deliberate in difficult situations. By making intelligence and morality effective in public affairs, they can help the world evolve in more enlightened ways.

The major differences between informative and persuasive speaking are summarized in Figure 14.1.

The Types of Persuasive Speaking

Persuasion helps us deal with the uncertainties reflected in the following questions:

- What is the truth?
- How should I feel about a situation?
- What should I do about it?

These questions in turn invite three basic types of persuasive speaking: speeches that focus on facts, speeches that address attitudes, beliefs, and values, and speeches that advocate action and policy.

Speeches That Focus on Facts

People argue constantly over what the true state of affairs was, is, and will be. Such arguments generate **speeches that focus on facts**. Uncertainty can surround questions of past, current, and future facts.

Past Facts.   Did something actually happen? Did the celebrity commit murder? Did the CEO defraud her stockholders? Persuaders argue questions of past facts before juries in courtrooms and on newspaper editorial pages as well as on the public platform. Speeches concerning past facts try to shape the perceptions and memories of people and events. They will be successful if they do the following:

Speeches that focus on facts may need visual supporting materials to strengthen their claims.

- **Present facts that confirm what they claim.** In the text of his speech "Global Burning," reprinted in Appendix B, note how Josh Logan uses charts and statistics to confirm the growth of greenhouse gases over the past thousand years.

- **Present supporting testimony from recent, respected expert sources.** To support his factual claims about global warming, Josh cites the "United Nations Intergovernmental Panel on Climate Change, reporting during the early part of this year." He describes this study as an "authoritative, thousand-page report, which correlates and tests the work of hundreds of environmental scientists from countries all around the globe."

▶ **speeches that focus on facts** Speeches designed to establish the validity of past or present information or to make predictions about what is likely to occur in the future.

- **Re-create a dramatic, credible narrative of how events in a dispute may have happened.** The renowned Roman orator Cicero, who was also one of the greatest courtroom lawyers who ever lived, was superb in creating narratives of past events that seemed to establish their reality. For an especially spicy example, which also implies the moral depravity of many people in the Rome of several thousand years ago, see his forensic speech, *Pro Caelius.*[2]

- **Current Facts.** What is actually going on? Is a certain rogue nation developing weapons of mass destruction? Questions involving current facts are incredibly important to the fate of nations and individuals. On the basis of our perceptions of current facts, we develop plans of action. Policymakers in the Bush administration decided that Iraq was vitally engaged in efforts to develop weapons of mass destruction. That perception of current facts confirmed their conclusion that Saddam Hussein was an intolerable threat to the security of the United States. That conclusion, in turn, led to their policy decision to invade Iraq and to remove Saddam from power. Clearly, persuasive speeches on current facts can start a chain reaction of important events.

At times, questions of past and current facts turn not on whether something happened or is happening, but on the *definition* of events. Yes, sexual activity occurred in the encounter between the sports star and the woman, but the sex was "consensual, not rape." Yes, Nation X possesses the alleged weapons, but they exist "for mass protection, not for mass destruction." To control the definitions of events is to control the feelings that people have about their meaning.

Future Facts. What will the future bring? And how should we plan for it? Persuasive speeches regarding future facts are **predictions** based on readings of the past and present. Should we invest in a certain company? One persuader may argue that the past record of company earnings justifies a strong vote of confidence in the future. Another may answer that much of this past success occurred under different leadership and that current management has yet to prove itself. The first offers an enthusiastic "buy" recommendation; the second advises caution. It's up to you as a potential investor to weigh the evidence and test the soundness of their reasoning.

Speeches That Address Attitudes, Beliefs, and Values

The world of uncertainty in which we live often underlies **speeches that address attitudes, beliefs, and values**. As we noted in Chapter 5, at the heart of our *attitudes* are feelings we have developed toward certain subjects. For example, Cherie's intense dislike for "ethnic cleansing"—the removal and persecution of entire populations on the basis of religious faith or ethnic affiliation—represents an attitude. *Beliefs* represent what we know or think we know about the world. Cherie's belief that ethnic cleansing is widely practiced in the world gives urgency to her attitude about it. *Values* are underlying principles that support our attitudes and beliefs. Cherie's attitude and belief both rise out of her commitment to a world in which people tolerate, respect, and appreciate one another's differences.

Ideally, our attitudes, beliefs, and values should be in harmony, creating a coherent worldview. However, these elements are sometimes undeveloped, disconnected, or even opposed to one another, leaving that inner world fragmented or

▶ **predictions** Forecasts of what we can expect in the future, often based on trends from past events.

▶ **speeches that address attitudes, beliefs, and values** Speeches designed to modify these elements and help listeners find harmony among them.

FINDING YOUR

voice   Harmonizing Attitudes, Beliefs, and Values

Can you think of situations that might represent inconsistency among attitudes, beliefs, and values? How might you frame persuasive speeches that could restore harmony among these elements? Report your thoughts in class discussion.

confused. When we become aware of this inner disarray, we experience what psychologists call **cognitive dissonance**, the discomfort we feel (or should feel) because of conflict among our attitudes, beliefs, and values. Persuasive speakers have the opportunity to create or restore consistency and harmony for us by recommending appropriate changes in attitude and belief. For example, if Cherie suspects that her listeners are indifferent to ethnic cleansing, even though they strongly value tolerance, she has the opportunity to encourage appropriate feelings and awareness about ethnic cleansing through an effective persuasive speech. By exposing her audience to evidence and powerful proofs, she can expand their moral universe and restore its harmony.[3]

Because values are an integral part of our personality, deep changes in them can have a real impact on how we live. Therefore, we don't change values as readily as we change attitudes and beliefs. Speeches that attempt to change values may seem radical and extreme. For this reason, such speeches are rare, usually occurring only in desperate times and situations. The Great Depression of the 1930s, the civil rights struggle of the 1960s, the Vietnam War of the 1960s and 1970s, and more recent conflicts have all inspired persuasive speeches critical either of American values or of policies that relate to them.

Speeches That Advocate Action and Policy

Speeches that advocate action and policy often build on earlier speeches that affirm facts or activate values. Therefore, in addition to bringing harmony to our inner world of attitudes, beliefs, and values, persuasive speeches can promote coherence between what we say and what we do. Persuasive speakers remind us that we should practice what we preach.

Such was the goal of Amanda Miller, who presented a powerful indictment of the Western Hemisphere Institute for Security Cooperation, better known as the "School of the Americas." Amanda argued that this institute, conducted for many years at Fort Benning, Georgia, under U.S. sponsorship, had been "implicated in gross human rights violations in Latin America." The school, she said, trained its students in "techniques for torture, false imprisonment, extortion, and intimidation" and had been "responsible for the deaths of many thousands of people and countless acts of terrorism." Amanda painted a vivid picture of the contradiction between American values and American actions, and she urged her listeners to "support the cause" of shutting down the Institute. In the process, they would be restoring coherence to the world of morality and action.

▶ **cognitive dissonance**   The discomfort we feel because of conflict among our attitudes, beliefs, and values.

▶ **speeches that advocate action and policy**   Speeches that encourage listeners to change their behavior either as individuals or as members of a group.

The actions proposed by such speeches can be simple and direct, or they can involve complex policy plans, depending on the nature of the problem. To meet the challenge of global warming, Josh Logan developed an elaborate solution that called for listeners' direct personal action as well as their support for changes in government policy. On a less complex issue, Betsy Lyles urged her listeners to donate hair to Locks of Love, an organization that offers hairpieces to impoverished children who are suffering from long-term medical hair loss.

When a speech advocates group action, the audience must see itself as having a common identity and purpose. As we noted in Chapter 11, the speaker can reinforce group identity by using inclusive pronouns (*we, our, us*), by telling stories that emphasize group achievements, and by referring to common heroes, opponents, or martyrs. Anna Aley used an effective appeal to group identity as she proposed specific actions:

Speeches that advocate action can help raise support for worthy causes. Here actor Danny Glover speaks out on behalf of the National Kidney Foundation.

What can one student do to change the practices of numerous Manhattan landlords? Nothing, if that student is alone. But just think of what we could accomplish if we got all 13,600 off-campus students involved in this issue! Think what we could accomplish if we got even a fraction of those students involved!

Type	Function	Techniques
Speeches that focus on facts	Establish true state of affairs	Strengthen claims of past, present, and future fact by citing experts and other supporting evidence. Create lively pictures of the contested facts that reinforce their reality.
Speeches that address attitudes, beliefs, and values	Harmonize attitudes with beliefs, and beliefs with values	Reawaken appreciation for values through stories, examples, and vivid language. Show listeners how to put these values to work. Encourage them to form and re-form attitudes and beliefs consistent with these values.
Speeches that advocate action and policy	Propose programs to remedy problems and put values into action	Show that the program of action will solve the problem by mentioning previous successes in similar situations. Prove that the plan is practical and workable. Picture audience enacting the plan of action. Show the consequences of acting and not acting. Visualize success.

FIGURE 14.2 The Work of Persuasive Speeches

By identifying and uniting them as victims of unscrupulous landlords, Anna encouraged her listeners to act as members of a group.

Speeches advocating action can involve some risk and inconvenience. Therefore, you must present good reasons to overcome your audience's natural caution. The consequences of acting and not acting must be clearly spelled out. Your plan must be practical and reasonable, and your listeners should be able to see themselves enacting it successfully.

The Persuasive Process

William J. McGuire, professor of psychology at Yale University, suggested that successful persuasion is a process involving up to twelve phases.[4] For our purposes, these phases may be grouped into five stages: awareness, understanding, agreement, enactment, and integration (see Figure 14.3). Familiarity with these stages helps us see that persuasion is not an all-or-nothing proposition. A persuasive message can be successful if it moves people through the process toward a goal.

Awareness

Awareness involves knowing about a problem and paying attention to it. This phase is sometimes called *consciousness raising*.[5] In her speech "Honduras: Paradise or . . .?" Alexandra McArthur raised awareness for her cultural critique of the tourism industry in Honduras by creating a vivid contrast between the dream picture painted for tourists and the reality she had experienced:

> The magazine written by the Institute of Tourism highlighted Honduras' hotels, beaches, restaurants, and shopping, while never mentioning the extreme poverty or violence in the country. It described Honduras as "One Small Country: Three Wide Worlds (Tropical Nature, Maya Renaissance, and Caribbean Creation)." In contrast, the land I knew combined the three worlds of superficial tourism, underdeveloped lands, and unequal distribution of wealth.
>
> The people I met on service trips were not the happy, smiling faces on tourist brochures. Instead, far too many of them suffer from malnutrition, and have little access to medicines, running water, or electricity.

Creating awareness is especially important when people do not believe that there actually is a problem. Before advocates could change the way females were

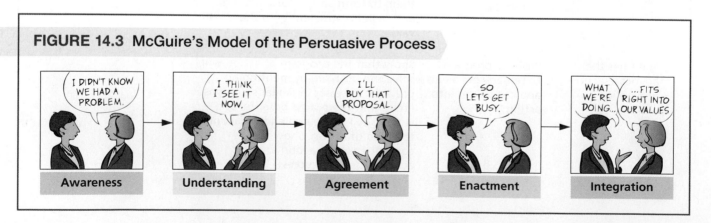

FIGURE 14.3 McGuire's Model of the Persuasive Process

Awareness · **Understanding** · **Agreement** · **Enactment** · **Integration**

▶ **awareness** This first stage in the persuasive process includes knowing about a problem and paying attention to it.

depicted in children's books, they first had to convince listeners that always showing boys in active roles and girls in passive roles could thwart the development of self-esteem and ambition in young girls.[6]

Understanding

The second phase of the persuasive process is **understanding**. Listeners must grasp what you are telling them and know how to carry out your proposals. Amanda Miller encouraged understanding of her School of the Americas message by citing a number of examples:

> In El Salvador, the United Nations Truth Commission found that of twelve officers responsible for the massacre of nine hundred villagers at El Mozote, ten of them were graduates of the School of the Americas.
>
> I wish this were a solitary case. But according to an Inter-American Commission on Human Rights, School of the Americas graduate Raphael Samundio Molina led a massacre at the Colombian Palace of Justice, and three years later was inducted into the School of the Americas hall of fame. In the same country, an International Human Rights Tribunal found that of two hundred and forty-six officers cited for various crimes, one hundred and five of them were School of the Americas graduates.
>
> Finally, the School has produced at least twelve Latin American dictators in countries such as Peru, Bolivia, Argentina, and Ecuador. This is the distinguished record of the School of the Americas that we continue to fund with our taxpayer dollars.

Because her examples were so controversial, Amanda had to document them carefully, using a variety of sources to heighten their credibility.

Agreement

The third stage in the persuasive process is **agreement**, the acceptance by listeners of your position. As they listen to you, audience members should go through a series of *affirmations*, such as: "He's right, this is a serious problem. . . . That's striking evidence; I didn't know about that. . . . I see how this can affect my life. . . . I've got to do something about this. . . . This plan makes sense. I believe it will work." These affirmations should build on each other, developing momentum toward agreement at the end of the speech. Any doubt, any hesitation over the validity of a claim or the soundness of evidence or the accuracy of reasoning, will weaken the process of agreement.

Speakers themselves become important models for agreement. When Dolapo Olushola described the plight of orphans in her native Nigeria, she seemed a strikingly authentic spokesperson as she asked for audience support:

> Did you know the current number of orphans in the world would make a circle around the world's equator three times, if they were all holding hands? Do you know that every 15 seconds another child in Africa becomes an AIDS orphan?

Then when listeners learned that Dolapo had helped form a service club dedicated to relieving the plight of orphans in sub-Saharan Africa, it was clear she had already walked the path she wanted them to take. As she painted word-pictures of these small abandoned humans, she invited listeners to share her passion and sympathy.

▶ **understanding** This second phase in the persuasive process requires that listeners grasp the meaning of the speaker's message.

▶ **agreement** The third stage in the persuasive process, which requires that listeners accept a speaker's recommendations and remember their reasons for doing so.

She convinced them that her cause deserved not just their agreement but their commitment. She had given them a living model for their response.

Agreement can range from small concessions to total acceptance. Lesser degrees of agreement could represent success, especially when listeners have to change their attitudes, beliefs, or values, or risk a great deal by accepting your ideas. During the Vietnam War, we often heard classroom speeches attacking or defending the U.S. involvement in that conflict. Feelings about the war ran so high that just to have a speech listened to without interruption was an accomplishment. If a reluctant listener were to nod agreement or concede, "I guess you have a point," then one could truly claim victory.

Enactment

The fourth stage in the persuasive process is **enactment**. It is one thing to get listeners to accept what you say. It is quite another to get them to act on it. If you invite listeners to sign a petition, raise their hands, or voice agreement, you give them a way to enact agreement and to confirm a commitment. The speaker who mobilized his audience against a proposed tuition increase brought a petition to be signed, distributed the addresses of local legislators to contact, and urged listeners to write letters to campus and local newspapers. He helped transform their agreement into constructive action.

Converting agreement to action may require the use of emotional appeals. Stirring stories and examples, vivid images, and colorful language can arouse sympathy. In an especially interesting use of narrative technique, Beth Tidmore asked her listeners to imagine themselves helping as volunteers for a Special Olympics weekend. As she told them the heartwarming story of what they would experience, she in effect invited them to transform this imaginative adventure into reality.

Integration

The final stage in the persuasive process is the **integration** of new commitments into listeners' previous beliefs and values. For a persuasive speech to have lasting effect, listeners must see the connection between what you propose and their important values. Josh Logan urged listeners not just to accept his recommendations but to *become* the solution he advocated. He asked for total integration of attitudes, beliefs, values, and actions.

All of us seek consistency between our values and behaviors. For example, it would be inconsistent for us to march against substandard housing on Monday and contribute to a landlord's defense fund on Tuesday. This is why people sometimes seem to agree with a persuasive message and then change their minds. It dawns on them later that this new commitment means that they must rearrange other cherished beliefs and attitudes.

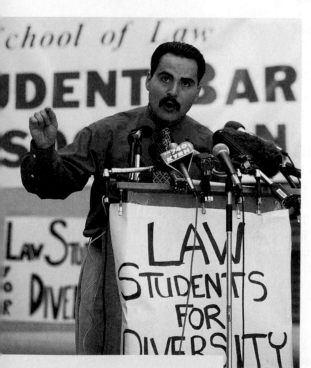

Persuasive speakers must often entice a reluctant audience to action, remove barriers to commitment, and move listeners to participate.

To avoid a delayed counterreaction, try to anticipate such problems as you design your speech. Don't attempt too much persuasion in a single message. Remember that dramatic change may require a campaign of persuasion in which any single speech plays a small but vital role. Be content if you can move listeners just a small distance in a desirable direction. To learn more about how speakers persuade, see the Web site developed by Kelton Rhoads, University of Southern California (www.workingpsychology.com/intro.html).

Persuasion, it is now clear, can be a complicated process. Any persuasive message must focus on the stage at which it can make its most effective contribution: raising

▶ **enactment**   The fourth stage of the persuasive process, in which listeners take appropriate action as the result of agreement.

▶ **integration**   Final stage of the persuasive process, in which listeners connect new attitudes and commitments with previous beliefs and values to ensure lasting change.

awareness, building understanding, seeking agreement, encouraging action, or promoting the integration of beliefs, attitudes, and values. To determine where to focus your persuasive efforts, you must consider the challenges of the specific situation.

The Challenges of Persuasive Speaking

The challenges that persuaders face range from confronting a reluctant audience to preparing messages that meet the most demanding ethical tests. As you plan a persuasive speech, you must consider the audience's position on the topic, how listeners might react to you as an advocate, and the situation in which the speech will be presented. The information and techniques concerning audience analysis that we introduced in Chapter 5 are crucial to success.

Begin preparing your speech by considering where your listeners stand on the issue. Might they hold differing attitudes about the topic, or are they more likely to be united? If listeners are divided, you might hope to unify them around your position. If listeners are already united—but in opposition—you might try to divide them and attract some toward your position.

Also consider how your listeners regard you as a speaker on the subject. If you do not have their respect, trust, and goodwill, use an abundance of supporting testimony from sources they do trust. Evaluating the relationships among the audience, the topic, and you as the speaker will point you to strategies for effective persuasion.

SPEAKER'S
notes   Uniting a Divided Group

Use the following strategies to unite a divided group:

1. Bring to life images of common heroes and enemies.
2. Describe group traditions they may have forgotten.
3. Depict the deeper values they share.
4. Picture common problems.
5. Illustrate goals they share.

6. Spell out the first step they can take together, and urge them to take it.
7. Speak the language of inclusion, such as using family or team metaphors.

Enticing a Reluctant Audience to Listen

If you face an audience that opposes your position, you should be happy with small achievements, such as simply getting thoughtful attention. One way to handle a reluctant audience is to adopt a **co-active approach**, which seeks to bridge the differences between you and your listeners.[7] The major steps in this approach are as follows:

1. *Establish identification and goodwill early in the speech.* Emphasize experiences, background, beliefs, and values that you share with listeners. Communication consultant Larry Tracy suggests you should try to meet with or telephone key members of your audience before you speak, establishing personal contact and seeking their advice. Then you should mention them favorably as you speak: "Nothing is so sweet to the human ear as the sound of his or her name, especially if it is mentioned positively before others."[8]

2. *Start with areas of agreement before you tackle areas of disagreement.* Otherwise, listeners may simply "turn off and tune out" before you have a chance to state your position.

3. *Emphasize explanation over argument.* By explaining your position more than refuting theirs, you avoid provoking defensive behavior and invite listeners to consider the merits of your position. As Tracy notes, "You cannot persuade people to change their mind; they must persuade themselves." Help them by providing the information they need.

4. *Cite authorities that the audience will respect and accept.* If you can find statements by such authorities that are favorable, you can gain "borrowed ethos" for your case. When he spoke before the Harvard Law School Forum, the late Charlton Heston, president of the National Rifle Association, attempted to disarm a chilly audience by citing his high regard for Dr. Martin Luther King Jr. and mentioning his attendance at King's "I Have a Dream" speech.[9]

5. *Set modest goals for change.* Don't try to push your audience too far, too fast. If reluctant listeners have listened to you—if you have raised their awareness and built a basis for understanding—you have accomplished a good deal.

6. *Make a multisided presentation that compares your position with others in a favorable way.* Show respect for opposing positions and understanding of the reasons why others might have supported them. Then reveal how these positions may not merit such support. Your attitude should be not to challenge listeners but to help them see the situation in a new light.

Let's consider how you might apply these steps in a speech against capital punishment before an audience of reluctant listeners. You could build identification by pointing out the values you share with the audience, such as, "We all respect human life. We all believe in fairness." It might also help to take an indirect approach in which you sketch your reasoning before you announce your purpose.

> What if I were to tell you that we are condoning unfairness, that we are condemning people to death simply because they are poor and cannot afford a good lawyer? What if I were to show you that we are sanctioning a model of violent behavior in our society that encourages more violence and more victims in return?

▶ **co-active approach** A way of approaching reluctant audiences in which the speaker attempts to establish goodwill, emphasizes shared values, and sets modest goals for persuasion.

As you present evidence, cite authorities that your audience will respect and accept—for example, "FBI statistics tell us that if you are poor and black, you are three times more likely to be executed for the crime of murder."

Keep your goals modest. Ask only for a fair hearing. Be aware that reluctant listeners may not *want* to give you a fair hearing. Such listeners may distort your message so that it seems to fit what they already believe. Or they may simply deny or dismiss it, saying that it doesn't apply to them. Or they may discredit a source you cite in your speech, believing that any message that relies on *that* source cannot be taken seriously. Remember also that if you propose too much change, you may create a **boomerang effect** in which the audience reacts by opposing your position even more strongly.[10]

For all these reasons, to hope for a major change on the basis of any single persuasive effort is what McGuire calls the **great expectation fallacy**.[11] Be patient with reluctant listeners. Try to move them a step at a time in the direction you would like them to go. Give them information that may eventually change their minds:

> I know that many of you may not like to hear what I'm saying, but think about it. If capital punishment does not deter violent crime, if indeed it may encourage more violent crime, isn't it time we put capital punishment itself on trial?

Make a **multisided presentation**. Acknowledge the arguments in favor of capital punishment, showing that you respect and understand that position, even though you do not accept it.

> I know that the desire for revenge can be strong. If someone I love had been murdered, I would want the killer's life in return. I wouldn't care if capital punishment wasn't fair. I wouldn't care that it condones brutality. I would just want an eye for an eye. But that doesn't mean you should give it to me. It doesn't mean that society should base its policy on my anger and hatred.

A multisided approach helps make those you do persuade resistant to later counterattacks, because you show them how to answer such arguments. This is called an **inoculation effect**, because you "inject" your listeners with a milder form of the arguments they may hear later in more vehement forms from others.[12]

When you acknowledge and then refute arguments, you also help your credibility in two ways. First, you enhance your trustworthiness by showing respect for your opposition. You suggest that their position deserves consideration, even though you have a better option. Second, you enhance your competence by showing your knowledge of the opposing position—the reasons that explain why people may find it attractive and the reasons that reveal how it is defective.

After your speech, you should continue to show respect for the audience. Even if some listeners want to argue or heckle, keep your composure. To help you through such difficult moments, rehearse your speech before friends who pepper you with tough questions after your presentation. Try to anticipate these questions and prepare for them. Listeners may be impressed by your self-control and may be encouraged to rethink their position in light of your example.

We once heard a student speak against abortion to a class that was sharply divided on that issue. She began with a personal narrative, the story of how her mother had been given a drug that was later found to induce birth defects. Her mother was then faced with a decision on terminating the pregnancy. The student concluded by saying that if her mother had chosen the abortion option, she would not be there speaking to them that day. She paused, smiled, and said, "Although

---

▶ **boomerang effect**   A possible negative reaction to a speech that advocates too much change.

▶ **great expectation fallacy**   The mistaken idea that major change can usually be accomplished by a single persuasive effort.

▶ **multisided presentation**   A speech in which the speaker's position is compared favorably to other positions.

FINDING YOUR

voice   Persuasive Confrontations

Are there ever times when a speaker should give up trying to persuade a hostile audience and simply confront listeners directly with the position they appear to oppose? Why would a speaker bother to do this? Might speaker and audience gain anything from such a confrontation? Look for an example of such a speech. Do you agree with the strategy used in it? Discuss in class.

I know some of you may disagree with my views, I must say I am glad that you are here to listen and that I am here to speak. Think about it." If your reasons are compelling and your evidence is strong, you may soften the opposition and move waverers toward your position.

Do not worry if the change you want does not show up immediately. There often is a delayed reaction to persuasion, a **sleeper effect** in which change shows up only after listeners have had time to think about and integrate the message into their belief systems.[13] Even if no change is apparent, your message may sensitize your listeners to the issue and make them more receptive to future persuasion.[14] Finally, there is one special technique that can sometimes create identification between speakers and reluctant, even hostile, audiences. That technique is laughter. The French philosopher Henri Bergson has pointed out that shared laughter can be the beginnings of community. The late Ann Richards, former governor of Texas, told a story that illustrates how this technique can work. After she had been elected early in her career to the Travis County Commission, Ann paid a visit to a road maintenance crew at their worksite. As she entered the crew office, Ann noticed a particularly ugly dog stretched across the front door. She proceeded to make her presentation to a group of men whose popular male boss she had just defeated. After her speech, no one responded when she asked for questions. As she told the story:

> Finally, just to break the ice and get them talking, I asked them about their dog. Texas men will always talk about their dogs. Nothing. No one said a word. There was some shuffling of feet. I thought, "There must be something unseemly about the dog's name, it's the only answer." I looked around the room and they were ducking my gaze. "Let me tell you," I said, "that I am the only child of a very rough-talking father. So don't be embarrassed about your language. I've either heard it or I can top it. So what's the dog's name?"
>
> An old hand in the back row with a big wide belt and big wide belt buckle sat up and said in a gravel bass, "Well, you're gonna find out sooner or later." He looked right at me. "Her name is Ann Richards." I laughed. And when I laughed they roared. And a little guy in the front row who was a lot younger and smarter than most, said in a wonderfully hopeful tenor, "But we call her Miss Ann!" From then on those guys and I were good friends.[15]

Facing a reluctant audience is never easy. But you can't predict what new thoughts your speech might stimulate among listeners or what delayed positive reactions to it there might be.

▶ **inoculation effect**   Preparing an audience for an opposing argument by answering it before listeners have been exposed to it.

▶ **sleeper effect**   A delayed reaction to persuasion.

Removing Barriers to Commitment

If you sense that your audience is largely uncommitted, you have to ask yourself why. Are my listeners undecided because they need more information? Do they not yet see the connection between the issue and their own interests? Are they not certain that they can trust my judgment?

Provide Needed Information. Often, a missing fact or unanswered question stands in the way of commitment. "I know that many of you agree with me but are asking, 'How much will this cost?'" Supplying the necessary information can help move listeners toward your position.

Apply Audience Values. You must show listeners that your proposal agrees with principles they already accept. For example, if your listeners resist an educational program for the financially disadvantaged because they think that people ought to take care of themselves, you may have to show them that your program represents "a hand up, not a handout." Show them that your proposal will lead to other favorable outcomes, such as reductions in crime or unemployment.

As we noted earlier, values are resistant to change. If you can reason from the perspective of your listeners' values, using them as the basis for your arguments, you will encourage their commitment to your position.

Strengthen Your Credibility. When audiences hesitate because they question your credibility, you can "borrow ethos" by citing expert testimony. Call on sources that your listeners trust and respect. Uncommitted audiences will scrutinize both you and your arguments carefully. Reason with such listeners, leading them gradually and carefully to the conclusion you would like them to reach and providing supporting material each step of the way. Adopt a multisided approach in which you consider all options fairly to confirm your ethos as a trustworthy and competent speaker.

When addressing uncommitted listeners, don't overstate your case. Let your personal commitment be evident through your sincerity and conviction, but be careful about using overly strong appeals to guilt or fear. Such appeals might cause cautious listeners to resist, resent, and reject both you and your message.[16] Don't push uncommitted listeners too hard. Help them move in the desired direction, but let them take the final step themselves.

FINDING YOUR
voice Adapting to Controversy

Select a controversial subject for your persuasive speech. What makes it controversial? Summarize the persuasive approach you might make, depending on whether the audience is reluctant, uncommitted, or favorable. What approach do you finally choose, and why? Explain your strategy at the end of the formal outline you prepare for your speech.

Persuasive speeches often must arouse strong feelings to move people to action.

Moving from Attitude to Action

Just as opponents may be reluctant to listen, sympathetic audiences may be reluctant to act. It is one thing to agree with a speaker and quite another to accept the inconvenience and risk that action may require. Listeners may believe that the problem does not affect them personally. They may not know what they should do or how they should do it.[17]

To move people to action, you must give them reasons to act. You may have to arouse their enthusiasm, remind them of their beliefs, demonstrate the need for their involvement, present a clear plan of action, and make it easy for them to comply.

Spark Their Enthusiasm. To move people to action, you may have to arouse feelings. Announce your own commitment, and ask listeners to join you. Once people have voiced their commitment, they are more likely to follow through on it. In her speech inviting listeners to become Special Olympics volunteers, Beth Tidmore anticipated that her listeners already agreed with her—*in principle*. But she had not yet won their hearts. Beth decided that the best way to arouse enthusiasm would be to help listeners imagine themselves enacting her proposal. Here is the way she approached this challenge:

I've had so many great experiences, but these are hard to describe without overworking words like "fulfilling" and "rewarding." So I'm going to let you experience it for yourself. I want everybody to pack your bags—we're going to the Special Olympics summer games in Georgia! . . .

Some of the athletes will be a little bit scared—it will be their first time away from home. All you've got to do is smile and reassure them that they'll have a great time—and you know they will. . . .

Now we'll go to opening ceremonies. You walk onto a big field, and there's a huge tent, and they're playing loud music. All of the kids start dancing—they've never had such a moment! After that, each county marches by with a banner, and when your county comes by, you'd better be up and cheering.

And then you hear something in the distance: a siren. Police cars and fire engines . . . and it's getting louder and louder. Soon it comes into the courtyard, and you catch your first glimpse of the Olympic torch runner. And as the runner gets closer, the Special Olympics theme blares louder on the speakers, and the sirens are just absolutely piercing. They make a final hand-off, and one chosen athlete will light the cauldron. And the flame goes up in this huge whoosh. It's just incredible. All of the athletes cheer, and they're so proud to be part of this moment. . . . Then the athletes get very serious, because they know it's time to take the Special Olympics oath. . . .

After the games are over, you get to see them all on the podium, because everyone gets a medal or a ribbon, everyone places. And it's great, because they're smiling and they're so proud, and there are flashbulbs going off, and the anthem is playing. And they turn and they congratulate their fellow competitors. . . .

Sunday is a sad time, because you have to send them back home to their parents. But when they run off the buses to show their parents their medals, and their parents walk up to you, their simplest "thank you" is a great reward. And in the end your vocal chords are shot, you have a second degree sunburn on most of your body. Your feet hurt, your back aches, and you feel like you could sleep for a week. But you just can't stop smiling, because you know that you've just taken part in something very special.

When Beth distributed commitment cards to her listeners at the end of her speech, it was clear that she had moved her listeners to action.

Revitalize Shared Beliefs and Values.   When speakers and audiences celebrate shared beliefs and values, the result is often a renewed sense of commitment. Such occasions may involve telling stories that resurrect heroes and heroines, giving shared beliefs new meaning. At political conventions, Jefferson, Lincoln, Roosevelt, Kennedy, and Reagan are often invoked in speeches. These symbolic heroes can help bridge audience diversity by bringing different factions together.

In her speech, Beth Tidmore relied on and revitalized the values of benevolence, generosity, and magnanimity—those large-hearted virtues that come into play when we reach out to those who do not share all of our blessings.

Demonstrate the Need for Involvement.   Show your listeners how the quality of their lives depends on action, and demonstrate that the results will be satisfying. It often helps if you can associate the change with a vision of the future. In his final speech, Martin Luther King Jr. said, "I may not get there with you, but I can see the Promised Land." King's vision of the Promised Land helped justify the sacrifice called for in his plan of action.

Present a Clear Plan of Action.   Listeners may exaggerate the difficulty of enacting a proposal or insist that it is impossible. To overcome such resistance, tell them how others have been successful using the same approach. Develop examples or narratives that show them completing the project successfully. Stress that "we can do it, and this is how we can do it."

SPEAKER'S notes   Moving People to Action

To move listeners to action, follow these guidelines:

1. Remind listeners of what is at stake.
2. Provide a clear plan of action.
3. Use examples and stories as models for action.
4. Visualize the consequences of acting and not acting.
5. Demonstrate that you practice what you preach.
6. Ask for public commitments.
7. Make it easy for listeners to take the first step.

Be Specific in Your Instructions and Make It Easy to Comply.   Your plan must show listeners what to do and how to do it. Instead of simply urging listeners to write their congressional representatives, provide them with addresses and telephone numbers, a petition to sign, or preprinted and addressed postcards to

FIGURE 14.4 Audience Considerations for Persuasive Speaking

Audience Type	Strategies
Reluctant to listen, possibly hostile	Seek common ground and establish good will. Quote sources they respect. Explain more than you argue. Limit your goals: try for a fair hearing, and ask little from listeners. Try to weaken their resistance. Acknowledge opposing arguments, but show tactfully why you have a different commitment.
Uncommitted, even uninterested	Provide information needed to arouse their interest and encourage their commitment. Connect their values with your position. Become a model of commitment for them to follow.
Friendly, but not yet committed	Remind them of what is at stake. Show them why action is necessary now. Give them clear instructions and help them take the first step. Picture them undertaking this action successfully.

complete and return. Beth Tidmore passed out information and cards at the end of her speech to help listeners confirm their commitment.

The Challenge of Ethical Persuasion

Ours is a skeptical and cynical age, made more so by large-scale abuses of communication ethics. Advertisers assure us that their products will make us sexier or richer, often with no foundation in fact. Persuasive messages disguised as information appear in "infomercials" on television. They try to slip into our minds under the radar of critical listening. So-called "think tanks" try to bribe experts into supporting their points of view, thereby contaminating a major source of responsible knowledge.[18] Public officials may present suspicious statistics, make dubious denials, or dance around questions they really don't want to answer. Little wonder that many people have lost trust in society's major sources of communication.

As a consumer of persuasive messages, you can at least partially protect yourself by applying the critical thinking skills we discussed in Chapter 4. As a producer of persuasive messages, you can help counter this trend toward unethical communication. Keep three simple questions in mind as you prepare your persuasive speech:[19]

- What is my ethical responsibility to my audience?
- Could I publicly defend the ethics of my message?
- What does this message say about my character?

As we noted in Chapter 1, an ethical speech is based fundamentally on respect for the audience, responsible knowledge of the topic, and concern for the consequences of your words.

Designs for Persuasive Speeches

As we noted in Chapter 9, evidence, proof, and patterns of reasoning are not effective until they are framed into a design for your speech.

Many of the designs used for informative speeches are also appropriate for persuasive speeches. Josh Logan used a categorical design when he proposed three categories of technological improvements in his plan to counter global warming. In addition, the sequential design can outline the steps in a plan of action to make it seem practical. The comparative design works well for speeches that concentrate on developing proposals for action. Following this pattern, you might compare the superior features of your proposal with less adequate features of competing proposals.

Three designs, however, are especially suited to persuasive speeches: the problem–solution design, the motivated sequence design, and the refutative design.

Problem–Solution Design

The **problem–solution design** first convinces listeners that there is a problem and then shows them how to deal with it. The solution can involve changing attitudes and beliefs or taking action.

It is sometimes hard to convince listeners that a problem exists or that it is serious. People have an unfortunate tendency to ignore problems until they reach a critical stage. You can counteract this tendency by vividly depicting the crisis that will surely occur unless your audience makes a change.

As you focus on the problem, use substantive evidence and combinations of proof to demonstrate that a serious problem exists. Reason from the reality of the situation by using presentation aids, dramatic examples, and colorful imagery to make the problem loom large in the minds of listeners. Reasoning from principle can help justify a solution ("Because better health care means a better future for our children, we must pass health care reform"). Analogical reasoning can help convince listeners that a proposed solution will work ("Here's how Massachusetts addressed this problem. . . ."). We shall say more about persuasive uses of these patterns of reasoning in the next chapter.

When a problem is complex, you must examine its causes. Doing so enables you to argue that your solution will work because it deals with the underlying causes.

▶ **problem–solution design**   A persuasive speech pattern in which listeners are first persuaded that they have a problem and then are shown how to solve it.

A problem–solution speech opposing a tuition increase at your university might build on the following general design:

Thesis statement: We must defeat the proposed tuition increase.

I. Problem: The proposal to raise tuition is a bad idea!

   A. The increase will create hardships for many students.

      1. Many current students will have to drop out.

      2. New students will be discouraged from enrolling.

   B. The increase will create additional problems for the university and the community.

      1. Decreased attendance means decreased revenue.

      2. Decreased revenue will reduce the university's community services.

      3. Reduced service will mean reduced support from contributors.

      4. The ironic result will be: another tuition increase!

II. Solution: Defeat the proposal to raise tuition.

   A. Sign our petition against the tuition increase.

   B. Write letters to your state legislators.

   C. Write a letter to our local newspaper.

   D. Attend our campus rally next Wednesday and bring your marching shoes!

When the problem can be identified clearly and the solution is concrete and simple, the problem–solution design works well in persuasive speeches.

As you are planning your problem–solution speech, be sure to take into account **stock issues**, those generic questions that a thoughtful person will ask before agreeing to a change in policies or procedures. Be certain that your speech can answer these questions to the satisfaction of such critical listeners. Stock issues are explored in Figure 14.5.

Motivated Sequence Design

The **motivated sequence design** offers a practical, step-by-step approach when speakers wish to move from the awareness through the enactment phases of the persuasive process in a single speech.[20] The design offers five steps to persuasive success:

   1. *Arouse attention.* As in any speech, you begin by stimulating interest in your subject. Vivid stories or examples, surprising claims, striking facts and statistics, eloquent statements from admired speakers—all can arouse the interest of your listeners.

   2. *Demonstrate a need.* Show your listeners that the situation you want to change is urgent. Arrange evidence so that it builds in intensity and taps into audience motivations to help listeners see what they have to win and lose with regard to your proposal. By the end of this demonstration, listeners should be eager to hear your ideas for change.

► **stock issues** The major general questions a reasonable person would ask before agreeing to a change in policies or procedures.

► **motivated sequence design** A persuasive speech design that proceeds by arousing attention, demonstrating a need, satisfying the need, visualizing results, and calling for action.

The stock issues in persuasion center around the following questions:

I. Is there a significant problem?

   A. How did the problem originate?

   B. What caused the problem?

   C. How widespread is the problem?

   D. How long has the problem persisted?

   E. What harms are associated with the problem?

   F. Will these harms continue and grow unless there is change?

II. What is the solution to this problem?

   A. Will the solution actually solve the problem?

   B. Is the solution practical?

   C. Would the cost of the solution be reasonable?

   D. Might there be other consequences to the solution?

III. Who will put the solution into effect?

   A. Are these people responsible and competent?

   B. What role might listeners play?[21]

FIGURE 14.5 Stock Issues in Persuasion

3. *Satisfy the need.* Present a way to satisfy the need you have demonstrated. Set out a clear plan of action and explain how it will work. Show how this plan agrees with audience principles and values. Offer examples that show how your plan has already worked successfully in other situations.

4. *Visualize the results.* Paint verbal pictures that illustrate the positive results listeners can expect. Show them how their lives will be better when they have enacted your plan. A dramatic picture of the future can help overcome resistance to action. You could also paint a picture of what life will be like if listeners *don't* enact your suggestions. Place these positive and negative verbal pictures side by side to strengthen their impact through contrast.

5. *Call for action.* Your call for action may be a challenge, an appeal, or a statement of personal commitment. The call for action should be short and to the point. Give your listeners something specific that they can do right away. If you can get them to take the first step, the next will come more easily.

Simone Mullinax used a motivated sequence design to convince her University of Arkansas listeners to become mentors:

Big Brothers is an effective mentoring program staffed by volunteers.

1. *Arouse attention*   Let me share with you a simple statistic: 20% of our nation's children—that's one in every five kids—is now "at risk." What does that mean? It means they have no one to trust, no

one to turn to. It means expectations for them are low—our expectations, more importantly, theirs.

2. *Demonstrate a need*   These are the so-called "problem kids"—the ones who drop out of school, and drop into lives that are unproductive, unsuccessful, and often mired in crime. These are wasted lives, wasted humanity, and society has to pay profoundly for their failures.

3. *Satisfy the need*   So what is the answer? I'll tell you about one I know that works because I've tried it. It's called "mentoring," a person-to-person program to become that friend someone doesn't have, that person who cares. It may involve only an hour or two a week, but the mentor is a troubled child's connection to a better, more healthy and hopeful world.

4. *Visualize the results*   Put yourself in this picture. (she tells the story of her mentoring relationship with one child). Mentoring helps us reclaim our children, one child at a time. I'll tell you someone else who has benefited—me!

5. *Call for action*   Best part about mentoring is that it's so easy: can you send an e-mail? Can you make a phone call? Can you talk to your younger sibling's friends? Can you take a child to a ball game or to the movies? Then you have the qualifications to be a mentor! Here's how you can get started (she names an organization, address, and phone number, and hands out material). I urge you, join me in this program. The good things we do in our lives radiate out from us and become magnified. The little fires we light can together help warm the world!

The motivated sequence design has helped generations of persuasive speakers achieve success.

Refutative Design

The **refutative design** is appropriate when you need to challenge other views. In this design, the speaker raises doubt about a position by revealing its inconsistencies and weaknesses. The point of attack may be illogical reasoning, flimsy evidence, self-interest, or hidden agendas. However, you should avoid personal attacks unless credibility issues are central and inescapable. Above all else, be fair. Five steps in developing an effective refutation are as follows:

1. State the point you are going to refute and explain why it is important.
2. Tell the audience how you are going to refute this point.
3. Present your evidence, using facts and figures, examples, and testimony. Cite sources and authorities that the audience will accept as competent and credible.
4. Spell out the conclusion for the audience. Do not assume that listeners will figure out what the evidence means. Tell them directly.

▶ **refutative design** A persuasive design in which the speaker challenges other views.

5. Explain the significance of your refutation—show how it discredits or damages the opposing position.

See if you can identify each step in this pattern in the following refutation of an argument opposing sex education in public high schools:

> Our well-intentioned friends would have you believe, and this is their biggest concern, that birth-control information increases teenage sexual activity. I want to share with you some statistical evidence that contradicts this contention—a contention that is simply not supported by the facts.
>
> The latest study on this issue by the Department of Health, Education, and Welfare compared sexual activity rates in sixty high schools across the United States—thirty with sex education programs and thirty without. Their findings show that there are no significant differences in sexual activity rates between these two groups of schools.
>
> Therefore, the argument that access to birth-control information through sex education programs increases sexual activity simply does not hold water. That's typical of the attack on sex education in the schools—to borrow a line from Shakespeare, it's a lot of "sound and fury, signifying nothing."

You can strengthen this design if you follow your refutation by proving a related point of your own, thus balancing the negative refutation with a positive demonstration. The result gives the audience an alternative belief to substitute for the one you have refuted. Use the same five-step sequence to support your position. For example, you might follow the preceding refutation with the following demonstration:

> I'm not going to try to tell you that birth-control information reduces sexual activity. But I want to tell you what it does reduce. It reduces teenage pregnancy. There is reliable evidence that fewer girls become pregnant in high schools with sex education programs. The same study conducted by Health, Education, and Welfare demonstrated that in high schools with sex education programs, the pregnancy rate dropped from one out of every sixty female students to one out of ninety within two years of the program's going into effect.
>
> Therefore, sex education is a good program. It attacks a devastating social problem—the epidemic of children having children.
>
> Any program that reduces unwanted teenage pregnancy is valuable—valuable to the young women involved, valuable to society. We all pay in so many ways for this personal and social tragedy—we should all support a program that works to reduce it. And we should reject the irrational voices that reject the program.

Design Combinations

Combinations of designs often work well in persuasive speeches. Amanda Miller's speech urging the close of the School of the Americas developed primarily in a problem–solution pattern, with the school itself constituting the problem and legislative proposals to close it providing the solution. But as she depicted what a serious problem the school had become, Amanda found it necessary to answer those who continued to defend it. In this section of her speech, she developed a refutative pattern within the larger problem–solution design:

> Those who argue in favor of the School claim that for many it is their only source of military education. But what kind of education are we providing?

I've already shown you what the textbooks teach—and that does not fit my idea of education. The School began as a line of defense against the U.S.S.R. in the Cold War. And with the Cold War long since completed, I can see little reason to continue spending millions of dollars each year funding a school that produces such negative results. That money might better be spent on real education, or health care, or the environment.

A second argument in favor of the School is that the techniques taught are necessary for "self-defense" against civil wars. But what kinds of selves are these people defending? Are they themselves civil? In 1993, an International Human Rights Tribunal revealed that over one hundred School of the Americas graduates had committed war crimes. Among these crimes were heading the concentration camps in Villa Grimaldi in Chile, organizing the Ocosingo Massacre in Mexico, and participating in drug trafficking and assassinations. How exactly do these activities qualify as "self-defense," in any legitimate sense of the word?

Having completed the refutative part of her speech, Amanda was ready to move on to her solution.

FIGURE 14.6 Selecting Persuasive Speech Designs

Design	Use When
Categorical	• Your topic invites thinking in familiar patterns, such as proving a plan will be safe, inexpensive, and effective. Can be used to change attitudes or to urge action.
Comparative/ Contrast	• You want to demonstrate why your proposal is superior to another. Especially good for speeches in which you contend with opposing views.
Sequential	• Your speech contains a plan of action that must be carried out in specific order.
Problem-Solution	• Your topic presents a problem that needs to be solved and a solution that will solve it. Good for speeches involving attitudes and urging action.
Motivated Sequence	• Your topic calls for action as the final phase of a five-step process that involves, in order, arousing attention, demonstrating need, satisfying need, visualizing the results, and calling for action.
Refutative	• You must answer strong opposition on a topic before you can establish your position. The opposing claims become main points for development. Attack weakest points first, and avoid personal attacks.

FINAL
reflections   The Case for Persuasion

Some people seem reluctant to persuade others. It's not right, they argue, for me to impose my views on someone else. How can I justify asking them to change because *I think* I know a better way?

The argument is interesting, but shaky. If my friends are ignorant of knowledge I have acquired, and that ignorance could cost them dearly, how can I justify *not* persuading them to consider and possibly apply what I have learned?

Recall the words of Isocrates that began this chapter. For Isocrates, the impulse to persuade was vital to the emerging nature of humanity, making possible what we now call "cultural evolution." Persuasion, he felt, lifts us above the "wild beasts" in that it allows us to exercise our humanity by inspiring one another and resolving our disputes by words rather than by fists. Persuasion makes possible community by encouraging cooperation and consent to come together and live in communities governed by laws rather than by brute strength. Persuasion promotes commercial arrangements, the specialization of labor, and the pursuit, accumulation, and advancement of knowledge. For Isocrates, persuasion was the key to civilization.

A final justification for persuasion is that we persuade because we have an ethical duty and imperative to speak. In finding our voice, we find causes to support and meaning for our lives. Not to speak, not to persuade, would deny our reasons for being.

A SAMPLE PERSUASIVE SPEECH

The persuasive speech that follows reflects a moment of self-discovery as Katie Lovett found her topic and her voice simultaneously. As Katie tells the story: "My persuasive speech topic came about after I attended a screening of the internationally acclaimed documentary 'Flow: For Love of Water' which addresses the global water crisis. Immediately after the film ended, I knew that I wanted to design a speech persuading people against buying bottled water. The research process for that speech was incredibly interesting and I am actually now getting more involved in the Davidson Environmental Action Coalition (EAC) as a result of our COM 101 speech assignment."

The Price of Bottled Water

KATIE LOVETT

Have you heard the tired old joke about the salesperson who could sell ice cubes to Eskimos? If you think about it, that's not only a tribute to sales skills but also says a lot about our attitudes toward Native peoples—and how superior we feel towards them. These stupid people (it implies) are buying something they have no use for.

But consider this: In today's society, huge corporations like Coca-Cola, Pepsi, and Nestle are marketing their own "ice cubes" to us with immense success. Water, a natural resource that has historically been viewed as free and open to the public, is now being bottled and sold for profit by large multinational corporations.

> *Katie sets up a refutative design which first identifies the shallow attitudes about bottled water that are induced by advertisers. She will then proceed to challenge these attitudes.*

Why are we buying water? And what are the consequences of it? These are the questions I want to consider today. We will examine marketing strategies, consumer misconceptions, and the environmental impact of our behavior.

Let's begin by considering how the bottled water industry sells its own "ice cubes" to us. Consumers gravitate towards bottled water instead of tap water for two reasons: what's in it and what's not in it. What could possibly be inside a 20-ounce bottle of water that would compel someone to pay $3 and beyond for it? According to *The Journal of Consumer Culture,* "bottled water is a form of cultural consumption, driven by everything from status competition to a belief in magical curing." Clever advertisers feed these feelings. Since bottled water has become an affordable status symbol in today's society, companies can appeal to social distinctions of wealth and class to sell their product.

> *Katie makes effective use of humor to debunk buying behaviors, and connects her speech to the "god terms" used by advertisers to make bottled water seem attractive.*

Take a look at some of the brands currently on the market: There are vitamin waters, nicotine waters, caffeine waters, electrolyte enhanced SmartWater, the "orbtastic" Aquapods that target kids, Bling H_2O which sells for $35 a bottle, "Hello Kitty" water for cats, and yes, even a "diet" water called "Skinny." And according to *The Journal of Consumer Culture,* "new water brands are entering the US market at the rate of about eight per month." Now tell me, how can we possibly feel superior to Eskimos?

Another main reason people want to buy bottled water is for what is *not* in it. The purity of water is the key theme for the bottled water industry. Bottlers seize upon public anxiety over municipal tap water supplies, supposedly offering us the safety that tap water cannot. As a result, the National Resources Defense Council has found that 'pure,' 'pristine,' and 'natural' are some of the most commonly used god-terms found in marketing and on labels.

> *Katie uses factual evidence to attack impressions of greater safety surrounding bottled water. She engages the persuasive process at the awareness phase, expanding audience consciousness and raising doubts about safety.*

So these are some of the fantasies and feelings that support the bottled water industry. Are they justified? Unfortunately, contrary to widespread belief, bottled water is not necessarily cleaner, safer, or purer than the water you get from your faucet. The perception is that if it is off the shelf, it is somehow cleaner and tastier. But *The Bulletin of Science, Technology & Society* argues that bottles of water become "petri dishes of germs." The bottles are loaded into trucks, driven down polluted highways, and transported by many different sets of hands before sitting around gathering dust and germs in storage houses.

In a recent four-year scientific study, the Natural Resources Defense Council tested more than 1,000 bottles of 103 brands of bottled water. In its publication, "Bottled Water or Tap Water?" the Council concluded that "there is no assurance that bottled water is any safer than tap water." In fact, a third of the brands tested were found to contain contaminants such as arsenic and carcinogenic compounds. Some of these samples contained levels of these harmful contaminants that exceeded state or industry standards. So much for "pure" and "pristine"!

Another important misconception involves the regulation of tap water and bottled water. The journal *Environmental Health Perspectives*, in its article "The Price of Bottled Water," reveals the startling fact that city tap water in the United States undergoes more rigorous testing than bottled water. The Environmental Protection Agency (EPA) oversees the treatment of tap water while the Food and Drug Administration (FDA) regulates bottled water. But the FDA's standards for bottled water are actually no stricter than the EPA's health standards for public tap water: the FDA merely adopted the EPA's public drinking standards, which were first set forth in the Clean Water Act of 1978.

You may be asking, what about these reports showing that thousands of people get sick and more than one hundred of them die annually from tap water? Isn't it true that the bottled water industry has a relatively clean record in terms of outbreaks of illnesses?

According to the *Bulletin of Science, Technology & Society*, the reason for this dramatic discrepancy is that while the federal government requires all municipal water authorities to report even the mildest illnesses within 24 hours, there is no requirement for reporting sickness from bottled water. *Flow: For Love of Water*, an internationally acclaimed documentary concerning the global water crisis, also makes the shocking point that there is only one person in the FDA regulating the entire multi-billion dollar bottled water industry.

So while you are laying out the big bucks, thinking that you are protecting your health by drinking bottled instead of tap water, keep in mind that bottled water has not been proven to be any cleaner or better for you.

What about the environmental consequences of the bottled water industry? Consider that it takes an enormous amount of energy to produce a bottle of water. The process of manufacturing, transporting, and recycling plastic bottles drains fossil fuels and contributes to greenhouse gases. The bottles are often filled far away, shipped overseas, transported across the country in trucks, and then stored in refrigerators at your local convenience store. Compare that environmental impact to just turning on your kitchen faucet and we can begin to see the even larger price of bottled water.

The article "5 Reasons Not to Drink Bottled Water" warns that bottled water produces up to 1.5 million tons of plastic waste per year, since over 80% of plastic bottles are simply thrown away rather than recycled. By doing what you can to reduce that enormous pile of plastic bottles, filling a reusable bottle with tap water instead, you can make your own contribution to the quality of the environment.

I hope now, after this speech, that you will be a little less susceptible to the marketing techniques of the bottled water industry. Remember, at the very least bottled water is not safer than tap water, and instead the opposite may be true. And finally, remember the negative impact on the environment.

We pay too much—and in too many ways—for our fantasies concerning bottled water. It's time to put away these childish things. It's time to turn on our faucets instead of opening our wallets!

◀ Katie clearly has uncommitted listeners in mind as she extends her argument on safety to include lack of regulation. She hopes to supply the facts these listeners will need to commit to her position.

◀ Katie assumes that her listeners are sensitive already to the importance of protecting the environment. Through her speech she hopes to create greater harmony between their environmental beliefs and their consumer behaviors.

THIS CHAPTER WILL HELP YOU

1 Use evidence and proofs to build sound arguments
2 Appreciate the ethical importance of reasoned argument
3 Develop effective patterns of reasoning
4 Avoid defects of evidence, proof, and reasoning

15 Building Sound Arguments

> *There's a mighty big difference between good, sound reasons and reasons that sound good.*
>
> —BURTON HILLIS

At the beginning of the last chapter, we noted that the memorable student persuasive speeches we have heard have one thing in common: they all arose out of strong feeling. There is one other trait these excellent speeches have in common: they build on a sturdy platform of argument that justifies the changes they call for.

■ Austin Wright demonstrated a thorough grasp of the government's use of fraudulent data banks. As the speech at the end of this chapter demonstrates, Austin built powerful proofs to bolster his case for reform.

■ Katie Lovett and Alexandra McArthur called on facts and expert testimony to unmask deception in the bottled water and tourism industries. They demonstrated mastery of the art of evidence.

■ Delapo Olushola and Beth Tidmore revealed their own powerful commitment to the causes they promoted. Their proofs combined personal ethos and expert knowledge.

Some persuasive efforts lift and inspire us, while others can seem degrading. What is the critical difference? There is a kind of persuasion—**manipulative persuasion**—that has become part and parcel of life in media America. Such persuasion creates a fantasy world made up of colorful images, appealing music, and attractive spokespersons. It reveals itself in thirty-second television commercials that sell us everything from deodorant to political candidates. In his book *The Assault on Reason*, Al Gore argues that contemporary politics especially attracts the manipulator and compromises the quality of persuasive discourse:

> Voters are often viewed mainly as targets for easy manipulation by those seeking their "consent" to exercise power. By using focus groups and elaborate polling techniques, those who design these messages are able to derive the only information they're interested in receiving *from* citizens—feedback useful in fine-tuning their efforts at manipulation.[1]

Such persuasion sidesteps a careful consideration of supporting evidence and proofs. *It avoids the ethical burden of justification.*

There is another kind of persuasion that is part of the Western tradition reaching back over several thousand years to the speeches of Pericles and Demosthenes in ancient Greece. **Reasoned persuasion** builds arguments out of carefully constructed evidence and proofs. It displays patterns of reasoning for critical inspection and justifies the critical listener's agreement and action. It is not *always* ethical, because evil speakers can sometimes twist evidence and disguise bad reasoning, deceiving even careful listeners. But typically, it accepts the burden of justification, addresses our judgment rather than our impulses, and honors the intellectual behaviors that make us human.

To find your voice in any genuine sense, you must also find respect for the intellectual qualities that make your listeners' commitment meaningful, and respect for the processes of argument that make public deliberation productive and civil. Reason without feeling can surely be cold and heartless, but feeling without reason is shallow and ephemeral. It is the *blend* of these qualities—passion and reason—that makes finding your voice possible.

Reasoned Persuasion

Reasoned persuasion is the business of this chapter. We consider ways *to build powerful arguments that deserve respectful attention from thoughtful listeners.* We show how to develop evidence and proofs, build patterns of effective reasoning, and avoid defects of evidence, proof, and reasoning.

Building Evidence

In persuasive speaking, supporting materials function as **evidence**, the foundation of ethical argument.

- Facts and figures often justify asking us to believe or act.[2] They can be especially important during the awareness phase of the persuasive process when they reveal a reality that calls for action. Research has confirmed the importance of statistical evidence in persuasion.[3] We Americans love numbers—or at least we hold them in high regard.

▶ **manipulative persuasion** Persuasion that works through suggestion, colorful images, music, and attractive spokespersons more than through evidence and reasoning. It avoids the ethical burden of justification.

▶ **reasoned persuasion** Persuasion built on evidence and reasoning.

▶ **evidence** Supporting materials used in persuasive speeches, including facts and figures, examples, narratives, and testimony.

- Examples can put a human face on situations. Austin Wright's speech at the end of this chapter is an impressive display of knowledge about the law and reality surrounding fraudulent databases. But at the beginning of his speech, Austin uses an example to introduce the human importance of his subject. He demonstrates that examples can empower the facts by bringing situations into sharp, living focus for listeners. Whenever listeners ask, "Can you give me an example?" they are asking for this kind of clarification and authentication.

Good stories can perform the same function. Recent research confirms that narratives can be a powerful form of evidence, perhaps because they are so vivid.[4] Moreover, when they are effective, examples and stories enjoy a special advantage in persuasion because listeners find them hard to refute.[5] We can dispute the meaning of facts and figures, and even debate them. But a good example or story is hard to deny and lingers in memory.

When you use testimony in a persuasive speech, you call on experts as witnesses to support your position. Expert testimony is most effective when (1) the audience knows little about the issue because it is new or complicated; and/or (2) listeners lack the ability or motivation to analyze the situation independently.[6] Introduce your witnesses carefully, pointing out how they are qualified to give expert testimony.

Witnesses who testify *against* their apparent self-interest are called **reluctant witnesses**. They provide some of the most powerful evidence available in persuasion. Democratic critics of President Obama's policies often have more impact because they appear to be speaking against their political affiliations.

In ethical persuasive speaking, you should rely mainly on expert testimony. Use prestige or lay testimony as secondary sources of evidence. These three types of testimony are discussed in detail in Chapter 8. You can use prestige testimony to stress values you want listeners to embrace. You can use lay testimony to relate an issue to the lives of listeners. Keep in mind that when you quote others, you are associating yourself with them. Be careful with whom you associate!

Reasoned persuasion often depends on expert testimony.

As you search for evidence, keep an open mind. Consider different points of view, so that you don't simply present one perspective without being aware of others. Gather more evidence than you think you will need so that you have a wide range from which to choose. Be sure you have facts, figures, or expert testimony for each of the major points you want to make. Use multiple sources and types of evidence to strengthen your case.

Developing Proofs

To build strong arguments, persuaders must develop powerful proofs. *A **proof** is an array of evidence, combined in a way that drives thoughtful listeners toward a conclusion.* For example, a certain proof might offer a number of vital facts, combined with examples and expert testimony, to entice you toward agreement with the speaker.

▶ **reluctant witnesses** Witnesses who testify against their apparent self-interest.

▶ **proof** An array of evidence that drives thoughtful listeners toward a conclusion.

YOUR ethical VOICE   Guidelines for the Ethical Use of Evidence

To earn a reputation for the ethical use of evidence, follow these rules:

1. Provide evidence from credible sources.
2. Identify your sources of evidence.
3. Use evidence that can be verified by experts.
4. Be sure such evidence has not been corrupted by outside interests.
5. Acknowledge disagreements among experts.

6. Do not withhold important evidence.
7. Use expert testimony to establish facts, prestige testimony to enhance credibility, and lay testimony to create identification.
8. Quote or paraphrase testimony accurately.

How do proofs work? That question has been studied since the Golden Age of Greece more than two thousand years ago. In his *Rhetoric*, Aristotle offered three answers that are deeply rooted in our humanity. *The first arises from our rational nature.* We are, or at least like to think we are, reasonable creatures. When speeches make good sense to us, when they are grounded in strong factual evidence validated both by experts and our own personal experience, and when they move logically to their conclusions, we find them hard to resist. Aristotle described proofs that emphasize the rational side of humanity as based in what he called **logos**.

Aristotle's second answer recognizes that we are also creatures of feeling. We can be touched by appeals to personal feelings such as fear, pity, and anger. Examples and narratives often provide the evidence this kind of proof emphasizes, just as Austin Wright aroused feelings of indignation over the unfair treatment received by Maher Arar. Aristotle describes proofs that emphasize such appeals to personal feeling as based in **pathos**.

Aristotle's third answer arises from our need for and attraction to leadership. Leaders are vital to our survival, and those who speak to us are assuming leadership positions. We measure their leadership potential, Aristotle noted, in terms of their competence, character, goodwill, and dynamism. When these qualities seem positive, we *want* to agree with them. When these qualities seem negative or are lacking, speakers will have a hard time winning us over. Aristotle described proofs that depend more on perceptions of the speakers themselves as based in **ethos**. We are also affected by the ethos of those whom you cite in a speech. If we trust and are impressed by the people you quote, we will listen respectfully to their testimony. If we are not impressed by them, you have just created a problem for yourself.

In our time, the work of many scholars has confirmed the presence of a fourth dimension of proof, which arises out of social feelings we develop as members of groups, communities, and nations. Feelings of group pride, loyalty and patriotism, often developed by legends and folktales that nurture them, become vital to our identity. They can anchor our traditions and values.[7] When Alexandra McArthur argued that ignoring the fierce poverty that afflicts many nations is behavior unworthy of Americans, she was appealing to powerful feelings of social identity. We call these appeals to social feelings and group identity proof by **mythos**.

A persuasive speech rarely relies on a single kind of proof. Each type of proof brings its own coloration and strength to the fabric of persuasion. But in manipulative

▶ **logos**   A form of proof that appeals to reason based largely on facts and expert testimony presented logically.
▶ **pathos**   Proof relying on appeals to personal feelings.

▶ **ethos**   A form of proof that relies on the audience's perceptions of a speaker's leadership qualities of competence, character, goodwill, and dynamism.

▶ **mythos**   A form of proof grounded in the social feelings that connect us powerfully with group traditions, values, legends, and loyalties.

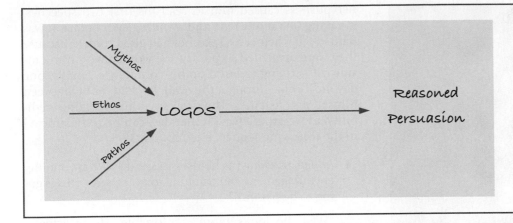

FIGURE 15.1 Proof Priorities in Reasoned Persuasion

persuasion, ethos, pathos, and mythos may be tapped more frequently than logos. Fast-food and automobile commercials rarely treat us as reasoning creatures.

On the other hand, reasoned persuasion stresses logos and assigns supporting roles to ethos, pathos, and mythos. Even if these latter forms of proof are vital in adding energy, color, and human interest to persuasion, they supplement the basic appeal to our rational nature. These priorities among the forms of proof are indicated in Figure 15.1

In the section that follows, we discuss in greater depth ethos, pathos, and mythos as we build up to the consideration of logos. We discuss the strengths and qualities of these proofs so that you may weave them effectively into your own persuasive speech.

Proof by Ethos.   Social scientists have discovered that credibility is a dynamic, not a stable quality: It can change during a speech.[8] As you stand to speak, listeners may already have some impressions of your character, ability, goodwill, and confidence. This is the **initial credibility** that you bring to a speech.

As you are actually speaking, your **emerging credibility** begins to build. We recall a student who, as a result of some very unpleasant speaking experiences before taking our class, suffered from acute communication apprehension. His

FINDING YOUR

voice   Case Study in Reasoned Persuasion

Find a news story that interests you. Using the information in the story,

■ show how you might use this material as evidence in a persuasive speech,
■ indicate how this evidence might be used to develop a proof, and

■ explain how this proof might function as part of a pattern of reasoned persuasion.

Present your findings in class.

▶ **initial credibility**   The audience's assessment of your ethos before you begin your speech.

▶ **emerging credibility**   The changes in the audience's assessment of ethos that occur during your speech.

When persuaders find their voices, the moment is often quite dramatic and illuminating.

nervousness caused him to read his first two speeches, speaking in a monotone and avoiding eye contact. It was hard to tell whether his speeches had good content because they were presented so poorly. We worked with him outside class, trying to build up his confidence. Finally, one day he broke through the wall he had built between himself and listeners. The process of his emerging credibility, as we experienced it that day, can be reconstructed in the following sequence of moments:

1. *Initial credibility* (as he rises to speak): We are smiling encouragement, but thinking to ourselves, "This is going to be painful."

2. "Well, he looks more comfortable. He is actually making eye contact! He is even smiling. Lights up the room."

3. "He clearly cares a lot about arts education. Didn't know he was capable of such feeling."

4. "Wow, he really knows his stuff. That's effective testimony, and impressive facts and statistics. Moving example too. The way he just used language—very good."

5. "That makes good sense. I'll go along with those recommendations."

6. (As the speech concluded in a congratulatory round of applause): "Well, we've got ourselves a speaker!"

The speaker's emerging credibility either changes or confirms initial credibility, resulting in **terminal credibility**. Your terminal credibility when one speech concludes becomes your initial credibility when you present another.

The interesting thing is that more than the audience changed its assessment of credibility that day. What we have described is a dramatic moment in which a speaker found his voice. It was also a dramatic moment in his discovery of his own worth as a human being. Such moments make all the work and all the discomfort of the public speaking class worthwhile.

If you enjoy high ethos in the eyes of listeners, all your other proofs will be more effective as well. Your examples and stories will have more impact, and your facts and figures will be more believable. Even the words you use can be more intense and colorful, and such language itself can assure greater persuasive effects.[9] In sum, your personal ethos can be the key to whether you succeed or fail as a persuasive speaker.

The sources of information you cite provide another type of proof by ethos. Proof based on the testimony of reliable, competent, and trustworthy sources is extremely important in persuasive speaking. *Identify your sources and point out why they are qualified to speak on the subject.* It is also helpful if you can say that the testimony is recent. For maximum effect, quote experts directly rather than paraphrasing them.

Proof by Pathos.   People usually respond strongly when they feel angry, afraid, guilty, excited, or compassionate toward others. If used ethically in a context of reasoned persuasion, appeals to personal feelings can help change attitudes or move people to act for good causes.[10]

▶ **terminal credibility**   The audience's assessment of ethos after a speaker has made a presentation.

When speakers tell personal stories, emotional appeals can be especially effective. Personal narratives blend the power of feeling with strong credibility. During a congressional debate on handgun control legislation, James Brady, the presidential press secretary who was shot during an assassination attempt on President Reagan, testified before the U.S. Senate Judiciary Subcommittee. Speaking from his wheelchair, he said:

> There was a day when I walked the halls of this Senate and worked closely with many of you and your staffs. There was a wonderful day when I was fortunate enough to serve the President of the United States in a capacity I had dreamed of all my life. And for a time, I felt that people looked up to me. Today, I can tell you how hard it is to have people speaking down to me. But nothing has been harder than losing the independence and control we all so value in life. I need help getting out of bed, help taking a shower, and help getting dressed.
>
> There are some who oppose a simple seven-day waiting period for handgun purchases because it would inconvenience gun buyers. Well, I guess I am paying for their convenience. And I am one of the lucky ones. I survived being shot through the head. Other shooting victims are not as fortunate.[11]

Often, appeals to emotions are the only way to convince people of the human dimensions of a problem or the need for immediate action. So how can you use proof by pathos persuasively? Consider again the section on motivation in Chapter 5. Effective appeals to pathos often connect the speaker's points in personal ways with this underlying pattern of motives. Figure 15.2 illustrates how such connections might be made to relevant motives.

As powerful as emotional proof may be, it should be used with caution. If an appeal to feeling is too obvious, audiences may suspect you are trying to manipulate them. Appeals to negative emotions such as fear or guilt are especially tricky because they can boomerang, causing listeners to discredit both you and your speech. When you use appeals to feeling, justify them with solid evidence. In your presentation, let your voice and body language understate rather than overstate the emotional appeal. Don't engage in theatrics.

Proof by Mythos. Appeals to the values, faith, and feelings that make up our social identity can be a powerful source of proof. Such appeals, often expressed in traditional stories, sayings, and symbols, assume that audiences value their membership in a culture and share its heritage. Communication scholar Martha Solomon Watson has

Motives	Personal Emotions	Possible Connection	
Health/Safety	Fear/Security	Does my subject affect the personal well-being and safety of listeners?	**FIGURE 15.2** **Connecting Pathos with Motives**
Nurturance/ Altruism	Sympathy/Caring for others	Does my subject invite feelings of sympathy and benevolence for the fate of others?	
Family/Significant Others	Love	Might my subject ignite feelings for loved ones?	

The Western frontier is a major source of mythos in American speeches. *American Progress*, a painting by American artist John Gast, portrays many icons and ideographs. Which ones can you identify?

noted, "Rhetoric which incorporates mythical elements taps into rich cultural reservoirs."[12]

Appeals to cultural identity often call on patriotism and remind us of our heroes or enemies. They may gain power from political narratives, such as the story of George Washington's harsh winter at Valley Forge. Or they may be embedded in folk sayings, as when speakers remind us that ours is "the land of opportunity."[13] Appeals to mythos also may be grounded in economic legends, such as American stories of success through hard work and thrift that celebrate the rise to power from humble beginnings. Such stories justify economic power in our society while assuring the powerless that they too can make it if only they have "the right stuff."

Appeals to cultural identity may also draw on religious narratives. Sacred documents, such as the Bible, provide a rich storehouse of parables, used not only in sermons but also in political speeches.[14] For example, references to the Good Samaritan are often used to justify government efforts to help those who are in need. Stories need not be retold in their entirety each time they are invoked. Because they are so familiar, allusions to them may be sufficient. The culturetypes discussed in Chapter 11 are often called into service, because they compress myths into a few provocative words. Words like *progress, science,* and *education* have positive mythic overtones, and *terrorist, pollution,* and *weapons of mass destruction* are negatively charged. In his speech accepting the Democratic presidential nomination in 1960, John F. Kennedy called on the myth of the American frontier to move Americans to action:

> The New Frontier of which I speak is not a set of promises—it is a set of challenges. It sums up not what I intend to offer the American people, but what I intend to ask of them.[15]

This appeal to cultural identity emerged as a central theme of Kennedy's presidency. He didn't need to refer directly to the legends of Daniel Boone and Davy Crockett or to the tales of the Oregon Trail to meet the challenges that lay ahead—he was able to conjure up those thoughts with the phrase "the New Frontier."

FINDING YOUR
voice   Proofs in Advertising

Bring to class advertisements that emphasize each of the four forms of persuasive proof: logos, pathos, ethos, and mythos. What factors in the product, medium of advertising, or intended audience might explain this emphasis in each example? Do the advertisements combine other forms of proof as well? How effective is each advertisement? Present your findings and your answers to these questions in class discussion.

Motives	Group Emotion	Possible Connection
Maintain Control/ Stability	Respect for/love of tradition	Does my proposal reaffirm traditions that my listeners want to protect?
Honor Affiliations	Feelings of group pride/patriotism	Does my subject connect with audience feelings of loyalty to a group and pride in membership?
Preserve Group Identity	Respect for heroes/great deeds	Does my speech connect with models of heroism and memories of great events? Does my speech call upon values that are vital to group identity?

**FIGURE 15.3
Connecting Mythos with Motives**

How can you use proof by mythos in a classroom speech? Once again, we return to the earlier discussion of motivation in Chapter 5. The social motives discussed there, which tend to engage group emotions, may also suggest guides to the development of proof by mythos. Figure 15.3 shows how connections might be made between mythos and motives.

The unique value of appeals to cultural identity is to help listeners understand how the speaker's recommendations fit into the total belief and value patterns of their group. An appeal that accomplishes this goal gives such proof a special role in the persuasive process we discussed in Chapter 14. It can help integrate new attitudes and action into the group's culture.

Like appeals to personal feeling, appeals to cultural identity can be a great good or a considerable evil. At their best, such appeals heighten our appreciation of who we are *as a people* and promote consistency between cultural values and public policy. However, when misused, these appeals can make it seem that there is only *one legitimate culture*. Some of those who argued for introducing democratic government to Iraq and Afghanistan seemed to base their arguments on the United States' model. To the extent they implied that our system is superior to all other options, no matter what the circumstances, they may have been guilty of ethnocentrism, an abuse of mythos that we discussed in Chapter 1. Appeals to cultural identity can also devalue those who choose *not* to conform to the dominant values or who belong to marginalized groups.

SPEAKER'S notes   When and How to Use Proof

As you decide how to align your proofs for maximum effectiveness, follow these guidelines:

1. To increase awareness and understanding, use rational appeals based on facts, statistics, and expert testimony (*logos*).

2. To communicate the human dimensions of a problem, stir listeners with moving examples and stories (*pathos*).

3. To reassure listeners that you are a credible speaker, convince them that you know what you are talking about, that you are fair and honest, and that you have audience interests at heart (*ethos*).

4. To connect a problem with group culture, show how it relates to popular traditions, legends, and symbols (*mythos*).

The Master Form of Proof

Reasoned persuasion comes to focus ultimately on one critical question: *is this a logical speech?* All the evidence and proofs that a speech develops must fit together finally in patterns of reasoning that thoughtful listeners find acceptable, convincing, and compelling. The connection between our idea of *logic* and the ancient conception of *logos* is evident, and it suggests that *in reasoned persuasion, logos is the master form of proof.*

In applying this standard, critical listeners consider the following tests:

- Have central issues and terms been clearly and fairly defined?
- Does the speech reason from sound principles?
- Is the speech firmly anchored in reality?
- Does the speech reason acceptably from similar or parallel cases?

In the sections that follow, we consider each test, explain its meaning, and indicate how you might pass it successfully en route to finding your voice.

Definitions of Central Concepts

The Greek philosopher Socrates was one of the first to insist that ethical persuasion begins with a clear understanding of the meanings of important terms. Have you ever had a heated discussion with someone, only to discover later that the two of you were not even talking about the same thing? If speakers and listeners don't share such understanding from the outset, it is difficult to communicate. When the speaker and audience come from different backgrounds, careful definitions are even more important. Opening his speech on "gender bending," Brandon Rader was careful to offer the following definition: "If you are a gender bender, you dress or act or think or talk like people in your community assume someone of the opposite sex would do or act or talk or dress." Having shared this understanding, Brandon went on to argue that most assumptions about gender benders are quite wrong. Definitions like Brandon's take a term that may be unfamiliar to many audience members and translate it into simpler, more familiar language.

Not all definitions involve translating technical language into familiar terms. Some of the most interesting definitions offered by speakers are efforts to change listeners' perspectives so that they will be more sympathetic to the arguments that will follow. Should alcohol be defined as a drug? Should a fetus be defined as a human being? Definitions that affirm or deny such questions can prepare the way for elaborate arguments advocating different kinds of public policy.

In the 1968 Memphis sanitation strike, which led to the assassination of Dr. Martin Luther King Jr., the workers marched carrying signs that read, "I AM A MAN." This simple definitional statement was actually the tip of a complex underlying moral argument.

The sanitation workers whose strike provided the setting for Dr. King's assassination wore their arguments defining themselves around their necks.

FINDING YOUR

voice   Controversies over Definitions

More than fifty years ago, in *The Ethics of Rhetoric*, Richard Weaver observed that frequent controversy over the definitions of basic terms in public arguments are a sign of social and cultural division. Look and listen for examples of lively disagreement over the definitions of the following terms in contemporary argument:

a. liberalism   **d.** abortion

b. marijuana   **e.** the role of government

c. gun rights

Do these disagreements reflect the kind of social division Weaver suggested? Bring your discoveries and thoughts to class for discussion.

The strikers were claiming they had *not* been treated like men in social, political, and economic terms.

As such examples make clear, definitions can be *the fundamental issues at the heart of controversies*. If you attempt to redefine your audience's perspective on a subject, you may have to defend your effort with all the evidence, appeals, and credibility you can muster.

Reasoning from Principle

As we absorb the folkways of our culture, we acquire principles that guide the way we think and live. For example, "freedom of speech" is written into the Constitution of the United States as a principle of government. As we are growing up, we learn about that principle in action as we study the words of those who have exercised that freedom.

When we **reason from principle**, we use such guides to justify our value judgments and calls to action. Such **deductive reasoning**, as it is sometimes also called, starts from some rule or principle and draws out of it a conclusion about how we should act. Consider a hypothetical example. A speaker begins by reminding listeners of a principle she believes they all accept: "We all believe in freedom of speech." In logical terms, such a principle is known as the **major premise**. Next, the speaker relates a specific issue to that principle, creating what is called the **minor premise**: "Melvin would like to speak." Finally, the speaker reaches her **conclusion**: "We should let Melvin speak." Because of their respect for the principle expressed in the major premise, many listeners would nod assent, even though they might not particularly like Melvin.

In logic this pattern of major premise/minor premise/conclusion is called a **syllogism**. Aristotle described such reasoning as vital in the persuasion of everyday life. Carmen Johnson based the reasoning in her speech praising the United Negro College Fund on the major premise: *The mind is a terrible thing to waste.* Carmen assumed her University of Nevada Las Vegas audience would accept that

---

▶ **reason from principle**   Reasoning from shared principles, values, and rules. Sometimes called deductive reasoning.
▶ **deductive reasoning**   Arguing from a general principle to a specific case.

▶ **major premise**   The general principle on which an argument is based.
▶ **minor premise**   Relating a specific instance to the general principle that supports an argument.

▶ **conclusion**   Meaning drawn from the relationship between the major and minor premises.
▶ **syllogism**   Pattern of deductive reasoning as it develops in reasoned persuasion.

premise without question. Dolapo Olushola based her powerful proof by pathos in defense of Nigerian orphans on the major premise: *children have the right to food, clothing, medical care, and loving care.* Again, she assumed her listeners would be deeply sympathetic.

Because it begins by reminding listeners of shared values, reasoning from principle is useful for establishing common ground. Such reasoning can also point out inconsistencies between beliefs and behaviors—the gap between what we practice and what we preach. For example, if you can show that the censorship of song lyrics is inconsistent with freedom of speech, then you will have presented a good reason for people to condemn such censorship. *We are more likely to change a practice that is inconsistent with cherished principles or values than we are to change the principles or values.* Because people like to be consistent and maintain the integrity of their values, reasoning from principle becomes a powerful way to achieve harmony among attitudes, beliefs, and values.

Occasionally, the pattern of reasoning in a syllogism is not entirely visible in a speech. For example, the major premise may not be stated: Speakers may simply assume that the principle it expresses is already accepted by listeners. When offered appropriate cues, listeners will think of these principles and complete the speaker's line of thought on their own. As she spoke of the problems of Native Americans, Ashley Roberson spent much of her time demonstrating the reality of "social injustice on reservations," which functioned as the minor premise in her syllogism. She did not think it necessary to state the implied major premise, *Social injustice in the United States should not be tolerated.* Instead, she felt justified in concluding, "We must eradicate social injustice on reservations."

We should realize, however, that not all members of the audience might accept principles that seem to us beyond question. For example, some researchers have discovered that if you read the Bill of Rights to people without telling them it is part of the United States Constitution, an alarming percentage will describe it as "radical" or "communistic." Therefore, you should not take such principles for granted. You may have to explain and defend them to reinforce your listeners' belief in them.

Another point critical to such reasoning comes when a speaker tries to show that a condition or situation—the minor premise—actually exists. People may not argue passionately about the *principle* of environmental protection, but assertions about a specific case of pollution can generate a good deal of heat. Your persuasive efforts may have to focus on that issue, emphasizing the kind of reasoning we discuss in the next section.

As you develop a principled pattern of reasoning for your speech, keep these cautions in mind:

- *Be certain your audience will accept the major premises on which your arguments are based.* Remind listeners why they believe as they do.

- *Demonstrate the existence of relevant conditions.* This, as we shall see in the next section, is where practical reasoning joins with principled reasoning to build convincing arguments.

- *Explain the relationship between principles and conditions (the major and minor premises).* Don't expect your audience to get the point automatically. Listeners may not see the connection between their responsibility to maintain the natural beauty of their country and specific environmental conditions that need reform. Help them by making the point explicitly.

- *Be sure your conclusion offers a clear direction for listeners.* Don't leave them foundering without a clear idea as to what you want them to do.

- *Be certain your reasoning is free from flaws and fallacies.* We discuss such problems of argument in the final section of this chapter.

Reasoning from Reality

Persuasive speakers must have an accurate grasp of the situation they are discussing. **Reasoning from reality** depends either on the speaker's personal experience or on knowledge provided by experts. This knowledge is reflected in the facts, statistics, examples, and testimony used in the speech. Reasoning from reality is sometimes called *inductive* because it draws general conclusions from particular instances. **Inductive reasoning** is the classic method of scientific investigation, and science remains a "god term" for many listeners in our culture:[16] if you can show that "science supports my argument," you will have strengthened your case for most audiences.

Austin Wright, in the prize-winning persuasive speech at the end of this chapter, demonstrated mastery of inductive reasoning from reality. He proved he was familiar with expert knowledge concerning the use and misuse of faulty databases, highlighting this information by startling statistical comparison and contrast and by breathing life into the data through his lively uses of language. The following passage reflects his skill at argumentation:

> The *Los Angeles Times* of January 27, 2006, explains that these companies also have a reputation for losing information. In 2005, for instance, Choicepoint's data system was breached by con artists, compromising more than 19 billion individual files, including social security numbers and financial histories. Although a 2007 Javelin Strategy and Research report finds that identity theft costs victims an average of $5,000, the government forced Choicepoint to pay out a mere $15 million in damages. That's an average of less than one tenth of one cent for each person whose private information was leaked by Choicepoint.

Although reasoning from principle and reasoning from reality may seem quite different, they actually work together. Reasoning from reality can reinforce principles so that they don't appear to be simply items of blind faith. For example, if we can demonstrate empirically that "free and open discussion actually results in better public decisions," then we bring both morality and practicality to the support of freedom of speech.

Reasoning from reality is critical for demonstrating the truth of the minor premise in a syllogism. Is the censorship of song lyrics an actual threat, or is it merely some bogeyman in the minds of liberals? Again, testimony from those who wish to censor and who have the power to censor would authenticate the threat. Similarly, Ashley Roberson had to prove with facts, statistics, and examples that the problems existing on Native American reservations were of such magnitude that they constituted "social injustice." Clearly, reasoning from reality can empower reasoning from principle in persuasive speeches, and the two forms are often found woven together. Reasoning from reality also implies an understanding of cause–effect relationships.

As you incorporate reasoning from reality into your arguments, keep in mind these basic requirements:

- You must be objective enough to see the situation clearly. Do not let your biases warp your perceptions. Look at an issue from as many perspectives as possible.

▶ **reasoning from reality** Emphasis on factual evidence in guiding one's general conclusions and decisions. Often called inductive reasoning.

▶ **inductive reasoning** Reasoning from specific factual instances to reach a general conclusion.

- You must compile a sufficient number of observations. One or two isolated incidents cannot justify reality claims.

- Since situations surrounding relevant issues are constantly changing, you must be sure your observations are up-to-date.

- Your observations must be truly representative of the situation. The exception does not prove the rule.

- Your observations must actually justify your conclusion. They must be relevant to the claim you wish to demonstrate.

- If your inductive exposure comes indirectly from library or Internet research, don't just accept the testimony of the first expert you encounter. Read more widely to see whether experts agree with each other. If they disagree, decide which of them are most credible. Be prepared to justify and defend your evaluation of evidence in your speech.

- As you present facts, statistics, examples, and testimony, be sure to introduce the experts who are the sources of the evidence. Establish their credentials to reassure thoughtful listeners. Beginning speakers often neglect this important requirement of successful persuasion.

Reasoning from Parallel Cases

When we deal with a problem by considering a similar situation and drawing lessons from it, we are **reasoning from parallel cases**. Such **analogical reasoning**, as it is sometimes called, can be useful to frame an unfamiliar, abstract, or difficult problem in terms of something that is more familiar, more concrete, or more easily understood. It also can be used to dramatize the speaker's claim: "If we don't deal with global warming, our children will inherit a degraded environment. Just like the tiger and the elephant, our habitat is in crisis."

Dr. Richard Corlin, in a presidential address before the American Medical Association on gun violence, used a vivid analogy to underscore the importance of video games in acclimating susceptible young minds into America's culture of gun violence. Reasoning from parallel cases helped him both magnify the problem and bring it into the understanding of listeners:

> I want you to imagine with me a computer game called "Puppy Shoot." In this game, puppies run across the screen. Using a joystick, the game player aims a gun that shoots the puppies. The player is awarded one point for a flesh wound, three points for a body shot, and ten points for a head shot. Blood spurts out each time a puppy is hit—and brain tissue splatters all over whenever there's a head shot. The dead puppies pile up at the bottom of the screen. When the shooter gets to 1,000 points, he gets to exchange his pistol for an Uzi, and the point values go up.
>
> If a game as disgusting as that were to be developed, every animal rights group in the country, along with a lot of other organizations, would protest, and there would be all sorts of attempts made to get the game taken off the market. Yet, if you just change puppies to people in the game I described, there are dozens of them already on the market—sold under such names as "Blood Bath," "Psycho Toxic," "Redneck Rampage," and "Soldier of Fortune."[17]

▶ **reasoning from parallel cases** Presenting a similar situation as the basis of an argument. Often called analogical reasoning.

▶ **analogical reasoning** Creating a strategic perspective on a subject by relating it to something similar about which the audience has strong feelings.

As useful as analogical reasoning can be in dramatizing arguments, it can be even more useful in persuading listeners to accept solutions. For example, in the continuing debate over our nation's drug policy, those who favor legalizing "recreational" drugs frequently base their arguments on an analogy to Prohibition.[18] They claim that the Prohibition amendment caused more problems than it solved because it made drinking an adventure and led to the rise of a criminal empire. They then claim that our efforts to outlaw recreational drugs have had the same result. The reason, they say, is that it is impossible to ban a human desire—that to try to do so simply encourages contempt for the law. Moreover, they assert that legalizing drugs would help put the international drug dealers out of business, just as the repeal of Prohibition helped bring about the downfall of the gangster empires of the 1930s. Finally, they argue, if drug sales were legal, it would be easier to control the quality of drugs, thus reducing the danger to users (parallel to the health problems associated with bootleg whiskey during Prohibition).

As this example shows, analogical reasoning emphasizes strategic points of comparison between similar situations. People on both sides of an issue will focus on these points, using evidence and proofs to defend or attack them. Opponents to legalizing drugs claim that there are many important differences between drugs and alcohol.[19] They say that alcohol is not as addictive for casual users as heroin or cocaine. They contend that legalization would multiply the drug problem, not reduce it, because it would make drugs more accessible and make them seem acceptable. They further suggest that since many drug abusers are prone to violence, the cost to society would increase. Thus, the public debate rages on over these crucial points of comparison.

What makes analogical reasoning work? It is similar to inductive reasoning from reality in that it seeks insight through careful observation. Analogy, however, concentrates *on one similar situation* rather than ranging across many. This means that although analogical reasoning may seem more concrete and interesting than some forms of inductive reasoning (such as that based often on statistical evidence), it can also be less reliable. Before you decide to develop an analogy as part of your argument, be sure that the important similarities outweigh the dissimilarities. If you must strain to make an analogy fit, rely on other forms of reasoning.

SPEAKER'S notes   Developing Powerful Arguments

To build arguments that will influence thoughtful listeners, follow these guidelines:

1. Provide clear definitions of basic terms.

2. Justify arguments by reasoning from accepted principles.

3. Remind listeners of why they honor these principles.

4. Convince listeners that your arguments are based in reality.

5. Create a vivid sense of problems.

6. Use a similar situation as a model from which to draw comparisons that illustrate and favor your position.

7. Build arguments to answer questions reasonable listeners might ask.

YOUR
ethical VOICE Building Ethical Arguments

To earn your reputation as an ethical persuader, observe the following guidelines:

1. Emphasize logical reasoning built on facts, statistics, and expert testimony.

2. Always supplement proof by pathos with hard evidence.

3. Never allow proof by mythos to become a mask for intolerance or an excuse to attack the rights of individuals who resist group values and culture.

4. Test the ethics of any persuasive strategy by considering how it will be judged by a thoughtful listener.

5. Strive to maintain consistency among attitudes, beliefs, values, and actions.

6. Acknowledge conditions that might disprove your argument.

7. As you research a problem, keep an open mind so that you can understand the various sides in a dispute.

Avoiding Defective Persuasion

It takes a lot of work to prepare a persuasive speech—analyzing your audience, researching your topic, designing your speech, and developing powerful arguments that will convince careful listeners. Don't ruin all your hard work by committing **fallacies**, or errors of reasoning. Fallacies may crop up in the evidence you use, the proofs you develop, or the reasoning in your arguments. There are also fallacies particular to some speech designs. In this section, we identify some of these major errors so that you can guard against them, both as speaker and as listener.

Defective Evidence

Evidence is defective if the speaker misuses facts, statistics, or testimony, or uses evidence inappropriately.

Misuse of Facts.   The **slippery slope fallacy** assumes that once something happens, it will establish an irreversible trend leading to disaster. The slippery slope fallacy often involves oversimplification and outlandish hyperbole. For example, a prominent religious leader once suggested that feminism was "a socialist, antifamily political movement that encourages women to leave their husbands, kill their children, practice witchcraft, destroy capitalism, and become lesbians."[20] In the slippery slope fallacy, it is not logic but rather our darkest fears that drive the prediction of events.

A second misuse of facts involves the **confusion of fact and opinion**. A factual statement is objective and verifiable, such as "Most Republican governors support the lowering of taxes." An opinion is a personal interpretation of information: a statement of belief, feeling, attitude, or value. Normally, factual and opinion statements stay in their proper places. The problem comes when speakers make impassioned claims based on opinions, such as "The Republicans have done it now! They're going to toss children out into the cold." Or, on the other side: "These Democrats are going to set up 'death panels' with their so-called health care reform. They're going to say, 'Too bad, grandpa! You've had a good life and it's time to go.'"[21] Opinions can be useful in persuasive speeches when they represent careful interpretations that are supported by

---

▶ **fallacies**   Errors in reasoning that make persuasion unreliable.

▶ **slippery slope fallacy**   The assumption that once something happens, an inevitable trend is established that will lead to disastrous results.

▶ **confusion of fact and opinion**   A misuse of evidence in which personal opinions are offered as though they were facts, or facts are dismissed as though they were opinion.

evidence. However, wild accusations that treat opinions as facts, and facts as opinions, are the source of many problems in public communication.

At one time, hunters used to distract their dogs from a trail by dragging a smoked herring across it. In our time, the **red herring fallacy** occurs when persuaders try to draw attention away from the real issues in a dispute, perhaps because they feel vulnerable on those issues or because they see a chance to vilify the opposition. Often, the "red herring" they use is some sensational allegation. In the ongoing abortion controversy, some pro-choice advocates tried to discredit their opponents by associating them with terrorists, assassins, and bombers. In return, some pro-life advocates tried to smear their opposition by suggesting that abortion clinics were underwritten by "mafia money." Such charges from both sides divert attention from the central issues of the controversy.

When listening to spectacular speakers, be on the alert for fallacies.

Statistical Fallacies. Audiences are often intimidated by numbers. We've all been taught that "figures don't lie" without being reminded that "liars figure." Speakers can exploit this tendency by creating statistical deceptions. For example, consider the **myth of the mean**. If you've ever vacationed in the mountains, you know that a stream may have an "average depth" of six inches, yet a person could drown in one of its deep pools. A speaker could tell you not to worry about poverty in Plattsville because the average income is well above the poverty level. Yet this average could be skewed by the fact that a few families are very wealthy, creating an illusion of well-being that is not true for most people. Averages are useful to summarize statistical information, but be sure they do not mask the reality of a situation.

Another statistical fallacy occurs when we offer **flawed statistical comparisons** that start from unequal bases. Suppose you have two salespersons, George and Maria, working for you. George has just opened a new account, giving him a total of two sales. Maria has opened three new accounts for a total of thirteen. George comes to you and asks for a promotion, arguing, "My success rate this year rose by 100 percent, while Maria's rose only 30 percent." George would be guilty of fallacious reasoning, if not bad salesmanship.

Defective Testimony. Testimony can be misused in many different ways. Speakers may omit *when* a statement was made to hide the fact that the testimony is dated. They may leave out important facts about their experts, intimidating us with titles in statements such as "*Dr.* Michael Jones reported that smoking does not harm health." What the speaker *didn't* reveal was that Dr. Jones was a marketing professor who was writing public relations material for the Tobacco Growers Association. Speakers also abuse testimony when they cite words out of context that are not representative of a person's actual position. This can happen when a qualifier is presented as though it represented a concession, misquoting a statement such as "unless the growers are no longer using herbicides" as "Ah hah! He admits—and I quote him—'growers are no longer using herbicides.'" As we noted in Chapter 8, prestige and lay testimony can be misused if they replace expert opinion when facts must be established. Finally, the "voice of the people" can be easily misrepresented, depending on *which* people you choose to quote.

▶ **red herring fallacy** The use of irrelevant material to divert attention.

▶ **myth of the mean** The deceptive use of statistical averages in speeches.

▶ **flawed statistical comparisons** Statistical reasoning that offers fallacious conclusions by comparing unequal or unlike situations.

Inappropriate Evidence. Other abuses occur when speakers deliberately use one form of evidence when they should be using another. For example, you might use facts and figures when examples would bring us closer to the human truth of a situation. Welfare statistics are sometimes misused in this way. When a speaker talks about poverty in terms of abstract numbers only, it distances listeners from the human reality of the problem. George Orwell once complained that such language "falls upon the [truth] like soft snow, blurring the outlines and covering up all the details."[22]

On the other hand, speakers may use provocative examples when what is needed is the dispassionate picture provided by facts and figures. Gail Collins, writing in the *New York Times*, offers a whimsical instance of this fallacy:

> When I was a teenager, [banker Charles] Keating came to my Catholic girls high school in Cincinnati in his capacity as the founder of Citizens for Decent Literature, an anti-pornography group. His theme was the evil of wearing shorts in the summertime.
>
> Keating said he knew a young mother who took her child for a walk while wearing Bermuda shorts. A motorist, overwhelmed with lust at the sight of the back of her uncovered calves, lost control of his car and slammed into them. Everybody was killed, and it was all her fault. We were then asked to sign pledge cards promising to conform to standards of modesty that would have satisfied the Taliban.[23]

Needless to say, Collins was not persuaded by this display of illogic.

Defective Proof

Any element of proof can be defective. We have already pointed out the danger when appeals to feelings overwhelm judgment and cloud the issue. Speakers might also misuse appeals to cultural identity to promote intolerance, such as "When are Native Americans going to start being *good* Americans?"

Similarly, speakers may abuse appeals to credibility by attacking the person instead of the problem. This is called an **ad hominem fallacy**. Such persuaders try to avoid issues by calling the opposition derogatory names. For example, during an environmental dispute, one side charged that its opponents were "little old ladies in tennis shoes" and "outside agitators." Not to be outdone, the other side labeled their antagonists as "rapists of public parkland."[24]

Senator Zell Miller of Georgia laced into *New York Times* columnist Maureen Dowd, a major critic of the religious right, in the following way: "The more Maureen Loud [sic] gets on 'Meet the Press' and writes those columns, the redder these states get. I mean, they don't want some highbrow hussy from New York City explaining to them that they're idiots and telling them that they're stupid." Miller also suggested "that red-headed woman at the *New York Times*" should not mock anyone's religion: "You can see horns just sprouting up through that Technicolor hair."

Dowd responded: "I'm not a highbrow hussy from New York. I'm a highbrow hussy from Washington. Senator, pistols or swords?"[25] Presumably, the public was not much enlightened by this exchange.

Proof by ethos also can be abused when speakers overuse it—when they try to intimidate listeners by citing an overwhelming list of authorities while neglecting to present information or good reasons for accepting their claims.

Finally, speakers neglect their responsibility to prove their points when they merely assert what they have not proved, thereby **begging the question**. Those who

---

▶ **ad hominem fallacy** An attempt to discredit a position by attacking the people who favor it.

▶ **begging the question** Assuming that an argument has been proved without actually presenting the evidence.

beg the question usually rely on colorful language to disguise the inadequacy of their proofs so that the words themselves *seem* to establish the conclusion. Critics who shout, "It's amazing how much money we're wasting on education these days" suggest wild and excessive spending without really proving the allegation. A similar abuse may occur when the speaker taps into the mythos of the audience without adequate justification or preparation. A conclusion such as "Be *patriotic*! Support the *American way of life*! Speak out against gun control!"—tacked onto a speech without further explanation—begs the question, because the speaker has not proved that being against gun control is a form of patriotism.

Defective Patterns of Reasoning

Major fallacies may infest the basic patterns of reasoning in persuasion. It is unethical to commit them purposely, irresponsible to commit them accidentally. In your role as critical listener, be on guard against them at all times.

Errors of Reasoning from Principle.   Reasoning from principle can be only as good as the underlying premise on which it is built. In the **shaky principle fallacy**, the premise is not sound. *If the principle is faulty, the entire argument may crumble.* We once heard a student begin a line of argument with the following statement of principle: "College athletes are not really here to learn." She was instantly in trouble. When her speech was over, the class assailed her with questions: How did she define *athletes*? Was she talking about intercollegiate or intramural athletes? How about the tennis team? How did she define learning? Was she aware of the negative stereotype at the center of her premise? Wasn't she being unfair, not to mention arrogant? It's safe to say that the speaker did not persuade many people that day. To avoid such a fiasco, be sure that you can defend each word in the principle that underlies your reasoning.

    Omitted qualifier, another fallacy common to reasoning from principle, occurs when a persuader claims too much, in effect confusing probability with certainty. The logic of everyday life is rarely certain. Suppose a friend from the Tau Beta fraternity calls you to set up a blind date. If the principle "Tau Betas are handsome" holds about 90 percent of the time in your experience, and if you are about 90 percent certain that your blind date is a Tau Beta, then your conclusion that your date will be attractive is an assumption qualified by at least two factors of uncertainty. It is better to say: "There is a *good chance* that my date will be handsome." If you point out the uncertainty factor in advance through proper qualification, you may not lose the audience's trust if a prediction does not come true.

Errors of Reasoning from Reality.   An error common to reasoning from reality is *assuming that if something happens after an event, it was caused by the event.* This **post hoc fallacy** confuses association with causation. It is the basis of many superstitious beliefs. The same people who wear their lucky boots and shirts to ball games may also argue that we should have a tax cut because the last time we had one we avoided war, increased employment, or reduced crime. One of our students—usually quite bright—fell into the post hoc trap when she argued that low readership of certain books in areas where the books are banned in public schools proves that the bans are effective. There may be many reasons why people don't read books—banning them in school libraries may or may not be among those reasons. It is just as likely that the book bans themselves are simply symptoms of deeper cultural conditions

▶ **shaky principle fallacy**   A reasoning error that occurs when an argument is based on a faulty premise.

▶ **omitted qualifier**   Fallacy occurs when speakers exaggerate the strength of a claim, confusing probability with certainty.

▶ **post hoc fallacy**   An inductive error in which one event is assumed to be the cause of another simply because the first preceded the second.

and that the bans might actually create curiosity about their objects of censure, resulting in more readership than might otherwise have happened. A speaker must demonstrate that events are causally connected, not just make the assumption on the basis of association.

Another error common to such reasoning is a **hasty generalization** that is based on insufficient or nonrepresentative observations. Suppose a student reasoned, "My big sister in Alpha Chi got a D from Professor Osborn. The guy who sits next to me in history got an F from her. I'm struggling to make a C in her class. Therefore, Professor Osborn is a tough grader." To avoid hasty generalization, you would need to know what Professor Osborn's grade distribution looks like over an extended period of time and across courses, plus how her grades compare with other professors teaching the same courses.

Finally, an error common to both reasoning from principle and reasoning from reality is the **non sequitur fallacy**. It occurs when the principle and the reality discussed don't really relate to each other, when the conclusion does not follow from the relationship between them, or when the evidence presented is irrelevant.

The late Marge Schott, an owner of the Cincinnati Reds baseball team, put in her bid for the cockeyed non sequitur logic award when she told a Denver radio audience that she would rather see children smoke than take drugs. Her reason? "We smoked a peace pipe with the Indians, right?"[26] Challenging her for that dubious award was Dixy Lee Ray, former chair of the Atomic Energy Commission, who offered this defense for atomic energy: "A nuclear power plant is infinitely safer than eating, because 300 people choke to death on food every year."[27]

Defective Analogy. A **faulty analogy** occurs when the things related are dissimilar in ways that would invalidate any lessons to be learned by comparing them. Former Rep. Tom DeLay, who owned an exterminating business, once urged his colleagues not to ban the use of chlordane, a cancer-causing chemical, in the control of termites. He argued: "This bill reminds me of legislation that ought to be introduced to outlaw automobiles on the grounds that cars kill people."

Critics argued against the analogy on grounds that banning cars would be socially and economically disruptive in a way that banning chlordane would not. Further, they argued that other pesticides were available to replace chlordane, while few modes of transportation could take the place of cars for many people in many places. Finally, they pointed out that cars play a role in society far more important for most people than does controlling termites in homes.

FINDING YOUR

voice Find the Fallacies

Look for examples of fallacies in the letters-to-the-editor section of your local newspaper, or in opinions expressed in blogs that you visit over a week's period of time. Bring these specimens to class for discussion and analysis.

▶ **hasty generalization** An error of inductive reasoning in which a claim is made based on insufficient or nonrepresentative information.

▶ **non sequitur fallacy** Occurs when conclusions do not follow from the premises that precede them or from irrelevant evidence.

▶ **faulty analogy** A comparison drawn between things that are dissimilar in some important way.

Fallacies Related to Particular Designs

In addition to fallacies of evidence, proof, and argument, there are at least two major fallacies related to particular persuasive designs. **Either-or thinking**, sometimes called a *false dilemma*, makes listeners think that they have only two mutually exclusive choices. This fallacy is attractive because it is dramatic: It satisfies our

FIGURE 15.4
Gallery of Fallacies

Kind	Nature of the Problem
1. Evidence fallacies	
A. Slippery slope	• Arguing that one bad thing will result in many others
B. Confusing fact with opinion	• Asserting opinions as though they were facts, or discrediting facts as opinions
C. Red herring	• Distracting listeners with sensational, irrelevant material
D. Myth of the mean	• Using an average to hide a problem
E. Flawed statistical comparisons	• Using percentage increases or decreases to distort reality
F. Defective testimony	• Omitting when a statement was made or a speaker's credentials; quoting out of context
G. Inappropriate evidence	• Using facts when examples are needed, or examples when facts are needed, or an intimidating list of authorities as a substitute for information
2. Flawed proofs	
A. Ad hominem	• Attacking the person rather than the point
B. Begging the question	• Assuming as decided what has actually not been proved
3. Defective arguments	
A. Shaky principle	• Basing an argument on an unsound assumption
B. Omitted qualifiers	• Confusing probability with certainty by asserting a conclusion without qualification
C. Post hoc	• Assuming because one event follows another, it was caused by it
D. Non sequitur	• Reasoning in which principles and observations are unrelated to each other or to the conclusion drawn
E. Hasty generalization	• Drawing conclusions based on insufficient or nonrepresentative observations
F. Faulty analogy	• Comparing things that are dissimilar in some important way
4. Persuasive design fallacies	
A. Either-or thinking	• Framing choices so that listeners think they have only two options
B. Straw man	• Belittling or trivializing arguments to refute them easily

▶ **either-or thinking**   A fallacy that occurs when a speaker suggests that there are only two options, only one of which is desirable.

need for conflict and simplicity. It occurs in statements such as, "We can either promote jobs or protect the environment—not both" or "If we pay down the debt, we will sacrifice social security." Either-or thinking blinds listeners to other options, such as compromise or creative alternatives not yet considered. Such thinking often infests problem–solution speeches when speakers oversimplify the choices.

People with gardens sometimes make a "straw man" to scare off crows. From this practice comes the **straw man fallacy**, creating a "likeness" of an opponent's view that makes it seem trivial, extreme, and easy to refute. The straw man fallacy understates and distorts the position of opponents and is unethical. Reducing health care reform to a "government take-over" of medical care, or the regulatory reform of banking practices to "socialism," are recent cases. As an ethical persuasive speaker, you have an obligation to represent an opposing position fairly and fully, even as you refute it. Only then will thoughtful listeners respect you and your arguments. The straw man fallacy is an implicit admission of weakness or desperation and can damage what may well be a legitimate case.

To learn more about the fascinating subject of fallacies, go to "Fallacy Files" (http://fallacyfiles.org), an interactive site containing an extensive collection of fallacies and bad argument. Developed by Gary N. Curtis, the site offers definitions and examples, and is well organized and entertaining. See especially "Stalking the Wild Fallacy," offered under the "Examples" feature on the Menu.

Persuasion is constantly threatened by flaws and deception. In a world of competing views, we often see human nature revealed in its petty as well as its finer moments. As you plan and present your arguments or listen to the arguments of others, be on guard against fallacies. Figure 15.4 lists and defines the fallacies we have been discussing.

FINAL
reflections Persuasion That Has Legs

The manipulator is interested only in influencing the momentary, shallow commitments that drive our everyday decisions. Some of these commitments may seem of rather limited consequence—the choice of one shampoo over others, one insurance company over others, perhaps even of one automobile over others. But once we leave the area of mundane personal choices, and enter the arena in which we are asked to support or reject government policies and decide among competing political candidates, such impulsive, shallow commitments are inappropriate, and the role and rule of the manipulator should come to an end.

Instead, for these more important decisions, we need a persuasion that respects the power of evidence and the importance of proofs, a persuasion that develops patterns of reasoning in which all these vital elements are arranged into sound and compelling arguments. This kind of grounded, reasoned persuasion is vital to the long-range impact of your ideas.

Finding your voice means more than discovering your call to a cause and learning how to make your voice heard. It has to do also with how long your voice will be heard, with its staying power, with the extent of its influence. Reasoned persuasion pursues the kind of commitment that endures. It has legs.

▶ **straw man fallacy** Understating, distorting, or otherwise misrepresenting the position of opponents for ease of refutation.

A SAMPLE SPEECH

This outstanding persuasive speech, presented during Honors Day in the Department of Communication Studies at the University of Texas at Austin, went on to win the National Championship for Persuasive Speaking presented by the National Forensic League. It is noteworthy for its reliance on reasoned persuasion, developing an array of proofs and evidence that emphasize facts and expert testimony, carefully documented to reassure critical listeners. Adding color and human interest to the speech are judicious uses of example, metaphor, and appeals to fear and fairness.

Keep Big Brother Off Your Back

AUSTIN L. WRIGHT, UNIVERSITY OF TEXAS AT AUSTIN

On September 26, 2002, Canadian citizen Maher Arar boarded a flight home from a family vacation in Tunisia. During a layover in New York City, American authorities detained Arar, interrogating him for the next twelve days. After repeatedly denying any connection to Al Qaeda, Arar was shackled and loaded onto a private, unmarked jet headed for Syria, where he was tortured for the next ten months.

As the *Electronic Privacy Information Center* or EPIC writes in an *amicus* brief presented before the U.S. Supreme Court on May 16, 2008, the U.S. government justified Arar's torture using patently false information. As the brief further explains, two American databases—the Department of Homeland Security's Automated Targeting System and the FBI's National Crime Information Center—track tens of millions of Americans and foreign nationals each year for things as simple as suspicious credit card charges and questionable Internet searches. Indeed, EPIC claims our government uses these databases for searches 2.8 million times every day!

Yet, these databases contain widely documented errors that the government has no intention of fixing. And, in 2007 the Department of Justice folded to pressure from the private intelligence companies and granted both databases blanket immunity over the accuracy of their contents, meaning no one can sue the government for the unlawful use of false information provided by private corporations.

In short: the information that our government uses to detain, interrogate and torture suspected terrorists can be fabricated on a whim. But with more Americans being tracked as suspected terrorists than at any other point in our nation's history—writes *The USA Today* of March 10, 2009—the danger of false data to all of us is too grave to ignore.

So today we will discuss how these error-ridden databases are protected, examine the dangers they pose to our personal liberties, and discuss some ways they might be corrected.

According to *The New York Times* of January 15, 2009, the Supreme Court ruled that evidence found in faulty databases may be used to charge someone with a crime, real or imagined. These databases pose a threat to the prohibition on unreasonable search and seizure, but they are protected by the government in two ways: constraints on the exclusionary rule and the use of private companies to sidestep restrictions.

◀ The speech opens with an example that raises issues of fairness over the government's use of false information and its complicity in torture. Implied in the example is a sense of violated mythos: should the United States, which prides itself over protecting individual rights, be engaged in such egregious violations of these rights?

◀ The speech offers a clear preview of what is to come, and promises to develop within a categorical design.

Initially, as the *Wisconsin Law Journal* of January 26, 2009 writes, the Supreme Court passed down a decision seriously limiting the scope of the exclusionary rule in the case of Herring v. United States. The exclusionary rule protects Americans from evidence acquired through an illegal search and seizure. But, in deciding the fate of Bennie Herring—an Alabama man who was pulled over and searched using an erroneous warrant—the Court amended the exclusionary rule, writing off the government's use of false information as "reasonable" since Herring was guilty of a crime. While this new legal doctrine may sound appealing, it does expose innocent Americans as well to unreasonable search, seizure and detention.

Additionally, the federal government hires private companies, like Choicepoint and LexisNexis, to develop these databases to circumvent legal restrictions on domestic intelligence gathering. Washington Post reporter Robert O'Harrow's 2005 book *No Place To Hide* clarifies that the law regulating private intelligence gathering is the Fair Credit Reporting Act. If private companies don't sell credit ratings, however, their techniques do not trigger oversight under the law, meaning that companies can use literally any means to gather information and are not legally required to verify its accuracy. As a June 1, 2007. *Salon.com* expose contends, the federal government is outsourcing domestic spying to private companies that can gather any information about anyone, using any means, without any consequences for releasing false information.

> The example that follows provides another perspective on false databases: not only are they dangerous—they are sometimes patently absurd. The sardonic humor provides a touch of color and lightness in the otherwise somber wordscape of the speech.

When Ron Peterson, a man from California, asked Choicepoint for his private information in 2005, he was told he was a female prostitute in Florida named Ronnie, an incarcerated murderer in Texas, a stolen goods dealer in New Mexico, a witness tamperer in Oregon and a sex offender in Nevada. All of which, thankfully, were not true. But just imagine how this so-called "information" might have been misused by a government investigator prepared already to believe the worst about Mr. Peterson!

Beyond such flagrant inaccuracies, these flawed databases threaten each of us in two ways: legal malfeasance and information leaks. Initially, given the Supreme Court's recent decision, false information contained within these databases has the same force of law as accurate information. Since the Department of Justice built a legal force field around these databases in 2007, writes the *Wisconsin Law Journal*, LexisNexis and Choicepoint are legally free to disseminate false information that can be used to fill these databases and to execute searches, seizures and false arrests, all without a shred of truth or actual legal merit.

These databases and the private companies hired to make them are also dangerously prone to information leaks. The *North Country Gazette* of January 14, 2009, writes that a former NYPD sergeant was able to access a database through his police status and leaked top-secret documents to help a friend win a divorce battle. What's more, the *Los Angeles Times* of January 27, 2006, explains that these companies also have a reputation for losing information. In 2005, for instance, Choicepoint's data system was breached by con artists, compromising more than 19 billion individual files, including social security numbers and financial histories. Although a 2007 Javelin Strategy and Research report finds that identity theft costs victims an average of $5,000, the government forced Choicepoint to pay out a mere $15 million in damages. That's an average of less than one tenth of one cent for each person whose private information was leaked by Choicepoint.

While we may not be able to change the way the Supreme Court treats the use of false information, we can cut this problem off at its source by pressuring the private intelligence companies hired by our government and checking the information they sell. As O'Harrow explains, LexisNexis has built a virtual monopoly on American intelligence gathering. Since 9/11, LexisNexis bought most of the companies hired by the federal government to build the Automated Targeting System and NCIC, including Choicepoint. What's even worse, the CEO of Choicepoint told the Washington Post in 2005 that his company won't tolerate regulation under the Fair Credit Reporting Act; meaning LexisNexis subsidiaries are using any means to gather even false information without any legal consequences.

LexisNexis charges our school about a $1.50 fee every time we use their search engine. So here's a radical idea: let's refuse to use it! And let's ask our librarians and our college officials to cancel their contracts with LexisNexis and its subsidiary companies until they clean up their act. When I found out LexisNexis makes about $5,000 a year off my speech team, I asked my teammates to start using alternative search engines like Google News and Google Scholar. I prepared this speech using only sources taken from Google News. As an academic community that makes heavy use of their tools, we are in a unique position to pressure LexisNexis for change. And we at the University of Texas—this large and prestigious university—can start a movement for reform that can sweep across this country!

If you want to take more immediate action, send a letter to Choicepoint, demanding access to your information. You can either visit their website or take one of the request forms I have printed off. All you have to do is fill in the blanks and make a copy of your driver's license and a recent bill you have paid that contains your address. If you happen to discover false information in your folder, don't hesitate to send a certified letter to Choicepoint requesting a revision of your file. Choicepoint is legally required to comply with your demands and correcting even minor errors could help keep Big Brother off your back.

When Maher Arar was illegally detained in 2002, the dual threats posed by the Automated Tracking System and the NCIC may have seemed isolated. But today, the stakes for tens of millions of Americans are greater than ever before. We must act and act now to pressure private intelligence companies to mend the information crisis they have created. With government conducting ten searches every second using faulty data, we literally don't have a second to lose.

◄ Austin concludes by raising a specter of government as a potentially abusive Big Brother, an image that might appeal to both liberals and conservatives He offers a nice sense of closure by tying back in to his initial example of a tortured citizen, and appeals for immediate action.

◄ Austin anticipated the question of what listeners might do to counter the vast injustice he had described by offering his own personal action as a model. He also appealed to the pride of his Texas listeners by offering a metaphorical vision of a movement for reform starting on their campus that might then "sweep across the country."

THIS CHAPTER WILL HELP YOU

1 Appreciate the value of ceremonial speaking
2 Master the techniques of ceremonial speaking
3 Prepare and present the most common types of ceremonial speeches
4 Act as a master of ceremonies
5 Develop a ceremonial speech using narrative design

16 Ceremonial Speaking

> *[People] who celebrate ... are fused with each other and fused with all things in nature.*
>
> —ERNST CASSIRER

Ceremonial speeches are offered on special occasions that are often vital to the meaning of our lives.

- Simone Mullinax described the significance of baking a key lime pie with her grandmother, whom she honored in her speech of tribute (see following this chapter).
- Ashley McMillan paid tribute to her dwarf cousin, whose indomitable spirit was much larger than her body (see Appendix B).
- John Bakke accepted his university's Martin Luther King Jr. award with remarks that morphed quickly into a speech of tribute to Dr. King and then into a speech of inspiration for his audience (see Appendix B).

Ceremonial speeches and speakers offer tribute to people and accomplishments, confer and accept awards, introduce featured speakers, evoke laughter and merriment during after-dinner occasions, celebrate happy occasions such as weddings and sports achievements, present memorials, and inspire listeners. In the process they often reinforce deep values that bind people together in communities.[1] The philosopher John Dewey observed that people "live in a community in virtue of the things which they have in common; and communication is the way in which they come to possess things in common. What they must have in common . . . are aims, beliefs, aspirations, knowledge—a common understanding."[2] It is ceremonial speaking that celebrates and reinforces our common aims, beliefs, and aspirations.

As you participate in these important rituals, you also can celebrate your success in finding your voice. Part of that success is discovering that you can now make a contribution, when the occasion arises, to your family, to a mentor or friend, or to the life of your community.

From Frederick Douglass's "What to the Slave Is the Fourth of July?" to Ronald Reagan's "Challenger Disaster Address," many of the greatest or most studied speeches in American history were delivered on ceremonial occasions. We remember them because they provide rich portraits of Americans struggling to reconcile a shared sense of purpose with moments of great testing and trial.

Ceremonial speaking addresses four questions of vital importance to any community: Who are we? Why are we? What have we accomplished? and What can we become together? In answering these questions, ceremonial speakers help to create an "ordered, meaningful cultural world."[3]

Of course, few of us will ever become towering historical figures, but there are many practical benefits as well of developing your ceremonial speaking skills. During your speaking career there will be many occasions for such skills. You might well be asked to "say a few words" upon the retirement of a former teacher or mentor, to present an award to an outstanding coworker, to celebrate the memory of a beloved friend, to offer a toast at a wedding reception, or act as the master of ceremonies at a banquet. And, as observers have noted since Aristotle, when you speak successfully on these occasions, it enhances perceptions of your competence, character, and leadership potential. When you find your voice, you often find your future.

There are as many kinds of ceremonial speaking as there are ceremonial occasions. They range from the serious or solemn in tone to the lighthearted and even humorous. In this chapter, we help you rise to the various challenges of ceremonial speaking.

FINDING YOUR

voice   Basic Ceremonial Questions

The speeches in Appendix B by John Bakke, Ashley McMillan, and Elie Wiesel are ceremonial addresses. How do they relate to the basic questions: Who are we? Why are we? What have we accomplished? and What can we become together? What values do these speeches celebrate? Discuss your take on these questions in class.

▶ **ceremonial speeches (ceremonial speaking)**   Speaking that celebrates special occasions, such as speeches of tribute, inspiration, and introduction, eulogies, toasts, award presentations, acceptances, and after-dinner speeches.

Techniques of Ceremonial Speaking

Two techniques, identification and magnification, are basic to ceremonial speaking.

Identification

Identification occurs when a speech creates the feeling that speaker and listeners share goals, values, emotions, memories, motives, and cultural background. Kenneth Burke, a leading communication theorist of our time, suggested that identification was the key term of public speaking.[4] People who *feel* together on issues will also reason and act together. Because ritual and ceremony draw people together, identification is also the heart of ceremonial speaking. Three common and sometimes overlapping strategies for promoting identification in ceremonial speaking are the use of narrative, the recognition of heroes and heroines, and the renewal of group commitment.

The Use of Narrative. As we noted in Chapters 3 and 8, storytelling can be an effective means of developing identification with an audience.[5] For example, if you were preparing a speech for a fundraising celebration at your university, you might recall things that happened during those long evenings when student volunteers were making calls. You might remember moments of discouragement, followed by other moments of triumph when the contributions were especially large or meaningful. Your purpose would be to draw listeners close together as they remember the shared experience. While you should be careful not to belittle or offend anyone, stories that evoke laughter can be especially effective because laughter itself is a shared phenomenon.

In her student speech printed in Appendix B, Ashlie McMillan told the inspiring story of her cousin Tina's accomplishments as a dwarf. In her introduction, she asked listeners to close their eyes and imagine themselves shrinking to help them identify more closely with the challenges Tina faced on a daily basis. This identification prepared the audience to accept Ashlie's eloquent conclusion: "You too may seem too short to grasp your stars, but you never know how far you might reach if you stand upon a dream." We discussed how to design effective narratives in Chapters 3 and 8, and shall have more to say about it later in this chapter.

The Recognition of Heroes and Heroines. Another strategy for promoting identification in ceremonial speaking is to invoke the words and deeds of heroes and heroines as role models. Depending on the nature and purpose of the celebration, speakers might invoke such figures as Thomas Jefferson, Martin Luther King Jr., Mother Theresa, or Elizabeth Cady Stanton. These figures embody and personify such virtues as dedication, steadfastness, sacrifice, and grand achievements against the odds. The lives they have lived—as we remember them—represent hope, for having lived once, they can live again in our actions and deeds.

Renewal of Group Commitment. Ceremonial speaking is a time both for celebrating what has been accomplished and for renewing commitments. Share with your listeners a vision of what the future can be like if their commitment continues. Plead with them not to be satisfied with present accomplishments. Renew their identity as a group moving toward even greater goals.

To reinforce this emphasis on group renewal, ceremonial speakers often depict a challenging present against the backdrop of an idealized past, then create a moral

▶ **identification** The feeling of closeness between speakers and listeners that may overcome personal and cultural differences.

FINDING YOUR

voice   The Uses of Heroism

Identify five heroes or heroines who are often mentioned in ceremonial speeches. Why do speakers refer to them so frequently? What occasions call them forth? What does this tell us about the nature of these admired persons, about the needs of contemporary audiences, and about the ceremonial speech situation? Be prepared to discuss these topics in class.

vision to guide listeners through the present into the future. In his "Gettysburg Address," delivered to commemorate the costliest battle of the costliest war in American history, Abraham Lincoln used this technique to substantially redefine America's moral identity as a nation.

Lincoln opened with a clear reference to an idealized past: "Four score and seven years ago our fathers brought forth on this continent, a new nation, conceived in Liberty, and dedicated to the proposition that all men are created equal." He then moved directly to the troubled present: "Now we are engaged in a great civil war, testing whether that nation, or any nation so conceived and so dedicated, can long endure." After expounding on the sacrifices of the "brave men, living and dead, who struggled here," Lincoln closed by offering a stunning vision to guide the American future: "that this nation, under God, shall have a new birth of freedom—and that government of the people, by the people, for the people, shall not perish from the earth."[6]

SPEAKER'S

notes   Promoting Identification

Use the following techniques to promote identification among listeners:

1. Tell stories that remind listeners of shared experiences.

2. Enjoy laughter: Listeners who laugh together are bonding with each other.

3. Create portraits of heroes and heroines as shared role models.

4. Revive legends and traditions that remind listeners of their shared heritage and values.

5. Offer goals and visions to inspire listeners to work together.

Magnification

In his *Rhetoric*, Aristotle noted that when speakers select certain features of a person or event and then dwell on those qualities, the effect is to magnify them until they fill the minds of listeners.[7] Such **magnification** comes to represent the meaning of the subject for listeners. It focuses attention on what is relevant, honorable, and praiseworthy.

For example, imagine that you are preparing a speech honoring Jesse Owens's incredible track and field accomplishments in the 1936 Olympic

▶ **magnification**   A speaker's selecting and emphasizing certain qualities of a subject to stress the values they represent.

Games. In your research, you come up with a variety of facts:

1. He had a headache the day he won the medal in the long jump.

2. He had suffered from racism in America.

3. He did not like the food served at the Olympic training camp.

4. He won four gold medals in front of Adolf Hitler, who was preaching the racial superiority of Germans.

5. Some of his friends did not want him to run for the United States.

6. After his victories, he returned to further discrimination in America.

If you used all this information, your speech might seem rambling and aimless. Which of these items should you emphasize, and how should you proceed? To make your selection, you need to know what themes are best to develop when you want to magnify the actions of a person. These themes include:

Jesse Owens was both a great Olympic hero and a great inspirational speaker.

■ Triumph over obstacles

■ Unusual accomplishment

■ Superior performance

■ Unselfish motives

■ Benefit to society

As you consider these themes, it becomes clearer which items about Jesse Owens you should magnify and how you should do so. To begin, you would stress that Owens had to overcome obstacles such as racism in America to make the Olympic team. Then you would point out that his accomplishment was unusual. No one else had ever won four gold medals in Olympic track and field competition, and his performances set world records that lasted many years. Because Owens received no material gain from his victories, his motives were unselfish, driven solely by personal qualities such as courage and determination. Finally, you would demonstrate that because his victories repudiated Hitler's racist ideology, causing the Nazi leader public humiliation, Owens's accomplishments benefited our society. The overall effect would be to magnify the meaning of Jesse Owens's great performances, both for himself and for his nation.

In addition to focusing on these basic themes, magnification relies on effective uses of language to create dramatic word-pictures, as we saw in Chapter 11. Metaphor and simile can magnify a subject through creative associations, such as "He struck like a lightning bolt that day." Parallel structure, the repetition of key words and phrases, can also help magnify a subject and embed it in our minds. For example, if you were to say of Mother Teresa, "Whenever there was hurt, she was there. Whenever there was hunger, she was there. Whenever there was desperation, she was there," you would be magnifying her dedication and selflessness.

Magnification also favors certain speech designs over others. Comparison and contrast designs promote magnification by making selected features stand out. For example, you might contrast the purity of Owens's motives with the crassness of those of today's well-paid athletes. Chronological designs used to relate the history of a situation enhance magnification by dramatizing certain events as stories unfold over time. As Simone Mullinax sketched certain incidents in her childhood, she gradually revealed and magnified the fascinating character of her grandmother. The causation design promotes magnification when a person's accomplishments are emphasized as the causes of important effects. For example, a speaker might suggest that Jesse Owens's victories refuted Nazi propaganda for many people. The narrative design, which helps to dramatize events and accomplishments, is a natural for ceremonial speaking.

Whatever designs ceremonial speeches use, it is important that they build to a conclusion. Speakers should save their best materials and language use for the end of the speech. Ceremonial speeches should never dwindle to a conclusion.

SPEAKER'S notes Magnification

Use the following strategies to magnify a person or accomplishment:

1. Show how people have overcome obstacles to success.
2. Point out how unusual the accomplishments are.
3. Underscore superior features of the performance.
4. Emphasize unselfish motives behind the achievement.
5. Show how listeners and society as a whole have benefited.
6. Use the techniques of magnifying language power that are discussed in Chapter 11.
7. Use speech designs—comparison, chronological, causation, and narrative—that promote magnification.

Types of Ceremonial Speeches

As we noted earlier, there are ceremonial speeches for all occasions. In this section, we consider the types you will most likely present in your personal and professional lives: speeches of tribute (award presentations, eulogies, and toasts), acceptance speeches, introductions, speeches of inspiration, after-dinner speeches, and speaking as master of ceremonies (see Figure 16.1).

Type	Use When
Tributes	You wish to honor a person, group, occasion, or event. Subtypes include award presentations, eulogies, and toasts.
Acceptance	You need to acknowledge an award or honor.
Introductions	You must introduce a featured speaker in a program.
Inspiration	You want to motivate listeners to appreciate and commit to a goal, purpose, or set of values; this may be religious, commercial, political, or social in nature.
After-Dinner	You want to entertain the audience while leaving a message that can guide future behavior. Here, as elsewhere, brevity is golden.
Master of Ceremonies	You must coordinate a program and see that everything runs smoothly. The master of ceremonies sets the mood for the occasion.

FIGURE 16.1 Types of Ceremonial Speeches

The Speech of Tribute

In magnifying the importance of accomplishments, the **speech of tribute** endorses the values of individual responsibility, striving, and achievement. For example, you might be called on to honor a former teacher at a retirement ceremony, present an award to someone for an outstanding accomplishment, eulogize a person who has died, or propose a toast to a friend who is getting married.

Speeches of tribute can serve several important purposes. If you have presented a series of speeches on related topics in your class, the speech of tribute gives you a chance to extend your efforts at informing and persuading listeners. For example, Holly Carlson chose the banning of books in public schools as the topic area for all her speeches. In her informative speech, she demonstrated how books are banned in schools all over the country, and she listed the books and authors most often targeted. In her persuasive speech, she offered a stirring plea for intellectual freedom, urging her listeners to support the right to read and think for themselves. Then, for her ceremonial speech, she offered a tribute to one of the most frequently banned authors of the twentieth century, J. D. Salinger. Her tribute to Salinger made her listeners want to read his works themselves. It also dramatized how hurtful censorship could be. Thus, all of Holly's speeches were woven into one pattern, which gave focus to her semester's work. She found her voice cumulatively and forcefully.

Speeches of tribute blend easily with inspirational speeches. John Bakke's speech accepting the University of Memphis Martin Luther King Jr. Human Rights Award quickly developed into a speech of tribute to that great leader, then transformed into a speech of inspiration for his listeners. Simone Mullinax's tribute to her feisty grandmother offered a conclusion that inspires appreciation for family love and tradition.

Praiseworthy accomplishments are usually celebrated for two reasons. First, *they are important in themselves*: The influence of a teacher may have contributed to the

▶ **speech of tribute** A ceremonial speech that recognizes the achievements of individuals or groups or commemorates special events.

The raising of the American flag at Iwo Jima during World War II became an important symbol for courage and fortitude, themes echoed in the similar photograph of the raising of the flag by firefighters over the wreckage of the World Trade Center.

success of many of her former students. Second, *they are important as symbols*. The planting of the American flag at Iwo Jima during some of the most intense fighting of World War II came to symbolize the fortitude of the entire American war effort; it represented commitment, and it was more important as a symbol than as an actual event. Sometimes the same event may be celebrated for both actual and symbolic reasons. A student speech honoring the raising of $60,000 for victims of the 2010 Nashville flood celebrated this achievement both as a symbol of generosity and for the actual help it brought to many people. When you plan a speech of tribute, you should consider both the actual and the symbolic values that are represented.

Developing Speeches of Tribute. As you prepare a speech of tribute, keep the following guidelines in mind:

- **Do not exaggerate the tribute.** If you are too lavish with your praise or use too many superlatives, you may embarrass the recipient and make the praise unbelievable.

- **Focus on the person being honored, not on yourself.** Even if you know what effort the accomplishment required because you have done something similar, don't mention that at this time. It will come across as conceit when the focus should be on the honoree.

- **Create vivid images of accomplishment.** Speeches of tribute are occasions for illustrating what someone has achieved, the values underlying those achievements, and their consequences. Tell stories that make those accomplishments come to life.

- **Be sincere.** Speeches of tribute are a time for warmth, pride, and appreciation. Your manner should reflect these qualities as you present the tribute.

When you honor a historical figure, your purpose will often be to promote values represented by the person's life. In his speech accepting the Human Rights award, John Bakke paid tribute to Dr. King's faith in nonviolence and to his holding fast to that faith, even in the face of criticism from friends as well as enemies. Bakke gave new life to the concept of nonviolence by expanding and exploring its meaning for our time. Note in particular his use of parallel structure and antithesis and his challenge to listeners to redefine their roles in the political process:

> Taylor Branch has asserted, "Nonviolence is an orphan among democratic
> ideas" but "Every ballot is a piece of nonviolence. . . ."
> It's time to make that ballot the effect of full democratic participation.
> It's time to reclaim our democratic processes. It's time to make the

voice Paying Tribute

Select a public figure whom you admire and prepare a speech of tribute honoring that person. Which aspects of your subject's life did you choose to magnify, and why? How did you accomplish magnification? Were you also able to promote identification with this person among your listeners? Either present your speech in class and answer these questions when you have concluded, or prepare a written report based on this assignment.

democratic processes work in America just as we are trying to make them work for Iraq.

That means more than voting. It means informed voting. It means supporting candidates and policies of our choice. It means commitment to the communication processes that give life to democracy. It means thinking of ourselves more as citizens than as just taxpayers. It means full-time citizenship. If campaigns are now permanent, citizenship cannot be cyclical. Democracy and "the vote" will always be open to criticism if people do not vote or do not know what they are voting for.

Award Presentations. When you present an award, you often accompany it with a speech of tribute. An **award presentation** recognizes the achievements or contributions of those on whom the award is bestowed. Most award presenters have two main points: they explain the nature of the award, and they applaud what the recipient did to qualify for it.

If an award is already well known, such as the Nobel Peace Prize, you can focus on why the recipient deserves such prestigious recognition. Thus, when Elie Wiesel received the 1986 Nobel Peace Prize, Egil Aarvik, Chairman of the Norwegian Nobel Committee, focused on Wiesel's unique accomplishments. Wiesel had not only survived the Nazi death camps—he had become a champion of the human spirit (see his moving acceptance speech in Appendix B):

> From the abyss of the death camps he has come as a messenger to mankind— not with a message of hate and revenge, but with one of brotherhood and atonement. . . . Elie Wiesel is not only the man who survived—he is also the spirit which has conquered. In him we see a man who has climbed from utter humiliation to become one of our most important spiritual leaders and guides. . . . The Holocaust was a war within a war, a world in itself, a kingdom of darkness where there existed an evil so monstrous that it shattered all political and moral codes. . . .
>
> His mission is not to gain the world's sympathy for the victims or the survivors. His aim is to awaken our conscience. Our indifference to evil makes us partners in the crime. . . . We know that the unimaginable has happened. What are we doing now to prevent it happening again?. . .
>
> It is in recognition of this particular human spirit's victory over the powers of death and degradation, and as a support to the rebellion of good against the evil in the world, that the Norwegian Nobel Committee today presents the Nobel Peace Prize to Elie Wiesel.[8]

▶ **award presentation** A speech of tribute that recognizes achievements of the award recipient, explains the nature of the award, and describes why the recipient qualifies for the award.

Republican Senator Orrin Hatch eulogized Democratic Senator Ted Kennedy at his funeral.

This tribute demonstrates well what you must do in justifying an award's presentation. You should emphasize the uniqueness, superiority, and benefits of the recipient's achievements and provide examples that illustrate these accomplishments and explain their meaning.

Eulogies. Earlier we asked you to imagine yourself preparing a speech to honor Jesse Owens. Following his death in 1980, many such speeches were actually presented. A speech of tribute presented on the death of a person is called a **eulogy**. The following comments by Thomas P. O'Neill Jr., then Speaker of the United States House of Representatives, illustrate how some of the major techniques we have discussed can work in a eulogy:

O'Neill's opening highlights the themes of unusual and superior accomplishment. He begins with the actual value of Owens's victories, and then he describes their symbolic value.

These comments magnify the values represented by Owens's life and develop the theme of benefit to the community. That Owens remained a patriotic American in the face of racism and indifference magnifies his character.

O'Neill's conclusion emphasizes the symbolic, spiritual values of Owens's life.

I rise on the occasion of his passing to join my colleagues in tribute to the greatest American sports hero of this century, Jesse Owens. . . . His performances at the Berlin Olympics earned Jesse Owens the title of America's first superstar. . . .

No other athlete symbolized the spirit and motto of the Olympics better than Jesse Owens. "Swifter, higher, stronger" was the credo by which Jesse Owens performed as an athlete and lived as an American. Of his performances in Hitler's Berlin in 1936, Jesse said: "I wasn't running against Hitler, I was running against the world." Owens's view of the Olympics was just that: He was competing against the best athletes in the world without regard to nationality, race, or political view. . . .

Jesse Owens proved by his performances that he was the best among the finest the world had to offer, and in setting the world record in the 100-yard dash, he became the "fastest human" even before that epithet was fashionable. . . .

In life as well as on the athletic field, Jesse Owens was first an American, and second, an internationalist. He loved his country; he loved the opportunity his country gave him to reach the pinnacle of athletic prowess. In his own quiet, unassuming, and modest way—by example, by inspiration, and by performance—he helped other young people to aim for the stars, to develop their God-given potential . . .

As the world's first superstar, Jesse Owens was not initially overwhelmed by commercial interests and offered the opportunity to become a millionaire overnight. There was no White House reception waiting for him on his return from Berlin, and as Jesse Owens once observed: "I still had to ride in the back of the bus in my hometown in Alabama."

Can one individual make a difference? Clearly in the case of Jesse Owens, the answer is a resounding affirmative, for his whole life was dedicated to the elimination of poverty, totalitarianism, and racial bigotry; and he did it in his own special and modest way, a spokesman for freedom, an American ambassador of goodwill to the athletes of the world, and an inspiration to young Americans. . . . Jesse Owens was a champion all the way in a life of dedication to the principles of the American and Olympic spirit.[9]

▶ **eulogy**   A speech of tribute presented upon a person's death.

When you are asked to present a eulogy at a funeral or memorial service, you often confront a special challenge. In addition to dealing with natural anxiety about speaking, you must also control your own feelings of grief. Plan your eulogy with these thoughts in mind:

■ While eulogies should acknowledge a shared sense of grief, remember that your primary purpose is to offer comfort to the living. Remind them of how much they meant to the deceased. Try to provide words that will continue to console them in the days, months, and years later.

■ Share stories that highlight the humanity of the person. Use gentle humor to recall his or her endearing qualities.

■ Focus on how wonderful it was to have shared the life of the person more than on the pain of the loss. Make the eulogy a celebration of life.

■ Focus on the meaning of the person's life for those who live on.

Toasts.   A **toast** is a ceremonial speech in miniature, offered as a tribute to people and what they have done, as a blessing for their future, or simply as lighthearted enjoyment of the present moment. You might be asked to toast a coworker who has been promoted or a couple at a wedding reception, or simply to celebrate the beginning of a new year. The occasion may be formal or informal, but the message should always be eloquent. It simply won't do to mutter, "Here's to Tony, he's a great guy!" or "Cheers!" As one writer has said, such a feeble toast is "a gratuitous betrayal—of the occasion, its honoree, and the desire [of the audience] to clink glasses and murmur, 'Hear, hear,' in appreciation of a compliment well fashioned."[10]

Because toasts are (or certainly should be!) brief, every word must count. Plan your toast well in advance of the occasion. Although most speeches are best presented extemporaneously, a toast should be memorized. Practice presenting your toast with glass in hand until it flows easily. If you have difficulty memorizing your toast, it is probably too long. Some years ago we attended a dinner for graduating seniors. One of the speakers offered a memorable toast:

> As you graduate, I'm offering you a gift of wisdom
> that some say originated with Mark Twain.
> Twenty years from now you'll be more disap-
> pointed by the things you didn't do than by the
> things you did. So throw off the bowlines, sail
> away from the safe harbor, and catch the trade winds. Explore, dream, learn,
> grow, and discover. Here's to the adventurous life that awaits you!

A toast, a ceremonial speech in miniature, is offered as a tribute to people, as a blessing for their future, or simply in light-hearted enjoyment of the moment.

While a touch of humor is often appropriate, a toast should never embarrass or humiliate the honoree.[11] For example, it would certainly be inappropriate at a wedding reception to say, "Here's to John and Mary. I hope they don't end up in divorce court the way I did!" Figure 16.2 offers some additional sample toasts.

▶ **toast**   A short speech of tribute, usually offered at celebration dinners or meetings.

FIGURE 16.2 Sample Toasts

- May you have warm words on a cold evening, a full moon on a dark night, and a road downhill all the way to your door. (Irish blessing)

- Here's looking at you, kid. (Humphrey Bogart toasting Ingrid Bergman in *Casablanca*)

- I drink to your charm, your beauty, and your brains—Which gives you a rough idea of how hard up I am for a drink. (Groucho Marx)

- To get the full value of joy, you must have someone to divide it with. (Mark Twain)

- May you have the hindsight to know where you've been, the foresight to know where you're going, and the insight to know when you're going too far.

- As you ramble through life, whatever be your goal, keep your eye upon the doughnut, and not upon the hole. (Offered by Sid Pettigrew)

- May the road rise to meet you.
  May the wind be always at your back.
  May the sun shine warm upon your face.
  And rains fall soft upon your fields.
  And until we meet again,
  May God hold you in the hollow of His hand. (Irish blessing)*

* From "Tom's Toasts: Irish Toasts and Blessings," March 1998. http://zinnia.umfacad.maine.edu/~donaghue/toasts01.html (16 Dec. 1998).

The Acceptance Speech

If you are receiving an award or honor, you may be expected to respond with a **speech of acceptance**. A speech of acceptance should express gratitude for the honor and acknowledge those who made the accomplishment possible. It should be humble, should focus on the values the award represents, and should use language that matches the dignity of the occasion.

When Elie Wiesel was awarded the Nobel Peace Prize, he began his acceptance speech with these remarks: "It is with a profound sense of humility that I accept the honor you have chosen to bestow upon me."[12] Follow his lead and accept an award with grace and modesty.

As you accept an award, express your awareness of its deeper meaning. In his acceptance speech Mr. Wiesel stressed the value of freedom and the importance of involvement—of overcoming hatred with loving concern.

Finally, be sure the eloquence of your language fits the dignity of the moment. Wiesel told the story of a "young Jewish boy discovering the kingdom of night" during the Holocaust. This personal, metaphorical narrative was introduced early in the speech and repeated in the conclusion when Mr. Wiesel remarked, "No one is as capable of gratitude as one who has emerged from the kingdom of night." Although you may not be so eloquent, you should make a presentation that fits the dignity of the occasion.

▶ **speech of acceptance** A ceremonial speech expressing gratitude for an honor and acknowledging those who made the accomplishment possible.

The Speech of Introduction

One of the more common types of ceremonial speeches is the **speech of introduction**, in which you introduce a featured speaker to the audience. The importance of this speech can vary, depending on how well the speaker is already known. At times, a formal introduction may seem quite unnecessary. For example, when Madonna introduced Muhammad Ali at a gathering of New York sports personalities, she simply said:

> We are alike in many ways. We have espoused unpopular causes, we are arrogant, we like to have our picture taken, and we are the greatest.[13]

A good speech of introduction usually does three things: makes the speaker feel welcome, establishes or strengthens the ethos of the speaker, and prepares the audience for the speech that will follow. You make a speaker feel welcome both by what you say and how you say it. Deliver your words of welcome with warmth and sincerity.

As soon as you know you will be introducing someone, find out as much as you can about the person. Talk with him or her about what you might emphasize that would be most helpful to the speech. Avoid making dangerous assumptions. One of our favorite stories has to do with the famous Western artist, writer, and cowboy, Charles M. Russell. Russell did not particularly enjoy public speaking, but on one occasion his wife, Nancy, talked him into speaking at a civic gathering in Montana. The toastmaster did not bother to talk to Charlie before the speech, and decided on his own to introduce him as a "famous pioneer." As Western historian Bob Doerk described the event in a public lecture, this is how Charlie responded:

> "I have been called a pioneer. In my book a 'pioneer' is a man who comes to a virgin country, traps off all the fur, kills off all the wild meat, cuts down all the trees, grazes off all the grass, plows the roots up, and strings ten million miles of barbed wire. A pioneer destroys things and calls it 'civilization.' I wish to God that this country was just like it was when I first saw it and that none of you folks were here at all."
>
> About this time he realized that he had insulted his audience. He grabbed his hat and, in the boots and desperado sash that he always wore, left the room.[14]

So much for assuming that you know the speaker's values and the culturetypes they honor!

It may seem obvious, but be sure also that you at least know how to pronounce the speaker's name. We have heard John Bakke speak many times, and we have heard introducers butcher his name on more than one occasion.

The following guidelines will help you build the speaker's ethos and lay the groundwork for speaker–audience identification:

- Create respect by magnifying the speaker's main accomplishments.

- Don't be too lavish with your praise. An overblown introduction can be embarrassing to the speaker and can create unreasonable expectations for the speech.

▶ **speech of introduction** A ceremonial speech in which a featured speaker is introduced to the audience.

- Mention achievements that are relevant to the speaker's message, the occasion on which the speech is being presented, or the audience that has assembled.

- Be selective! Introducers who drone on too long can create real problems for the speakers who must follow them.

The final function of an effective introduction is to tune the audience. In Chapter 5, we discussed how preliminary tuning can establish a receptive mood. You tune the audience when you arouse anticipation for the message that will follow. However, don't try to preview what the speaker will say. Let the speaker present the speech.

SPEAKER'S notes

Introducing Featured Speakers

When you are called on to introduce a featured speaker, keep the following in mind as you prepare your remarks:

1. Be sure you know how to pronounce the speaker's name.
2. Find out what the speaker would like you to emphasize.
3. Focus on aspects of the speaker's background that are relevant to the topic, audience, and occasion.
4. Announce the title of the speech and tune the audience for it.
5. Make the speaker feel welcome. Be warm and gracious.
6. Be brief!

The Speech of Inspiration

The **speech of inspiration** arouses an audience to appreciate, commit to, and pursue a goal, purpose, or set of values or beliefs. Speeches of inspiration help listeners see subjects in a new light. These speeches may be religious, commercial, political, or social. When a sales manager introduces a new product to marketing representatives, pointing up its competitive advantages and its glowing market potential, the speech is both inspirational and persuasive. The marketing reps should feel inspired to push that product with great zeal and enthusiasm. Speeches at political conventions that praise the principles of the party, such as keynote addresses, are inspirational in tone and intent. So also is that great American institution, the commencement address. As different as these speech occasions may seem, they have important points in common.

First, *speeches of inspiration are enthusiastic.* Inspirational speakers accomplish their goals through their personal commitment and energy. Both the speaker and the speech must be active and forceful. Speakers must set an example for their audiences through their behavior both on and off the speaking platform. They must practice what they preach. Their ethos must be consistent with their advice.

Second, *speeches of inspiration draw on past successes and frustrations to encourage future accomplishment.* At a Catalyst Awards dinner, Sheila W. Welling, the organization president, evoked vivid memories of what the past was like for women as she urged continued progress toward equality in the workplace:

> One hundred years ago, at the dawn of the last millennium, our bustled Victorian great-grandmothers could not run for a bus, let alone for Congress. If the race—as the Victorian poet claimed—went to the swift, women lost.

▶ **speech of inspiration** A ceremonial speech directed at awakening or reawakening an audience to a goal, purpose, or set of values.

Girdled, corseted, enveloped in yards of gingham and lace, women were balanced precariously on their pedestals.

. . . Women couldn't vote when my mother was born. Every time I think about it, it startles me: Even as Edith Wharton wrote her novels, as Helen Keller graduated from Radcliffe with honors, even as women manufactured the arms that led to victory in World War I and the nation's move to global primacy, women still could not vote.[15]

Third, *speeches of inspiration revitalize our appreciation for values or beliefs*. Such speeches can strengthen our sense of mythos, the distinctive code of values underlying our society. In the later years of his life, when his athletic prowess had faded, Jesse Owens became known as a great inspirational speaker. According to his obituary in the *New York Times*, "The Jesse Owens best remembered by many Americans was a public speaker with the ringing, inspirational delivery of an evangelist. . . . [His speeches] praised the virtues of patriotism, clean living and fair play."[16]

In his inspirational speeches to budding athletes, Jesse Owens frequently talked about his Olympic achievements. The following excerpts, taken from a statement protesting America's withdrawal from the 1980 Summer Olympic Games, illustrate his inspirational style. Jesse Owens was unable to deliver this message personally. He prepared it shortly before his death from cancer.

What the Berlin games proved . . . was that Hitler's "supermen" could be beaten. Ironically, it was one of his blond, blue-eyed, Aryan athletes who helped do the beating.

> Owens's introduction suggests the larger meaning of his victories and sets the stage for identification.

I held the world record in the broad jump. Even more than the sprints, it was "my" event. Yet I was one jump from not even making the finals. I fouled on my first try, and playing it safe the second time, I had not jumped far enough.

The broad jump preliminaries came before the finals of my other three events and everything, it seemed then, depended on this jump. Fear swept over me and then panic. I walked off alone, trying to gather myself. I dropped to one knee, closed my eyes, and prayed. I felt a hand on my shoulder. I opened my eyes and there stood my arch enemy, Luz Long, the prize athlete Hitler had kept under wraps while he trained for one purpose only: to beat me. Long had broken the Olympic mark in his very first try in the preliminaries.

> Note the use of graphic detail to recapture the immediacy of the moment.

"I know about you," he said. "You are like me. You must do it all the way, or you cannot do it. The same that has happened to you today happened to me last year in Cologne. I will tell you what I did then." Luz told me to measure my steps, place my towel 6 inches on back of the takeoff board and jump from there. That way I could give it all I had and be certain not to foul.

> Owens's use of dialogue helps listeners feel they are sharing the experience.

As soon as I had qualified, Luz, smiling broadly, came to me and said, "Now we can make each other do our best in the finals."

And that's what we did in the finals. Luz jumped and broke his Olympic record. Then I jumped just a bit further and broke Luz's new record. We each had three leaps in all. On his final jump, Luz went almost 26 feet, 5 inches, a mark that seemed impossible to beat. I went just a bit over that and set an Olympic record that was to last for almost a quarter of a century.

I won that day, but I'm being straight when I say that even before I made that last jump, I knew I had won a victory of a far greater kind—over something inside myself, thanks to Luz.

> This narrative leaves open the meaning of Owens's "inside" victory: Perhaps it was over self-doubt or over his own stereotype of Germans. Perhaps it was over both.

This scene presents an inspirational model of international competition.

Owens shows how individuals can rise above ideologies, as Long's final message invites identification.

Owens ends with a metaphor of the "road to the Olympics."

The instant my record-breaking win was announced, Luz was there, throwing his arms around me and raising my arm to the sky. "Jazze Owenz!" he yelled as loud as he could. More than 100,000 Germans in the stadium joined in. "Jazze Owenz, Jazze Owenz, Jazze Owenz!"

Hitler was there, too, but he was not chanting. He had lost that day. Luz Long was killed in World War II and, although I don't cry often, I wept when I received his last letter—I knew it was his last. In it he asked me to someday find his son, Karl, and to tell him "of how we fought well together, and of the good times, and that any two men can become brothers."

That is what the Olympics are all about. The road to the Olympics does not lead to Moscow. It leads to no city, no country. It goes far beyond Lake Placid or Moscow, ancient Greece or Nazi Germany. The road to the Olympics leads, in the end, to the best within us.[17]

The After-Dinner Speech

Occasions that celebrate special events or that mark the beginning or end of a course of action often call for special dinners and provide the setting for an **after-dinner speech**. Political rallies, award banquets, the kickoff for a fundraising campaign, or the end of the school year may constitute such occasions.

The after-dinner speech is one of the great rituals of American public speaking and public life. If you are the leader of the group holding the dinner or have won some special recognition that makes people look up to you or simply have the reputation for being an entertaining speaker, you may be invited to give such a speech. As these qualifications suggest, the purpose of such a speech may vary from celebrating group accomplishments and setting new goals to simply enjoying the company of the moment and the laughter that can enrich lives and bond groups more closely together.

Almost all after-dinner speeches, however, share certain features. In keeping with the nature of the occasion, they should not be too difficult to digest. Speakers making these presentations usually do not introduce radical ideas that require listeners to rethink their values or that ask for dramatic changes in belief or behavior. Nor are such occasions the time for anger or negativity. Rather, they are a time for people to savor who they are, what they have done, or what they wish to do. A good after-dinner speech typically leaves a message that can guide and inspire future efforts.

The Role of Humor. Humor is appropriate in most after-dinner speeches. In the introduction, humor can place both the speaker and the audience at ease.[18] Enjoying lighter moments can remind us that there is a human element in all situations and that we should not take ourselves too seriously.

Communication scholar Diane Martin has identified a range of functions that humor can serve in speeches.[19] For example, humorous stories can create identification by building an "insider's" relationship between speaker and audience that draws them closer together. In sharing humor, the audience becomes a community of listeners.[20] Another study has discovered that the use of humorous illustrations helps audiences remember the message of the speech.[21]

As we noted in Chapters 8 and 9, however, speakers should play to their strengths, and humor should not be forced on a speech. If you decide to begin with a joke simply because you think a speech should start that way, the humor may

▶ **after-dinner speech** A brief, often humorous, ceremonial speech, presented after a meal, that offers a message without asking for radical changes.

seem contrived and flat. Rather, humor should be functional, relevant, and useful in making a point.

The humor in a speech is best developed out of the immediate situation. Dick Jackman, director of corporate communications at Sun Company, opened an after-dinner speech at a National Football Foundation awards dinner by warning those in the expensive seats under the big chandelier that it "had been installed by the low bidder some time ago."[22] Such references are often made more effective by a touch of self-deprecation.[23] In the spring of 2007, with his approval ratings lower than any sitting president in over twenty-five years, President George W. Bush used humor to poke fun at himself and his situation as he spoke at an annual dinner for media correspondents:

> Well, where should I start? A year ago, my approval rating was in the 30s, my nominee for the Supreme Court had just withdrawn, and my Vice President had shot someone. [laughter] Ahh, those were the good old days. [laughter and applause][24]

Humor requires thought, planning, and caution to be effective. If it is not handled well, it can be a disaster. For example, religious humor is dangerous, and racist or sexist humor is unacceptable. In general, avoid any anecdotes that are funny at the expense of others.

Developing an After-Dinner Speech. After-dinner speeches are more difficult to develop than their lightness and short length might suggest. Like any other speech, they should be carefully planned and practiced. They should have an effective introduction that commands attention right away, especially since some audience members may be more interested in talking to table companions than listening to the speaker. After-dinner speeches should be more than strings of anecdotes to amuse listeners. The stories told must establish a mood, convey a message, or carry a theme forward. Such speeches should build to a satisfying conclusion that conveys the essence of the message.

Above all, perhaps, after-dinner speeches should be mercifully brief. Long-winded after-dinner speakers can leave the audience fiddling with coffee cups and drawing pictures on napkins. After being subjected to such a speech, Albert Einstein once murmured: "I have just got a new theory of eternity."[25]

Steve Martin and Alec Baldwin use humor as they emcee the Academy Awards Ceremony.

Master of Ceremonies

Quite often, ceremonial speeches are part of a program of events that must be coordinated with skill and grace if things are to run smoothly. It takes at least as much careful planning, preparation, and practice to function effectively as a master of ceremonies as it does to make a major presentation. As the **master of ceremonies**, you will be expected to keep the program moving along, introduce participants, and possibly present awards. You will also set the tone or mood for the program.

If at all possible, you should be involved in planning the program from the beginning. Then you will have a better grasp of what is expected of you, what events

▶ **master of ceremonies**   A person who coordinates an event or program, sets its mood, introduces, and, provides transitions.

have been scheduled, what the timetable is, who the featured speakers are, and what special logistics (such as meal service) you might have to contend with. The following guidelines should help you function effectively as a master of ceremonies:[26]

- **Know what is expected of you.** Remember, as master of ceremonies (emcee) you are not the star of the show. You are the one who brings it all together and makes it work.

- **Plan a good opener for the program.** Your opening remarks as an emcee are as important as the introduction to a major presentation. You should gain the attention of the audience and prepare them for the program. Be sure that the mood you set with your opener is consistent with the nature of the occasion.

- **Be prepared to introduce the participants.** Find out all you can about the speakers in advance: Search the Internet, check *Who's Who*, and examine local newspaper clipping files. Ask them what they would like you to emphasize and determine how you might best tune the audience for their speeches. Be sure you know how to pronounce the speakers' names.

- **Know the schedule and timetable so that you can keep the program on track.** Also, be sure that the participants get this information. They need to know how much time has been allotted for them to speak. Review the schedule with them well before the program and work out some way to cue them in case they should run overtime. If time restrictions are severe (as in a televised program), be ready to edit and adapt your own planned comments if need be.

- **Make certain that any prizes or awards are kept near the podium.** You shouldn't be left fumbling around looking for a plaque or trophy at presentation time.

- **Plan your comments ahead of time.** Develop a key-word outline for each presentation on a running script of the program. Print the name of the person or award in large letters at the top of each outline so that you can keep your place in the program.

- **Practice your presentation.** Although you are not the featured speaker, your words are important (especially to the person you will introduce or who will receive the award you present). Practice your comments the same way you would practice a speech.

- **Make advance arrangements for mealtime logistics.** Speak with the maître d' before the program to be sure the waiters know the importance of "silent service."

- **Be ready for the inevitable glitches.** Remember Murphy's Law: If anything can go wrong, it will. Be ready for problems like microphones that don't work or that squeal, trays of dishes being dropped, and people wandering in and out during the course of the program. As you respond to these events, keep your cool and good humor.

- **End the program strongly.** Just as a speech should not dwindle into nothingness, neither should a program. Review the suggestions for speech conclusions in Chapter 9. When ending your presentation, thank those who made the program possible, and then leave the audience with something to remember.

Narrative Design

In Chapters 8 and 9 we discussed how storytelling helps structure and support a speech. In ceremonial speaking, narrative plays an especially important role. **Embedded narratives**—stories within speeches—can build identification and magnify character and action. Vicarious experience and master narratives develop within narrative designs that structure the ceremonial speeches in which they appear. Because of this special pertinence to ceremonial speaking, we shall delve a little more deeply into narrative design in this section. For more on narrative design as used in multimedia presentations, see www.multimediacreative.com.au/articles/narratives.htm.

You will recall that **vicarious experience narratives** invite listeners *into* the speech, asking them to imagine themselves participating in the action as it unfolds. Note how President Ronald Reagan encouraged listeners to *enter* the story he recounted in his second inaugural address:

> Hear again the echoes of our past.
> A general falls to his knees in the harsh snow of Valley Forge; a lonely President paces the darkened hall and ponders his struggle to preserve the Union; the men of the Alamo call out encouragement to each other; a settler pushes West and sings a song, and the song echoes out forever and fills the unknowing air.
> It is the American Sound. It is hopeful, big-hearted, idealistic—daring, decent and fair. That's our heritage. That's our song.[27]

In the **master narrative**, the entire speech becomes a story that reveals some important truth. We saw a good example of this as Jesse Owens told of his experience at the 1936 Olympic games.

The **narrative design** developed in such speeches differs markedly from other speech design formats. Whereas the categorical, causation, problem–solution, and other designs associated with informative and persuasive speaking typically follow a linear pattern, the narrative design follows a dramatic pattern of development. Speeches that build on narrative design do not make points so much as they present selected scenes in a mini-drama. Such design features three major components: prologue, plot, and epilogue.

Prologue

The **prologue** of narrative design sets the scene for what will follow. It is the counterpart of the introduction in other speech designs. The prologue orients listeners to the context of the action so that they can make sense of it. It foreshadows the meaning and importance of the story that will follow. It also introduces the important characters that will enact the story and whose ethos will develop as the story unfolds.

To see these elements in action, consider again the prologue to Jesse Owens's speech on the 1936 Olympics:

> What the Berlin games proved . . . was that Hitler's "supermen" could be beaten. Ironically, it was one of his blond, blue-eyed, Aryan athletes who helped do the beating.
> I held the world record in the broad jump. Even more than the sprints, it was "my" event. Yet I was one jump from not even making the finals. I fouled on my first try, and playing it safe the second time, I had not jumped far enough.

▶ **embedded narrative**   Stories inserted within speeches that illustrate the speaker's points.

▶ **vicarious experience narrative**   Speech strategy in which the speaker invites listeners to imagine themselves enacting a story.

▶ **master narrative**   Form of speaking in which the entire speech becomes a story that reveals some important truth.

voice Narrative Design in Action

Analyze Ashley Smith's "Three Photographs" (at the end of chapter 11) as a speech built on narrative design. Can you identify the prologue, plot, and epilogue and the scenes of the speech? Who is the major character developed by the narrative? Might the narrative have been improved? Bring your ideas to class for discussion.

The first two sentences in this prologue foreshadow the meaning of the story. They help prepare listeners for the actions that will unfold within the plot. They also anticipate the major character who will develop within the speech, Luz Long. The final four sentences present the context and setting of the story, the fact that Owens held the world record and was favored and the crisis he now had to confront.

Plot

The **plot** functions as the body of a speech organized by narrative design. Within the plot of a successful speech, two important things must happen. First, *the action of the story unfolds in a sequence of scenes designed to build suspense until there is a moment of climax.* Colorful detail, lively dialogue, and graphic imagery help this action come alive for listeners. Second, *the characters that are central to the story gain complexity by the way they participate in the action.* They develop an ethos that often makes them idealized portraits that live on in our memories after the speech is over.

Consider again the Owens speech. The plot develops in a sequence of three closely connected scenes: (1) the moments before the actual competition, (2) a description of the competition, and (3) the aftermath of the competition.

In the first scene, we watch a crisis of self-doubt, as Owens kneels to pray. We are also introduced to the generous spirit of Luz Long, who appears on cue as though he were the answer to Owens's prayer, and who offers the advice Owens needs to qualify for his event. Owens re-creates the immediacy of the moment by using actual dialogue as Long speaks.

The second scene, which describes the competition itself, is summarized rather quickly. It might have been quite colorful, had Owens wished to dwell upon it.

But he hurries on to the third scene, the aftermath, because the real business of this speech is to portray the ethos of Luz Long as an Olympic ideal. The fact that Long is German, even that he represents a Nazi ideology, adds irony to this portrait. Owens's point is that good sportsmanship transcends both national origin and political affiliation and joins people as brothers and sisters. Thus we behold the extraordinary spectacle at the conclusion of the competition when Luz Long raises Owens's arms to the sky as he leads the throng of Germans in chanting "Jazze Owenz."

Epilogue

The **epilogue** of a story reflects on the meaning of the action and offers final comments on the character of those who participated in it. It is the counterpart of the

---

▶ **narrative design** Speech structure that develops a story from beginning to end through a sequence of scenes in which characters interact.

▶ **prologue** An opening that establishes the context and setting of a narrative, foreshadows the meaning, and introduces major characters.

▶ **plot** The body of a speech that follows narrative design; unfolds in a sequence of scenes designed to build suspense.

conclusion in other speech designs. When used in ceremonial speeches, the epilogue often conveys a moral lesson for the present audience and situation. Thus, in the Owens example, we see the nobility of Luz Long reaffirmed in the final scene of the story:

> Luz Long was killed in World War II and, although I don't cry often, I wept when I received his last letter—I knew it was his last. In it he asked me to someday find his son, Karl, and to tell him "of how we fought well together, and of the good times, and that any two men can become brothers."

What Owens doesn't quite tell us, but we can infer it from what he says, is that Long and Owens had become good friends, that they corresponded often, and that Long knew that his end was near. These inferences only strengthen the underlying lesson for the audience Owens addressed in 1980:

> That is what the Olympics are all about. The road to the Olympics does not lead to Moscow. It leads to no city, no country. It goes far beyond Lake Placid or Moscow, ancient Greece or Nazi Germany. The road to the Olympics leads, in the end, to the best within us.

Just as the Olympic spirit could thrive in the bigoted atmosphere of Nazi Germany in 1936, so also could it blossom in the Cold War atmosphere of Moscow in 1980. Owens's speech, apparently commemorating a long-past moment and honoring an obscure sports competitor, becomes finally an argument criticizing the action taken by the United States in boycotting the 1980 games.

FINAL
reflections   And in Conclusion Let Us Say

We began our book by toasting your quest to find your voice. We hope that quest has been successful and that you have benefited, are benefiting, and will benefit from it. We end our book with our own speech of tribute, this time to you. Public speaking may not have always been easy for you. But it is our hope that you have grown as a person as you have grown as a speaker. Our special wishes, expressed in terms of the underlying vision of our book, are that

- you have learned to climb the barriers that people sometimes erect to separate themselves from each other and that too often prevent meaningful communication.

- you have learned to weave words and evidence into eloquent thoughts and persuasive ideas.

- you have learned to build and present speeches that enlighten others in responsible and ethical ways.

- above all, that you have found subjects and causes worthy of your voice.

And so we propose another toast: *May you use your new speaking skills to improve the lives and lift the spirits of all who may listen to you.*

▶ **epilogue**   The final part of a narrative that reflects upon its meaning.

SAMPLE CEREMONIAL SPEECH

Simone Mullinax presented this speech of tribute to her grandmother in a public speaking class at the University of Arkansas. The speech develops a master narrative based on an extended metaphor and paints an endearing portrait of a complex person who–like key lime pie— combines the qualities of sweetness and tartness.

Baked-In Traditions

SIMONE MULLINAX

▶ This brief opening does a great deal of work. Simone opens with a rhetorical question and a definition, and establishes her personal ethos. She then hints of a clever categorical design that will follow the three main ingredients of a pie.

▶ This paragraph completes the sketch that introduces Simone's grandmother. Simone paints this portrait by offering a few glimpses of her grandmother in action, small slices of life that depict character.

▶ As she tells us more about pies, Simone also reveals more about herself. We learn that she has been a beauty pageant contestant who has a particular fondness for key lime pies.

▶ This begins an elaboration of the pie as extended metaphor in order to reveal the value and values of her grandmother. Family connectedness is an underlying theme.

Have you ever baked a pie? No, I don't mean one you get from the freezer section at the grocery store—I'm talking about one you bake from scratch. I learned to bake a pie at an early age. And what I learned, early on, is that there are three things you have to master: the crust, the filler, and the topping. You can't have a pie if you lack any of these.

So where do you start? You start of course in the kitchen, which is where I meet my grandmother every time we get together. I would like to tell you she's that sweet, picturesque, grandmotherly grandmother you see on television, but she's not. Rather, she's that opinionated, bold, "her-way-or-the-highway" type that scares some people off. Her salvation is that she's also insanely funny and you fall in love with her stories, her cooking, and her opinions, even when you don't agree with all of them. Just when you're ready to pack up and move on, she does or says something that makes you want to hang around.

She's the woman who marches to the front of the line when her "babies" don't get what they need. She's the woman who sends us care packages made up of "goodies" from Dollar General. She's the woman who offers her opinions to everyone on any occasion, whether they want them or not. She's also the woman who gathered all the family recipes together—some of them unique and over a hundred years old—and gave them to me for a Christmas present. She's my grandmother and my best friend.

But back to baking pies. My signature pie is a key lime pie. It really isn't my signature at all because I frequently forge my grandmother's. People often think of it as a hot weather treat, but every time we are together, even if it's 23 degrees outside, we make that key lime pie. Last year before I competed in the Miss Oklahoma pageant, a reporter called and asked what I was most looking forward to eating after the competition, and I said, "A key lime pie. A whole key lime pie." It was in bold headlines the next day: "Miss Tulsa looking forward to eating a pie." For weeks afterwards people asked me, "So did you get your key lime pie?" And I was able to answer, "Sure did." Because after the pageant my grandmother had two pies sitting on the counter, one for now, and one for later.

Grammy taught me you can't have the pie without the crust. Everything in her life is built on a firm foundation, from the love of her family to the strength of her husband and the companionship of her friends. She stands behind her word, her love, and her family. She is the crust that keeps us all together, and also—I might add—all in line. Many times I have called Grammy with problems or confessions, and then I will hear advice like, "Oh, you don't need to do that, honey." And I know that, but her reminding me makes my own foundation that much stronger. Nothing crumbles in her key lime pie, especially the crust.

What would a pie be without the filling? Some are lemon or pecan or pumpkin or chocolate or apple or—of course—key lime. But that is what makes each pie unique when you take that first delicious bite. Grammy fills her own life with meaning: one of her favorite sayings is, "Comfort the afflicted and afflict the comfortable." She believes in character-building, and in the value of striving for improvement: "Struggle to get better, struggle to succeed," but "Don't let success prevent you from struggling to get even better." The key lime, like her advice, is sweet—but it definitely has a bite to it!

The best part of the pie is the topping. Sometimes it's another layer of crust, sometimes it's meringue or whipped cream. The topping is that something extra that finishes the pie off. For Grammy, it's doing a little bit more than is necessary, a little bit more than what's expected. Part of it is literally going that extra mile. She and I walk together at 6:30 in the morning, because she says it's the only time of day when the sun doesn't beat you down. I am barely awake for some of these walks, and that extra mile she loves to walk is often uphill! Beyond that, Grammy's favorite toppings are good words, good deeds, and high expectations.

Years from now I will teach my own granddaughter to build a perfect key lime pie. As we make it I will be thinking about the woman whose love seeps into every crust holding me together. We will mix the fillings together and we will know just what to top it off with to make it perfect. And we will bake pies like friends hold conversations, the intricacies hidden beneath the taste and the impressions lasting beyond the words.

◀ These discussions of the filling and the toppings offer Simone an opportunity to develop other aspects of her grandmother's character— her urge to help others build character and her willingness to go beyond the ordinary in order to accomplish worthwhile purposes.

◀ Inspired by her grandmother, Simone can see herself in the distant future baking pies with her own granddaughter and holding the same kinds of conversations. Her conclusion offers extraordinary poetic appreciation for this kind of pie-baking.

Communicating in Small Groups

Many of the important communication interactions in your life occur in small groups. In school you may be assigned to a team for a special assignment. At work you may be appointed to a committee to plan a project. In your community there may be problems that can only be solved by people working together. All of these situations require effective group communication skills. Moreover, members of a group often make public presentations promoting their recommendations after the group has completed its work. To understand how groups communicate, we need to consider the nature of a group.

Is any gathering of people a group? Not necessarily. For example, a gathering of people waiting for a bus would not be considered a group. *To be considered a* **group,** *a gathering of people must actively interact with one another over a period of time to reach a goal or goals.*

Let's suppose that the same people have been meeting at the bus stop every workday for several months. They may chat with one another while waiting for the bus, but this casual interaction does not make them a group. Now, suppose that the Metropolitan Transit Organization (MTO) announces in the morning paper that it wants to raise fares from $2.00 to $3.00 each way for the trip downtown. That morning when the people get together, they begin to express their outrage about the problem that confronts them. One of them suggests that they gather at her apartment that evening to come up with a plan to persuade the MTO to reconsider its proposal. When these people get together that evening, they will be interacting as a group.

Participating in a group can also help you find your voice. You will be exposed to different points of view on an issue, which can help you clarify your own position. You will be called on to use all of the public communication skills you learn in this course and thus will see the benefits of those skills in action. In this appendix we discuss how groups function and how good public communication skills can make you a better participant or leader in groups. We also consider the various types of group presentations that you may be called upon to make.

Advantages and Disadvantages of Group Problem Solving

When we listen to a single speaker, we hear only one version of a situation or problem. That perspective may be biased, based on self-interest, or simply wrong. When a topic is important, it often helps to assemble a group to investigate the situation and make recommendations concerning it.

▶ **group** Gathering of people who interact with one another to reach goals.

Group problem solving has many advantages over individual efforts. When people share their various ways of seeing a problem, they begin to see things as others see them. Misconceptions and bias may come to light. Listening to others' points of view can stimulate creative thinking about solutions. In well-managed problem-solving groups, people on all sides of an issue have a chance to discuss the similarities and differences of their viewpoints. Through such discussions, they may uncover areas of agreement that can help resolve differences.

Although working in groups has many advantages, it also has some disadvantages. **Cultural gridlock**—communication problems based on deep cultural differences—may arise in groups when members come from different backgrounds. For example, people in the marketing departments and in the research and development departments of an organization may bring conflicting expectations to a meeting. Participants from dissimilar social backgrounds may bring different perspectives, agendas, priorities, procedures, and ways of communicating to meetings. These differences may sidetrack constructive discussions.

Dealing with cultural gridlock is never easy, but the following guidelines will help minimize its impact:

1. Allow time for people to get acquainted before starting to work.

2. Distribute an agenda before the meeting so people know what to expect.

3. Summarize discussions as the meeting progresses. Post key points of agreement.

4. Avoid using jargon that some participants may not understand.

5. Be sensitive to cultural differences in how people relate to one another and to nonverbal communication norms.[1]

Another disadvantage that can occur in problem-solving groups is **groupthink,** the uncritical acceptance of a position.[2] Groupthink is most likely to occur when participants place a higher value on harmonious interactions than on performing effectively. Other factors that contribute to groupthink include a dynamic leader's preference for a certain position or the lack of a clear set of procedures for working through problems.

In the realm of public affairs, groupthink can be dangerous because outsiders may assume that a group has deliberated carefully and responsibly when it has not. Groupthink may lend itself to an inadequate investigation of the problem and an incomplete consideration of alternative solutions.

Dealing with groupthink is difficult, but there are some steps you can take to guard against it. First, groups need to be aware that groupthink can be a problem. The major symptoms of groupthink include pressuring dissidents within the group and censoring their ideas, defending opinions more than exploring alternate ways of thinking, and asserting the group's own moral righteousness while attacking the character of opposing groups.

Once a group is aware that groupthink is a problem, the leader can take action to minimize its effects. The leader should encourage the group to set standards for investigation and appraisal that discourage uncritical thinking and hasty conclusions. The following leadership behaviors can help reduce groupthink problems:

- Insist that participants evaluate the support behind recommendations.

- Urge members to delay decisions until all have expressed their views.

▶ **cultural gridlock**   A problem that occurs when the cultural differences in a group are so profound that they create tensions that block constructive discussion.

▶ **groupthink**   Occurs when a single, uncritical frame of mind dominates group thinking and prevents the full, objective analysis of specific problems.

- Encourage critical questions from participants.
- Encourage debate of all recommendations.

Group Problem-Solving Techniques

Group deliberations that are orderly, systematic, and thorough help members reach better decisions. To function effectively, problem-solving groups can use a variety of methods, the most common of which is called reflective thinking.

Reflective Thinking and Problem Solving

The reflective thinking approach used in problem-solving groups is a modification of a technique first proposed by John Dewey in 1910. This systematic approach has five steps: (1) defining the problem, (2) generating potential solutions, (3) evaluating solution options, (4) developing a plan of action, and (5) evaluating the results.

Step 1: Defining the Problem.   Sometimes what the group initially thinks is the problem is actually only a symptom of the problem. A group that starts with what it thinks is a problem of insufficient support for public education may discover that the actual problem is far more complicated. For example, the real problem may involve the lack of clear educational goals, poor communication with the public about education in the community, or inadequate public participation (parents and others) with the schools. All problem-solving groups should take time to define the problem carefully before looking for solutions. The following guidelines can help a group define the problem it needs to work on:

1. Describe the problem as specifically as possible.
2. Gather enough information to understand the problem.
3. Explore the causes of the problem.
4. Investigate the history of the problem.
5. Determine who is affected by the problem.
6. Consider the outcomes if the problem is solved or not solved.

Step 2: Generating Potential Solutions.   Once the problem has been defined, the group can begin looking for solutions. One useful technique for generating possible solutions is **brainstorming**. Brainstorming encourages all group members to contribute their ideas for solutions.[3] During the brainstorming process, members do not evaluate the potential solutions or decide which option to follow. The following rules should govern brainstorming sessions:

- Present your ideas enthusiastically.
- Contribute all your ideas, no matter how outrageous they may seem. The more options the group generates, the more ideas the group has to work with toward a solution.
- Don't evaluate the ideas as they are presented. Keeping the process free of criticism helps the group generate more and better potential solutions.

▶ **brainstorming** Technique that encourages the free play of the mind.

- Try combining ideas to come up with additional options.

- Be sure that everyone contributes.

Once all participants understand the ground rules, the process of brainstorming proceeds as follows:

1. The leader asks each member in turn to contribute an idea during each round. A member who does not have an idea may pass. At this stage, the emphasis is on full participation and the number of ideas advanced.

2. A recorder writes all ideas on a flip chart or marker board so everyone can see them.

3. Brainstorming continues until *all* members have contributed an idea or passed.

4. The suggestions are reviewed for clarification, adding new options, or combining options.

5. The group identifies the most promising ideas.

6. The leader appoints members to research each idea and to bring additional information to a later evaluation meeting.

7. The process of gathering solution possibilities should remain open during this break. Additional ideas should be considered during the next phase of the problem-solving process.

If time is short or if face-to-face interaction may inhibit the open expression of ideas because of cultural or status differences among group members, the group may use **electronic brainstorming,** in which participants generate ideas online before meeting face-to-face.[4] One advantage of initial electronic explorations is that leaders can encourage participants to bring additional supportive materials to the meetings to clarify options.

Step 3: Evaluating Solution Options.   When the generation of options comes to an end, a meeting to evaluate the ideas should be scheduled. Between meetings, members can gather information on each potential solution. During the evaluation session, the following evaluation criteria should be used:

- Costs of the options being enacted

- Probability of success

- Ease or difficulty of enacting options

- Time constraints

- Additional benefits of options

- Potential problems of options

Evaluations of each option should be placed on a flip chart and posted so that members can refer to them as they compare options. As options are considered, some will be dropped, and others will be strengthened and refined. The group also may combine options to generate new alternatives. For example, if the group is caught between option A, which promises improved efficiency, and option B, which promises lower cost, it may be possible to combine the best features of each into option C.

▶ **electronic brainstorming**   A group technique in which participants generate ideas in computer chat groups or by e-mail.

After all of the options have been considered, the group then ranks the solutions in terms of their acceptability. The option receiving the highest overall rank becomes the proposed solution.

Participants often become personally caught up with their own solutions. During the evaluation phase, the leader must keep the group focused on the ideas advanced. Differences of opinion and conflict are a natural and necessary part of problem solving. Discussing the strengths of an idea before talking about its weaknesses can help take some of the heat out of the process.

Step 4: Developing a Plan of Action.   Once the group has selected a solution, it should figure out how the solution can be implemented. For example, to improve company morale, a group might recommend a three-step plan:

1. In-house training programs to increase opportunities for promotion

2. Pay structure that rewards success in training programs

3. More employee participation in decision-making.

As the group considers the plan, it should consider what might help or hinder it, what resources will be needed to make it work, and what type of timetable it will need. If the group cannot develop a plan of action for the solution or if insurmountable obstacles crop up, the group should return to step 3 and reconsider other options.

Step 5: Evaluating Results.   A problem-solving group must also decide how to evaluate results of the plan's enactment. They should establish evaluation criteria for success, a timetable of when results are expected, and contingency plans to use if the original plan fails. For example, to monitor the ongoing success of the three-part plan to improve employee morale, the group would have to determine benchmarks of progress for each stage. That way, the company could detect and correct problems as they occur, before they damage the plan as a whole. Having a scheduled sequence of benchmarks provides a way to determine results while the plan is being enacted, rather than having to wait for the entire project to be completed.

Other Approaches to Group Problem Solving

When a group consists of people from very different backgrounds, **collaborative problem solving** may work best.[5] For example, in many urban areas, coalitions of business executives and educators have worked together on plans to train people for jobs in the community. In such situations, the problems are usually important and the resources are typically limited. Because there is no established authority structure and the factions may have different expectations or goals, these diverse participants may have problems working together. To be effective, such groups need to spend time defining the problem and exploring each other's perspectives. This should help them recognize their interdependence while preserving the independence of each. In such groups, the participants must come to see themselves *not* as members of group A (the executives) or group B (the educators), but as members of group C (the coalition). Leadership can be especially difficult in such groups.

One useful approach in such situations is **dialogue groups.** According to William Isaacs, director of the Dialogue Project at the Massachusetts Institute of Technology Center for Organizational Learning, "Dialogue is a discipline of collective

---

▶ **collaborative problem solving**   In group communication, an approach that gathers participants from separate areas of public or private sectors for their input on a problem.

▶ **dialogue groups**   A group assembled to explore the underlying assumptions of a problem but not necessarily to solve it.

thinking and inquiry, a process for transforming the quality of conversation, and, in particular, the thinking that lies beneath it."[6] Dialogue groups stress understanding the different interpretations of the problem that participants bring to the interaction. Their purpose is to establish a dialogue from which common ground and mutual trust can emerge.

Leadership is critical in dialogue groups. According to Edgar Schein of the MIT Center, the facilitator must take the following steps:

1. Seat the group in a circle to create a sense of equality.

2. Introduce the problem.

3. Ask people to share an experience in which dialogue led to "good communication."

4. Ask members to consider what leads to good communication.

5. Ask participants to talk about their reactions.

6. Let the conversation flow naturally.

7. Intervene only to clarify problems of communication.

8. Conclude by asking all members to comment however they choose.[7]

The dialogue method is not a substitute for other problem-solving techniques, such as the reflective thinking process presented earlier. Instead, the dialogue method may be used to provide an opportunity for members to understand each other well enough to be talking the same language as they work on solutions to problems.

When an organization wants to explore the feelings or motivations of customers or clients, they often hold a **focus group**.[8] Focus groups typically have six to ten members carefully selected to provide the type of information sought. In a focus group the moderator asks questions and encourages all of the participants to respond. Advertisements, brochures, other printed materials, or video clips may also be used to stimulate discussion. Interactions between members of the group often provide the most valuable information. The sessions are recorded on either audiotape or videotape for later analysis. Focus groups are typically face-to-face encounters, but they may also be conducted through telephone conference calls, on the Internet, or through videoconferencing.

Participating in Small Groups

To work effectively in a small group, you must understand your individual responsibilities. You should also be prepared to assume leadership when called upon to do so.

Working as a Group Member

Becoming an effective group participant means you must accept the following responsibilities:

■ First, come to meetings prepared to contribute. This means reading background materials and completing any tasks assigned by the group leader before attending a meeting.

▶ **focus group**   A small group formed to reveal the feelings or motivations of customers or clients.

■ Second, be open to learning from others. Contribute but don't dominate discussions. Don't be defensive if challenged. Be willing to admit when you may be wrong. Willingness to change your position is not a sign of weakness, and obstinacy is not a strength.

■ Third, listen constructively. Don't interrupt others. Speak up if you feel consensus is forming too quickly. You might save the meeting from groupthink.

Analyzing your group communication skills can help you become more effective in groups. Use the self-analysis form in Figure A.1 to steer yourself toward more constructive group communication behaviors.

As you participate in groups, you should also keep in mind the following questions:

■ What *is* happening now in the group?

■ What *should be* happening in the group?

■ What *can I do* to make this come about?

If you notice a difference between what the group is doing and what it should be doing to reach its goals, you have the opportunity to demonstrate leadership behavior.

Leading Small Groups

For many years, social scientists have been studying leadership by analyzing group communication patterns. This research suggests that two basic types of leadership behaviors emerge in most groups. The first is **task leadership behavior,** which directs the activity of the group toward a specified goal. The second is **social leadership behavior** (sometimes called maintenance leadership), which helps build and maintain positive relationships among group members.

Task leaders direct group communication toward a goal. They give and seek information, opinions, and suggestions. A task leader might say, "We need more information on just how widespread sexual harassment is on campus. Let me tell you what Dean Johnson told me last Friday." Or the task leader might ask, "Gwen, tell us what you found out from the Affirmative Action Office."

Social leaders express agreement, help the group release tension, and provide support. A social leader often gives compliments: "I think Gwen has made a very important point. You really helped us by finding that out." Sincere compliments help keep members from becoming defensive and help maintain a constructive communication atmosphere. In a healthy communication climate, the two kinds of leadership behavior support each other and keep the group moving toward its goal. When one person combines both styles of leadership, that person is likely to be highly effective.

Leadership has also been studied in terms of the way a leader handles the task and maintenance functions. An **autocratic leader** makes decisions without consultation, issues orders or gives direction, and controls the members of the group through the use of rewards or punishments. A **participative leader** seeks input from group members and gives them an active role in decision-making. A **free-rein leader** lets members decide on their own what to do, how to do it, and when to do it. If you were working in an organization, you would probably say you "worked *for*" an autocratic leader, "worked *with*" a participative leader, and "worked *in spite of*" a free-rein leader.

▶ **task leadership behavior**   A leadership emphasis that directs the attention and activity of a group toward a specified goal.

▶ **social leadership behavior**   Occurs when leaders focus upon building and maintaining positive, productive relationships among group members.

▶ **autocratic leader**   A leader who makes decisions without consultation, issues orders or gives direction, and controls the members of the group through the use of rewards or punishments.

FIGURE A.1 Group Communication Skills Self-Analysis Form

	Need to Do Less	Doing Fine	Need to Do More
1. I make my points concisely.	☐	☐	☐
2. I speak with confidence.	☐	☐	☐
3. I provide specific examples and details.	☐	☐	☐
4. I try to integrate ideas that are expressed.	☐	☐	☐
5. I let others know when I do not understand them.	☐	☐	☐
6. I let others know when I agree with them.	☐	☐	☐
7. I let others know tactfully when I disagree with them.	☐	☐	☐
8. I express my opinions.	☐	☐	☐
9. I suggest solutions to problems.	☐	☐	☐
10. I listen to understand.	☐	☐	☐
11. I try to understand before agreeing or disagreeing.	☐	☐	☐
12. I ask questions to get more information.	☐	☐	☐
13. I ask others for their opinions.	☐	☐	☐
14. I check for group agreement.	☐	☐	☐
15. I try to minimize tension.	☐	☐	☐
16. I accept help from others.	☐	☐	☐
17. I offer help to others.	☐	☐	☐
18. I let others have their say.	☐	☐	☐
19. I stand up for myself.	☐	☐	☐
20. I urge others to speak up.	☐	☐	☐

▶ **participative leader**   A leader who seeks input from group members and gives them an active role in decision-making.

▶ **free-rein leader**   A leader who leaves members free to decide what, how, and when to act, offering no guidance.

More recent work on leadership suggests that leadership styles are either transactional or transformational. **Transactional leadership** takes place in an environment based on power relationships and relies on reward and punishment to accomplish its ends. **Transformational leadership** appeals to "people's higher levels of motivation to contribute to a cause and add to the quality of life on the planet."[9] It carries overtones of stewardship instead of management. Transformational leaders have the following qualities:

- They have a vision of what needs to be done.
- They are empathetic.
- They are trusted.
- They give credit to others.
- They help others develop.
- They share power.
- They are willing to experiment and learn.

In short, transformational leaders lead with both their hearts and their heads. According to John Schuster, a management consultant who specializes in transformational leadership training, "The heart is more difficult to develop. It's easier to get smarter than to become more caring."[10] Transformational leadership encourages communication from subordinates because they are less intimidated by their superiors and more willing to ask for advice or help.[11]

Consider how effective leadership relates to the major components of **ethos** (see the discussion of ethos in Chapter 3). An effective leader is *competent*. This means the leader understands the problem and knows how to steer a group through the problem-solving process. An effective leader has *integrity*. This means the leader is honest and places group success above personal concerns. An effective leader is perceived as a person of *goodwill*, concerned less about the self and more about those the group serves. Finally, an effective leader is *dynamic*. Dynamic leaders are enthusiastic, energetic, and decisive. Most of us have these qualities in varying degrees and can use them when the need for leadership arises. To be an effective leader, remember two simple goals: *Help others be effective* and *get the job done.* Cultivate an open leadership style that encourages all sides to air their views.

Planning Meetings. In many organizations, meetings are seen as time wasters. This may be because the people who conduct them do not know when to call meetings or how to run them.[12] Meetings should be called when people need to:

- discuss the meaning of information face-to-face.
- decide on a common course of action.
- establish a plan of action.
- report on the progress of a plan, evaluate its effectiveness, and revise it if necessary.

▶ **transactional leadership** A leadership style based on power relationships that relies on reward and punishment to achieve its ends.

▶ **transformational leadership** A leadership style based on mutual respect and stewardship rather than on control.

▶ **ethos** These characteristics that help a speaker seem competent, honest, and dynamic.

More than just knowing when to call meetings, you need to know how to plan them. The following guidelines should help you plan effective meetings:

- *Have a specific purpose for holding a meeting.* Unnecessary meetings waste time. If your goal is simply to increase interaction, plan a social event rather than a meeting.

- *Prepare an agenda and distribute it to participants before the meeting.* Having an agenda gives members time to prepare and assemble information they might need. Solicit agenda items from participants.

- *Keep meetings short.* After about an hour, groups get tired, and the law of diminishing returns sets in. Don't try to do too much in a single meeting.

- *Keep groups small.* You get more participation and interaction in small groups. In larger groups, people may be reluctant to ask questions or contribute ideas.

- *Select participants who will interact easily with each other.* In business settings, the presence of someone's supervisor may inhibit interaction. You will get better participation if group members come from the same or nearly the same working level in the organization.

- *Plan the site of the meeting.* Arrange for privacy and freedom from interruptions. A circular arrangement contributes to participation because there is no power position. A rectangular table or a lectern and classroom arrangement may inhibit interaction.

- *Prepare in advance.* Be certain that you have the necessary supplies, such as chalk, a flip chart, markers, note pads, and pencils. If you will use electronic equipment, be sure it is in working order.

Conducting an Effective Meeting.   Group leaders have many responsibilities. Leaders must encourage deliberations that proceed in good faith toward constructive ends. They should also be well informed on the issues so that they can answer questions and keep the group moving toward its objectives. The following checklist should be helpful in guiding your behavior as a group leader:

- Begin and end the meeting on time.

- Present background information concisely and objectively.

- Lead, don't run the meeting.

- Be enthusiastic.

- Get conflict out in the open so that it can be dealt with directly.

- Urge all members to participate.

- Keep discussion focused on the issue.

- At the close of a meeting, summarize what the group has accomplished.

As a group leader, you may need to present the group's recommendations to others. In this task, you function mainly as an informative speaker. You should present the recommendations offered by the group, along with the major reasons for making these recommendations. You should also mention reservations that may

---

FIGURE A.2 Behaviors That Enhance or Impede Decision Making

Enhancing Behaviors	Impeding Behaviors
Opinions are sought out.	Members express dislike for others.
Creativity is encouraged.	Members personally attack others.
Participation is encouraged.	Members make sarcastic comments.
Opposing views are encouraged.	Leader sets criteria for solution.
Members provide information.	Leader makes the decision.
Group analyzes suggestions.	Leader intimidates members.
Members listen to one another.	Meeting becomes a gripe session.
Members respect others' ideas.	Disagreements are ignored, not aired.
Members support others' ideas.	Disagreement is discouraged.
Problem is thoroughly researched.	Members pursue personal goals.
Group sets criteria for solution.	
Members are knowledgeable on issue.	
Evidence for suggestions is presented.	
Group focuses on task.	

---

have surfaced during deliberations. Your job in making this report is not to advocate, but to educate. Later, you may join in any following discussion with persuasive remarks that express your personal convictions on the subject.

Finally, as you conduct meetings, keep in mind behaviors that either advance or impede group effectiveness.[13] Better group decisions are made when all group members participate fully in the process; when members are respectful of each other and leaders are respectful of members; and when negative emotional behaviors are kept in check. More specific details of these findings are listed in Figure A.2.

Guidelines for Formal Meetings

The larger a group is, the more it needs a formal procedure to conduct meetings. Also, if a meeting involves a controversial subject, it is wise to have a set of rules to follow. Having clear-cut guidelines helps keep meetings from becoming chaotic and helps ensure fair treatment for all participants. In such situations, many groups follow **parliamentary procedure**.

Parliamentary procedure establishes an order of business for a meeting and lays out the way the group initiates discussions and reaches decisions. Under parliamentary procedure, a formal meeting proceeds as follows:

1. The chair calls the meeting to order.

2. The secretary reads the minutes of the previous meeting, which are corrected, if necessary, and approved.

▶ **parliamentary procedure**   A set of formal rules that establishes an order of business for meetings and encourages the orderly, fair, and full consideration of proposals during group deliberation.

3. Reports from officers and committees are presented.

4. Unfinished business is considered.

5. New business is introduced.

6. Announcements are made.

7. The meeting is adjourned.

Business in formal meetings goes forward by **motions,** or proposals set before the group. Consider the following. The chair asks: "Is there any new business?" A member responds: "I move that we allot $500 to build a Homecoming float." The member has offered a main motion, which proposes an action. Before the group can discuss the motion, it must be seconded. The purpose of a **second** is to ensure that more than one person wants to see the motion considered. If no one volunteers a second, the chair may ask, "Is there a second?" Typically, another member will respond, "I second the motion." Once a motion is made and seconded, it is open for discussion. It must be passed by majority vote, defeated, or otherwise resolved before the group can move on to other business. With the exception of a few technical motions (such as, "I move we take a fifteen-minute recess" or, "Point of personal privilege—can we do anything about the heat in this room?"), the main motion remains at the center of group attention until resolved.

Let us assume that, as the group discusses the main motion in our example, some members believe the amount of money proposed is insufficient. At this point, another member may say: "I move to amend the motion to provide $750 for the float." The **motion to amend** gives the group a chance to modify a main motion. It must be seconded and, after discussion, must be resolved by majority vote before discussion goes forward. If the motion to amend passes, then the amended main motion must be considered further.

How does a group make a decision on a motion? There usually is a time when discussion begins to lag. At this point the chair might say, "Do I hear a call for the question?" A motion to **call the question** ends discussion, and it requires a two-thirds vote for approval. Once the group votes to end discussion, it must then vote to accept or reject the motion. No further discussion can take place until the original or amended original motion is voted on.

Sometimes the discussion of a motion may reveal that the group is confused or sharply divided about an issue. At this point a member may move to **table the motion** instead of calling the question. This is a way to dispose of a troublesome motion without further divisive or confused discussion. Once a motion is tabled, it can only be reconsidered if the member who called for the table moves to rescind that motion. At other times, the discussion of a motion may reveal that the group lacks information to make an intelligent decision. At that point, we might hear from a member: "In light of the uncertainty over costs, I move we postpone further consideration until next week's meeting." The **motion to postpone consideration** gives the chair a chance to appoint a committee to gather the information needed. The **move to adjourn** presented by a member ends the meeting.

These are just some of the important procedures that can help ensure that formal group communication remains fair and constructive (see Figure A.3). For more information on formal group communication procedures, consult the latest edition of *Robert's Rules of Order*.

▶ **motions**   Formal proposals for group consideration.

▶ **second**   A motion must receive a "second" before group discussion can proceed; ensures that more than one member wishes to have the motion considered.

▶ **motion to amend**   A parliamentary move that offers opportunity to modify a motion presently under discussion.

FIGURE A.3 Guide to Parliamentary Procedure

Action	Requires Second	Can Be Debated	Can Be Amended	Vote Required	Function
Main Motion	Yes	Yes	Yes	Majority	Commits group to a specific action or position.
Second	No	No	No	None	Assures that more than one group member wishes to see idea considered.
Move to Amend	Yes	Yes	Yes	Majority	Allows group to modify and improve an existing motion.
Call the Question	Yes	No	No	Two-thirds	Brings discussion to an end and moves to a vote on the motion in question.
Move to Table the Motion	Yes	No	No	Majority	Stops immediate consideration of the motion until a later unspecified time.
Move to Postpone Consideration	Yes	Yes	Yes	Majority	Stops immediate discussion and allows time for the group to obtain more information on the problem.
Move to Adjourn	Yes	No	No	Majority	Formally ends meeting.

Making Group Presentations

After a group has completed its work, it may need to present its findings and recommendations to a larger audience. To plan this presentation, the group leader should:

- Designate which group members will present which parts of the report.
- Assign other duties such as preparing or coordinating presentation aids
- Develop an outline or agenda for the presentation
- Determine who should handle questions and answers
- Schedule and oversee a rehearsal of the group presentation.

Often, a designated spokesperson will simply present an **oral report.** This report is basically an informative speech which follows a specific design. The introduction

▶ **call the question** A motion that proposes to end discussion and bring a vote.
▶ **table the motion** A parliamentary move to suspend indefinitely the discussion of a motion.

▶ **motion to postpone consideration** A motion that defers discussion until some specified time.
▶ **motion to adjourn** A motion that calls for the meeting to end.

▶ **oral report** Presentation that summarizes the deliberations of a small group to inform a larger audience of decision-makers.

briefly reviews the problem, introduces the members of the group (including their credentials) if they are not well known to the audience, and describes the process used by the group to study the problem. The body of the report covers the major findings or recommendations for action. The conclusion summarizes the findings and may make suggestions for further work. The report should be as brief as possible and should allow for questions and answers following the formal presentation.

In addition to a simple oral report, group presentations may follow four other formats: a symposium, a panel discussion, a roundtable presentation, or a forum.

A **symposium** features a moderator and members of the problem-solving group as presenters. This group should be selected on the basis of the participants' special competencies and communication skills. The primary role of the moderator is to introduce the topic and speakers at the beginning of the symposium and to summarize the findings as the presentation draws to a close. Each symposium speaker will typically cover one aspect of the topic, making a short (well-prepared and rehearsed) report on the group's findings or recommendations in that area. The moderator enforces time limits and keeps the presentations on track. The symposium is usually followed by a question-and-answer session.

A **panel discussion** is less formal than a symposium. It also has a moderator who introduces the topic and the participants, but it does not feature prepared speeches. Rather, it is a planned pattern of spontaneous exchanges. Following the brief introductions, the moderator asks questions of the group. Participants respond with brief impromptu answers. The moderator guides the discussion and keeps the group in focus. He or she should also see that no single participant dominates the discussion and that all panelists participate.

Although responses in a panel discussion are impromptu, the participants should be told in advance what general types of questions may be asked so that they can prepare with these in mind. Panelists should think back through what went on in the group and organize their ideas in advance of the discussion. They should be prepared for tough follow-up questions either from the moderator or from the audience.

A **roundtable** presentation is an interactive way of publicly exchanging information, ideas, or opinions.[14] All members of the group are considered equal and are encouraged to participate openly and fully in the proceedings. There are no formal opening statements or prepared speeches. The leader helps generate discussion, makes certain the speakers stay on track and adhere to time limits, and encourages a nonjudgmental dialogue. In late 2006 the Sierra Club conducted a roundtable on the climate crisis that included business and political leaders as well as environmental activists.[15] An abridged transcript of the proceedings is available in the May/June 2007 issue of *Sierra*.

In a **forum** presentation, questions come from the audience rather than from the moderator. The basic job of the moderator of a forum is to keep the discussion on track. The moderator may introduce the topic and participants, and during the course of the forum, he or she recognizes audience members who wish to ask questions. At times, the moderator may also have to actually "moderate"—act as a referee if questions or answers become heated on emotional topics. If the group anticipates controversy, it may wish to arrange for a parliamentarian to help keep the meeting constructive. Participants should follow the guidelines suggested for handling questions and answers in Chapter 12.

▶ **symposium**   Group presentation in which speakers address different areas of an issue.
▶ **panel discussion**   A group presentation featuring organized exchanges among speakers, directed by a moderator.

▶ **roundtable**   Interactive way of informally exchanging ideas, information, or opinions within a small group before a larger audience.

▶ **forum**   Presentational format in which a group of specialists in different areas of a subject respond to questions from an audience.

B Speeches for Analysis

Self-Introductory
Sandra Baltz *My Three Cultures*
Elizabeth Tidmore *Lady with a Gun*
BJ Youngerman *To Toss or Not to Toss: The Art of Baseball Umpiring*

Informative
Cecile Larson *The "Monument" at Wounded Knee*
Joseph Van Matre *Video Games*
Michael Anthony Parker *To Clone or Not to Clone*

Persuasive
Joshua Logan *Global Burning*
Anna Aley *We Don't Have to Live in Slums*
Betsy Lyles *Fairly Traded Coffee*

Ceremonial
John Bakke *Remarks on Accepting the Martin Luther King Jr. Human Rights Award*
Elie Wiesel *Nobel Peace Prize Acceptance Speech*
Ashlie McMillan *Reach for the Stars!*

Self-Introductory Speeches

My Three Cultures

SANDRA BALTZ

Sandra Baltz first presented this self-introductory speech many years ago at the University of Memphis. She addressed the themes of cross-culturalism and family values long before these became fashionable. Sandra's deft use of comparison and contrast, and her example of foods illustrating how three cultures can combine harmoniously, are instructive. As her speech developed, she built her ethos as a competent, warm person, highly qualified to give later informative and persuasive speeches on issues involving medical care. Presented at a time when tensions in the Middle East were running high, Sandra's speech served as a gentle reminder that people of goodwill can always find ways to enjoy their differences and to reaffirm their common membership in the human family.

Several years ago I read a newspaper article in the Commercial Appeal in which an American journalist described some of his experiences in the Middle East. He was there a couple of months and had been the guest of several different Arab families. He reported having been very well treated and very well received by everyone that he met there. But it was only later, when he returned home, that he became aware of the intense resentment his hosts held for Americans and our unwelcome involvement in their Middle Eastern affairs. The journalist wrote of feeling somewhat bewildered, if not deceived, by the large discrepancy between his treatment while in the Middle East and the hostile attitude that he learned about later. He labeled this behavior hypocritical. When I reached the end of the article, I was reminded of a phrase spoken often by my mother. "Sandra," she says to me, "respeta tu casa y a todos los que entran en ella, trata a tus enemigos asi como a tus amigos."

This is an Arabic proverb, spoken in Spanish, and roughly it translates into "Respect your home and all who enter it, treating even an enemy as a friend." This is a philosophy that I have heard often in my home. With this in mind, it seemed to me that the treatment the American journalist received while in the Middle East was not hypocritical behavior on the part of his hosts. Rather, it was an act of respect for their guest, for themselves, and for their home—indeed, a behavior very typical of the Arabic culture.

Since having read that article several years ago, I have become much more aware of how my life is different because of having a mother who is of Palestinian origin but was born and raised in the Central American country of El Salvador.

One of the most obvious differences is that I was raised bilingually—speaking both Spanish and English. In fact, my first words were in Spanish. Growing up speaking two languages has been both an advantage and a disadvantage for me. One clear advantage is that I received straight A's in my Spanish class at Immaculate

Conception High School. Certainly, traveling has been made much easier. During visits to Spain, Mexico, and some of the Central American countries, it has been my experience that people are much more open and much more receptive if you can speak their language. In addition, the subtleties of a culture are easier to grasp and much easier to appreciate.

I hope that knowing a second language will continue to be an asset for me in the future. I am currently pursuing a career in medicine. Perhaps by knowing Spanish I can broaden the area in which I can work and increase the number of people that I might reach.

Now one of the disadvantages of growing up bilingually is that I picked up my mother's accent as well as her language. I must have been about four years old before I realized that our feathered friends in the trees are called "birds" not "beers" and that, in fact, we had a "birdbath" in our backyard, not a "beerbath."

Family reunions also tend to be confusing around my home. Most of my relatives speak either Spanish, English, or Arabic, but rarely any combination of the three. So, as a result, deep and involved conversations are almost impossible. But with a little nodding and smiling, I have found that there really is no language barrier among family and friends.

In all, I must say that being exposed to three very different cultures—Latin, Arabic, and American—has been rewarding for me and has made a difference even in the music I enjoy and the food I eat. It is not unusual in my house to sit down to a meal made up of stuffed grape leaves and refried beans and all topped off with apple pie for dessert.

I am fortunate in having had the opportunity to view more closely what makes Arabic and Latin cultures unique. By understanding and appreciating them I have been able to better understand and appreciate my own American culture. In closing, just let me add some words you often hear spoken in my home—*adios* and *allak konn ma'eck*—goodbye, and may God go with you.

Lady with a Gun
ELIZABETH TIDMORE

Beth Tidmore presented this self-introductory speech to her honors class in oral communication at the University of Memphis. The speech, offered as a tribute to her mother's faith in her, describes her dramatic development into a shooting champion. Beth's speech is noteworthy for its use of narrative design, especially dialogue. Her graphic descriptions, engaging her listeners' senses of sight, sound, touch, and smell, also helped her establish a vital, direct contact with her audience and transported them to the scenes she depicted. By the end of that semester, Beth had won the National Junior Olympic Championship Women's Air Rifle competition and had been named to the All-America shooters team.

I'm sure everybody has had an April Fool's joke played on them. My father's favorite one was to wake me up on April first and tell me, "School's been canceled for the day; you don't have to go," and then get all excited and say "April Fools!" I'd get up and take a shower . . .

Well, on April first, 2000, my mother said three words that I was sure weren't an April Fool's joke. She said, "We'll take it." The "it" she was referring to was a brand-new Anschutz 2002 Air Rifle. Now, this is $2,000 worth of equipment for a sport that I'd been in for maybe three months—not long. That was a big deal! It meant that I would be going from a junior-level to an Olympic-grade rifle.

Someone outside of the sport might think, "Eh, minor upgrade. A gun is a gun, right?" No. Imagine a fifteen-year-old who has been driving a used Toyota and who suddenly gets a new Mercedes for her sixteenth birthday. That's how I felt.

And as she was writing the check, I completely panicked. I thought, "What if I'm not good enough to justify this rifle? What if I decide to quit and we have to sell it, or we can't sell it? What if I let my parents down and I waste their money?" So later in the car I said, "Momma, what if I'm not good enough?" She said, "Don't worry about it—it's my money." Okay . . .

So my journey began. Most shooters start out when they're younger, and they move up through different rifles. Most of my peers had at least four years' experience on me. I had to jump right in and get a scholarship. And to get a scholarship I had to get noticed. And to get noticed I had to win, and to win, I had to shoot great scores immediately.

So my journey was filled with eight-hours-a-day practice, five days a week. On weekends I shot matches and I traveled. I had to take my homework with me to complete it before I got back to school. I had to do physical training, I had dietary restrictions. When all my friends were out at parties and at Cancun for Spring Break, I was at the shooting range. My free time—if I had any—was spent lifting weights and running.

At times I really resented my friends, because I thought they must have all the fun. But you know what, it was worth it! My friends don't know what it's like to feel the cold, smooth wood of the cheekpiece against your face. And they don't know the rich smell of Hoppe's No. 9 [oil] when you're cleaning your rifle. And they've never been to the Olympic Training Center in Colorado and seen how they embroider the little Olympic logo on *everything* from the mattresses to the plates. And they don't know the thrill of shooting in a final and having everyone applaud when you shoot a ten or even a center ten, or standing on the podium and having them put a medal around your neck, and being proud to represent your school, your country. . . .

There's a bumper sticker that says, "A Lady with A Gun Has More Fun." After three years in this sport, I have had so much fun! I've been all over the U.S., I've been captain of a high school rifle team, I've been to matches everywhere, I've won medals, I've been to World Cups and met people from all over the world. And I've gotten to experience so many different people, places, and events through my participation in shooting sports.

So not long ago, I asked my mother, "Mom, how did you know?" She said, "Ah, I just knew." I said, "No, Mom—*really*. How did you know that you weren't going to waste your money?" She got very serious and she took me by the shoulders and she squared me up. She looked me right in the eye and she said, "When you picked up that gun, you just looked like you belonged together. I knew there was a sparkle in your eye, and I knew that you were meant to do great things with that rifle."

So, thanks, Mom.

To Toss Or Not to Toss: The Art of Baseball Umpiring

BJ YOUNGERMAN

BJ Youngerman presented this speech in his class at Davidson College. It illustrates the use of an activity as the starting point for a self-introductory speech. BJ combines effective narrative, animated gestures, and vocal contrast to carry listeners to the scene of an umpiring situation and to create the setting for his speech. He offers an impressive array of expert testimony in support of his own extensive experience to create an authentic, highly credible speech.

> *Me:* "He's out!" [with hand motion].
>
> *Coach:* "You've got to be kidding me, Blue! He was a good 10 feet beyond the base before the ball got there. That's horrible!"
>
> *Me:* "Coach, shut up, you know you're being ridiculous. Get back to your dugout."
>
> *Coach:* "Blue, that was the worst call I've ever seen. You're totally blind."
>
> *Me:* "Coach, you're just a sore loser: Get in the dugout."
>
> *Coach:* "Well just because you got cut in Little League doesn't mean you have to take it out on these kids!"
>
> *Me:* "That's it! You're done!" [*swings arms to signify ejection of coach*].

Although umpiring is often considered to be a job where the sole purpose is to make judgment calls, in fact, the work includes many complexities, especially when you're dealing with angry players, coaches, and spectators. In the next few minutes, I will look into the importance of maintaining order, the importance of professionalism, and the necessity of making the right call the *first* time when working as a baseball umpire. But first let me tell you a little about my background as an umpire.

My first umpiring experience occurred with Little League when I was 13. By the time I was 16, I had been certified by the High School Federation Board and now have umpired three seasons for well over 200 games.

Some of you may be wondering: What exactly is the role of an umpire? According to Kathryn Davis, author of *The Art of Sports Officiating*, "Referees [Umpires] are the decisive directors of the game. They rule, punish, guide, and educate, all in the same split second." The U.S. Department of Labor estimates that there are roughly 16,000 umpires, referees, and other sports officials nationwide. Fred Frick, a writer for *The Baseball Almanac*, provides the "10 Commandments of Umpiring," which include the following: First, keep your personalities out of your work. Second, Forgive and forget and avoid sarcasm. Don't insist on the last word. Third, never charge a player, and above all, no pointing your finger or yelling. Finally, he advises to always keep your temper, as a decision made in anger is never sound.

Another important aspect of the art of umpiring is in maintaining order throughout the game. Rich Coyle and Arnie Mann, president and commissioner respectively for the Greater New Haven Baseball Umpires Association, offer several different techniques to use in maintaining order. Coyle recommends defusing the situation by walking away. Mann also made the infamous comment, "Don't look for boogers," or you'll encounter problems. Both Coyle and Mann agree that if someone starts attacking you personally, then eject him or her. One of the ways to avoid ever getting to the point of potentially having to eject someone is to always remain professional.

Why is it important to maintain professionalism? First and foremost, because image is crucial to success. Davis points out that you must establish your initial image at the pre-game conference. You ought to explain any new or difficult rule interpretations and ask if there are any questions. Another aspect of professionalism is the uniform, as it is a major part of your image. Davis notes, "Groomed appearance exudes competence, confidence and pride in the profession." According to Travis Hamilton, an expert on professionalism, the uniform must be tucked in and shoes must be shined. Rich Coyle jokingly comments that you can get through the first three innings even if you're the most horrible ump in the world, so long as you look good.

Attitude is also a part of image. You should be friendly but reserved. Davis says, "Coaches notice an official's rapport with the players, punctuality to the game, proper game equipment, enthusiasm, and effort." Finally, knowledge and competence are incredibly important as well, as they are components of professionalism. Aside from looking good, the other important part of professionalism is doing your job correctly. This brings up the question: How are you to make the right call and when, if ever, should you make the decision to change it?

In terms of making the right call, Rudy Raffone, rules interpreter for the Greater New Haven Chapter of the High School Umpires Federation board, suggests, "Replay the play in your head so you don't simply react, but instead actually think." Additionally, Rich Coyle recommends selling the call by showing loud verbal and physical signs.

Changing a call is a much more difficult decision. Jay Miner of *Referee* magazine asks, "When is a judgment call not a judgment call? Is it when an umpire second-guesses his own call, consults with a colleague, and changes it?"

I once encountered a similar situation to this. At age 16, I was a new umpire working a game in which the players were also 16. There was a close call at third base from which I was shielded. I made a call, but immediately went to my home plate umpire for help. After discussing the play with my co-umpire, he told me that I made the wrong call, so I did what I thought was the logical and right thing, and reversed the call. Though I probably did end up making the right decision by changing the call, my credibility was immediately gone, as the coaches, fans, and players now assumed I would overturn almost any call. Jerry Crawford, a Major League Baseball umpire says, "You don't waver . . . and that's how I would deal with [a close call]; there was no backing off. You've got to maintain that sense about you all the time. Your job is to maintain control out there and being weak-kneed, there's no place for that on a baseball field." It certainly seems that a Major League umpire should know best, having worked his way through the whole system.

In conclusion, umpiring requires so many different elements that one must constantly stay focused both on the game as well as on maintaining order, remaining professional, and making the right call the first time.

With this information in mind, let's do a little reenactment of the scene I portrayed a few minutes ago:

> *Me:* "He's out!" (*with hand motion*).
> *Coach:* "You've got to be kidding me, Blue! He was a good 10 feet beyond the base before the ball got there. That's horrible!"
> *Me:* "Coach, it's a judgment call. I called it like I saw it. Please get back to your dugout."
> *Coach:* "Blue, that was the worst call I've ever seen. You're totally blind."
> *Me:* "Coach, this is your final warning: Get in the dugout."
> *Coach:* "Well just because you got cut in Little League doesn't mean you have to take it out on these kids!"
> *Me:* "That's it! You're done!" (wave arm)

The first scene was me, rookie umpire. The second is me, veteran umpire. In this case, the result on the field did not change. But I carried away from that second scene the knowledge that I was serving the game I love in just the right way.

Informative Speeches

The "Monument" at Wounded Knee
CECILE LARSON

Cecile Larson's speech informs listeners about a shameful episode in American history. The speech follows a spatial design. Cecile's vivid use of imagery and the skillful contrasts she draws between this "monument" and our "official" monuments create mental pictures that should stay with her listeners long after the words of her speech have been forgotten.

We Americans are big on monuments. We build monuments in memory of our heroes. Washington, Jefferson, and Lincoln live on in our nation's capital. We erect monuments to honor our martyrs. The Minuteman still stands guard at Concord. The flag is ever raised over Iwo Jima. Sometimes we even construct monuments to commemorate victims. In Ashburn Park downtown there is a monument to those who died in the yellow fever epidemics. However, there are some things in our history that we don't memorialize. Perhaps we would just as soon forget what happened. Last summer I visited such a place—the massacre site at Wounded Knee.

In case you have forgotten what happened at Wounded Knee, let me refresh your memory. On December 29, 1890, shortly after Sitting Bull had been murdered by the authorities, about 400 half-frozen, starving, and frightened Indians who had fled the nearby reservation were attacked by the Seventh Cavalry. When the fighting ended, between 200 and 300 Sioux had died—two-thirds of them women and children. Their remains are buried in a common grave at the site of the massacre.

Wounded Knee is located in the Pine Ridge Reservation in southwestern South Dakota—about a three-hour drive from where Presidents Washington, Jefferson,

Theodore Roosevelt, and Lincoln are enshrined in the granite face of Mount Rushmore. The reservation is directly south of the Badlands National Park, a magnificently desolate area of wind-eroded buttes and multicolored spires.

We entered the reservation driving south from the Badlands Visitor's Center. The landscape of the Pine Ridge Reservation retains much of the desolation of the Badlands but lacks its magnificence. Flat, sun-baked fields and an occasional eroded gully stretch as far as the eye can see. There are no signs or highway markers to lead the curious tourist to Wounded Knee. Even the *Rand-McNally Atlas* doesn't help you find your way. We got lost three times and had to stop and ask directions.

When we finally arrived at Wounded Knee, there was no official historic marker to tell us what had happened there. Instead there was a large, handmade wooden sign—crudely lettered in white on black. The sign first directed our attention to our left—to the gully where the massacre took place. The mass grave site was to our right—across the road and up a small hill.

Two red-brick columns topped with a wrought-iron arch and a small metal cross form the entrance to the grave site. The column to the right is in bad shape: cinder blocks from the base are missing; the brickwork near the top has deteriorated and tumbled to the ground; graffiti on the columns proclaim an attitude we found repeatedly expressed about the Bureau of Indian Affairs—"The BIA sucks!"

Crumbling concrete steps lead you to the mass grave. The top of the grave is covered with gravel, punctuated by unruly patches of chickweed and crabgrass. These same weeds also grow along the base of the broken chainlink fence that surrounds the grave, the "monument," and a small cemetery.

The "monument" itself rests on a concrete slab to the right of the grave. It's a typical, large, old-fashioned granite cemetery marker, a pillar about six feet high topped with an urn—the kind of gravestone you might see in any cemetery with graves from the turn of the century. The inscription tells us that it was erected by the families of those who were killed at Wounded Knee. Weeds grow through the cracks in the concrete at its base.

There are no granite headstones in the adjacent cemetery, only simple white wooden crosses that tell a story of people who died young. There is no neatly manicured grass. There are no flowers. Only the unrelenting and unforgiving weeds.

Yes, Americans are big on monuments. We build them to memorialize our heroes, to honor our martyrs, and sometimes, even to commemorate victims. But only when it makes us feel good.

Video Games
JOSEPH VAN MATRE

Joseph Van Matre presented this informative speech to his Fundamentals of Communication class at the University of Arkansas, taught by Lynn Meade. He reports that the idea for the speech "just popped into my head" after listening to a report on National Public Radio. The speech opens very effectively by using rhetorical questions, and features timely and interesting research that develops in a categorical pattern.

If I say the word "gamer," what words come to mind? Antisocial? Geek? Dropout? Well, how about fitness guru, educator, or intelligence analyst?

I'm not a hardcore gamer, but I do enjoy a round of Mario Smash Bros. every now and then. So when I heard on National Public Radio one day that video games can actually help in the business world, I was intrigued and did some research. What I discovered was quite surprising.

While there have been many stereotypes associated with video games and those who play them, today I'm going to show you some of the very real benefits video games can bring to the health, education, military, and business worlds. By the end of my presentation, some of you may even be ready to break out your Game Boy!

While many people think that video games contribute to inactivity, and therefore to health problems, video games have actually helped many gamers become more active. In fact, new input systems in the twenty-first century have encouraged many players to climb off the couch. Dance Dance Revolution, for example, has become popular with many physical educators. As the *New York Times* of April 2007 reported, the West Virginia Department of Education and the Los Angeles Unified School System both use DDR as a part of their PE programs. The game "requires players to dance in ever more complicated and strenuous patterns in time with electronic dance music." Dr. Linda Carson, distinguished professor at West Virginia University, reported her first encounter with the game: "I was in a mall walking by the arcade and I saw these kids playing D.D.R., and I was just stunned. There were all these kids dancing and sweating and actually standing in line and paying money to be physically active. . . . It was a physical educator's dream." In followup studies, Dr. Carson and her colleagues have found significant health benefits for overweight children who play the game regularly.

New technologies developed by NASA can also promote mental health. While this is a little complicated, as one plays a video game, the controller gets easier to use when the player brings a healthy brainwave pattern to the game. Thus the game becomes both diagnostic and therapeutic. According to Dr. Olafur Paisson, professor of psychiatry at Eastern Virginia Medical School, "With this new [biofeedback] technology, we have found a way to package this training in an enjoyable and inherently motivating activity."

Now that you know how video games can help keep you healthy, let's consider how they can make you smarter. First, video games can be effective educational tools. A study by the British Government showed that playing games such as SimCity and Rollercoaster Tycoon can help develop creativity, critical thinking, and math skills. When played in a group, they can also develop interpersonal skills. Then if you add correct economic and human behavior algorithms, you can make these games even more effective for economics and business education.

Video games can also help people develop a knowledge of history. For example, many people are fascinated by World War II, but it's hard for them to imagine what fighting in that war must have been like. But if you place them right in the middle of simulated battle situations in which they receive the combat orders just as soldiers of that time received them under actual conditions, their imaginations are stimulated. They must act and think and fight for survival. Playing such battle games makes it so much easier to motivate them to learn about the countries and causes and underlying cultural conditions involved in the many battlefields of that war. All these types of interactive education "games" are being developed right now.

Now that you see how video games can be used in education, let's look at how they also can function in the worlds of business and national defense. Businesses are finding great uses for video games to enhance training. In 2008, for example, UPS spent over $5.5 million on new training centers that integrate "on-line learning, 3-D models, podcasts, and videos with traditional classroom learning." These training programs are effective, according to the *Emerging Technologies Center*, because they are "immersive, require the player to make frequent, important decisions, have clear goals, adapt to other players individually, and involve a social network." Obviously, these cultivate important skills in the business world.

Finally, the military is using video games to enhance training, lower costs, assist in rehabilitation, and perform dangerous tasks. Converting war games into video games allows training to focus on specific goals and can lower costs dramatically. Southern California's Institute for Creative Technologies has shown that using X-box type games can help soldiers returning from the Middle East and Afghanistan to cope with PTSD (Post-traumatic Stress Disorder). Working with video games, trainees develop skills that can help them control drone planes and tanks on the battlefield. As Dr. Alan Pope of Langley Air Force Base has reported, "Flight simulators are essentially very sophisticated video games." By developing such games, training is simplified and accelerated, and mistakes can be corrected without devastating on-site consequences.

So have you begun to change your mind about video games and gamers? We've seen that video games can make us more healthy, smarter, better trained for the business world, and more secure from international threats. The next time you see people playing World of Warcraft or Halo, try not to think of them as "geeks" or as "dropouts." Those "geeks" may have their hands on the future!

To Clone or Not to Clone
MICHAEL ANTHONY PARKER

Michael Parker presented this informative speech in an Oral Communication class at the University of Memphis, taught by Kimberly Johnson. Because cloning is such a controversial subject, Michael decided to inform his listeners of the major arguments for and against cloning, leaving them to make up their own minds. The speech starts with good attention material, focuses nicely on a central question, and defines the subject carefully and clearly. The speech seems well researched, but needs to document its sources of information more carefully.

Most of us have seen one of those cheesy, awful, B-rated science fiction movies from the 1980s that peer clumsily into the future. The flying cars they predicted are still a no-show and the food replicators are nowhere to be found. However, one aspect of the future often talked about in these dreadful movies has become a reality, or at least a real possibility.

What is he referring to, you ask? The answer to this question is simple, even if the process involved or the controversy surrounding it is not. I am speaking of human cloning. Those of you who have seen these dismal movies of yesteryear may have sometimes asked yourselves, what would it be like to have a clone of myself, an exact duplicate of me, running around?

None of us may ever know what it would be like to have a carbon copy of ourselves out there in the world. Why? Because religious and political opposition has resulted in laws in our country that prohibit or severely restrict funding for research, let alone actual experiments. Nevertheless, this is a free country, and we are free here to consider the central question in this controversy: should cloning be legalized in the United States?

Today I want to define what cloning means, give you a brief history of recent events in the controversy, and examine a few of the arguments on both sides.

Merriam-Webster's dictionary defines a clone as "an individual grown from a single somatic cell or cell nucleus and genetically identical to it." With human cloning there are two types to consider: reproductive and therapeutic. Reproductive cloning, also called artificial twinning, "involves removing one or more cells from an embryo and encouraging the cells to develop into a separate embryo with the same DNA as the original," according to B. A. Robinson of the American Medical Association. Therapeutic cloning, also called research cloning, is related to reproductive cloning in that both procedures involve the use of an embryo. The differences comes when the "resultant embryo would be allowed to grow for 14 days. Its stem cells would then be extracted and encouraged to grow into a piece of human tissue or a complete human organ for transplant," states Robinson.

Turning to recent history, cloning a human being has been a controversy for a little more than a decade now. In 1997, the United States National Bioethics Advisory Commission (NBAC) advised former President Bill Clinton that there should be a ban on human cloning. That next year, in 1998, the Prohibition of Cloning Human Beings Act was introduced in Congress, mandating "that no federal funds be allocated for human cloning." Among the questions driving this debate was whether a clone might be regarded as fully human. This concern comes "from the underlying fear that clones would be denied the same rights as other individuals in society," says the Council on Ethical and Judicial Affairs of the American Medical Association.

In April 2001, Senator Bill Campbell of Colorado, with the full blessing of President Bush, offered a law that not only prevented federal funding of research, but also make it illegal to attempt to clone humans. Violations of these laws carried penalties of up to ten years in jail and a fine of $10 million. Universities around the country quickly got in step with these prohibitions.

And yet the controversy continues. To better understand it, let's consider the arguments on both sides of the dispute, starting with the opponents of human cloning.

Many religious opponents declare that cloning is not only morally and ethically wrong, but that it is unnatural and sacrilegious. Their main complaint centers on scientists "playing God." Human life, they argue, must originate naturally from the mother's womb, and not from a test tube. Other opponents ask whether clones would be fully functioning members of society, and whether they would know the difference between right and wrong. Can clones feel emotions? Will they be able to function independently, or will they be slaves? Will the clone have a soul?

Probably the champion of those opposing cloning was President George W. Bush. In April of 2002, President Bush held a press conference in which he publicly condemned cloning in both its reproductive and therapeutic forms. Said Bush, "I believe all human cloning is wrong, and both forms ought to be banned."

Proponents of human cloning research view the situation quite differently. They are outraged by the Federal government summarily dismissing this issue without so much as considering its possible long-term benefits. Proponents such as Nathan Myhrvold, columnist for *Slate* magazine, posed a question early in the dispute that centered cloning on a fundamental right of human beings: the right to procreate. Myhrvold said, "Start by asking whether human beings have a right to reproduce. I say yes. I have no moral right to tell other people they shouldn't be able to have children, and I don't see that Bill Clinton has that right either."

Probably the strongest argument of proponents comes with the promise of therapeutic cloning for creating new organs and tissues. There is no doubt that collecting stem cells from artificially created embryos can destroy potential life for the sake of those who are actually living, even though such embryos are destined to be discarded anyway. Some scientists consider this to be an acceptable loss given all the good that can come from creating hope for those desperately in need of the new organs and tissues. In an address in front of Like-Minded Scientists for Cloning Advancement (LMSCA) members, Dr. Gene Krupkauer sad, "There is still resistance to cloning out there, but that is of no consequence. The world we envision is as inevitable as it is beautiful—it is a world from which every one of us stands to benefit."

So there's the controversy: it's there and it won't go away. Where do you stand on it? That question is up to you. But whether or not you think it would be cool to have a mirror image of yourself going to school with you each day, working next to you at your job, or helping you with the household chores, that decision—currently at this time—is not up to you. Laws are in place that make it illegal to do research, let along perform experiments. Whether you want a clone or not is irrelevant. Or is it?

Persuasive Speeches

Global Burning
JOSHUA LOGAN

Josh Logan presented this persuasive speech on the theme of global warming in his class at the University of Memphis. "Global Burning" focuses on the problem and attempts to arouse awareness, share understanding, and secure agreement. Its strategy is to magnify the reality of global warming and its meaning for listeners. Its challenge is to remove barriers that might stand in the way of their commitment. To achieve his goals, Josh used colorful, graphic language, a presentation aid, and effective examples. His presentation reflected his passion, sincerity, and commitment on this topic.

Ten years ago, five years ago, reasonable people could still argue and even disagree over some tough environmental questions: Is there really such a thing as "global warming"? Is the world really getting hotter at a rapid pace? And is it being fanned by humans? Are we really responsible for environmental conditions?

Now there's little room left for argument. The answer to all these questions is clearly YES. This definitive answer has been provided by the United Nations Intergovernmental Panel on Climate Change, reporting during the early part of 2007. This authoritative report, which correlates and tests the work of hundreds of environmental scientists from countries around the globe, concludes that the process of global warming is now in motion and is accelerating. And the fire is fed largely by humans: the IPCC supports this conclusion at a 90 to 99% level of confidence. The United States especially, with about 4% of the world's population, accounts for 25% of all global warming. We are the ones with our foot on the accelerator.

Today I want to sketch the dimensions of this problem, and what it might mean for you and your children. I will first track the causes of global warming, then trace its recent path and project its future. As recently as 2006, polls tell us that many people in the United States were in denial about global warming: yes, we believe it exists and, yes, we are concerned, but we're not that much concerned. Fifty-four percent of us think global warming is a problem for the future—but not now! Global warming is still something of an abstract, distant problem for us, and we can't see the future all that clearly.

That's the challenge I want to try to meet today. We must recognize global warming for what it is, the monster we are creating by all our action and inaction. We must become scared—really scared! We must be willing to think green and act green, from the personal everyday decisions we make on disposing trash to the big consumer decisions we make on which cars to buy, to the political decisions we make on which candidates to support. We must understand that this hot world is starting to catch fire—and we must be willing to pay the price to help put the flames out. We must be committed to the proposition that global warming must not become global burning.

Global warming begins with greenhouse gases—the tons of carbon dioxide that belch out of our smokestacks and our automobile exhausts; the vast clouds of methane gas that rise from our farms and ranches and landfills; the nitrous oxide from fertilizers, cattle feed lots, and chemical products. The world's forests are supposed to absorb much of this industrial and agricultural output, but guess what? We've also been busy cutting the rainforests and clear-cutting our own forests. We're tying nature's hands behind her back at just the wrong moment. So all these deadly gases mix and accumulate in the atmosphere, where they magnify the heat of the sun.

Now let's gain some perspective on where we now actually stand. I want to show you a chart that traces the human influence on the atmosphere over the past thousand years of history. This chart summarizes the history of greenhouse gases, according to the IPCC's *Summary for Policymakers*. Notice that the bottom border divides the time frame into two-hundred-year periods. The side frame measures the amount of the gas pouring into the atmosphere. Notice that for about eight hundred of these years, this amount is stable and even—almost a straight line. Then as the nineteenth century dawns on the Industrial Revolution, the lines begin to climb, at first gradually, then increasingly steeper until they almost reach the vertical during the past half-century. The dry technical language of the summary, speaking to carbon dioxide alone, carries the message of this chart with sharp clarity: "The atmospheric concentration of carbon dioxide (CO_2) has increased by 31 percent since 1750. The present CO_2 concentration has not been exceeded during the past 420,000 years and likely not during the past 20 million years. The current rate of increase is unprecedented during at least the past 20,000 years."

Now what does all this mean in human terms, especially if these lines continue to climb on the charts of the future? Well get your fans out, because it's going to be hot. Very hot. According to *National Geographic News* of July, 2006, eleven of the last twelve years have been the hottest on record, probably reaching back for at least a thousand years. But that record won't last for long. The UN congregation of the world's scientists predicts that the earth's surface temperature could rise at least five degrees over the next hundred years—just in the last generation it has already risen two degrees on average. Can you imagine what it will be like to add five degrees to the average summer day in Memphis?

Beyond that, the world's agriculture will be profoundly changed. Fertile lands will become deserts, and vast populations will be forced to relocate. As you might imagine, and as *Time* magazine of April 2006 confirms, it is the poorest and least flexible populations—such as those one finds in Africa—who will be hardest hit initially. *Science* magazine adds that major forest fires in the West and South are more numerous and more devastating than they were a generation ago. The average land burned during a given year is more than six times what it was a generation ago.

Moreover, it will soon get more lonely here on planet earth. The latest word is that more than one-third—that's one-third—of all species in several parts of the world could be destroyed over the next fifty years. Chris Leeds, conservation biologist of the University of Leeds, says: "Our analyses suggest that well over a million species could be threatened with extinction as a result of climate change." That's over a million species.

The story becomes more tragic when we contemplate the fate of the oceans. Some scientists had previously discounted global warming because some of the most dire predictions about rising temperatures had not come true. What they forgot was the capacity of the oceans to absorb heat and smother some of the immediate impact of global warming. But a recent issue of *Science* magazine has published reports that—as they put it—"link a warming trend in the upper 3,000 meters of the world's oceans to global warming caused by human activities."

As the oceans grow warmer, especially in the Gulf of Mexico area, the threat of hurricanes grows more ominous. In its summary of conditions in 2006, *Time* reported that over the past thirty-five years, the number of category 4 & 5 hurricanes has jumped 50%. But these reports truly threaten all living creatures. In particular, they confirm the IPCC predictions that most coral reefs will disappear within thirty to fifty years. And as the oceans continue to warm and melt the great ice shelves in the polar regions, the rise in sea level—as much as three feet over the next century and perhaps even more—will wipe out vast lowland areas such as the Sundarbans in India and Bangladesh, the last, best habitat for the Bengal tiger. Large parts of Florida and Louisiana will surrender to the sea—sell your beach property soon! The barrier islands off Mobile Bay, where my parents took me camping as a boy and where I hope to take my own children, will gradually recede into memory. These are just fragments, mere glimpses, of the future global warming has in store for us, our children, and grandchildren.

Well, I hope I have gained your attention today. We have a problem here that threatens the quality of life here on earth. Can we do anything about it? I would like to give you a happy, simple answer to this question, but it is a complex one. It's not like we can just take our foot off the greenhouse accelerator, and bring the bus to a halt. Once it is heated, the ocean does not cool quickly. Once they have accumulated, greenhouse gases can linger for a long time. But there are things we can do to change this scenario. The future is not an either-or proposition, and we can mitigate some of the worst possibilities. We can cool the fires under global warming to prevent it from becoming global burning. In my next speech I hope to show you how.

The clock is ticking, but I don't think it's too late. I hope that what I've said in the last two speeches has gained your attention. Get involved! Together we can cool the fever, and turn down the heat under our planet.

We Don't Have to Live in Slums
ANNA ALEY

Anna Aley was a student as Kansas State University when she presented this persuasive speech. It is noteworthy for its vivid language; its effective use of supporting materials, especially narrative; and the way in which it focuses listeners on a program of action.

Slumlords—you'd expect them in New York or Chicago, but in Manhattan, Kansas? You'd better believe there are slumlords in Manhattan, and they pose a direct threat to you if you ever plan to rent an off-campus apartment.

I know about slumlords; I rented a basement apartment from one last semester. I guess I first suspected something was wrong when I discovered dead roaches in the refrigerator. I definitely knew something was wrong when I discovered the leaks: the one in the bathroom that kept the bathroom carpet constantly soggy and molding and the one in the kitchen that allowed water from the upstairs neighbor's bathroom to seep into the kitchen cabinets and collect in my dishes.

Then there were the serious problems. The hot water heater and furnace were connected improperly and posed a fire hazard. They were situated next to the only exit. There was no smoke detector or fire extinguisher and no emergency way out—the windows were too small for escape. I was living in an accident waiting to happen—and paying for it.

The worst thing about my ordeal was that I was not an isolated instance; many Kansas State students are living in unsafe housing and paying for it, not only with their money, but their happiness, their grades, their health, and their safety.

We can't be sure how many students are living in substandard housing, housing that does not meet the code specifications required of rental property. We can be sure, however, that a large number of Kansas State students are at risk of being caught in the same situation I was. According to the registrar, approximately 17,800 students are attending Kansas State this semester. Housing claims that 4,200 live in the dorms. This means that approximately 13,600 students live off-campus. Some live in fraternities or sororities, some live at home, but most live in off-campus apartments, as I do.

Many of these 13,600 students share traits that make them likely to settle for substandard housing. For example, many students want to live close to campus. If you've ever driven through the surrounding neighborhoods, you know that much of the available housing is in older houses, houses that were never meant to be divided into separate rental units. Students are also often limited in the amount they can pay for rent; some landlords, such as mine, will use low rent as an excuse not to fix anything and to let the apartment deteriorate. Most importantly, many students are young and, consequently, naive when it comes to selecting an apartment. They don't know the housing codes; but even if they did, they don't know how to check to make sure the apartment is in compliance. Let's face it—how many of us know how to check a hot water heater to make sure it's connected properly?

Adding to the problem of the number of students willing to settle for substandard housing is the number of landlords willing to supply it. Currently, the Consumer Relations Board here at Kansas State has on file student complaints against approximately one hundred landlords. There are surely complaints against many more that have never been formally reported.

There are two main causes of the substandard student housing problem. The first—and most significant—is the simple fact that it is possible for a landlord to lease an apartment that does not meet housing code requirements. The Manhattan Housing Code Inspector will evaluate an apartment, but only after the tenant has given the landlord a written complaint and the landlord has had fourteen days to remedy the situation. In other words, the way things are now, the only way the Housing Code Inspector can evaluate an apartment to see if it's safe to be lived in is if someone has been living in it for at least two weeks!

A second cause of the problem is the fact that campus services designed to help students avoid substandard housing are not well known. The Consumer Relations Board here at Kansas State can help students inspect apartments for safety before they sign a lease, it can provide students with vital information on their rights as tenants, and it can mediate in landlord–tenant disputes. The problem is, many people don't know these services exist. The Consumer Relations Board is not listed in the university catalogue; it is not mentioned in any of the admissions literature. The only places it is mentioned are in alphabetically organized references such as the phone book, but you have to already know it exists to look it up! The Consumer Relations Board does receive money for advertising from the student senate, but it is only enough to run a little two-by-three-inch ad once every month. That is not large enough or frequent enough to be noticed by many who could use these services.

It's clear that we have a problem, but what may not seem so clear is what we can do about it. After all, what can one student do to change the practices of numerous Manhattan landlords? Nothing, if that student is alone. But just think of what we could accomplish if we got all 13,600 off-campus students involved in this issue! Think what we could accomplish if we got even a fraction of those students involved! This is what Wade Whitmer, director of the Consumer Relations Board, is attempting to do. He is reorganizing the Off-Campus Association in an effort to pass a city ordinance requiring landlords to have their apartments inspected for safety before those apartments can be rented out. The Manhattan code inspector has already tried to get just such an ordinance passed, but the only people who showed up at the public forums were known slumlords, who obviously weren't in favor of the proposed ordinance. No one showed up to argue in favor of the ordinance, so the city commissioners figured that no one wanted it and voted it down. If we can get the Off-Campus Association organized and involved, however, the commissioners will see that someone does want the ordinance, and they will be more likely to pass it the next time it is proposed. You can do a great service to your fellow students—and to yourself—by joining the Off-Campus Association.

A second thing you can do to help ensure that no more Kansas State students have to go through what I did is sign my petition asking the student senate to increase the Consumer Relations Board's advertising budget. Let's face it—a service cannot do anybody any good if no one knows about it. The Consumer Relations Board's services are simply too valuable to let go to waste.

An important thing to remember about substandard housing is that it is not only distasteful, it is dangerous. In the end, I was lucky. I got out of my apartment with little more than bad memories. My upstairs neighbor was not so lucky. The main problem with his apartment was that the electrical wiring was done improperly; there were too many outlets for too few circuits, so the fuses were always blowing. One day last November, Jack was at home when a fuse blew—as usual. And, as usual, he went to the fuse box to flip the switch back on. When he touched the switch, it delivered such a shock that it literally threw this guy the size of a football player backwards and down a flight of stairs. He lay there at the bottom, unable to move, for a full hour before his roommate came home and called an ambulance.

Jack was lucky. His back was not broken. But he did rip many of the muscles in his back. Now he has to go to physical therapy, and he is not expected to fully recover.

Kansas State students have been putting up with substandard living conditions for too long. It's time we finally got together to do something about this problem. Join the Off-Campus Association. Sign my petition. Let's send a message to these slumlords that we're not going to put up with this any more. We don't have to live in slums.

Fairly Traded Coffee
ELIZABETH LYLES

This persuasive speech by Betsy Lyles was presented in her class at Davidson College. It relies heavily on an impressive array of facts and figures to convince listeners of the ethical importance of buying fairly traded coffee. The speech might have benefited from a greater use of motivational appeals and narratives to make it come alive more powerfully for listeners.

How many of you began the morning with a cup of coffee? Many, if not most of you buy coffee every day. This daily purchase amounts to about $500 a year that you might spend on coffee. Based on a very conservative estimate that 10% of Davidson students drink coffee daily, collectively we as a student body invest more than $75,000 in the coffee industry per year.

The money we spend on coffee can go to either of two markets—the fair trade coffee market and regular trade coffee market. Today I want to urge you to support fairly traded coffee because it promotes both sustainable development and a decent life style for coffee farmers in those regions that are dependent upon the export of coffee for income. I will help you gain an understanding of what fair trade is, the effect of fairly traded coffee on workers and the environment, and how you can support fairly traded coffee here on campus.

Let's start by discussing how most coffee is produced. Most coffee is produced in ways that are harmful to both the farmer and the environment. According to an article by Don Wells in *Herizons* magazine, it is grown on plantations where trees have been cut down to allow more space to plant coffee beans. After the crop is harvested the soil is depleted.

Most coffee produced this way is sold by the farmers to a big supplier. The supplier then sells it separately to importers. This means there are two more people who share the profit and the coffee farmers themselves get very little money for their work. The article in *Herizons* goes on to say that of the $7 we might pay for a pound of coffee, the coffee farmers might get 3 cents while the coffee corporations get 86 cents of every dollar consumers spend on coffee. With coffee farmers losing most of their profits to the "middle man" it creates a strain on their families, making it hard for them to maintain a sustainable lifestyle.

Now let's look at how being associated with fair trade helps the coffee farmers and the environment. Fair trade helps workers develop a lifestyle that is both sustainable and comfortable. Fair trade pays coffee farmers more per pound than they would be paid otherwise.

Andrew Downie reported in the *New York Times* last month that fair trade coffee farmers in Brazil are paid at least $1.29 a pound, compared with the regular market rate of roughly $1.05 per pound. That might not sound like much to you, but consider it from the point of view of a small farmer in Brazil, trying to raise a family. The difference mounts up into something really substantial! Downie also goes on to say that fair trade policies also create price floors to make sure that farmers will make a reasonable amount even if the coffee prices go down. The price floor is always set above the regular coffee market rate.

Coffee workers can see a noticeable difference in lifestyles as a result of fair trade. As Wells noted, coffee importers who trade fairly provide low-interest loans and credit to farmers, which helps them stay out of debt to local lenders. In a book by Alex Nicholls, *Fair Trade: Market-Driven Ethical Consumption*, a farmer from Belize remarked about how his lifestyle had changed:

> "I used to live in a thatch hut with a mud floor. Now I have two concrete houses and I have been able to educate my children. . . . They had to work in a shrimp farm when they were younger [to support the family], but now my children only go to school. We don't need them to work."

Another benefit of fair trade coffee is that it's grown organically, which means it has a lower environmental impact than mass produced coffee. Organic farming methods are less likely to deplete the soil and do not contribute to pollution and land and water resources.

So far we have learned what constitutes fair trade coffee farming and how it helps both the farmer and the environment. Now let's look at ways that you can personally support fair trade. There are many opportunities, right here in Davidson.

To begin, it's not hard for you to buy fairly traded coffee. According to the Davidson College Dining Services web site, both the Commons and the Union serve S&D coffee, which is a fair trade supplier. So we've already supported fair trade coffee, if we've bought our coffee on campus. One hundred percent of Summit Coffee is fairly traded, so by purchasing this coffee you are supporting farmers. Even if you don't like coffee, even if you never drink coffee, you can still support fair trade enterprises, because our Ben & Jerry's sells fairly traded ice cream.

A second contribution you can make is to promote awareness of fairly traded coffee. Only 3.3 percent of coffee sold in the United States last year was certified fair trade, but even that was more than eight times the level in 2001. The online campaign "Join the Big Noise" has produced a huge part of this increase, and by going online to maketradefair.com you can join the campaign to promote fair trade. Additionally, according to a study conducted last year by the New York based National Coffee Association, 27% of Americans said they were aware of the fair trade movement, up from the 12% claiming to be aware of it just a few years earlier. I challenge every one of you to participate in making those numbers increase even more significantly.

Now you understand how fair trade is an ethical alternative, how it positively affects the workers and the environment, and what you can do to support it right here in Davidson. I will leave you with the words of Bruce Crowther of the Fairtrade Foundation:

> People see [fair trade] as charity, but it is not, it is justice. We have to get rid of the charity way of thinking. I see doing fair trade as doing two things: one, it is helping people immediately and changing their lives; then there is the bigger picture where it is a protest tool, a way of registering your vote. But now we are not boycotting something, we are supporting something positive.

Every time you drink coffee remember the coffee farmer. Buy fairly traded coffee.

Ceremonial Speeches

Remarks on Accepting the Martin Luther King Jr. Human Rights Award

JOHN BAKKE

Professor John Bakke presented this thoughtful speech in 2006 in ceremonies held at the University of Memphis. Dr. Bakke used his acceptance speech to breathe new life into Dr. King's principle of nonviolence. Rather than a dated tactic in a long-ago civil rights struggle, nonviolence, by Bakke's interpretation, now demands full participation in the political process and acceptance of one's obligations as a citizen. Thus, what begins as an acceptance speech for an award quickly becomes a speech of tribute to Dr. King and finally a speech of inspiration to his listeners.

Thank you. It seems to me that many acceptance speeches begin with the words, "I've received many awards before, but . . ." Well, the truth is that I have not received many awards before, but of all the awards I have not received, this is the one I always wanted. What is more important in our lives than our rights as human beings? And who in our lifetime has done more to extend human rights than Dr. King? I'm overwhelmed by the honor. So please indulge me for a few minutes while I thank some people who are special to me before I say a few words in honor and memory of the person whom we all have reason to thank today. Dr. Martin Luther King Jr. gave me the courage to practice what he preached as best I could in and out of academia at critical points in my own life and in the life of this university and our community. And for that I am most thankful. . . . [Dr. Bakke acknowledges his family and friends, as well as his colleagues at the University of Memphis who shared his values and supported his work.]

We came to Memphis in 1967 and I was fortunate to be part of a progressive department at a university in a community ready for positive change. It is no accident that four members of that department, then called Speech and Drama, were previous recipients of this Martin Luther King Award. . . . And finally, thanks to all the seekers and holders of elected office who have given me the opportunity to work with them as well as to all the wonderful people whom I have worked with as a partisan in the political process. I got into campaign communication to help good people become more competitive in the campaign arena. I am proud of all these people for what they have done for human rights.

Dr. Martin Luther King Jr. gave to human rights his last full measure of devotion. He was devoted to nonviolence as a political strategy and as a personal philosophy because he knew the effects of violence even on those who commit violent acts as a means of necessary self defense or in a just cause. But when King was nearing his last days on earth, as Taylor Branch has recently written, in his commitment to nonviolence, King "found himself nearly alone among colleagues weary of sacrifice."

In 1968 King was increasingly under attack from all sides, by friends and foes alike. He was criticized by the Johnson Administration for opposing the war in Southeast Asia. He was under intense scrutiny by J. Edgar Hoover and the FBI. He was criticized by the white liberal establishment for his proposed Poor People's March. He was criticized by militant Black Power advocates for his nonviolent tactics and his coalitions with whites. And many of his closest friends just wanted him to back off for a while and by all means stay out of Memphis where a sanitation workers strike had been going on since February 2nd.

All such criticism came together and reached a crescendo after King's march in Memphis on behalf of the sanitation workers was disrupted by violence. The criticism came from all over, from the *New York Times* and *Washington Post* as well as the *Atlanta Constitution*, the *Dallas Morning News*, and, yes, the local *Memphis Commercial Appeal* and *Press Scimitar* newspapers. In editorials entitled "King's Credibility Gap" and "Chicken a la King," the *Commercial Appeal*, for example, said that "King's pose as the leader of a non-violent movement has been shattered" and "The Real Martin Luther King . . . [is] one of the most menacing men in America today." The *Press-Scimitar* said that King's "rhetoric has lost its spell" and the *Dallas Morning News* called him "a headline hunting high-priest on non-violent violence," "a press agent protester," "a marching militant" willing to "wreck everything for a spot on the evening newscast" and a "peripatetic preacher" who "could not allow the troubled waters to go unfished when there was a chance that the fisher might pick up a little publicity." You can imagine what was being said on the street at the time.

From all corners, the message was clear. "Martin Luther King! Go home! Go back where you came from. Get back in your place! At worst, you're dangerous. At best, you're history." Believe me! James Earl Ray was not the only American who wanted King out of the way. On the eve of April 4, in such a climate of violence in Memphis, Martin Luther delivered his "Mountaintop Speech" at Mason Temple. Like Socrates at his trial, like Jesus before Pilate, like Luther at Worms, King, virtually alone, had to stand up and be who he was: Dr. Martin Luther King Jr., the true apostle of nonviolent direct action.

I spent much time as a graduate student studying great speeches. I also read many treatises on the nature of eloquence. Thus I can say, personally and professionally, history knows no more eloquent speaker than Martin Luther King Jr. I never understood what Longinus meant when he wrote that "eloquence was the concomitant of a great soul" until I heard Dr. King in a context in which I knew what he was up against and what he was asking for. His last speech in Memphis was more than speech. It was "eloquence," once described by the great orator Daniel Webster as "action . . . noble, sublime, godlike action."

In the peroration of what became his last speech, King mentioned the threats and uncertainties that surrounded his life, but announced that he had been to the mountaintop. And from that lofty eminence he had seen "the Promised Land," a vision that would redeem all the years of pain and suffering. He might not get there with them, but assured listeners "that we as a people will get to the Promised Land."

It was perfect communication. All in his presence were filled with King's conviction and what they felt was his "truth." The striking sanitation workers would get what they deserved and so too would they as a people. That WAS more than speech. It WAS action. In Webster's words: "noble, sublime, manly, godlike action." Martin Luther King, you see, was more than just a "dreamer," more than someone who simply walked on troubled waters turning the other cheek. King was America's conscience and a powerful force for change.

In his *Ethics of Rhetoric*, published in 1953 before King became a national figure, Richard Weaver wrote that the discourse of the noble orator is about "real potentiality or possible actuality," whereas that of the "mere exaggerator" is about "unreal potentiality." In his famous "I Have a Dream" speech, King said—remember it was 1963—that he had a dream that the sons of former slaves and former slave owners would be able to sit down together at the table of brotherhood. Unreal potentiality or possible actuality? He said little black boys and black girls would be able to join hands with little white boys and girls and walk together as sisters and brothers. Possible actuality or unreal potentiality? And he said that his four children would one day live in a nation where they would be judged not by the color of their skin but by the content of their character. A dream? Or real vision? And what about "We as a people will get to the promised land"? What about that one? Where are we on that one today? And if we are not where we want to be, whose fault is it? Certainly not Martin Luther King's nor the legitimacy of his vision.

In the last volume of his great trilogy, *America in the King Years*, Taylor Branch begins with the assertion that today "nonviolence is an orphan among democratic ideas." He says, "It has nearly vanished from public discourse even though the basic element—the vote—has no other meaning." In homage to King and for the good of ourselves, Branch strongly suggests that we commit the same time, energy, and resources to the nonviolent means of change as we now commit to the violent ones. "Every ballot is a piece of nonviolence," he says, "signifying hard-won consent to raise politics above fire power and bloody conquest."

It's time to make that ballot the effect of full democratic participation. It's time to reclaim our democratic processes. It's time to make the democratic processes work in America just as we are trying to make them work for Iraq.

That means more than voting. It means informed voting. It means supporting candidates and policies of our choice. It means commitment to the communication processes that give life to democracy. It means thinking of ourselves more as citizens than as just taxpayers. It means full-time citizenship. If campaigns are now permanent, citizenship cannot be cyclical. Democracy and "the vote" will always be open to criticism if people do not vote or do not know what they are voting for.

I don't care how much we spend on voting technology. I don't care how much we restrict campaign contributions. Special interests will always have special influence as long as we the people are not especially interested. Voting two dead people certainly was bad [in a recent local election], but over 90% of live voters staying home was a whole lot worse.

If we work to make the democratic processes work for us at home as well as around the world, we will be on the true path—the nonviolent path—to the kind of homeland security that will keep us moving toward the Promised Land. It is nonviolence that makes civilization civil and it is through the nonviolent participation in democracy that we can live out the true meaning of OUR creed. We will be keeping alive the hope of the American dream of our founding fathers and the real potentiality in the vision of Dr. Martin Luther King Jr.

Nobel Peace Prize Acceptance Speech
ELIE WIESEL

Elie Wiesel delivered the following speech in Oslo, Norway, on December 10, 1986, as he accepted the Nobel Peace Prize. The award recognized his lifelong work for human rights, especially his role as "spiritual archivist of the Holocaust." Wiesel's poetic, intensely personal style as a writer carries over into this ceremonial speech of acceptance. He uses narrative very effectively as he flashes back to what he calls the "kingdom of night" and then flashes forward again into the present. The speech's purpose is to spell out and share the values and concerns of a life committed to the rights of oppressed peoples, in which, as he put it so memorably, "every moment is a moment of grace, every hour an offering."

It is with a profound sense of humility that I accept the honor you have chosen to bestow upon me. I know: your choice transcends me. This both frightens and pleases me.

It frightens me because I wonder: do I have the right to represent the multitudes who have perished? Do I have the right to accept this great honor on their behalf? I do not. That would be presumptuous. No one may speak for the dead, no one may interpret their mutilated dreams and visions.

It pleases me because I may say that this honor belongs to all the survivors and their children, and through us, to the Jewish people with whose destiny I have always been identified.

I remember: it happened yesterday or eternities ago. A young Jewish boy discovering the kingdom of night. I remember his bewilderment, I remember his anguish. It all happened so fast. The ghetto. The deportation. The sealed cattle car. The fiery altar upon which the history of our people and the future of mankind were meant to be sacrificed.

I remember: he asked his father: "Can this be true? This is the 20th century, not the Middle Ages. Who would allow such crimes to be committed? How could the world remain silent?"

And now the boy is turning to me: "Tell me," he asks. "What have you done with your life?"

And I tell him that I have tried. That I have tried to keep memory alive, that I have tried to fight those who would forget. Because if we forget, we are guilty, we are accomplices.

And then I explained to him how naive we were, that the world did know and remain silent. And that is why I swore never to be silent whenever and wherever human beings endure suffering and humiliation. We must always take sides. Neutrality helps the oppressor, never the victim. Silence encourages the tormentor, never the tormented.

Sometimes we must interfere. When human lives are endangered, when human dignity is in jeopardy, national borders and sensitivities become irrelevant. Wherever men or women are persecuted because of their race, religion or political views, that place must—at that moment—become the center of our universe.

Of course, since I am a Jew profoundly rooted in my people's memory and tradition, my first response is to Jewish fears, Jewish needs, Jewish crises. For I belong to a traumatized generation, one that experienced the abandonment and solitude of our people. It would be unnatural for me not to make Jewish priorities my own: Israel, Soviet Jewry, Jews in Arab lands.

But there are others as important to me. Apartheid is, in my view as abhorrent as anti-Semitism. To me, Andrei Sakharov's isolation is as much a disgrace as Iosif Begun's imprisonment. As is the denial of Solidarity and its leader Lech Walesa's right to dissent. And Nelson Mandela's interminable imprisonment.

There is so much injustice and suffering crying out for our attention: victims of hunger, or racism and political persecution, writers and poets, prisoners in so many lands governed by the left and by the right. Human rights are being violated on every continent. More people are oppressed than free.

And then, too, there are the Palestinians to whose plight I am sensitive but whose methods I deplore. Violence and terrorism are not the answer. Something must be done about their suffering, and soon. I trust Israel, for I have faith in the Jewish people. Let Israel be given a chance, let hatred and danger be removed from her horizons, and there will be peace in and around the Holy Land.

Yes, I have the faith. Faith in God and even in His creation. Without it no action would be possible. And action is the only remedy to indifference: the most insidious danger of all. Isn't this the meaning of Alfred Nobel's legacy? Wasn't his fear of war a shield against war?

There is much to be done, there is much that can be done. One person—a Raoul Wallenberg, an Albert Schweitzer, one person of integrity, can make a difference, a difference of life and death. As long as one dissident is in prison, our freedom will not be true. As long as one child is hungry, our lives will be filled with anguish and shame.

What all these victims need above all is to know that they are not alone: that we are not forgetting them, that when their voices are stifled we shall lend them ours, that while their freedom depends on ours, the quality of our freedom depends on theirs.

This is what I say to the young Jewish boy wondering what I have done with his years. It is in his name that I speak to you and that I express to you my deepest gratitude. No one is as capable of gratitude as one who has emerged from the kingdom of night.

We know that every moment is a moment of grace, every hour an offering; not to share them would mean to betray them. Our lives no longer belong to us alone; they belong to all those who need us desperately.

Thank you Chairman Aarvik. Thank you members of the Nobel Committee. Thank you people of Norway, for declaring on this singular occasion that our survival has meaning for mankind.

Reach for the Stars!
ASHLIE McMILLAN

In her speech of tribute to her cousin, Ashlie McMillan, a student at Vanderbilt University, makes use of both identification and magnification, the major techniques of ceremonial speaking. By asking her listeners to imagine themselves as dwarfs, Ashlie develops a narrative based on vicarious experiences.

Please close your eyes. Imagine now that you are shrinking. Can you feel your hands and feet getting smaller, your arms being pulled in closer to your shoulders? Can you picture your legs now dangling off the edge of your seat as your legs shrink up closer to your hips? Now you are only three feet tall. But don't open your eyes yet. This is your first day of being a diastrophic dwarf.

You wake up and get out of bed, which is quite a drop because the bed is almost as tall as you are. You go to the bathroom to wash your face and brush your teeth, but you must stand on a trash can because the faucet is out of your reach. Now you go back to your dorm room, and you're ready to put on your clothes. But again you can't reach the clothes hanging in your closet because you're too short. You have to struggle to get dressed.

Now you have errands that you must run. But how are you going to do them? If you walk, it will take you a long time because you must take many short steps. And you can't drive a car because you can't reach the pedals, much less see over the steering wheel. Finally you get to the bank. But it takes you about five minutes to get the teller's attention because she can't see you below the counter. Next you go to the grocery store. This takes forever because you can't push a cart. You're forced to use a carry basket and to find people who will reach high items for you. Frustrated yet? Okay, open your eyes.

In 1968 my cousin, Tina McMillan, was born. Today she's in her twenty-ninth year as a diastrophic dwarf. What does that mean? It means that she'll never be taller than three feet. It means that her hands will never be able to bend this way [gestures] because she will never have joints in her fingers or toes. She'll always have club feet, and she had to have a rod put in her spine because all diastrophic dwarfs are plagued with scoliosis.

So what does her dwarfism mean to my cousin? Nothing. When you first meet Tina, you might be a little shocked at how tiny she is. But after a while you forget her physical size because her personality is so large and her spirit is so bright. Today I want to tell you the story of how this small person is reaching for the stars. Her life is a miracle that should teach us never to let obstacles stand in the way of our goals and dreams.

When my aunt and uncle were told that they were going to have a baby who was a diastrophic dwarf, they prepared themselves. They were ready to tell their child that she would never be able to have a Great Dane dog because it would be three times the size that she was. That she would never be able to ride a horse. That she would never be able to drive a car. And that she might not be able to attend college because the dormitories and other facilities were not built for people three feet tall.

What my aunt and uncle were *not* prepared for was a child with a physical disability who refused to see herself as disabled. I can tell you that growing up with Tina was quite an experience. She was always the ham of the cousins, always the center of attention. I remember going over to her house and playing with her *three* Great Dane dogs in the backyard. I remember every Sunday when my grandpa would take us out to the farm and we would fight over who got to ride the horses. And Tina would even fight my grandfather so she could get up on the horse all by herself. And I remember the day, some time after her sixteenth birthday, that she slid behind the wheel of a car. She had teamed up with some engineers down in Texas to have the pedals extended as well as hand gears made on the steering wheel so that she could drive herself. But perhaps my proudest and fondest memory was watching my cousin walk across the graduation stage at Texas Christian University in 1991. She not only got her degree in English, but she went on to get a master's degree in anthropology from TCU. After she graduated, the university invited her to come back to teach in the English Department. But by this time Tina had a new challenge: She declined the teaching job so that she could enter politics as campaign manager for the mayor of Dallas.

Tina has never stopped challenging the perception that she is disabled. Next April she will be marrying a person of normal stature, and once again she will defy society's assumption that something must be wrong about such a marriage. And then in the fall she plans on attending the University of Texas law school. Want to bet against her there?

Somehow, against the odds, my cousin has led a normal life. To many people, what she has accomplished might not seem that exceptional. To me, however, she is an inspiration. Whenever I think I've got problems that are too much for me, I think of her and of what she has done, this large and vital person stuffed into such a small body. I think of how she refuses to use her disability as a scapegoat or excuse. And I remember how she does not even consider quitting if something stands in her way. She simply views the obstacle, decides the best way to get around it, and moves on. And although she will lose the ability to walk, probably by the age of forty, I believe that she will still find the way to keep moving toward her goals.

The next time a large obstacle stands in your way, remember Tina, my small cousin, who has achieved such noteworthy things. You too may seem too short to grasp your stars, but you never know how far you might reach if you stand upon a dream.

Glossary

accuracy   Criterion for evaluating the correctness of information by checking it against other information.

acronym   A word composed of the initial letters of a series of words.

ad hominem fallacy   An attempt to discredit a position by attacking the people who favor it.

advocacy Web site   A Web site whose major purpose is to change attitudes or behaviors.

after-dinner speech   A brief, often humorous, ceremonial speech, presented after a meal, that offers a message without asking for radical changes.

agreement   The third stage in the persuasive process, which requires that listeners accept a speaker's recommendations and remember their reasons for doing so.

alliteration   The repetition of initial consonant sounds in closely connected words

amplification   The art of developing ideas by restating them in a speech.

analogical reasoning   Creating a strategic perspective on a subject by relating it to something similar about which the audience has strong feelings.

analogous color scheme   Colors adjacent on the color wheel; used in a presentation aid to suggest both differences and close relationships among the components.

antithesis   A language technique that combines opposing elements in the same sentence or adjoining sentences.

articulation   The manner in which individual speech sounds are produced.

attitude adjustment   Shifting your focus from yourself to your listeners and message.

attitudes   Feelings we have developed toward specific kinds of subjects.

audience   Includes those whom speakers would like to listen, as well as others who actually listen.

audience demographics   Observable characteristics of listeners, including age, gender, educational level, group affiliations, and sociocultural background.

audience dynamics   The motivations, attitudes, beliefs, and values that influence the behavior of listeners.

authority   Criterion for evaluating the credentials of the source of information.

award presentation   A speech of tribute that recognizes achievements of the award recipient, explains the nature of the award, and describes why the recipient qualifies for the award.

awareness   This first stage in the persuasive process includes knowing about a problem and paying attention to it.

balance   Suggests that the introduction, body, and conclusion receive appropriate development.

bar graph   A graph that shows comparisons and contrasts between two or more items or groups.

begging the question   Assuming that an argument has been proved without actually presenting the evidence.

beliefs   What we know or think we know about subjects.

body   That part of a speech where main points are developed and the message is supported.

body language   Communication achieved using facial expressions, eye contact, movements, and gestures.

boomerang effect   A possible negative reaction to a speech that advocates too much change.

brainstorming   Technique that encourages the free play of the mind in finding a topic.

brief example   A concise illustration of a point.

briefing   A short informative presentation offered in an organizational setting that focuses upon plans, policies, or reports.

bulleted list   A presentation aid that highlights ideas by presenting them as a list of brief statements.

categorical design   Arranges the main ideas of a speech by natural or customary divisions.

causation design   Addresses the origins or consequences of a situation or event, proceeding from cause to effect or from effect to cause.

ceremonial speeches (ceremonial speaking)   Speaking that celebrates special occasions, such as speeches of tribute, inspiration, and introduction, eulogies, toasts, award presentations, acceptances, and after-dinner speeches.

chronological design   Explains events or historical developments in the order in which they occurred.

co-active approach   A way of approaching reluctant audiences in which the speaker attempts to establish goodwill, emphasizes shared values, and sets modest goals for persuasion.

cognitive dissonance   The discomfort we feel because of conflict among our attitudes, beliefs, and values.

cognitive restructuring   Replacing negative thoughts with positive, constructive ones.

communication anxiety   Those unpleasant feelings and fears you may experience before or during a presentation.

comparative design   Arranges a speech by exploring the similarities or differences among things, events, and ideas.

competence   The perception of a speaker as being informed, intelligent, and well prepared.

complementary color scheme   Colors opposite one another on the color wheel; used in a presentation aid to suggest tension and opposition.

computer-generated presentation   The use of commercial presentation software to blend audio, visual, textual, graphic, and animated components.

conclusion   Summarizes your message and offers concluding remarks. Meaning drawn from the relationship between the major and minor premises.

confusion of fact and opinion   A misuse of evidence in which personal opinions are offered as though they were facts, or facts are dismissed as though they were opinions.

connotative meaning   The emotional, subjective, personal meaning that certain words can evoke in listeners.

constructive listening   Search for the value that messages may have for your life, despite their defects.

context of interpretation   Helps shape the meaning of a fact by offering a way of looking at it.

contrast   Attracts attention and sharpens perspective by highlighting the differences between opposites.

coordination   The requirement that statements equal in importance be placed on the same level in an outline.

critical listening   Listening for careful appreciation and evaluation of a message.

critique   An evaluation of a speech that emphasizes strengths as well as weaknesses and that focuses on how a speaker might improve.

cultural sensitivity   The respectful appreciation of diversity within an audience.

culturetypes   Terms that express the values and goals of a group's culture.

deductive reasoning   Arguing from a general principle to a specific case.

denotative meaning   The dictionary definition or objective meaning of a word.

dialect   A speech pattern associated with an area of the country or with a cultural or ethnic background.

dialogue   Having the characters in a narrative speak for themselves, rather than paraphrasing what they say.

direct quotation   Repeating the exact words of another to support a point.

discovery phase   Identifying large topic areas that might generate successful speeches.

disinformation   Information that has been fabricated or distorted in order to advance a given agenda.

distance   Principle of proxemics involving the control of the space that separates speaker and audience.

doublespeak   Words that point in the direction opposite from the reality they supposedly describe.

dynamism   The perception of a speaker as confident, decisive, and enthusiastic.

either-or thinking   A fallacy that occurs when a speaker suggests that there are only two options, only one of which is desirable.

elevation   Principle of proxemics dealing with power relationships implied when speakers stand above listeners.

embedded narrative   Stories inserted within speeches that illustrate the speaker's points.

emerging credibility   The changes in the audience's assessment of ethos that occur during your speech.

empathic listening   Phase of listening in which we go beyond rationality to encompassing the human and humane aspects of a message.

enactment   The fourth stage of the persuasive process, in which listeners take appropriate action as the result of agreement.

enduring metaphors   Metaphors of unusual power and popularity that are based on experience that lasts across time and that crosses many cultural boundaries.

enunciation   The manner in which individual words are articulated and pronounced in context.

epilogue   The final part of a narrative that reflects upon its meaning.

ethnocentrism   The tendency of any nation, race, religion, or group to believe that its way of looking at and doing things is right and that other perspectives have less value.

ethos   A form of proof that relies on the audience's perceptions of a speaker's leadership qualities of competence, character, goodwill, and dynamism.

eulogy   A speech of tribute presented upon a person's death.

euphemism   Words that soften or evade the truth of a situation.

evidence   Supporting materials used in persuasive speeches, including facts and figures, examples, narratives, and testimony.

examples   Verbal illustrations of a speaker's points.

expanded conversational style   A presentational quality that, while more formal than everyday conversation, preserves its directness and spontaneity.

expert testimony   Citing the words of people (or institutions) qualified by training or experience to speak as authorities on a subject.

exploration phase   Examining large topic areas to pinpoint more precise speech topics.

extemporaneous presentation   A form of presentation in which a speech is carefully prepared and practiced, but not written out, memorized, or read.

extended example   A more detailed example that speakers develop with their messages.

facts   Statements that can be verified as true or false by independent observers.

factual example   An example based on something that actually happened or really exists.

fallacies   Errors in reasoning that make persuasion unreliable.

faulty analogy   A comparison drawn between things that are dissimilar in some important way.

feedback   Your perception of how audience members react to the message as you speak.

figurative analogy   A comparison drawn from subjects from essentially different fields of experience.

figurative language   Words used in surprising and unusual ways that magnify the power of their meaning.

flawed statistical comparisons   Statistical reasoning that offers fallacious conclusions by comparing unequal or unlike situations.

flip chart   A large, unlined tablet, usually a newsprint pad, that is placed on an easel so that each page can be flipped over the top when is full.

flow chart   A visual method of representing power and responsibility relationships, or describing the steps in a process.

formal outline   Represents the completed plan of your speech, offering an overview of its major components and how they fit together and listing the research sources that support it.

full outline   A full-sentence outline of a speech.

gender stereotyping   Generalizations based on oversimplified or outmoded assumptions about gender roles.

general purpose   The speaker's intention to inform or persuade listeners, or to celebrate some person or occasion.

general search engine   An Internet search engine that allows you to enter a keyword and find related Web sites.

goodwill   The dimension of ethos by which listeners perceive a speaker as having their best interests at heart.

graphics   Visual representations of information, such as sketches, maps, graphs, charts, and textual materials.

great expectation fallacy   The mistaken idea that major change can usually be accomplished by a single persuasive effort.

habitual pitch   The vocal level at which people speak most frequently.

hasty generalization   An error of inductive reasoning in which a claim is made based on insufficient or non-representative information.

hypothetical example   An example not offered as real but as representative of actual people, situations, or events.

identification   The feeling of closeness between speakers and listeners that may overcome personal and cultural differences.

ideographs   Compact expressions of a group's basic political faith.

immediacy   A quality of successful communication achieved when the speaker and audience experience a sense of closeness.

impromptu speaking   Speaking on the spur of the moment in response to an unpredictable situation with limited time for preparation.

inductive reasoning   Reasoning from specific factual instances to reach a general conclusion.

inferences   Assumptions based on incomplete information.

information   Using facts or statistics to support a point.

information cards   Research notes on facts and ideas obtained from an article or book.

information literacy   The skills one needs to locate information efficiently and to evaluate what one learns.

information Web site   A Web site designed to provide factual information on a subject.

informative speaking   Functions to enlighten by sharing ideas and information.

informative value   A measure of how much new and important information or understanding a speech conveys to an audience.

initial credibility   The audience's assessment of your ethos before you begin your speech.

inoculation effect   Preparing an audience for an opposing argument by answering it before listeners have been exposed to it.

integration   Final stage of the persuasive process, in which listeners connect new attitudes and commitments with previous beliefs and values to ensure lasting change.

integrity   The quality of being ethical, honest, and dependable.

intensity   Refers to the extent to which aspects of a speech have the quality of being striking or standing out.

interest chart   Visual display of a speaker's interests, as prompted by probe questions.

interference   Distractions that can disrupt the communication process.

internal summary   A transition that reminds listeners of major points already presented in a speech before proceeding to new ideas.

introduction   That part of your speech that should capture listeners' attention, establish your ethos, and preview your message.

inversion   Changing the normal order of words to make statements memorable.

jargon   Technical language related to a specific field that may be incomprehensible to a general audience.

key-word outline   An abbreviated version of a formal outline that may be used in presenting a speech.

lay testimony   Citing the words or views of everyday people on a subject.

line graph   A visual representation of changes across time; especially useful for indicating trends of growth or decline.

literal analogy   A comparison drawn between subjects from the same field of experience.

logos   A form of proof that appeals to reason based largely on facts and expert testimony presented logically.

magnification   A speaker's selecting and emphasizing certain qualities of a subject to stress the values they represent.

main points   The most prominent ideas of the speaker's message.

major premise   The general principle on which an argument is based.

malapropisms   Language errors that occur when a word is confused with another word that sounds like it.

manipulative persuasion   Persuasion that works through suggestion, colorful images, music, and attractive spokespersons more than through evidence and reasoning. It avoids the ethical burden of justification.

manuscript presentation   A speech read from a prepared text or teleprompter.

master narrative   Form of speaking in which the entire speech becomes a story that reveals some important truth.

master of ceremonies   A person who coordinates an event or program, sets its mood, introduces speakers, and provides transitions.

maxims   Brief and particularly apt sayings.

media and Internet prompts   Sources such as newspapers, magazines, and the electronic media that can suggest ideas for speech topics.

memorized text presentations   Speeches that are committed to memory and delivered word for word.

message   What speakers wish to accomplish.

metaphor   Brief, concentrated form of implied comparison. Often connects subjects that are not usually related in order to create a surprising perspective.

mind mapping   Changes customary patterns of thinking to encourage creative exploration.

minor premise   Relating a specific instance to the general principle that supports an argument.

mirror questions   Questions that repeat part of a previous response to encourage further discussion.

monochromatic color scheme   Use of variations of a single color in a presentation aid to convey the idea of variety within unity.

motivated sequence   Expanded version of the problem-solution design that emphasizes attention, need, solution, visualization, and action steps.

motivation   An energizing psychological dynamic that explains why people behave as they do.

multisided presentation   A speech in which the speaker's position is compared favorably to other positions.

myth of the mean   The deceptive use of statistical averages in speeches.

mythos   A form of proof grounded in the social feelings that connect us powerfully with group traditions, values, legends, and loyalties.

narrative   A story that conveys an idea or establishes a mood.

narrative design   Speech structure that develops a story from beginning to end through a sequence of scenes in which characters interact.

narrative fidelity   The extent to which a narrative "rings true" with the knowledge, interests, and experiences of your listeners.

narrative probability   Measures the skill of the speaker in blending scene, characters, and action into a compelling story.

neologism   An invented word that combines previous words in a striking new expression.

non sequitur fallacy   Occurs when conclusions arise from irrelevant evidence or do not follow from the premises that proceed them.

novelty   The quality of being new or unusual.

objectivity   Criterion for evaluating whether a source is free from bias.

occasion   Why speakers and listeners gather to present and listen to speeches.

omitted qualifier   Fallacy occurs when speakers exaggerate the strength of a claim, confusing probability with certainty.

onomatopoeia   Words that sound like the subjects they signify.

opinions   Expressions of personal attitude or belief offered without supporting material.

optimum pitch   The level at which people can produce their strongest voice with minimal effort and that allows variation up and down the musical scale.

oral citations   References to supporting materials during the speech that strengthen the credibility of the speech and support controversial and surprising claims.

order A consistent pattern used to develop a speech.

parallel construction Wording points in a repeated pattern to emphasize their importance and to show how they are both related and contrasted.

paraphrase Rephrasing or summarizing the words of another to support a point.

pathos Proof relying on appeals to personal feelings.

personal Web site A Web site designed and maintained by an individual.

personification A figure of speech in which nonhuman or abstract subjects are given human qualities.

persuasion The art of gaining fair and favorable consideration for our points of view.

pie graph A circle graph that shows the size of a subject's parts in relation to each other and to the whole.

pitch The position of the human voice on a scale ranging from low and deep to high and shrill.

plagiarism Presenting the ideas and words of others as though they were your own.

plot The body of a speech that follows narrative design; unfolds in a sequence of scenes designed to build suspense.

post hoc fallacy An inductive error in which one event is assumed to be the cause of another simply because the first preceded the second.

predictions Forecasts of what we can expect in the future, often based on trends from past events.

preliminary tuning effect The effect of previous speeches or other situational factors in predisposing an audience to respond positively or negatively to a speech.

PREP formula A technique for making an impromptu speech: state a point, give a reason or example, and restate the point.

presentation Delivering a speech to an audience, integrating the skills of nonverbal communication with the speech content.

presentation aids Visual and auditory illustrations intended to enhance the clarity and effectiveness of a presentation.

prestige testimony Citing the words of a person who is highly admired or respected but not necessarily an expert on your topic; similarly, citing a text in this way.

preview The part of the introduction that identifies the main points to be developed in the body of the speech and presents an overview of the speech to follow.

probes Questions that ask someone being interviewed to elaborate on a response.

problem–solution design A persuasive speech pattern in which listeners are first persuaded that they have a problem and then are shown how to solve it.

prologue An opening that establishes the context and setting of a narrative, foreshadows the meaning, and introduces major characters.

pronunciation The use of correct sounds and of proper stress on syllables when saying words.

proof An array of evidence that drives thoughtful listeners toward a conclusion.

proxemics The study of how human beings use space during communication.

public speaking ethics Standards for judging the rightness or wrongness of public speaking behaviors.

quoting out of context An unethical use of a quotation that changes or distorts its original meaning.

rate The speed at which words are uttered.

reality testing Subjecting negative messages you send yourself to rational scrutiny.

reason from principle Reasoning from shared principles, values, and rules. Sometimes called deductive reasoning.

reasoned persuasion Persuasion built on evidence and reasoning.

reasoning from parallel cases Presenting a similar situation as the basis of an argument. Often called analogical reasoning.

reasoning from reality Emphasis on factual evidence in guiding one's general conclusions and decisions. Often called inductive reasoning.

red herring fallacy The use of irrelevant material to divert attention.

refinement phase Framing the general and specific purposes of a speech topic and a thesis statement.

refutative design A persuasive design in which the speaker defends a disputed claim and attacks the reasoning and evidence of opposing views.

reinforcer   A comment or action that encourages further communication from someone being interviewed.

relevance   Refers to the extent to which a speech relates to an audience's specific needs, interests, or concerns.

reluctant testimony   Invoking the words of sources who appear to speak against their own interests.

reluctant witnesses   Witnesses who testify against their apparent self-interest.

repetition   Repeating sounds, words, or phrases to attract and hold attention.

responsible knowledge   An understanding of the major features, issues, information, latest developments, and local applications relevant to a topic.

retention   The extent to which listeners remember and use a message.

rhetorical questions   Questions that have a self-evident answer, or that provoke curiosity that the speech then proceeds to satisfy.

rhythm   Rate and stress patterns of vocal presentation within a speech.

selective relaxation   Practicing muscle control techniques to help you reduce physical tension by relaxing on cue.

self-awareness inventory   A series of probes that allow speakers to explore their individuality so they can prepare a speech of self-introduction.

sequential design   Explains the orderly steps of a process.

setting   Physical and psychological context in which a speech is presented.

sexism   Allowing gender stereotypes to control interactions with members of the opposite sex.

sexist language   Making gender references in situations in which the gender is unknown or irrelevant, or using masculine nouns or pronouns when the intended reference is to both sexes.

shaky principle fallacy   A reasoning error that occurs when an argument is based on a faulty premise.

simile   A language tool that clarifies something abstract by comparing it with something concrete; usually introduced by "as" or "like."

simplicity   Suggests that a speech has a limited number of main points and that they are short and direct.

slang   The language of the street.

sleeper effect   A delayed reaction to persuasion.

slippery slope fallacy   The assumption that once something happens, an inevitable trend is established that will lead to disastrous results.

source cards   Records kept of the author, title, place and date of publication, and page references for each research source.

source citations   Abbreviated references in a formal outline that show how research supports the points made.

spatial design   Arranges the main points of a speech as they occur in physical space.

speakers   Those who present oral messages for public consumption.

specific purpose   The speaker's particular goal or the response that the speaker wishes to evoke.

speech of acceptance   A ceremonial speech expressing gratitude for an honor and acknowledging those who made the accomplishment possible.

speech of demonstration   An informative speech that shows the audience how to do something or how something works.

speech of description   An informative speech that uses vivid language to illustrate an activity, object, person, or place.

speech of explanation   An informative speech that offers understanding of abstract and complex subjects.

speech of inspiration   A ceremonial speech directed at awakening or reawakening an audience to a goal, purpose, or set of values.

speech of introduction   A ceremonial speech in which a featured speaker is introduced to the audience.

speech of tribute   A ceremonial speech that recognizes the achievements of individuals or groups or commemorates special events.

speeches that address attitudes, beliefs, and values   Speeches designed to modify these elements and help listeners find harmony among them.

speeches that advocate action and policy   Speeches that encourage listeners to change their behavior either as individuals or as members of a group.

speeches that focus on facts   Speeches designed to establish the validity of past or present information or to make predictions about what is likely to occur in the future.

statistics   Facts that are measured mathematically.

statistics   Numerical information.

stereotypes   Generalized pictures of a race, gender, or group that supposedly represent its essential characteristics.

stock issues   The major general questions a reasonable person would ask before agreeing to a change in policies or procedures.

straw man fallacy   Understating, distorting, or otherwise misrepresenting the position of opponents for ease of refutation.

subject directory   An organized list of links to Web sites on specific topics.

subordination   The requirement that material in an outline descend in importance from the general to the specific—from main points to subpoints to sub-subpoints, etc.

subpoints   The major divisions of a speech's main points.

sub-subpoints   Strengthen subpoints by supplying relevant supporting materials.

supporting materials   The facts and figures, testimony, examples, and narratives that are the building blocks of substantive speech-making.

syllogism   Pattern of deductive reasoning as it develops in reasoned persuasion.

symbolic racism   An indirect form of racism that employs code words and subtle, unspoken contrast to suggest that one race is superior to another.

synecdoche   Represents a subject by focusing on a vivid part of it or on something clearly associated with it.

terminal credibility   The audience's assessment of your ethos after you have made a presentation.

testimony   Citing the words of others to support your ideas.

textual graphics   Visuals that contain words, phrases, or numbers.

thesis statement   Summarizes in a single sentence the central idea of your speech.

threshold listening   Phase of listening in which we focus on, understand, and interpret the verbal and nonverbal aspects of messages.

toast   A short speech of tribute, usually offered at celebration dinners or meetings.

topic analysis   Using questions often employed by journalists to explore topic possibilities for speeches (who, what, why, when, where, and how).

topic area inventory chart   A means of determining possible speech topics by listing topics you and your listeners find interesting and matching them.

transitions   Connecting elements that cue listeners that you are finished making one point and are moving on to the next.

trigger words   Words that arouse such powerful feelings that they interfere with the ability to listen critically and constructively.

understanding   This second phase in the persuasive process requires that listeners grasp the meaning of the speaker's message.

universal listeners   Listening as though one represents all who might be affected by a message.

values   The moral principles that suggest how we should behave or what we see as an ideal state of being.

verifier   A statement by an interviewer confirming the meaning of what has just been said by the person being interviewed.

vertical file   A library resource containing local materials.

vicarious experience narrative   Invites listeners to imagine themselves enacting a story.

visualization   Systematically picturing yourself succeeding as a speaker and practicing your speech with that image in mind.

vocal distractions   Filler words such as "er," "um," and "you know" used in the place of a pause.

well-being   A sense of satisfaction with one's life.

working outline   A tentative plan showing the pattern of a speech's major parts, their relative importance, and the way they fit together.

works cited   List that supplies complete relevant information about sources of research actually cited in the speech.

works consulted   List that supplies complete relevant information about all sources of research considered in the preparation of the speech.

Notes

Chapter 1

1. Richard M. Weaver his *Ideas Have Consequences* (Chicago: University of Chicago Press, 1948) and *The Ethics of Rhetoric* (Chicago: Henry Regnery Company, 1953).

2. Press Release, National Association of Colleges and Employers, 15 March 2007, www.naceweb.org/ press/display.asp?year=2007& prid=254 (accessed 7 May 2007).

3. Press Release, National Association of Colleges and Employers, 29 January 2009, www.naceweb.org/ press/display.asp?year= 2009&prid=295 (accessed 22 October 2009).

4. "Employers Complain about Communication Skills," *Pittsburgh Post-Gazette*, 6 February 2005, www.post-gazette.com/pg/pp/05037/453170.stm (accessed 7 May 2007).

5. Jill J. McMillan and Katy J. Harriger, "College Students and Deliberation: A Benchmark Study," *Communication Education* 51 (2002): 237–253.

6. Roderick P. Hart, "Why Communication? Why Education? Toward a Politics of Teaching," *Communication Education* 42 (1993): 101.

7. From Kathleen Peterson, ed., *Statements Supporting Speech Communication* (Annandale, VA.: Speech Communication Association, 1986).

8. Elizabeth Lozano, "The Cultural Experience of Space and Body: A Reading of Latin American and Anglo American Comportment in Public," in *Our Voices: Essays in Culture, Ethnicity, and Communication*, eds. Alberto Gonzalez, Marsha Houston, and Victoria Chen (Los Angeles: Roxbury Publishing, 2004), p. 275.

9. T. Harry Williams, ed., *Abraham Lincoln: Selected Speeches, Messages, and Letters* (New York: Holt, Rinehart and Winston, 1964), p. 148.

10. See the discussion in James A. Herrick, *The History and Theory of Rhetoric: An Introduction*, 3rd ed. (Boston: Allyn & Bacon, 2005).

11. Pericles, "Funeral Oration," in *Thucydides on Justice, Power, and Human Nature*, ed. and trans. Paul Woodruff (Cambridge, MA: Hackett Publishing Company, 1993), p. 42.

12. Michael and Suzanne Osborn, *Alliance for a Better Public Voice: The Communication Discipline and the National Issues Forums* (Dayton, OH: National Issues Forums Institute, 1991).

13. Learn more about this nonpartisan organization at its website http://www.nifi.org/about/index.aspx.

14. Aristotle, *On Rhetoric*, trans. George A. Kennedy (New York: Oxford University Press, 1991).

15. Cicero, *De Oratore*, trans. D. W. Sutton and H. Rackham (Cambridge, MA: Harvard University Press, 1988).

16. Plato, *Gorgias*, trans. Benjamin Jowett, http://philosophy.eserver.org/plato/gorgias.txt (accessed 8 May, 2007).

17. *The Dialogues of Plato*, trans. Benjamin Jowett, in *Great Books of the Western World*, vol. 7 (Chicago: Encyclopaedia Britannica, Inc., 1952). See also the analysis by Richard M. Weaver, "The *Phaedrus* and the Nature of Rhetoric," in *Language Is Sermonic*, eds. Richard L. Johannesen, Rennard Strickland, and Ralph T. Eubanks (Baton Rouge: Louisiana State University Press, 1970), pp. 57–83.

18. *Quintilian, Institutes of Oratory: Education of an Orator* (12 books), trans. John Selby Watson (London: George Bell & Sons, 1892), http://honeyl.public. iastate.edu/quintilian/index.html (accessed 7 May 2007).

19. Michael Scherer and Jay Newton-Small, "Welcome to the Fun House," *Time*, 9 November 2009, pp. 40–41.

20. See especially Burke's discussion of identification and consubstantiality, "The Range of Rhetoric," in *A Rhetoric of Motives* (Berkeley: University of California Press, 1969), pp. 3–43.

21. Martin Luther King, Jr., "I Have a Dream," www.americanrhetoric.com/speeches/mlkihaveadream.htm (accessed 8 May 2007). Copyright 1963 Dr. Martin Luther King Jr., copyright renewed 1991 Coretta Scott King.

22. Credo of Ethical Communications; National Communication Association. Reprinted by permission of the National Communication Association. www.natcom.org.

23. Tom Teepen, "Twisting King's Words to Give His Antagonists Comfort," *Minneapolis Star Tribune*, 14 July 1997, p. 9A.

24. Lawrence M. Hinman, "How to Fight College Cheating," *Washington Post*, 3 Sept. 2004, http://ethics.sandiego.edu/LMH/op-ed/CollegeCheating/index.asp (accessed 29 June 2006).

25. *Spectra*, newsletter of the National Communication Association (Sept. 2008), pp. 28–29.

26. This theme develops in Richard L. Johannesen, *Ethics in Human Communication*, 5th ed. (Long Grove, IL.: Waveland Press, 2002).

Chapter 2

1. Elizabeth Quinn, "Why Do So Many Athletes Have Superstitions and Rituals?" 28 Oct. 2008, http:// sportsmedicine.about.com/od/sportspsychology/a/superstitions.htm (accessed 4 November 2009).

2. Cited in Dave Weiss, "Performance Anxiety—Is It Really a Syndrome?" 6 April 2006, http://www.healthcentral.com/diet-exercise/c/36/1557/anxiety. (Accessed 10 November 2009)

3. "Michael Jackson's Stage Fright!" http://www.waleg.com/celebrities/archives/005799.html. (Accessed 8 November 2009)

4. Simran Khurana, "Elvis Presley Quotes," undated, http://quotations.about.com/od/stillmorefamous people/a/elvispresley1.htm. (Accessed 4 November 2009)

5. Robert L. Leahy, *Cognitive Therapy Techniques* (New York: The Guilford Press, 2003).

6. Harvard University, Public Speaking Home Page, http://gseweb.harvard.edu/~westma/pubspeak.htm/ (accessed 28 July 1999).

7. Robert L. Leahy, *Anxiety Free: Unravel Your Fears Before They Unravel You* (New York: Hay House, 2009), p. 44.

8. H. Dennis Beaver, "Got Stage Fright?" Resource Library, Graduate School of Banking, University of Wisconsin-Madison, www.gsb.org/articles/ Stage_Fright.htm (accessed 15 February 2007).

9. Joe Ayres and Brian L. Heuett, "The Relationship Between Visual Imagery and Public Speaking Apprehension," *Communication Reports* 10 (1997): 87–94.

10. Joe Ayres, "Speech Preparation Processes and Speech Apprehension," *Communication Education* 45 (1996): 228–235.

11. Randolph W. Whitworth and Claudia Cochran, "Evaluation of Integrated Versus Unitary Treatments for Reducing Public Speaking Anxiety," *Communication Education* 45 (1996): 306–314.

Chapter 3

1. James C. McCroskey and Mason J. Teven, "Goodwill: A reexamination of the Construct and Ira Measurement," *Communication Monographs* 66 (1999): 90–103.

2. Kenneth Burke, *A Rhetoric of Motives* (Berkeley: University of California Press, 1969), pp. 20–23.

3. Barack Obama, "Reclaiming the Promise to the People," *Vital Speeches of the Day* 70 (1 Aug. 2004), p. 625.

Chapter 4

1. Tony Hillerman, *Coyote Waits* (New York: Harper Paperbacks, 1990), pp. 176–177.

2. Cited in Clifton Fadiman, ed., *The Little Brown Book of Anecdotes* (Boston: Little Brown, 1985), pp. 475–476.

3. "Listening Skills in Business," *Business Encyclopedia, http://www.answers.com/ topic/listening-skills-in-business* (accessed 13 April 2010).

4. Professor Halley discussed this "Triggering Stimuli Assignment" on the Web site of the International Listening Association in 1998. The article is no longer available online.

Chapter 5

1. *The Rhetoric of Aristotle*, trans. George Kennedy (New York: Oxford University Press 1992), Book 2, Chs. 11–14, pp. 163–169.

2. Richard E. Petty and Duane T. Wegener, "Attitude Change: Multiple Roles for Persuasion Variables," in *Handbook of Social Psychology*, eds. Daniel T. Gilbert, Susan T. Fiske, and Gardener Lindzey, 4th ed., vol. 1 (Boston: McGraw-Hill, 1998), p. 358; Milton Rokeach, *The Open and Closed Mind* (New York: Basic Books, 1960); and T. R. Tyler and R. A. Schuller, "Aging and Attitude Change," *Journal of Personality and Social Psychology* 61 (1991): 689–697.

3. Cited in Allison Adato and Melissa G. Stanton, "If Women Ran America," *Life* (June 1992): 40.

4. "College Degrees by Gender," http://www.realonlinedegrees.com/college-degrees-by-gender, undated (accessed 22 May 2010).

5. John W. Wright, ed., *The New York Times Almanac* (New York: Penguin, 2010), p. 347.

6. K. Stenner, *The Authoritarian Dynamic (New York*: Cambridge University Press, 2005); J. F. Dovido, P. Glick, and L. A. Rudman, eds., *On the Nature of Prejudice: Fifty Years After Allport* (Malden, MA.: Blackwell, 2005).

7. "'Socialism' Not So Negative, 'Capitalism' Not So Positive: A Political Rhetoric Test," http://pewresearch.org/pubs/1583/political-rhetoric-capitalism-socialism-militia-family-values, 4 May 2010 (accessed 20 May 2010).

8. Henry A. Murray, *Explorations in Personality* (New York: Oxford University Press, 1938). Interest in Murray's research continues, and the Radcliffe Institute for Advanced Study maintains a Web site for the Murray Research Center at www.radcliffe.edu/.

9. Abraham H. Maslow, *Motivation and Personality*, 2nd ed. (New York: Harper & Row, 1970).

10. Tom Rath and James K. Harter, *Wellbeing: The Five Essential Elements* (Gallup Organization, 2010).

11. Rushworth M. Kidder, *Shared Values for a Troubled World* (San Francisco: Jossey-Bass, 1994), pp. 1–19. See also the Web site for Kidder's Institute for Global Ethics, www.globalethics.org/ (accessed 20 April 2007).

12. Associated Press, "Gore Promotes Benefits of Good Story-telling," *Memphis Commercial Appeal* (8 Oct. 1995): B2.

13. Humphrey Taylor, "Americans Believe That Over Half the World's Population Speaks English," Harris Poll (Nov. 1998).

Chapter 6

1. Robert J. Kriegel, *If It Ain't Broke … Break It!* (New York: Warner, 1991), pp. 167–168.

2. Cited in Judith Humphrey, "Executive Eloquence: A Sevenfold Path to Inspirational Leadership," *Vital Speeches of the Day* 64 (15 May 1998): 469.

3. The concept of mind mapping takes somewhat different directions in books that develop the technique. See, for example, Joyce Wycoff, Steve Cook, and Michael J. Gelb, *Mindmapping: Your Personal Guide to Exploring Creativity and Problem-Solving* (New York: Berkley Publishing Group, 1991), and Tony Buzan and Barry Buzan, *The Mind Map Book: How to Use Radiant Thinking to Maximize Your Brain's Untapped Potential* (New York: Plume Books, 1996).

4. Corporate mind mappers often refer to this space as "landscape." They think of the central concept as a tree and its associated ideas as "branches."

5. Rudyard Kipling, *Just So Stories* (Garden City, N.Y.: Doubleday, 1921), p. 85.

6. Wayne C. Booth, Gregory G. Colomb, and Joseph M. Williams, *The Craft of Research* (Chicago: University of Chicago Press, 1995), p. 42.

7. Ibid., p. 38.

Chapter 7

1. Association of College and Research Libraries, "Information Literacy," http://www.ala.org/ala/mgrps/divs/acrl/illues/infolit/index.cfm, posted 2010 (accessed 5 June 2010).

2. Sharon A. Weiner, "Information Literacy: A Neglected Core Competency," *EDUCAUSE Quarterly*, Vol. 33, Number 1, 2010 (available online at http://www.eucause.edu/EDUCAUSE+ Quarterly/EDUAUSEQuarterly).

3. Janet E. Alexander and Marsha Ann Tate, *Web Wisdom: How to Evaluate and Create Information Quality on the Web* (Mahwah, NJ: Lawrence Erlbaum, 1999).

Chapter 8

1. Richard Weaver, "Ultimate Terms in Contemporary Rhetoric," in *The Ethics of Rhetoric* (Chicago: Henry Regnery, 1953), pp. 211–232.
2. U.S. Department of Labor, "The Employment Situation – February 2010," 5 Mar. 2010, http://www.bls.gov/news.release/archives/empsit_03052010.pdf (accessed 28 May 2010).
3. Anne P. Mintz (ed.), *Web of Deception: Misinformation on the Internet* (Medford, NJ: CyberAge, 2002), p. 8.
4. William L. Benoit and Kimberly A. Kennedy, "On Reluctant Testimony," *Communication Quarterly* 47 (1999): 376–387.
5. "Kay: No Evidence Iraq Stockpiled WMDs," CNN.com, 26 Jan. 2004, http://www.cnn.com/2004/WORLD/meast/01/25/sprj.nirq.kay (accessed 16 May 2010).
6. Bill Moyers, "Best of Jobs: To Have and Serve the Public's Trust," keynote address at the PBS Annual Meeting, 23 June 1996, reprinted in *Current*, 8 July 1996.
7. Michael Calvin McGee, "In Search of 'The People': A Rhetorical Alternative," *Quarterly Journal of Speech* 61 (1975): 235–249.
8. "Barack Obama's Speech on Race," the *New York Times*, http:// www.nytimes .com/2008/03/18/us// politics/18text-obama.html (accessed 19 March 2008).
9. "To a Higher Level: Barack Obama's Appeal to Reason," *Arkansas Democrat Gazette*, 22 Mar. 2008, p. 10B.
10. "On the Campaign Trail," *Reader's Digest*, March 1992, p. 116.
11. Bono, "Remarks to the 2006 National Prayer Breakfast: February 2, 2006," 15 Mar. 2007, http://usliberals.about.com/od/faithinpubliclife/a/ BonoSermon.htm (accessed 19 May 2007).
12. Jane Goodall, "Dangers to the Environment," *Vital Speeches of the Day*, 15 Nov. 2003, p. 77. Reprinted by permission.
13. Walter R. Fisher, *Human Communication as Narration: Toward a Philosophy of Reason, Value, and Action* (Columbia: University of South Carolina Press, 1987).
14. From Norman Mailer, *The Spooky Art*, excerpted in *Newsweek*, 27 Jan. 2003, p. 64.
15. Dale Bumpers, "Closing Defense Arguments at the Impeachment Trial of William J. Clinton delivered January 21, 1999," transcribed by your authors from the live C-Span broadcast.
16. Fisher, pp. 62–69.

Chapter 9

1. Patricia Kearney, Timothy G. Plax, Ellis R. Hayes, and Marily J. Ivey, "College Teacher Misbehaviors: What Students Don't Like About What Teachers Say and Do," *Communication Quarterly* 39 (1991): 309–324.
2. The concept was introduced in Alan Monroe, *Principles and Types of Speech* (New York: Scott, Foresman, 1935).
3. Cited in Arthur M. Schlesinger Jr., *A Thousand Days: John F. Kennedy in the White House* (Boston: Houghton Mifflin, 1965), p. 733.
4. Full text and video of Martin Luther King Jr.'s "I Have a Dream" are available online at www.americanrhetoric.com. Copyright 1963 Dr. Martin Luther King Jr., copyright renewed 1991 Coretta Scott King.

5. Henri Bergson, *Laughter: An Essay on the Meaning of the Comic*, trans. Cloudsley Brereton and Fred Rothwell (London: MacMillan, 1911), pp. 56.

6. Martin Luther King Jr., "The Drum Major Instinct," *A Knock at Midnight*, ed. Clayborne Carson and Peter Holloran (New York: Warner Books, 2000), pp. 185–86.

7. *MLA Handbook for Writers of Research Papers*, 7th ed. (New York: The Modern Language Association of America, 2009).

Chapter 10

1. Elisabeth Bumiller, "We Have Met the Enemy and He is PowerPoint," *New York Times*, 26 Apr. 2010, http://www.nytimes.com/2010/04/27/world/27powerpoint.html.

2. "Dyslexia," *Black's Medical Dictionary*, 42nd ed., http://ezproxy.lib.davidson.edu:3668/entry/blackmed/dyslexia.

3. Cheryl Hamilton and Cordell Parker, *Communicating for Results*, 6th ed. (Belmont, CA.: Wadsworth, 2001), p. 396.

4. Robert Heinich, Michael Molenda, and James D. Russell, *Instructional Media and the New Technologies of Instruction*, 4th ed. (New York: Macmillan, 1993), p. 66.

5. See the classic study conducted by Wharton Business School's Applied Research Center and the Management Information Services Department of the University of Arizona, cited by Robert L. Lindstrom, "The Presentation Power of Multimedia," *Sales and Marketing Management*, Sept. 1994.

6. Lisa Collier Cool, "Danger in the Dorm," *Family Circle*, 17 Feb. 2004, p. 15.

7. Cited in Laurence J. Peter, *Peter's Quotations: Ideas for Our Time* (New York: Bantam, 1979), p. 478.

8. An excellent resource on understanding, preparing, and using charts and graphs is Gerald Everett Jones, *How to Lie with Charts* (Lincoln, NE: iUniverse, 2000).

9. Our thanks for this example go to Professor Mary Katherine McHenry, Northwest Mississippi Community College, Senatobia, Mississippi.

10. Rebecca Ganzel, "Power Pointless," *Presentations*, February 2000, pp. 53–58.

11. Ricky Telg and Tracy Irani, "Getting the Most Out of PowerPoint," Agricultural Education Magazine, April 2001, p. 11. The Apple version of PowerPoint is Keynote.

12. Dave Paradi, "Results from the 2009 PowerPoint Survey" and "Survey Shows How to Stop Annoying Audience with Bad PowerPoint," www.thinkoutsidetheslide.com/articles/ (17 May 2010 and 14 Mar. 2004).

13. Peter Norvig, "The Gettysburg PowerPoint Presentation" and "The Making of the Gettysburg PowerPoint Presentation," http://norvig.com/Gettysburg/ and http://norvig.com/Gettysburg/making.html (Accessed 18 May 2010).

14. Garr Reynolds, *PresentationZen: Simple Ideas on Presentation Design and Delivery* (Berkeley, CA.: New Riders, 2008), p. 68. See also Reynolds' Web site at http://www.garrreynolds.com/, and William Earnest, *Save Our Slides: PowerPoint Design That Works* (Dubuque, Iowa: Kendall/Hunt, 2007).

15. Farhad Manjoo, "No More Bullet Points, No More Clip Art," 5 May 2010, http://www.slate.com/id/2253050/.

16. Professor Scott Titsworth, Ohio University, CRTNET posting #11325, 10 May 2010. Reprinted by permission of Scott Titsworth, Director of the School of Communication Studies at Ohio University.

17. Alex White, *The Elements of Graphic Design: Space, Unity, Page Architecture, and Type* (New York: Allworth Press, 2002), ix.

18. Gerald Everett Jones, *How to Lie with Charts* (Lincoln, Neb.: iUniverse, 2000).

19. Lee Berton, "Deloitte Wants More Women for Top Posts in Accounting," *Wall Street Journal*, 28 Feb. 1993, p. B1.

20. Cornelia Brunner, "Teaching Visual Literacy," *Electronic Learning* (November–December 1994), p. 16.

21. "NPPA Calls *Newsweek*'s Martha Stewart Cover 'A Major Ethical Breach,'" National Press Photographers Association, 9 March 2005, www.nppa.org/news_and_events/news/2005/03/newsweek.html (accessed 20 May 2010).

22. Gloria Borger, "The Story the Pictures Didn't Tell," *U.S. News & World Report*, 22 Feb. 1993, pp. 6–7; and John Leo, "Lapse or TV News Preview?" *Washington Times*, 3 Mar. 1993, p. G3.

Chapter 11

1. William Raspberry, "Any Candidate Will Drink to That," *Austin American Statesman*, 11 May 1984, p. A–10.

2. Ollie Reed, "Corsicans, Navajo Weave Ties," Scripps Howard News Service, 3 July 2001. *Commercial Appeal (Memphis)*, www.gomemphis.com (accessed 5 July 2001).

3. Among the most recent of these studies is that reported by Peter A. Andersen and Tammy R. Blackburn, "An Experimental Study of Language Intensity and Response Rate in E-Mail Surveys," *Communication Reports* 17 (no. 2) Summer 2004, pp. 73–82.

4. Jerry Tarver, "Words in Time: Some Reflections on the Language of Speech," *Vital Speeches of the Day*, 15 Apr. 1988, p. 410.

5. These powers of language were first explored in Michael Osborn, *Orientations to Rhetorical Style* (Chicago: Science Research Associates, 1976), and are developed further in Michael Osborn, "Rhetorical Depiction," in *Form, Genre, and the Study of Political Discourse*, eds. Herbert W. Simons and Aram A. Aghazarian (Columbia: University of South Carolina Press, 1986), pp. 79–107.

6. 5 Apr. 1996, http://www.v-j-enterprises.com/astro2.html (accessed 17 June 2008).

7. Based on the account in Claire Perkins, "The Many Symbolic Faces of Fred Smith: Charismatic Leadership in the Bureaucracy," *Journal of the Tennessee Speech Communication Association* 11 (1985): 22.

8. Adapted from *The American Heritage Dictionary*, 2nd ed. (Boston: Houghton Mifflin, 1985), p. 92.

9. Speech on Race, presented March 18, 2008, in Philadelphia, PA, http://www.nytimes.com/ 2008/03/18/us/politics/18text-obama.html?ei=5087&em=&en=ee.

10. Nikki Giovanni, "We Are Virginia Tech," 17 April 2007, www.americanrhetoric.com/speeches/nikkigiovannivatech-memorial.htm (accessed 14 May 2007). © 2007 Nikki Giovanni. Reprinted by permission.

11. Listeners whose lives seem dull and unrewarding are especially susceptible to such dramas. See the discussion in Eric Hoffer, *The True Believer: Thoughts on the Nature of Mass Movements* (New York: Harper, 1951).

12. Ronald Reagan, "Second Inaugural Address," *Vital Speeches of the Day*, 51 (1 Feb. 1985): 226–228.

13. AOL News, 13 June 2008, http://news.aol.com/story/ _a/flood-puts-city-at-gods-mercy/ 20080612191009990001.

14. "TennCare Offset Fee Gets Backing," *The Memphis Commercial Appeal*, 12 March 2010, p. C1.

15. "Presidential Ecospeak," *New York Times*, Editorials/Op-Ed, 18 Oct. 2003, www.truthout.org/cgi-bin/artman/exec/view.cgi/15/2355 (accessed 29 Oct. 2003). From *The New York Times*, © October 18, 2003, The New York Times. All rights reserved. Used by permission and protected by the copyright laws of the United States. The printing, copying, redistribution, or retransmission of the material without express written permission is prohibited.

16. Bill Gates, "High Schools Are Obsolete: Teaching Kids What They Need to Know," *Vital Speeches of the Day* 71 (15 April 2005): 396–397.

17. "Malapropisms Live!" *Spectra*, May 1986, p. 6.

18. Haven E. Cockerham, "Conquer the Isms That Stand in Our Way," *Vital Speeches of the Day*, 1 Feb. 1998, p. 240.

19. "Swim Club President Apologizes, NBC Philadelphia, 10 July 2009 http://www.nbcphiladelphia.com/news/local-beat/Swim-Club-President-Apologizes-About-Pool (accessed 15 March 2010).

20. Antoinette M. Bailey, "Bow Wave," *Vital Speeches of the Day*, 1 June 2001, p. 502.

21. Memphis *Commercial Appeal*, 26 January 2010, p. A9.

22. For additional discussion of such metaphors, see Michael Osborn, "Archetypal Metaphor in Rhetoric: The Light-Dark Family," *Quarterly Journal of Speech* 53 (1967): 115–126, and "The Evolution of the Archetypal Sea in Rhetoric and Poetic," *Quarterly Journal of Speech* 63 (1977): 347–363.

23. George W. Bush, "Inaugural Address," *Vital Speeches of the Day*, 1 Feb. 2001, p. 226.

24. See another side of this image in J. Vernon Jensen, "British Voices on the Eve of the American Revolution: Trapped by the Family Metaphor," *Quarterly Journal of Speech* 63 (1977): 43–50.

25. Barack Obama's Speech on Race, http://www.npr.org/templates/story/story .php?storyId=8847867

26. For an insightful discussion of the metaphors we use to construct our ideas about illness, see Susan Sontag, *Illness as Metaphor* (New York: Vintage Books, 1979), and *AIDS and Its Metaphors* (New York: Farrar, Straus and Giroux, 1988).

27. See Robert Ivie, "Images of Savagery in American Justifications for War," *Communication Monographs* 47 (1980): 279–294.

28. Michael Osborn, "Patterns of Metaphor Among Early Feminist Orators," in *Rhetoric and Community: Studies in Unity and Fragmentation*, ed. J. Michael Hogan (Columbia: University of South Carolina Press, 1998), pp. 10–11.

29. Quoted from Dr. Seuss [Theodore Seuss Geisel], "How Orlo Got His Book," *The New York Times Book Review*, 17 Nov. 1957.

30. Wendi C. Thomas, "Spaced Out on Budget Priorities," *The Memphis Commercial Appeal*, 1 Jan. 2004, A1. (accessed 22 Jan. 2004).

31. Michael Calvin McGee, "The Origins of Liberty: A Feminization of Power," *Communication Monographs* 47 (1980): 27–45.

32. Osborn, *Orientations to Rhetorical Style*, p. 16.

33. Richard Weaver, "Ultimate Terms in Contemporary Rhetoric," in *The Ethics of Rhetoric* (Chicago: Henry Regnery, 1953), pp. 211–232.

34. Michael Calvin McGee, "The Ideograph: A Link Between Rhetoric and Ideology," *Quarterly Journal of Speech* 66 (1980): 1–16.
35. This example is adapted from Ronald H. Carpenter, *Choosing Powerful Words: Eloquence That Works* (Boston: Allyn & Bacon, 1999), pp. 14–15.
36. Bill Moyers, "Pass the Bread," a baccalaureate address presented at Hamilton College, May 20, 2006.

Chapter 12

1. Richard Conniff, "Reading Faces," *Smithsonian* 34 (January 2004): 49.
2. Quoted in Conniff, p. 47.
3. James C. McCroskey, *An Introduction to Rhetorical Communication*, 9th ed. (Boston: Allyn & Bacon, 2006).
4. Virginia P. Richmond and James C. McCroskey, *Nonverbal Behavior in Interpersonal Relations*, 5th ed. (Boston: Allyn & Bacon, 2004).
5. Howard Giles and Arlene Franklyn-Stokes, "Communicator Characteristics," in *Handbook of International and Intercultural Communication*, ed. Molefi Kete Asante and William B. Gudykunst (Newbury Park, CA: Sage, 1989), pp. 117–144.
6. Jon Eisenson with Arthur M. Eisenson, *Voice and Diction: A Program for Improvement*, 7th ed. (Boston: Allyn & Bacon, 1996).
7. Adapted from Stuart W. Hyde, *Television and Radio Announcing*, 10th ed. (Boston: Houghton Mifflin, 2003).
8. N. Scott Momaday, *The Way to Rainy Mountain* (Albuquerque: University of New Mexico Press, 1969), p. 5.
9. Carole Douglis, "The Beat Goes On: Social Rhythms Underlie All Our Speech and Actions," *Psychology Today*, November 1987, pp. 36–41.
10. William Price Fox, "Eugene Talmadge and Sears Roebuck Co.," in *Southern Fried Plus Six* (New York: Ballantine Books, 1968), p. 36.
11. Michael L. Hecht, Peter A. Andersen, and Sidney A. Ribeau, "The Cultural Dimensions of Nonverbal Communication," in *Handbook of International and Intercultural Communication*, ed. Molefi Kete Asante and William B. Gudykunst (Newbury Park, CA: Sage, 1989), pp. 163–185; Larry A. Samovar, Richard E. Porter, and Edwin R. McDaniel, *Communication Between Cultures*, 6th ed., Wadsworth Series in Communication Studies (2007).
12. Ralph Hillman, *Delivering Dynamic Presentations: Using Your Voice and Body for Impact* (Boston: Allyn & Bacon, 1999).
13. Betty Ren Wright, *Johnny Go Round* (NY: Tell a Tale Books, 1960) pp. 1–3.
14. *NBC Handbook of Pronunciation*, 4th ed. (New York: Harper, 1991).
15. William B. Gudykunst et al., "Language and Intergroup Communication," in *Handbook of International and Intercultural Communication*, ed. Molefi Kete Asante and William B. Gudykunst (Newbury Park, CA.: Sage, 1989), pp. 145–162.
16. Carolanne Griffith-Roberts, "Let's Talk Southern," *Southern Living*, February 1995, p. 82.
17. "Jeff Foxworthy: From Hootenanny to Hoosier," *Satellite TV Week*, 28 July–3 August 1996, p. l.
18. Samovar, Porter, and McDaniel, p. 177.
19. See Erving Goffman's discussion in *The Presentation of Self in Everyday Life* (London: The Penguin Press, 1969), pp. 1–14.

20. Peter A. Andersen, "Nonverbal Immediacy in Interpersonal Communication," in *Multichannel Integrations of Nonverbal Behavior*, ed. A. W. Siegman and S. Feldstein (Mahwah, NJ: Erlbaum, 1985).

21. Mark L. Knapp and Judith A. Hall, *Nonverbal Communication in Human Interaction*, 5th ed. (Belmont, CA: Wadsworth, 2002), p. 365.

22. Research psychologist Carolyn Copper has found that newscasters influence voters when they smile while speaking of candidates, further evidence of the power of facial expression ("A Certain Smile," *Psychology Today*, January–February 1992, p. 20).

23. Timothy Gura and Charlotte Lee, *Oral Interpretation*, 11th ed. (Boston: Houghton Mifflin, 2005).

24. Edouard Gasarabwe-Laroche, "Meaningful Gestures: Nonverbal Communication in Rwandan Culture," *UNESCO Courier*, September 1993, pp. 31–33.

25. The literature supporting this conclusion is reviewed by Virginia Kidd, "Do Clothes Make the Officer? How Uniforms Impact Communication: A Review of Literature," presented at the Visual Communication Conference at Pray, Montana, 8 July 2000.

26. Goffman, p. 21.

27. D. T. Max, "The Making of the Speech," *New York Times*, 7 Oct. 2001, http://select.nytimes.com/search/restricted/article?res=F40714FF39590C748CDDA90994 (accessed 18 May 2007).

28. David E. Sanger and Don Van Natta, Jr., "After the Attacks: The Events; In Four Days, a National Crisis Changes Bush's Presidency," *New York Times*, 16 Sept. 2001, p. 7, http://select.nytimes.com/search/restricted/article?res=F30714F63D5F0C758DDDA00894 (accessed 19 May 2007).

29. "Remarks to Police, Firemen, and Rescueworkers at the World Trade Center Site in New York City," *2001 Presidential Documents Online*, 14 Sept. 2001, http://frwebgate3.access.gpo.gov/cgi-bin/waisgate.cgi?WAISdocID=54051314900+24+0+ (accessed 18 May 2007).

30. Ken Ringle, "George Bush and the Words of War," *The Washington Post*, 9 Mar. 2003, http://pqasb.pqarchiver.com/washingtonpost/access/303554101.html?dids=303554101:303 (accessed 18 May 2007).

31. These guidelines for handling questions and answers are a compendium of ideas from the following sources: Stephen D. Body, "Nine Steps to a Successful Question-and-Answer Session," *Management Solutions*, May 1988, pp. 16–17; Teresa Brady, "Fielding Abrasive Questions During Presentations," *Supervisory Management*, February 1993, p. 6; J. Donald Ragsdale and Alan L. Mikels, "Effects of Question Periods on a Speaker's Credibility with a Television Audience," *Southern States Communication Journal* 40 (1975): 302–312; Dorothy Sarnoff, *Never Be Nervous Again* (New York: Ballantine, 1987); Laurie Schloff and Marcia Yudkin, *Smart Speaking: Sixty-Second Strategies* (New York: Holt, 1991); and Alan Zaremba, "Q and A: The Other Part of Your Presentation," *Management World*, January–February 1989, pp. 8–10.

32. Matthew Hutson, "How to Dodge a Question," *Psychology Today*, October 2009, p. 24.

33. "South Carolina Democratic Debate transcript," MSNBC, p. 7, 27 April 2007, www.msnbc.msn.com/id/18352397 (accessed 20 May 2007).

34. Adam Nagourney and Jeff Zeleny, "In Mostly Sedate Debate, Democrats Show More Unity than Strife," *New York Times*, 27 April 2007,

http://query.nytimes.com/gst/fullpage.html?res=9400E7DD123EF934A15
757C0A9619C8 (accessed 19 May 2007).

35. Commentaries, "Hardball with Chris Matthews," CNBC, April 27, 2007.

36. "Remarks by the President at GOP House Issues Conference," 29 Jan. 2010,
http://www.whitehouse.gov/the-press-office/remarks-president-gop-house-
issues-conference (accessed 21 Feb. 2010).

37. The authors are indebted to Professor Roxanne Gee of the television and
film area in the Department of Communication at the University of
Memphis for her assistance and suggestions in putting together this advice.

38. Illustrations of major video hand signals may be found in Stuart W. Hyde,
Television and Radio Announcing, 10th ed. (Boston: Houghton Mifflin, 2003).

39. Ralph R. Behnke and Chris R. Sawyer, "Public Speaking Procrastination as a
Correlate of Public Speaking Communication Apprehension and Self-
Perceived Public Speaking Competence," *Communication Research Reports* 16
(1999): 40–47.

40. Tony E. Smith and Ann Bainbridge Frymier, "Get 'Real': Does Practicing
Speeches Before an Audience Improve Performance?" *Communication
Quarterly* 54 (2006): 113.

41. Judith Humphrey, "Taking the Stage," *Vital Speeches of the Day*, 1 May 2001,
pp. 435–438.

42. Ibid., p. 436.

Chapter 13

1. Katherine E. Rowan, "Goals, Obstacles, and Strategies in Risk Communication:
A Problem-Solving Approach to Improving Communication About Risks,"
Journal of Applied Communication Research 19 (1991): 314.

2. Ibid.

3. Martin Luther King Jr., "I've Been to the Mountaintop," *americanrhetoric.com*,
2001–2010. 10 May 2010.

4. Paul Ashdown, "From Wild West to Wild Web," *Vital Speeches of the Day*,
1 Sept. 2000, pp. 699–701.

5. Paul R. Gamble and Clare E. Kelliher, "Imparting Information and Influencing Behavior: An Examination of Staff Briefing Sessions," *Journal of
Business Communication* (July 1999): 261.

6. Ancil B. Sparks and Dennis D. Staszak, "Fine Tuning Your News Briefing:
Law Enforcement Agency Media Relations," *FBI Law Enforcement Bulletin*
(December 2000): 22.

7. Howard Gardner, *Changing Minds: The Art and Science of Changing Our Own
and Other People's Minds* (Cambridge, MA: Harvard Business School
Publishing, 2006).

8. Representative is Timothy J. Koegel, *The Exceptional Presenter* (Austin, TX:
Greenleaf Book Group Press, 2007).

Chapter 14

1. Mark A. Hamilton and John E. Hunter, "The Effect of Language Intensity on
Receiver Attitudes Toward Message, Source, and Topic," in *Persuasion:
Advances Through Meta-Analysis*, eds. M. Allen and R. W. Preiss (Beverly Hills,
CA: Sage, 1998).

2. This speech is made available in English translation by the Perseus Digital Library, sponsored by Tufts University, www.perseus.tufts.edu/cgi-bin/ptext?doc=Perseus:text1999.02.0020:text=Cael.:section=1.

3. For a different view, which depicts persuasion in terms of manipulation and domination, see Sonja K. Foss and Cindy L. Griffin, "Beyond Persuasion: A Proposal for an Invitational Rhetoric," *Communication Monographs* 62 (1995): 2–18.

4. William J. McGuire, "Attitudes and Attitude Change," in *The Handbook of Social Psychology*, eds. Gardner Lindzey and Elliot Aronson (New York: Random House, 1985), vol. 1, pp. 258–261.

5. Roger Brown, *Social Psychology: The Second Edition* (New York: Free Press, 1986).

6. Gloria Steinem, *Revolution from Within: A Book of Self-Esteem* (New York: Little, Brown, 1992), p. 120.

7. Adapted from Herbert W. Simons, *Persuasion in Society* (Thousand Oaks, CA: Sage, 2001).

8. Larry Tracy, "Taming Hostile Audiences: Persuading Those Who Would Rather Jeer than Cheer," *Vital Speeches of the Day*, 1 Mar. 2005, p. 311.

9. Charlton Heston, "Winning the Cultural War," *Vital Speeches of the Day*, 1 Apr. 1999, pp. 357–359.

10. N. H. Anderson, "Integration Theory and Attitude Change," *Psychological Review* 78 (1971): 171–206.

11. McGuire, p. 260.

12. Joshua A. Compton and Michael W. Pfau, "Inoculation Theory of Resistance to Influence at Maturity," *Communication Yearbook 29*, ed. P. J. Kalbfleisch (Mahwah, NJ: Lawrence Erlbaum, 2005), pp. 97–145.

13. Mike Allen and James B. Stiff, "Testing Three Models for the Sleeper Effect," *Western Journal of Speech Communication* 53 (1989): 411–426; and T. D. Cook et al., "History of the Sleeper Effect: Some Logical Pitfalls in Accepting the Null Hypothesis," *Psychological Bulletin* 86 (1979): 662–679.

14. M. E. McCombs, "The Agenda-Setting Approach," in *Handbook of Political Communication*, eds. D. D. Nimmo and K. R. Sanders (Beverly Hills, CA: Sage, 1981), pp. 121–140.

15. As recounted in Diane M. Martin, "Balancing on the Political High Wire: The Role of Humor in the Rhetoric of Ann Richards," *Southern Communication Journal* 69 (2004): 278.

16. Franklin J. Boster and Paul Mongeau, "Fear-Arousing Persuasive Messages," in *Communication Yearbook 8*, ed. R. Bostrom (Beverly Hills, CA: Sage, 1984), pp. 330–377; and Richard E. Petty and Duane T. Wegener, "Attitude Change: Multiple Roles for Persuasion Variables," in *The Handbook of Social Psychology*, eds. Daniel T. Gilbert, Susan T. Fiske, and Gardner Lindzey, 4th ed. (Boston: McGraw-Hill, 1998), pp. 353–354.

17. Katherine E. Rowan, "Goals, Obstacles, and Strategies in Risk Communication: A Problem-Solving Approach to Improving Communication About Risks," *Journal of Applied Communication Research* 19 (1991): 322.

18. Steve Hargreaves, "Exxon Linked to Climate Change Pay Out," *Fortune (CNN.Money)*, 2 Feb. 2007 http://money.cnn.com/2007/02/02/news/companies/exxon_science/index.htm?cnn=yes (accessed 23 May 2007).

19. Adapted from Richard L. Johannesen, Kathleen S. Valde, and Karen E. Whedbee, *Ethics in Communication*, 6th ed. (Prospect Heights, IL: Waveland, 2007).

20. The motivated sequence design was introduced in Alan Monroe's *Principles and Types of Speech* (New York: Scott, Foresman, 1935) and has been refined in later editions.

21. The structure of the stock issues design has been adapted from Charles U. Larson, *Persuasion: Reception and Responsibility*, 12th ed. (Belmont, CA: Wadsworth, 2010), and Charles S. Mudd and Malcolm O. Sillars, *Public Speaking: Content and Communication* (Prospect Heights, IL: Waveland, 1991), pp. 100–102.

Chapter 15

1. Al Gore, *The Assault on Reason* (New York: Penguin Press, 2007), pp. 245–246.

2. Franklin J. Boster et al., "The Persuasive Effects of Statistical Evidence in the Presence of Exemplars," *Communication Studies* 51 (2000): 296–306.

3. M. Sean Limon and Dean C. Kazoleas, "A Comparison of Exemplar and Statistical Evidence in Reducing Counter-Arguments and Responses to a Message," *Communication Research Reports* 21 (2004): 291–298.

4. Thomas Hugh Feeley, Heather M. Marshall, and Amber M. Reinhart, "Reactions to Narrative and Statistical Written Messages Promoting Organ Donation," *Communication Reports* 10 (2006): 89–100.

5. Limon and Kazoleas, 291–298.

6. Shelly Chaiken, Wendy Wood, and Alice H. Eagly, "Principles of Persuasion," in *Social Psychology: Handbook of Basic Principles*, eds. E. Tory Higgins and Arie W. Kruglanki (New York: Guilford, 1996), pp. 702–742.

7. Representative of this scholarship is Ernest G. Bormann, "Fantasy and Rhetorical Vision: The Rhetorical Criticism of Social Reality," *Quarterly Journal of Speech* 58 (1972): 396–407; Walter F. Fisher, "Narration as a Human Communication Paradigm: The Case of Public Moral Argument," *Communication Monographs* 51 (1984); 1–22; Michael C. McGee, "In Search of 'The People': A Rhetorical Alternative," *Quarterly Journal of Speech* 61 (1975): 235–249; Michael Osborn, "Rhetorical Depiction," in *Form, Genre and the Study of Political Discourse*, eds. Herbert W. Simons and Aram A. Aghazarian (Columbia: University of South Carolina Press, 1986), pp. 79–107; and Janice Hocker Rushing, "The Rhetoric of the American Western Myth," *Communication Monographs* 50 (1983): 14–32.

8. The discussion that follows is based on James C. McCroskey, *An Introduction to Rhetorical Communication*, 9th ed. (Boston: Allyn & Bacon, 2006). We use the term *emerging credibility* in place of McCroskey's *derived credibility* to emphasize the dynamic, interactive nature of the process.

9. Peter A. Andersen and Tammy R. Blackburn, "An Experimental Study of Language Intensity and Response Rate in E-Mail Surveys," *Communication Reports* 17 (2004): 73–82.

10. Antonio R. Damasio, *Descartes' Error: Emotion, Reason, and the Human Brain* (New York: Putnam, 1994).

11. From a brochure distributed by Handgun Control, Inc., 1990.

12. Martha Solomon, "The 'Positive Woman's' Journey: A Mythic Analysis of the Rhetoric of STOP ERA," *Quarterly Journal of Speech* 65 (1979): 262–274.

13. Rushing, pp. 14–32.

14. Roderick P. Hart, *The Political Pulpit* (West Lafayette, IN: Purdue University Press, 1977).

15. John Fitzgerald Kennedy, "Acceptance Address, 1960," in *The Great Society: A Sourcebook of Speeches*, ed. Glenn R. Capp (Belmont, CA: Dickenson 1969), p. 14.

16. Richard M. Weaver, "Ultimate Terms in Contemporary Rhetoric," in *Language is Sermonic: Richard M. Weaver on the Nature of Rhetoric*, eds. Richard L. Johannesen, Rennard Strickland, and Ralph T. Eubanks (Baton Rouge: Louisiana State University Press, 1970), pp. 92–93.

17. Richard F. Corlin, "The Secrets of Gun Violence in America," *Vital Speeches of the Day*, 1 Aug. 2001, p. 611. Reprinted by permission of Richard Corlin.

18. Lisa M. Ross, "Buckley Says Drug Attack Won't Work," *Commercial Appeal (Memphis)*, 14 Sept. 1989, p. B2.

19. Mortimer B. Zuckerman, "The Enemy Within," *U.S. News & World Report*, 11 Sept. 1989, p. 91.

20. Gilbert Cranberg, "Even Sensible Iowa Bows to the Religious Right," *Los Angeles Times*, 17 Aug. 1992, p. B5.

21. "False 'Death Panel' Rumor Has Some Familiar Roots," *The New York Times*, http://www.nytimes.com/2009/08/14/health/policy/14panel.html (accessed 15 Mar. 2010).

22. George Orwell, *Shooting an Elephant and Other Essays* (London: Secker and Warburg, 1950), p. 97.

23. Gail Collins, "Clearing the Ayers," the *New York Times*, http://www.nytimes.com/2008/10/09/ opinion/09collins.html?hp=&pagewanted=print (accessed 15 Mar. 2010). From *The New York Times*, © October 8, 2008, The New York Times. All rights reserved. Used by permission and protected by the copyright laws of the United States. The printing, copying,redistribution, or retransmission of the material without express written permission is prohibited.

24. Michael M. Osborn, "The Abuses of Argument," *Southern Speech Communication Journal* 49 (1983): 1–11.

25. http://www.readersread.com/blog/11100401 (accessed 21 May 2010).

26. *Commercial Appeal (Memphis)*, 6 Sept. 1996, p. C1.

27. Bruce Felton, *What Were They Thinking? Really Bad Ideas throughout History* (Guilford, CT: Globe Pequot Press, 2003), p. 180.

Chapter 16

1. Celeste Michelle Condit, "The Functions of Epideictic: The Boston Massacre Orations as Exemplar," *Communication Quarterly* 33 (1985): 284–299; Gray Matthews, "Epideictic Rhetoric and Baseball: Nurturing Community Through Controversy," *Southern Communication Journal* 60 (1995): 275–291; Randall Parrish Osborn, "Jimmy Carter's Rhetorical Campaign for the Presidency: An Epideictic of American Renewal," Southern States Communication

Association Convention, Memphis, March 1996; Ch. Perelman and L. Olbrechts-Tyteca, *The New Rhetoric: A Treatise on Argumentation* (South Bend, IN: University of Notre Dame Press, 1971), pp. 47–54; and Richard M. Weaver, *The Ethics of Rhetoric* (Chicago: Henry Regnery, 1953), pp. 164–185.

2. John Dewey, *Democracy and Education* (New York: Macmillan, 1916), p. 4.

3. James W. Carey, "A Cultural Approach to Communication," *Communication* 2 (1975): 6.

4. See Burke's discussion in "The Range of Rhetoric," in *A Rhetoric of Motives* (Berkeley and Los Angeles: University of California Press, 1969), pp. 3–43.

5. Walter R. Fisher, *Human Communication as Narration: Toward a Philosophy of Reason, Value, and Action* (Columbia: University of South Carolina Press, 1989).

6. *Selected Speeches and Writings by Abraham Lincoln* (New York: Vintage Books, 1992), p. 405.

7. See the discussion in *The Rhetoric of Aristotle*, trans. Lane Cooper (New York: Appleton-Century-Crofts, 1932), I.7, I.9, l.14 (pp. 34–44, 46–55, 78–79).

8. The Nobel Peace Prize 1986. Presentation speech by Egil Aarvik, *www.pbs. org/eliewiesel/nobel/presentation.html*.

9. *Congressional Record*, 1 Apr. 1980, pp. 7459–7460.

10. Owen Edwards, "What Every Man Should Know: How to Make a Toast," *Esquire*, January 1984, p. 37.

11. The advice that follows is adapted from Jacob M. Braude, *Complete Speaker's and Toastmaster's Library: Definitions and Toasts* (Englewood Cliffs, NJ: Prentice Hall, 1965), pp. 88–123; and Wendy Lin, "Let's Lift a Glass, Say a Few Words, and Toast 1996," *Commercial Appeal (Memphis)*, 28 Dec. 1995, p. C3.

12. Elie Wiesel, "Nobel Peace Prize Acceptance Speech," *New York Times*, 11 Dec. 1986, p. A8.

13. *Commercial Appeal (Memphis)*, 23 Oct. 1995, p. D2.

14. Frank Dobie, "The Conservatism of Charles M. Russell," in *Charlie Russell Roundup: Essays on America's Favorite Cowboy Artist*, ed. Brian Dippie (Helena: Montana Historical Society Press, 1999), p. 256.

15. Sheila W. Welling, "Working Women: A Century of Change," *Vital Speeches of the Day*, 15 June 1995, pp. 516–517.

16. *Congressional Record*, 1 Apr. 1980, p. 7249.

17. Ibid., p. 7248.

18. Roger Ailes, *You Are the Message* (New York: Doubleday, 1988), pp. 71–74.

19. Diane M. Martin, "Balancing on the Political High Wire: The Role of Humor in the Rhetoric of Ann Richards," *Southern Communication Journal* 69 (2004): 273–288.

20. For more on the social function of laughter, see Henri Bergson, *Laughter: An Essay on the Meaning of the Comic*, trans. Cloudsley Brereton and Fred Rothwell (London: Macmillan, 1911).

21. Robert M. Kaplan and Gregory C. Pascoe, "Humorous Lectures and Humorous Examples: Some Effects upon Comprehension and Retention," *Journal of Educational Psychology* 69 (1977): 61–65.

22. Dick Jackman, "Awards Dinner of the National Football Foundation and the Hall of Fame," *Harper's Magazine*, March 1985.

23. Charles R. Gruner, "Advice to the Beginning Speaker on Using Humor—What the Research Tells Us," *Communication Education* 34 (1985): 142–147; and Christie McGuffee Smith and Larry Powell, "The Use of Disparaging Humor by Group Leaders," *Southern Speech Communication Journal* 53 (1988): 279–292.

24. "President Bush Attends Radio and Television Correspondents' Annual Dinner," 28 March 2007, www.whitehouse.gov/news/releases/2007/03/20070328–6.html (accessed 23 May 2007).

25. *Washington Post*, 12 Dec. 1978.

26. Adapted from Joan Detz, *Can You Say a Few Words?* (New York: St. Martins, 1991), pp. 77–78.

27. Ronald Reagan, "Second Inauguration Address," *Vital Speeches of the Day* 51 (1 Feb. 1985): 226–228.

Appendix A

1. Adapted from Marc Hequet, "The Fine Art of Multicultural Meetings," *Training* (July 1993): 29–33.

2. For additional insights on groupthink, see the following articles: Judith Chapman, "Anxiety and Defective Decision Making: An Elaboration of the Groupthink Model," *Management Decision*, 2006, vol. 44, 1391–1404; Jack Eaton, "Management Communication: The Threat of Groupthink," *Corporate Communications*, 2001, vol. 6, 183–192; and Steve A. Yetiv, "Groupthink and the Gulf Crisis," *British Journal of Political Science*, 2003, v. 33, 419–442.

3. For more information on face-to-face brainstorming see J. M. Hender, et.al., "Improving Group Creativity: Brainstorming versus Non-brainstorming Techniques in a GSS Environment,"*Proceedings of the 24th Annual Hawaii International Conference on System Sciences, 2001*; Thomas, J. Kramer, Gerard P. Fleming, and Scott M. Mannis, "Improving Face-to-Face Brainstorming Through Modeling and Facilitation," Small Group Research, Vol. 32 (2001); and Paul B. Paulus, et.al. "Social and Cognitive Influences in Group Brainstorming: Predicting Production Gains and Losses," *European Review of Social Psychology*, vol. 12, Jan. 2002.

4. For additional information on electronic brainstorming see Nicolas Michinov and Corine Primois, "Improving Productivity and Creativity in Online Groups Through Social Comparison Process: New Evidence for Asynchronous Electronic Brainstorming," *Computers in Human Behavior* 21 (2005), 11–28.

5. Roz D. Lasker and Elisa S. Weiss, "Broadening Participation in Community Problem Solving: A Multidisciplinary Model to Support Collaborative Practice and Research," *Journal of Urban Health*, March 2003, 14–47; Nikol Rummel and Hans Spada, "Learning to Collaborate: An Instructional Approach to Promoting Collaborative Problem Solving in Computer-Mediated Settings," *Journal of the Learning Sciences*, Vol. 14 (2005), 201–241.

6. William M. Isaacs, "Taking Flight: Dialogue, Collective Thinking, and Organizational Learning," *Organizational Dynamics* (Autumn 1993): 24–39.

7. Edgar H. Schein, "On Dialogue, Culture, and Organizational Learning," *Organizational Dynamics* (Autumn 1993): 40–51. For additional information

on dialogue groups see Joseph H. Albeck, Sami Adwan, and Dan Bar-On, "Dialogue Groups: TRT's Guidelines for Working Through Intractable Conflicts by Personal Story Telling," *Peace and Conflict: Journal of Peace Psychology*, Vol. 8 (2002), pp. 301–322.

8. David W. Stewart, Prem N. Shamdasani, and Dennis W. Rook, *Focus Groups: Theory and Practice*, 2nd ed. (Thousand Oaks, CA: Sage, 2006); Thomas L. Greenbaum, *Moderating Focus Groups: A Practical Guide for Group Facilitation* (Thousand Oaks, CA: Sage, 2000); and Claudia Puchta and Jonathan Potter, *Focus Group Practice* (Thousand Oaks, CA: Sage, 2004).

9. John P. Schuster, "Transforming Your Leadership Style," *Association Management* (January 1994): 39–43.

10. *Ibid.*

11. Svjetlana Madzar, "Subordinate's Information Inquiry: Exploring the Effect of Perceived Leadership Style and Individual Differences," *Journal of Occupational and Organizational Psychology* (June 2001): 221–232.

12. Much of the material in this section is adapted from Gregorio Billikopf, "Conducting Effective Meetings," August 2005, www.cnr.berkeley.edu/ucce50/ag-labor/7labor/11.pdf (accessed 30 June 2007); Don Clark, "Meetings," 20 May 2007, www.nwlink.com/~donclark/leader/leadmet.html (accessed 30 June 2007); and Carter McNamara, "Basic Guide to Conducting Effective Meetings," copyright 1997–2007, www.managementhelp.org/misc/mtgmgmnt.htm (accessed 30 June 2007).

13. Michael E. Mayer, "Behaviors Leading to More Effective Decisions in Small Groups Embedded in Organizations," *Communication Reports* (Summer 1988): 123–132.

14. "Roundtables," 4 Dec. 2003, www.sdanys.org/Archive_Round/NYPWAGuidelines.htm (accessed 30 June 2007).

15. Marilyn Berlin Snell, "Climate Exchange," *Sierra*, May/June 2007, 44–53. 73–74.

Appendix B

1. Page 408, John Bakke, *Remarks on Accepting the Martin Luther King Jr. Human Rights, 2006.* Reprinted by permission of John Bakke.

2. Page 410, Elie Wiesel, *Nobel Peace Prize Acceptance Speech,* December 10, 1986. © The Nobel Foundation 1986.

Photo Credits

Index

Note: *f* indicates figures.

A

Aarvik, Egil, 363
Able speaker, 10
About.com, 132
"About Us" links on Web sites, 139
Abstract ideas
  concrete, continuum of abstract to, 238*f*
  presentation aids for, 202–203
  supporting materials for, 166
Abyskera, Neomal, 206
Academic dishonesty, 19–20
Academic Search Premier, 131
Acceptance speeches, 361*f*, 366
Accuracy of Internet resource, 138
Achievement
  needs, appeal to, 94
  as universal value, 98
Acronym graphics, 211, 211*f*
Actions, persuasive speeches advocating,
  306–307, 307*f*
Adaptation
  to audience, 82–83
  in classroom speeches, 74
  ethical adaptation, guidelines for, 105
Additions, transitions indicating, 179, 181*f*
Ad hominem fallacy, 346, 349*f*
Adjourn, motion to, 390, 391*f*
Advertising, proofs in, 336
Advocacy Web sites, 135–136
  home page, example of, 136*f*
Affirmations in persuasive speaking, 309
After-dinner speeches, 361*f*, 370–371
Age of audience, 84–85
Agreement in persuasive speaking,
  309–310
Alexander, Janet E., 138
Aley, Anna, 16, 97, 188, 234–235, 301, 302,
  404–406
All in the Family, 240
Alliteration, 248, 249*f*
  in informative speech, 286
Almanacs, consulting, 127
Alternative perspectives, acknowledgment
  of, 72–73
Amend, motions to, 390, 391*f*
American character, 8
American Fact Finder, 133
American Progress (Gast), 336
American Psychological Association
  (APA), 194
American Red Cross Web site, 137
American Rhetoric, 133
Amplification, 237
Analogical reasoning, 342–343
Analogies
  defective analogies, 348
  in explanatory speeches, 283

faulty analogy fallacy, 349*f*
  in informative speech, 289–290
Analogous color schemes, 220–221, 221*f*
Analogy, use of, 46
Analysis of topic, 113–115
Ancient writing, 11, 11*f*
Anderton, Melissa, 40–41
AND in Internet searches, 133
Angelou, Maya, 161, 184
Annenberg Center for Public Policy, 139
Anthologies, guide to citing, 195*f*
Antithesis, 247, 249*f*
  in tribute speech, 362–363
Anxiety. *See* Communication anxiety
Apathy, words overcoming, 232–233
Arar, Maher, 332
Arguments, 329–353. *See also* Fallacies; Proofs;
  Reasoned persuasion; Reasoning
  defective arguments, 349*f*
  ethical arguments, building, 344
  powerful arguments, developing, 343
Aristotle, 10–11, 84, 201, 235, 332, 358
  on ethos, 40
  on metaphors, 242
  on reasoning, 339
Articulation, 260
Ascending emphasis of main points, 172–173
Ashdown, Paul, 289
Assault on Reason (Gore), 330
Atlantic Monthly, 135
Attention
  introductions capturing, 182–185
  main points drawing, 175
  in motivated sequence design, 320
Attitudes
  adjustments, 30–31
  of audience, 89–90
  information-gathering about, 90
  persuasive speeches addressing,
    305–306, 307*f*
  presentation and, 254–255
  survey questionnaire on, 90–91, 91*f*
Audience, 13. *See also* Audience demographics;
  Audience dynamics; Feedback;
  Informative speaking; Persuasive
  speaking
  adaptation to, 82–83
  analysis worksheet, 104, 104*f*
  contact with, 52
  context of speech and, 103–105
  diversity of, 96–101
  importance of, 82
  introductions and, 182–183
  occasion of speech and, 102–103
  pandering to, 82–83
  place of speech and, 102
  as predatory listeners, 28

preliminary tuning effect, 103
recent events, effect of, 104–105
rhetorical land mines, 99–101
setting of speech and, 103–105
size of, 103
supporting materials for diverse audiences,
  97–98
time of speech, effect of, 101–102
topics involving, 108–109
understanding of, 105
universal values, applying, 97, 98
Audience demographics, 83–88
  age of audience, 84–85
  educational level, 85
  gender of audience, 85
  group affiliations and, 85–87
Audience dynamics, 88–96
  attitudes, 89–90
  beliefs, 89
  motivation of, 90–96
  values, 89
Audio resources, 214–215
Authenticity of presentation aids, 203
Authority of Internet resource, 138
Autocratic leaders, 385
Award presentations, 363–364
Awareness in persuasive speaking, 308–309

B

Bachmann, Michelle, 14
Bacon, Francis, 231
Bailey, Antoinette M., 242
"Baked-In Traditions" (Mullinax), 376–377
Bakke, John, 361, 362, 367, 408–410
Balance, 172–173, 173*f*
  in presentation aids, 220
  for short presentations, 173
Baldwin, Alec, 371
Baltz, Sandra, 54–55, 162, 165, 245, 253,
  394–395
Bar graphs, 209–210, 209*f*
  misleading bar graphs, 223–224
Barriers to commitment, removing, 314
Baruda, Paul, 5
Baudelaire, 107
Beaver, H. Dennis, 28
Begay, D. Y., 228
Begging the question fallacy, 346–347, 349*f*
Behaviors
  enhancing/impeding behaviors, 389*f*
  reasoning from principle and, 340
  social leadership behavior, 385
  task leadership behavior, 385
Beliefs
  of audience, 89
  inspiration speeches addressing, 369
  maxims, use of, 240